THE
Courts
OF
Babylon

TALES OF GREED AND GLORY
IN A HARSH NEW WORLD
OF PROFESSIONAL TENNIS

PETER BODO

SCRIBNER

NEW YORK LONDON TORONTO SYDNEY TOKYO SINGAPORE

SCRIBNER
1230 Avenue of the Americas
New York, NY 10020

SCRIBNER and design are trademarks of Simon & Schuster Inc.

DESIGNED BY ERICH HOBBING

Manufactured in the United States of America

1 3 5 7 9 10 8 6 4 2

Library of Congress Cataloging-in-Publication Data

Bodo, Peter.
The courts of Babylon : tales of greed and glory in a harsh new
world of professional tennis / Peter Bodo.
p.   cm.
Includes index.
1. Tennis. 2. Tennis players. I. Title.
GV995.B6832   1995
796.342'64—dc20   95–14760
CIP

ISBN 0-684-81296-7

This book is for Marion Gengler,
whose copious knowledge of tennis was the least of it.

CONTENTS

ACKNOWLEDGMENTS

THE PLEASURE OF WRITING this book was qualified by the death of two wonderful people for whom the earthly pleasure of reading may be incomparable to the joy they now know. One of them was my mother, Elizabeth, who did not attend a single pro tennis event in her entire life. She did watch the game on television, but only because she considered it some kind of game, or challenge, to catch a glimpse of me in the crowd. That's a mother for you.

The other was Arthur Mann, the father of my agent Carol Mann. Devoted father, inspiring teacher, and passionate tennis nut, Arthur had a knowledge of the game that was formidable, and his support will always be greatly appreciated.

My friend Boris Becker once remarked that one should measure the age of a tennis player in "dog years." And while that observation doesn't necessarily apply to tennis journalists, my two decades in the game and tennis community seem like a very long time indeed, particularly when I think about all the people who helped me to develop my understanding of this rich, complex, colorful sport. They include players, coaches, business managers, administrators, fellow reporters, camp followers, parents . . . you get the drift. Any effort to individually and meaningfully acknowledge their help, cooperation, and kindness would be doomed from the start. I just hope that some small or large portion of this book brings them pleasure and makes them feel appreciated.

However, I would like to mention and thank three chief editors at *Tennis* magazine, the publication for whom I have worked almost exclusively from the beginning of my so-called career in 1976. Shep Campbell, a prime mover in the initial success of *Tennis*, gave me the kind of support, freedom, and trust that every neophyte journalist dreams of. His successor, Alex McNab, whose understanding of the way the game is played remains unparalleled, also shared my overall vision of tennis and backed my efforts to bring it to print. Donna Doherty, the current editor at *Tennis,* is another member of the cognoscenti. More important, she is a journalist of great integrity, and an executive who has never allowed her position of authority to corrupt her capacity for compassion and decency.

9

I would also like to thank E. Digby Baltzell, who opened my eyes to powerful sociological forces that have shaped the transition from amateur to professional tennis, and who remains the single most important influence on my interpretation of the game. Carol Mann, she of the nuclear forehand, who found me the right editor in Edward T. Chase ("Ned," to the titans with whom he struggles on courts throughout this great land). Ned not only bought this ambitious book, he patiently and wisely curbed some of my more feverish intellectual impulses as I tried to get it all down on paper. Hamilton Cain saw the project through to its conclusion, and as any barroom brawler can tell you, finishing something can be a whole lot tougher than starting it.

God bless you all.

AUTHOR'S NOTE

"It was the best of times, it was the worst of times . . ."
—Charles Dickens,
A Tale of Two Cities

I DON'T KNOW ABOUT YOU, but I never really understood that line or any other in that popular first paragraph of Dickens's epic. In fact, for a long time I thought it was one of the most overrated and abused chestnuts in our entire canon of recorded wisdom. It said everything, it said nothing. It was grand, it was empty. It was true of the time about which Dickens was writing, but it could have been written about any other time in history, too, as a zillion literary rangers have proven. Go ask a Weimar dandy or a peace protester from the late 1960s. The quotation covered all the bases, and that was exactly what was bogus about it.

Then, after writing about half of this book, I had a crisis. And I came out of it thinking that maybe Dickens's opening line wasn't so bombastic and overgeneralized after all. You see, I found that I was writing a highly critical book about a game and a class of people I had more or less happily spent twenty years getting to know. One of the chief reasons that those years were happy was that I quickly developed a reputation as a friend of tennis and those who played the game. The bulk of my magazine journalism reflected that. It also earned me easy and virtually unlimited access to players, administrators, and others, most of whom believed I was fair and sympathetic to my subjects. So, as this book evolved, it was only natural to ask if at some level it didn't represent an act of betrayal.

The answer to that question comes in two parts. First, the only true reason for a person in my position to write a book like this is to make tons of money and to get on "Larry King Live." But seriously, while I do think about such things, the true reason is that writing this book gave me a chance to sit down and say what I really think. And that was slightly problematic.

In the "personality profiles" that became my specialty for *Tennis*

11

magazine, I always felt that my first obligation was similar to that of a portrait painter. I was commissioned to capture essences, to bring people to life at their best (and I don't mean their prettiest) and most complex at specific junctures in their lives. I never went against my instincts or rational conclusions, but I sometimes bit my tongue—a discipline I highly recommend to anyone who would aspire to find out how any community as insular as tennis truly works.

The extended profiles of the players in this book are sharper and more analytical than some of my previous ones. Magazine articles catch and freeze a moment; the essays in this book represent a long look back and an overview. I like most tennis players. In fact, I like most people, even many of the ones with whom I habitually disagree. But in the overall context of this book, which attempts to show how tennis players' specific identities as professionals affected them, I came to realize that my feelings and thoughts about them were more complex than I had imagined. In the big picture, I see them in the same way that combat correspondents often come to view soldiers. They might hate war and what it does to soldiers, but they don't hate soldiers.

That brings me to the second part of the answer. I have always believed that a book of this kind works best when it has a unifying theme. Mine is the evolution, nature, and impact of professionalism on what was until very recently an amateur sport, and how that radical change affected the tennis community. My misgivings about the nature of professionalism also created a conflict. The opportunities created by the aggressive commercialization of tennis gave me gainful employment, brought me into contact with many delightful people, and ultimately put me in a position to write this book. Life is funny. Let's leave it at that.

One more thing. We're living in a time of moral neutrality, when many people are loath to make judgments, take positions, or believe in anything that is in conflict with other beliefs. My own nature and the spirit of this project are incompatible with such neutrality. I believe that making a considered judgment is not a mean-spirited indulgence but an obligation. At the same time, I don't confuse my opinions with gospel truth. Things would be much easier if I could.

I will undoubtedly be criticized for many of my opinions and observations about the women's tour. However, I believe that the degeneration and corruption of that tour, a process that began with the premature retirements of Tracy Austin and Andrea Jaeger, has been the most underreported story in tennis in our time. Sure, the escapades of Jennifer Capriati and the brutalization of Monica Seles generated plenty of sensational copy. But nobody has grappled with the social, historical, and institutional elements that have played a part in turning the women's tour into an ugly, smoking battlefield of abuse, greed, and venality. I know that some of my friends on the women's tour are bound to take offense at my analysis, and that saddens me.

Finally, many readers may feel that I am overly kind to such friends as Evonne Goolagong Cawley and Boris Becker and overly critical of people I merely know, such as Martina Navratilova or Bjorn Borg. But that's how it works in this kind of a book, and that's what makes it my book.

An opinion can be a terrible thing to have.

INTRODUCTION

THE COMMISSION TO BUILD the "Courts of Babylon" was issued in 1968, the year the amateur establishment that ruled tennis yielded to popular demand and embraced full-blown professionalism. But as anyone who has ever tried to build anything more complex than a doghouse will tell you, nothing ever gets finished on time.

In the case of tennis, it took the architects of the new professional era almost a decade to fight their turf wars, clear out the dead wood, round up the lawyers, and lay the foundations for the new era. The courts of Babylon were finally ready for play by the mid-1970s, and the unofficial opening ceremonies took place at the U.S. Open in 1976.

That was the year after the West Side Tennis Club in Forest Hills, Queens, New York, the traditional site of the U.S. Open (né the U.S. Nationals), reluctantly ripped out its grass courts and replaced them with a green clay surface called Har-Tru. In those heady days, so influenced by the egalitarian revolution of the 1960s, grass was not a substance on which you played tennis but an illicit weed that you smoked. You were Everyman. So was everybody else. And grass, or marijuana, was the recreational drug of choice, the egalitarian medication.

While almost everybody smoked grass, people no longer wanted to play tennis on it anymore. Grass-court tennis smacked of tradition, exclusivity, and elitism. The vestigial grass-court game was okay at Wimbledon, where they also had royalty, double-decker buses, and judges in powdered wigs who liked getting spanked by schoolgirls dressed up as French maids. But in America in the 1970s, tradition, exclusivity, and elitism were loaded words that helped turn the tide of opinion against amateur tennis.

In 1976 the United States Tennis Association, which owns the U.S. Open, got rid of tournament director Bill Talbert, whose links with the amateur era were politically incorrect. The USTA also brought in the marketing firm of Capital Sports Inc. to improve and sell the new U.S. Open. Capital improved the infrastructure (we're talking toilets and water fountains), planted plastic shrubs, and imported designer foods such as bacon and Gruyère quiche. In other words, the new "populist" crowds would no longer have to subsist on the "elitist" fare that had been so popular at Forest Hills, the common hot dog.

Capital Sports also banished the once beloved Mr. Peanut, a guy who walked around in costume on behalf of Planter's. You might have thought that Mr. Peanut's nature as a promotional gimmick would have saved him. He certainly represented the old guard's deepest bow to the advances of commercialism and marketing. But, alas, Mr. Peanut was another victim of the purge.

The cause of professionalism was aggressively promoted by the unemployable bums, idiot savants, and gifted athletes who wanted nothing more than the chance to make a living from the thing they loved to do best: play tennis.

For the record, I'll point out that world-class tennis players in the amateur era were not unable to make a living from tennis. They merely failed to become filthy rich in the life span of your typical mayfly. So they owned modest homes, decided to eat pasta at least once a week, and worried about how they were going to put their kids through college. Hey, welcome to the real world. In fact, the real world often treated amateur-era tennis players much more kindly than it would their lavishly compensated pro successors. The knowledge that tennis offered limited financial opportunities led many amateur-era players to cultivate catholic interests and social abilities. The list of amateur-era players who went on to become successful in other enterprises, from banking to real estate development, is long and distinguished. René LaCoste (yes, the shirt), Dick Savitt, Ham Richardson, Fred Perry, Jack Kramer, and many others prospered. Lesser lights did as well or even better. The only development that has saved many of the pro era players from practical midlife crises is that tennis has become an industry that a good player never has to leave. Senior tours, cushy resort appointments, and a burgeoning tennis establishment allow pros to be tennis players for life.

Proto-professional players also complained that it was degrading to get paid under the table. The Australian former champion and popular television commentator Fred Stolle once told me an amusing story about his countryman Mervyn Rose. When Rose entertained guests, he liked to give them a tour of the house he had built. When Rose showed off his spacious, elegantly furnished living room, he would say, "This room was built and furnished by the British Lawn Tennis Association." This was an oblique reference to covert cash payments or convertible goods that he had received for playing in various British tournaments. Rose's handsome dining room was provided by the French Tennis Federation, and his den by the USTA. Rose invariably ended the tour at the john, bitterly commenting that it represented the stingy contribution made by his native Australian Lawn Tennis Association.

Nevertheless, as soon as full-blown pros began to make big money, the first thing many of them did was hire agents and accountants whose job descriptions often included drumming up illicit cash appearance fees and perks, and finding hollowed-out tree trunks in which to hide money from the tax man. In that sense the pros are just like you and me.

You'll notice that I haven't mentioned any women players yet. Back in the amateur era, when gender roles and opportunities were more limited, all but the very top players implicitly understood that they would play on the international tour until they were ready or able to set up shop as homemakers. For many of these women, their brief tennis careers represented the best—or at least the most carefree—of times because they were able to follow what may be the most valuable piece of advice anyone can receive: Always leave a party while you're still having a good time.

Women who had fewer traditional aspirations, including the lesbians who constitute an identifiable class in tennis, were big winners as a result of the professional movement. They were empowered as players-for-life by their chief icon, Billie Jean King. And the nature of the women's pro tour has been so radical, so averse to traditional roles and aspirations, that at times during the pro era the majority of women in the world's top ten were lesbians. In some ways the pro tour reflected the nature and values of society at large, but particularly for the women, it also became a society unto itself.

Some of these remarks may lead you to think that I resent the rich and envy the staggering amounts of money tennis players in the pro era have been able to earn. For now, let me just say this: I'm so pro-wealth that I wish *everybody* could be rich. It sure would eliminate a lot of whining from people who would rather see everybody poor than some people rich, not to mention the subterranean envy felt most acutely by the people who are *almost* rich. The way I see it, the only problem we'd have if everybody were rich is that you couldn't tell the tennis players from everybody else.

Anyway, the pro era was conceived at the advent of Open tennis in 1968, but the gestation period lasted nearly a decade. And when the infant finally popped out, it had all the charisma of Rosemary's Baby. The exact time and date of delivery was 4:21 P.M. on Friday, September 3, 1976 (I'm not making this up, I checked my watch), a minute during which the following events transpired:

At the entrance to the press marquee, a stubborn cop refused admittance to transsexual Renee Richards. It seems she didn't have the right

credentials, a charge that would be repeated time and again as she liti-
giously lobbied her way into acceptance as a female tennis player.

On a nearby redwood bench framed by plastic shrubs, two urchins
were hawking out-of-focus prints of Bjorn Borg. High in the air, the
Goodyear blimp was making its first strafing run over the stadium. It
waddled through the sunshine, so close to the ground that its shadow
sucked along like a massive storm cloud, blotting out whole sections of
the crowd, cameras fixed on the extraordinary scene playing out on the
green dirt floor of the stadium.

There, the German player Hans-Jurgen Pohmann had just taken the
second set from the Romanian Ilie Nastase. Pohmann, wild-eyed and
caked from head to toe with green clay, thrust his fist in the air, and
pandemonium broke out. Some people threw coins and crushed paper
cups into the arena. Nastase turned to the players' guest box, petrified.
He was a small creature cornered by a beast, one he had provoked out of
the long slumber of the amateur era by poking it with his famous middle
finger. And like most monsters, when it wasn't sleeping, it was eating.

The U.S. Open of 1976 was the wildest and woolliest tennis tournament I've ever attended. Through twelve wacky, seething days, tennis
lurched and staggered into a new era like a drunken sailor, knocking
down everything in its path. The 1976 Open was about gender confusion, commercial sponsorship, cheating, Wagnerian posturing, television, sellout crowds, overmanned quiche troughs, and inadequate
officiating. It was about a beastly crowd that devoured everything
thrown its way in an egalitarian orgy that made up for all the restraints
of the amateur era in one prolonged feeding frenzy. In its own ghastly
way it was great theater, prefiguring a new age in tennis. It was the best
of times, it was the worst of times.

"My God, it's like a bullring out there," an awestruck Marty Reissen
whispered to his opponent as they waited in the wings to play their
third-round match. "They're waiting for the kill."

The men's singles title eventually went to Jimmy Connors, in the
waning days of his early mastery of Bjorn Borg. Connors's love affair
with New York began in the heat and green dust of that 1976 tournament. Think what you will of Connors, but this is for sure: He has
never been anybody's fool. In 1976 he crawled through the draw on his
belly, careful not to antagonize anyone despite his image as the new
era's first punk-at-large.

So when the body parts were finally cleared away and the smoke settled, Connors stood there grinning. "Hey, we're *professionals* now," he
said. "You've got to let the crowd participate. New Yorkers want blood,
and I didn't want to give them any of mine yet. But you won't get me

saying anything about this crowd because I'm going to have to face them for a while."

Fifteen years later, in a new incarnation as a folk hero, Connors would say, "New Yorkers want you to spill your guts, and I'm willing to do that. *That's* why they love me, and that's why I love them."

To everything, Jimbo, turn, turn, turn.

Still, the most relevant match of that 1976 tournament was the brawl between Nasty and Pohmann—not because of its cheap horror quotient but because it personified the clash between the vestigial amateur ethic and the new values of professionalism.

The fireworks began during an otherwise close and entertaining match when a spectator made an "out" call during a point that Pohmann won in the first set tiebreaker. Nastase immediately protested, got a ruling to replay the point, and won it. The crowd of twelve thousand didn't much like that, and they grew even more upset when Nastase went on to win the set.

In the second set, after Nastase made a ruckus over another line call, all hell broke loose. Nastase freaked out and spat at spectators, threatened courtside photographers, and trotted out every vulgar gesture and obscenity in his formidable repertoire. The crowd responded in kind with gusto, beginning a sustained dialogue that Nastase—who, unlike his protégé Connors, has at various times been everybody's fool—got sucked into.

Later, while serving to even the match at 6-all in the third set, Pohmann was stricken by cramps. He collapsed three times but, keenly aware of the crowd's sympathy, managed to find his legs. At one point umpire George Armstrong called for a doctor. It was a humane gesture, but it violated the rule book.

"Is not football," Nastase screamed at the umpire while the doctor examined Pohmann and the crowd roared. "No time-outs."

By then the crowd, the match, and the players were out of control. Nastase ranted and raved indiscriminately, finding time here and there to save a few match points. Pohmann, lacking only a steel helmet with horns sticking out to complete his impersonation of a Wagnerian god, worked the frenzied crowd and staved off four match points before succumbing to Nastase.

When it was over, Pohmann refused to shake Nastase's trembling hand. Nastase spit at him and called him names. Armstrong also refused to shake Nastase's hand, so Nastase gave him the same treatment. Nastase abused the spectators nearby, one of whom had to be restrained from coldcocking the Romanian.

I beat it back to the small, overcrowded locker room just a few steps ahead of the players. There, Nastase rushed at Pohmann and screamed, "Fuck you, Hitler. Fuck you."

"It's the animal," Pohmann retorted. "Fuck you, animal."

Nastase lunged at Pohmann, shoving him against a locker, whereupon Pohmann demonstrated that he was a true visionary gazing out at the bright, burning horizon of the professional era. He looked Nastase straight in the eye and, with bystanders restraining both men, shouted, "I'm going to *sue* you."

Okay, there was an element of farce in all this, but then the same could be said about the sight of Nikita Khrushchev hammering away with his shoe on the table at the United Nations. It doesn't make it any less important.

The Nastase-Pohmann match showed that once you start throwing buckets of money around, notions of fair play and standards of conduct vanish. You end up fighting an endless battle to make the game child-proof, tamper-proof, and lawyer-proof—none of which can be done. But in the course of trying to do those things, you can make the game a bureaucratic nightmare and drastically alter what it means to be a tennis player.

At the end of the first twenty-five years of Open tennis, the game was full of extremely rich and extremely unhappy superstars, some of voting age and most of greater interest for what they hated about the game than for what they loved about it. I'll put it another way: How many tennis players in the first quarter century of Open tennis, besides Jimmy Connors, are famous for their passion for tennis?

You could put the whole Nastase-Pohmann imbroglio down to bad or incompetent officiating, but there was an interesting reason for the systemic failures of the early Open era. Before that time, tennis didn't need much officiating because it operated on a kind of honor system. That, more than snooty class attitudes, explains why tennis had a tradition of using eighty-five-year-old narcoleptics in straw boaters as linesmen and umpires. Nobody got bent out of shape if they messed up, and it gave the old boys something to do.

In the amateur era you were obliged to follow a largely unwritten code of conduct inspired by notions of personal honor and sportsmanship. When the regulations of the game were printed, they were in pamphlet form, and the "rules" included the mandate that if you weren't sure if a ball hit by your opponent was in or out, you were honor-bound to give him the point.

After twenty-five years of Open tennis, the "official" ATP Tour Code of Conduct is a 230-page tome that covers everything from the protocol for going to the toilet when you have the runs, as Connors did during the final of the 1986 Open, to the maximum size and dimensions of the advertising patch you can wear on your shoulder, or the nature of the product whose logo you stencil on the strings of your racket. Still, tennis players are famous for arguing line calls, breaking rackets, and violating rules.

One man who really has a grip on this is E. Digby Baltzell, the distinguished University of Pennsylvania sociologist and author of the seminal work, *The Protestant Establishment: Aristocracy and Class in America*. Baltzell has played and watched tennis for most of his life, and the sociology of the professional game comes to life like a 3-D comic book when you look through his magic glasses. He's a great believer in personal rather than legislated morality and the concept of sportsmanship. He speaks eloquently about dehumanization. This may make you wonder if he wears a beret, fancies performance art, and sleeps with his students. Ixnay on all three counts.

According to Baltzell, the concept of the gentleman was a secular compromise with the Christian ideal embodied by the celibate priest. And he is quick to point out that unlike communism or the secular materialism that increasingly characterizes American culture, Christianity and democracy are both systems of thought in which process rather than result is paramount. That is, they stress the means over the ends.

It was the ideal notion of the gentleman and his conduct that gave us the traditional concept of sportsmanship. But the only way the "gentleman" fits into today's culture is as the object of its resentment. He's white, he's male, he's Western, and he's directly responsible for everything that's wrong with your life. He's also a little bit nuts in that, among other antiquated notions, he actually believes that sports is a tool for developing character.

Baltzell likes to cite the opinion that Don Budge, the first man to win a Grand Slam, held about the legendary Australian coach Harry Hopman. "According to Budge, Hopman didn't achieve his spectacular success as a Davis Cup captain because of his knowledge of tennis but because of his knowledge of discipline, especially self-discipline."

One of the most convenient but absurd charges brought against tennis on the brink of the professional era was that the game needed to be liberated from an ethic foisted on it by the rich, who were the only ones who could afford to play or get any good at it. The simple truth is that most great tennis players sprang from the lower and middle classes, and they became masters of the sport because they loved everything about it, including its patrician values.

Fred Perry, the last great English champion, was a working-class boy whose father stood as a member of Parliament for Labour. The American Frank Parker set new standards for gentlemanly conduct, despite having grown up in the slums of Milwaukee. Rod Laver was a farm boy from Queensland, Australia. Delightful Evonne Goolagong was an aborigine who spent her childhood sleeping on a dirt floor. Chris Evert's father, Jimmy, dated Gloria Connors way back when both of them were middle-class college students who shared a passion for tennis. Gottfried von Cramm, that quintessential gentleman, did happen to be a German aristocrat.

"Most of the great players in the amateur era were not from the upper class, but they embraced a class ethic," Baltzell said. "In today's egalitarian society, nobody wants to pick up a class ethic. It's understandable that Perry, an outsider in a rigid class society, was a tough, accomplished gamesman who flouted the conventions of sportsmanship. But it's ironic that John McEnroe along with a lot of the other kids playing today can be lousy sports despite coming from privileged backgrounds."

In other words, go ahead and eat the rich. Just make sure you pick the right guy.

Unfortunately, snobbery also became part of the old amateur order. The elitists blew it for themselves when they began to believe that superiority was based on things like class or color rather than the only worthwhile standards: individual distinction and adherence to a code of conduct that can neither be written into "law" nor enforced by it. Let's face it, anybody who observes a higher standard of conduct than the one that obtains in his society is an elitist, a value snob. He wants to be less, rather than more, like everybody else.

Thus, the ATP Tour Code of Conduct is not a simulacrum of the Sumerian code but a benumbing body of rules and regulations that spell out things that ought to be ordained by any knucklehead's sense of dignity and fair play. The funny thing about this is that the Code of Conduct not only makes it impossible to be a bad sport, it also denies the individual the opportunity to be a good one.

The proliferation of laws also makes the breaking of any one law that much easier. Forget how the government spends your money—the way it collects it, via a byzantine system of tax write-offs, breaks, and shelters, is probably the most powerful inducement anybody can have for cheating on his taxes when it comes time to pony up for Uncle Sam. John McEnroe once told me that he felt less like an outlaw than a maze rat in the complex bureaucracy of pro tennis.

"The system stinks," McEnroe said. "There've been matches when my behavior was so outrageous that I should have been defaulted, but I'm such a big drawing card that no tournament director is going to shoot himself in the foot by defaulting me. So they came up with this suspension plan that sits you down if you accumulate so many dollars in fines over a given period.

"Even then, you don't get kicked out when you go over the limit but later, and even that can be appealed. The system was there to be manipulated, and a lot of times I played it to the hilt. A part of me was always aware of how far I could go and what it might cost me down the line. What I didn't realize then was how much damage I could do to myself along the way by playing the system."

There is an even more direct way to look at this. At heart, the totalitarian man or woman is essentially one-dimensional—whether he's an ex-Soviet apparatchik or a Wharton sharpy in wing tips whose primary purpose in life is ringing the cash register. Now let me ask you this: What word comes to mind when you see or read about a sixteen-year-old tennis pro who hasn't done anything since kindergarten but play tennis? Professional? One-dimensional?

Professional tennis players are rarely well-rounded individuals. Many of them are result-oriented, rule-addled, lavishly compensated victims of a totalitarian way of life. That's probably why we love them and hate them at the same time. This condition is exacerbated with every passing day, and by the incremental drop in the average age at which pros begin—and end—their careers.

Most of the leading "institutions" in tennis facilitate this process. The Women's Tennis Association quickly and shamelessly abandoned the moral high ground it staked out on age limitation rules when the legal guardians of Jennifer Capriati made it clear that the way they saw it, Capriati had a right to play on the tour just as soon as she wanted. And when you came right down to it, the renowned Nick Bollettieri's Tennis Academy is basically a veal farm. I'd like to go on record saying that I like Bollettieri, despite his uncritical willingness to embrace and advance some of the more dehumanizing aspects of the professional ethic.

This brings me to another vital element in the beleaguered and changing sensibility of democracy, the time-honored tradition of agreeing to disagree. In a healthy democratic society, opponents are just opponents—not enemies. But tennis players in the pro era have become just as susceptible to enemy-mongering as politicians. Neither John McEnroe and Ivan Lendl nor Monica Seles and Steffi Graf have ever had dinner together, despite their shared experiences and goals. In fact, I'm not sure any of them ever even mouthed the tepid courtesy phrase, "Nice shot," to the other during a match.

McEnroe and Jimmy Connors played on the same Davis Cup team together, against Sweden in 1984. They barely spoke a word to each other, and their behavior before, during, and after matches disgraced their sport and nation. The sad thing about all this is that their way of life prevented these fiercely competitive, proud champions from being friends with the only people with whom they have a lot in common—each other. Thus, their celebrity, wealth, and one-dimensional life-styles were not enriching but dehumanizing. Their fame and privileges and wealth did not bring them closer to their peers but served only to increase their self-obsession and isolation. They may realize this, but they are often powerless against it.

For instance, Boris Becker's commitment to leading a "normal" life has been amply documented, yet he is forever being asked when he is going to win another big tournament and when he is going to retire. This is the essence of dehumanization because it denies Becker any status other than that of a title machine and a potential burnout case.

The dehumanization of tennis players is accelerated by their itinerant way of life. Say what you will about the joys of room service, telephones alongside toilets, or free all-night movies featuring nymphets like Emmanuelle, but traveling for any other reason than the sheer pleasure of it gets old quickly and robs you of a life.

Over the years I've interviewed a lot of tennis players at their homes. These were often palatial residences, but they were almost always so new that they still smelled of paint. Their decor usually made me think of nothing more cozy than the furniture section of a chic department store or the suite in a good hotel. This makes perfect sense, given the amount of time players spend in hotels. They become habituated to the ambience.

A few years ago Steffi Graf bought a lavish duplex in a new, fashionable building near Union Square in Manhattan. This was a remarkable choice for a thoroughly German girl going on twenty-three whose only other personal residence was a room upstairs in the enormous house she built for her family in her native Bruehl, Germany—a room that her agent Phil De Picciotto once described as "a really, really neat room."

Having bought her new place in Manhattan, Graf immediately hired a decorator, partly because she didn't have time to do things like poke around furniture stores. Graf's head undoubtedly rested on a lush down pillow, and she probably loved the wonderful view, the unbelievable sound system, and the multizone climate-control system. But because she couldn't spend more than a few weeks of the year in the residence, the first thing she would probably have to do upon her return was dig out the floor plans in order to locate the bathroom or the linen closet.

Unfortunately, Graf could hardly have done it any other way. The pro tennis player's way of life is characterized by luxury that has no context and cannot be truly appreciated. Usually, a blue-chip player is wedded to this bizarre way of life before he or she is aware of its pitfalls. The opportunities and demands facing top players are such that they don't even know what they're missing—things such as adolescent fun, an education, the sheer joy of participating in sports. Tennis is their business, and they become successful at it so quickly that they are left with nothing to look forward to other than the curious afterlife represented by retirement, by which time they can hardly be expected to make up for all the lost time.

This overall loss of innocence was prefigured some fifty years ago and documented in 1981 in the Academy Award–winning movie *Chariots of Fire*. The film so sharply defined the changing values that foreshadowed the end of the amateur era and the rise of professionalism that Baltzell often used it in the classroom. The movie, which is based on a true story, is about two Olympic-calibre runners, Eric Lidell and Harry Abrahams. Lidell, a devout Christian, tries to reconcile his pursuit of excellence with his faith. He runs to honor his God, and he refuses to run for the same reason when the 100-meter Olympic final is scheduled to take place on a Sunday.

Abrahams, a Jew who feels the bitter sting of anti-Semitism even as he cuts a swath through WASP culture, runs for personal vengeance and exoneration. His decision to hire Mussobini, an Italian coach, brings him into direct conflict with his mentors at Cambridge, whose amateur ethic is violated by Abraham's "professional" approach. And later yet, his obsessive desire to win at almost any cost nearly ruins his greatest competitive triumph.

The movie often borders on the clairvoyant. The characterization of the American Olympic athletes is a deft, economic portrait of a cheerfully eclectic, secular, proto-professional society naively perched on the brink of its heyday. And Mussobini is at heart so evocative of Nick Bolletieri that all you can do is sit back and laugh.

This brings us in a roundabout way back to 1976 and a better understanding of how tennis changed and why. Let's go back to Ilie Nastase for a moment. Born and raised in the totalitarian hellhole that was Romania, he was part of a culture in which beating the system was not merely a popular pastime but an honorable one. It was inevitable that Nastase would opportunistically abuse and manipulate rules that relied so heavily on individual conscience and notions of gentlemanly conduct. Romania had neither an amateur ethic nor, at the time Nastase was born, a classic tradition in tennis. In fact, the game was considered a decadent imperialistic pursuit, and the Romanian autocrats probably would not have allowed Nastase to play tennis abroad if it were not for the game's new professional nature. But tennis had suddenly become a way to raise hard Western cash for the ruling elite of a nation whose own currency was about as valuable as beetle dung.

Nastase could not be expected to understand the residual ethics of the amateur era or even the professional mandate to at least play fair. Ultimately, he was saved by his personal charm and the flowering of his own eccentric, unpredictable conscience—an evolution that was accelerated by the willingness of any number of his victims to punch out his lights if he got out of line.

But a group of individuals will eventually see that establishing and observing standards of conduct makes a certain amount of sense—hence the Code of Conduct. It's also hard to extinguish totally a human being's inborn ability to tell right from wrong. Ion Tiriac, Nastase's Romanian Davis Cup partner, was frequently accused of being a cheat. But he has evolved into a successful entrepreneur and man of conscience. Ivan Lendl swiftly transcended his totalitarian Czech roots to become an individual who understands the beauty of the American dream more profoundly than many of his American peers.

Nevertheless, Nastase was the keynote performer at the opening ceremonies for the courts of Babylon. And he wasn't that hard an act to follow.

PART 1

CHAPTER I

AUSTRALIA
So Golden It's Almost Freakish

Here was a country of indolent climate, general prosperity, and a philosophy of happiness; it was a wonderful set-up for choice and indulgence. Yet life was dismal and such public enjoyment as occurred often degenerated into rowdiness. A pall of ennui spread over the suburbs at night and at weekends. There was all this life to lead and nothing much to lead it with. Apart from the pleasures of family life three main diversions were open to the people—drink, sport, and money.

—Donald Horne,
The Lucky Country, 1964

NO NATION ON EARTH is more drastically different from the image it projects than Australia. If you go by coffee-table books, movies, and beer commercials, Australia is a land of picaresque crocodile hunters, ruggedly independent sheep farmers who own "stations" the size of Rhode Island, and pubs filled with friendly, weathered locals who lift their tinnies of lager, wink, and say, "G'day." All that, and cover girls who bodysurf, too.

In reality, 88 percent of Australia's population lives in cities along the coast, and an alarming number of them manufacture nothing. Think about it: What Australian product have you ever lusted for besides the boxed sets of Mel Gibson's Mad Max film trilogy? Even those airline commercial featuring bronzed Matildas holding adorable koala bears turn out to be bogus. The few Australians who really *are* from the country know better than to cuddle with these nocturnal creatures. Koalas are perpetually whacked-out on eucalyptus, and comatose during the daylight hours when they pee at whim and often.

I first went to Australia to check out the spanking-new, state-of-the-art National Tennis Center, a facility that was built in 1989 and intended to restore the glory of the Australian Open. The tournament, which takes place in mid-January, is the first of the four Grand Slam events that remain the foundation of the game. The other three are the French Open, Wimbledon, and the U.S. Open. I also wanted to find out how the Australians managed to destroy their remarkable tennis tradition overnight and to see if the new site, and some highly publicized new programs of Tennis Australia, the governing body of the game Down Under, were going to change that. I didn't really understand the answers to those questions until I learned a little more about this baffling nation.

Australians, whose only conscious national dogma is informality, like to call their nation "Oz." Being a literal bunch, the Aussies don't appreciate how accurate—and funny—that characterization is. But the problem with Oz—or other fantasy lands such as Disney World—is that spending too much time there becomes, well, boring. You might be oblivious to that fundamental fact of life if you live there, but it is brought home dramatically when you visit. Spend enough time in Oz, and you can feel the boredom creeping into your days with tidal consistency. That's when you realize that there are disadvantages to developing as Australia did, in natural isolation from the peppery cross-influence enjoyed by the other, contiguous continents.

On the surface, Australian people seem a lot like Americans. They inhabit a vast, underpopulated nation rich in natural resources and they have a rich store of frontier myths and sprawling suburbs. The Australians exterminated aborigines, the continent's indigenous people, with a relish that even American settlers were hard put to match.

Besides, while walking around in some quaint European city, you could easily mistake an Aussie for a Yank at fifty yards. They share an affinity for ghastly T-shirts, short pants, white socks pulled up to the knee, and running shoes that allow you to see if not hear them coming from a mile away.

Australians surf. They drink beer. They barbecue. They drink beer. They like their own elementary version of football (Aussie rules). And they like to live in one-story, ranch-style houses with big garages and little windows that look out on identical setups where other people barbecue and drink beer.

A lot of Australians, fueled by the anti-Western agenda of many intellectuals, now like to consider themselves an organic Pacific basin nation—white socks, tract homes, and all. But they can't quite wean themselves away from the British roots they refuse to recognize, or the cutting-edge attitudes generated in places like New York, London, Paris, and Los Angeles.

Most Australians have always been sports nuts. But even at the best of times, sports fulfilled a deeper and more unusual role for Aussies than for other people. Recognizing the twin threads of conformity and sports worship in the Aussies, visionary sociologist David Horne, author of *The Lucky Country*, concluded: "For many Australians, playing or watching sport gives life one of its principal meanings. The elements of loyalty, fanaticism, pleasure-seeking, competitiveness, ambition, and struggle that are not allowed precise expression in non-sporting life (although they exist in disguise) are stated precisely in sport."

Like many aggressive and confident nations, Australia once took great pride in its sporting achievements, particularly in the team sports that so often required near-militaristic discipline and cooperation. Aussies born and raised before or during the World War II era also embraced the British concept of amateur sports as a vehicle for building character, and character was an essential ingredient in men who would go on to build the nation.

As a result, Australia dominated international tennis in the 1960s and 1970s, on the brink of the professional era. When John Newcombe won Wimbledon in 1971—year four of the pro era—the feat represented the nineteenth All England men's singles title taken by an Aussie. Margaret Smith Court and Evonne Goolagong, Australia's last great female champions, won five Wimbledon titles between them, extending the Aussie tradition. Goolagong was the first mother to win the singles title at Wimbledon, a feat she accomplished at the age of twenty-eight in 1980. She was the last of the great Australians and a friend about whom I'll write more.

Between 1950 and 1971, Australian men took twenty-eight of forty-two places in the Wimbledon singles final. They included such legendary players as Rod Laver, Lew Hoad, Roy Emerson, Fred Stolle, Tony Roche, and Ken Rosewall. In that period of twenty-one years, an Aussie failed to reach the Wimbledon final only three times. But since 1971, only two inhabitants of Oz reached the final—Ken Rosewall (at age forty in 1974) and the 1987 champion Pat Cash.

But the epitome of Australian success during the golden age was the Davis Cup squads that prevailed in the premier international team competition seventeen times in twenty-seven years, ending in 1977. Granted, some of those victories were facilitated by the decision of many top American players to play on proto-professional tours—a choice that made them ineligible for Davis Cup play because of the amateur establishment's taboo against professionals.

The chief factor in Australia's Davis Cup dynasty was that nation's unique notion of fraternalism. Aussies don't call every Tom, Dick, and Harry "mate" for nothing. The word symbolizes and evokes one of the most striking social traditions of Australian life. Here's Horne again:

> The doctrine of fraternity, still largely meaningless in most countries, has received great ideological attention in Australia. . . . In the narrower sense, "mates" are men who are thrown together by some emergency in an unfriendly environment and have become of one blood in facing it. In this sense, its use is strongest in the unions and armed forces. Mates stick together in their adversity and their common interest. Mateship of this kind is not a theory of universal brotherhood but of the brotherhood of particular men. However, the emphasis on adversity can lend a suggestion of theatricality at a time when there is not much adversity: a mate situation of this kind can become paranoid when mates all get drunk together and express their suspicions of a conspiring world.

Australian fraternalism and postwar wealth facilitated success in a quintessentially Anglo sport at a time when most Australians still cherished their ties to the mother nation of England. But those ties weakened, and the world beyond Australia continued changing, too.

"In the fifties, Australia was very sporty," Paul McNamee, who won the Wimbledon doubles title two times in the early 1980s, told me. "It wasn't a very intellectual culture, so it accepted competition and the regimentation of sports at face value. Since then, Europe has grown athletically while Australia has gotten more intellectual. That's probably one of the reasons why the situation changed so fast."

Indeed, back in the 1950s, the two things you could find in even the smallest of Australian towns were a pub and a tennis court, of which only the pub can be said to be an intellectual institution. When the Davis Cup Challenge Round was played between Christmas and New Year's, the entire nation was transfixed. The radio in every living room and holiday cottage was on, and even the hordes of sunbathers at the beach tuned in to the exploits of Laver, Rosewall, et al. The competition attracted close to twenty thousand spectators, and temporary stands had to be erected at major facilities such as White City in Sydney and Melbourne's Kooyong.

The conditions in fraternal, sports-crazy Australia allowed a man of great vision and ambition to take all of that raw athletic material and mold it into a dynasty, in a vivid episode that raises the old question of whether man makes history or history makes the man. In this case the man was an avid player turned journalist turned taskmaster turned national hero. Harry Hopman was not exactly a poor paperhanger from

Austria, but his ascent was equally improbable. He will always be remembered as the true wizard of Oz.

Like so many other wizards, Hopman had seemingly uncanny powers. He was also a fastidious man, a stern disciplinarian of slight stature with an iron will. Some might argue that he had a Napoleon complex to go with his Napoleonic record. Those players who didn't hit it off with Hopman—including Bob Hewitt and Marty Mulligan, both of whom emigrated from Australia because Hopman didn't take a shine to them—would wholeheartedly agree. Nevertheless, Hopman inspired a loyalty that bordered on reverence in most of his protégés. He was one of those endangered Aussies whom Horne characterized as a "man of will," and he expertly tapped into the quasi-militaristic, fraternal tradition of his nation.

Hopman's record and character survived the changing times. He remained a beloved coach and teacher long after his expatriation, a move that left him holed up in a mildly depressing, prefabricated golf and tennis development in Bradenton, Florida. Vitas Gerulaitis, one of his last protégés, was utterly devoted to Hopman despite an insistence on leading his life as if he were a self-destructive rock star. Gerulaitis called his mentor "Mr. Hopman" until the day the wizard of Oz quietly went on to his greater reward in 1985.

Hopman had an eerie ability to identify talent. When he first spotted Rod Laver, the redheaded youngster was firing away, spraying balls over the net, over the baseline, and over the fence surrounding the court. When an observant journalist pointed this out to Hopman, he replied, "No worries, mate. One day every one of those balls will fall inside the court."

The wizard of Oz also knew how to handle talent without caving in to its demands. Young John McEnroe was another protégé, at a time when Hopman ran his "academy" under the auspices of the Port Washington Tennis Club on Long Island, New York. During one close and chaotic junior match, McEnroe began showing flashes of the temper that would eventually come to define him. Conscious of Hopman's strict standards, one of the assistant pros brought McEnroe's antics to Hopman's attention. "Let him be," Hopman decided. "He has so much talent that it would be a shame to break him."

As former touring pro Bob "Nails" Charmichael said, "Hop could look at two eighteen-year-old kids who seemed virtually identical as players and pick out the one who would go on to be a world champion. It was uncanny."

But Hopman's real strength was not in his formidable ability to spot talent, and it most certainly wasn't in his technical or tactical vision of the game. He personified nothing more complicated than the ability to instill in his players remarkable stores of self-discipline, motivation, pride, obedience, and fraternal unselfishness. Most of the champions he developed were country boys who responded to his leadership like true "mates." They were eager recruits listening to an officer on the eve of a battle, back in the days when being a good soldier was considered a distinction.

On the practical side, Hopman's agenda was supported by the Australian Lawn Tennis Federation (the amateur establishment), which still exercised unilateral control of the players' activities. Thus Hopman enjoyed absolute authority over a group of young men who, even if they had been inclined to buck the system, didn't have the power to do so.

Ray Ruffels is a delightful guy who never won a Grand Slam title, so he will always be remembered not as part of the flame that was Australia's golden age but as a wisp of smoke that marked its extinction. As a reserve on one of Hopman's last Davis Cup squads, he remembers the day that Hopman ordered him to squeeze juice out of oranges for the A team. After diligently filling a pitcher, Ruffels brought it to Roy Emerson. The Australian star drank the juice, smacked his lips, and turned to Hopman. "Gee, that was good," he said. "I'd like to have a little more of that." Whereupon Hopman turned and nodded to Ruffels, who then trotted off to squeeze more oranges.

Among the other glamorous jobs reserved for junior members of the Davis Cup squad was the chore of painting everybody's shoes white before a match.

Neale Fraser, the 1960 Wimbledon Champion and the Aussie Davis Cup captain through most of the 1980s, said, "Today you're lucky if you can get one of the guys in a doubles team to do a simple chore for the good of his partner. It's just a different era, mate."

Elitism undoubtedly fostered success and distinction, and its exclusionary nature forecast an end to the party. Critics of the former Australian establishment believe that it fostered an English-style old-boy network that, once out of Hopman's grip, would end up being manned by old boys who didn't know what the hell they were doing.

In late 1992 the former pro John Alexander set his sights on Neale Fraser's job as Davis Cup captain. Alexander passionately believed that after more than a decade at the helm, Fraser had evolved into just another tired administrator doing his job by rote. The Aussies did surprisingly well with limited talent in the 1980s, but that was mostly because Pat Cash was a remarkable competitor and inspirational leader. Once Cash called it quits after a series of debilitating leg and back injuries, the Aussie teams sank back into mediocrity. None of the Aussie players took a stand, but Alexander said what many were thinking when he charged that the team was lousy, poorly selected, and in desperate need of newer, younger leadership. I tend to agree that the job had become a sinecure for Fraser ever since an Australian friend told me of a scene that took place right before a crucial Davis Cup match between Australia and Italy.

When the Australians arrived at the site of the match in Rome, the Italian squad, featuring singles players Adriano Panatta and Paolo Bertolucci, were just finishing practice. My friend asked Fraser if he could do anything to help the Aussies prepare, whereupon Fraser shrugged and said, "No thanks, mate. Just tell me, which bloke is Panatta and which one is Bertolucci?"

Alexander ultimately forced the issue and rallied enough support to bring the matter of the captaincy to a vote within the federation. After some clandestine wheeling and dealing, the establishment squelched Alexander and issued a vote of confidence in Fraser.

Paul McNamee maintains that important coaching jobs in Australia are basically perks reserved for past champions or, at best, good players who were never outspoken critics of the Australian system. But now, most of the top players of the early Open era—such as Laver, Newcombe, Stolle, and Emerson—don't want the job because the pay is low and the old-boy network is deadly. The kids, having grown up professional, are pampered and independent in ways that would drive the old guard nuts. Who needs it? Most of the Australian legends expatriated to the United States for long periods, and in some cases for good. They can stay busy with endorsements, senior tours, resort deals, and fantasy camps.

One of the fine Aussie coaches who believed he was shut out of the system because he wasn't a top player is Bob Brett, a former assistant to and protégé of Hopman. Brett bears a strong resemblance to Hopman, physically and temperamentally. Ironically, Brett sat in the stands with tears welling in his eyes as Boris Becker, the first player he took on as a full-time personal coach, seized the number one world ranking in 1991. Ironically, Becker did it at the Australian Open.

Brett had emigrated from Australia long before that day because he was never taken seriously by the establishment. "I was judged too small and too lacking in weapons to be a top prospect in the great Aussie tradition," he told me. "That left me out in the cold from the start. The interesting thing about that is that the attitude is already a big departure from the Hopman tradition. Mr. Hopman's judgments were subjective, arbitrary, and autocratic. But they were generally spot on.

"You know, Australia is a great country to live in but not to find opportunity in. I had to go to the United States for that, because the system here just didn't have room for someone like me to work my way up."

Like Hopman, Brett may be remembered not just for his record as a coach but as a player on the losing side in the battle for Australia's sporting soul.

Australia's current tennis woes create a vivid portrait of a society that has deep-sixed many of its traditions and plunged unselfconsciously into the post-modern, nuclear-free, Pacific basin age. Many Aussies, even those who were witnesses to the Hopman era, seem to have no use for myths or habits of the old Australia. This becomes clear when you ask them: So what happened?

"We were big fish in a small pond back then," Neale Fraser told me. "Over the years, everybody else slowly caught up."

Barry McMillan, recently the administrator of a massive junior development program for the national tennis association, Tennis Australia, put it this way: "Our golden age was so golden it was almost freakish. It had to end, and it's hard to imagine something like it happening again."

Ray Ruffels, now a coach laboring on behalf of Tennis Australia, was more blunt: "Australians got rich, and tired of being great. The wind just went out of everybody's sails."

Broaching the subject of Australia's former glory these days seems to embarrass rather than fire up its tennis community, to the extent that it often seems Aussies who lived the golden days would just as soon forget them. The transformation in the Australians' attitude toward tennis was vividly clear when the new National Tennis Center opened in 1989. There, in one fell stroke, the tennis establishment rejected and probably betrayed the past in the name of progress.

For most of the modern era, the Australian Open was contested in Melbourne on the grass courts of the Kooyong Club. The private club was comparable to the two main venues of the amateur era, the All-England Lawn Tennis and Croquet Club, also known as Wimbledon, and the West Side Tennis Club, site of the U.S. Open. The continuity was traditional, based on the English model. But for a variety of reasons, Kooyong did not flourish with the advent of Open tennis. Throughout the late 1970s and the early 1980s, the Australian Open steadily declined. With tennis booming worldwide, professional opportunities blossoming everywhere, and the Aussie dynasty in eclipse, most of the top foreign players couldn't be bothered making the long trip Down Under anymore.

Furthermore, the Australian Open was usually played during the Christmas holiday season, which had suddenly become the logical time for top players to take a break from an increasingly crowded schedule. As a result, the winners of the tournament included such modest talents as the Australian Mark Edmondson (1976), Brian Teacher (1980), and Johan Kriek (1981 and 1982).

When it became clear that Australia could no longer beat mother England and the American colonies at their own game, the Australian establishment decided to build the better mousetrap. It went into partnership with the city of Melbourne to create the new National Tennis Center. The new venue featured a rubberized asphalt surface called Rebound Ace, and the showcase of the NTC complex was a state-of-the-art stadium with a retractable roof. By abandoning the grass-court tradition, Australia took away a powerful home-court advantage for its players and overlooked one cardinal rule in tennis: that the mental aspects of the game will almost always be more decisive than the physical ones.

Rod Laver and the other country boys grew up playing on courts of pulverized anthills or compacted dung but had taken to grass courts like ducks to water. Grass looks cushy and soft and it smells great, but it also requires a constant bending and lunging that taxes a body more while stressing it less than other surfaces. Trained by Harry Hopman, the Aussies were often fitter and better prepared for grass-court tennis.

The Aussies were also practitioners of the attacking serve-and-volley game that works best on fast, low-bounce surfaces like grass; if they could serve and volley on crushed dung, they could certainly do so on grass. Besides, they had global athletic vision and recognized that the most important tournaments of all were contested on grass. Like true provincials with something to prove, the Aussies also got a kick out of beating a lot of Yanks and British. Even the string of journeymen players who followed the golden age often became Masters of the Universe on grass, simply because they thought they could. All of these factors helped to create a great grass-court tradition in Australia.

Tennis Australia officials told me that they considered keeping the Australian Open on grass, but it was both outdated and impractical to do so. Actually, that was a euphemistic way of saying that they couldn't afford grass. In order to get the NTC built, Tennis Australia had to go into partnership with a government whose bureaucrats wanted to build a venue that could generate revenue in a variety of ways. What they really wanted was to get in the entertainment business, with the Australian Open featured as one of many big shows.

The sad thing about the NTC is that there isn't a single testament to the golden age of Australian tennis on the premises—nothing comparable to, say, Yankee Stadium's outfield monuments to Lou Gehrig, Babe Ruth, and Joe DiMaggio, or Wimbledon's "Fred Perry" gate, or the retired numbers and divisional championship flags that hang from the rafters of every basketball and hockey arena in the United States.

The halls of the NTC are lined with pictures of people who have played there, but their names aren't Laver, Rosewall, Newcombe, Stolle, or Roche. They're Sting, Ozzie Osbourne, Rod Stewart, Elton John, and Metallica. Granted, the drummer for Metallica is Lars Ullrich, whose father Torben was a gifted and colorful player in the 1950s, but somehow it isn't quite the same.

As a result of this show-business sensibility, the Australian Open has become a spectacle more like a rock concert or a circus than an international athletic event in which Australians play a major role. Watching rather than playing tennis has become the Australian pastime, giving this observation by Donald Horne an aura of prophecy: "They [young Australians] seek more variety. They may be about to turn sport worship upside down, treating outdoor activity as a pleasurable diversion rather than a nation-building institution. They may not care to win the Davis Cup or the [cricket] Tests."

But even before Australia departed from its traditions, another factor began to come into play. While Australians always had a healthy tendency to look askance at people who took themselves or their missions too seriously, they have also developed an ingrained hostility toward individual achievement, a reflex commonly called "the tall poppy syndrome." This willingness to cut down and discredit achievers who towered over their peers helped to ruin the career of the only Aussie champion since the golden age, Pat Cash.

Cash won just one Grand Slam title in his career, but it was a doozy—Wimbledon, in 1987. He was also the runner-up at the Australian Open in 1987 and 1988, and a semifinalist at Wimbledon and the U.S. Open in 1984. In general, he was limited by the lack of a big weapon. Cash was a light heavyweight fighting up, and he often gave the big boys conniptions.

Cash climbed as high as number four in the world rankings (May 1988), but he was also plagued by an assortment of injuries throughout a career characterized by fits and starts, agonizing bouts of rehabilitation (mostly for his chronic back injuries), and long, lonely struggles to work his way back up through the rankings after each layoff. A quick run through his resume suggests that he might have been named not Pat but Job:

1982: Cash wins the junior Wimbledon and U.S. Open titles and is
          runner-up at the junior French Open (on clay, no less).
1983: Cash leads Australia to its first Davis Cup title since 1977.
1984: Cash cracks the top ten after reaching the U.S. Open semifinals
          (he held two match points against Ivan Lendl before losing).

1985: A chronic back injury sidelines Cash for eight months.

1986: Ready to play again, Cash undergoes an emergency appendectomy in London just three weeks before Wimbledon. Nevertheless, he receives a wild card and advances to the quarterfinals. His subsequent leap in the rankings, from number 413 to number 99, is the biggest jump since the computer rankings were adopted in 1973. He also leads Australia to another Davis Cup title.

1987: Cash reaches the final of the Australian Open, and he wins Wimbledon.

1988: Cash reaches the final of the Australian Open again, losing one of the most memorable matches in the history of that event to Mats Wilander, 8–6, in the fifth set.

1989: Cash reaches the fourth round at the Australian Open, then severs his Achilles tendon soon thereafter. His ranking falls to number 368.

1990: Cash, in his first tournament back, wins the doubles title in the Sydney/New South Wales Open with countryman Mark Kratzmann. A month later he is runner-up at the Korean Open, and the following week he wins the singles and doubles titles in Hong Kong. He climbs back to number 113 but never cracks the top 100 again.

There was nothing flukey about Cash's victory at Wimbledon. Although he lacked a heavy serve, he had extraordinary reflexes, the quickness of a cat, and an unrivaled ability to play from the low crouch demanded by grass. His forehand was sometimes shaky, but Cash's ground strokes always had purpose: They were pinpoint placements, creating the impression that he was not hitting a tennis ball as much as throwing darts.

Cash's greatest asset was an invisible muscle, his heart. Like his renowned predecessors, Cash was, in the tabloid patois of Oz, a "true-blue Aussie battler"—a courageous, cool player who feared nobody and played relentless, attacking tennis, come what may. If I had to pick a guy to play a tennis match for my life, I'd consider choosing a healthy Pat Cash, if for no other reason than knowing he wouldn't let my life go without surrendering his in the effort.

Cash won only six titles in his career, and his friend, the former pro Paul McNamee, put that curious statistic into perspective when he told me: "The guy is so much the 'superstar' type that he may find it difficult to find the trigger for his ambition in a typical event. But get him in a big match or a huge tournament, and there's a different Pat Cash out there. The guy thrives on pressure. The more precarious and risky the situation, the more likely it is that Pat will be the guy left standing when the smoke clears."

The essence of Cash's attitude dawned on me in 1986, the year before he won Wimbledon. During an interview I brought up the subject of Wimbledon and asked if he felt he had a good chance to win the tournament someday. His hazel eyes glittered, and he replied in a shrewd, slow drawl: "Every dog has his day, know what I mean, mate?"

I'll always remember that moment fondly, and not just because I subsequently went around predicting that Cash was going to win Wimbledon, and felt like a genius when he did so. The exchange personified Cash as a simple and confident fellow unfazed by the intimidating mystique of Wimbledon—in short, Cash was the vanishing Aussie Everyman. A mate.

The ultimate proof of Cash's Aussie identity was his success as a team player. He led Australia to victory in the preeminent team competitions staged at every age level: the Avennire Cup for under-sixteen players, the Galea Cup for under-seventeens, and, the following year, the prized Davis Cup.

But unlike Laver and company, Cash was not the product of provincial Australia, nor did he embody its conservative values—not even cosmetically. Cash was a thoroughly contemporary rock 'n' roll animal, complete with a shag haircut, assorted earrings, and an abiding contempt for the good manners and personal restraint practiced by his forerunners. He had an unquenchable taste for heavy-metal music and a robust appetite for the nightlife.

A friend of mine once interviewed Cash before a critical Davis Cup match at the Portland, Oregon, hotel where the Australian squad was staying. In the middle of the interview, Cash spotted a young lady who had just walked into the lobby. He winked at my friend and excused himself, claiming that he had a "prior engagement." He collected the young lady and disappeared into the elevator with her. It was his third such "prior engagement" of the day.

If Cash had a fatal flaw as an Aussie, it was the individualism that coexisted with his sense of mateship. The player he most admired was John McEnroe, and the parallels between the two players were striking. Both were Irish Catholic boys who grew up in the suburbs. Their parents, John McEnroe, Sr., and Pat Cash, Sr., were both lawyers who ended up managing their sons. Both players had children out of wedlock, wore diamond-stud earrings, and insisted on abusing electric guitars. But because McEnroe was an American, he got away with it. Cash did not—at least not at home. Although Cash fit the Australian model in the most important ways, he simultaneously stood as the intriguing embodiment of a culture in transition. His nonconformist tendencies, along with his rough edges, disturbed many Aussies. They wanted Cash to be heroic in the manner of Laver, and they refused to acknowledge the extent to which the creation of another Laver had become impossible. They wanted Cash to be a conformist of the kind once created by Harry Hopman, but they did not see how they had rendered such men anachronistic. Even the most "progressive" of Aussies chose to see Cash not as a vivid symbol of the new Australia but as a tall poppy, someone who needed to be cut down to size.

Ironically, Cash's troubles began at the very moment he led Australia to its first Davis Cup title in the post–golden age. Cash won the cup for Australia by defeating Joakim Nystrom of Sweden in the fourth rubber of the 1983 final round, but the conditions surrounding the match were acrimonious. Always a temperamental player, Cash shocked Australians who expected self-disciplined, well-mannered players. Cash bucked the authority of Davis Cup captain Neale Fraser, flouted tennis etiquette, and did nothing to hide his contempt for reporters.

"Pat's problems really became insurmountable at the start of that 1983 Davis Cup tie, with the infamous 'sandwich in the mouth' press conference," the Australian journalist Mark Fogarty once told me. "He had lost the first rubber to Wilander, and then he made the press wait an hour and fifteen minutes before he showed up in the interview room. Then he sat back, put his feet up, and talked with his mouth full. At one point he had little bits of sandwich dribbling out of the corners of his mouth.

"It was so bad that a few people actually left the room. It was truly a shame, because Pat just never understood that everybody was looking for a hero. He was just too young, too uneducated, too inarticulate, too much the product of a different society to know what was going on around him. Basically, he was a very un-Aussie type of guy, a new breed that nobody was accustomed to or prepared to accept. They still wanted Rosewall and Laver and Newcombe. They still wanted it the way it used to be."

Cash was shocked and embittered by the criticism and ridicule heaped on him after Australia's triumph. Taking his cues from the new generation of players rather than his Aussie antecedents, he embarked on a career-long battle against the press and the critics, known in the rough Aussie parlance as "the knockers."

"We had plenty of good players coming up over the years," he told me, ever faithful to his mates. "But the big problem is always the knockers. As soon as a junior gets a little attention, he gets knocked to death. Look at Mark Kratzmann. He's a great player—you just watch how well he'll do in the long run. But when he loses a match, they just knock him. You're never good enough for the knockers. I was lucky, awfully lucky, to make it to the top of the game quickly. I'd hate to have to fight the knockers for years on end. The best part of getting good results for me has had nothing to do with rankings or money or fame. The best part is the relief, the great relief of getting some of the knockers off my back."

But ultimately the "knockers" carried the day, and the final, ugly battle between Cash and his critics took place at the Australian Open early in 1989, in the waning days of Cash's fluctuating career. Cash played Stefan Edberg in an eagerly anticipated fourth-round match that year. Having been a runner-up in Melbourne on two previous occasions and showing good signs of full recovery from his various ailments, Cash seemed ready to make one more serious attempt at his national title.

Unfortunately—and unknown to most observers—Cash had been stricken by gastroenteritis the day before his match with Edberg, and he still felt the effects of the illness when he took the court. Looking listless and sick, Cash succumbed meekly, 6–4, 6–0, 6–2.

Cash arrived at the post-match press conference in an uncommunicative, truculent mood. As the tension in the room mounted, he proudly—and stupidly—refused to offer any explanations or excuses for his lackadaisical performance. In a curious way this represented his allegiance to a cardinal element of the traditional Aussie credo: If you're fit enough to step onto the court, you're fit enough to take a beating without making excuses afterward.

Regrettably, other elements of Cash's performance before the press were not nearly as traditional. Pressed from all sides, and especially by those who could barely disguise their glee at having witnessed the debacle, Cash made two infantile remarks. He said that his apparent listlessness was caused by menstruation. He later amended that and blamed his performance on "the jack," or venereal disease.

The few women in the room were outraged. Their male colleagues also felt insulted. It got ugly, but Cash refused to give an inch. When he finally stood up to go, the reporters all rushed off to describe the match and its appalling aftermath. The result was a three-day media feeding frenzy to rival anything in Australia's voluminous shark lore. Camera crews hunted down Cash, who had gone into seclusion. Psychiatrists, pop and clinical, trotted out grand theories on news and talk shows. Columnists all over Australia reviled Cash, characterizing him as offensive, vulgar, boorish, and an embarrassment to his nation. The tall poppy finally came crashing down, with a sundering of limbs and a massive thud that could be heard throughout Oz.

My own feeling was that while Cash's performance in the interview room had indeed been vulgar and boorish, the press just couldn't have been happier—either because they had the ingredients of a sensational story, or because they relished the opportunity to cut Cash down for good. The bottom line, in my opinion, was that Cash had done nothing unseemly during or immediately after the match in front of the Australian public. He had made an ass out of himself in the interview room, but that was behind closed doors, in an environment where an assembly of professionals might have exercised more judgment and—heaven forbid—even showed a little compassion.

Cash was devastated by that loss. He was obliged to give an interview against his wishes, and he had made a huge mess of it. I didn't think the Australian public cared very much for how Cash got on with the press, but that sorry relationship became the focus of a national firestorm in the last Australian Open in which Pat Cash, the last great Australian player, ever loomed as a contender.

Before I bring the sad saga of Australian tennis to an end, I have to backtrack to a fellow named Mark Kratzmann—the player Cash so hotly defended in his criticism of Australia's abundance of "knockers."

As it turned out, Kratzmann did not become nearly the player that Cash and some others predicted he would, and the reason "Kratzie" never rose above journeyman status may have had a lot to do with attitudes and even delusions fostered in the new Australia, and the way the nation has gone about trying to develop its tennis talent.

Responding to the paucity of tennis players and a general shortfall of gifted Australian athletes in the late 1970s, the Australian government created the Australian Institute of Sport. The job of the AIS was to identify talent and then to whisk it away to a central location in Canberra, where all the technology of sports science and all the accumulated wisdom of the administrators could be brought to bear on the challenge of creating great athletes.

Although the AIS has had some success in other sports, its record in tennis has been dismal. Kratzmann and most of the other Aussie players on the tour in the early 1990s were products of the AIS. They were the elected Aussie tennisjungen, and they seemed to fall victim to the honor. They became "mates" in the institutional sense, judging their progress against that of their peers rather than the world-at-large, moving through the netherworld of the rankings in concert, settling for the role of small poppies in the field of international tennis. Armed with the blessing of the AIS, they were entrenched in the national tennis establishment, lulled into the worst kind of conformity, and good enough to make a nice if undistinguished living.

Australia's failure to produce a new wave of champions despite the proactive role of the AIS triggered a spirited public debate, and one of the secret pleasures of visiting Down Under recently has been the chance to catch up on the dialogue. It has become a curious combination of bloodletting and witch-hunting among Aussies who don't know who they are anymore and disgruntled romantics who remember who they once were.

The great climax in this debate occurred in early 1992 when tennis tour veterans, including Tony Roche and John Alexander, publicly vilified the AIS and its national director of coaching, Denis Colette. The former players questioned the qualifications of Colette, a fifty-year-old academic type whose resume as a player is so modest that, by comparison, Bob Brett is a regular Rod Laver.

In 1992, Colette was at the top of the bureaucratic heap at the AIS. His response to the criticism of Roche and others was to accuse them of never having attended his seminars. It turns out that Colette is a sports science fanatic whose major contribution to the AIS effort was deciding that the key to successful tennis was the "multisegmented forehand," a stroke he identified after extensively studying films of Ivan Lendl. His game plan for an Australian renaissance was to put a multisegmented forehand in the palm of every Aussie junior player.

The controversy over the multisegmented forehand provided me with the final piece of the puzzle, and it left me feeling that I finally knew what was wrong with Australian tennis. Despite all the evidence both in their own nation and abroad, the Aussies somehow came to the conclusion that the development of a tennis player could be institutionalized. This conclusion came naturally in a highly socialistic nation infatuated with "progressive" postnuclear, Pacific basin verities, but the bald truth is that no system has ever created a great tennis player. The "system" that created a bumper crop of Swedish champions in the early 1980s was nothing more than a tennis boom in a nation with a social system that made tennis, and modest amounts of coaching, available to the general population. To wit: Stefan Edberg didn't ride his bicycle to determine his aerobic capacity for some indifferent technician in a lab coat. He rode it to get to the nearest tennis club so that he could play. The beauty of the Swedish "system" was that tennis courts were as available to eager young players as basketball courts or baseball diamonds to American kids.

Likewise, the idea that the great Czech players were produced like so many Frankensteins in some secret, biomechanical lab deep in the woods is patently absurd. The Aussies can't appreciate the extent to which the development of players from eastern Europe was accelerated not by the availability of some sophisticated development system but by the urge to escape a comprehensive sociopolitical one. Players from nations such as Czechoslovakia, Poland, and Romania wanted to escape an environment of scarcity. They wanted to drive cars, wear blue jeans, and eat food that didn't cause terminal flatulence. Becoming world-class, professional tennis players was just one way for the most gifted ones to achieve that.

On the flip side of the socioeconomic spectrum, Boris Becker, Michael Stich, and the other fine German players were the products of an energetic, increasingly prosperous, bourgeois society whose constituents could afford the considerable investment required to provide their children with coaching and court time. And when those players began to show world-class promise, the German tennis federation stepped in, providing opportunities for high-caliber competition and individual help on a case-by-case basis.

The latest wave of American champions, including Jim Courier, Michael Chang, Pete Sampras, and others, rose from the muck and mire of the private sector. In many cases their parents and coaches begged, borrowed, and stole help from anywhere they could get it. The parents of these kids made some extraordinary sacrifices long before the USTA offered them some help.

The funniest thing about all this is that Pat Cash was once recruited by the AIS, too. But he walked away from a free ride at the AIS gulag because of its stifling, conformist atmosphere. This exposed Cash and his family to considerable financial risk, but it also paid off for the Cash family in the form of Pat's Wimbledon title.

The promise of a free lunch can degenerate into an ugly thing. The recent generation of Australian players is not as much a lousy generation as an abandoned and lost one in search of a multisegmented forehand. Which leaves me with one piece of advice for the parents of gifted young tennis players in Oz. Someday a nice gray sedan with government plates might pull into your driveway in Sydney, Wagga Wagga, Adelaide, or Mundiwindi. A pleasant-looking man in a dark suit will get out of the car, carrying a briefcase. He works for the AIS. When he rings your doorbell, don't act like you just won the lottery. In fact, you'd better draw the blinds, stuff the family into the closet, dial 911, and then hide under the bed. He has come for your children, mate.

CHAPTER 2

Ivan Lendl
A Spartan in Babylon

IVAN LENDL, tennis champion, family man, fitness fanatic, and closet spiritualist, has a lot in common with the German shepherd police dogs that he loves to breed. Like his dogs, Lendl has been much respected but rarely loved by anyone outside of his immediate family.

This is too bad, because Lendl is a unique personality lacking only the charisma of a John McEnroe, a Boris Becker, or an Andre Agassi. Instead, he has a fascinating history. It is the story of a boy whose temperament and environment, both cultural and domestic, drove him to excel at tennis with robotic precision.

It is also the story of a youth who overcame his athletic shortcomings to become a great player, and a host of dehumanizing circumstances to become a man of conscience and responsibility. Despite his achievements he was never a darling in Babylon, partly because he still looks grumpy and says "Vimbledon" instead of "Wimbledon."

Like many of my buddies in the media, I, too, was once an enthusiastic Lendl-basher. Frankly, Lendl seemed to deserve it during his early years on the tour, when he was often snotty and cold in a way that reminded me less of a nascent tennis star than one of those thirteen-year-old rocket scientists who knows that he's smarter than everybody else. But back in those days (before 1985), Ivan routinely lost his nerve and choked in big matches. This was a man who lost in three consecutive U.S. Open finals before he won one and whose won-lost record in Grand Slam finals at one point was 1–6. For a while, watching Lendl gag was a popular and entertaining pastime.

Besides, Ivan was a guy whose idea of a good joke was to invite you up to his home in exclusive Greenwich, Connecticut, and then tell you that he was doing it so that he could watch his dogs tear you apart and devour your liver. A guy like that ought to be able to back up that kind of talk in a bar fight, never mind the serene confines of a tennis court.

I took Lendl up on an invitation to visit his home around Christmas in 1991. As a human being I was curious to know how this intelligent but often difficult man had ripened with age. As a journalist I wanted to know how Lendl felt about his adventures in Babylon. And as a dog lover I wanted to meet the shepherds of which he so often and so proudly spoke.

One thing I wouldn't do was put a tennis ball in my pocket at Lendl's request. When Gunther Bresnick, a former coach of Jakob Hlasek and Boris Becker, did that during a visit, Lendl gave his dog Cayden a covert fetch command. Cayden bolted from the margin of the court and pounced on the ball, which was still situated in the front pocket of Bresnick's track suit. I like that kind of humor—provided some other guy is in the track suit at the time.

Ivan was there to meet me just inside the electrically operated security gates surrounding his sixteen-thousand-square-foot stone Georgian mansion. Lendl was flanked by Cayden and another shepherd, Todd, who greeted me with nothing more menacing than a lick of the hand. Ivan's gracious and introverted wife, Samantha, was in the kitchen, occupied by the couple's infant twins, Caroline and Isabelle.

I was given a tour of the house, which had a few distinctly Lendlesque touches: All of the art in the rooms I saw were the work of the brilliant Czech poster artist Mucha. Ivan's legendary single-mindedness obviously was not confined to his tennis career. Ivan and Samantha's bedroom was neat and uncluttered; a few portraits of Samantha were mixed in with pictures of Ivan at various stages of his career. The only trophies on display were replicas of the ones handed out to the singles champions by the Grand Slam tournaments: four from the French Open, three from the U.S. Open, two from the Australian Open, and one . . . well, that was a problem.

"It would be nice to have one from Vimbledon," Lendl said wistfully, alluding to the only major title he had failed to win. He seemed to perceive this problem the way he understood most of the others he has encountered: partly as one of logic or symmetry. "Four, three, two, one. The balance would be perfect, but what can I do?"

Lendl's office was full of technological goodies: a computer at which he mostly played Scrabble against the machine. Fax machines. A Versa-Climber fitness machine standing on a thick sheet of polyethylene to protect the lush carpet from flying sweat, blood, and tears.

The Lendls' grand dining room contained a magnificent table that would easily seat fifteen. But when I remarked that it seemed like a great set-up for throwing dinner parties, Lendl just shrugged. "We don't really entertain," he said. "When we're here, we just go out to eat. Or we eat in the kitchen with the kids."

Top tennis players have the resources to live in a grand style and, at least in the Lendls' case, good taste that translates to elegance rather than ostentatiousness. But the itinerant nature of their lives, their tendency to surround themselves with people who qualify as support staff rather than simple friends, and their own inexperience at nonprofessional life—which includes such high-risk activities as making friends—often leaves them seeming socially uninterested or inept. Unless players make an effort, they end up living in opulent quarantine. Their only real community is the other people in the tour's shifting show, and often their only hedge against the boredom that accompanies being home is the knowledge that in five or eleven days they'll be taking off for London, Melbourne, or Tokyo. You can accuse tennis players of lots of things, but fear of flying isn't one of them.

Many players also shun hobbies that aren't portable or can't be pursued in the confines of a hotel room or on a long flight. Hobbies constitute a serious threat to a player's need to concentrate and remain focused on his pro mission. And everyone around a player obsequiously "understands" and accepts that the only way to approach an evening match is to lay around in a hotel room all day, eating food from room service and watching television. That's why playing electric guitar has become such a popular pastime on the tour: You can pick at the grapes, the remote tuner, and your guitar strings, all without getting up from the couch.

But dedicated, obsessive Ivan Lendl became a dog breeder, and he did so despite having suffered a fairly serious injury from a dog bite when he was a teenager. It was the kind of experience that often leaves people fidophobic. While staying at an apartment in France, Lendl was attacked by a Doberman. The dog took a chunk out of Ivan's thigh, but he nevertheless flew to Barcelona the same day and played in a Europe-versus-USA exhibition match. He had a bitter, three-set struggle with Vitas Gerulaitis, prevailing by 11–9 in the third set. By the end of the match, the heavy bandage on Lendl's leg had soaked through and he was a bloody mess.

Just a few years later, Lendl was busy setting up his own kennel operation. He chose the name "Quantum Kennels" because Lendl wanted his dogs to be quantums, which are "units of bursting energy." Lendl talks about his dogs with characteristic frankness and the kind of icy logic that makes some people shudder. This is how he explained his interest in breeding dogs that he would donate to local police departments: "If a crook running through the bushes shoots a dog, it's sad. But it's still better than having an officer shot. I'm not interested in the profit, but because I like the challenge of breeding a type of dog so special that only eight of a hundred from even the best bloodlines qualify. I want to do it because I love dogs, I want a good supply for myself, and I want to help the police."

Although Lendl has appeared on plenty of magazine covers in his day, he is proudest of the one on a fanzine for dog lovers. The cover shows Lendl with Cayden, perched in a tree eight feet above the ground. Lendl considers Cayden's willingness to climb the tree a sign of the confidence and trust the dog feels for its owner.

Knowing that Lendl is a realist, I couldn't resist asking him what he felt was the difference between people and dogs—other than that it's safer for your health to kiss a dog, and that no dog will ever tell you that the check is in the mail.

"Well, not that much," Lendl replied. "Dogs have personalities just like people. Some are more consistent than others, some are more moody or playful. I had dogs before I had a family, and all of them have been great companions. You need to talk to them, to take care of them, and to play with them. But unlike children, when you get sick of them, you can just say enough and close the door behind you."

Almost every household has an issue that won't go away. In some, it's the amazing inability of the male homo sapien, which is generally blessed with great manual dexterity, to perform a task as simple as washing a dish. In others, it's the indiscriminate conversion of gold cards into revolving debts, or the serial dawn battle over who gets to use the bathroom first. But for Ivan and Samantha Lendl, the issue at the time of my visit was the library.

Ivan was showing off his library, a clubby, dark room with somber wood paneling and elaborately carved mantels, when Samantha joined us. I complimented them on the room, whereupon Samantha frowned and suggested that it was too dark.

"Samantha, a library is for reading and studying," Ivan said in his clipped, hard accent. "The darkness creates a comfortable atmosphere."

"But it can be dark without being grim," Samantha replied—for the umpteenth time, I felt. "It doesn't have to be *Gothic.*"

Samantha left the room, and Ivan described the various classes of books he owned, from hokey golf instruction manuals to handsome leather-bound classics, including some by Czech writers. Then, in a conspiratorial tone, he asked, "Do you want to know where I go when I really want to learn something—where I can find . . . *everything?*"

I scanned the shelves quickly, looking for some ponderous, crumbling volume of *Ars Poetica* or Spengler's *Decline of the West.*

Lendl then pointed to a shelf containing the *Encyclopaedia Britannica.*

"Whenever I want to learn something, I just come over here," Lendl said cheerfully. "The encyclopedia is fantastic. And I bought it from a guy who one day just came to my door."

Imagine that—a guy who just came to the door!

The dynamics of the marital relationship and the challenges of parenthood have been a constant if private theme in Lendl's adult life. And while he appears to be a hard man, he is by no means a thoughtless one.

It may have been Providence that gave Ivan and Samantha Lendl four little girls—at least the veteran Aussie player John Fitzgerald would like to think so. When Fitzgerald's firstborn child turned out to be a girl, Lendl loved to rag him. "You're not man enough to have a boy," Lendl said. "Better try again, girly-man." Having a girl and then two others in one drop shut Lendl up but good.

If you wanted to be cynical about the Lendl family, you could say that having four girls was Samantha Frankel's revenge on Ivan Lendl. She was barely a teenager attending an exclusive Manhattan girls' school when she began dating Lendl, and their subsequent romance was conducted in great secrecy. In public appearances Samantha seemed painfully shy. She was a constant fixture in the players' guest box, elegant and poised, watching her boyfriend and then her husband play with an invariably impassive expression. On one occasion when she left the box to visit the ladies' room, Lendl reportedly chewed her out for abandoning her post.

Such incidents, combined with Samantha's retiring personality, led many critics to perceive her as something of a Stepford wife—a submissive child bride who became the suppressed partner of a domineering, egocentric man. Somehow that never rang true for me. Samantha seemed to prize Lendl's consistency as well as his conventional vision of romantic and domestic life.

The Lendls have a traditional family set-up, but it hasn't prevented them from confronting the issues that inevitably pop up in many marriages. Although Ivan has never had trouble expressing his desires or opinions, he has often found it difficult to express his feelings. And while Samantha graciously accepted a subordinate role in a relationship in which her husband's needs always came first, she was not always willing to air her grievances when they mounted up.

"Samantha's great strength is her flexibility," Lendl told me. "And I don't care if people think that is just a nice way to say that I can push her around. But sometimes people like that don't want to tackle a problem head-on. The important thing is knowing how to say what it is that you want, and then having to deal with the fact that sometimes you want different things.

"It's been tough for Samantha in this American environment, where being a career woman is so popular," Lendl said. "But I would like to give my kids what I know how to do best. Obviously, changing diapers and feeding them is not what I know best. I kid Samantha about this, but the way I see it, the mother takes care of the children when they're babies, and the fathers get more involved when they get old enough to start doing things like sports.

"But the toughest times are probably over, and it will get better if I play less. As a top tennis player, my career had to come before almost everything else. If we had a problem, she had to deal with it. If the baby was sick and crying, I had to close the door to get my rest and leave her with the child. The hard part for me was blocking those things out, and I'm sure the hard part for her was accepting that role because it isn't the best role. Unfortunately, I don't see how it could be any other way for a top player."

The Lendls are equal partners in making decisions about the future of their children, and that's probably a good thing. Lendl knows that he can go overboard on issues such as discipline and behavior. Ivan had always planned to take his children to the Czech Republic one day, just to show them that not every nation was like America. But he also came to realize that such lessons might be lost on them, or on anyone else who had not experienced hardship and deprivation firsthand. Also, Ivan didn't want his children to feel guilty about having grown up in privileged circumstances. He wanted them to feel loved and provided for, to feel lucky without feeling overly indebted. Such considerations have been particularly acute for Lendl because of his own background and formative experiences.

"I promised myself that if I ever forbade my kids from doing something, the reason would never be, 'Because I said so.' I hated it when anybody said that to me. I don't really want to criticize my parents, but I really did come from the school where children were expected to obey their parents like little machines, and I vowed to do things differently. I believe that the best way to make somebody do what you want is to explain the good sense of it."

Samantha Lendl has watched this dialectic play out in her husband with curiosity, wonder, and even amusement. An accomplished equestrienne, a watchful introvert, and a patient wife and mother, she has a good grasp of the conflicts bred by her husband's all-consuming profession, his reflexive rigidity, and his desire to be a warm, loving partner and father. She has helped him resolve those internal disputes, which is why she has been indispensable to him.

But it hasn't been easy. When I got around to talking horses with Samantha, I asked if Ivan shared her passion for them. When she said he didn't, I asked, "Why not?" She smiled benignly, and I felt as if I had asked the dumbest question possible. She said, "He doesn't like them because he can't control them."

Writing about the U.S. Open final of 1985, I tried to create the most honest and accurate internal monologue Ivan Lendl might have conducted with himself when he stepped up to the baseline to serve for the match against John McEnroe:

> You have been Weird Ivan Lendl for too long now, and this is your best chance, perhaps your last chance, to alter that identity. You have been arrogant and cold, but when you stood in this place in the past, the sawdust lying at your feet looked like stuffing leaking out. You have boasted of how fast you drive your Porsche and how strong your dogs are, but you have not been perceived as swift or powerful. Now you stand four points from maturity. You stand four points from becoming a fully realized champion. You stand four points from exoneration, and if you believe that the idea is too simple to be true, you had better pretend to believe otherwise.

That paragraph still sounds harsh, and it still rings true. In light of subsequent events, it even sounds fair. And I wouldn't go back in time and change a word of it because even though I know a lot more about the pride and character of Lendl now than I did then, he had unwittingly dug himself into a pretty deep hole, pretty quickly, after he took the tennis world by storm at age twenty in 1980.

In the four years after 1980, Lendl was considered the most promising and dangerous young player on the tour. But in that stretch, he was the runner-up in four Grand Slam tournaments before he finally won one, the French Open in 1984. And the key feature in that performance was its improbability. John McEnroe led Lendl by two sets and 5–2 in the third before he went ballistic because of the noise created by the motor drive of a photographer's camera in the sideline photo pit. The tantrum proved to be the turning point of the match and the turning point in Lendl's career. Suddenly the man jokingly referred to in the pressroom as "the choking dog" mounted one of the great comebacks of the Open era, in a Grand Slam final against a player who was not only gifted and fearsome, but Lendl's chief rival.

Looking back, Lendl considers this comeback victory over McEnroe something of a fluke, a match he had no right to win. "A lot of it was just plain dumb luck," he told me when he was at the peak of his powers in 1989. "But the good thing that came out of it was that the public began to think of me as a fighter, a potential champion."

All things considered, it would have been easy for Lendl to continue to just take the money and run well beyond the four-year period that ended in 1984. Many other players had done just that, deciding that the challenge of making that final breakthrough just wasn't worth the effort, pain, and sacrifice. Instead, Lendl drew on his reserves of pride and applied logic as if tennis were just another elaborate math problem. He flung himself into cross-training, scientifically designed diet programs, and sports psychology. He performed mental-focus drills with slightly sinister sounding names like "witnessing" and "visualization," administered by a Florida psychologist, Alexis Castori.

Lendl also hired a racket guru by the name of Warren Bosworth to fine-tune his sticks, which had the swing weight of sledgehammers. Soon he was taking a fresh frame right from its plastic wrapper on every ball change during a match. A five-set match that goes the distance without being a titanic battle contains about fifty games, during which Lendl would unsheath a freshly strung and tuned racket at least six times. Lendl used custom-made, super-thin gut strings, which he had Bosworth install at a tension of exactly seventy-two and a half pounds. And when Lendl signed a deal to play with an Adidas frame, his contract stipulated that the company would buy all the molds used to manufacture Lendl's original racket at Kneissel, as well as the rights to work with the engineer who had designed the original frame.

During tournaments, Lendl was so fastidious about his fitness program that he refused to drink anything but pure water. As he put it, "Normal water goes through fastest and comes out cleanest." Besides, Lendl had learned that the body has to work harder on carbonated drinks (including fashionable mineral waters) because the oxygen discharged by the bubbles in the drink takes up valuable space that should be reserved for oxygen generated by normal expansion within the blood.

Still, at one point Lendl had won only one of seven Grand Slam finals. He was working on adding another match in the lost column when he found himself down 2–5 in the first set to McEnroe in the 1985 Flushing Meadow final. Whether or not Lendl actually conducted a monologue similar to the one I created for him is anybody's guess; however, he did step up to win the match, clearing the final hurdle to his ascendancy.

"The year it all came together in my mind was 1985, no matter what anybody says. I have my own truth, both good truth and bad truth, about myself. And I've always gone by that. So even when I began to dominate and people talked about how I thrive on pressure or how tough I am or how systematically I win, I didn't put much stock in it. The fact is, I'm not that different now from ever before. A lot of it was just a question of maturity."

Ultimately, Lendl would win eight Grand Slam titles, one more than his lifelong tormentor, John McEnroe, and the same number as his other major rival, Jimmy Connors. He would contest nineteen Grand Slam finals, appearing in the championship match in at least one of the Big Four tournaments for a solid decade beginning in 1981. Lendl led Czechoslovakia to a Davis Cup victory in 1980, but the lack of a supporting cast and his expatriation to the United States in 1984 prevented him from becoming a great performer in that competition.

Lendl was ranked in the top ten for 13 consecutive years, a streak surpassed only by Connors (16 successive years). He won 94 sanctioned titles in his career, 17 more than McEnroe but 15 fewer than Connors. Between 1985 and 1988, Lendl held the world's number one ranking for 157 consecutive weeks, second only to Connors's 160-week run. But Lendl has spent the most total weeks in the number one position (270 weeks—2 weeks longer than Connors). Thus, he has a legitimate claim to being the top player of the Open era.

The most extraordinary thing about Lendl may be that he can make that claim despite getting off to a slow start and despite conspicuous physical limitations. Lendl was not a great natural talent, and he often appeared awkward and clumsy on the court. If you closed your eyes during a match between McEnroe and Lendl, it was easy to tell which man occupied either side of the court. McEnroe's footfalls were as silent as those of a cat, while Lendl made an astonishing amount of noise—as if he were moving furniture, complete with all the requisite thudding and scraping.

One of the enduring mysteries of tennis is how Lendl managed to retrieve as many balls as he did and then hit penetrating ground strokes or pinpoint passing shots in reply. The only explanation is eye-hand coordination that had nothing to do with his ungainly footwork or his stiff torso. Watching Lendl play was almost an exercise in seeing how a man could hit great strokes and play out complex points in spite of his biophysical profile. I still believe that if he had not learned the game on slow red clay, he never would have become a dominant player.

Lendl's assets were a heavy, consistent serve and abundant power and consistency off both wings on his accurate ground strokes. His forehand was particularly devastating, struck with such timing that the balls appeared to be launched from a slingshot. Lendl's attempts to volley or to serve and volley completely exposed his shortcomings as an athlete. He was neither quick nor flexible enough to win at Wimbledon, and under pressure his volley was always erratic.

And finally, there was Lendl's toughness. It was partly the result of his maniacal conditioning regiment, but some of it was also an innate willingness to suffer and absorb punishment. This capacity was amply demonstrated at the Australian Open after the change to hard courts in 1988. The heat in Melbourne during the tournament is always blistering, and the hard courts sometimes become as hot as skillets underfoot. One year a camera crew broke an egg on a field court, and the thing eventually fried. On other occasions the rubberized asphalt became so tacky that players blew out the side of their shoes or turned ankles on the hot, sticky Rebound Ace.

Lendl thrived under those brutal conditions, making only one concession to the heat: He took to wearing a goofy legionnaire's hat, a funky-looking thing with panels of cloth hanging off the back to protect his neck from the heat. Lendl reached the Australian Open final for three consecutive years (1989–91), winning the title on the first two of those occasions. His performance in 1989 was especially noteworthy. The temperature was 130 degrees and the air was absolutely still when Lendl played his semifinal against the Austrian strongman Thomas Muster. Lendl won the first two sets but then appeared to wilt. Muster won the third set and remained even with Lendl in the fourth until the games reached 5-all. Marshaling his resources, Lendl broke Muster and served out the match.

Afterward, Muster repaired to the trainer's room with blisters the size of silver dollars on the soles of both feet. Lendl staggered into the locker room and spotted a principal in the next semifinal, the Swede Jan Gunnarson.

"Lendl looked like he was dead, he was so pale," Gunnarson said of their meeting. "He looked at me and said, 'Have fun out there. Good luck.' Then he started laughing. He was gone, I mean completely gone. But in a way I think he took pleasure in it. He liked to think of himself as a machine, and that seems accurate. He just changes the oil and keeps going."

Occasionally, the frequent comment that Lendl was an automaton, a high-tech robojock, bothered him, but not that much. He knew all along that part of him was indeed like that, and the best thing he could do was put it to good use and go about building himself one heck of a record as a tennis player, one heck of a nice life.

❖   ❖   ❖

Lendl's own analysis of his career, particularly his early trials, is a little different from that of most critics. Citing the experience of his countrywoman Martina Navratilova, Lendl points out that unlike her, he did not "go to pieces" when he expatriated to the United States. But he also believes that his critics did not appreciate the radical nature of his move to the United States at age twenty.

"I left a repressive, poor country and went to the most liberal, richest one on earth," Ivan told me. "Most of the criticism I got came in the three or four years after I made the move. That was a period when I had to decide where to live and who my friends were going to be. I think I made it look pretty smooth on the top, but on the bottom there were some pretty big storms. Most of the important things that were happening to me were not happening on the tennis court. Everybody thinks I turned my career around when I started to win big matches, but I know that I started to win big matches because I finally turned my life around and got a little settled."

Lendl was born in 1960 in the Czech city of Ostrava, an industrial center whose smokestacks were so busy that folks called it "the black city." Think of it as Gary, Indiana, without football or pickup trucks. At the time, Czechoslovakia was in the apparently terminal grip of the Soviet Union. If the communist system had been just a little bit better at putting food on the table, Lendl might have grown up to be the ideal totalitarian man: cold, efficient, single-minded, and ruthlessly hostile toward open or critical thinking.

Ironically, the lack of essentials such as money, consumer goods, drugs, and MTV ensured that the family was the main source of a child's values or lack of them. For Lendl, this proved to be a mixed blessing. He came from a very close, happy family, but he was simultaneously sheltered and dominated by his mother, Olga Lendlova. She was the second-ranked woman tennis player in Czechoslovakia at one time and also played basketball on the national level. She had great ambitions for her only child and the will to make him do as she pleased. She put a timer on Ivan to make sure he ate the vegetables he so detested. She made him hang up his clothes and wash his dishes every day. When he was a toddler, she put him in a wagon alongside the tennis court. When he invariably tipped the wagon over, she would tether him to a net post. "My Life as a Dog" is not always so different from the more glamorous version, "My Life as a Champion."

When Ivan was a little older, Olga allowed him to be her ballboy. This was a job he enjoyed. It was better than the disciplined exercise of tennis, for which Olga was carefully grooming her son.

"It was always the nicest for me to be with my parents," Ivan told me.

"I really enjoyed being ballboy for my mother, even though she always wanted the same ball when she won a point, and so I would have to run all over the court for it."

Lendl's father, Jiri, was a solid player and a prominent lawyer who went to too many meetings, ate too much sausage, and didn't spend as much time with his only child as Ivan would have liked. As an official in the Czech tennis federation, Jiri Lendl traveled to many tennis tournaments abroad. Whenever he returned from a trip, young Ivan would refuse to go to sleep until his father told him rambling, vivid tales about the great Rod Laver, dashing John Newcombe, or silky Ken Rosewall.

"I used to sit by the window, watching for my dad to come home," Lendl remembered. "If he didn't have to go out to meetings or something, we would play table soccer or hockey. And on a weekend, if there was going to be a big hockey or soccer match on the television, we would play it out first on the dining room table and then watch it together.

"I even went to watch my father play chess, which I guess is kind of boring. But I enjoyed it because most of all I loved family activities. If my mother was playing a match, with my father watching her and me being the ballboy, that was great. I couldn't imagine anything better."

When Ivan was old enough to swing a racket, he played mostly with his father. He would have to earn the right to play with his mother, who beat him every single time they played until Ivan was fourteen years old. She also coached him, which proved to be a disastrous enterprise.

"One of us always ended up in tears," Lendl said. "She because I wouldn't listen, or me because I thought she was being too rough on me. In the end it was the similarity between us rather than the difference that caused all the problems. One part of me told me that my mom really loved me. The other part didn't understand why she was doing certain things. Now I can understand why she was doing certain things. Now I can understand it and accept it as I get older. It was all part of the way she was educating me for tennis."

Lendl's parents continued to give him advice right up to the tail end of his tennis career, often over the intercontinental telephone lines. "Can you believe it?" he once asked me. "Neither of my parents has ever played on grass, and here they are, trying to coach me long distance for Vimbledon."

Finally, Lendl came up with a strategy for dealing with those brainstorming sessions. He would tell his parents to hold on and pass the phone to his coach Tony Roche. The beauty of that approach was that since neither of Lendl's parents speaks English, they would soon grow annoyed and hang up. At other times, Lendl would just set the phone down on the side table, read for a few minutes, and then pick up the receiver and say, "You know, I think you're right about that."

Emerging from this hothouse atmosphere and a brutalized society whose only link to the modern world was its history in happier times, Lendl had a lot of catching up to do. This was a kid who had gotten off the plane on his first trip to Australia and, on seeing the doomsday-sized headlines announcing the murder of pop star John Lennon, asked, "Who is John Lennon?" This was a kid whose first record album was *Chipmunk Punk,* featuring the Chipmunks' interpretation of punk-rock classics.

But Lendl did not lose control when he was set loose in the West with a hefty bank account. He didn't scramble helter-skelter for acceptance with the in-crowd, nor did he tailspin into a horrendous slump. Lendl's only excesses were taking up roller-skating and devotedly watching the popular dadaist television show "That's Incredible."

Carrying a normal load of testosterone and being a budding tennis star to boot, Ivan did discover his appeal to American women. According to a former associate, Lendl's agent, a savvy fellow called Jerry Solomon, would take his protégé to Bloomingdale's where they cruised the cosmetics department and picked up girls. The notorious bank robber Willie Sutton would have appreciated the simple beauty of this strategy. After all, he was the one who, upon being asked why he robbed banks, answered, "Because that's where the money is."

Lendl soon fell under the influence of the former Polish touring pro Wojtek Fibak. Here was a man who could understand and help the naive young boy from Ostrava. The son of a Polish lawyer, Fibak himself had one day packed up a sputtering, lurching Volkswagen and, with his fiancée Eva in tow, set out to become a tennis pro in the West. He accomplished that dream and enjoyed a strikingly successful career, mostly as a doubles player.

Fibak was well educated for a tennis player, and he enjoyed being described as a cultured man with a taste for fine art and mastery of seven languages. He was also shrewd and crafty, a born wheeler-dealer. This did not always sit well with his peers, some of whom held Fibak in contempt. They felt that he traded a little too heavily on his image as a man of culture and worked a little too hard at presenting himself as a consummate sportsman when he was also an accomplished games-man—a player who covertly manipulated and intimidated linesmen and umpires, even while he was winning applause with overt gestures of sportsmanship.

Fibak also had a reputation as a lothario. According to the wife of a fellow pro who happened to be a good friend of mine, Fibak once tried to seduce her. She resisted his aggressive advances, but Fibak pressed on, claiming that everybody knew she slept around. She claims that he accused her of recently having had a torrid affair with an Italian pro. You can imagine her surprise when the name he threw at her was that of one of the few known homosexuals on the men's tour!

After Fibak faded from the pro tour, he became a successful art dealer. He wore snappy designer suits, bought a beautiful Parisian home stuffed with antiques, and became something of a political activist. After the Iron Curtain fell, Fibak became an entrepreneur in the new Europe. All in all, he made himself into a man of the world in some of the best—and worst—senses of the term.

Lendl learned a great deal under Fibak's wing. On the plus side, he stopped wearing the black shoes and gear that made him look less like a tennis player than an exemplary worker in the Socialist People's Union of Dry Wall and Sheet Metal Fabricators. Fibak also introduced Ivan to art and provided him with a surrogate family, complete with an East European sensibility and a cook who whipped up homemade dumplings to help alleviate his homesickness.

On the minus side, Fibak at that time seemed to be an Ion Tiriac wannabe. As the coach of Ilie Nastase and Guillermo Vilas (this was before Tiriac discovered Becker), Tiriac was perceived as a Machiavellian gangster who would stop at nothing to toughen up his protégés and propel them to the top. Fibak talked a good game about helping Lendl become more open and comfortable, but privately he owned up to fueling Lendl's childish desire to project a menacing image.

"Look, everybody is watching to see what Ivan is thinking," Fibak once remarked as we sat together during a match. "Maybe looking so stern, so serious always, is a help. He is not really a close friend to anyone, but that's the way tennis is going today. Just by the way he is, Ivan gets a lot of free points. The guy on the other side knows that if he is at the net and he gives Ivan an easy shot, Ivan will hit him with it, even in the face. Ivan is an intimidator, but fair. I pushed him that way, it's true."

Lendl paid for his own arrogance long before he even knew it existed. No matter what he says about sorting out his life and even his renowned dedication to training, some of the problems he experienced between 1980 and 1984 could be blamed on karma. Interestingly enough, Lendl ultimately severed relations with the two most important influences on his early career: the agent Solomon and the coach Fibak.

After a nice lunch at Lendl's home during my visit to Greenwich, we went to Hartford to watch his beloved Whalers play a hockey game. I'm one of those people who believes that there are only two surefire ways to get to know a person with whom you aren't sleeping. One of them involves huddling together in a foxhole; the other, which is a lot more pleasant, involves spending four hours together in moderate traffic in a sleek Turbo-Porsche. It says here that the real key to world peace and understanding is carpooling.

Reflecting on a lifetime spent in Babylon, Ivan felt that it was poor preparation for life for most players. He recognized the way of life on the pro circuit as a fool's paradise that even in his own time grew more and more lavish and seductive than anyone could imagine.

"We really are pampered, there's no two ways about it," he said. "We get picked up at the airport, the hotel room is taken care of, and if we need something, we just pick up the phone and the tournament people will do it—anything. It isn't just the top guys, either. It's for everybody now. And a lot of them don't realize how that's different from the real world.

"Nothing about tennis except maybe the on-court competition prepares these guys for real life anymore. A good player who also happens to be smart can secure his future with a few good years. That's the plus side. But a lot of these guys get bad advice. They surround themselves with 'yes' men and the kinds of people who are so intimidated or starstruck that they'll tell a guy exactly what he wants to hear just to be able to keep hanging around, or to keep making money off it. In that way you have to sympathize with a good tennis player because nobody is going to read him his rights. If he isn't prepared and willing to take a good, long, hard look at himself, he may never really know what he is all about."

Lendl learned his own lessons painfully, and the price of his ambition can be measured partly in unmade friendships, as well as opinions and attitudes that make him the ultimate example of the tough, archconservative, self-made man. Although he got along well with that consummate sportsman, Stefan Edberg, he has never had dinner with McEnroe, his relationship with Connors has never been anything but cool, and he was always puzzled by the antagonism he sensed in the popular and friendly Boris Becker.

At the same time, Lendl expressed some sympathy for McEnroe and Becker because each of them became a world star at a very young age. In retrospect, Lendl felt lucky that he didn't hit his peak until relatively late in his career. "John and Boris often talked about the pressures of being number one," Lendl mused. "And I'd say they have personality problems that reflect those pressures that came on them so soon. I was much luckier. I can honestly say that I enjoyed my time at the very top. I enjoyed every minute of it."

Lendl made a ton of money in his career, and he invested it wisely. But despite his avowed love of capitalism, he has no wish to become a CEO, or to build an edifice called the "Ivan Lendl Tower." With his love of hockey, his Czech background, and his apprenticeship as a board member of the Hartford Whalers, Lendl would be a natural in the hockey business. But despite the services he has performed as a go-between for Czech players and the National Hockey League, along with the advice he has given many NHL players, he lacks a taste for the business. Lendl had the opportunity to get in on the ground floor when the changing political climate made it possible for the NHL to secure the services of players from the former Soviet Union, but he shied away from the offers. It struck him as an ugly business, a flesh-peddling practice that he likened to the sale of Africans into slavery.

Lendl may not have grand ambitions, but his mania for organization churns away constantly and its fruit can be . . . let's just say amusing. Having to pass some Yugo rolling along at a solid 45 in the fast lane on the Merritt Parkway, he unveiled a traffic-control plan that Rube Goldberg would have admired. Lendl would like to identify drivers and cars in three classes each, corresponding to beginner, intermediate, and expert. The category of the car would be designated by a colored stripe, and drivers would have to qualify through testing and pay through the nose for the higher-class licenses. In this way all those Yugos, Datsuns, and Hyundais with their presumably yellow stripes would have to poke along at under 55 in the slow lane. Meanwhile, a blue-striped Lexus or Taurus could zip along at a happy 65 in the center lane, while red-striped Porsches and Corvettes could burn along at 90 in the fast lane while their owners talked on a cellular phone and sent faxes to Hollywood.

Lendl has a similar plan for gun control, but I'm sure you get the idea.

A knowledgeable tennis fan reading this might nod and say, "Yep, that's our Ivan." But very few people would believe that this same logical and fastidious man would entrust himself to a Filipino faith healer in an effort to find a cure for his chronic shoulder problems. And nobody could be expected to believe that the man performed the surgery successfully without the benefit of anesthetics or a scalpel. Hey, even I find it hard to believe—even though Lendl told me the story in deadly earnest in the locker room of the U.S. Open in 1990.

About fifteen years ago, Tony Roche, who would end up as Lendl's coach, had chronic tennis elbow. When none of the traditional remedies worked, a desperate Roche went to see this faith healer in Baguio City in the Philippines. He swore that the treatment worked, and when he went public with his story, the tabloid newspapers jumped all over it.

Shortly after Lendl lost a marvelous five-set U.S. Open final to Mats

Wilander in 1988, he began to have trouble with his collarbone. An esteemed specialist diagnosed the condition as a muscle problem that would require a layoff of twelve to fourteen months. Unwilling to wait that long, Lendl asked Roche if he would accompany him to Baguio City to visit the same faith healer that had cured his coach.

They found the faith healer, who performed an operation on Lendl without even cutting him open. According to Lendl, the man simply passed his hand over Lendl's shoulder and the skin opened up. The faith healer then removed all sorts of matter and closed the wound with another pass of his hand. When Lendl offered to pay, the healer just asked for a small donation to his church.

When Lendl returned to the United States, he paid a visit to his specialist, Dr. Frank Jobe. He examined the small red scar on Lendl's shoulder and listened to his story. He thought it was an elaborate hoax, but when he probed the wound with an orthoscope, he found Lendl's shoulder in perfect condition. Lendl wound up this unlikely story by saying, "Since then, other people have made videos of the man performing an 'operation.' They can slow down the tape to 1/32 speed and actually see the guy's hand in there, up to the wrist. I can't explain it, but it worked. At least it did for me."

Not long after Lendl's experience, the marvelous Slovak player Miloslav Mecir began to suffer the back problems that would prematurely end his career. Lendl encouraged Mecir to visit the man in Baguio City, and Mecir finally relented. He was in Baguio City when the massive earthquake that devastated the Philippines a few years ago struck, killing thousands and making instant headlines around the world. Watching the news, Lendl saw the remains of the hotel where Mecir was supposedly staying. The place had collapsed, killing most of the people in it. He frantically began calling around to find out if Mecir had survived. "They were some of the toughest hours of my life," Lendl said. "But it turned out that Mecir had changed his plans and gone before the earthquake. He was home, and the only bad part was that he didn't get much relief from the visit."

Despite this thoroughly un-Lendlesque tale, Ivan has little use for alternative medicine, alternative life-styles, or alternative anything else. He's a conservative, and a peculiarly American version of one. It's easy for an American who has been spoiled by a cushy life-style and an education administered by politically correct bozos to scoff at Lendl's high regard for the United States. He really does go around saying things like, "Most Americans don't know how lucky they are, and I wish some of the more loudmouthed critics had gone to live in East Germany for just a few years."

I was once skeptical of Lendl's patriotic fervor for his adopted country. Given his lofty status, it sometimes seemed like a blind rant—the flip side of Martina Navratilova, his countrywoman, broadcasting the entire canon of liberal pieties. But I changed my mind after a curious experience in 1989 on a hot and sultry day in Washington, D.C., thanks to a salesman called Griffin.

At the time I was researching a story on Lendl. I had flown down with him to Washington, D.C., where he was to conduct a clinic as part of his endorsement deal with Hertz. While Ivan exchanged forehands with a bunch of baffled but generally contented and slightly awestruck dynamos from the Hertz marketing force, I wandered out to the parking lot for a smoke. A guy approached me from the haze and humidity across the lot. He was a disheveled sort, with a little Hitleresque mustache and a paunch protruding from a white T-shirt defaced with a stain made by chocolate ice cream. I was surprised when he addressed me by name and introduced himself as the marketing rep for some company or other.

It turned out that citizen Griffin was on the lam from his day job selling ad time on cable TV because he had heard that Lendl was going to be in the area. And he really wanted Lendl to try the product manufactured by the company for which he was moonlighting. Griffin then showed me the product, the Exer-Stik. It was a foot-long piece of pipe with a foam rubber grip at each end. By adjusting the tension and twisting the grips, you could do a variety of wrist and arm strengthening exercises.

Griffin showed me a binder full of ringing endorsements, picked my brain about the potential uses of the product for tennis, and finally asked if I could get him together with Lendl, seeing as how he himself hadn't actually been invited to the Hertz function. This seemed like a good way to see if Lendl was willing to put his money where his mouth was when it came to all those wonderful things he had been saying about entrepreneurial capitalism. I told Griffin that if he sneaked into the locker room right away and waited, he might be able to buttonhole Lendl before lunch.

A few hours later, while Ivan was deep in a schmooze-fest with the Hertz people, Griffin appeared at my side, grinning from ear to ear.

"How'd it go?" I asked.

"Great," he blurted. "Unbelievable. A lot of these celebrity types, they look at me like I'm from Mars or something. Most of them wouldn't give me the time of day. But Lendl was great. Man, he looked me right in the eye, and he listened. I gave him an Exer-Stik, and he put it in his locker and said he was going to try it out. I was so pumped up that I called my wife and said, 'Honey, this Lendl guy, he's okay. He's great. He's a regular dude.'"

At the end of the day Lendl and I went back to the locker room to collect his things. The Exer-Stik was lying on the top shelf of the locker. Lendl grabbed his bags. He was about to slam the door when he saw the Exer-Stik. He briefly examined the object before he shrugged and stashed it in his bag.

"You never know," he said. "It's always worth trying something new and different. And it's always worth giving a guy a break."

Which, of course, is what Ivan Lendl often did not get in his sojourn in Babylon.

CHAPTER 3

Privileges and Perks
in the Global Tennis Community

NDUKA ODIZOR may be a mere pawn on the global board of international pro tennis, but when he returns to his home in Lagos, Nigeria, it is as a chieftan king. The role suits Odizor, a well-spoken, charismatic man with indigo skin and a penchant for wearing colorful embroidered pillbox caps that imbue him with an appropriate aura of royalty.

"Hey, hey, Chief," the baggage handlers and airplane mechanics at Lagos International Airport call out, recognizing Odizor on one of his visits home.

The customs agents also hail the Chief and dramatically, magnanimously wave him through. So does passport control, and when was the last time anybody you know got through that gauntlet without standing for forty minutes in what turns out to be the longest and slowest of eight lines?

In fact, if you travel to Nigeria with Odizor, don't even bother to get a visa because you won't need it. With a broad sweep of his hand, Odizor will part the bureaucratic waters not only for himself but for any of his guests as well. That's something not even Boris Becker or John McEnroe can do for you in his respective homeland.

So what's all this fuss about a guy whose ranking the last time I checked was number 254 on the IBM ATP Tour computer—and still heading south? Only this: At the time, he was the number one player in Nigeria. He was ambassador-at-large to the glamorous world of pro tennis. He was *the chief.*

"It is so nice to live in the USA now," the Chief told me with a world-weary sigh. "It's so nice not to be recognized, not to be bothered."

Indeed. One of the charms of pro tennis is that the pecking order established by the world rankings is not the ultimate yardstick of success or celebrity. The honor of being a nation's top player or the star of a national team such as the Davis Cup or women's Federation Cup teams engenders great social and financial privileges.

By virtue of his top ranking in Nigeria, the Chief was looking at a starting spot in the last Barcelona Olympics. The same could not be said for the American Michael Chang, a former French Open champion and fixture in the world Top Ten. Clearly, there are advantages in being what the top Finnish woman player Petra Thoren described as "a big fish in a leedle lake."

Of course, the conditions vary from leedle lake to leedle lake when it comes time to trade on a top ranking or to obtain endorsements, sponsorships, or guaranteed fees for playing in exhibition matches. It's nice to be a top player from a big nation with a strong tennis tradition. It's gratifying to be the top cat in a tiny but sophisticated nation like Israel, where folks get all fired up when one of their own can go toe-to-toe with the best in the world. It's fun to be a big tennis star in a country where most of the population doesn't even know how to keep score in the game. But you can't beat being a medium-sized fish in a medium-sized lake filled with endorsements and other commercial forage—a France, let's say, or Argentina.

You don't necessarily want to be a Boris Becker in Germany or a Bjorn Borg in Sweden because once you've won a couple of big titles, a lot of people who didn't know a volley from a rally before you came along set themselves up as experts who inevitably expect you to win everything all the time. And when you don't, the press takes you on a sensational roller coaster that plunges from the peaks of adulation to the deepest valleys of contempt, where your struggles are blamed on rampant fornication, drug abuse, flawed character, laziness, or plain old greed. This is called pressure.

It's far more desirable to be, say, Guy Forget of France. As of this writing, Forget has never won a Grand Slam tournament—fortunately for him, no other active French player has, either, not since Yannick Noah triggered a tennis boom by winning at Roland Garros in 1983. However, Forget was the hero of the unforgettable French upset of the USA in the 1991 Davis Cup finals in Lyon, France, and he has won a number of big indoor meetings, a few of them in France. This is called good timing. These triumphs enabled the personable, clean-cut Frenchman to become a multimillionaire and celebrity without having to get down in the big pit and come out triumphant against the likes of Becker or Edberg (although he has beaten the top players occasionally in lesser events or preliminary rounds at Grand Slam tournaments). They also represent the payoff of a good investment many folks had made in Forget long before it was clear that he would do so well.

In the early 1980s, potential sponsors and product manufacturers lavished money on any French player with even a glimmer of talent, with the hope of backing a potential winner. One of the first results of the spend-a-thon was an unfortunate phenomenon that might be called the Tulasne complex, after the French youngster Thierry Tulasne. Here was a kid who, thanks to a few good results when he hit the pro circuit for the first time, raked in over half a million dollars in endorsement guarantees alone. Great things were predicted for Tulasne, and for a while he kept his game at a decent level that enabled him to bank some big bucks in prize money and exhibition fees. But when he began to falter, many French critics charged that he was spoiled, that the money heaped on him had blunted his will, his motivation, and his work ethic.

My own feeling was Tulasne had been a risky investment from the start. The surfeit of topspin in Tulasne's game and his limited physical gifts were obstacles that he wouldn't be able to overcome, no matter how hard he worked. In fact, excessive practice posed a certain danger to his game in that enthusiastic baseliners who rip the ball with heavy topspin often lose both pace and penetration in their mind-bogglingly dull quest for consistency. That's close to what happened to Tulasne—and many others—who believed that the ultimate player was a human backboard. This belief was based on a complete misreading of Bjorn Borg's game, in which swiftness, counter-punching ability, and a willingness to put the ball away when the opportunity presented itself were no less important than consistency. Tulasne was just a kid lucky enough to be standing at the station when the gravy train pulled up. You can hardly hold it against him, but many people did.

Forget was better raw material. He had a lot more firepower and a much more adventurous game than Tulasne. As a top international junior player in 1981, he was positioned much like Tulasne, at the right siding to meet the gravy train. At age sixteen Forget's clothing and shoe contracts alone were worth a guaranteed $100,000, with bonus incentives that amounted potentially to another $30,000. It sounds modest compared to just ten years later when Andre Agassi would be earning a million dollars a month from nontournament sources before he had even won a Grand Slam tournament.

"It was crazy for a kid," Forget admitted. "But it wasn't our fault that we got so much. And it wasn't our fault that some of us didn't make it as far as people expected. The only blame, if anything like that is in order, is on the system. We were products in which businessmen trafficked and speculated."

You could say that Forget was a successful exception in an otherwise vulgar and even harmful bout of money-burning. It did not hurt Forget that he was not only intellectually sophisticated and financially conservative but also armed with the good sense that many of his fellow court rats lacked.

Forget worked hard and lived right, and he finally cracked the top ten in 1991, setting the stage for his Davis Cup heroics and his breakthrough at important tournaments. This was good news to the sponsors who had faith in his measured rise, who in 1993 included Gatorade, Onet (a conglomerate with interests as diverse as industrial cleaning and surveillance), the obligatory deodorant deal, and a racket, shoes, and clothing deal with LaCoste.

Forget could also pull down $35,000 per night for an exhibition, but he made it a policy to restrict himself to four or five of those a year. And two of them were for the charity set up by his friend Yannick Noah, Les Enfants de la Terre.

"A lot of people in France know me," Forget said, "where a lot of Americans never had any idea of who Brad Gilbert was, even though Brad was consistently ranked higher than me. So it should not be surprising that I earned more money than Brad even though my ranking was lower. The amount of money we players make is an issue in France, as it is everywhere else in the world. But once you're honest with yourself and put in all the work, you don't feel guilty about it. I know that I don't, and I don't see why I should."

In wealthy, enthusiastic tennis nations such as France and Germany, well-endowed national tennis federations also act as de facto sponsors. They underwrite travel and coaching for talented juniors, hoping that the goodwill they generate will keep the players coming back to compete in domestic tournaments and to represent their nations in Davis or Federation Cup competition.

Given the money it takes to even attempt to make the cut as a pro player these days, the funding provided by the various national federations is a critical economic factor. This is how the tournament system works in the pro era: Grand Slam tournaments and ATP Tour or WTA Tour events accept players on the basis of their world rankings, which are generated by sophisticated computer programs. The higher a player's ranking, the better his chance of being accepted into the field, or "draw." The only exceptions to that rule are qualifiers and wild cards (more about them later) who can take places held open after the main draw has been filled by the highest-ranked players seeking entry.

A two-week Grand Slam event has a draw of 128, while a typical one-week tour events has a draw of 32. Of those 128 places in a Grand Slam draw, 16 are reserved for qualifiers and 8 for wild cards, leaving 104 places that are filled solely in order of world rankings—rankings that are generated by a complex formula worked out to rate a player's performance over the previous twelve months. Events with smaller draws have proportionately fewer places for qualifiers and wild cards.

Thus, the number seventy-five player in the world is assured of a place in the draw of Wimbledon, but whether or not he is "straight in" in a popular one-week ATP Tour event with a draw of thirty-two is questionable. It all depends on the cutoff number, which is a function of how many players want to play the event and how high their rankings are. During a week when there are two or three tournaments in progress in different parts of the world, the number seventy-five player has a good chance of getting into an event with a draw of thirty-two, even though he is not one of the top thirty-two players in the world. It all depends on how many of the players ranked above him are playing elsewhere or not at all.

So the maximum number of players in any tournament is 128, yet the ATP and WTA tours rank 500 players each, and behind them are thousands of other players who would love to get a shot at playing the pro tour. That's where qualifiers, wild cards, and the plethora of "satellite" circuits and Challenger tournaments come into it. Theoretically, anybody can have a wild card into Wimbledon or the U.S. Open, and that includes you and me. Wild cards are rendered at the discretion of the promoter or tournament director, but they are generally given to promising junior players, aging champions who remain gate attractions despite being in semi or full retirement, and quality players who have lost their rankings because of unusual circumstances such as a long layoff because of injury. The competition for wild cards is fierce. Promoters use them to enhance the marquee value of their events. Player agents wheel and deal with promoters to get them for promising juniors, and each of those parties uses the wild cards as a tool for building credibility with the prodigy and his or her parents.

Qualifying is the real door to the big time for players who do not automatically earn entry into tournaments because their rankings are not high enough. The sixteen places reserved for qualifiers at Grand Slam events go to players who earn the berths in the qualifying event that immediately precedes the tournament. With five hundred players holding official rankings, the qualifying competitions can be fierce, but they enable a player to leapfrog over those ranked above him, right into the big time, if he or she has the game to do so.

For instance, John McEnroe vaulted from the Wimbledon qualifying tournament into the semifinals of the main tournament in three enchanted weeks in June and July of 1977. By virtue of that feat, he never had to play a qualifying event again. Even if he had not backed up his Wimbledon debut with fine performances in subsequent events, he probably would have been granted wild cards for months on end because of the celebrity—and notoriety—he had gained.

One of the most remarkable feats of the pro era was turned in by Andrea Jaeger, a fourteen-year-old prodigy, in 1980. Although she was touted as a future star, even her most ardent supporters could hardly have anticipated her performance during the four weeks in February and March of that year. Jaeger did not have enough computer points to qualify for even the qualifying tournament of the Avon Futures of Las Vegas, a tournament that was part of a mini-circuit designed to feed upcoming players into the main Virginia Slims Tour. So she entered the prequalifying event (her junior record and ranking earned her the opportunity) and ended up winning thirteen consecutive matches (the equivalent of winning two one-week tournaments and reaching the quarterfinals at a third) to take the Las Vegas title.

The victory guaranteed her a place in the draw at the next event on the main tour, the Virginia Slims of Chicago. Jaeger promptly declared that she was turning pro, and she won her first pro match before falling to veteran Kathy Jordan in the second round. The following week in Seattle, Jaeger beat three formidable tour regulars (Rosie Casals, Wendy Turnbull, and Sue Barker) before Tracy Austin stopped her in the semifinals. The feat was a tribute not only to Jaeger but to a system that is truly open and liquid.

Although the system hasn't turned out a Jaeger or a McEnroe recently, it remains pretty much the same with a few noteworthy differences. Today's qualifying events offer tennis as good as anything you're likely to see in the main draw, and most of the time you can go and watch them for free if you want a dose of world-class tennis up close and personal. At the higher levels of tournament play, qualifying events have become overflow tournaments, lacking only the pizzazz created by the presence of the very top players.

There are five levels of pro tournaments for men these days. They are, in descending order of importance, Grand Slam events, followed by four stages of ATP Tour play: the lucrative Championship Series events, World Series tournaments, Challenger events, and Satellite "segments." These consist of five tournaments that offer about $10,000 each in prize money, and the top performers qualify for a Masters-style playoff at the end of each segment where they earn a little more money and all-important computer points.

Most of the lesser pro events also have their own qualifying events to prevent a bottleneck at any level of the system. The USTA and other national federations also stage Satellite- and Challenger-style events, working in conjunction with the ATP Tour to create job opportunities and a flow of players that never seems to end. That's where the support from a national federation or even a private sponsor comes in handy, enabling aspiring players to travel to the far-flung and remote tennis outposts where these tournaments are held. The competition these days is so intense that a gifted young player must travel the world in order to prep his or her game for the big time.

But any German can tell you that there are certain advantages to staying home should a player lose his appetite for knocking around the foothills of the Andes or the plains of central India in search of computer points. That is the Bundesliga, a national club competition that offers no computer points but dangles serious money and outrageous perks in front of recruits. The engine driving the competition is the pride of the individual clubs and the gusto with which they try to put together the best team money can buy in order to lord it over rival clubs. A player can earn close to $100,000 and pull down such perks as a free apartment for year-round use just for representing a club in a total of ten matches. Granted, this might not appeal to an Andre Agassi or a Goran Ivanisevic, but it's an awfully nice way for journeyman players of any nationality to spend the summer in one place without suffering a loss of income or worrying about how a loss might affect their computer rankings.

Players in Western nations driven by market economies do a brisk business trading on their celebrity, but the same does not apply to socialistic or Third World nations, even those such as India that have a solid tennis tradition. India's Ramesh Krishnan has been a quarterfinalist at both the U.S. Open and Wimbledon, and he comes from a distinguished tennis lineage: His father, Ramanthan, was a Wimbledon semifinalist in 1960 and 1961. You would think that being a well-known pro and the best tennis player in a nation of millions would present unlimited opportunities, but it isn't so, not by a long shot.

"My name is much more of a calling card for expatriated Indians in other countries than it is at home," Krishnan told me. "You see, the idea of sports as a business hasn't really caught on at home. For me, earning $2,000 for doing a television commercial that runs for an entire year is rather a big deal. And our currency restrictions make it a nightmare to try to put on exhibitions of any kind. I have just one sponsorship even though I've been a top twenty player. That deal is with Air India, and they don't even pay me. They just let me travel for free."

Of course, two grand in India buys a whole lot of curry, rice, and poori, so sometimes it really is relative. But contrast Krishnan's opportunities with those of Catherine Tanvier, a French woman who never

got past the fourth round at a Grand Slam tournament and who was
never ranked higher than number twenty in the world. But she did hold
the top domestic ranking in France at one point some years ago, and she
has dined out on it often.

Tanvier still has more than fifteen endorsement deals as well as two
"patch" deals that alone generate $40,000 a year plus bonuses. Patch
deals were the hottest thing going in the late 1980s when enterprising
sponsors and agents figured out that because the patches were sewn on
a player's sleeve, there was no way for a still or television camera to
avoid showing them. Although the ATP and the WTA have regulations
to control the size and placement of patches—presumably so that
nobody will confuse a real, live tennis player with a stock car that has
beer and chewing tobacco decals all over it—they do tend to proliferate.

My favorite patch was the one Derrick Rostagno wore during the
U.S. Open of 1991. It said simply MORENO, but it got plenty of exposure when the handsome Rostagno, a supremely casual player and colorful character, upset the Wimbledon champion Michael Stich.
Something about the patch looked weird, so I went up to Rostagno to
have a closer look at it after his official postmatch press conference. The
thing looked as if it was cut out of an old sheet, and it was obviously
handwritten with Magic Marker in a forced, scrawly script. "I made it
myself because Moreno's the best Italian restaurant in New York," Rostagno explained. "I just did it because I like the place so much. I didn't
ask them for a dime, either."

For those players who lack the flair of a pasta packer like Rostagno,
patch deals can bring in considerably more than a dime. A Sampras or
an Agassi can earn more than a quarter of a million dollars annually
from a patch deal, and up to half a million if the deal includes TV or
print advertisements and appearances.

The glory and potential payout offered by official team championships sponsored by national federations (Davis Cup and Federation
Cup, among others) has led to all kinds of shenanigans in the pro era.
Over the last decade we've seen a lot of people who qualify as "Cup
sluts," players who have exploited loopholes in the qualification and
residency rules to play for countries that can hardly qualify as their
own, no matter what the passports, birth certificates, or tax returns say.

Cup sluts have their own grand tradition in tennis dating back to the
time when a Czech Wimbledon champion, Jaroslov Drobny, expatriated to England and then a few chapters later ended up playing for the
Davis Cup for Egypt. Marty Mulligan, a talented Australian player at a
time when mere talent wasn't nearly good enough, left Oz and set up
shop in Italy where his maternal lineage promptly won him a place on

the Davis Cup squad. More recently, Francisco Gonzales of Puerto Rico represented Paraguay in the Davis Cup, and Eduardo Masso, an Argentine, is the big star of the Belgian Davis Cup squad.

Gigi Fernandez, another Puerto Rican, moved to the USA a long time ago. She was put under considerable pressure to represent Puerto Rico in the Federation Cup and even the Olympics, but she had a unique problem. She was a marvelous doubles player but an erratic performer in singles. It is unlikely that she would have brought Puerto Rico any glory in singles, and there wasn't another Puerto Rican woman player good enough to bring out the best of Fernandez in doubles. Consequently, she has always played doubles for the high-profile, well-compensated American teams that dominate international women's competition.

Matt Doyle, a former Ivy League player and, briefly, journeyman on the pro tour, put his sentiment where his mouth was and found a way to finagle himself into a place on the Irish Davis Cup team. This generated a fair amount of visibility for Doyle when an American team, led by another wild Irish boy by the name of John Patrick McEnroe, hit ye olde sod. Doyle became the ersatz master of ceremonies at that event, a condition that created some interesting situations. Emboldened by Guinness stout and an acquaintance with McEnroe, Doyle knocked on the door of McEnroe's room late at night on the eve that the match was to begin in Dublin. A sleepy McEnroe opened the door, and Doyle staggered in. As McEnroe told it: "Matt was kind of wasted from some party, and for a while he just stood there, rocking back and forth, smelling like a brewery. He finally came out and asked me to give him a racket or a pair of shorts or something for a charity auction. The whole thing was kind of funny. He was all sentimental about Ireland and all this other stuff that I wasn't really into myself. Of course, I was happy to give him what he wanted. It was still bizarre, to say the least, to think that the next day I'd have to play this other American guy in a 'big' Davis Cup match. It was all kind of a farce."

Playing in the Davis Cup competition for your country—or even somebody else's country—is still both a privilege and a thrill. Call it the Jamaican bobsled team phenomenon: Whether you win, lose, or get crushed like a bug has nothing to do with it. Not that many people can claim to have played in Davis Cup competition, and being one who can gives you a certain cachet at cocktail parties, in a boardroom, or when you're down on your knees before a bank mortgage officer.

The level of remuneration fluctuates wildly for players pressed into national service on tennis courts. When Jim Pugh and Rich Leach teamed up to play doubles for the USA's successful 1990 Davis Cup campaign, they walked away from the series with $210,000 each from guarantees and profit-sharing. On the other hand, if the key issue in this competition were money, the powerhouse Swedish teams of the 1980s never would have existed, much less won the Cup several times. Mats Wilander and Stefan Edberg were paid little, and it speaks well of them that they didn't just tell their federation to take a hike when they got a look at the offering.

"If I play and win two singles matches through all four rounds it takes to win the Cup, I get a grand total of $25,000 for those eight victories," Edberg told me in 1991. "That's less than I can make in a one-night exhibition tournament, for more victories than it takes to win Wimbledon, and more time than it takes to win *two* Grand Slam tournaments. But I'm not complaining. I believe in playing for my country and in supporting my federation."

All of this provides some consolation for Nigeria's Nduka Odizor, who ruefully told me, "The Davis Cup is just chicken change for me, but I suppose that if this is also so for Stefan Edberg, I can hardly complain very much. I only get $500 or $700 for a tie, and it isn't often that we last long enough to play more than one of them. In my situation, it's probably better for me if we don't win our first tie because then we don't have to play again. But in reality I am happy to win for Nigeria, even for such amounts, on any occasion. But what does bother me is the totally amateur attitude of our association. They just tell me to be in Cairo for a tie, and I have to book my own flight and then fight to get reimbursed for it. In fact, the Davis Cup costs me money. I'm still waiting to get my money back for a flight I paid to Vienna some years ago."

So while the Chief may be able to stroll through metal detectors without removing the fingernail clippers from his pockets, while he can grin broadly and wave at the customs agents without breaking stride on his way out of the terminal, he, too, has to suck it up when the smiling man from the Nigerian Tennis Federation says, "Don't worry, Chief. The check is in the mail."

It's awfully difficult to dislike the sweet, albeit sometimes gloomy, Bulgarian, Manuela Maleeva-Fragniere. But if anybody could whip up a resentment of her, it would have to be Emanuela Zardo. Who? you ask. Precisely my point.

"When I was a little girl, the thing I most wanted was to be number one in Switzerland," said Zardo, who, at five feet four inches and 111 pounds can still be said to be a little girl. "But when Manuela married a Swiss man and moved here, my hopes became impossible. I don't really know what the Swiss people think, but I imagine they're happy. In

Manuela they have an international star. Our federation team now has a chance to win against many other good teams, and she makes tennis more popular, which helps the rest of us who are trying to make our way as international players."

At the time we spoke, Zardo had modest endorsement contracts with Adidas and Head. Although she knew that she would be worth more as the number one player in wealthy Switzerland, her real earning potential was still dampened by her modest world ranking of 31.

The Swiss federation helped to develop and support Zardo by paying some of her expenses, picking up the tab for her practice sessions at the National Tennis Center in Berne, and underwriting the coaching she received from the Swedish expatriate Roy Sjogren. In exchange, Zardo had to be available for Federation Cup competition, the Swiss national championships (winner's prize: $2,000), Queens Cup (a Europe-only version of the Federation Cup), and any sanctioned domestic tournaments for which she qualified by virtue of ranking.

"Sure, Emanuela would get more money from contracts if she were the Swiss number one," Sjogren said, "but with Manuela playing Federation Cup, Zardo gets more prize money because the team does better. She is also more recognizable because of Manuela's impact on the popularity of the game. I think it evens out."

It may have evened out financially, but Zardo will never be able to tell her grandchildren that she was recognized as the best player from her country, nor could she hope to attain much celebrity in the long shadow cast by Maleeva-Fragnieri. She had to be content with a profile that is high only in her hometown of Giubasco, where she couldn't take a stroll in the street without being recognized. Nor could anyone else, for that matter, in the sleepy mountain village of seven thousand.

Manuela Maleeva-Fragnieri's romantic defection to Switzerland not only stole Zardo's thunder but left her younger sister Katerina Maleeva at both ends of a good-news, bad-news joke—namely, that Katerina had a chance to be number one, but got it at the worst of all times—when Bulgaria had no economy to speak of.

And if any of you budding pros out there are thinking that on the strength of your relation to some third cousin in Kibutsky you might move to Bulgaria and be number one in the event Katerina breaks a leg or retires, forget about it. Sister number three of the marvelous Maleeva family—Magdalena Maleeva—was waiting patiently in the wings to take over from Katerina when her time came. The Maleevas are a unique and often overlooked family: At one point all three of them were in the world's top ten.

Katerina Maleeva told me it meant nothing to her to become number one in Bulgaria, which was an understandable attitude for a girl who was not even number one in her own family. But there were other reasons as well, all of them related to Bulgaria. The Maleevas were closet anti-communists who were utterly repelled by the corruption and misery that characterized life in their homeland.

"We always stayed out of the system when I was growing up because it's so bad, and everyone at the time was involved with the government," Katerina said. "But it wasn't a situation where the federation could help a little, because they had no money. And also my mother was very, very careful about asking them for anything but the right to travel and to try to play on the tour. The less we had to do with the federation, the happier we were."

Conditions in Bulgaria were so bad recently that Katerina considered her own quest for success in tennis a trivial matter compared to the battle her fellow Bulgarians fought for everyday survival. Nevertheless, she would ritually return home even in the worst of times, to the streets without electric light, the dilapidated houses, the sausages made of grease and gristle. The level of suffering in Bulgaria was so high while the Maleevas were perched atop the tennis rankings that they lived the opposite experience of most people from minor nations where international success is a ticket to domestic stardom. Most Bulgarians didn't even recognize the Maleevas, and when they did, they couldn't be bothered acknowledging them.

Katerina remembered one month in 1992 when food was in such short supply that the "official" ration per person per month was six eggs, one kilo of sugar, one liter of cooking oil (made from a substance that she couldn't identify), one kilo of cheese, and five hundred grams of butter.

"For people living with that, our good fortune as tennis players was unbelievable," Katerina told me. "And I mean literally unbelievable. They could not even imagine how good our lives were. In my country there was only one way to have money—by cheating. And people still can't imagine having money from actually working. So most people thought that what success we had came because we were clever enough to find some way to steal money, or from privileges. Tennis had nothing to do with it."

Yet Katerina always refused to take advantage of any privilege extended to her because of her celebrity. When she went to the store, she took her place at the end of the inevitable long line, despite offers to have her whisked to the front. If she went to a local tennis club, she would calmly wait her turn for a meager allotment of court time. And when Katerina visited home, she made it a habit to drive the family car, a Russian-made Lada, despite the Mitsubishi her sister Manuela had won in Tokyo and presented to her parents.

There are no severe shortages in England, but, surprisingly, there isn't much opportunity, either, for the flower of England's tennis youth. Although the Brits have the greatest tennis tournament on earth, Wimbledon, they have produced very few successful players in the Open era. As a result, many Brits see their tennis players as a bunch of lazy, incompetent sods standing on the dole queue of the game. The state of tennis in England is so awful and the debate over it so hilarious that I'll take a closer look at it in another chapter. For now, let's just say that the state of English tennis is such that their top players through the 1980s, Jeremy Bates and Jo Durie, struggled to stay in the world's top one hundred. This condition caused Durie some embarrassment when she pulled up to a stoplight in her Vauxhall automobile and the folks in the next lane craned their necks to read the following message on the door of the car: JO DURIE, BRITAIN'S NUMBER ONE TENNIS STAR.

"Sure, I felt funny," Durie told me, "but then, it was a free car."

The British have no players, but they have Wimbledon, a year-round industry and point of public fascination that ensures a massive British press presence. Right now, somewhere in the world, some English hack is busy putting together a story that will draw its credibility partly, if not wholly, from the fact that it has something to do with Wimbledon. One side effect of this is that the likes of Durie and Bates get more press coverage than some Top 10 performers from other nations. The key word here is coverage—not respect or encouragement or even sympathy.

The prime tormentors are notorious tabloids such as London's *Sun*, a rag that features women clad in cheap nylon teddies, or sometimes nothing at all, on the famous Page Three. The *Sun* devotes the rest of its space to elaborate search-and-destroy missions, targeting everyone from prominent politicians to football hooligans. While there's something to be said for a paper that ridicules philandering MPs in a strikingly appropriate, vulgar way and publicly humiliates bubbleheaded royals like Sarah Ferguson, it isn't very much.

But you won't convince Durie or Bates of even that. When they won the Wimbledon mixed doubles title in 1987, the win was one of the woefully few high points for British tennis in the Open era. The *Sun* chose to celebrate by devoting its back page to a picture of Durie with a fake tape measure superimposed on her waist. The paper dubbed her "Roly-Poly Jo." They also observed the great English journalistic tradition of fabricating a quote to go along with the picture, alleging that Bates declared, "I shan't play with Jo again unless she sheds two stone."

"It's a very, very sick situation," Bates told me, "so don't ask me about commercial support. British players don't even get coaching or moral support. All we get is a routine rubbishing by a barbaric press."

Life is a lot easier for the top players farther south in sunny, happy-go-lucky Portugal where two equally talented pros, Nuno Marques and Joao Cunha-Silva, both placed in the world's top one hundred in the early 1990s. Their relation to the domestic press was educational rather than confrontational, and after matches their formal "interview" often consisted of instructing the Portuguese pencils in both the nuances and the basics of tennis. "The press is ignorant," Marques said. "You feel lucky if the guy knows that if you miss your first serve, you automatically get a second one."

If Marques does eventually crack the world's top fifty, he will qualify as an official national sports hero. And the folks at BMW might actually give him a splendid 325i sports sedan instead of just letting him drive one for a while.

It is for just such reasons that Petra Thoren was content to be a big fish in a "leedle" lake. Make that a pond. Actually, a pothole may be more apt. Like Marques and Cunha-Silva, Thoren barely cracked the top one hundred. But that was enough to land her contracts with Canon, Mazda, the manufacturer of candy called Chymos ("They are good," she claimed, "maybe a little too good for my ranking"), and the big daddy of common Finn products, the scissors-maker Fiskars.

As we all know, free is tough. Deep discount is easier, and the players are well aware of it. Sure, there's something cheesy about telling a player that you respect him enough to "knock a little something off" because he knows that it really means, if you were a little more famous, we might give it to you for free. But being offered a deep discount by anyone other than the guy walking down your street at night with a television on his shoulder is flattering and seductive, even though most tennis pros can afford almost anything anybody bothers to manufacture short of a Stealth bomber. On big-ticket items such as, say, a Porsche, a deep discount works out to five figures, as the Italian Rafaella Reggi happily discovered. Mercedes is another car company that has offered deep discounts to those pros who play in the events they sponsor. The same goes for Volvo, which at one point engaged a pro player as an on-tour salesman who happily took orders for cars from his buddies.

"I would never go into a shop and say, 'Hi, I'm Sabine Appelmans. I want a discount,'" Belgium's number one female player told me. "But if they offered it, I wouldn't say no. I went to buy a Gucci watch not long ago, and the lady recognized me. She knocked off one hundred U.S. dollars from the price. That's good, no?"

It's good, but it's even better when you come from a place where the ability to negotiate is considered a gift, not a character flaw. Amos Mansdorf, who was probably the most famous athlete in Israel in the late 1980s, always had a few irons in the fire. At various times he endorsed orange juice, men's clothing, and Gali shoes. He was routinely invited to play with all kinds of tennis nuts, including the former Israeli minister of defense, Itzak Rabin, and various wealthy Israelis who make up the hardcore tennis establishment of about two thousand people. The schmoozing paid off.

"If I play doubles with some car dealer guy," Mansdorf said, "I usually get a little break on a car. That's just how it goes. Israel is a place where you're always making deals, but that can hurt you, too. Some people don't care if you're a big tennis player, they'll try to rip you off anyway. But basically I have it good. In the USA being number ten in the world doesn't do that much for you. But in Israel, people want to associate with me even though my ranking wasn't nearly that high. I get good tables in the best restaurants. In Israel, the word "Mansdorf" means success."

Which brings us back to Nigeria's Nduka Odizor. The Chief grew up playing barefoot and subsisting on one meal a day. He was, in his own words, "a ghetto child," and that was at a time when a can of tennis balls in Nigeria cost about $15. The funny thing about privileges, perks, and even deep discounts is that they are usually wasted on the rich, as youth is wasted on the young, so it's nice to hear about a guy like the Chief who came from hunger and appreciates his charmed life. "I take a religious point of view," Odizor said. "I believe God aligned it so that I would have an opportunity. I have no other explanation to offer."

The Chief was spotted as a teenager in Lagos by a professor at the University of Houston who sponsored him as an exchange student. Odizor was a tennis all-American in 1976, 1980, and 1981, and he reached the semifinals of both the singles and doubles at the 1981 NCAA championships. Odizor also ran track and competed in the long jump, all of which earned him honors as the University of Houston's Athlete of the Year in 1981. The Chief also earned degrees in international marketing and finance, but he planned to spend his future not on the floor of some money market but in the pulpit of a church, either in the United States or Nigeria.

"In my heart I feel first of all Nigerian," he said. "Because of my education, I am a member of the elite in a country where education equals status. I also speak three of the five native languages, which means that

I can speak one thousand different dialects [a claim that even the cultured Pole Fibak would be hard put to make!]. If I am conducting business, I don't have to bribe a clerk to carry the papers from one office to the next. I have been offered handsome sums to leave Nigeria and play Davis Cup for some other countries, but I would never do that.

"Everybody at home wants a piece of my time, and if I don't give it, they decide that I'm a spoiled brat. Some people at my club in Lagos have concluded also that I am a snob because I don't associate with them. But the truth of this position is that I have problems of conscience associating with some of them because of the way they conduct their affairs."

The Chief paused to reflect.

"It's all relative, I know that. Some people might look at my world ranking, somewhere around 200, and think, 'How can this guy feel successful?' But I was a boy who went to sleep hungry many nights, and now I can eat lobster, steak, or salad every night if I choose. In Nigeria, I never even saw salad."

CHAPTER 4

The Gals of Babylon, Part One

IF YOU HAVE A PROBLEM with the title of this chapter because it sounds like some awful *Playboy* magazine pictorial that makes you think of heavy lip gloss and women called Sherri and Tanya wearing just cowboy boots, then you've missed my point—but not by much.

These days we aren't supposed to call women "girls," but the so-called women's tour has become an entity featuring mostly female adolescents—youths, children, kids . . . *girls*. Sure, there are always a few adult warhorses knocking around, but their longevity proved one thing above all else: Only exceptionally talented female players are able to hang in there and play pro tennis until they actually reach an age when they can choose, understand, and appreciate what they do.

The adultification of children has been an ongoing theme in the pro era of tennis, but it wasn't really brought home in a tidy package for me until the Lipton International Players' Championships in Key Biscayne in 1991.

Saturday, March 16, turned out to be a perfect afternoon for a game of tennis. The sun was so strong that even the shadows looked like solid objects. Inside the stadium, a crowd of twelve thousand looked like some restless pointillist painting consisting of fluorescent dots, fluorescent being the color of choice for tennis wear and accessories in the early 1990s.

After twenty years of women's professional tennis it had come down to this: The women's final was being contested by two girls whose cumulative age made them just three years older than Evonne Goolagong Cawley was when she won her last Wimbledon title. One of the finalists was a slender girl of seventeen from Yugoslavia, Monica Seles. The other player was raw-boned and ponderous, a devout fan of

Bart Simpson, and a millionaire a few times over at age fourteen, Jennifer Capriati.

The way that any of us plays tennis tells a little, and often a lot, about our personalities. And these girls played the game as it were some kind of growing pain. They lashed out at every ball with shots that were more like roundhouse punches thrown in a bar fight, and they punctuated their efforts with an assortment of mighty grunts, sighs, and shrieks.

The match was very, very close. On the other hand, it wasn't very good—at least not in the technical sense. A good tennis match has a plot that is spontaneously created by the clash of two players who have different skills and personalities. There's an ebb and flow to a good match, conflicts and resolutions determined by the skill, or will, of the participants, played out against a backdrop of shot variety and selection. At its best, a good match is like a tightly plotted novel: You traipse merrily along from the mutilated corpse to the breathless blonde to the tough-but-honest cop to the car chase . . .

The basic problem with the Seles-Capriati match was that there was no plot; it was all car chase. This was most easily explained by the youth of the participants. Their struggle was a series of points that were equally meaningful—and thus equally meaningless—played out with unmodulated aggression, at an astonishing level of competence, without imagination. You know how it is when kids go at it. Oh, there was a brutal majesty about that match. That's one of the reasons I remember it so clearly. In a way it was like those first few murky feet of film shot on the night in 1991 when the allies began to bomb Baghdad. Call me a cynic if you like, but a certain amount of firepower will impress anybody.

After the girls split sets and maintained the helter-skelter pace through the early stages of the third set, the fans grew frenzied. Gray-haired, paunchy men in short pants hooted and hollered. Women who wore more ostentatious jewelry than clothing clapped and leaped to their feet, screaming out, "Go, Jen. . . . Wooooooo," or, "Do it, Monica."

The air on the floor of the stadium was dead still. The outside temperature had long since edged over the one hundred-degree mark. Inevitably, Capriati and Seles got involved in yet another atomic rally. Each girl was pulled full stretch a few times before the point ended with Capriati making a futile, headlong dash after another Seles winner. The stadium erupted again.

The dejected fourteen-year-old retreated to the scant shade offered by the wall of the baseline grandstand. She was sweating heavily, gasping for air, staring off into space. My reporter buddies were scribbling furiously. I glanced over at the players' guest box where Capriati's parents, Denise and Stefano, were having a hard time observing the unspoken proscription against cheering too vociferously. When Jennifer looked toward them, Denise clenched her fists and hissed encouragement.

Suddenly the unthinkable flashed through my mind: *What if Capriati dies out there?* What if this goofball kid's big young heart just explodes because it's too hot and too tense and too damned tough out there? It may sound melodramatic, but it happens to young race horses and certain breeds of dog. It periodically happens to some high school boy during football practice in the September heat. Like many healthy young animals, fourteen-year-olds are blissfully unaware of their own mortality.

Fortunately, no such tragedy occurred, but I'm pretty sure that it could have, effectively killing women's tennis for decades. We reporters, so busy reveling in the drama and tension of a match, so accustomed to a string of ever-younger prodigies, would suddenly find ourselves trying to sort out just how such an awful event could have occurred and what it said about us and our culture. Then most of us would have tried to piece together the explanation by interviewing all the parties who could be held responsible for Capriati and Seles having been on that court on that day, when most other kids of their age were frolicking by a swimming pool or just hanging around, in no mortal danger from anything save boredom.

The chain of accountability lay there, and it handily defines just what women's professional tennis has become two decades after the floodgates were thrown open. It is the story of ambitious and often avaricious parents, tough agents who accept a cut but not responsibility, marketing forces, and the public's apparently unslakable thirst for novelty and celebrity. It is both a perfect example of free market forces at work and an indictment of the process.

Stefano Capriati and Karolj Seles, the fathers of Jennifer and Monica, represented a new breed in tennis. Up through the early part of the Open era, when young women played on the pro tennis tour, they were most often chaperoned by their mothers. This was true of Chris Evert and Tracy Austin as well as such lesser lights as Barbara Potter and Bettina Bunge. But as the stakes in professional teens rose, a new breed emerged on the women's tour to supplant the traditional stage mother: the scary, aggressive tennis dad.

There had always been a few maniacal tennis dads around. Back when Dick Stockton and Harold Solomon were promising juniors, their fathers once got into a fistfight while the boys were playing a match. But generally fathers remained breadwinners and mothers handled the logistics of organized athletics.

This tradition was shattered dramatically as tennis grew. Sniffing big money and celebrity, many men abandoned their own careers and decided to roll the dice on their daughters' potential. For instance, Mary Pierce's father Jim sold his home, packed his family into the Cadillac, and set out on a road intended to make his daughter a champion. There was a curious testosterone factor implicit in this role reversal, as if the new breed of tennis father were saying to his wife, "Honey, this job is too big and too rough to be left in the hands of a woman. I'm taking over from here."

As the 1990s began, Stefano Capriati stood as the state-of-the-art example of this phenomenon, and his biography personifies many distinct and even radical changes in the role of parents in the pro era. These are the basic facts: Stefano Capriati is an Italian immigrant who, when asked about his past, says he played pro soccer and worked in real estate. He met his American wife, Denise, a former flight attendant, while she was lounging beside a swimming pool in Spain. When their firstborn, Jennifer, began to show signs of prodigy at age eight, Stefano became her manager.

Society is simultaneously envious of and curious about anyone who gets rich and famous, even at one remove. Thus, being the proud albeit unemployed father of a tennis prodigy is not only legitimate but it's a ticket to minor celebrity. And within the closed society of tennis, starstruck functionaries, cynical agents, and even the conscientious damage-control specialists who really do have the best interest of the kids at heart treat tennis fathers with the deference due a pasha. This does not prevent any of them from telling exquisite horror stories about the selfsame men.

Tennis fathers also have proliferated because, unlike almost any other industry (including the "progressive" film business), tennis is blissfully free of sticky child labor laws. Players as diverse as Seles, Andrea Jaeger, Mary Joe Fernandez, Andrea Temesvari, Mary Pierce, and Steffi Graf all have one thing in common: Their fathers stopped working when it became clear that their little girls stood a better chance of bringing home the bacon—and bigger, fatter slabs of it—than they could ever hope to provide. A lot of them had just that scenario in mind from the get-go. Others, like Karolj Seles, truly seemed to have no choice.

These fathers tend to be a funny and predictable lot. For instance, I've yet to meet one who didn't claim to have been some kind of world-class jock who just didn't happen to make the Olympics or Wimbledon because of blah-blah-blah. Furthermore, when you ask why they're walking around at tennis tournaments in short pants eating ice cream cones instead of working, they come up with tennis's version of the

Twinkies defense: The sheer talent of their kids, combined with their need for guidance, unfortunately forced them to abandon the glowing prospects of their former lives.

You might even believe the malarkey some of these tennis fathers come up with if you didn't know your tennis. James Evert, Kenneth Goolagong, and George Austin not only kept their day jobs while their daughters were kids, they even hung on to them long after Chris, Evonne, and Tracy were wealthy and famous. And it wasn't because any of them was rich. The only thing they had in common was a capacity for being gainfully employed in industries ranging from rocket science to sheep shearing, rather than the occupation of marketing and living off their celebrated children.

On paper, Jimmy Evert had all the makings of the tennis father from hell. He loved the game, but he never became a world-class player. He was from a modest, middle-class background. When his children were born, he was teaching the game on the public courts of Fort Lauderdale, Florida, and he continued to do so until long after retirement age. Chris Evert was very much the product of her father's theories and ambitions, but she never became the victim of them. She has often said that for most of her career she was driven by the need to win her father's approval. That she never soured on that ambition said a great deal about his own motives and hopes.

Jimmy Evert was a devout Catholic, a disciplinarian, and a man who cherished family values. Naturally, his kids—being kids—caused him plenty of heartache and aggravation. As a tennis nut, Jimmy must have reveled in visions of his attractive daughter winning Wimbledon and ruling tennis, but he mostly saw those achievements as a way for her to distinguish herself while leading a clean and healthy life. He believed that if his daughter was able to maximize her talent as a player—by playing the game the way he taught her—the rest of it would take care of itself.

Jimmy Evert did not even attend the tournaments in which his daughter played until late in her career, when on a few important occasions she asked that he show up to provide her with inspiration. Chris's mother, Colette, who freely admitted that she neither knew very much about nor cared excessively for tennis, chaperoned Chris for many years as a dutiful mom. She was a gracious presence on the tour, and she had a kind word for everyone, including her daughter's most threatening rivals.

The Austins were also very traditional. George Austin really was a rocket scientist, working as a nuclear physicist until he reached retirement age. He never appeared to get much more than a good chuckle—

and a massive hit of pride—from the exploits of his gifted children, particularly Tracy. His wife, Jeanne, was a certified tennis nut whose idea of a good time was ferrying her kids from the club to lessons to tournaments and somehow squeezing in a few sets of tennis with friends for herself. She even made many of Tracy's dresses, a rather quaint tradition that much to Tracy's embarrassment never went unmentioned in the press.

This unlikely triumvirate was completed by Kenneth Goolagong. He was an Australian aborigine, an itinerant sheep shearer who continued to work until the day he was struck and killed by a car while walking home from work on a badly lit country road. Although he saw Evonne whisked away at a tender age by an obsessive coach from the big city, Kenneth never tried to hop on the gravy train. A country man, he remained supportive, baffled, and bemused by Evonne's spectacular success. Evonne helped the family financially over the years, but her father was not the sort of man who asked for it.

The one thing these radically different men do have in common is that their daughters survived all the pitfalls of pro tennis to become successful, well-adjusted women. Evert and Goolagong enjoyed great longevity and ultimately started families. Austin's career was cut short by injuries, but she segued nicely into everyday life along the same path as the other two players. A traditional family life may not be the ultimate measure of success or happiness, but those three women will tell you that for them it is, particularly when it follows on the heels of having been the best woman player on the planet.

This is not to say that Capriati, Graf, or Seles will not end up leading healthy, normal lives. It's just that they will have a lot of catching up to do when they finally get their fathers off their backs and out of their subconsciouses.

Okay, that was then, this is now. Times change, and so do the ways in which we do business. The pioneer of the contemporary tennis father was Roland Jaeger whose daughter, Andrea, reached the finals at both the French Open (1982) and Wimbledon (1983), losing to Martina Navratilova on both occasions. Andrea was the youngest woman ever to crack the world's top ten, which she did at the age of fifteen in 1980. She was for all intents and purposes finished with tennis by 1984 when she played in only one Grand Slam event, losing in the first round of the French Open.

At the time that Jaeger left the game, the American social crisis of the month was something called "burnout." She found herself embroiled in that issue, and while she had experienced problems of motivation and adjustment to life on the women's tour, she was also plagued by chronic shoulder problems that required surgery on six different occasions. At the age of twenty-four she complained to me of her inability to perform a task as simple as lifting a bag of groceries.

Back in 1980, some weird fit of clairvoyance led me to dub Jaeger the Tatum O'Neal of tennis. I did this long before either John McEnroe or I had met Tatum, and what moved me to the comparison was Jaeger's affected toughness along with her unconvincing cynicism. And like O'Neal, Jaeger had a complex and difficult relationship with her father.

Roland Jaeger and his wife, Ilsie, emigrated to the United States from West Germany in 1956 when he was nineteen. In his youth Jaeger had been a boxer, but once he settled near Chicago he became a bricklayer, a barkeep, and a part-time drag racer of the family Corvette. Roland and Ilsie did not take up tennis until after the birth of their daughters, Susy, who was born three years after the Jaegers emigrated, and Andrea. Soon thereafter, Roland and Ilsie were smitten by the tennis bug. They became a good, club-level mixed-doubles team. Before long, Roland also became a teaching pro at a club near their home, Courts on 22.

Susy, the older girl, became a good junior player who ultimately distinguished herself as an athlete and student at Stanford. But Andrea was the pistol, the adorable tomboy who learned her first valuable lesson in life when, at the command of her father, she went and punched out a little boy who had taken off with her bicycle.

"I guess for a little girl I did stuff that was pretty bad," Jaeger told me when she was fifteen. "Snowball fights during recess, a few brawls. You could say I got into trouble. And a lot of it was because boys couldn't stand me. I guess they were mad because a girl could do something better than them."

A combination of athletic skills and precocious toughness helped Andrea set the junior tennis record books ablaze, and her pugnaciousness led many people to observe that the apple hadn't fallen far from the tree. In fact, Andrea played the game as if it were governed not by the Rules of Lawn Tennis but by those of the Marquess of Queensberry. On changeovers, Jaeger would stroll around the netpost and forgo the pleasure of sitting down to catch her breath, as did her exhausted and often terrified opponent. Instead, Andrea would march to the baseline and stand there, one hand on her hip, tapping a foot, glaring at the umpire as if to say, "If this chump can't come out for the next round, why don't you just stop the fight?"

Jaeger was so eager that she could not abide the leisurely pace that still characterized the game back then. Most kids mimicked the pace at which adults played the game—a pace that defined tennis as a game of nuance, carefully measured strategy, and delicious stillnesses between even the most thunderous of exchanges. Between points, Jaeger would stand at the baseline, impatiently twirling her racket as if it were a drum majorette's baton. As the perceptive television commentator and former touring pro Mary Carillo once remarked, "She plays like she's double-parked."

Chuck Bennett, an International Management Group (IMG) agent with both a tough side and a poetic streak, described Jaeger this way when she was fifteen: "You can tell that inside she's tough as nails. You look at her in the third set of a tough match, after she just lost serve, and you can see the tears standing in her eye. Her jaw is slack, her face is red, and she's scowling. She looks like a fighter who just got her jaw broken, but she's coming out for round fifteen. And you know it's not a put-on. For her, it's a war. And that's where her father comes in. He gave her a fighter's outlook on life, and it's buried so deep in the kid that it's a real part of her personality."

Such shenanigans, combined with tales of Roland's capacity for physical intimidation and even abuse, created a tempest of controversy around the Jaegers. In 1979, just months before she would turn pro, Jaeger was given a wild card into the U.S. Open. Ironically, she drew formidable Tracy Austin as her first-round opponent and lost the match. Witnesses said that when that night match was over, Roland Jaeger did not even allow his daughter to shower and say good-bye to anyone. He hustled her into the family van and immediately set out on the long drive back to Lincolnshire, Illinois. He did not even stop to call to explain to the family that had been gracious enough to provide hospitality (meaning room, board, and use of the washing machine) to the Jaegers.

Such tactics generated both publicity and notoriety for Roland and Andrea long before they actually hit the big time. When Andrea finally turned pro and joined the tour at the age of fourteen, Ana Leaird, the publicist for the Women's Tennis Association, said, "Everybody but everybody was waiting, frozen, to see what this man Roland Jaeger was really like."

Roland had a soup-bowl haircut, a craggy face, the compulsory crooked nose, and the kind of raspy tenor voice that allows some actors to make a good living as Truly Evil People in B-movies. Roland dressed badly, and he couldn't give a hoot about quality food, cultivating a suntan, or hitting up tournament promoters for perks and privileges. All in all, he was an okay guy except for the fact that he was a tennis father. He came fully equipped with paranoia, and he sensed a raw deal lurking around every corner. Sometimes Roland's suspicions were justified, even if his crude way of expressing them was not. The women's tour always has been an insular entity, with its own pecking order and a good deal of jockeying for an appropriate place in it. As a man afoot in an environment dominated by women, Roland automatically commanded a certain amount of wariness and respect, and he was not above taking advantage of it.

I suppose there was an unexpected but real advantage to being a tennis father. Few women would have gotten away with barging into a tournament director's office, pounding on the desk, and demanding a fair shake. But when Roland did it in the women's tour, the administrators listened. And much to their credit, they generally didn't seek revenge on Andrea herself.

There is a little bit of the child in any parent whose relationship to his offspring is extraordinarily close, probably because no other adult would be as adept at, or interested in, practicing the kind of manipulation that drives such relationships. And manipulation is the right word for it.

"My father doesn't really get mad at me when I lose a match," Jaeger told me after a loss early in her career. "It's just that he gets . . . upset. And it's not like we go yelling at each other for the rest of the day. He can yell at me for half an hour, and then we go and get an ice cream cone."

By the age of eighteen Jaeger understood how her father had pushed and pulled her to a position of preeminence. Continuing a long habit of comparing herself to her father, she told me, "One of the big similarities between us is that we're both always on tiptoes, expecting the worst things to happen. At home I'd sneak around and listen to Dad and Mom talk about tennis. I once heard him say, 'I wonder if she can make it through the prequalifying rounds in the Las Vegas tournament. I don't know, she may not be good enough. She may not be ready.' So that was the event where I not only got through the prequalifying event, but I went all the way and won the tournament. It was kind of the thing that made me turn pro even though I was only fourteen. Looking back at that, I think maybe he wanted me to hear that conversation. That was always his way.

"He always wanted to help me, but he was new to most of the things that came with that job. He didn't understand some things because of the way I was, too. I always had the talent, so as a little girl I tended to slide by, to get away with stuff. That made him always try to figure out ways to push me harder. He had all these little tricks that worked perfectly when I was starting out. But I caught on to them, and then I'd come up with some little way to get around things."

In 1983 when Jaeger had reached number three in the world and seemed poised to win a Grand Slam title and challenge for the top ranking, Chris Evert said, "Mr. Jaeger was always a man who used reverse psychology on Andrea, and sometimes even on others. I don't even know if he was doing it on purpose or not, but the result was always the same. If Andrea got to, say, the semifinals of a tournament and had to play me next, he'd come up to me and say something like, 'This is fine for her, but now she has to play you, and there's no way she can beat you.' I don't want to be uncharitable, but deep down I always felt that it wasn't exactly what he was thinking and feeling."

As things turned out, agent Chuck Bennett might have been wrong about one element in his analysis of Roland's imprint on Andrea—his contention that the mentality of the amateur fighter was "buried deep" in Andrea's personality, When Jaeger left the tour, she was something of a misfit. She settled near Tampa and worked at a secretarial job for Time Inc. She told me she had trouble finding a boyfriend who wasn't interested in her because of her name, or who wasn't preoccupied with her anatomy rather than her personality. She soon followed a host of other tennis players out to Aspen but said she did not feel entirely comfortable in that cliquish, gay community.

Jaeger reminded me of certain Vietnam war veterans or child stars who had no success as adults. Ghosts and shadows flitted over her soul; she seemed to have problems adjusting to life away from tennis. But slowly things turned around for her. She applied herself to creating a foundation for disadvantaged children with help from people like John McEnroe. It appears to have become her life's calling.

It's too early to tell what lies in store for Jennifer Capriati, who abruptly quit tennis in late 1993 and then became the focus of a sensational drug bust in early 1994. But there are striking similarities in the burdens she and Andrea shared, many of them rooted in the way their fathers—and a host of other tennis dads—came to the game, and what they brought with them.

Men like Roland, Stefano, Peter Graf, Karolj Seles, Jim Pierce, and Otto Temesvari—the Hungarian whose daughter, Andrea, precociously leaped into the top ten only to run into a firestorm of problems—have a few striking things in common. None of them was a tennis player or a member of the tennis community at large. Jaeger and Graf both did some boxing, while Capriati played soccer, Temesvari played and coached basketball, and Seles competed in track and field before he became a prize-winning cartoonist in Yugoslavia. In different ways, all six men began as hungry outsiders looking in at the glamorous and exciting world of pro tennis. Three of them (Jaeger, Seles, and Capriati) moved to America to further their family ambitions. Some of them were afflicted by the ambitious, uneducated immigrant's desire to have too much, too soon.

The curious thing about Stefano, and the quality that makes the Capriati tragedy so poignant, is that among all the tennis fathers under discussion, he seemed the most hardy and well equipped for Babylon. Roland Jaeger was all rough edges, a man doomed to pace around the edges of the tennis community. Peter Graf insisted on remaining at arm's length from the establishment, and he must have sat around nights trying to outguess and outfox the untold legions who, he imagined, were plotting against him and his Steffi. Karolj Seles barely spoke a word of English, and he often seemed merely to be along for the ride mapped by his willful daughter. Jim Pierce, a convicted felon, was legally barred from attending tournaments because of his menacing ways.

Stefano Capriati, on the other hand, was a more visible presence at tournaments than even his own once-sprightly daughter. He was often gruff, vulgar, and demanding, and he had no compunctions about throwing his weight around when it came to demanding all the perks that the players and their entourages traditionally extort from tournament promoters. In an amusing reversal of the scenario in which the spoiled rich kid throws his daddy's name around, Stefano went around bullying people and demanding regal treatment using his daughter's name. To his credit, though, Stefano was relatively gregarious and merely greedy in an environment where some of his peers were deluded and antisocial.

But in the end, reality caught up with Stefano, as it did with Roland Jaeger. These days Roland is living with his wife, Ilsie, in Florida, happily teaching other people's kids how to play tennis. From the reports I get, he's a patient, attentive, clever teacher who knows how to get the most out of the little devils. He has the experience, and he knows how kids think.

Andrea also knew how Roland thought, or at least she figured it out. Maybe the same thing will be said one day for Jennifer Capriati.

Ironically, one of the prominent guests in the players' box during that Capriati-Seles match at Key Biscayne was Chris Evert's brother, John, who was nominally Capriati's agent on behalf of the firm for which he worked, IMG. The agents of IMG, along with those of the other major firms (ProServ and Advantage International) and a handful of independent operators, are what pros in the alcohol and drug rehab business call "enablers." That is, they seek budding talent and then proceed to make the players offers that they cannot refuse, at an age at which most of them cannot even drive. Agents do this, of course, in cahoots with the parent of the promising players in question.

Agents are often cast as the whipping boys and girls of the professional era. The most interesting thing about this agent phobia is what it says about the way many of us perceive parents today—not as the ultimate sources of authority and culpability but as mere players on a board populated by other players. Theoretically, most tennis parents are reasonably well educated adults whose primary purpose is to ensure their children's well-being. So if the agents can be cast as flesh peddlers, parents have to be defined as the providers of the bodies. The only mitigating circumstance is that a prodigy sometimes really is a giant infant raging out of control, casting a shadow in which parents cower.

Parents want to make the right decision but sometimes are afraid to lay down any law that might hamper the development of the child into the next Wimbledon champion. The naive gusto of the child often makes it that much harder to resist the beck and call of professionalism, and the rewards for turning pro are documented in dollar signs by agents, which sends a powerful all-systems-go message. Parents often hear that if they show restraint or unilaterally act on principles that may be in conflict with the tennis agenda, their children may lose interest in the game or forfeit some vital, developmental edge. As a result, parents cave in, step by step.

Question: If God wanted agents to run these kids' lives, why did he make parents?

Answer: Because somebody has to carry the rackets.

But no agent ever signed a minor without the consent of his or her parents. At least that part is written in stone because while no child labor laws obtain to tennis, so far we still choose to "discriminate" against youth by insisting that they are minors who cannot enter into legal contracts.

Securing the right to represent a player these days can be a long, arduous process. Agents feel obliged to establish contacts with the prospect and the prospect's family long before even the most precocious kid is ready to turn pro. This involves a lot of downtime spent at junior tournaments and in restaurants, wining and dining parents and pretending to be interested in their lives, not just in their kids' future as athletes. Agents don't really represent kids anymore, they represent families. In that sense they're probably underpaid no matter how much they make.

Agents know that it doesn't hurt to try to get into a kid's good graces, either. Coming up with some tickets to a rock concert or giving her a Nintendo game helps, although these days agents leave a lot of that stuff to the tournament promoters with whom many of them strike shifting, informal alliances. Promoters like to establish good relations with potential champions early on. The undisputed master of this is the establishment renegade John Korff, the promoter of a lucrative exhibition played in July in Mahwah, New Jersey. Korff's event is the closest thing tennis has to a county fair or a carnival. Though proud of his Barnumesque sensibilities, he has no delusions about how to succeed in the current tennis environment.

"A lot of what I do is driven by the fact that these players are still kids," Korff told me. "When Jennifer [Capriati] first came to play my event, we sent a ton of supermarket food to her room. We had a huge Nabisco display, a pop-a-shot display, and two huge squirt guns. So what does that cost us, like $1, $8, $12? But the thing is, Jennifer *herself* isn't interested in a check for a zillion dollars. She's just a kid. She's interested in having fun with a squirt gun or a basketball hoop in her own room."

I said that John Evert was "nominally" Jennifer Capriati's agent because being a mere fourteen did not prevent her from having a slew of them with duties known almost exclusively only to one another. Bear with me while I describe how the commercial net was thrown over Capriati by this particular team of fishermen.

Bob Kain, the president of IMG's tennis division, is tough and honest and loyal—qualities that helped him establish and maintain a long-standing relationship with Chris Evert. Jennifer Capriati grew up in south Florida where her reputation was such that Evert quite naturally took an interest in her. In fact, Jimmy Evert quietly kept an eye on Jennifer and advised the Capriatis as she developed.

Meanwhile, halfway around the world, Cino Marchese had secured for himself a position as the capo of Italian tennis. Inevitably, he would become an operative for IMG, a firm that was not only routing the competition in the agent biz but fast becoming a worldwide force in promotion and event management as well as player representation. It was only natural that Marchese befriended Stefano Capriati because they had two languages in common: Italian and Financial. Soon Cino and Stefano had a handshake deal for Jennifer to play the Italian Open—a tournament of which Marchese happened to be director—when Jennifer was nine.

In the ensuing years Cino steered Stefano toward IMG. He also nudged the Capriatis toward the Italian shoe and clothing firm Diadora when it came time for Jennifer—make that Stefano—to strike a deal. In those key years before Jennifer turned pro, every agent (including the shrewd and intelligent Ion Tiriac) was sniffing around the family. But IMG was slowly and inevitably drawing tight the net.

It wasn't as if this transpired under the cover of night, either. Whenever little Jennifer was pounding yet another hapless junior foe into oblivion, Cino could be seen sitting patiently with Stefano on the uncomfortable aluminum bleachers, knees up to his chin. They were an odd couple indeed: squat Stefano in his shorts and sneakers, eating ice cream, and the regal Cino in his natty tailored suits, with his shock of white hair, delivering commentary in his basso profundo voice.

The Evert family had no ulterior motive in befriending the Capriatis. Jimmy was a purist who loved the game of tennis, and Chris was old enough to be gracious toward younger players. But there was a sensible way for the Capriatis to thank the Everts, which was by allowing Chris's younger brother, John, to become involved in the management of Capriati's career.

Because of Chris's fame, John had experienced a rocky adolescence. At junior and collegiate tournaments his opponents took particular pleasure in beating him. Some of them even taunted John with the nickname "Chrissie." Wrestling with what appeared to be an identity crisis, John engaged in a fair amount of reckless and irresponsible behavior before he decided to become an apprentice in the agent game. Although the Capriatis liked and trusted John, the deal still represented a coup for IMG. Having John in place would allow Kain, a family man himself, to oversee the Capriati industry from his Cleveland office. It would also strengthen IMG's relationship with one of their prime clients, Chris. And the deal would allow Chris to repay John for some of the indignities she had inadvertently caused him to suffer.

Fourteen-year-old Jennifer Capriati ended up with what really amounted to four agents: Stefano, her father, legal guardian, and de facto manager who exercised unilateral control over her career, but lacked the savvy and clout to run the show himself; Kain, the man who knew the tennis business inside and out but no longer had the stomach to rock a client's cradle or baby-sit her parents; Marchese, a trusted friend and advisor; and John Evert, who was young enough to put up with all the minutiae that comes with actually representing Jennifer Capriati, which included staying in the same hotel as Jennifer wherever she was playing and her parents were watching, ever ready to act out one of those "jump/how high?" scenarios.

As the point man for the Capriatis, Evert didn't exactly land that far from the psychological territory where he had encountered so much grief as Chris's brother. Some members of the media contemptuously dubbed him "the Colonel," a reference to the notorious Colonel Parker who managed—and fleeced—Elvis Presley. Every time someone greeted John as "the Colonel," you could see the color rise in his cheeks. The nickname wasn't fair because John was just a middleman who stood in the direct line of fire.

John had a realistic view of his job and his position among the power and money brokers around him. He understood the absurdities and ironies of the situation and shared them with those he trusted. As far as apprenticeships went, it was a pretty good deal. And it wasn't a bad shake for the Capriatis, either, because their decision to go with IMG made them exactly what the Jaegers never became: legitimate members of the official tennis family, complete with the blessing of Chris Evert.

Supported by a few good men and beyond financial cares thanks to incipient long-term contracts with, among others, Diadora and Prince, Capriati faced only one big problem at age thirteen. There was suddenly no place where she could officially play the game. Which brings us to the next link in the chain of accountability, the Women's Tennis Council—the body that ostensibly governs the women's game.

Back in the mid-1980s, the controversial, premature retirements of Austin and Jaeger, and the attendant outcry over "burnout," led the Council to create a formula that would limit the number of pro tournaments a girl could play based on her age. This was relatively painless, the equivalent of throwing a bucket of water on a blaze that had already burned out. But new wisps of smoke were already visible on the horizon.

At the time, the conscientious administrator Trish Faulkner told me a tale that had drifted overseas from Europe. An eleven-year-old named Seles had just won the International Tennis Federation's Sports Goofy World Championships, only to return to Yugoslavia for two operations, one on her knee and the other for an ulcer. The bit about the operations was baloney, but the report of Seles's extraordinary potential were not. And down in Florida, Capriati was already being hailed as a can't-miss prodigy.

Capriati fulfilled her junior potential in 1989, winning the French and U.S. Open junior titles. Clearly, she was ready to try the pro tour. In fact, she needed to do so in order to feel properly challenged. The question was how much she should play, and nobody on the tour believed for a moment that Stefano and company would exercise the same restraint that Jimmy Evert had shown after his sixteen-year-old daughter's run in the semifinals of the U.S. Open in 1971.

The Council felt obliged to take police action. It soon passed the first of the rules that John Feinstein, author of the recent book *Hard Courts,* would mischievously call the "Capriati Rules." The rule set an age limit of fourteen years for kids wishing to play on the pro tour. But for a host of reasons the Capriatis liked the idea of Jennifer making her pro debut in a women's tournament in Boca Raton, just up the road from the Capriati domicile at Saddlebrook, Florida. Unfortunately, Capriati would not actually turn fourteen until March 29, three weeks after the start of the event. The Council decided to accommodate the Capriatis. The Council quickly passed an amendment saying that you didn't have to *be* fourteen at the time of the pro tournament you wished to play. It was okay if you turned fourteen sometime later in that month.

The bottom line was this: The council did not want to face a nasty restraint-of-trade lawsuit brought by the Capriatis and their powerful representatives nor waste any more time looking for a little messiah who could deliver the game from the pleasant but repetitious prospect of more Evert-Navratilova finals. Thus, Capriati made her debut where her handlers intended, at age thirteen.

At the next level in the great chain of accountability, the lines often blur between administrators, sponsors, promoters, and a host of public relations functionaries. Most of them work hand in hand, week in and week out, at the tournaments that constitute the wetlands of pro tennis. There, in the mud and muck, life is created and sustained for both the bottom feeders and the big shots in tennis.

The Women's Tennis Association (WTA), like its counterpart among the men, the Association of Tennis Professionals (ATP), began as a player's union created to give the pros a voice in how the game was run. But while the ATP ultimately wrested control of the world tour—but not the preeminent Grand Slam events and the Davis Cup—away from the traditional tennis establishment, the WTA's attempt to pull off a similar coup failed in 1992.

Although the WTA Tour became a reality, the organization remained accountable to the Women's Tennis Council, an umbrella group under which all representatives of the game (the ITF, tournament promoters, and players) had a voice.

So the WTA Tour continues to process tournament entries, write rules, issue rankings, represent the players before the WTC, and create an elaborate support system for the players. It also acts as the go-between for players and media. At each tournament there are at least two pleasant WTA Tour "public relations coordinators" on hand to escort the players from the court to the locker room and then to the press interview room. They do this cheerfully and efficiently, but with the covert alertness of wardens making sure that the jailbirds don't make a break for it en route to the chapel.

Attendance at post-match press conferences is obligatory. These group sessions make it easier for reporters to do their jobs, and they are a good public relations tool for the tour. But mandatory press conferences can be farcical, dehumanizing experiences for all concerned. Legislated intercourse can breed dishonesty, manipulation, contempt, and hostility.

Imagine being Jennifer Capriati at sixteen, forced to sit before fifty reporters who are mostly strangers to you, and having to answer questions about how you blew a match, how you feel about your parents, how much pressure you feel to win a big one. Needless to say, you quickly develop a cunning if transparent way to answer any question with guarded platitudes, clichés, and generalities. It's a hell of a way to learn about human communication.

The WTA aides also screen and pass along requests for private interviews, and they stand by as general escorts when the press conferences end, just in case an overzealous fan decides to run up and ask Gabriela Sabatini for her panties or a disgruntled expatriate tries to pin down the Russian Natalia Zvereva on how she really feels about the Uzbek independence movement.

Because of the peculiar working conditions faced by girls who are increasingly younger and often undereducated, the WTA periodically conducts a special "school" in which it attempts to teach kids like Capriati how to handle themselves in public and how to use the language in a way that will both effectively hide and make up for their appalling ignorance of it.

These seminars are spawned with the best intentions and characterized as "educational" services. But that's something of a reach in that they mostly alert the kids to the dangers implicit in telling reporters what they really feel about both private and tour issues, and they teach players how to act as their own spin doctors in order to make themselves, and the tour, more marketable.

The women's tour also has a heavy sponsor representation, a tradition established when Virginia Slims pretty much ran the whole shooting match. This trend was maintained when Kraft-General Foods, another division of Philip Morris, took over sponsorship of the world tour. The Virginia Slims people not only created women's professional tennis, they wrote the book on public and media relations.

The women's tour has always had a dazzling number of personnel on hand to make sure that everybody remains happy. This involves a lot of schmoozing and entertaining of parents, players, media, and tournament officials. The public relations staff provides an impressive flow of up-to-the-minute information covering everything from complete career records to biographical tidbits, and they hand out voluminous media guides, T-shirts, umbrellas, calendars, free cigarettes, and even reporters' notebooks. This can add up to a lot of fun but not necessarily for the out-to-lunch fourteen-year-old prodigy at the center of it all.

Jennifer Capriati did not die at Key Biscayne on that day in 1991. She didn't even get sick and throw up even though a couple of times it looked as if she might. She did cry after losing that match to Seles, but you would be forgiven for crying, too, if you had been Capriati on that day, or on almost any other day over the next few years. At age fourteen Capriati was a small, teetering stone placed by fate at the top of an enormous pyramid. This edifice was composed of literally thousands of human beings who were either directly or indirectly responsible for her position in the last place any child should be: high atop a very steep and slippery slope.

As a reporter I also felt like a block in the base. Thus it was with some sense of unease and regret that I watched what Capriati subsequently went through. Instead of keeping her appearances limited to important Grand Slam events and judiciously chosen tour stops, the Capriati brain trust allowed or coerced her into playing too often and in too many unworthy places for no good reason other than the income and publicity her appearance generated. Being a child, she loved every minute of it because she was indulged by every official, functionary, and fan along the way.

One of the unfortunate by-products of this full-blown debut was that Capriati very quickly established herself in the upper reaches of the top ten, where she hit a wall. She certainly had the talent to win a Grand Slam event, and the competitive mettle as well. But she was not quite mature or experienced enough, and soon she looked as if she was playing by rote. A moodiness crept into her game, and at times it seemed as if she didn't really differentiate important tournaments from any other playing "opportunities." It was all of a piece to her; she was just a tourist in Babylon, watching all those places and faces slide by in a pleasant blur.

It all came to a head almost as quickly as it began, with Jennifer in deep rebellion against her parents and her job by the time she was sixteen. After competing in the Australian Open of 1992, she was scheduled to play in exhibitions against Gabriela Sabatini and then in a tournament in Tokyo. She fought her way through the Orient, homesick for her friends in Florida and sick of her parents.

In Tokyo she locked herself in her hotel room and refused to talk. She finally resorted to a weapon that was her own equivalent of a nuclear warhead, her tennis game. She played and lost a dispirited early-round match in Tokyo, packed her bags, and declared that she would never play there again. Hearing of the incident, Martina Navratilova remarked, "I'd won Wimbledon three times before I went around blowing off whole cities."

The first time I saw Capriati after her Australian/Asian swing of 1992 was at the Lipton tournament at Key Biscayne—right back where this whole discourse started. The big news when I arrived was that the Capriatis had just redecorated their home only to have Jennifer, who had discovered the neo-hippie aesthetic, suddenly decide that she wanted her quarters done over in black. Given her age, it wasn't an unusual request. Besides, she had paid for the renovation in the first place, so she was entitled to requesting that the whole house be turned into a crash pad complete with strobe lights, water coolers full of electric Kool-Aid, and an endless loop of Grateful Dead tunes reverberating throughout every room.

I looked in on one of Capriati's press conferences in Key Biscayne early that week, and it was almost painful to behold. In what seemed like just months, Capriati had turned from a cute, bouncy kid with an amber glow to her skin into a moody, reticent, overweight girl who eschewed slick, upscale, boring clothes—namely, the ones she was contracted to wear—in favor of a retro-hippie wardrobe.

Clearly, Capriati didn't understand, or simply chose to ignore, the entire sticky web of commercial commitments in which she was entangled. The Oil of Olay people may have been in an even worse position than Capriati. Suddenly their radiant poster girl had the same complexion as all those hormonally whacked-out mall rats and nervous eaters whom she was supposed to be recruiting for Oil of Olay in the first place. And worse yet, she wanted nothing more than to be one of them.

The tragicomedy of pimples is difficult for kids to handle even in the most conventional school and home environments, never mind under the microscope of public scrutiny. And no matter how oblivious Capriati may have been to so many of the other issues surrounding her youth and status, you can bet she was painfully aware of this problem.

I've rarely seen anyone, of any age, tune out the world as effectively as Capriati did in that press conference after a routine win. She sat in the press tent gazing off into the distance. She mumbled a few inanities to a few predictable questions, chewing her gum so assiduously that the sound thundered through the microphone and over the PA system in the interview room. When it was clear that the desultory proceedings were winding down, I couldn't help but ask:

"Jennifer, what kind of gum are you chewing?"

"Trident," she answered, absolutely deadpan. "Sugarless."

As laughter erupted through the tent, I was stricken by the feeling that I'd embarrassed the child. But I quickly realized that it had all gone over her head, that she hadn't even bothered to look up. She couldn't care less. Sitting there answering questions, her face a stony mask of disinterest, was just something she had to do, like listening to some boring old teacher tell her how important it was to know about American history.

Capriati was not the first or last kid to have a rough puberty, but she was one of the few who had to face it with the harrowing, debilitating freedom of a little Caligula. The endless privileges heaped on her invited

Capriati to test the boundaries of her freedom and power, and discovering that they were virtually limitless could not have helped her.

By the time Korff's exhibition in Mahwah rolled around in July, Jennifer was fed up with her omnipresent parents. She insisted on making the trip to Mahwah without them, and they reluctantly agreed to let her go solo. Korff was a trusted friend, John Evert would be there as a minder, and a host of Virginia Slims people in nearby New York could be counted to keep an eye on her.

When Evert missed his flight to New Jersey, Capriati got busy testing her newfound freedom. She made a beeline for a local bar, either under the mistaken impression that nobody there would recognize her—or perversely hoping that everybody would. When I heard about the incident, I sought out Korff and asked if he had known about Jennifer's excellent adventure.

"No," he replied, shaking his head. "Not until it was too late. I was in my office when I got a call from the place, and this bartender said, 'You're never going to believe who I've got in here. Jennifer Capriati. What do you want me to do?'

" 'Don't serve her,' " Korff said. " 'Somebody will be right there.' "

After Capriati had been brought to heel, Korff told her that she couldn't go sneaking around while he was trusted to look after her. He told her that she could go anywhere she liked as long as John Evert or Jim Fusie (a Virginia Slims employee who had become another of Capriati's minders) went with her.

When Capriati's parents learned of this escapade, they went ballistic. Evert was briefly fired for arriving in Mahwah late, but he was soon brought back on board. He spent a good part of the rest of the week trying to control a loose cannon. Capriati nagged him about going to Manhattan, a short trip that might have been a pleasant diversion. Only Jennifer didn't want to go to a Broadway show, a trendy pasta joint, or the museum. She wanted to go "where the hippies were."

Evert had fits of anxiety as he entertained visions of chasing Capriati through the streets of the East Village while she tried to score pot from the dozens of street vendors who operate there. Reinforcements came pouring in from a vast network of tennis folks who felt personally or professionally obliged to "protect" Capriati from herself.

One of the more hilarious aspects of this charade was to get a pile of tickets for a concert by the notorious rock band Guns N Roses. One of the Virginia Slims public relations people even called me and suggested that I go along. I have to admit that I like some of Guns N Roses' songs, but not enough to wade into a sea of bikers and headbangers from New Jersey in the company of a couple of fifteen-year-old girls and a troupe of conservative, nicely dressed executives whose own taste in music doesn't get much further from the mainstream than Michael Bolton or Whitney Houston.

More importantly, I knew that going to see Guns N Roses with an entourage of tennis types would have been a massive bummer for Capriati. When the architects of this plan ran it by her, she reacted in a predictable way.

According to one of them, Capriati demanded, "Why do *you* all want to go? So you can be spies for my mom?"

Well, the kid was learning . . .

The field trip to see Guns N Roses did finally happen, although I was not part of it. Monica Seles, who was also playing at Mahwah that week, did go, but not with Capriati. And being as mature as Capriati was callow, Seles was unencumbered by spies masquerading as Axl Rose groupies. The day after the show, Fusie saw Seles and asked her how she liked the concert.

"It was great," Monica replied. "Where were you guys sitting, anyway?"

"We had second-row seats," Capriati said. "What about you?"

"I was in the sound booth," Seles said. "We had backstage passes."

Upon hearing this, Capriati marched off to argue with the woman who had procured the precious tickets, Korff's assistant Robin Gellman.

It had indeed been a rough week for Gellman. Capriati had insisted on chewing gum and rocking in her chair during her press conferences, which had forced Gellman to resort to guerrilla tactics. She moved the chair back to the wall so that it was physically impossible to rock it back and forth. Then she filled the water cup on the table with lime juice and mixed in water and ice chips.

When I asked Gellman about the special drink she was concocting, she smiled impishly. "I figure that if you're chewing gum and you take a bunch of ice in your mouth, the ice will freeze the gum, and that takes care of the gum-clicking problem. Sometimes you just have to improvise."

By August 1992 people in tennis were sick of Capriati and her growing pains. They were also sick of her parents, which was one thing they had in common with the struggling prodigy. Few people expected anything from Capriati at the Olympics in Barcelona. She seemed too embroiled in her own emotional problems to loom as much of a threat in an event that was bigger than, and different from, even the most prestigious of tennis tournaments.

So Capriati went and won the gold medal. She did it by playing a strong, patient, mature match against an opponent who had already collected a gold medal four years earlier in Seoul, Korea—Steffi Graf. And she was moved to do it by the unique Olympic ambience in which Capriati was just one among thousands of athletes. Instead of traveling from hotel to practice court to stadium to hotel, usually in the company of her parents, Capriati was free to run amok and get lost in Barcelona, where she was not the girl in the spotlight but one of thousands in a floodlight. She watched other athletic events and socialized with the other competitors in the cafeteria of the Olympic Village. She even saved up her lunch money, stashing her $10 per diem meal allotment because, as she said, 'at the end of two weeks it adds up."

This is how Capriati summed up her Olympic experience: "This has been the most fun two weeks for me, especially away from the tennis. I love the feeling in the Olympic Village. You just flop down in the cafeteria and start talking to the other athletes. You find out what country they come from, what sport they play. You take a picture with them. It's totally cool. It's so different from being on the tour. Seeing all those other athletes who work like crazy for four years just to get one crack at one race or event that could be over in ten seconds, I realized how lucky I am to be in a sport that's so publicized, where I can make a lot of money and play in important matches all the time, not just once in four years."

In Barcelona it seemed that Capriati had come to see how much she had taken for granted. But the realization wasn't enough to make her rush back to tennis and pursue her career with Spartan dedication. As she told Robin Finn of *The New York Times,* "On the tour, the main thing was that I was supposed to be smiling all the time, no matter what, and for the first year it wasn't so hard, because everything was new and fun. But this [tour] life gets kind of old. The Olympics were different for me because they were fresh.

"Maybe I did some extreme things on the tour, but it was never meant to hurt anybody. I mean, if I like black fingernails, I'm going to do it. If I like to dress in tie-dye, what's the problem? I don't have blond hair and blue eyes, and I'm not the next Chris Evert. I'm different. I'm me."

Finally, Capriati seemed to be coming around, figuring out who she was and what she wanted. Everyone was poised to see a quick, happy ending written to the saga of Jennifer Capriati. Everyone should have known better. If anything, the Olympic experience—one that represents the last, threatened bastion of the amateur sensibility to which Capriati was never exposed—helped sour Capriati on pro tennis for good. We all know what happened soon thereafter.

Will Capriati's still unfinished history change the way people do business in tennis? I doubt it. Big rewards call for big risks, right? And the ante is constantly being upped in a game in which a seemingly endless number of tennis fathers are willing to play, using their daughters' physical, psychological, and emotional well-being as markers. The administrators of the game are not pleased by this, but their history has been one long story of capitulation.

In Barcelona at Capriati's enchanted Olympics, Ion Tiriac told me about a conversation he'd had with the parents of a promising twelve-year-old. The father was a former Olympic rower from Germany; the mother was a successful Romanian economist. The talent of their child was so evident that the family had moved at great expense to a city where they could be close to first-rate coaching. Soon they had a manager who was willing to finance the further development of the girl—if the family would sign an eight-year management contract, with a hefty guaranteed income for the family for six of those years.

"I told them to resist if they could," Tiriac said. "If the problem was money for travel to tournaments, I offered to give them $5,000 to cover it. What is the point of sending out a twelve-year-old and risk breaking her heart before she's even old enough to know she has one? Let them have a few years of childhood instead of facing a situation where at fifteen they are failures at life.

"I am definitely for some kind of rule about who can play professional. The question is where you put such a rule. Do you base it on height, on weight, or only on playing statistics? If I had to decide right now, I would make the cutoff at fifteen years and make no exceptions."

About a month after we had that conversation, I ran into Heather MacLachlan, an agent who left the large American management firm of ProServ to work for Tiriac. She told me that during the U.S. Open she walked into the fashionable Manhattan restaurant Bice one evening just after midnight. She recognized Anna Kurnokova, a promising Russian junior apparently just over from Moscow, having dinner with her mother and a few agents from a leading firm. At the time Anna was ten years old.

To understand how this state of affairs has come to pass, we have to look at the evolution of the women's tour—a process that, in an era of feminist consciousness, was simultaneously conventional and radical, attractive and controversial. Stay tuned.

CHAPTER 5

EVONNE GOOLAGONG
The Nose of the Kangaroo

EVONNE GOOLAGONG and her husband, Roger Cawley, who became my closest friends in tennis during the late 1970s, called me one wintry day in New York and invited me for drinks at Trader Vic's in the Plaza Hotel. This was to be a sentimental celebration because it was at Trader Vic's in London that Roger and Evonne plotted her break with Vic Edwards, the Australian coach and father figure who was a major fixture in her life until she was twenty four, in 1975.

After a painful break with Edwards, Roger and Evonne married, moved to Hilton Head Island, South Carolina, and shortly had two lovely children, Kelly Inala and Morgan. Like many exceptional people with unusual backgrounds, Evonne would pursue a conventional life with a vengeance.

If you've ever been to a Trader Vic's, you know that they specialize in exotic drinks served in goldfish bowls and hurricane glasses the size of vases, festooned with umbrellas, skewered fruits, and plastic baubles. The smooth fruity taste of the drinks, along with the accoutrements, make it easy to forget the lethal amounts of alcohol that go into them, although you're not going to catch me writing to my congressman about this problem.

We whiled away a couple of hours chatting and drinking. At one point we couldn't help but notice a fat guy standing alone at the bar, staring at us. When Evonne got up to visit the ladies' room—the "dunny," as she invariably called it in Australian slang—the man intercepted her. There was no reason to panic because Evonne knew how to take care of herself. As it turned out, the "fat guy" was the opera star Placido Domingo. He was a fan of Evonne's, as were any number of people in the arts, from Liza Minnelli to Kenny Rogers to the classical pianist Misha Dichter, all of whom would become her friends. No player captured the imagination of artistic people more fully than Evonne, whose achingly graceful style, poise, and natural beauty transcended tennis and put her on an equal footing with ballet dancers and other performing artists. She was so down to earth, however, that I'm not sure she ever realized it, and I know she didn't trade on it. All of which only added to her appeal.

Evonne returned after having a chat with Domingo. We ordered another round, having by that time forgotten all about dinner (a fairly common occurrence at that time in our lives). Anyway, the drinks hit me like a ton of bricks. I vaguely remember excusing myself, walking into the men's room, and with my back against the tiled wall, just sliding down into a heap on the floor.

The next thing I remember was coming to, with a hand gently shaking me by the shoulder. It was Evonne; she had become concerned when I failed to return to the table and took it upon herself to find me. She then got hold of my two hundred-pound carcass and pushed me back up along the wall. She dipped her shoulder under one of my armpits and, with a healthy heave-ho, proceeded to carry me out of the men's room. She didn't want to drag me through the crowded lounge, so she hefted me up the stairs and left me with an astonished, liveried staff member of the Plaza Hotel. Evonne went back for Roger, and together they carried me out into the street.

Evonne was that great creation, the consummately natural person. The unselfconscious celebrity. Some people put this down to her aboriginal ancestry, but through Evonne I met quite a few aboriginal people who were as self-conscious and tied up inside as your everyday angst-ridden German intellectual.

Evonne played a marvelous tennis game short on power but long on finesse. If the game of her major rival, Chris Evert, personified will, Evonne's represented instinct. Her unique game often came and went like a summer breeze, accounting for the famed "walkabouts" that sportswriters—particularly the cheesy poets of the British tabloid press—loved to chronicle. In a sport requiring mental discipline, this condition cost Evonne some titles. Still, she won seven Grand Slam singles titles: four at the Australian Open (1974–77), one at the French Open (1971), and two at Wimbledon (1971 and 1980). The nine-year gap between her Wimbledon titles is the longest in the Open era in women's tennis. With her second Wimbledon victory, she became the first mother to win the title since Dorothea Douglass Lambert Chambers sixty-six years earlier.

But despite Evonne's grace, dignity, and the communicable delicacy that became the trademark of her game, she had a remarkably high threshold for pain. This became clear in the latter half of her career. For

reasons that she ultimately ascribed to the changes wrought by child-
birth, she became susceptible to a seemingly endless series of lower-
body injuries, including one that incapacitated her on the Centre Court
at Wimbledon in 1978 while she was engaged in a titanic semifinal struggle with Martina Navratilova.

Before that match, Evonne had taken an injection of the anesthetic
Xylocaine to quell the pain in the Achilles tendon of her left foot. She
won the first set handily, but then she went "walkabout" and allowed
Martina to take a 4–0 lead in the second set. During the rest of the second set both women played brilliantly, with Martina prevailing, 6–4.
Early in the third set the Xylocaine began to wear off, and Evonne began
to favor her left leg. Limping visibly, she still managed to hold two break
points for 4–2, but Martina fended them off and held for 2-all.

In the next game, Evonne hit a winning lob at game point and simultaneously cried out in pain. She sank to her knees and clutched her
lower calf. The rest of the match was played before a hushed, compassionate crowd. Martina held easily for 4-all, and although Evonne was
able to mount surprising resistance in the next game, she was ultimately
broken. Martina served out the match to win, 1–6, 6–4, 6–4.

Evonne left the court that day as a gimp, but she spent the night
drinking champagne and hobbling around the dance floor at the exclusive London disco, Tramps.

Although Evonne personified femininity throughout her career, she
was a person whose gender never seemed to matter. She was the sort of
game, adventurous woman who was comfortable in a man's world. If we
were in Miami and the surf was up late at night, she was the first one to
suggest a midnight swim. Evonne loved to fish, and she had no fear of
wading barefoot through the tidal flats of South Carolina, despite the
plethora of crabs, sharks, and other things that lived there. She had
grown up poor in rural Australia, and the process of becoming a celebrated and wealthy tennis star did not kill the country girl in her.

Evonne, as a successful member of a disfranchised minority and a
magnificent athlete, was a powerful role model for women. Yet at the
time she was never heralded or embraced as such. There certainly were
some practical reasons for this. As an Aussie and an aborigine, Evonne
was, wittingly or not, perceived as an exotic. She also lacked intellectual
interests or pretensions, and she never craved publicity or power. At
heart she was like a farm mother or a wife who was too busy taking care
of her family and doing the chores to develop what elitist, urban intellectuals, forced by circumstances to spend their spare time analyzing
Woody Allen movies, would call her "feminist consciousness." Only
after her career was over and her stock as a celebrity had diminished

everywhere but in Australia did she become increasingly active as a spokeswoman for aborigines—a role she has continued to pursue.

In a way, Chris Evert faced a problem similar to Goolagong's. Thus, early in their careers, both Goolagong and Evert were often at odds with founders of the women's tour, including Billie Jean King, the feminist paragon in tennis. You could say that King was a tireless champion for women's rights and female equality. Her battle to get women equal prize money and her struggle to help create a viable women's pro tour certainly support that claim. At the same time, King was a professional athlete in the fullest sense, working as a tireless promoter for the growth of an enterprise—the business of pro tennis—in which she had a direct fiduciary stake that often extended much further than the prize-money checks she collected at tournaments. I wouldn't burn her at the stake for that, but it's handy to keep in mind.

Evert and Goolagang were different, and their lack of broad popularity among urban intellectuals was an indirect comment on the degree to which the feminist movement of the time was—or wasn't—truly representative of most women and their aspirations. But it also sheds light on the process by which the women's tour has evolved into an unhealthy organism featuring too many lonely or half-formed adults, venal men, and exploited children.

There is one more parallel to be drawn before we take a closer look at Evonne's life. One of Evonne's most noteworthy distinctions was her impeccable sense and practice of sportsmanship. Although there have been a number of great sports in the game, I can think of only one player whose own code of court conduct was similar both in kind and expression to that of Evonne: the late Arthur Ashe. My own first take on this comparison is a double-take. Arthur was a man of both deep and catholic intellectual interests; Evonne had almost none. Arthur was characterized by, and affectionately renowned for, a certain stiffness, both in his personal bearing and in his game; Evonne was legendary for her spontaneity and informality.

But Arthur and Evonne shared similar anxieties, and they developed similar defense mechanisms for coping with them. It was a subject that we discussed often, mostly in private.

"I probably seemed natural on the court because that's how I am as an athlete, and the tennis court was the one place where I was always totally comfortable with what I was doing," she once told me. "But it was always different in life. Off the court, I didn't ever really know how I was coming off, and I was concerned with how I did come off. Instead of asking myself how I felt about a certain issue or question, I would ask myself how I was *supposed* to feel. It took me a long, long time to get over that."

Nobody in tennis understood that mentality more clearly than Arthur Ashe. Like Evonne, he was partly shaped by his racial identity and status as an outsider. Both of them traveled far from their roots at early ages, and there was a haunting similarity in their self-control and vigilant reserve, although those qualities were not as evident in superficially blithe, happy-go-lucky Evonne. Each of them was also deeply traditional, a quality reflected in their successful marriages and in their devotion to their children.

Both Evonne and Arthur, Australian aborigine and African American, were exemplary tennis players, distinguished citizens, and personally conservative individuals in an era when those traits were not particularly fashionable. For a long time there was a subtle but genuine bias against Ashe and Goolagong among the progressive elite. They were often perceived as products and representatives of an old, repressive order—victims and survivors rather than autonomous vital personal forces.

Evonne Goolagong was the last great champion produced by Australia, and like so many of the other Aussie luminaries, she came not from an urban or suburban background but from a rural one. She was born in Griffin, New South Wales, in 1951, and she spent a good deal of her youth living in an aboriginal mission, in a hut with a dirt floor, where the most effective and commonly used insect repellent was compressed, ignited cow dung.

Evonne was the third of eight children (four of them boys) born to Kenneth and Melinda Goolagong. Ken supported the family on his modest income as a sheepshearer. Although a few of Evonne's siblings chose to live traditional small-town life, one of her sisters made the dramatic move to urban Sydney to become an office worker. A brother, Ian, had enough talent to overcome a very late start in tennis and became a player on the pro satellite circuit. He eventually married an Australian girl and settled in as a teaching pro in Melbourne. Another brother, Mully, showed great promise as a golfer, but after a stint in the United States, he returned to Australia with an American bride to work at a civic post.

Imaginative journalists have written that Goolagong means "tall trees by still water," but Evonne once confided that her name actually means "nose of the kangaroo." To this day I don't know if she was pulling my leg or not, but she did have the good sense to choose a less exotic middle name for her daughter Kelly. "Inala" indisputably means "a peaceful place" in aborigine dialect.

Not long after Evonne was born, the Goolagongs moved to Barellan, which was about as peaceful as a place can get; in fact, Evonne has described it as lonely and desolate, made tolerable for her mostly by the size and closeness of her family, the only aborigines in the community.

Barellan, like many Australian towns, had at least one pub and one tennis court. Evonne's introduction to tennis was on a court of parched red earth surrounded by the rusted shells of abandoned cars and peppercorn bushes whose dried berries rustled and rattled with every breeze. She was fascinated by tennis—or, rather, by tennis balls—from the get-go. When the family jalopy finally broke down and the seats were removed for salvage, Ken found a stash of two dozen tennis balls left under the rear seat by little Evonne.

Bill Kurtzman, a local resident, spotted young Evonne peering through the fence around that court one day and encouraged her to take up the game. Her natural talent was evident from the outset, and soon she was participating in local tournaments. Before long, Evonne was spotted by two assistants of Vic Edwards, the proprietor of a tennis school in Sydney, who were on a scouting trip to the bush country. Edwards traveled to Barellan to look for himself, and he was so smitten by Goolagong that he persuaded her parents to allow her to further her tennis education in Sydney. At thirteen, in 1967, Evonne moved into Edwards's home, became a doubles partner of Edwards's daughter, Patricia, a student in the local secretarial school, and a champion in the making. The making did not take long.

On her second world tour, at age nineteen, Goolagong won the 1971 French Open in her first appearance at Roland Garros. A month later she won the Wimbledon title with a 6–4, 6–1 victory over her childhood idol, Margaret Court. She would ultimately win four Australian Open singles championships, two singles titles at Wimbledon, and one at the French Open. She was also the runner-up at the U.S. Open four years in a row, beginning in 1973, and the winner at the season-ending Virginia Slims Championships twice, in 1974 and 1976. All in all, she won forty-three singles titles in a fifteen-year career during which she was rarely far from the top of the game.

Years later Evonne would look back on her modest background with the same attitude as some other athletes who hailed from similar circumstances. She knew that rural poverty was more benign than urban destitution and felt that poverty was not a crime or a curse, nor some extraordinary state created so that New York socialites could throw themselves elaborate charity balls.

"About the only question I've been asked regularly that I really don't like is 'So what was it like to grow up poor?' " Evonne told me. "I don't know the answer to that because I never thought about it when I was young. I had no idea what it meant to be rich or to be poor. I just know that I had fun when I was playing outside, and when I had something to eat when I was hungry, I felt satisfied even if it was just a bowl of cereal or a Vegemite sandwich."

On one occasion a talk-show host really threw her for a loop by flipping the B-side of the poverty issue. He asked her what it felt like to be so rich when most aborigines were destitute.

"I didn't really know what to answer," she said years later. "But unlike a lot of other questions, this one really bothered me, because it made me feel like I was guilty or something. I thought about it for a long time afterwards. I realized that there were a lot of other aboriginal kids who had a lot of talent. A lot of them didn't really have the opportunity to develop their skills, and in that way I was just a lot luckier than they were. But that wasn't all there was to it.

"There really was no reason for me to feel guilty about my success because a lot of the other kids didn't have the determination to succeed. It's nothing they should be blamed for, and it shouldn't be put down to them being aborigines. Thousands of white kids don't make it, either, despite having all the advantages, so what does that line of thinking say about them?

"I reckon some people think that Mr. Edwards plucked me out of Barellan and, presto, I became a Wimbledon champion. The thing that still bothers me about that question is that it gives me no credit as a person. The guy who asked it was just looking at me like I was some little abo girl who'd just gotten lucky and won the lottery. Like I was a novelty."

Evonne was a young woman who always knew what she wanted, and she still cites that surety as the greatest of gifts. She was lonely when she first went to Sydney, and accepting the discipline of training became her way of cultivating an identity. Recognizing this spared her the agonies visited on other dislocated kids whose principal desire was to "fit in" a new neighborhood or school at any cost. Evonne was a shy girl who became popular with her peers, but she always stood apart. This became especially difficult when her hormones began to kick in.

"The 'boy' stage came pretty quickly after I went to Sydney, but Mr. Edwards was very strict and conservative about that. There were school dances every weekend, and the girls would invite me to go along and I was dying to go. But I realized that I had to train, get the right amount of rest, and concentrate on tennis and school. So after a while the girls stopped asking me along to dances because I never said yes. But I watched them go through the boy stage, and sometimes I envied their freedom."

Nevertheless, Evonne was consoled by her rapid development as a player. In 1974, Evonne won the Australian Open and reached the final of the U.S. Open. In the short span of four years she had appeared in ten Grand Slam finals and won three of them. And at twenty-three she was ready to quit tennis. By then Evonne had begun to bridle against the authority of the man who played Henry Higgins to her Eliza Doolittle. As attractive as her story was on the surface—it certainly was a dream for sportswriters—Evonne felt stunted and oppressed. Edwards's fatal flaw was a relentless desire to control and manipulate Evonne's life in order to eliminate any threat that, in his Victorian mind, endangered her tennis. Shopping was okay, and so was listening to the American Motown music that Evonne adored. But socializing on her own was just as taboo as it had been back in secretarial school. Dating men was definitely out.

Still, Evonne had met a persistent young man named Roger Cawley at a party in 1972. He was a man about town and an aspiring entrepreneur in London whose interests ranged from the sale of comic books to dealing in scrap metal and minerals. Roger and Evonne began to correspond regularly. Then they began to meet clandestinely.

Deceiving "Mr. Edwards" weighed heavily on Evonne, who had a strong sense of loyalty as well as an understandable fear of destroying a relationship that, no matter how unhealthy, had also been at the root of her success. Still, it took a seemingly extraneous event in 1975 to move Evonne into a confrontation with Edwards. That was the death of her father, Kenneth. Feeling depressed and isolated after that tragedy, Evonne decided it was time to make a life for herself with Cawley.

When Evonne told Edwards that she wanted to marry Cawley, the elderly coach hit the roof. This was a grotesque overreaction, given the seemliness of the match. Roger not only loved tennis, but as a gifted player and former junior competitor, he was also of the community. The best spin that could be put on Edwards's opposition to the marriage was that he was motivated by pure if foolhardy reasons.

Edwards's rebuff stung Evonne, but at first she refused to simply cut him off. She bore him no ill will, and she genuinely loved the Edwards clan as much as she did her own family. The young couple tried to reason with Edwards, but each of their meetings degenerated into an ugly confrontation. Accustomed to having absolute authority, Edwards succumbed to the ultimate conceit of the autocrat: He began to believe that he was absolutely indispensable to Evonne. He finally gave Evonne a "him or me" ultimatum, and it proved to be no choice at all.

I got to know Roger and Evonne at about the time that all this transpired, after *Tennis* magazine asked me to write a profile of Evonne on the heels of these events. I pieced together what I could without any private access to either Evonne or Roger, whose desire to avoid publicity over the break led them to politely decline requests for interviews. I wrote a highly interpretive piece in which my theory was that Evonne had always played for others—for Edwards, for aborigines, for Australia, for anybody but herself. And my only conclusion was that she had decided to take control of her own life, and we were just going to have to see if she enjoyed playing tennis for herself and her husband.

At a tournament a few months after the story appeared, a tennis functionary came to me in the pressroom and said that Roger Cawley was standing outside waiting to see me. This often means that you're about to get an earful, the content of which will determine whether or not you actually end up rolling around on the floor punching each other. But Roger just wanted to compliment me on the story, and we were soon gabbing away about tennis in general. We hit it off, and I was impressed by his knowledge of, and enthusiasm for, the game and its players. A few nights later I had dinner with Roger and Evonne, and we became friends. Over the years I watched dozens of matches with Roger, some of them excruciatingly tense affairs in which his wife was a party. He never once lost his cool or failed to acknowledge a brilliant point, no matter who won it.

Over the next few years Evonne did indeed get a life, one in which she blossomed, and one that made her genuinely happy. She had two children, and she would win three Grand Slam titles through the long and prosperous second stage of her career. I doubt that she would have enjoyed such success and longevity if she had succumbed to Edwards's ultimatum, but one thing continued to strike me for years afterward. No matter how close we grew and how many unguarded moments we spent together, Evonne almost never spoke about Vic Edwards. I finally came to understand that it was out of deference to the rest of his family, with whom she remained close. She maintained her silence about her mentor even after he died. I don't know if she had entirely wiped the memory of him from her mind, but her reticence always struck me as highly dignified.

When the Cawleys married, Evonne's success and celebrity did not eliminate the problems that face a tennis player who doesn't hail from the two chief tennis locations: the United States and Europe. In fact, it exacerbated them. The Cawleys were already immersed in a web of opportunities and the obligations that came with them. And like any young couple, the Cawleys wanted to make hay while the sun shone, a desire that almost precluded living anywhere but in the United States.

The Cawleys finally settled on Hilton Head Island, a resort community that sprang up almost overnight off the southern coast of South

Carolina. This was a peculiarly American phenomenon that extended the mall sensibility to encompass all of life. The developments on resort islands like Hilton Head were tightly planned communities featuring private homes, time-share condominiums, golf courses, and clothing and cookie boutiques.

Many of these residential-resort communities, consciously playing to the cachet of the aristocratic, genteel old South, were called "plantations." They also had aggressive marketing strategies based on hosting televised golf and tennis events. The theory was that if you lured enough celebrity players—and celebrity-player worshipers—to the plantations for tournaments, you could move lots of real estate even if it was perpetually damp. As a result, the Mayflower families at Hilton Head included many golf and tennis pros, with such luminaries as the former Wimbledon champion Stan Smith and his wife, Margie, the eldest girl in a distinguished tennis family from Locust Valley, New York. The Smiths, devout Christians, liked Hilton Head because it was simultaneously conservative, semirural, and conveniently upscale.

It was easy to see why life on Hilton Head was attractive to tennis players. It was a healthy, sporty environment despite the golf balls that periodically went whizzing by your head. The brand-new condos, private homes, and nautical-theme restaurants were pleasantly bland variations on the kinds of places where tennis players worked and lived on the road. But the marketing strategy worked only too well. The hype surrounding Hilton Head quickly triggered a land rush among upwardly mobile types who hankered to live next door to the Smiths or the Cawleys. The end result was human and natural pollution. By the 1980s, runoff from the developments and road construction had ruined many of the rich shellfish banks and wetlands on an island that for most of its history had been a humid, mosquito-infested marshland of great fertility but no great beauty. Ultimately, the Smiths made the radical decision to educate their children at home.

Like the Smiths, the Cawleys arrived at Hilton Head before the frenzy, and they settled into a healthy domestic routine on Port Royal Plantation. Evonne trained for tennis, and Roger dabbled in real estate. The Cawleys barbecued dinner on their patio overlooking the tidal flats of Calibogue Sound, and the main course was often fish that the Cawleys had caught themselves.

When I annually went to cover the Family Circle Cup, a successful tournament on Hilton Head, I stayed with the Cawleys. Being a sport fisherman, some of my fondest memories are of evenings spent with Evonne and Kelly on the network of tidal pools and creeks that ran through the local golf links and undeveloped housing tracts. Evonne seemed absolutely at home, tramping through the brush and alluvial muck, ever alert for snakes and even alligators.

However, the Cawleys were not nearly so conservative as the Smiths. They were a spirited young couple who liked to socialize and made friends easily—a little too easily, I came to believe. Neither of them had a critical temperament, so if an acquaintance seemed like fun, he or she almost immediately became a friend. One of Evonne's appealing qualities, the blithe indifference to her own celebrity, became a liability in that it made her accessible to people who, with their necks craned, were looking to pull into life's fast lane.

The Cawleys socialized with an assortment of hipsters and swingers: people who were millionaires one day and broke the next; expatriate doctors from California who ended up wrapping their Corvettes around trees in drunk-driving episodes; couples who thought that sniffing cocaine off the naked butt of their best friends' wives was good clean fun; couples who segued, seemingly overnight, from marital bliss to ugly divorce.

One night we were out late in a local bar with a woman friend of the Cawleys who had set up shop as a real estate agent on the island. Loosening up after a few drinks, this woman began to rail at me about the "New York Jews" who were descending on Hilton Head and buying up everything in sight. At closing time this woman snapped to attention and, with tears in her eyes, sang along to a rendition of "Dixie." I saw her the next day, eagerly showing the floor plans of model condominiums to a group of New York Jews.

Occasionally I would drop remarks about various members of this crowd, but you know how it is when it comes to criticizing friends for the friends they choose. Mostly I watched, with drink in hand. And sometimes I saw Evonne and Roger in a peculiar way, as two kids, really, cut loose from their roots, with not much to buffer them from corruption besides their love for each other and their children. Thankfully, the Cawleys' own excesses were benign, but I did worry about them when they opened a nightclub called "Evonne's" on the island. They survived that experience, partly because it was short-lived.

Another element that simultaneously kept the Cawleys youthful but also put them at risk was the domestic dilemma faced by any couple in which a spouse is a top player. The subordinate partner in the relationship is almost always forced to surrender any semblance of his or her own career. The combination of incessant travel and the level of both practical and emotional support demanded, often unconsciously, by even the most unselfish of players is overpowering. Men who marry women players almost invariably drift into coach-manager roles, often because it is the only work they're free to undertake. This role is fraught with dangers, but it has one valuable function: It can protect players from the very agents who bring so much opportunity their way. Many agents have compassion, but all of them live on commission, and they are not only tempted but duty-bound to generate as much revenue as they can for their clients and for themselves. Often, a spouse is a player's most reliable hedge against the dangers of playing too much or becoming involved in too many transactions that ultimately damage his or her motivation or ability to perform on court. The grace and good sense with which Roger accepted his role as a tennis spouse, and the couple's love for their children, ultimately protected them from becoming hedonists or victims of their own celebrity. But they certainly traveled in interesting circles.

On one of her solo trips to New York, Evonne called and invited me over to Liza Minnelli's apartment for coffee. When I arrived, the women were in the kitchen, where Liza was testing her new microwave oven on multicolored popcorn. Although I wasn't a big fan of the type of music Liza sang, I had always admired the absolute power of her voice and told her so. She replied that it was not a natural gift as much as an ability developed by muscle isolation and control. She then took my paw and put it on her chest. She sounded a note and held it so that I could feel her diaphragm reverberating like a drum—an exercise that was almost as disconcerting as the placement of my hand.

Minnelli and her husband at the time, Mark Gero, a tennis nut, also threw the most star-studded party I've ever attended at their capacious Upper East Side apartment—a giant maze of rooms and hallways, each one exquisitely decorated. It was a birthday party for Liza, and I was invited through the Cawleys along with my friend Liz Nevin.

At most fashionable parties in New York you might see a Danny DeVito here, a Julian Schnabel there, maybe a Meryl Streep or a John F. Kennedy, Jr. Everybody else stands around whispering things like, "Look, that's Danny DeVito stuffing down the oysters. He looks just like in the movies, only shorter."

At Liza's party everybody was a celebrity except for me and Liz. The range of people was astonishing: Lucille Ball, Robert DeNiro, Bianca Jagger, Al Pacino, Halston, Truman Capote, Andy Warhol, and raw youngsters like Kevin Kline and Christopher Walken. And that's the short list.

On another evening, at Elaine's restaurant, Woody Allen passed by our table on his way out. He hesitated and then hurried away. The next time I saw Elaine, she told me that Woody had really wanted to introduce himself, but he was such an ardent admirer of Evonne's that he was simply struck dumb. Andy Warhol had no such problems, because his remoteness was intrinsic. After he met and chatted with Evonne, she just shrugged and, with classic Aussie understatement, remarked, "He's a bit different now, isn't he?"

As Evonne's career wound down, she slipped out of the celebrity circuit just as easily and spontaneously as she had entered it. She took her career at face value, as a wild ride. And when the roller coaster came to a grinding halt, she didn't freak out. She just got out and walked away without looking back.

But the end of a player's career always poses a difficult transition, both materially and psychologically. As Evonne's playing days decreased and her income declined, the Cawleys reviewed their resources, aims, and options. A developer in Naples, Florida, a resort community not unlike what Hilton Head Island had once been, offered them a deal. The Cawleys sold their house at Port Royal and moved into a home that had been created by combining two condominium units. In the winter of 1989, at a time when I\ was having problems of my own, the Cawleys sent me a round-trip air ticket so that I could escape the decadent environment of New York and spend New Year's Eve with them.

Roger picked me up at the airport in the vehicle that had replaced the Rolls-Royce, the Porsche, the grocery warrior, and even the little Mercedes convertible that the Cawleys had once owned. It was a jet-black van with reclining seats, drink holders, a television, plastic Venetian blinds, and wall-to-wall carpeting. It was the ultimate "Let's go to Disney World!" vehicle.

I was happy to see that their family life was stronger than ever. But something was also coming to an end, and their new home made me aware of it. Their old house on Hilton Head had been big, comfortable, full of daily life. The new condominium was all marble floors and high-tech gadgets of chrome and black steel. Much to the delight of the kids, the main fixture in the living room was a pool table. In many ways the place represented a final fling with the giddy life of fun and games. It was a candy store reflecting a way of life that was coming to an end.

Soon thereafter, the Cawleys moved back to Australia. I always felt that Australia was where Evonne really belonged, and her sojourn in the United States was a long detour and an interesting study in the tremendous sacrifices that some tennis players have to make for their careers.

Back at home, Evonne became increasingly interested in her aboriginal roots. Back in 1985, Evonne had been deeply stung when a prominent aboriginal spokesman had written a bitter, highly publicized poem that essentially accused Evonne of turning her back on her people. It had moved her to a greater consciousness of her roots, and one result of that was a potential project that we hatched together in 1987.

I suggested that Evonne host a television documentary about aboriginal history and culture, and that she do it the simple but authentic way—traveling about Australia in a Land Rover with as small a crew as possible, moving as close to the heartbeat of the land and its people as she could get. But at the time, everybody still wanted a piece of Evonne. Roger thought the whole project would be a lot more workable if they sold international rights to commercial television, brought in major sponsors like Ford, and flew Evonne into various locations as her time allowed. I lost interest in the project, which was never realized.

I really miss the Cawleys, but I gather from our brief telephone conversations that Evonne is happy to be home at last. It doesn't surprise me, because she never did outgrow the values of rural Australian life—values that are rapidly vanishing Down Under, and in most other places where they were once held dear. Those values made Evonne a flexible but strong woman hampered only by the lack of a formal education and a suspicion of the intellect.

But there are still worlds for Evonne to understand and conquer, including those right outside her doorstep. She has accepted a place in the state sports' establishment and has become increasingly active in aboriginal issues. Roger is overseeing the publication of her official biography, and in our last conversation he told me that they were busy reviving the concept of the documentary that we talked about and argued over so long ago. I still hope she does it the simple way.

PART 11

CHAPTER 6

FRANCE
Of Jerry Lewis, Philippe Chartrier, and the Alphabet Wars of the Open Era

AH, SPRINGTIME IN PARIS. Ascending hemlines, descending tourists. Cobblestones on the rue des Arts shining with the fine mist that passes for rain, sidewalks mined with neat piles of steaming poop in this city where bichons frises, schnauzers, and even lowly mutts are no less revered than Yannick Noah, Mickey Rourke, or Jerry Lewis.

Say what?

Jerry Lewis. Show me a true Parisian, and I'll show you a man whose veins are clogged with cholesterol sludge and whose heart harbors a secret passion for the accordion. I'll show you a woman who's got a little thing for Rodney Dangerfield. Don't ask why, *c'est la vie*.

Ah, springtime in Paris. The tulips are in full bloom in the Tuileries, and a waiter in a stinky shirt takes your order for *steak frites* with an attitude suggesting that he'd just as soon bring you a neat pile of steaming— After all, *vous êtes un Américain*, which pretty much means that if you're not Mickey Rourke, Jerry Lewis, or a member of the pop band Supertramp, *vous êtes un chien*. And not one of the four-legged ones they like, either.

In the morning the empty tables at the cafes on the boulevard Saint-Germain beckon you with promises of cafe au lait, croissants, and more calories than you can count. You trot out your high school French in an effort to create international goodwill, and you are regarded as if you have just violated French air space on your way down from Pluto. Don't ask why. It's just, well, *comme il faut*.

Ah, springtime in Paris. You partake of the Parisian ritual of going

121

for ice cream to Bertoli's on the Ilie Saint-Louis. The pouty, drop-dead gorgeous student in the obligatory motorcycle jacket sitting at the next table fires up a Gauloise, and your companion faints from what the health fascists have dubbed "secondary smoke." The very notion is laughable when it comes to Gauloise or Gitanes, whose smoke would roust a gopher out of its den. After you resuscitate your friend, you buy some charming old prints from the *bouquinistes* along the Seine, and you end up giving them to a third cousin for Christmas. You go to the Louvre, but there are so many Japanese tourists waiting to see the *Mona Lisa* that you wander off into the Medieval Thimble Wing. You end up lost, but a search party led by the Japanese, who are used to such occurrences, rescues you. Don't ask why. *Plus ça change, plus c'est la même chose.*

Just fifteen years ago most Americans visiting Paris in early June assumed that Roland Garros was the name of some typical dog-walking, Jerry Lewis–loving, chain-smoking Frenchman, and they could not be blamed for wondering why everybody in Paris was talking about him. But the French Open has grown so big and so important that almost any visitor to Paris knows that Garros was a French aviator who was killed in action during World War I. The French named the stadium and grounds where their national championships are played in his honor, and they refer to both the tournament and the site simply as "Roland Garros."

The French are renowned for their style, which explains much of why their tournament may be the best of the Grand Slam events. The Australian Open is fun and it's easy—a little too easy in that the space and the casual ambience at Flinder's Park prevent the tournament from generating the electricity that is created at the other, crowded Grand Slam sites when important matches are in progress.

Wimbledon provides the most wrenching drama, but the omnipresent, disheartening signs of English class distinction and snobbery are in evidence everywhere, compounding the feeling that at Wimbledon you are just a lucky trespasser on the hallowed grounds of the All-England Lawn Tennis and Croquet Club. Who needs that kind of hooey?

The U.S. Open is free of British formality, but because the U.S. Open is primarily a made-for-TV show, the site at Flushing Meadow is appallingly short on character and aesthetics. The heat and humidity are often brutal in New York in late August. If the sensibility is more democratic, it is so in the peculiar way summed up by that charming New York maxim, "Money talks, bullshit walks." I still haven't figured out which is worse: reserving your best seats, as Wimbledon does, for pale English aristocrats who actually think they're somebody, or selling them to the loud, upwardly mobile bond traders who make up the corporate entertainment crowd that seems to occupy most of the best seats at the U.S. Open.

The French Open strikes just the right balance between elitism and conviviality. There is plenty of posing and posturing, but that comes with the territory in France, where not too far below the surface of almost any old person is a prince or princess who likes what he likes and knows what he knows. It has nothing to do with social position or money, which eliminates a lot of the silly resentments and class hang-ups that abound in London and New York.

And of course there is the food. The underlying principle of French national unity is a common appreciation of good food, and the French Open is the epicurean's tournament. The kiosks feature crepes filled with apricot jam and dusted with powdered sugar, and ice cream bars flavored with Grand Marnier liqueur. The "sandwich jambon," a thin slice of cured ham on a hunk of buttered baguette, is another deceptively simple specialty that evolved from centuries of respectful doting on the sensitive receptacle that, for unenlightened folks who don't like the accordion or Jerry Lewis, passes for a mere stomach.

The ascendancy of the French Open has a complex subtext that reflects the changing values and leadership of the Open era. Back in 1968 the French Open was the most vulnerable of all the Grand Slam events. For one thing, Roland Garros was the only Grand Slam event that was not based on purely Anglo sensibilities and traditions. For another, the fatal flaw in the Grand Slam calendar was, and remains, the scheduling of Roland Garros and Wimbledon less than one month apart. The dates alone reveal the extent to which the French Open was initially perceived as an equal-but-different Grand Slam. After a couple of lagers, almost any member of England's old-boy network might wink and say, "It's quite a nice little event, but they do play the thing on that bloody clay. It is, after all, *French*."

The French Open is the only Grand Slam event contested on clay (the other three were all played on grass until well into the Open era). In the Anglo-centric world, real men and women played on grass and considered the spring clay-court circuit culminating at Roland Garros a pleasant way to play themselves into shape for the truly important summer "meetings" in London and New York.

Until the Open revolution, most tennis stars hailed from Australia, Great Britain, or the United States, but the French did produce one of the most gifted and successful generations in tennis history in the 1920s. That was the famed Musketeers—Henri Cochet, Jean Borotra, Jacques Brugnon, and René LaCoste. Those men dominated the all-important Davis Cup competition for seven years running, beginning in 1923. LaCoste himself won seven Grand Slam singles titles between 1925 and 1929. But between 1933 and 1983, the only Frenchman to win the singles title at Roland Garros was Marcel Bernard in 1946.

Yannick Noah turned in one of the great upsets of the Open era when he beat the Swede Mats Wilander for the 1983 title at Roland Garros, 6–2, 7–5, 7–6. But Noah could hardly be considered a typical Frenchman. He was born to a French mother and Cameroonian father in Sedan, France, but he spent his formative years in Africa. He might have become a pro soccer player were it not for Arthur Ashe, who discovered Noah and convinced the French Federation to underwrite Noah's development.

The only other Frenchman to contest a Roland Garros final in the Open era was Henri LeConte, a dazzling shotmaker who lost the championship match to Mats Wilander in 1988, 7–5, 6–2, 6–1. The best explanation I've ever heard for the modest results the French posted in their own championships was the one offered by my friend Philippe Bouin, the tennis correspondent for the French sports daily *L'Équipe.* "The verb 'to compete' does not exist in the French language," Bouin told me. "We have only 'to play' or the more serious 'to battle.'

"We are not good at sport," Bouin maintains. "In our culture we are taught to stress doubt, even self-doubt, over confidence and certitude. In school, sports were never accorded the same status as in other nations. The facilities are poor, and sport was thought to be only for the idiots in society."

Significantly, Noah and a handful of other French players who cracked the world's top twenty were the product of a developmental program instituted by the French Federation of Tennis. The program integrated education and tennis training in a way that no French school would have tolerated.

And if you're wondering how a society indifferent to sports produced *L'Équipe,* the most distinguished sports daily in the world, the answer is easy. "We exist only because 'serious' French papers paid no attention to sports," Bouin explained. "*L'Équipe* is like a national sports section that you buy separately from your favorite newspaper."

Thus, the rehabilitation of the French Open was a challenge much larger than bringing one of four equal events up to speed. And if the history of the pro era is the tale of the decline and dissolution of a quintessentially Anglo game and its values, the success of the French Open is a vivid testament to the breakdown of that old order.

In the big picture, there were three important factors in the rise of Roland Garros: the success of Bjorn Borg, changes in equipment that altered the way the game on clay is played, and the leadership provided by Philippe Chartrier.

Before a massive renovation effort in the late 1980s, there was a vaguely martial quality to Roland Garros. The permanent structures, including the stadium (Stade Roland Garros) resembled ivy-covered bunkers with floors of *terre battu*, which translates to broken earth but actually means red clay. The mood has since been softened by a discreet, well-executed expansion that hasn't ruined the atmosphere of the original site. Unlike Americans, the French don't subscribe to the scorched-earth theory of renovation.

The militaristic spirit of the original site was appropriate because at one time playing the French Open *did* bear a resemblance to the death march at Bataan. Early in the Open era, Europe and then South America were full of players who waged wars of attrition on the slow red clay surface that put a premium on defensive, consistent play from the baseline. These grinders were further encouraged when the U.S. Open, seeking a unique identity, opted to stage the competition on clay for a three-year span in the mid-1970s.

This cadre of new professionals turned the game into an exercise in trench warfare. Lobs and looping, topspun ground strokes fell like mortars everywhere, only to be returned like unexploded ordnance in a benumbing exercise of patty-cake. The battles that began while late-risers were still nibbling croissants on the boulevard Saint-Germain often lasted long into the lingering dusk, which in Paris ends after 9 P.M.

Anybody who has ever sat through a five-set, second-round battle between two unseeded unpronounceables on Court Whatever on a cold, overcast day at Roland Garros staggered away when the match ended with a new grasp of the word "torture." It was enough to make the Medieval Thimble Wing at the Louvre seem like a happening place.

And then came Bjorn Borg. His impact on the French Open and the grinders who populated it was similar to the influence of the Beatles on pop music. Borg was the first European superstar of the new Open era and the first clay-court player to dominate the world game in that period, more or less legitimizing clay-court tennis and its premier championship at a crucial time in tennis history. Whether or not Borg was the greatest player ever is a matter of debate, but his superiority on clay is not. He was one class above his rivals for the duration of his career on that surface.

Borg won the French Open six times in the nine years between 1973 and the year he abruptly retired, 1981. (Borg skipped the French because of World Team Tennis in 1977.) His match record was 49–2. One of Borg's two losses was in his first appearance at Roland Garros, when he was a fourth-round loser in 1973 at age sixteen. His only other loss was in the quarterfinals in 1976. He won at Roland Garros from 1978 to 1981 and at Wimbledon from 1976 to 1980, and while his Wimbledon triumphs were characterized by an almost supernatural ability to survive close matches, at Roland Garros he simply woofed down the competition. The French Open was a gimme for Borg; the prize money was just chump change, and the thrill of victory was blunted for him only by a laughable absence of the agony of defeat.

Changes in technology also played a vital role in the renaissance in Paris. At just about the time Borg retired, the same engineers who created a breakthrough by enlarging the head of the standard racket were experimenting with various synthetic materials to create rackets that were virtual cannons made of graphite, Fiberglas, and Kevlar. Borg was the last French Open champion to use a standard-sized wooden racket. The next generation, trained and armed with the early oversized and midsize rackets, was ready to move into the upper echelon of the game and to alter the way it was played on clay.

Early in the 1980s, the traditional clay-court specialist was still a grinder, a steady stroker who derived power from his legs and lungs. But in the mid to late 1980s, players began to find new power in their equipment. The classic wooden racket was the equivalent of a governor on an internal combustion engine, setting a mechanical ceiling on speed and power. As in racing, once the governor was removed, the nature of the competition changed.

When Mats Wilander, wielding a midsize graphite racket, won his first French Open title in 1982, he camped at the baseline and hit moonballs to Guillermo Vilas until the Argentine player's arm nearly fell off. When Wilander won his second French title in 1985, he attacked and volleyed his way past Ivan Lendl. Wilander, a supremely versatile, intelligent player, was forced to take that tack partly because Lendl, armed with an advanced racket, had already taken the baseline game to a new peak of aggression. A few years earlier, Wilander might have been able to outlast and outrun a big and relatively awkward player like Lendl, but Lendl's new racket allowed him to put many more balls away, even from the backcourt. The message was clear: Never again would the baseline be the impregnable fortress of the past.

In 1984, John McEnroe served and volleyed his way to the final at Roland Garros, not long after abandoning his Wilson wooden racket for a graphite-composite midsize job made by Dunlop. He led Lendl by two sets and a break in what would devolve into the most heartbreaking loss of McEnroe's entire career. Since then, such serve-and-volley luminaries as Stefan Edberg (a finalist in 1989 and a quarterfinalist in

1991), Boris Becker (a semifinalist three times), Michael Stich (a semi-finalist in 1991), and Petr Korda, finalist in 1992, have established their credentials on clay. The success of these pros, along with a host of other power players, is evidence of a minimalist trend that has affected play on every surface.

On grass and indoor carpet, the game is no longer serve and volley, but serve and return. On medium to fast hard courts and indoor Supreme courts, serve-and-volley tennis pays off handsomely. On slow cement and European clay, tennis reaches its most pleasing form as a short-rally game. While there will always be defensive, counter-punching specialists around, the long-rally wars of attrition that once characterized Roland Garros are history.

Ah, springtime in Paris. Like the city itself, tennis on the clay of Roland Garros suddenly appears timeless, romantic, elegant, *civilized*—a word that can't be used to describe the slam-bang game you see these days on fast courts. On the soft, packed clay, the most punishing serve from the most advanced racket becomes the strong opening statement in a dialogue rather than a fierce and final expletive. The clay absorbs atomic ground strokes and asks a little more: an interesting angle here, an off-pace backhand there. Even the baseline players who do well at Roland Garros these days hit the ball very hard and go for the winning placement when the opportunity arises. Jim Courier won the tournament twice operating on that premise.

The third factor in the renaissance in Paris was a man of vision and will who, by the end of the 1980s, was burned out by the tennis wars and saddled with a nagging sense of defeat. Philippe Chartrier was a pivotal figure not only at Roland Garros but in the notorious "alphabet wars" between World Championship Tennis (WCT), World Team Tennis (WTT), the International Tennis Federation (ITF), the Association of Tennis Professionals (ATP), the Men's Tennis Council (MTC), and even the International Olympic Committee (IOC).

In a way, Chartrier could be defined as the ultimate bureaucrat. He played an important role in erecting the political roadblock that may have prevented Jimmy Connors from winning a Grand Slam. Some will always remember him as the man who hung Guillermo Vilas. But Chartrier was much more than an administrative power broker. He liked power, but he wasn't corrupted by it. He was not motivated by greed, either. Chartrier worked to promote a traditional vision of the game, one that was under assault from engineers of the new professionalism.

Chartrier, the son of a moderately successful stockbroker, was born near Paris in 1928. He was eighteen and the top-ranked junior in France when his father died, whereupon Madame Chartrier went to work, partly to enable her son to pursue his interest in tennis. Chartrier ultimately achieved the number six ranking in France, which was good enough to get him on the Davis Cup squad but not good enough to get him playing time (although later he would serve as the French Davis Cup captain).

Chartrier knocked around on the international circuit and got a foothold in journalism, which led him at age twenty-five to quit tennis and start the magazine *Tennis de France*. One of his main purposes in that enterprise was to light a fire under the Fédération Française du Tennis (FFT), whose attitude and vision Chartrier characterized as "appalling." Like patrician federation types in most countries, the leadership of the FFT appeared oblivious to the rapidly changing tennis landscape surrounding it, a situation that calls for a little explanation.

As the sport of tennis became popular in England and an export to foreign lands during the colonial era, tennis nuts created national federations to administer and promote the game by staging "sanctioned" competitions, issuing rankings, and embracing a missionary agenda. These federations ultimately came under the umbrella of the International Tennis Federation, which soon became the ultimate authority in the amateur game, which was then the only game.

At the top of the federation pyramid in each nation were the Davis Cup and Federation Cup teams, along with the official national championships staged by each nation. The federations' operating expenses were covered by modest membership fees (you must be a member of the federation to play in sanctioned tournaments for rankings), donations, endowments, and whatever revenue the federations could generate at their showcase events.

The seeds of professionalism began to take root after the turn of the century, and they quickly flowered in such sports as soccer, baseball, and football. But the amateur establishment retained control in tennis, and the players who pioneered the pro game in tennis did so outside the purview of the ITF and its affiliates. When top players turned pro, they said good-bye to the lawns of Wimbledon and Forest Hills, and they went on barnstorming tours outside the amateur circuit. But inevitably the movement to allow pros to compete at the most important and traditional tennis events picked up steam, culminating in the genesis of the Open era in 1968. Although the ITF and its affiliates still controlled the Grand Slam event and operated a traditional circuit, they suddenly found themselves engaged in the competitive business of staging, managing, and promoting professional tournaments.

The great handicap of the ITF and its national affiliates, including the FFT and the USTA, was their nature as volunteer organizations. Federation officials fell into roughly two categories—the superstars of the old-boy network and old-fashioned do-gooders. The single thing most of them had in common, apart from the desire to put something back into the game they played, was a high tolerance for the elephantine nature of huge not-for-profit organizations.

The advent of professionalism did not profoundly affect the way the federations functioned in places such as Uruguay, Nigeria, or even Sweden, but in the four lucky nations whose national championships formed the Grand Slam, there was suddenly mind-boggling potential for revenue from ticket sales, sponsorships, and the sale of broadcast rights. At the same time, the Grand Slam tournaments were threatened by the new independence of the players and competition from new events and tours.

The tennis nuts who ran the amateur game would be challenged by entrepreneurs whose expertise gave them a leg up in the free-market scramble for players eager to assert their independence, and in the burgeoning industry of tennis promotion.

Wimbledon was poised to survive this transition relatively well for a curious and crucial reason: While the national federations in the three other Grand Slam nations owned and operated their national championships, Britain's federation, the Lawn Tennis Association, did not own Wimbledon. The event is the property of the club at which the event is staged, the All-England Lawn Tennis and Croquet Club. The AELTC supports the LTA with a voluntary contribution of about $10 million a year, and the federation is wise enough not to grouse about the setup.

Of course, the AELTC is run by OBN types, but they have always put the good of Wimbledon ahead of all else. Thus, the AELTC broke ranks with the ITF in the struggle to suppress professionalism and unilaterally declared in 1967 that it would allow professionals to play at Wimbledon. This was the turning point in the drive to establish professional tennis and, presented with a fait accompli, the other ITF constituents fell into line.

The French, sitting on a Grand Slam event that was already different and in many ways less prestigious than others, floundered. Armed with a progressive entrepreneurial mind and the credibility of an establishment insider, Chartrier took the French federation to task in editorials, and he ran *Tennis de France* so well that he soon secured his financial independence. Responding to overtures from the establishment, he joined the FFT as an official in the first year of the Open era, 1968. Chartrier was motivated partly by the conviction that the federations could be saved only by can-do activists and partly by the allure of the new age in tennis.

Securing the presidency of the French Federation would prove a lot easier for Chartrier than getting rid of it. He got the nod in 1972, after just four years of service, and it was soon apparent that he had stumbled into one of those president-for-life deals. He remained in office until 1993. Just five years after he came to power in France, Chartrier was elected president of the ITF.

"My long tenure in the FFT is easily explained by the role I played in the French Open," Chartrier told me, "but I've always been a little surprised by how long I lasted in the ITF presidency, from 1977 to 1992. I believe that is because the ITF came to understand that the power in tennis was shifting. There would be waves of players and growing tennis interest from Latin countries, from Scandinavia, from the Third World and Asia. In many ways I could be a bridge—the Latin guy who could live with the Anglo-Saxons but who also would be more flexible in dealing with the others."

Chartrier brought the French up to speed by acknowledging that, despite the prestige implicit in the Grand Slam events, the days when the player had no choice but to compete in them were over. Wimbledon and the U.S. Open were probably too important to pass up, but early in the Open era the French and Australian Opens were not as critical. So, first and foremost, Chartrier needed to build strong player fields for Roland Garros. This job increasingly entailed catering to the wishes of the players and their managers in ways that most OBN types would have considered beneath their dignity. Players of the new era were courted with flattery, under-the-table appearance money, and perks that were often thinly veiled attempts to skirt the prohibition against appearance fees. As a former player, businessman, and realist, Chartrier knew what was required, and he was willing to roll up his sleeves. But as a man with designs on the reigns of the establishment, his hands had to be clean when he held them up for inspection.

Chartrier's most brilliant stroke was one of those statist deals that leave free traders crying "foul" or "protectionism." He got the French government to kick back to the players a massive 33 percent of the withholding taxes usually slapped on the income earned in France by foreigners. Obviously, tennis players weren't considered your garden-variety "guest workers," and the French government approved the plan because of the prestige and potential revenue a strong French Open would generate.

In order to obviate the ITF's official policy against paying appearance fees, Chartrier offered perks that included free lodging in first-class hotels for players as long as they were in the tournament.

Chartrier also had to convince the powerful Anglo-based media that Wimbledon and Forest Hills were not the only tournaments that mat-tered. Philippe wasn't one of those newshounds who graduates to public relations or business and then goes around lambasting journalists. He knew how to woo the media, and at times he even appeared to take some kind of sentimental satisfaction from the drill. My firsthand experiences of this were frequent and amusing.

Chartrier approached me one day at the U.S. Open of 1978 and asked if I was planning to cover Roland Garros. I told him that I wasn't sure. He then offered to pick up my airfare, a proposal that I took back to my editor at *Tennis,* Shep Campbell. If the invitation had been issued to cover some tournament created to help sell condominiums at some new resort, we would have passed on it. But the French Open was a legitimate Grand Slam event that warranted coverage. I was not on the magazine's staff at the time, so I was not subject to *The New York Times*'s strict guidelines about freebies. Shep decided that accepting Chartrier's offer presented no ethical problems, but we weren't going to rely on his largess. I booked and paid for a commercial flight.

During the tournament Philippe reminded me to go around to his office to collect the airfare. When I did so, one of his assistants said she would meet me in front of the FFT offices in a few minutes. She came out and handed me an envelope containing French francs worth about $1,200. As she turned on her heels and disappeared back inside, I had the uneasy feeling that I had been transformed into a Haitian customs official or, even more alarming, a U.S. congressman.

I don't know if you'd call this a bribe, but it sure felt like one. And like most good bribes, it represented an interesting mutation of the honor system. Obviously I could do anything I wanted with that money. It was cold, hard cash, given with no questions asked. Over the ensuing years I would learn that this practice was deeply ingrained in tennis and almost religiously practiced by promoters looking for more or better press coverage. Europe is a hotbed of such honor systems. Incidentally, I squared all accounts with *Tennis* when I got home. I think Philippe would have been proud of me.

Chartrier was also a shrewd judge of character. At the FFT he surrounded himself with able, bright people who not only understood his methods but believed in his vision of the game. If Chartrier were to be judged on his record at the FFT alone, he would be acknowledged as an administrator and promoter of unqualified genius. But the larger battle always beckoned, and Chartrier always rose to the call.

Chartrier's first significant battle in the war between the new entrepreneurs of the pro era and an ITF establishment struggling to retain power was waged on the *terre battu* of his beloved French Open. In the early 1970s an American consortium threw money into an enterprise

called World Team Tennis, the brainchild of Billie Jean King. The enterprise might have succeeded if it were not for the greed of the players
and agents, the profligate ways of the owners, and King's stubborn insistence that WTT would employ a radical format and be played under
conditions as different as possible from typical tennis tournaments.

The WTT owners knew that the players would not pass on Wimbledon or the U.S. Open in order to play team matches in silly uniforms
before tennis-ignorant audiences in places like Phoenix, Cleveland, and
Pittsburgh. But they felt that they could compete with the French
Open for players, so they created a two-part season conveniently sandwiched around Wimbledon.

Ultimately, King, Bjorn Borg, Jimmy Connors, Chris Evert, Evonne
Goolagong, and others took the big money offered by WTT and either
skipped Roland Garros or played WTT under the provision that they
could fly over to Paris and compete in the tournament if they chose.

Chartrier was not yet ITF president, but he recognized the threat
WTT posed to the establishment and to his own tournament. He soon
became the point man in the battle against WTT, and in 1974 he persuaded the ITF to lock WTT participants out of the French Open even
if they were willing to play. The ban was in force long enough to keep
Connors from playing Roland Garros in 1974. As a result, Connors
may have been prevented from becoming the first man since Rod Laver
in 1969 to complete a Grand Slam by winning the four major tennis
events of the year.

Although Chartrier's first skirmish put him at loggerheads with the
players, one of his subsequent crusades constituted a form of self-interested restitution. By 1983, Chartrier was also chairman of the Men's
Tennis Council, or Pro Council, the body that organized and policed
the official game in an attempt to satisfy all its constituents. And if it
were not for Chartrier's political clout in that office, Yannick Noah
would not have won the 1983 French Open—thus averting one of the
most delicious moments of the pro era.

Noah had the bad judgment to pull out of a clay-court warm-up for
Roland Garros, the World Team Cup event in Dusseldorf, Germany, at
a time when the Pro Council was in a mood to crack down on all kinds
of hanky-panky, from the payment of guarantees (appearance fees) to
last-minute withdrawals from events. Thus, the Pro Council's administrator, Marshall Happer III, was under considerable pressure to sus-
pend Noah, a move that would have pleased law-and-order types and
sent a clear signal to players and agents. But Chartrier mounted a furious lobbying effort on behalf of Noah. As the promoter of the French
Open, Chartrier knew that Noah's absence would have been a real blow

to his own event and a huge disappointment to the French fans. So Chartrier prevailed upon Happer to make the suspension effective after the French Open, when the only thing on Noah's mind would have been his chronic inability to make any kind of impact at Wimbledon.

Although there was a clear conflict-of-interest issue in play, Happer agreed to Chartrier's plan, and Noah went on to win the French Open. He was only the second black man (after Arthur Ashe) to win a Grand Slam title. His triumph generated worldwide interest in tennis and raised tennis awareness in France to heights unknown since the heyday of the Musketeers.

The fallout for Chartrier from this affair was minimal: The three player representatives on the Pro Council were by definition pro-player; the three tournament representatives hoped that the precedent might be useful to them if any of their number ever stood to lose a top drawing card; and the three ITF representatives on the Pro Council were supporters and minions of Chartrier.

For his efforts, Chartrier got nothing but a cold shoulder from Noah who thought any suspension was unfair. The two men didn't speak for eight years, but it was typical of Chartrier that he ultimately extended the olive branch in a unique and powerful way. At the end of the 1980s he offered Noah, a legendary free spirit, the Davis Cup captaincy. The move might have produced a debacle in that Noah, at twenty-nine, hardly seemed ready to take on the dull, thankless responsibilities that accompany the Davis Cup captaincy. But the end result was France's second greatest episode of the Open era, as Noah, a principal in the first one, led the Davis Cup squad to an upset of the United States in Grenoble in 1991.

The image of Chartrier and Noah locked in an embrace just moments after the tie ended was both touching and symbolic. It became the graceful epilogue to Chartrier's brilliant career in France. The results of his work on the larger, international stage on behalf of the ITF did not proceed nearly as smoothly, nor did they end on a similarly happy note.

On a bright, breezy day during the Australian Open of 1991, I strolled around the grounds at Flinder's Park looking for a quiet spot to smoke a cigar and watch a couple of players in the junior competition. I settled on a court surrounded by nearly empty stands, and as I went around to the emptiest spot, I happened to bump into Chartrier, who stood with his arms folded, watching the match.

By then the major battle for control of the pro game was over, and Phillipe had been the field marshal of the losing side. The nine-member

Pro Council (on which the ITF, the players, and the tournament promoters had equal voices in running the men's professional game) lay in
smoking ruins. There was something sad about the failure of this organization, as there is about the ruin of any group in which the principals
try to put aside self-interest in the quest to govern by consensus. In this
case, The Association of Tennis Players, the union of pro players, ultimately conspired with tournament directors (and, allegedly, the agents)
to freeze out the ITF and seize control of the pro tour. From 1991 on,
the pro circuit would be called the ATP Tour, and it would operate in
competitive coexistence with the ITF. Significantly, many of the gener-
als on the winning side, such as former U.S. President Jimmy Carter's
aide Hamilton Jordan, were either absolute outsiders who knew little
about tennis, or men whose exclusive interest was the commercial success of the pro tour.

Although the ITF had lost the war, its constituents had not been
forced to relinquish their homelands. They still owned and controlled
the four most important tournaments on the calendar, the Grand Slam
events, and they were busy re-entrenching for a potential siege, with the
member federations working together as they had rarely done in the
past to protect their stake in the game. They had formed the Grand
Slam Committee in order to develop strategies for protecting the four
major events and the ITF.

In 1989 the Grand Slam Committee gave its blessing to an extraordinary and controversial tournament, the Grand Slam Cup, for which
12 players qualified on the basis of their results in Grand Slam events.
The prize money was staggering, with a $2 million check going to the
champion for winning as few as three matches. Ironically, one of the
distinguishing features of a Grand Slam event is that, unlike a typical
one-week, thirty-two-draw event on the circuit, it features a draw of
128 players. A Grand Slam champion must win seven consecutive
matches during the two-week competition. Thus, endorsing the small-
field, restricted-entry, insanely lucrative Grand Slam Cup had put the
ITF into the business of promoting exactly the kind of "special event"
that it had so adamantly opposed back in the days of unity.

Anyway, Phillipe looked melancholy that day in Oz. He had been
crushed by the defeat and the destruction of the Pro Council. He spoke
slowly and softly as we watched an artistic young Indian player with
marvelous touch struggle against the straightforward Teutonic power
game of a German youth.

"It's wonderful, isn't it?" Chartrier mused. "This boy from India is
playing against a German in Melbourne, Australia. This is truly a world
community full of cultural variety. Each of these boys represents ten

years' worth of investment and development by the ITF. Each of them is the product of a system that found them, gave them a playing structure, and even financial support. Each of them may become a millionaire by the time he is twenty-one years old. In return, the ITF gets absolutely nothing except the voluntary participation of these boys and girls in their events. Who else could do this in tennis? Who else would *want* to?"

I knew exactly what Chartrier meant, and it was why I had come down on the side of the ITF in many political battles. When the men and women who work in the pro tennis industry say that their entrepreneurial skills and business acumen promote interest in the game, they're right. But it's spectator interest, and it's entirely driven by commercial values. Pro sports are an end unto themselves because they define "success" in strictly commercial terms.

Amateurism also stressed participation, which was the ITF's primary mandate. By contrast, the pro establishment has no real interest or any infrastructure to promote the grass-roots growth of tennis. I think there's something creepy about living in a society of spectators, content to watch professionals doing something they could just as easily be doing themselves. I rationalize my spectator interest in pro football on the grounds that I'd have to be a real knucklehead to play the game in some Sunday league at age forty-plus. It's also tough to get eighteen people together for a casual game of baseball. But tennis is different. As the USTA claimed in a recent recruiting campaign, tennis is a sport for a lifetime, and it's also one in which men and women can participate together. Tennis is more like running than any contact sport, and it doesn't present the logistical problems of securing a large field and teams of players. Sure, your skill level will be a lot lower than that of the pros, but your entertainment quotient may be higher. And playing the game really enhances your appreciation as a spectator.

In the best situation, pro sports are an extension of the amateur game. That's why college sports, despite the special problems posed by abuses of the amateur system, are so valuable. On paper, if not always in reality, prospective pro athletes are offered the opportunity to get as good an education as they care to pursue. They can spend more time being young, prepare for life after sports, and have better tools with which to make career choices—including the decision to become a pro athlete.

In this context, it's odd that tennis, which is so often perceived as an Ivy Leaguish enterprise, has made a dramatic break with that tradition and pioneered one-dimensional professionalism. And one of the tragedies of the Open era has been the way the pro establishment has, wittingly or not, laid waste the college game. This is doubly ironic because tennis has a lot more in common with "minor" college sports (golf, track, lacrosse) than it does with football or basketball. The logistics of fielding a team are easy, and the expense is relatively minimal. The structure of the collegiate game gives players a great opportunity to experience—perhaps for the last time in their lives—the joys of team competition and the camaraderie it breeds, a sense of fellowship they will never experience on the insular, individualistic pro tour.

Before you put this down as so much idealistic or sentimental hogwash, take a roll call of the last American generation to exploit the college experience: Dennis Ralston, Bob Lutz, Arthur Ashe, Stan Smith—all of them had distinguished pro careers, and all of them became well-adjusted adults. Some of them went on to become People Who Matter. But in today's environment, it is unlikely that an Arthur Ashe would go on to college (never mind serve in the army). The next generation of pros, led by Bjorn Borg, became fantastically rich, and that may be all you can say for them. Some of them later withered as irrelevant celebrities and experienced great pains adjusting to life after they had retired.

So let's assume for a moment that the ATP Tour, armed with its own sense of mission, continues to grow and gain power. Inevitably, this new establishment will press for an ever-larger slice of the action at the Grand Slam events. If the ITF is forced to make those concessions, its revenues will be slowly but inexorably diminished, funneled into the burgeoning bureaucracy of the pro game and the pension funds of players who have earned small fortunes before people of the same age can afford to buy their own homes. Meanwhile, the ITF will be left with dwindling resources to foster the game at the grass roots.

This may sound alarmist, but in the end the tennis community may evolve into nothing more notable than a Hollywood-style establishment that services millions of curious spectators through the labors of a privileged class of extraordinarily rich tennis stars. These stars will be developed from a diminishing pool of kids whose parents are fortunate enough to finance the high cost of lessons. One of the other great ironies in this scenario is that you end up having exactly the sort of elite, remote establishment that the populist pro movement in tennis was supposed to destroy. And you have an establishment with entirely self-serving values, with its success or failure measured in nothing more dynamic than gate receipts.

If you really think about it, the ITF is an extraordinary body, and its massive infrastructure is a great testament to the good that people motivated by the public spirit can accomplish. And if you look at the worldwide tennis community as an organic whole comparable to a human body, shutting out the ITF has to be seen as a trauma comparable to the loss of a limb. The body doesn't have to die, but if wounds don't heal properly, it will anyway.

One small glimmer of hope issued on this horizon in 1994 when the ATP Tour finally abandoned its fixation on "glamour" charities (important as they are) and decided to throw its charity apparatus into a cause that was actually tennis-related: junior development. I hope this signals an increased awareness on the part of the ATP Tour of the importance of the grass-roots game. Unfortunately, it's probably too late to revive the collegiate game. Most of the world is committed to the concept of cradle-to-grave professionalism, and the United States is falling into lockstep. You can hardly expect a promising young American player to opt for college, knowing that the decision would give his peers abroad a great developmental edge.

These issues took on a new, vibrant life during a heated debate over the "crisis" in tennis in 1994. Faced with declining sponsor revenues, falling TV ratings, and a general worldwide recession on both the recreational and professional fronts, the tennis community conducted a lengthy bout of soul-searching. The "crisis" in tennis proved that without strong, grass-roots support for the game, pro tennis is at the mercy of capricious spectators in a market glutted with sports, sponsors whose marketing strategies have nothing to do with the nature of, or values embodied by, the sport of tennis, and a coddled class of players who lack the education and experience to take a vigorous part in the debate, much less bring solutions to the table. The crisis of 1994 was brought about almost entirely by the professional sensibility, by a new establishment relentlessly obsessed with tennis as a mere spectacle, a popular entertainment.

Tennis politics have always been a real-life equivalent of what novelist John Le Carré, describing the shifting alliances and hidden agendas of the espionage community, called "a wilderness of mirrors." Uneasy alliances, subterfuge, and intense horse trading have been the engines driving the game no less mysteriously than one of those old-fashioned political machines assembled by a Chicago alderman. Thus it was hardly surprising that when the political operatives in the expanding game originally went head-to-head, they did so within the civilized structure of a committee. By forming the Pro Council in 1974, nine representatives of different and often conflicting groups within the tennis community agreed to try to resolve their differences and govern for the common good. The body then hired Marshall Happer as a nonvoting administrator whose mandate was to carry out Pro Council policy.

Just two years after Chartrier became ITF president in 1977, he became chairman of the Pro Council. He was one of the three ITF votes that represented the conservative, traditional side of the game. The promoters generally used their three votes to protect their own vested interests, either from predation by newcomers promoting lucrative exhibitions and nonsanctioned "special events" or from either player or ITF threats to the sub–Grand Slam world tour. The players' representatives tried to maximize opportunities and income for ATP members without destroying an "official" game that was founded on the concept of an international tour in which participation was based on merit (ranking) and prize money was awarded only for performance.

The minutiae of tour operation became one of the administrator's chief responsibilities. Happer was responsible for producing the original Code of Conduct. He policed the game, levying fines and suspensions when a player violated the Pro Council's code in any number of areas, ranging from verbal abuse of officials to late withdrawal from tournaments to violations of the official dress code. Happer's office was also responsible for mundane things such as the protocol for entering tournaments and the regulations pertaining to courtside advertising and signage.

But the big battles waged by the Pro Council were against Lamar Hunt and his World Championship Tennis Tour, against the increasing role of agents in staging and running tournaments, and against an issue that, ironically, began in the "shamateur" era and just wouldn't go away in the Open era. This was the paying of under-the-table appearance fees ("guarantees") to secure participation by top players in tournaments that were supposed to offer only prize money. This was the way Mervyn Rose built his home and the way kids like Jimmy Connors and Bjorn Borg partly accumulated fortunes.

Hunt's WCT Tour was a well-run, attractive, and in many ways revolutionary step forward at the dawn of the pro era. Hunt was a Texas oil billionaire and a visionary who wanted to organize and promote tennis in the manner of the National Football League. (He is the owner of the Kansas City Chiefs and a founder of the old American Football League.) Many of Hunt's ideas—ranging from encouraging the players to wear colored shirts because they were more telegenic to his attempt to develop a sensible, integrated television package—were subsequently implemented by the very people who drove him out of the game.

The greatest strength of the WCT concept proved to be its undoing, as the increasingly diverse members of the new establishment were scared off by the prospect of one man—Lamar Hunt—owning the entire professional tour and subcontracting tournaments out to pro-moters in individual cities. Thus the power brokers, driven by instincts of self-preservation, joined to do battle with the renegade Texan and establishment outsider. The battle began when the Pro Council decided to go with the Grand Prix system in which all the sanctioned pro tour-naments were linked in much the same way as events are in Formula 1 auto racing. Hunt was able to secure only a few dates on the calendar, and for a few years WCT remained a mini-tour within the main tour. But realizing that he was being squeezed out of the action, Hunt declared all-out war in 1982, setting up a new, full-blown WCT circuit to compete with the Grand Prix system.

The chief beneficiary of the conflict was the players. Ivan Lendl made over $2 million in prize money in 1982 without winning a Grand Slam title or reaching the world's number one ranking. Most of that income was provided by the lucrative WCT circuit, which he supported with gusto. But the WCT events took huge financial losses, and Hunt's bold, final move to seize control of the tennis circuit collapsed. He quickly faded from the picture, although his tour represented exactly the kind of progressive consistency and order that his successors would try unsuccessfully to impose on the game.

It's impossible to address the other two big-ticket items on the men's tennis circuit agenda without this preface: Tennis is a game that has been not only shaped by conflicts of interest but in many ways defined by them. I've already mentioned Chartrier's self-interested intervention on behalf of Yannick Noah in 1983. Chartrier also never relinquished his stake in the influential magazine he founded, *Tennis de France.* He surrendered editorial control when he threw in his lot with the FFT and ITF, but he retained a financial stake—a position whose advantages are clear enough.

In the big picture, this is certainly a small-potatoes conflict. I men-tion it only to show the degree to which almost all people of influence in the game had a closet full of hats to suit any occasion that required wearing one. But the Grand Master of conflicting interests was tennis's original superagent, Donald Dell.

Dell was a brash, vulgar man who had once been a lieutenant in the Kennedys' political machine. An amateur-era player, U.S. Davis Cup performer, and hard-nosed lawyer, Dell was a firmly entrenched, though controversial, member of the establishment. Unlike many of his peers, he was a highly ambitious character who loved to play hardball and was thus perfectly positioned to jump all over the opportunities kicked up by advancing professionalism. He began his career as an agent and nearly cornered the market on top players, particularly Americans. He was as loyal as he was tough, evidenced by his lifelong friendship with many clients, including Stan Smith and Arthur Ashe.

Dell's conflicts were considerably more disturbing than those of Chartrier. At the high point of his career, Dell's player clients virtually ran the ATP board of directors, and Dell himself was the union's chief legal counsel. Dell's right-hand man, Bob Briner, was executive director of the ATP, and Dell was deeply involved in running tournaments and representing sponsors, including the title sponsor of the Grand Prix tour itself, Volvo.

Sometimes Dell's conflicts assumed the dimensions of parody. For example, he enjoyed serving as a commentator on many tennis tele-casts, so he would package TV deals that included himself as part of the broadcast team. Dell was a serviceable if uninspiring talking head, but the problem was that he often ended up windbagging about matches in which both—or, worse yet, just one—of his clients participated.

The bitterest battle undertaken by the Pro Council, until it became embroiled in a simple, ultimately unsuccessful struggle for survival, was against the agents, including Dell (of ProServ) and Mark McCormack (of IMG). In the early days of the Pro Council, everyone had reason to fear the expanding influence of the firms that, after modest beginnings as talent management agencies, moved smoothly and voraciously into tournament marketing and promotion. The threat in this development was clear: When the very men who advise and often control players also stage or run events, they can easily make or break a tournament by pro-viding, or withholding, players. Independent tournament promoters feared they could not compete fairly against events that were run by agents. Agents would not only persuade players to participate in com-pany-run events but could come up with all kinds of baroque payola schemes that violated the "prize-money only" mandate of the Pro Council, throwing the whole system off track. And, finally, the ITF feared that without a built-in mandate for anything but their own finan-cial success, the agents would outspend and outmaneuver the ITF establishment, saddled as it was with volunteer leadership and a cum-bersome mandate to ensure "the good of the game."

The agents had an irrefutable response when these fears were voiced. They pointed out that they had not started their own tournaments but had either bought unsuccessful ones or been recruited by promoters who wanted to take advantage of their marketing and administrative expertise (not to mention their access to players). Bob Kain, head of the tennis divi-sion of IMG, is particularly proud of what his firm has done for the growth of women's tennis. Undeniably, one of the great weaknesses of the

ITF was its obdurate indifference to the potential of the women's game. The only good explanation for that blindness was simply sexism.

Furthermore, many of the agent-run tournaments were owned by ITF–affiliated national federations that were unable to market their events successfully. The agents had a field day. In some cases all they had to do was guarantee the anxious federations that their event would not lose money, and the agents were free to make as much as they could for themselves. The agents also claimed that their business skills and methods created growth and prosperity that rubbed off on all tournaments—including the Grand Slams—and all segments of the public. By definition that meant they were good for the game.

Still, the purist faction on the Council prevailed, due partly to Happer's vision of both his office and the game. A consummate rationalist as well as a lawyer given to brooding over ethics, Happer was almost obsessive about the conflicts of interest that ruled tennis. This, along with Happer's status as a former player and tennis community insider, put him in lockstep with Chartrier. Of course, as chairman of the Pro Council, Chartrier also happened to be Happer's boss.

Happer was instrumental in establishing and implementing policy. In the end he just couldn't square the role of agents as both player representatives and tournament promoters. He ended up leading the Pro Council's long and costly battle to define turf lines in the pro game. Armageddon was staged in the cozy confines of a well-appointed court of law, complete with bored security guards and stale, bottled water.

Actually, it was Volvo and Dell who began the war by filing a lawsuit in response to the Pro Council's objections to a stunt orchestrated by Dell. In 1985, Nabisco took over title sponsorship of the Grand Prix tour, replacing Volvo. Dell and his friends at Volvo were all hot and bothered by the defeat, so they put together a series of linked events that in myriad cheeseball ways (signage, advertising, and so forth) created the impression that Volvo was still the "official" sponsor of the tour.

Among other things, this episode spoke volumes about Dell's arrogance, and the degree to which being an "insider" armed him with a smug sense of righteousness—a conviction that was not at all threatened by the fact that his actions constituted, in my opinion, a remarkable abuse of his power and an extraordinary betrayal of his community.

In response, the Pro Council launched a campaign to censure Volvo/Dell and to assert its unilateral control of the official tour. When the MTC asserted its jurisdiction over the Grand Prix tour and told Volvo to stop running its knockoff tour, the aggrieved parties, supported by a host of allies (including rival management companies that

saw the advantages of weakening or destroying the Pro Council), filed
a suit accusing the Pro Council of violating the antitrust laws. The Pro
Council felt it could not only demonstrate a right to rule the game but
that it could utterly discredit Dell and his cohorts because of their outrageous and glaring conflicts of interest.

Federal Judge Kevin Duffy of the Southern District in New York
looked at Volvo/Dell's claims and pretty much chucked them out the
window. The dismissal of the suit acknowledged the Pro Council's right
to run the tour, which implied that its prohibitions against such things
as agents running tournaments were legitimate. This was the high-water
mark for Chartrier and the Pro Council, but the victory would be a
Pyrrhic one.

The agents recognized the massive threat that the newly empowered
Pro Council represented to their interests. They were also shrewd
enough to refrain from taking the offensive. As both advisors to and
representatives of the players, they knew that there was a grass-roots
movement among the players to take control of the game. So all the
agents had to do was pace the sidelines like so many football coaches,
directing the game and counseling the team when the players went up
against the Council.

The battle was decided as quickly as it was joined. Acting on a plan
developed under the leadership of the ATP's chief executive officer,
Hamilton Jordan, a man who came to tennis with no knowledge of the
game but plenty of experience in the back rooms of politics, the ATP
declared during the U.S. Open of 1988 that it would take over the ownership and operation of the men's pro tour. The official announcement
was made in the main parking lot at Flushing Meadow, with the players
bitterly complaining that the USTA had denied them the use of a room
on site to make their declaration. This grievance was one of the more
amusing—and disconcerting—elements in the scenario. Did the players
really believe that the USTA should have eagerly provided them with
the stage on which the players would declare war on the establishment?

When the smoke cleared after the ATP rebellion, the agents were
right back in the business of running tournaments. In fact, the victory
was particularly sweet for IMG. Although the nascent ATP Tour's
CEO Hamilton Jordan had vowed that he would not allow agents to
represent players, promote events, and market the tour, they wound up
doing just that. The deals that the agents put together were simply too
sweet to resist. Thus IMG ended up being the exclusive representative
of the ATP Tour when it came time to market the tour for television.
The $60 million guarantee offered to the ATP Tour for a television
rights package was far better than anyone else could deliver.

Ironically, one of the big losers in the battle to destroy the Pro Council was Grand Master Dell. By virtue of a good head start Dell had a strong grip on the top players and many events in the 1970s, but he was eventually blown out of the water by agent Mark McCormack and his firm, IMG, who had previously aligned themselves with Dell in many conflicts with the Pro Council. Playing out what amounted to a masterful divide-and-conquer strategy, IMG allowed Dell to turn on the establishment of which he was a part, and then it turned on Dell and gobbled him up.

Dell was too shortsighted to see what Chartrier had recognized: the diminishment of Anglo ascendancy in tennis. IMG, built on McCormack's highly successful partnership and friendship with golfer Arnold Palmer, had a much broader international vision. The company moved into tennis slowly, nibbling at the edges of Dell's empire by signing aging but marketable Australian stars, including John Newcombe, Rod Laver, and Evonne Goolagong.

The linchpin in IMG's success proved to be the first European megastar, Bjorn Borg. Signing the Swedish superstar was the official confirmation of IMG's emergence as a serious rival to Dell's organization, ProServ. As IMG mounted one client and marketing success after another, Dell's partners at ProServ, increasingly disgruntled by his autocratic ways, among other reasons, plotted a mutiny. Soon thereafter a few key ProServ personnel bolted and created a new management company, Advantage International. The split left IMG the dominant management company in tennis.

Dell still had plenty of scraps off which to feed (including the juicy one of his continuing role as negotiator of the USTA's U.S. Open television contract), but he was through as a majordomo in tennis. In a way, he simply outmaneuvered himself.

Conflicts of interest hit absurd levels in the issue of appearance money. Players wanted to be paid guarantees, agents felt both obliged and happy to secure them, and promoters were unwilling to suffer the consequences of not paying them. Still, everybody in the game supported the prohibition against paying guarantees. This was even true of many players and tournament directors who at one time had served on the Pro Council and sanctimoniously endorsed antiguarantee regulations! One former Pro Council member told me how in one meeting the South African promoter Owen Williams was vilified for paying Guillermo Vilas a whopping guarantee. Standing his ground, Williams dared all the other members to make an issue of it, knowing how almost every one of them had comparable transgressions on his record. "It was awful," Williams told me. "We were engaged in a total farce because nobody wanted to accept the reality of the situation. . . . All of us were guilty. In fact, the only people who wouldn't be hurt were the ones who were really operating underhandedly—you know, giving over money in cash in a brown paper bag, that kind of thing."

But as it turned out, when the Pro Council finally went to the mat over a guarantee case, it was indeed over a brown paper bag. Unfortunately, the major victim in the case was the otherwise exemplary and popular player Guillermo Vilas. He and his manager, Ion Tiriac, were legendary guarantee hounds whose demands were reported as gleefully and confidentially as ethnic jokes in a barroom. Still, they were not significantly different from the rest of the top players and their managers. Not only did guarantees remain a feature of the game after the Vilas case, but they have since become institutionalized on the ATP Tour. Whenever a top player loses in an early round in a tournament that is just below Grand Slam or ATP Tour championship series level, you can almost bet that he was just showing up to collect his appearance fee.

One of the great examples of this occurred in 1994 at the lucrative tournament staged in early January by the oil-rich nation of Qatar. The tournament offers a mere $525,000 in prize money and ranks as a mere world series tournament, meaning that it is allowed to offer appearance money. The top stars who have chosen to stop in Doha en route to the Australian Open include Boris Becker, Stefan Edberg, and Goran Ivanisevic, and no wonder: Players of their caliber are offered appearance fees that sometimes match the entire prize money pool for the tournament.

In 1994, Pete Sampras was guaranteed $500,000 to play in Doha. He showed up the day before he was supposed to play his first match in the desert heat, posed for the obligatory photo opportunities astride a camel and wearing a mullah, and proceeded to lose in the first round of the event to Kareem Alami. When he was criticized for failing to even disguise his lack of interest, the cheery, insouciant Sampras replied, "It wasn't as bad as some people made it sound. I arrived in Qatar *two* days before I was supposed to play."

In the current system, players are not only able to indulge in this kind of hanky-panky but are almost encouraged to do so by the notorious "Best of Fourteen" rule that the ATP Tour has created to balance the need for a ranking system based on sanctioned tournaments, the players' desire to maximize their earning potential, and the constant struggle to get the top players to play as often as possible.

Under the Best of Fourteen system, only the fourteen best tournament results of a player are used to calculate his ranking. The computer rankings are issued every two weeks on a "rollover" basis, with the results of the previous year dropped as the current ones are added. So, as long as a player has fourteen good tournaments in the electronic bank over a twelve-month period, he can maintain or improve his ranking.

In order to "defend" their rankings, players must post at least the same results in their fourteen "official" tournaments as they had in the previous year. The nightmare scenario for a player is losing in the first round of a tournament where, twelve months earlier, he had won the title. All the points he had earned with his outstanding performance fall off the computer, along with bonus points he may have earned for beating top players along the way. The only way for a player to make up the lost points and his subsequent drop in the rankings is by earning them back at another tournament. Top players like to have a few good tournament results in the bank as insurance. Journeymen often play week-in and week-out, hoping to hit a hot or lucky streak here or there to boost their rankings.

This system can therefore create artificially high rankings, but it is designed to make the top players participate in the official tour. Furthermore, tournaments below the championship series level (such as Doha) are allowed to pay appearance fees, which leads some top players to take the money and run. They sometimes turn in unprofessional performances, knowing that their rankings are protected by the Best of Fourteen rule. But tour officials don't seem to mind because the system has been effective against the threat posed by unofficial exhibition matches in which players can earn more in a weekend than they did for winning a sanctioned seven-day tournament.

And the players don't mind because they are not punished for bad losses as long as they have fourteen good results in the bank each year. A player who picks up a hefty appearance fee and then loses in the first round has just participated in a "competition" that may be even less meaningful than an exhibition, which does not even pretend to be "official" the way a sanctioned tournament does.

I don't like the Best of Fourteen system, but I believe that promoters who insist on throwing money at players should be allowed to do so. How they go about getting maximum value for their dollars is their business, not mine. But these realities also make me look back on the Vilas affair with a different perspective. In retrospect, it was one of the darkest hours in the history of the Pro Council. Chartrier and Happer hung Vilas, and it was a tragedy—not because Vilas was innocent but because the entire drill was a futile, sad, and ultimately wasteful attempt to enforce laws that were unenforceable, universally violated, and ultimately discarded.

The case broke when Happer received a letter from the city of Rot-

terdam, which had sponsored a Grand Prix event. It was on official sta-
tionery, town seal and all, and on reading it, Happer put down his
glasses and thought, "It looks as if we're going to the wall on this one."
The letter said that a post-tournament audit showed a shortfall of
$60,000, which the tournament director, Peter Bonthius, claimed he had
paid to Vilas's manager, Ion Tiriac, in cash as a guarantee for Vilas's
appearance. Naturally, he hadn't asked for a receipt.

In a typical tournament sponsored by a private company, the shortfall would have been considered an ordinary operating expense. But the
Rotterdam event was sponsored by the city itself, with public funds,
and the books could not easily be cooked. The disappearance of sixty
grand constituted an enormous problem, one that could potentially
erupt in a full-blown public scandal.

When Happer announced that he would pursue the investigation and
stage a hearing, most people in the tennis community cried scapegoat.
To this day Happer insists that the charge was unfair. "I hated the case
then, and I hate it now," Happer told me recently. "But people forget
that this wasn't an investigation we initiated or even a case developed
out of our desire to police the guarantee issue. It was a ticking time
bomb dropped right in our laps."

However, Happer couldn't have asked for a more appropriate case.
Although Vilas was considered a credit to the game, his manager, Tiriac,
did not share the same reputation. In those days the former Romanian
Davis Cup player was considered an unethical wheeling-and-dealing
renegade, an autonomous freelancer who flagrantly operated beyond
the pale of the tasteful cheating practiced by the rest of the agents and
promoters. Tiriac had also made a lot of enemies, dating back to his days
as a player who would stoop to the crudest forms of gamesmanship. In
the big picture Tiriac was a hungry outsider obsessed with playing hardball lest he miss out on the action or end up perceived as an East European bumbler with a horseshoe mustache. Although it's impossible to
call Tiriac a scapegoat, he was a politically correct target for the establishment.

Ironically, it was Happer himself who had secured Vilas's appearance
in Rotterdam. Part of his job as administrator of the Pro Council was
to find substitutes for top players who pulled out of official Grand Prix
tournaments at the eleventh hour. Thus, when Jimmy Connors pulled
out of Rotterdam just two days before the event was to begin, Happer
got on the horn with, among others, Tiriac. That was on a Friday
evening, and Tiriac told Happer he would get back to him. The following afternoon Tiriac called Happer back and said Vilas would play.

This was, to say the least, unusual. Players make their schedules up to twelve months in advance, and it takes a mighty inducement to make them depart from them. Tiriac didn't tell Happer that he was getting sixty grand for going to Rotterdam, but much later Happer would argue that Vilas's sudden decision to go could have been inspired by nothing less than a big payoff. Of course, this raises the interesting question of why Happer, the chief cop on the tour, didn't monitor the whole charade back when it transpired in the first place. It also raises the spectre of entrapment, although Happer still swears that there was no such plan or intent. In fact, Happer claims that he tried to do a deal with Tiriac to spare Vilas both embarrassment and the cost of litigation. He offered Tiriac an arrangement that would have amounted to the Romanian's turning state's witness. With Tiriac's help, Happer could have staged a roundup that corralled IMG, ProServ, and all the other agents, giving the Pro Council a historic opportunity to sit down with them and hammer out some kind of a workable policy about guarantees. But Tiriac refused to cooperate. He was the kind of guy who believed in honor among thieves.

The details of the case aren't important. It was a tawdry affair in which different parties gave different versions of physical facts and conversations. One of the things I learned sitting through the two-day New York portion of the hearing was that listening to men in $1,500 suits tell stupid lies about the simplest of things is sordid and depressing.

The piece of evidence that ultimately hung Guillermo Vilas was a tape recording of the conversation Tiriac had made of his chat with Bonthius on the same Friday night that Happer had called Tiriac. Tiriac would not have had to produce the incriminating tape on his own, and he only coughed it up in response to the very last question asked in the hearing by the Council's attorney, Roy Reardon.

But the content of the conversation eliminated any doubt in the minds of the three men on the panel responsible for rendering a final verdict. Happer himself had never doubted Tiriac's guilt or accepted his claim that Bonthius had simply kept the money. "If the guy hadn't given Tiriac the money," Happer said, "Vilas wouldn't have played. Tiriac may be a lot of things, but he wasn't a sucker."

The penalty for Vilas was a paltry fine of $20,000 (although his legal fees were considerably more) and a one-year suspension from competition in Grand Prix tournaments. Coming at a late stage in Vilas's career, the suspension clouded an otherwise brilliant, tranquil career and ended it on an incomplete note.

The lingering question is why Tiriac, a master of expedience, fought the case. His former companion and business partner, Heather MacLachlan, insists it was because Tiriac and Vilas truly did not take the money. "I think any of the other agents would have avoided the whole hearing by complying with Happer or by just paying a fine," MacLachlan told me. And she ought to know, having worked at various times for IMG as well as ProServ and Tiriac. "But Ion fought this with a lot of emotion. . . . Think about it. If he had taken the money, would he have gone to such lengths to prove that he hadn't? Only an idiot would do that."

Meanwhile, Happer is waiting for the day when Tiriac grows tired of stonewalling. "I don't think Ion even admits to himself that he took the money," Happer told me. "And I'm not even sure that Vilas knew he took it. I think one day Ion will come up to me and tell me the truth— I should say he'll *admit* the truth. He's even indicated to me on one fleeting occasion that he'll eventually talk to me about it."

"I'm not saying Guillermo would have pulled a Jimmy Connors and gotten to a Grand Slam semifinal at age thirty-eight," MacLachlan said, "but the suspension definitely hurt him the most. He was a pro who never took drugs, never drank, got along with everybody, and never created problems on the court. He was a positive role model, and these guys (the Pro Council) destroyed his career instead of letting him play his way into retirement."

Years later, Chartrier, president of the Pro Council when it hung Vilas, was unflinchingly honest about his role in the affair and about the general issues that tore apart the tennis community as the Pro Council fought to survive in the game.

"I have a guilty conscience about the Vilas affair, I'll tell you that right away," he said. "I was chairman of the Pro Council, and I was a tournament promoter. I was policing the same things that I was doing, and it was normal procedure. Absolutely."

Shortly after our conversation in Australia, Chartrier resigned the presidency of the French Federation. Henceforth he would devote all his efforts to the Olympic movement as a member of the International Olympic Committee. He swore to me that he would go to the wall in one battle and one battle alone—the fight to keep prize money out of the Olympics. Let the athletes be paid by their national athletic institutions, he said, or by shoe or clothing manufacturers. Let them earn bundles in endorsements and appearance fees, but let them compete in the Olympics just for the sheer joy of it and the honor of representing their nations, with nothing more at stake in those brief agonizing or triumphant moments than a medal and a national anthem. He somehow thought this struggle was different from the one he waged in tennis, and one that could be won. Unfortunately, a progressive case of Alzheimer's disease soon ended Chartrier's new role as a guardian of the Olympic spirit.

"I wouldn't want to go through it again the way I went through it in tennis," Chartrier told me in Australia. "That's for sure. I lost the war in tennis, but that was because the war ended up being about money. Money: It's everywhere, and it's nothing worth fighting over, I can tell you that. Now I don't even want to know about it. Even at the tournament I love so much, Roland Garros, I'd just as soon forget about it."

CHAPTER 7

BJORN BORG
Hey-doo, and Little Else

BJORN BORG'S ILL-FATED RETURN to professional tennis at Monte Carlo in 1991 may have been a generally miserable episode in the convoluted life of that magnificent athlete and baffling human being, but it sure represented a high point in my career.

The comeback attempt by Borg was the most mystifying event I've ever covered in tennis. For all kinds of people, including Borg, it was a wild-goose chase full of ghosts and insane hopes, delusions and mesmerizing echoes. For roughly a week everybody in and around Monte Carlo was enthralled by a resurrection driven not by divine ordinance but by Borg's conceit and, above all else, his distinctive willfulness. The Swede seemed to believe that time had actually stood still and waited while he took a hiatus from tennis that lasted for nearly a decade. And as anybody who has ever bought a computer will explain—usually for a lot longer than you're willing to listen—things change more in a decade nowadays than they did in the entire Bronze Age.

The comeback attempt explained many things about Borg, a man who had previously been unknowable because he was so unforthcoming. This character trait served him well in many ways. It kept him at arm's length from his rivals, it stymied the media, and it created about him a mysterious and glamorous aura. This spared him the indignity of being cast as what some cynics suspected that he was all along: a boring Swedish guy who went about winning all those Grand Slam titles with all the panache of a butcher slicing up half a pound of olive loaf. A blond Euro stud who was into chicks and money and not much else. A blue-eyed warrior from a cool hell.

Borg was always great to write about because he never really told you anything important about himself. That gave you license to play armchair psychologist and read anything you wanted into him. Anybody

150

could have a theory about Borg, and there was room aboard the arm-chair for everybody. And as the Borg comeback story unfolded and cul-minated, you could have accused him of just about anything *except* being a boring guy.

In Monte Carlo, which is Europe's version of Las Vegas *sur la mer,* Borg finally showed his hand. He revealed himself as a man alarmingly free of self-consciousness in the broad sense, a man with no sense of irony or any trace of what might be called analytical intelligence. For a brief, shining moment, Borg became a wildly romantic soul.

Borg's doomed comeback also said a great deal about how his iden-tity as a professional tennis player—the quintessential tennis player of the Open era—had influenced him for life.

I can't remember ever being as eager to cover an event when I arrived in Monte Carlo. I was booked into a five-star hotel (in that part of the world, they don't have hotels with soft-drink vending machines in the halls or sliding glass doors that open on a parking lot) in the village of Beausoleil, about thirty minutes away from the Monte Carlo Country Club. The draw was to be held late on the afternoon that I checked in, at a place called The Sporting Club. I dropped my bags in the room and dashed off to town to get my transportation for the week, a small motorbike.

By the time I got squared away I was running late. To make matters worse, the Sporting Club turned out to be an elaborate complex of banal modern buildings housing all kinds of restaurants, banquet spaces, and discotheques above a maze of dimly lit subterranean park-ing lots. I got utterly lost trying to find my way above ground, but when I finally emerged in a long, empty corridor, I heard a great commotion heading my way.

Suddenly a throng of people came bobbing toward me. Reporters were trying to write as they walked; paparazzi dodged back and forth, flashbulbs exploding. The fellow at the head of this parade was Bjorn Borg, walking briskly. I stopped and for one brief moment our eyes met. And then Bjorn laughed. He laughed out loud—a quick, unemo-tional laugh delivered on the run. Borg didn't even break stride and he was by me, leading his ragtag army out into the parking lot. I still don't know how to interpret that laugh. Maybe I looked comical, in a ratty bomber jacket and with road grime all over my hands. Maybe I just took him by surprise, and he was unable to fend off the absurdity of encoun-tering me in exactly the same way he had on myriad occasions in another time, a different life—as if I had staked out that exact spot a decade ago and stood patiently waiting, me and old Father Time, two people whom Borg didn't necessarily feel he had to acknowledge. I

don't know if Borg was laughing at me or with me, or merely expressing anxiety, because he had no idea of the forces he had set in motion
and how it was all going to end.

In 1978, when Borg was still at the peak of his powers, I went to interview him at the Hotel Roosevelt in New York. The scene I found there
became no less important an image to me than the memory of a resplen-
dent Borg hunched over and ready to deliver a lethal two-handed backhand, with his left foot distinctively placed in a slightly unnatural,
turned-out position evocative of a ballet dancer.

It was shortly after noon when Borg's lifelong coach, Lennart
Bergelin, opened the heavy oak door and invited me into their suite.
Bergelin, dressed in the trademark pinstriped Borg Line track suit by
Fila, smelled as if he hadn't bathed in a week. The curtains in the lavish
suite were drawn tight, shutting out the light and the magnificent view
of the Manhattan skyline. The coffee table was littered with half-eaten
fruit, a spray of wilted flowers, three empty bottles of Grolesk beer, and
a scattering of dishes, all encrusted with leftovers. Newspapers lay in
disarray on the table and in a nearby wing chair. Scraps of curled paper
bearing telephone numbers that would never be dialed littered the furniture and carpet.

We sat on the couch for a while, making small talk in hushed tones.
Although the Swedish coach Percy Rosberg had discovered Borg and
shown the good sense to leave his distinctive and radical strokes just as
they were, Bergelin was the man who had evolved into Borg's coach,
father figure, masseur, and gofer when the prodigy began to travel on
the international circuit at age sixteen.

Bergelin's role as coach was the first one to become superfluous.
Borg's game was simple and unimpregnable, his mind was as strong as
a steel trap and seemingly impervious to competitive pressure or anxiety. A player with that profile doesn't need a coach, but he does need a
companion to assume a variety of other roles. Bergelin fulfilled them
with the loyalty of a rottweiler, putting Borg above all other things for
over a decade.

In his own time, Bergelin had been one of a very few Swedish players good enough to play on the international circuit. He was best
known among his peers not for his wicked serve or rangy backhand but
for his individualistic verve. After one tour of Australia, Bergelin cashed
in his return ticket and bought himself a motorcycle. In short order he
found himself a comely Australian woman with whom he disappeared
into the Outback for a month.

Bergelin was thirty years older than Borg but wholly absorbed in his career. At heart he was a tennis nut who could not resist the siren song of the greatness that had eluded him. And Borg, like any other star who allowed nothing to come between him and his aspirations, unconsciously but completely sucked Bergelin and others into his life.

As we sat chatting about Borg in the hotel that day, I was struck by how haggard and pale Bergelin had grown over the few years I'd known him. I don't think he was capable of uttering three sentences in which Borg's name did not come up.

We were interrupted by the opening of the door to Borg's bedroom. In six or seven hours' time Borg would step onto the court in Madison Square Garden, dressed in immaculate tennis whites, his blond hair gleaming in the intense indoor light. But at the moment he was barefoot and his toes were gnarly. Although Borg was dressed in the latest upscale offering from Fila, a track suit in gray ultra-suede, the garment was so rumpled that I suspected Borg had slept in it—for days. The Swedish idol's face was unwashed, and his hair hung in oily strands. His eyes were sunken deep in ashen sockets. You could always tell how important a given tournament was to Borg by the number of blemishes on his face, and the Masters had produced a bumper crop. He looked less like the greatest tennis player on earth than the unhealthiest man alive, with Bergelin in close pursuit. I was reminded that in Swedish Bjorn means "bear" and that Borg's pulse rate of 35 was closer to that of a bear than the average human's, which is 70.

Bergelin's eyes followed Borg closely as his protégé puttered around the dark room, looking for something to drink. Borg wandered into the kitchen, where I heard him tear back the aluminum tongue of a soft-drink can. Then Borg came and settled into an overstuffed armchair. As if on cue, Bergelin quietly retreated into his own room.

"I'm feeling pretty good," Borg replied to my stock opening question. His eyes were already focused on the murky middle distance, as they always were during a formal interview, and he continued in a drone that I knew well. "But you know, it's a tough tournament, for sure. We just have to see what my chances are."

As the interview progressed, I was reminded of a remark an English friend of mine had made about Borg: "The bloke can say less, with fewer words, than anybody in the world."

On impulse I asked, "Bjorn, what do you think of Howard Hughes?"

"I don't know him," Borg replied. "He has a lot of money, huh? Anyway, he seems like a nice guy."

A clock on the end table ticked loudly. Neither of us spoke.

When Borg was at the peak of his powers, he had no reason to leave that suite for any reason other than to play a match. But I couldn't have guessed then that in an unexpectedly short time, radical changes would force him out of his sequestered, dimly lit life.

Bjorn Borg was the first European superstar of the professional era, a cradle-to-grave tennis player who was not taught or trained, or inclined to do much of anything else. Although a great deal of the commercial action early in the Open era was created and promoted in the United States, Americans had not fully embraced the idea that the sooner a promising kid can begin making money at sports, the better.

Europeans, unencumbered by powerful amateur traditions and institutions like the Amateur Athletic Union or the National Collegiate Athletic Association, accepted with much less equivocation the idea of the professional individual. If you wanted to quit school at twelve to play pro tennis, fine. If you could get a racket deal at age nine or a long-term clothing contract that financed your development as a junior, good for you.

Nothing in Borg's personal or cultural background prevented him from becoming a barbarian at the gate of tennis at the earliest age, which in his case was seven. That was when Bjorn's father, Rune, a salesman in a clothing store, won a tennis racket in a table tennis tournament and presented it to his only son.

Borg's talents developed like those of many other top players, in a highly competitive home environment. Games such as darts and pitching cards into a basket were prominent features of *en famille* Sunday outings. When Bjorn was a little older, Saturday was designated as his day with Rune. On many of those Saturdays, Bjorn was sent to bed early because of the tantrums he threw when he lost some childish competition to his father.

"I was always stubborn," Borg told me during a chat about his impeccable sportsmanship and competitive sangfroid. "I stayed that way for my life. But also as a little boy I had a very bad temper. When I first started playing, I was the worst—always throwing my racket, sometimes cheating, you know? I was cheating even in practice with my friends, I wanted to win so badly. My parents were very disappointed, very embarrassed. They would shake their heads and say, 'No way are you going to improve your game like that.' I used to come home every day with broken rackets. I was a madman."

After one of Bjorn's particularly wild tantrums, his parents took away his rackets and forbade him to play for a month. That incident has often been cited as a formative experience, but Borg cited another impetus for his evolution into an impassive player who became legendary for his ability to suppress his emotions. Early in his teens Borg watched a televised tennis match featuring Rod Laver, the standard against whom all modern players, including Borg, are measured. Taking a cue from Laver's cool conduct, Borg decided that anyone who could not control his temper would never become a great player. Years later when Borg described his feelings about Laver, he put it this way: "If Laver ever wanted to earn more money, he could be the greatest poker player in the world."

Table tennis, tennis, poker . . . they all ran together in the mix of ambitions, emotions, and influences that created Borg, the most extraordinary player of the Open era. If the soul of genius is simplicity, Borg was undeniably a genius. After all, his game was just tennis's version of the better mousetrap. He imposed a table tennis sensibility on the inflated proportions of a tennis court and, starting with Rune, proceeded to beat the pants off anybody who stepped up to play him over the next fifteen or so years.

Borg's style was an embarrassment to the formalists who have always dominated the coaching ranks. No coach would have taught Borg to play the way he did, but every coach on earth took a crack at analyzing why it worked so damned well. By the age of eighteen Borg was able to sum up his tennis philosophy like this: "I've tried to make tennis as simple and uncomplicated as possible. You try to hit the ball over the net one more time than your opponent does."

That, of course, is easier said than done. The strength of Borg's game was no more complicated than that, but the bulwark on which his style rested was unique and natural. Borg was blessed with great eyes, great anticipation, and superb feet. Most pro tennis matches are not really won or lost with the arm, but with the legs and feet. And Borg had the greatest wheels ever seen on a tennis player. Although Connors and McEnroe were as nimble as Borg, neither one was as fleet for extended periods of time, particularly on clay courts.

Borg also had an extraordinary constitution that carried him into eighty-eight sanctioned tournament finals (he won sixty-two of them). His right arm was the greatest testament to his durability because it was impervious to the remarkable strain created by his heavy, torqued, topspin strokes, the kind of strokes with which he developed his unsurpassed ability to keep the ball in play.

Borg also was able to play with a relatively heavy racket, so tightly strung (ninety pounds) that sometimes, in the middle of the night, one of his Donnay frames audibly caved in from the stress. Borg played his entire career with the equivalent of a cast-iron skillet and suffered few arm or shoulder injuries. Although Borg was almost a finished product by age sixteen, he did make one quantum technical leap that proved crucial to his success at Wimbledon. In the twelve months preceding June 1976, his serve evolved from a good stroke into a weapon.

All in all, Borg was an astonishing athlete who bent and shaped the physical laws that usually govern tennis. Not only could he run down almost any ball that wasn't an outright winner, he did so in time to return it with a penetrating, forcing shot. Although he played the perfect defensive, baseline game, he also dictated the flow and pace of the rallies. Borg's extra-physical assets were his concentration, his will, and his ironclad emotions—all of which served his quintessentially conservative, bullheaded, thou-shalt-not-pass style. But in the big picture, Borg's vaunted stubbornness was a mixed blessing in his game long before it led to disastrous consequences in his life. At the worst of times, Borg was not merely intractable but downright blind. And if his stubborn nature was one key to the brilliance of Borg's record, it also helped to explain its uneven nature.

All told, Borg played in twenty-seven Grand Slam events between 1973 and 1981. He reached the final in sixteen of them, winning eleven of those. None of the contemporary titans of tennis could match Borg's success ratio: Connors reached only one less Grand Slam final than Borg's fifteen, but he ended up with three fewer titles. More important, Connors competed in more than twice as many Big Four events (fifty-seven). McEnroe's numbers were forty-six events played, ten finals reached, and seven titles. And Lendl was fifty, nineteen, and eight.

At the French Open, Borg lost only one match after his debut in 1973 when he reached the fourth round. The loss was to Adriano Panatta in the quarterfinals of 1976. (But even that turned into a positive experience because it led to Borg's first date with the woman he would marry, Marianna Simionescu.) At Wimbledon, Borg won five times running (1976 to 1980).

The most extraordinary thing about Borg's statistical excellence, and the position it earned him in tennis history, is that he compiled it without ever having won two of the four Grand Slam titles. Borg played the Australian Open only once, losing in the third round. And he was jinxed at the U.S. Open even though he reached at least the fourth round in every year he played but one, 1974. He was four times the runner-up but never champion at Forest Hills and Flushing Meadow.

The nature of Borg's Grand Slam record dramatically qualifies any claim laid on his behalf as the greatest player of all time. Laver completed two Grand Slams, winning all four titles in the same year on two occasions: 1962, during the amateur era, and 1969, the second year of Open tennis. The only other male player to ever complete a Grand Slam was the American Don Budge in 1938.

Borg stubbornly believed that if he just hung in there and got the ball back into the court, he would prevail. And he did. He believed that he could beat Connors, his early nemesis, without changing his defensive baseline game. He did that, too. And Borg bucked conventional logic and believed that he could win Wimbledon five times running, with the style least likely to produce outstanding Wimbledon results. That, too, came to pass.

But then there was the flip side to Borg's willfulness, which sometimes manifested itself as overweening pride housed in an otherwise quiet, easygoing, modest man. Borg intensely disliked the U.S. Open for reasons both legitimate and silly, and it always damaged his chances. He often sulked like Achilles in his tent during the tournament, and he suffered the same disastrous consequences as the vain Greek hero.

Borg made four frustrating trips to the U.S. Open final, once when it was played on clay Har-Tru at Forest Hills and three times on the cement at Flushing Meadow. Some of his failures stemmed from bad luck, particularly in the three-year period when the Open was held at Forest Hills on clay, his best surface. In 1975, Borg was beaten in the semifinals by Connors. Borg was still intimidated by Connors when they met in the 1976 final, in a fine match won by Connors in four sets, 6–4, 3–6, 7–6, 6–4. Over the next twelve months Borg made great strides in his rivalry with Connors, but he had to pull out of the 1977 Open because of a bum shoulder. Guillermo Vilas, whose game never presented problems for Borg, then went on to upset Connors and win the tournament.

When the tournament moved to the cement at Flushing Meadow in 1978, Borg's problems were compounded. He dreaded playing the night match that each of the top names was forced to contest at least once during the tournament. Borg also felt that officials at Flushing Meadow stacked the deck against him in their compulsive desire to see an American champion. In 1978, Borg reached the final opposite Connors, but a badly injured thumb, a twilight start to the match, and his own pessimism contributed to his lethargic 6–4, 6–2, 6–2 loss.

Borg's disillusionment with the Open was not entirely the result of his pride, however, and his paranoia was not entirely unjustified. To a much greater degree than their counterparts at the other Grand Slam events, USTA officials *were* willing to tweak the system in order to favor or accommodate a top American player. They also allowed television producers to dictate the schedule, even when the decisions violated common sense or broad principles of fairness. The best example of the stop-Borg mentality that seemed prevalent at the U.S. Open occurred in 1979. When the schedule was announced on the evening before the quarterfinals, the featured night match was the one between Borg and the hard-serving American southpaw Roscoe Tanner. Media cynics, having seen this coming, howled with laughter. And coach Lennart Bergelin had a conniption.

Bergelin held an impromptu press conference in a hallway under the stadium. He bitterly denounced the USTA and then went on about how thoroughly Borg hated to play at night because of the radically different ambient conditions. Among other things, Borg felt that he couldn't pick up the ball coming off his opponent's racket nearly as well at night as during the day, and there he was, set up to meet the man with the most fearsome serve in the game!

I've never seen a coach expose a weak hand as freely and completely as Bergelin did that night, and I later asked Bergelin if he had done anything to avert or at least prepare for the pairing. He gave me a blank look instead of an answer.

It turned out that while all the other players and their handlers were scrambling and lobbying to find out when they would play at night and against whom, Borg had been stewing in a state of denial and Bergelin had been sitting nearby, night after night, wringing his hands while his stomach lining was being slowly eaten up by a fear that the worst-case scenario would come to pass. Which it did. By then it was pretty clear that if Tanner played any kind of match, he would beat Borg. Which he did.

Sadly for Borg fans, 1979 turned out to be his last great chance to win the Open. Within twelve months a kid named John McEnroe would be eating Borg's lunch—and in broad daylight, too. Worse yet for Borg, McEnroe's appearance on the scene set in motion a chain of events that echoed Greek tragedy. The fiery American became the catalyst of Borg's decline, not merely because of his superior play, but because McEnroe exposed the worst aspects of Borg's pride.

Borg appeared to have everything, when a one-two punch led him to throw it all away. In the Wimbledon final of 1981, McEnroe defeated Borg in one of the most exciting matches of the Open era, 4–6, 7–6, 7–6, 6–4. Two months later at the U.S. Open, McEnroe performed an encore, beating Borg in the final, 4–6, 6–4, 6–2, 6–3. Granted, Borg was one mightily tired tennis player by that time, but his decision to quit the game on the heels of those two losses revealed a disconcerting weakness. It suggested that Borg did not have a really good reason to keep at what he had done most of his life. Nor did he appear to appreciate or understand his craft, as Connors did. Borg suddenly seemed to find the focus of his entire youth and early adulthood burdensome.

Borg believed he could dismiss the threat of McEnroe without making any changes in his game or his approach to it, as he had in his rivalry with Connors. When he was unable to do that in less than two years, he abruptly quit the game. And he left under the delusion that his status as a beloved athlete who personified grace under fire and good sportsmanship would win him special concessions from the game's bureaucrats.

The blow dealt to Borg by the administrators of the game was a crucial and rarely cited component in the strange saga of Bjorn Borg. When Borg quit the game, the pro bureaucracy was creating lavish opportunities for the players and also demanding increasing control over their lives. In order to maintain the ranking on which tournament entries were based and in order to remain in good standing on the tour, players had to commit to playing a specific number of tour events. That was fine for journeymen, who could play every week, lose in the first or second round, and still make handsome sums of money, but the game was star-driven, and the top players faced much greater doses of physical, mental, and emotional fatigue than their happy-go-lucky peers. They also bridled at having to carry the establishment, as well as the rank-and-file players, on their backs.

In the months following his retirement, Borg petitioned the Pro Council and the ATP for a special dispensation that would allow him to play a reduced schedule without losing his ranking. He was politely but firmly turned down. He subsequently tried to call the establishment's bluff, to no avail. Perhaps most important, he felt betrayed and insulted by the game for which he had done so much just by virtue of his accomplishments.

The important thing is not that Borg was wrong about some things because he was right more often than he was wrong. It is also impossible to criticize him for wanting out of a life ruled by the discipline of his profession and filled with hotel suites where it was perpetually twilight. But these misadventures demonstrated that Borg saw most things in the same harsh black-and-white terms as the scores on a drawsheet. That penchant illuminated the dark side of Borg's makeup as a competitor, and it would also unleash the dark side of his personality.

In many ways Borg's reaction was understandable. The world has a fair number of ex-stockbrokers who chucked it all and settled down as faux ranchers or rock-climbing guides. But Borg didn't come to his realization until after he had fallen to number two, which suggested that Borg was much more interested in results than process. That's a good attitude in a tank battalion commander or anyone who is about to be strapped into a dentist's chair, but it's a terrible impediment to enjoying everyday life, much less a job.

At the time of his retirement Borg seemed like the ultimate one-dimensional man. Although the luster of his record remained untarnished, his nature as a competitor lost some of its depth and color. Borg lived in a jungle of winners and losers, but he could only survive as a winner. As it turned out, he was designed for the role of the hunter rather than the hunted. He was much better at doggedly following a trail than at breaking a new one, circling back, or concocting some other creative, evasive strategy for victory, for survival. Down deep, Borg was as inflexible as a stick of uncooked pasta.

The deadly companion piece to Borg's inflexibility was the hubris that led him to saw off the limb on which he had perched for so long, so high above the ground. I suppose that he looked forward to landing softly in the verdant lap of what most extraordinary people longingly characterize as "normal" life. Instead, Borg went into a free-fall that lasted for a decade, until he landed in debt, was hospitalized, unhappily married, and driven by the distinctly un-Borgian desire to return to a profession that he had forsworn.

Borg's ten-year hiatus from pro tennis cannot be recounted in narrative form. It's actually more like a picture puzzle, with pieces strewn across a few continents, thrown away over years of prosperity, lost over years of waste. Pieces of it can still be found stuck between the cushions of discotheques, clinging to mirrored surfaces in penthouse apartments, and shattered on the floors of various emergency wards where both Borg and his last wife, the lusty Italian pop star Loredana Berte, have done some time.

But the more pieces you collect, the more baffling and mysterious the puzzle becomes. Only one person on this earth was in a position to know what the completed puzzle looked like in 1991, and as usual he wasn't talking. But I doubt that even Bjorn knew what the whole picture looked like, either.

But if I had to start assembling somewhere, I would go back to something Borg told me when he was just sixteen: "I know from the history of the game, and from my own career, that if I ever settle down with a steady girlfriend, I might as well forget about my tennis dreams. Every day during my first Wimbledon, I saw friends and acquaintances together with women, often so-called steady girlfriends. Each time I saw this I thought to myself, 'Don't let it happen to me.' "

In the early stages of his career, Borg stubbornly clung to this curious vow, undoubtedly with the encouragement of his conveniently forgetful, skirt-chasing, motorcycle-riding mentor, Bergelin. For the first two or three years of his spectacular career, even the English tabloids during Wimbledon were stymied. All they could do was publish pictures of Borg leaping out of windows or being jostled by security guards as he tried to evade the hordes of starstruck schoolgirls who hounded him. One tabloid did publish a picture of Borg hiking up his trousers after an alleged tryst in a copse in Hyde Park, but the subject was just a look-alike, and nobody fell for the hoax.

Borg was a cautious, tennis-obsessed young man, but he was also understandably curious about women and was by no means innocent. He generally avoided women in his quest for greatness until an age when he began to hunger for more than the occasional tryst. In 1976 he was a highly accomplished but naive twenty-year-old embarking on his first, and perhaps most successful, marital relationship.

The details of Borg's meeting with the Romanian player Marianna Simionescu are telling. In May of that year, Borg was upset in the French Open by Adriano Panatta. That evening Bergelin, Borg, and his father Rune decided to go into Paris for a few beers. They piled into the complimentary Saab that Borg used, but upon reaching the Peripherique they realized that after a few drinks they might not be able to find their way back. So they returned to the Sofitel Hotel and called for a taxi. While they were waiting, Bjorn impulsively ran over to the house phones and called Simionescu, who was also playing in the tournament. They had never been introduced, but he knew her by sight. Simionescu went along on the boys' night out, and the two were soon inseparable. Marianna was not the typical girlfriend in a sport that abounds with chic, immaculately groomed and dressed women. She was a sturdy, voluptuous girl with a twinkle in her eye and a refreshingly natural air about her. Given Borg's dedication to tennis, she was a wise, appropriate choice.

At the time Bjorn and Marianna met, she was a solid performer on the women's tour, but much like Bergelin, she was soon sucked deeply into Borg's gravitational field. Bowing to Borg's genius, she surrendered her own aspirations and became the female half of the Bjorn Borg support group. Long before they married, the Borgs lived like a middle-aged couple. They rarely went out, particularly during tournaments. Bergelin screened calls, arranged practice times, and attended to such mundane matters as booking the airline tickets and hotel rooms. Simionescu cooked, washed, and ironed.

Reflecting on her relationships long after the Borgs divorced, Marianna told journalist Curry Kirkpatrick: "Lennart and I were like home to Bjorn. We were just Sweden. As a couple, Bjorn and I never had time to live like real people. All we had, since we were children, was *the game*. There was never anything but the game. We were very closed off."

Perhaps because Simionescu was such an important component in Borg's career and success, he would divorce her just about a year after he announced his retirement. The divorce was some time in the making, as Borg had been steadily nibbling at the edges of the nightlife and sybaritic pleasures available to a man of his status.

Borg's best friend at the peak of his career was the late Vitas Gerulaitis, a mercurial, fun-loving American player who maintained a world top-five ranking for years on no sleep and a quick, electric game, the kind of tennis you would expect from a hyperactive, wisecracking, free-spending New Yorker whose friends included Andy Warhol, Rolling Stones guitarist Keith Richards, and the original supermodel Cheryl Tiegs.

As a protégé of Vitas, Bjorn began to sample all of the pleasures available to celebrities in the era when Studio 54 was the hottest disco on the planet, cocaine was the recreational drug of choice, and the pro tour had no policy concerning substance abuse. But by and large Bjorn held his desire to be a party animal firmly in check while he was still the number one player, particularly in the weeks leading up to crucial Grand Slam events.

One of the most disastrous decisions Borg made when he decided to quit the game was to jettison everything and everyone that had come along with it. Bergelin, Gerulaitis, and Simionescu were three of the most obvious victims. Basically, Bjorn decided to start from square one, and he chose to do so in the place that represented the closest thing he had ever had in his adult life to a home: Monte Carlo. If you expand the definition of a hazardous waste site beyond geochemical boundaries, Monte Carlo could be called one. Apart from a few pockets, the place isn't even beautiful anymore, at least not as it was before the principality built a forest of high-rise apartment houses to accommodate the city's burgeoning population of tax dodgers, arms dealers, and zillionaires.

Nightlife in Borg's adopted city revolved around the international white trash set, and it transpired in places with names like Jimmy'z, a famous disco populated with unhappy South American heiresses, and perpetually tan party boys dressed in Armani suits and aviator shades. When you visit Monte Carlo, you can see why Princess Stephanie turned out the way she did, and when you see what else there is to choose from, you understand why she married one of her bodyguards. At least that guy was *supposed* to be in aviator shades, and he actually had a job.

Borg's choice of Monte Carlo as the place where he would conduct a "normal" life, a stupid idea in the first place, was rendered flat-out absurd by Borg's paucity of ordinary interests. Granted, he once professed to be excited about fishing, so much so that he took the trouble to tell me about Vikingshill, the idyllic island hideaway that he owned off the coast of Sweden until he was forced to give up the archipelago because of tax problems. But even on the few occasions when we got to talking about such mundane and delightful things, Bjorn's enthusiasm struck me as, if not exactly forced, once removed from true passion. Sadly, I think he truly wanted to love those things—the fishing, the country, the trek that he and Marianna took in Nepal on their honeymoon—but I don't believe he did because he dropped or gave up on them quickly and easily.

Borg's ambition to be "normal" was a little like the desire to be tall or naturally redheaded or African American. You either are or you aren't, and effort has nothing to do with it. Marianna saw the handwriting on the wall early, while it seemed they might still carve out a normal life in Monte Carlo. As she told Kirkpatrick, "Right from the beginning of his retirement, Bjorn didn't know what to do. He didn't know his place in life anymore, and that was very sad. Bjorn would watch television, and then he would go out with the night people. He wanted to have another life, but then he was always saying, 'What am I going to do now?' "

The catalyst for Bjorn and Marianna's separation was a beautiful blonde model from Stockholm, Jannike Bjorling, whom Borg had met while serving as a guest judge in a beauty contest. Marianna did not learn about this liaison until she read that Borg and the seventeen-year-old Bjorling were seen together in Hawaii in August 1984. When Marianna called Bjorn after reading the item, he simply told her that he was sorry but he wasn't coming home.

In 1985, Bjorling bore Borg a son, Robin. But the two were never married. By 1988 their split had turned from amicable to ugly. Bjorling vowed to wage an ugly custody battle, and she told the Swedish satirical magazine *Z* that Borg had been a cocaine abuser during their relationship. Although Borg won a $12,500 defamation suit against the magazine, he uncharacteristically went public a few years later and admitted to having tried the drug.

The first casualties of Borg's campaign to achieve normalcy were the very qualities that might have provided him with direction in his quest: his healthy life-style, his renowned self-discipline, and the firm grip he had always exerted on his emotions. Sometimes the fruits of his new feeling of license were comical, and at other times tragic.

Borg's decline seemed to fit a pattern that was best articulated by Gene Scott, the former Davis Cup player and publisher of the newspaper *Tennis Week*. We got to talking about Borg once, and he theorized that Borg had a very powerful urge to rebel against his nature as a cautious, straight-laced, and highly disciplined Swede. According to Scott, Borg was a fair-skinned child of the light who grew compulsively fascinated by the dark side of life, the forbidden fruit embodied by certain women and experiences that were dark, sensual, emotional, and exotic.

Bjorling was a great beauty, but Borg ultimately fell for a woman who may have represented his taste for the exotic far better, the Italian chanteuse Loredana Berte. She would happily accompany him to whatever darker realms he wished to explore. Berte had about ten years on Borg, who was thirty-one when they met in 1988. Borg first saw her on television in a music video in which Berte was busy trying to break the same ground that Madonna was plowing in America at about the same time. But it was much harder to shock Berte's native Italy, and there was also some inconvenient issue about Berte's actual talent. Many critics considered Berte a bit of Calabrian dross, trying a little too hard to make it as a pop star. Her trademark tune had been "Non Sono una Signora" (I'm Not a Lady), although it wasn't exactly a disclaimer she needed to issue to redress the public's misconception.

Borg learned who Berte was through his friend, the former Italian player and playboy Adriano Panatta. The first meeting between Bjorn and Loredana occurred on Ibiza, a chic Spanish island. The result was spontaneous combustion. As soon as the unlikely couple began appearing in the tabloids, Bjorling began to fire salvos from Stockholm, accusing Borg of being a cokehead and then promising to keep him from their son, Robin.

But Borg forged ahead and married Berte, appearing for the ceremony in a ludicrous suit of Lucifer red—matching the veil Berte had donned, presumably to offset her traditional white wedding gown. But the comical, made-for-the-tabloids adventure turned serious when, in February 1989, Borg was rushed to a hospital in Milan to have his stomach pumped after allegedly having taken an overdose of sleeping pills. Borg originally said that he contracted food poisoning from having eaten "bad fish," but later claimed it was because of an accidental combination of wine and sleeping pills. The Italian press fell into two camps on the incident: One attributed Borg's collapse to a coke binge, and one had him attempting suicide following a violent argument with Berte over Bjorling's attempt to keep Borg from seeing his son.

By then Bjorn could be forgiven for wanting to pull the plug on himself for a variety of other reasons as well, beginning with the sheer ennui that he seemed unable to escape, and ending with the losses he had absorbed in his failed attempt at so-called business. Bob Kain of IMG had handled most of the money Borg earned, parlaying $3.6 million in career earnings, plus millions more in endorsement deals and exhibition fees, into a fortune estimated at $75 million. But when Borg decided to venture into the business world, he turned his back on Kain, much as he had on most of the early friends and associates. According to Simionescu, Borg had a desire to succeed on his own and to do so in Sweden, where the press and public had begun to see him as a selfish, spoiled millionaire, a loafing playboy as radically estranged from his roots as he was from the sport that had made him an international celebrity. The best thing that can be said for Borg's subsequent activities was that they represented a sincere, albeit harebrained, attempt to create new ties with his heritage and his people at a time when he was adrift and alone.

It all began conventionally enough, with a holding company called Bjorn Borg Enterprises, which included such diverse ventures as a real estate firm and the Bjorn Borg Design Group, which created and marketed a Bjorn Borg signature line of sportswear, cologne, and aftershave. The clothes didn't sell and the world was not clamoring for Bjorn Borg after-shave, but that seemed less important or telling than the nature of the men Borg chose for partners.

Borg seemed unable to distinguish between potentially legitimate business associates and the smooth-talking, impeccably tailored, Eurotrashy opportunists whose only credentials as potential partners appeared to be their penchant for frequenting the same discos as Borg.

One of them was Christer Gustafsson, a public relations man whom Borg met in a disco. Another was Eric Steiner, a professional poker player who ran the White Elephant gaming club in London. Onni Nordstrom was an agent who recruited models and celebrities to parties he threw for Borg. If Nordstrom is ever nominated for a Nobel Prize, it will be for having signed the actor Don Johnson to endorse a Swedish ice cream. But the most notorious—and troublesome—of this lot was a fellow by the name of Lars Skarke. He was an office supply salesman turned sports marketing executive turned Borg business partner when he bought a 25 percent share of Bjorn Borg Enterprises. The Swedish press was all over this one, reporting that Skarke commonly went by the name *Skurke*, which is Swedish for "scoundrel."

When things began to turn ugly, Borg's lawyer, Henning Sjostrom, vented his feelings about Skarke to the Stockholm newspaper *Dagens Nyheter*. He charged that Skarke's partnership with Borg amounted to a swindle. "Those who played with Borg's assets have done it for their own personal use," Sjostrom said. "They have lived high on his money."

The list of improprieties attributed to Skarke was a long one, from using company funds to underwrite transportation by private jet and limousine, to spending Bjorn Borg money on jet-skis, stereos, luxury cars, and Arabian horses, some bestowed on others as "gifts" while the rest languished in the country manor Skarke inhabited on the Swedish island of Ekero. Not only did Skarke deny the charges of impropriety, but when Borg's venture into Swedish "business" collapsed, he slapped Borg with a lawsuit demanding $12 million in damages on the grounds that Borg had stolen Skarke's share of the business. The upshot of this sordid scandal was Borg's quiet retreat from an ill-conceived but probably sincere attempt to rekindle a relationship with his homeland. The attempt failed, and it probably ensured that Bjorn, the prodigal son, would never again feel comfortable in his homeland. The newspapers had a field day with the entire mess, and even when they were sympathetic toward Borg, all they could do was cast him as a deluded and pitiable failure.

This particularly saddened Marianna, who believed that Bjorn's problems were rooted in nothing more sinister than the combination of his stubborn nature and his remarkable naïveté.

Borg was eventually forced by his various creditors to liquidate his assets in Sweden at public auction. He sold off his Stockholm apartment, his speedboat, and the Vikingshill retreat that he once professed to love. Reports that Borg was broke raced through the press, but they were erroneous. According to Kain, Borg still had millions squirreled away in Bjorn-proof trust funds and other long-term investments. The auction was merely a rich man's way of conveniently divesting himself of the ties that bind.

Following the auction, the only connection Borg had left with Sweden was his estranged lover Bjorling and their son, Robin. By then, in late 1990, Borg was no longer getting along with Berte, either. Having drifted or broken from his friends, having severed his ties in Sweden, and possessing no real desire to return to Milan and a marriage that was unraveling a lot more quickly than his first one had, Borg had no place left to call home. No place, that is, no place except the dark hotel rooms, the airline seats, the crowded grandstands and liniment-scented locker rooms of the tennis circuit that he had quit. In August 1990, as the rest of his life was collapsing around him, Borg sneaked into London under cover of night and began to practice tennis again. Over the ensuing months he would turn up in Buenos Aires, Milan, and various other outposts, mimicking the itinerant life that he had come to hate when he quit the game.

Borg finally confirmed the growing rumors by announcing in early 1991, at age thirty-four, that he had asked for a wild card to compete in the main draw of the high-profile sanctioned tournament held in his domicile, Monte Carlo.

The morning after the draw was held at The Sporting Club of Monte Carlo dawned crisp, cool, and full of promise. I arrived very early at the Monte Carlo Country Club, just to soak up the atmosphere and to await the arrival of Borg, who was due to practice at 11 A.M.

The MCCC is a grand old place, hardly touched by the vulgarization of Monte Carlo. It is elaborately terraced into a sharp slope that leads down to the Mediterranean. Strolling the walkways around the maze of practice courts, I admired the traditional, sculpted cypresses that surround attractive villas perched on the distinctive knolls and promontories of the neighborhood. Beyond and below the imposing villa of Karl Lagerfeld lay the private beach where Princess Stephanie sunbathed. Beyond that shimmered the achingly blue Mediterranean.

By 10 A.M. the grounds of the club were abuzz with activity. Curious spectators hoping to catch a glimpse of the great Borg milled about. Here and there I ran into a journalist I hadn't seen in years, and one or the other of us inevitably laughed, just as Borg had done when I encountered him at the Racing Club. The anticipation and electricity in the air were palpable. Even the players, from Mats Wilander to Andres Gomez to Henri LeConte, were just standing in clusters talking to each other or to journalists about Borg—how he would fare and what he had been doing.

Borg had been practicing with a variety of players before I arrived, and many of the top players had offered their services both in homage and out of curiosity. According to them, the most distinctive feature of these practices was the compulsive pace at which Borg played. He never stopped to chat or to linger over the water cooler. With his trademark headband firmly in place, Borg hammered away briskly from the baseline. He actually trotted to pick up the balls. Just fifteen minutes after he had begun practicing with Borg, Goran Ivanisevic broke a heavy sweat and found himself wondering what he had gotten himself into. One practice partner after another walked off the court and said that one thing was for sure: Borg was fit enough to compete.

The players also agreed that Borg hit the ball well, off both wings, and they made it a point to say how honored they felt to practice with him and how they were all hoping he would win a few rounds in the tournament—as long as it wasn't at their expense. Boris Becker also told me the truth about his practice session with Borg.

"In the first set I played normal except for holding back on my serve. I won 6–1 in twenty minutes. In the second set I didn't hit any first serves, and I didn't come in to volley unless it would have been silly not to. I rallied with him from the baseline, and I won that set in half an hour, at 6–2. In the third set I began to hit hard from the baseline, and I was quickly ahead 3–0 when we quit. He hits the ball nice, he hits it clean. But his ball doesn't have any *druck* [a German word for force or pressure]."

Borg's first-round opponent was an obscure but very tough clay-court player, the Spaniard Jordi Arrese. The first man to reach Arrese after the draw was made had been the Swedish journalist Mats Olson. He found the shy Catalan on a practice court. Arrese didn't believe the news until another journalist showed up, whereupon Arrese feigned quaking in his boots. He said, "At least now I'll be famous for at least one day."

"Jordi is both the best and worst guy for Borg," said Becker's manager, Tiriac. "If the guy is overpowered by the occasion, he could lose to Borg. But if he plays his normal game, he could beat Borg two and one. What does Borg have? What did he ever have? He has a forehand and a backhand. No volley. No drop shot. No overhead. No serve. Not on clay. What he *did* have was speed, but now he is thirty-four years old. If he is only five percent slower, he will be twenty percent less effective."

Shortly after eleven o'clock I stood waiting on the sidewalk near the modest entrance to the club. Soon a sedan pulled up to the curb and began to disgorge an astonishing succession of characters, including two ballerinas (Tanya and Doreen), a doughty secretary whose identity was never revealed, and Tia Honsai, a seventy-nine-year-old, self-described master of martial arts and shiatsu massage. And lastly, the little car coughed up the man who had assembled this curious entourage through God knows what kind of convoluted logic or mystical yearning: Bjorn Borg. I hardly had a glimpse of Borg as the cocoon of security closed around his entourage and swept him away.

About twenty minutes later I found the court where Borg was practicing with another Swede, Jonas Svennson. The shoulder-length blond hair, the random fingers carefully wrapped with plain white adhesive tape, the signature tweaks and hitches that always marked his stroke production were as fresh as if they had been preserved like tennis balls in an airtight container. A wave of vertigo swept over me.

"It is like seeing a ghost," whispered the woman at my elbow, the Italian journalist Michaela Rossi.

The only changes in this otherwise timeless image of Borg were the loose V-neck sweater around his shoulders, a remnant of his venture into the rag trade, and the black, unmarked, conventional-sized wooden racket—a generic racket right out of a Dick and Jane book. Borg had the racket made covertly, at great expense, by Gray's, a manufacturer of esoteric rackets for squash and court tennis hidden deep in the English countryside. For all I knew, the racket had been made by elves. It certainly bore no resemblance whatsoever to the synthetic, mid- and oversized rackets that had been the norm on the pro tour for nearly a decade. Borg apparently felt no pressing need to exploit the technological changes that had revolutionized the game. This was typically Borgian, reflecting his utter indifference to the idea that things had changed, even technologically, since his salad days.

Watching Borg practice was alternately exhilarating and demoralizing, like an illogical dream—an impression abetted by the latest version of the Bjorn Borg support group. Once there had been the faithful Bergelin and the chipper wife, Simionescu. Now it was the cast of a Fellini movie. The new "coach," Honsai, whom Borg simply called "the Professor," was a Welshman who, depending on which sleuth you believed, was born either Ron Steward or Ron Thatcher. The Professor was dressed in black patent-leather shoes and black slacks, with a white patent-leather belt and a broad, white straw hat. You could be forgiven for mistaking this mighty master of the martial arts—and God knows what other forms of arcana—for a barber from Bensonhurst, Brooklyn, on his first trip to Disney World.

Early in the practice, Borg trotted over to the Professor, who instructed him briefly, with lavish hand gestures. Then the Professor settled in to watch, observing Borg through a pair of binoculars (even though Borg was less than thirty feet away), which he occasionally flipped around and used as a monocle. Now and then Honsai muttered something that the secretary, who had trouble negotiating the red clay because of her high heels, dutifully recorded.

I watched this session from a small cement grandstand on the uphill side of the court, across from the Professor. It soon became crowded, and I found myself standing alongside an ordinary man dressed in shades of brown and gray, wearing a pair of clunky, cheap-looking shoes. I recognized him as Rune Borg and said not a word.

After the practice session, a gang of pencils bushwhacked Honsai and forced him to hold a spontaneous press conference. He was a frail little man who attributed his interest in the martial arts to "having been punched in the nose too often as a weak little boy." The Professor could barely walk because of a bum knee, and despite an electronic aid, he had trouble hearing. But it's not like he needed to listen carefully to the questions posed to him in order to answer. Like many Masters of the Mysterious Realms, he communicated in epigrammatic generalities and dropped profundities that may have been as inscrutable to himself as to the rest of us.

Honsai claimed that he had worked with Borg since "before Wimbledon," as if their mysterious relationship had preexisted that august tournament. The Professor also declined to take credit for Borg's five victories in London, magnanimously declaring that "all honors go to Lennart Bergelin. I was merely by Borg's side in order to prepare his body."

Honsai denied being a guru; he claimed only "to know a little about the human body." When a newshound asked just what he knew about the human body, Honsai mournfully replied, "If I told you, you wouldn't understand."

Of Borg's chances, Honsai said, "He should go all the way. There's nothing to stop him, nothing at all." He claimed that under his tutelage, Borg had become a man with the corporeal powers of a twenty-two-year old. That much certainly appeared to be true, although it may have had less to do with the Professor's secret knowledge than Borg's own decision to clean up his act, a program that included swearing off booze and pills, practicing for a few hours each day, and going to bed by ten.

When an American magazine writer said that he understood Honsai had treated Ava Gardner and Ingrid Bergman, Honsai said, "I have treated the most famous and the most toughest and the most greatest people in the world. Who? I can't tell you."

A German television commentator asked what he should do for a bad back, to which Honsai replied, "Give up the wine."

When a London journalist asked Honsai if he was British, the Professor replied, "I've forgotten."

And when a Swedish radio reporter introduced himself, Honsai did not even allow him to pose his question. He merely interjected, "What is all this hate for Bjorn in Sweden? He doesn't hate you, he feels sorry for you. I think you should concentrate on his sport, not his character."

By that time the poor old man was teetering on his feet. He was whisked away by tournament officials, leaving the journalists to guffaw and compare notes on the Professor's pronouncements.

By then my own head was swimming. I kept thinking of how little had changed in the way Borg looked, the way he played. You could accuse Honsai of many things, but behaving like a typical tennis coach was not one of them. In fact, he admitted to knowing nothing about tennis.

Suddenly, I found myself thinking the unthinkable and hoping that it would come to pass. The very sight of Bjorn, coupled with the surreal ambience, had opened a door in my heart. Once that door was ajar, I couldn't get it closed again. I couldn't allow common sense, logic, or even the low comedy of the situation to threaten the skewed romance of it all. I found myself firmly believing, and even arguing, that anything, but *anything,* could happen when the ghost of Bjorn Borg returned to the red clay courts that he had once utterly ruled.

At about the same time that Honsai was facing the press, one member of that corps, a Swede named Lennart Ericksson, was driving back from Nice airport with a man whom everybody had been asking about, Lennart Bergelin. Ericksson was an excellent journalist and a decent man who had maintained friendly relations with Bergelin through the years—years that had not been very kind to Bergelin. He had suffered two heart attacks since the last time he saw or spoke with Borg, who probably did not even know about Bergelin's failing health.

Ericksson had gone to visit Bergelin shortly after Borg announced that he would be making a comeback. Bergelin sat on a sofa during their chat, holding a tennis racket and explaining that his teary eyes were the result of a bad cold. He tried to take a philosophical approach to the fact that Borg hadn't even called to tell Bergelin of his plans, saying, "Such is life." Bergelin told Ericksson that the saddest day of his life was the one when Borg decided to get some of his trusty rackets back from Bergelin, who had sentimentally kept a dozen of them over the years, just in case. Borg didn't bother to collect the rackets himself; he sent his "contact man," Ingmar Alverdal. Bergelin gave Alverdal six rackets and asked him to have Borg call, to explain what he was doing. But the telephone never rang.

Bergelin had not even been invited to Monte Carlo, but he decided to come anyway.

I was just about to leave the club after that enervating first day when Ericksson and Bergelin arrived. Bergelin was toting six more of Borg's old rackets—hostages, I suppose, to his desire to see Borg again. Bergelin also had a few models of a racket that he had developed and tried to market, the Protagon. It was a bizarre contraption with adjustable strings.

When Bergelin saw me, he waved and called out the popular Swedish greeting, "Hey-doo."

We found a vacant table in the cafe of the MCCC, where the Europeans around us smoked cigarettes endlessly and drank the strong coffee that seems to induce world-weariness along with sleeplessness. Not knowing how to start what would inevitably become a painful conversation, I asked about the Protagon.

"The first version was not so good because you needed a key to adjust the strings, *ya*? But on this one, you yust turn the handle, so," Bergelin said, demonstrating.

It was easy enough to get Bergelin talking about what had happened since Borg unceremoniously dumped him in 1981, after their twelve intense years together. Since then, Borg and Bergelin had seen each other only twice.

"Once, in Stockholm, Bjorn showed me his little boy," Bergelin recalled. But the light that briefly flickered in his eyes went out. "The other time was yust an accident, *ja*? We were each going out to some islands in boats, and we spoke a little across the water. Yust a quick hey-doo and little else."

Bergelin grew heated when I brought up the subject of Honsai and his ambiguous claim to having been Borg's trainer since "before Wimbledon." Bergelin denounced Honsai and insisted that Borg had met the Professor on only two occasions before his retirement. The first time was during Wimbledon in 1978, when Honsai was sought out not by Borg but by Marianna, because she'd heard that Honsai could help her quit smoking. The other occasion was during a subsequent Wimbledon tournament when Bergelin and Borg consulted Honsai on a sore muscle that had been plaguing Borg. Honsai allegedly touched Borg's quadricep and, pronouncing him fit as a fiddle, sent him on his way.

"The guy knows nothing," Bergelin added bitterly. "He was never there, he has no idea of what it is all about. For eleven, twelve years Bjorn and I were together twenty-four hours a day. When did he see this guy? When could he see this guy? Nobody knows this guy, *ya*? He is a complete fraud."

Our conversation was cut short by the intrusion of a few other journalists. I shook Bergelin's hand and left the club, falling into a lousy mood. It was hard to accept the way Bjorn had treated Bergelin, and my stubborn insistence that anything could happen over the next few days was challenged by my vague belief in karma. If that came into play, Arrese might just go out and kick Borg's butt and leave it lying there in the red dirt for all to see, and perhaps even for Bergelin to spit on.

Two more days would pass much like that first one, filled with rumors, speculations, and theories about Borg, the bizarre nature of his entourage, and the events unfolding in Monte Carlo. Honsai played hide-and-seek with an increasingly aggressive press. Borg failed to turn up for one scheduled practice session, and he called Ivanisevic's coach Bob Brett to cancel another one at the last minute, saying only that he had "something else to do."

The very idea was stupefying. Back home in Milan, apart from her husband for the seventh week in a row, Berte was coming apart at the seams. Having been told to stay home during Borg's preparations for his comeback, she suspected that he was not only preparing for battle but also philandering. She could do nothing but comb the tabloids for news of her husband's activities, and she frequently called Italian journalists in Monte Carlo, hoping to get the poop on Bjorn's activities.

The tension that had been building and crackling like heat lightning over all of Monte Carlo suddenly dissipated on the day Borg played Arrese. The hummingbirds were out early on that dry, clear morning, hovering over the scarlet and blaze-orange wildflowers, calmly and insatiably sucking the nectar out of them. An endless procession of spiffy luxury cars wound their way up the snaking road to the entrance of the MCCC and dropped off the well-heeled patrons who were lucky enough to hold tickets for the big day. Inside the stadium, the gathering crowd was subdued, reminiscent of churchgoers filing into their pews for a service.

In his heyday, Borg spent the mornings before his matches sequestered until it was time to slip into the locker room, get dressed, and wait for his match to be called. But on this long-awaited day, Borg, all dressed up to play, uncharacteristically walked into the dining room of the club. There, Honsai and his ballerinas were having lunch with the actor James Coburn and his comely female companion. Borg joined them, setting off a paparazzi orgy and a rush by young and old to get his autograph. He accommodated them patiently. Outside, a large contingent of fans chanted, "*Vive le roi, Borg est le roi*" (Long live the king, Borg is king).

A light blue haze hung over the Mediterranean, and a breeze whispered through the cypress trees when the competitors were finally announced. The steep grandstands were packed. There wasn't an empty seat in the royal marquee, presided over by Prince Albert, above the north baseline of the court.

Arrese came out of the tunnel leading to the court with visible trepidation, as timidly as some wild creature forced from his warren. He was followed closely by Borg, who walked with his brisk, rolling gait, head down, regarding things only peripherally.

There isn't very much to say about the match, which transpired in the worst way possible—predictably. Borg looked tentative, unsure of where to hit the ball. Arrese stayed way back at the baseline, feeding Borg balls with which he could do nothing. Neither Borg's serve nor his ground strokes appeared to have the sting, purpose, or penetration for which they had once been acclaimed. Most of the time Borg was kept busy just getting the ball back, like any second-rate baseline player whose success would be determined by how many balls he could retrieve, and how many of those balls led to unforced errors by his opponent. At his very best, Borg had once turned defensive tennis into an offensive tool. Against Arrese, Borg was a defensive player working overtime to contain the firepower of a man who didn't have much of it. He clearly lacked the confidence, the match experience, and, most strikingly, the aura of invincibility that once gave his game wings and thunder.

Arrese won the first set handily, 6–2.

The sky began to spit rain during the second set, and far below, the Mediterranean was not shimmering but simmering. All the sailboats were gone from the horizon. Honsai, who had apparently fallen asleep during the proceedings, came around with Borg trailing, 3–4, in the second set. He ponderously rose to his feet and bellowed, "Now, Bjorn, do it now!" Whereupon Borg hit a double fault.

Arrese won the second and final set, 6–3.

In less than twenty-four hours Berte, enraged over tabloid photographs of Borg and a female journalist, called an Italian newspaper and declared, "If there's another woman, I'll kill her." Instead, she tried to kill herself, taking an overdose of barbiturates. She was rushed to a hospital to have her stomach pumped, just as Borg had been early in their relationship.

Ah, *l'amour, l'amour. La publicité, la publicité.*

There was only one person I wanted to see after the match, and I found him standing at the bar in the cafe, drinking the coffee that he had been prohibited because of his heart ailment.

"It's not the way it should be," Bergelin said softly. "To me Bjorn is the world champion. I remember a champion, but today Bjorn was not even a real tennis player. He was scared to hit the ball. My heart was very heavy, *ya?*"

I wanted to tell Bergelin not to waste any more of his already overextended heart on Bjorn, but I knew that if Borg picked up the phone and called him the next day, Bergelin would be on the next plane to wherever Borg wanted him to turn up.

I wondered how I could have been so misguided in my expectations, so blind to logic and oblivious to what I understood as a cardinal rule of tennis: Anybody can look like a champion on the practice court, but it wasn't *tennis* until an umpire climbed up in the high chair and said, "Players ready? Play." Bjorn couldn't play anymore. He had played his last card in a tricky hand of high-low poker, gone for bust, and found that his high wasn't high enough, his low wasn't sufficiently low.

I felt bad for Bjorn, but there was one good thing about it all. The last question, one that he must have asked himself for years as one ambition, one relationship, and one enterprise after another kept collapsing around him, had finally been answered. He couldn't go back to the past even if he wanted to. He was finally and truly at rock bottom, and he could no longer harbor any delusions. In another new life he would have to make do without the help or encumbrance of his greatness. It was a separate thing now, just something called "reputation."

Bjorn was free. He had an adorable son. He still had plenty of money. There would always be women if he ever figured out what they were all about.

On the plane ride home I remembered the last words Tiriac said as we parted on the vacant, windswept veranda of the Monte Carlo Country Club: "Borg came back because he discovered that there is no life after death. What he will do now, who knows?"

I found myself hoping that somebody, anybody, would still care. Nobody deserves to be utterly alone.

CHAPTER 8

Style
Pajama Tops, Pukka Shells, and Bad Hair Days in Babylon

TWENTY-FIVE YEARS AGO everything that seemed silly about tennis to many people was pretty neatly summed up in the classic tennis sweater. You know the one I mean: the white, V-neck, cable-knit job with maroon and navy blue stripes on the neck and cuffs. It was worn by a kid whose first name was often a last name in disguise (Hamilton, Bowen, Taylor) and whose mummsy left him at the tennis club while she went off for a swim, a scoop, and a peek in the stud book—also known as the Social Register.

But after twenty-five years of unrelenting fashion errors committed by an increasingly desperate sportswear industry and a new breed of tennis fan yearning for just the right, upscale image, I find myself sorely missing that classic tennis sweater. It was elegant. It was simple. And it didn't hurt that in an era which would soon spawn the tissue-thin $200 Italian pullover, it was relatively cheap. The tennis sweater made a declaration of commonalty, not a statement of socioeconomic status. It was part of your tennis kit, and it represented the same ideal combination of form and function that made blue jeans, deck shoes, and, more recently, logging boots big fashion statements with people who had never spent a day wrangling (except with lawyers), sailing (except on drugs), or scaling conifers (except to place decorations on a fake Christmas tree).

Because that sweater was part of the typical tennis outfit, you wouldn't get all bent out of shape if someone else happened to show up dressed in one. Back when tennis clothes were just that, you didn't sit around all day agonizing over what to wear for your evening doubles match. You were free to think about better and more important things

175

if you were so inclined. Lastly, I miss that sweater because when you saw some hero at Wimbledon in it, you knew it was because he liked it, not because a subsidiary of a Japanese conglomerate had decided to crash the sportswear market and paid the player a small fortune to wear the garment.

This brings us to the only defense you can make for what passes for "style" in pro tennis these days: You can't accuse the players of having bad taste because what they wear has nothing whatsoever to do with taste. They wear what they're paid to wear. This is very weird in a couple of ways. Tennis is a sport of acute self-consciousness, but by dressing for bucks a player surrenders control over his most immediate and direct method of projecting personality. A pro with a clothing deal is also denied something that any mall monster would probably consider a fundamental human right: the prerogative to choose and buy the clothes you wear. When you come right down to it, tennis pros are among the few individuals in a consumer society denied the right to shop for the most important social events of their lives, Wimbledon and the U.S. Open.

On the other hand, Jim Courier received $4 million plus from Nike when he signed a multiyear deal with the company in 1991. No matter how you cut it, that's a hefty sum—even if it does demand that you walk around as Courier did, dressed in a neo–Boy Scout uniform.

The current endorsement system makes a tennis pro a promotional vehicle, and with the sleeve and shoulder "patch deals" that became popular in the 1980s, a tennis pro came to resemble nothing more closely than a stock car plastered with sponsor logos. I'm not sure exactly what this does to the concept of human dignity, but I'm happy that personality proves to be a pretty difficult thing to kill—even in the rag trade. A Boris Becker, Pete Sampras, or Andre Agassi can project all the sartorial disinformatzia in the world, but we still smoke out his character and come to conclusions about him. His clothes give us no help along the way.

However, some clothing manufacturers over the years did manage to get it right. I always felt that given his druthers, Bjorn Borg would have played tennis in a white T-shirt and standard-issue shorts. But Fila built a whole line of very expensive togs around Borg, and the stuff sold like hotcakes to *arriviste* plastic surgeons and tubby real estate brokers. Often the Borg line didn't suit their physiques, but it was decidedly right for Borg's.

Fila made another perfect match with Evonne Goolagong. The simple monochromatic tank tops and short, wrap-around skirts Goolagong wore were both minimalistic and elegant. They perfectly underscored her simple, natural game and personality. They didn't do bad things for her slender, boyish figure, either.

Similarly, the Ellesse line worn by Chris Evert tapped into her persona perfectly. Evert's roots were suburban and middle class. She was an icon to women who preferred to walk the middle of the road, somewhere between the boundaries set by *Vogue* and *Good Housekeeping*. The great thing about the Evert line was that, unlike Borg's kit, women of most sizes and shapes could get away with wearing it.

Ellesse goods were high priced and high quality, and they never challenged convention or threatened to upset the established order of things. In fact, the Ellesse line was curiously asexual. Most of the tops featured horizontal stripes in tame pastel colors, including lots of blues and pinks. Cut to expose very little, Ellesse tops bore a closer resemblance to the classic men's polo shirt than to anything you'd stumble on in a Victoria's Secret catalog.

More recently, Nike had the good sense to make a multi-million-dollar investment in Andre Agassi, a kid once given to wearing makeup and putting blue and red streaks in his hair. Agassi's youthful spunk, gender confusion, and agreeable exhibitionism gave Nike a great entree into the expanding youth culture and market.

The payoff for Nike came swiftly, culminating at the 1990 French Open. Speaking on behalf of the establishment, ITF president and French Open bigwig Philippe Chartrier suggested that Agassi's neon and lycra ensembles grotesquely violated the dress code of tennis. Quite a charge when you consider that the "dress code" in tennis was already gutted. Chartrier said that because of Agassi's costume (let's call a spade a spade), the French Open might adopt the "predominantly white" rule that still pertained at Wimbledon. Agassi's reaction was to call Chartrier and his ilk "a bunch of bozos," providing newspapers worldwide with a lively story. The interesting thing about this controversy was that while it was about flouting tradition, in a larger sense it was squarely in the tennis tradition. Bozogate was a tempest in a teapot, not unlike the one created in the early 1950s when couturier Ted Tinling put Gussie Moran in tennis panties trimmed with lace at Wimbledon.

The big difference between the two incidents is that Tinling's fashion statement made him persona non grata at Wimbledon for two decades. Agassi went his merry way while Chartrier and company sat around trying to figure out what the word "bozo" meant. All the other inhabitants of Babylon once again got to debate whether or not an industry preoccupied with such issues could properly be called a "sport."

But breaking new ground with Agassi put Nike in a curious bind. The company knew it was unlikely to sell flourescent pink Lycra bicycling tights over stone-washed black shorts to the host of aerospace engineers, arbitrage lawyers, and CEO types who also played tennis. So the job of promoting "conservative" tennis clothes for the adult market fell upon that paragon of adult restraint, John McEnroe. Now that was an interesting comment on where all the bare-knuckle competition had landed the tenniswear industry, and it pointed to the trade's appetite for self-destruction. Because in spite of some successful and intelligent campaigns, the history of the industry can be broadly interpreted as an aggressive, successful effort to destroy the very notion of tenniswear.

Classic style and understatement were out by the 1980s, blown away by an entire generation's exhibitionistic love affair with acquisition and with abstract issues of "quality" and "bestness." Even immutable, inexorable time was subject to judgment, creating the intrachronological particle called "quality time." The 1980s were the era of the $700 tennis racket, sunglasses that cost a C note, and tennis shoes resembling ski boots for the color blind. It was a time when you didn't really buy a car, a vodka, or a raincoat; you bought a BMW 321e, Absolut, or a Barbour, and that was supposed to say something important about you. The tennis shirt was replaced by the Fila, Tacchini, or Nike shirt, a garment that was only incidentally connected to tennis.

One of the great ironies of the Open era is that instead of making tennis more accessible and less expensive, it made the game ever more costly to play and watch. Tennis wasn't democratized nearly as much as it was consumerized, dragged from its modest traditions and turned into a battleground for self-expression and self-indulgence. Tennis in the amateur era may have been ruled by patrician values and tastes, but anybody could go and buy himself an elegant Fred Perry shirt for less than twenty bucks. Back in the late 1960s the price of tennis equipment, clothes, and shoes was hardly an issue for anyone living above the poverty line. Today your desire to take up the game might be severely dampened by the sheer cost of starting up.

Although the classic tennis sweater was an early casualty of the clothing wars, the concept of the tennis shirt lived on. It, too, was once a simple and elegant thing that lacked only one important feature for those times when you weren't playing tennis in it; a pocket. Surely you remember the heavy cotton, solid-color shirts produced by Perry or Chemise LaCoste?

But while blue jeans and cowboy boots became fashion staples for what they were, as they were, the tennis shirt was radically transformed from something comfortable, tasteful, and wonderfully basic into a bizarre accessory. It became a flimsy garment designed simply to catch the eye of the consumer while a famous person was wearing it, without even saying anything about the celebrity on whom it was hung, in order to trigger an impulse buy.

In 1990, Stefan Edberg (under contract to Adidas) wore a shirt that hardly suited this son of a policeman from the sleepy town of Vastervik, Sweden. Edberg was known for his gentle demeanor and his country-boy simplicity. He was literal-minded, meek, and law-abiding. He was Citizen Stef. Adidas put him in a shirt that seemed more appropriate for one of those intensely mental types who are so busy figuring out just who they are that they never get to find out. You may remember the shirt I'm talking about: The upper half was covered with complicated, swirling gray and blue lines and glyphs. Random-colored lines ran through this grid at whimsical angles. I asked a few people what the shirt "said" to them and received an interesting range of answers. It looked like Roquefort cheese but with more blue bits. It looked like the trail map for a ski resort. One person thought it resembled a satellite weather photo with computer-enhanced graphics. I finally asked Edberg himself, who told me that the shirt made him think of a map of the subway system in his adopted city, London.

This was not the only fashion error promulgated by Adidas, the German company that once produced tasteful, bold, and above all *sporty* clothes for characters as different as Stan Smith and Ilie Nastase. At about the same time that what-you-see-is-what-you-get Stef, Citizen Stef, was dressed like a walking Rorschach test, Adidas had leggy, pet-loving, family-centric Steffi Graf wearing shirts that came directly from the Salvador Dali school of design. One of those shirts appeared to be made from strands of genetic material, suggesting that maybe the Germans were up to their old tricks again, trying to revive some *Uberfrau* theme from their dark past. Another shirt created for Graf was adorned with checked stars and multicolored lines that zigzagged across her ample bust. When Graf's agent, Phil de Picciotto, asked an Adidas marketing honcho about the graphics, he was told that the pattern symbolized "daydreams." De Picciotto, a man who is not usually lost for words, said, "Oh."

In 1990, Boris Becker wore a Fila shirt with a dense blue-and-green pattern that evoked nothing more exciting than a shower curtain. Diadora was hawking a shirt decorated with shapes that resembled fluorescent orange Scrabble tiles (matching socks were optional). But my favorite was the shirt worn by the lanky, goofy Croatian chick magnet Goran Ivanisevic. This talented player had yet to make his mark at a Grand Slam tournament, but he was already famous for his flakiness and his patriotism—tendencies that came to a bizarre intersection when, during the height of the fighting in the former Yugoslav Republic, Ivanisevic passionately declared, "My racket is my gun. If you put a line of Serbs by that wall over there, I would shoot them all." Ivanisevic was contracted to Austral, and his signature shirt featured a pastel panoramic view of a mountain range, complete with the orange traces of a lurid sunset. It looked like a mural you might find spray-painted on the side of a van.

While all these shirts provided plenty of fodder for the pressroom, they also reflected an interesting transformation in the tennis community as well as the sportswear industry. Marty Mulligan of Fila told me that they represented a general effort to expand the role of tennis shirts. The manufacturers were trying to make shirts that were equally appropriate for a game of tennis, a Fourth of July picnic, and a Grateful Dead concert. Mulligan also confided that there was probably nothing quite as dangerous as a designer given a mandate to express himself rather than to create a garment that expressed the nature of the person who would be wearing it, often in front of millions of television viewers. What can you say about a bunch of people so creative that they would put a player like Jim Courier into olive shorts that became black when he perspired? The first commandment of tenniswear is, Thou shalt not create a garment that draws attention to sweat. Which was the main reason that tennis whites were once so popular in the first place.

The take-the-money-and-run sensibility of the players also facilitated their devolution into mannequins. Most of them couldn't be bothered to think about what they wore to work, provided they were handsomely paid. The cumulative effect on these trends was that by the 1990s the industry was driven by one simple mandate: Have your clothes noticed. Top whatever statement the competition was making with a louder one. Be remembered for any reason whatsoever. Score that impulse buy.

Image is *everything*.

That line, spoken by Andre Agassi in a television commercial for Canon cameras, was catchy, effective, and brilliant. The storyboard crew that thought it up unwittingly placed a shutter finger right smack on top of an issue that has haunted tennis forever.

Image and style go hand in hand, and style has always been central to tennis. It's one of the great things about the game, and it also explains some of the silliness surrounding it. Tennis aficionados care deeply about, say, whether the attack strategy is superior to the defensive baseline game. Tennis fans also care about the personal styles of the pro players. That's why, at any given tournament, you are just as apt to find two friends engaged in a spirited debate over Andre Agassi's hair as you are to overhear a lofty dialogue about Steffi Graf's topspin backhand or Pete Sampras's choice of a forehand grip.

Tennis is just as much about the people who play the game as it is about the game itself. That's why fans who have never met Sampras, Capriati, or Lendl insist on calling them Pete, Jen, and Ivan. Tennis fans empathize with their favorite players, and they are merciless toward those they dislike. Tennis is a personality-driven game partly because it is a sport of itinerants, an eclectic array of individuals whose styles of play and conduct are as unique as their fingerprints.

Agassi paid dearly and unfairly for his bold statement about image. It quickly became a statement about Agassi himself, a sinister confession taken seriously by those who profess to loathe image and the machinery that creates it, who happen to be some of the most reflexively image-conscious people of them all. But if Agassi were clever or manipulative enough to take all this image-is-everything bit seriously, he certainly wouldn't be stupid enough to admit it.

Francis X. Shields was by all accounts a wonderful player as well as an all-purpose party animal who did most of his damage to the sterling silver industry—and female hearts—back in the 1930s. Incidentally, he was also the grandfather of a young lady named Brooke who would revive the glamour associated with the Shields name some fifty years later and bring the circle around when she became Agassi's girlfriend in 1994.

Someone once asked Francis X. what he packed for a tennis weekend in the cradle of American tennis, Newport, Rhode Island. Shields wickedly replied, "A pair of pajama tops and a bottle of scotch."

So much for theories about guys with names like Bowen, Crocker, Davis, or Francis X. So much for the notion that before the dawn of Open tennis, the game was the exclusive domain of weak-chinned society boys. In fact, I'd say that tennis became a game geared toward fashion victims, practiced by too many coddled, spoiled, sheltered personalities, not before the advent of Open tennis but after it.

Shields's crack articulated an attitude characterized by many tennis players in the amateur era, and that weltanschauung had less to do with getting sloppy drunk and groping at women than it did with the felicitous idea that life was there to be lived—enjoyed, even. Like many of his contemporaries, Shields saw sport as a means rather than an end, even when that end had nothing to do with the development of character or leadership qualities. Show me a person who doesn't allow tennis to overwhelm his life, and I'll show you a person with style, whether it is generated by the flair of a Vitas Gerulaitis or Andre Agassi, the high-minded purpose of an Arthur Ashe, or the nutty activism of Martina Navratilova.

In the amateur era, players traveled the circuit because they loved to play, although hating to work may have had something to do with it, too. They were willing to live hand to mouth, burn through family fortunes, and crash in the spare bedrooms of strangers' homes in order to be where the tennis action was, to see the world, and to collect experiences and memories. Their possessions amounted to nothing more than a pair of rackets, a few sets of tennis whites, pajama tops, and a bottle of scotch.

These days if your daughter starts going out with a good tennis player, you can be forgiven for acting as if you just won the lottery. Back then you might have been more inclined to lay in wait behind the hedges with a shotgun as the fellow came to pick her up for a date. There was a certain doomed, romantic quality to being a tennis player in the old days, along with a healthy dose of notoriety. Tennis players had panache. They had style.

The Australian players who dominated the game in the 1950s and 1960s personified the happy-go-lucky tennis bum, but that image is not entirely accurate. They were also practical, proto-professionals from a rough democratic culture. They were beer-swilling country boys named Rod (Laver), Lew (Hoad), Kenny (Rosewall), and Roy (Emerson) whose nicknames were, respectively, Rocket, Hoady, Muscles, and Emmo. (Ever meet anybody at Newport called Muscles?)

These players drove the game relentlessly toward professionalism, but they were uniformly appalled when, some twenty years later, they saw what they had created. All they ever wanted was legitimacy, an end to the absurd distinctions between amateur and pro players, and a measure of security for the long years that would follow their retirement from competition—none of which demanded that you dress in costume, throw sawdust in the faces of fans, and pierce your nose.

But the excesses that came to characterize the Open era took root early, and they reflected broad cultural changes as well as transformations in the attitude and ethic of the elite international cadre of tennis players. At a time when tennis players wanted to be taken seriously, many took their cues from the Camp Beverly Hills school of fashion and grooming. The lure of materialism at the time was so strong that most players indulged in ostentatious fashion errors.

If you hung around the lobby of a hotel where the players stayed, circa 1974, you were apt to see Ashe walk by wearing clogs and carrying a little purse. The male handbag looked particularly queer when it was an accessory to a blue denim jumpsuit of the kind favored by Tom Okker, the Flying Dutchman. The jumpsuit look didn't last very long, but gold chains did. In the early 1980s, Herb Krickstein told me that his sixteen-year-old was into "macho" things. Like what, I wondered? Cockfights? Catfish wrestling? Chain saws? Herb leaned over close and whispered, "Gold chains. He loves them."

Male tennis pros in the 80s went nowhere without their blow driers, partly because so many of them had long hair. We're not talking about just plain long hair but high-maintenance cuts created by mononomial stylists. Exotic furs were all the rage at the time, and even Borg once showed up at some tournament in a coat made from the hide of a magnificent wolf. I'm sorry, but any male wearing fur ought to be carrying a spear, not a handbag.

I'll tell you exactly how bad it was. For a few months there, Rod Laver—the tight-lipped Rocket, winner of not one but two Grand Slams—wore a choker made from pukka shells. These necklaces have since gone the way of the mood ring and earth shoe, but at the time the tour was a nightmare of androgyny and bourgeois affectations. I confess that I, too, wore a necklace: a sterling silver necklace with a piece of turquoise hanging off it.

This nonsense, while fairly benign, did nothing to convince the public that tennis players meant business, except in the literal sense. Still, despite these cosmetic affectations, the ethic represented by Laver and his fellow proto-professionals, from the Aussies to Ashe to East Europeans like Jan Kodes, cast men's tennis in an appealing light. Soon that light would be replaced by the flashing strobe, as tennis became a sport characterized by the temper tantrum, bickering, and childish name-calling among a class of people once known for discipline and a sense of camaraderie.

But despite the climate of lawlessness early in the Open era, nobody ever resorted to seeking frontier justice. Well, almost nobody. Some guy once punched out the notoriously surly South African, Bob Hewitt, but that was at the dawn of the new era. The fellow happened to be a spectator, so he doesn't count. Clark Graebner, who played during the transition to the pro era, once grabbed Nastase by the throat during a hotly contested match. Another fellow head-butted Nastase and chipped his tooth, but that took place in a New York disco where Nasty had been unwise enough to make a pass at the guy's girlfriend. But by and large, serious confrontations rarely occurred during the Open era.

It may be tempting to interpret the half-cocked Gandhian ethic in tennis as a throwback to some concept of gentlemanly conduct, but a gentleman, if you can find one, will tell you that a code of honor not only contains a provision for taking a poke at somebody but it demands that you do so when nothing you might say would constitute satisfac-

tion. But be warned: The mandate to punch somebody in the nose usually kicks in when the offending party is a six-foot-four hairy-backed
Coke machine impersonating a human being in a tank top.

Taken cumulatively, the developments and trends of the Open era
did little to dispel the misgivings an inquisitive public had about tennis.
It was once perceived as a "sissy" sport practiced by aquiline-nosed
opera buffs with names like Ellsworth dressed in classic tennis sweaters.
In the Open era, the game molted into a glitzy variation of pro-
wrestling, practiced by a bunch of rule-bending, fit-pitching, earring-
wearing babies who earned millions of dollars.

The public and the media came to regard tennis players with the same
curious combination of contempt and fascination that they showed
toward other celebrities. Tennis players arouse more passion than they
should, and less respect. McEnroe personified this trend. He once told
me that his single overpowering ambition had been "to take the game
to another level, to put tennis players up there on a par with the top
names in the NBA or the NFL." But we all know that it didn't always
work out that way. Personal style is always the first—and foremost—
quality in determining the public's attitude toward a player. Tennis was
once interesting because it represented a way of life complete with its
own ethic and aesthetics. Now, even for the most down-to-earth players, it is a way of not living, characterized by isolation and demanding
commercial opportunities and obligations. Playing tennis isn't an
adventure anymore, it's a job. It requires a high degree of skill but very
little resourcefulness—or, for that matter, social skill.

There is no elite society of tennis players to pique interest anymore,
least of all where it is most needed: at the top of the game. Today's tennis players hole up in lavish suites, surrounded not by their peers but by
an inner circle of advisors, obsessing about how many computer points
they must earn in the incipient tournament in order to maintain their
electronically generated rankings, or which of the lucrative shoe and
clothing deals is most attractive. This has changed some with the emergence of a new, conservative American generation led by the likes of Jim
Courier, Michael Chang, Pete Sampras, and Todd Martin, but despite
their best intentions and standards, it seems unlikely that the tide will
be reversed. Too much has changed, from modes of travel to the lodes
of opportunity. Tennis once had characters, it now has showmen. And
when a player like Sampras or Courier declares that he has no desire to
play the clown, he is often characterized as a boring blight on the game.

Tennis is saturated with fashion, albeit bad fashion, but it may no
longer have style.

                    *   *   *

Not very much has been written in this chapter about women so far, even though they are generally more fashion conscious than men and the industry that targets them is larger, as well as more energetic and eclectic. But this industry, which leaves no stone unturned in its quest to engage taste and thereby move product, has been remarkably stagnant. There are a few curious reasons for this, the most important being the overall loss of identity suffered by women's tennis when the female tour became a mirror-image of the men's circuit. More about the "masculinization" of the women's tour in a later chapter.

In the pro era, tennis developed a unisex sensibility, with most of the cues coming from the masculine side of the fence. One of the first casualties of the trend was the traditional tennis dress. Tracy Austin wore a dress when she won the U.S. Open in 1981, but it was more than a decade until another top female player wore one in a Grand Slam event—the statuesque Franco-American Mary Pierce, in 1994. Pierce updated her fashion statement by wearing Lycra bicycling shorts instead of the classic tennis panties under her dress.

There was a powerful commercial reason for this trend: Separates (shirts and skirts) are much more versatile and salable. You can mix and match them for all sorts of occasions. The only thing you could do with the classic tennis dress was look divine in it. Furthermore, tennis dresses were sleeveless, and women players nowadays can't bare their tanned arms because you can't sew a promotional patch on skin. The difference in the image Gabriela Sabatini projects in her sleeved, patch-laden shirt and skirt combo and the appearance she would have projected in a sleeveless white tennis dress is a good indication of the extent to which women pros have been defeminized. The androgynous trend underscored the extent to which pro players began to think of themselves less and less as women or men who happened to make a living playing tennis than as *professional tennis players.* Talk about one-dimensional man, totalitarian woman, professional It!

Ted Tinling, the late couturier and ubiquitous man about tennis, was one of the most ardent supporters of the professional movement even though it would eventually put him out of the fashion business for good when sportswear manufacturers began to pay women to wear separates. But even Tinling was mortified when he saw the extent to which the pro sensibility defeminized women players, and he fought a long, futile, rearguard action against the trend. In addition to being a couturier, Tinling was a world-class bowler, a former British intelligence officer, and a liaison man at Wimbledon. He was also a spokesman for Virginia Slims, the ITF, and the International Tennis Hall of Fame, to which he was inducted shortly before his death in 1990. Tinling was a prominent gadfly, a social critic, and a designer of wedding gowns for English society ladies between the two world wars, not to mention Chris Evert on the occasion of her marriage to the skier Andy Mill.

But to most tennis fans in the 1980s, Tinling was merely the most conspicuous unknown man in tennis. That was because he also served as the emcee at numerous tournaments (including some Grand Slam events), and once you saw Tinling, you didn't forget him. A gangly, six-foot-seven Englishman, Tinling was as bald as a baby's behind. He wore a massive diamond stud earring, turquoise rings, and a gold bracelet that looked like the anchor chain off an eighteenth-century British frigate. On any given day the rest of Tinling's outfit was likely to be a garish Edwardian suit made of polyester, stuff that he insisted was going to save the world. He looked as if he had just stepped out of a Peter Max poster, circa 1969, and he fancied those outfits right up until the day he died at age eighty. And to bottom it all off, Tinling liked to be seen with black square-toed pirate shoes or red Converse high-top sneakers on his size fifteen feet.

Tinling was a freak and delighted in describing himself as such. He was an unflinchingly honest man with a wicked sense of humor and no patience whatsoever for pretense. I loved Ted, and if I knew him less well, I might have had a real problem with the fact that I literally interviewed him to death, even though that surely would have been the way he wanted to go.

Ted was already suffering from the lung condition alveolitis when I interviewed him in Miami for a long profile in March 1990. Seeing him gasping for breath and taking massive hits from an inhaler during the course of two evenings, I kept trying to cut short the interview. But Ted would have none of it. He collapsed after we finished on the second evening, and by the next morning he was in the hospital. He hung in there for a few weeks, but the end was near. It was typical of Tinling that during our last interview he talked about his impending death with the same unsentimental and keen vision that he had brought to his life.

"You can't go on forever with this process of thinking about the end," he said, waving one of his massive paws. "The reality of death comes to one slowly. At first it's a little bit overwhelming and one thinks, 'Oh, my God.' But then you think, 'So what?' "

While Tinling was very much the product of the amateur era (he was a fair player who competed at Wimbledon and the French Open), a gentleman in the trappings of a freak, and a dreamer who couldn't care less about money, he was one of the great proponents of the professional movement and an important force during its inception and growth. He hoped to see tennis ascend to unprecedented heights in the public consciousness, and he believed that the professional game would take it there.

Like many of the more interesting people in tennis, Ted came to the game accidentally. The son of a wealthy accountant, he developed respiratory problems at a young age. His mother, an ardent disciple of the famed spiritualist Madame Blavatsky, whisked young Ted away with her to the Riviera, where he would spend his formative years in the company of the idle rich. Tinling fell in love with tennis when he was called on to umpire a match for Suzanne Lenglen, who changed the face of tennis forever by bringing loads of charisma and theatrical flair to the game. As he put it decades later, "Suzanne . . . created an image for tennis, an image that nobody had ever heard of or thought possible. She revolutionized tennis by virtue of the fact that she made herself the first real star of the game."

Tinling's first brush with what we now call "star quality" dazzled him for life. He decided to become a couturier, and he built an important portfolio as a revolutionary designer, the fashion world's version of Buckminster Fuller or Marshall McLuhan.

In 1961, Tinling designed the first commercially marketed paper dress. He was also the first to design an outfit for a rock star, Tommy Steele, for his premier appearance with Bill Haley. Tinling was a pioneer in the relatively new field of uniform design. He designed the first uniforms worn by civilians as diverse as the staff of British Midland Airways, the Elizabeth Arden salon, the Maypole supermarket chain, and even the factory workers for Quaker Oats.

Tinling completely modernized golf attire with the uniform he created for the British women's golf team, and he outfitted the world champion British female archers. He broke new ground by pushing the boundaries in ice-skating costumes, and we've all seen where that has led. But the deepest mark Tinling made was on his first love among sports, tennis.

In 1949, Tinling fired one of the professional movement's first shots across the bow of the establishment's boat. The world was still in a somber mood following the horrors of World War II, and the ever-progressive Tinling was impatient with the climate. So he designed a pair of panties trimmed in lace, and he knew just the right woman for them: the chipper, earthy, American heartthrob, gorgeous Gussie Moran. By today's standards this was a bit of harmless fun. But the shock waves created by Moran's appearance at Wimbledon in the frilly panties were felt clear around the world. As a result of the stunt, Tinling was persona non grata at Wimbledon for two decades. That he returned from his exile with no hard feelings whatsoever was a tribute to Tinling's character as well as his affection for Wimbledon.

"I'm told that I have an instinct for getting to the heart of the matter—any matter—and that's what the lace panties were all about," Tinling told me many years later. "I'm like a scavenging animal that way. I
don't go sniffing around the cabbage leaves unless there's a juicy bone
hidden somewhere in there. In this case, it was that people were bored
out of their skulls after the war. It was the same old, same old. They
needed cheering up, they needed and wanted some kind of change.
They were ready for sex."

Tinling himself was gay, but he had contempt for people who talked
about their sexuality, considering such behavior vulgar. He knew people would want clothes made with sex appeal, and synthetics. In 1950,
Tinling created the first nylon dress and the first permanently pleated
tennis dresses. Two years later he made a dress out of a new fabric called
Orlon. The following year, he designed the first polyester dress. Later,
he became the fashion guru of the ground-breaking Virginia Slims pro
tour. The dresses he designed for the likes of Billie Jean King, Rosie
Casals, Margaret Court, and Evonne Goolagong were not only theatrical, they were often downright ugly. But they illustrated the new priorities of the Open era.

"All of the dresses I made for the pro tour were predicated on the
idea that they had to have an impact on people sitting hundreds of feet
away and in some cases up high in the dark reaches of some stadium.
That was one of the reasons for all the oversized collars, the rhine-
stones, and the vibrant colors. I had to surprise people without shocking them, and at the same time I tried to bear in mind that the first rule
of my occupation is physical flattery of the player wearing one of my
designs."

Of one of his favorite clients and favorite people, Billie Jean King,
Tinling said, "She looks her best in wildly elaborate things that are
strictly tailored. See, this suits her dual personality in that she always
wanted it both ways. She wanted to be one of the masses, and at the
same time she wanted to be a star. I gave her elaborations for the star
side, tailoring for the masses. You know, she's perfectly happy to sit
down and have a couple of hamburgers and a milkshake with a ballboy
if there's nobody better around. But she's happier yet when she's being
screamed at by five million people. To find a garment that suits both
qualities is my problem."

A spectator at the first match played between the veteran Rosie
Casals and the fifteen-year-old prodigy Tracy Austin might have been
forgiven for thinking that he had wandered into a Halloween party
instead of a tennis tournament. Casals chose to wear one of the most
outrageous garments Tinling ever created—a black-velvet, rhinestone-

studded, Lady Elvis costume. In stark contrast, Austin wore braces, braids, and the red gingham pinafore that had become her trademark. "What was going on there was simple," Tinling observed. "Tracy was being touted as the next great champion, and everybody knew that the image projected by her pinafores and ribbons was way out of line with her fierce competitive nature as a player. Rosie was just impersonating one of those exotic fish who puffs itself up at the first sign of danger."

One of Tinling's lasting regrets was that he never got the chance to dress Chris Evert, who landed a comprehensive clothing endorsement deal at the early age of seventeen. At the time, Evert was a shy, introspective, scared-to-be-different Catholic girl. She was so square that she probably would have signed to wear a dress made of sackcloth rather than be seen in one of Tinling's wild creations. Aptly enough, her first deal was with Puritan, a company that made proper, sleeveless tennis dresses.

Up to that point, Tinling had dressed every woman who counted in tennis, including ten successive Wimbledon champions (1952–61), and he chalked up a grand slam of his own when he clothed the winner of every major singles championship in 1963. Tinling did not begrudge Evert her contract because he saw the handwriting on the wall. He was also one of the first to recognize that she was anything but a bland suburban chick with wicked ground strokes.

"Ever since Chrissie was fourteen, she's had this ability to hit the nail right *bang* on the head, without any problems. It goes right through you, and I love that about her. Maureen Connolly had that same quality, which is definitely a star quality. She has this strange aloofness from conversation until it reaches a point where it touches something critical, and then you realize that she knows about everything that's gone on, because she makes the only apt comment that you haven't yet heard."

Tinling had an imagination that gravitated to the fantastic, and a remarkable grasp of character. His trenchant observations were as vivid and controversial as the garments he created, and toward the end of his life he became an irrepressible font of wit and wisdom. A reporter needing a juicy quote could always go to Tinling, and he delivered as reliably as the post office. Nobody could put tennis and the people who played it into as broad or socially resonant a context as Tinling did, every time he opened his mouth.

After Tinling's primary job had vanished into thin air because of the commercial garment wars, he continued to serve in various liaison positions, and no elderly person I've ever met was as sharp or observant as Tinling, right up to the day he died.

Of Steffi Graf and Boris Becker, Tinling said: "These kids make tennis relevant in the yuppie era. They play a game of instant gratification, hitting the ball without restraint. If it goes in, great. If it misses, so what? There's always another opportunity, another point, another match, and another tournament tomorrow."

In 1990, at a time when many of the women pros were adopting savage fitness regimens to enhance their strength, Tinling said, "I'm appalled by the conspicuous lack of intelligence in the game some women play. They have no feel for the important points, for the full use of court space. They see the men playing a smash-bang brand of tennis, and they feel obliged to do the same thing even though they can't. It's all because of some absurd feminist paranoia. The more time they spend on hitting the ball as powerfully as they'd like, the less they know about where to put it."

Tinling was most attracted to classic beauty and traditional femininity. He was contemptuous of women who felt obliged to abandon feminine traditions in order to prove themselves the equal of men. One practical manifestation of this was Tinling's frequent defense of the baseline game that was—and continues to be—the traditional style in women's tennis.

"If a woman doesn't serve and volley today, she's apt to feel that she is letting down the feminist side. It's almost a loss of social face in some quarters not to volley, which grows out of this wild illusion that unless you project a butch sensibility, you're inferior."

And while Tinling embraced and promoted the professional sensibility, he loathed many of the dehumanizing conditions it created. When the prodigy Jennifer Capriati arrived in the press interview room after a win over Helena Sukova, Tinling burst into applause. Our mutual friend, author John Feinstein, leaned over and reminded Ted of the professional journalists' prohibition against such behavior.

"Nonsense," Tinling replied. "The day you give priority to bogus ethics over human reactions, you become a loser. Human reactions are priceless. Rules should never, ever stifle emotions. Tennis is a very human game facing a great danger that it will be strangulated in a cat's cradle of unnecessary or inhumane rules."

Tinling was buffeted by such "rules" throughout his life, from the calcified affectations that helped give amateurism a bad name, to the commercial laws that ruled fashion in the Open era. But Tinling didn't mind being tossed from wave to wave because he was a sturdy craft. It was probably even fun for him.

I always wondered how Tinling was able to remain above it all without losing any of his taste for tennis. And it wasn't until I went back and

reviewed his history that the answer crystallized. Tinling was a visionary, although I wasn't sure I wanted to live in the kind of world that he
saw coming—partly because it was a world in which people like Tinling
would become redundant, much as he himself had. But Ted knew that,
and he was resigned to it. I guess he was too honest to swim against the
tide, and too fixated on the down side of an establishment that had
exiled him from Wimbledon because he had shown the audacity to put
an attractive tennis player in frilly bloomers.

Ted made his last trip to the Australian Open in January 1990. I spent
a fair amount of time with him then, but John Feinstein and our Australian
colleague, Rich MacKinnon, made an extra effort to keep an eye on him.

One morning, MacKinnon bumped into Tinling walking down the
hall in the National Tennis Center. "Ted," he asked, "how do you feel?"

"How do I feel?" Tinling shouted. "My God, I'm dying, young man.
How do you *think* I feel?"

Tinling was consoled in those waning days by his conviction that
there was indeed an afterlife. He even told me what he hoped to find
there: "I'm convinced that if I cross that great divide and manage to end
up in the right place, Suzanne [Lenglen] will be there to greet me. And
she'll say, 'Ted! What are *you* doing here?'" Tinling's ice-blue eyes lit up
as he continued: "And then, of course, she'll say, 'How can you possi-
bly have said that Steffi Graf uses the court better than I did? Were you
mad or merely stupid?'"

Given the degree to which Tinling had so often been right about the
future, I wouldn't be at all surprised to learn that it all happened just like
that.

So let's wind this up with a quick fashion tour of the contemporary tennis pro, from head to toe, and the fashion statement he or she manages to
make—or avoid—on that choice piece of real estate called a body.

You might know all you need to about the professional era by understanding that it went from being a game of the crew-cut to a game of
big hair. In the Open era, the discipline and clean living implied by the
crew-cut were no longer fashionable. The dominant hairdos were the
Prince Valiant bowl cuts, favored by players as diverse as Bob Lutz and
Jimmy Connors (the best one belonged to a fellow called Rick Fagel),
and the unkept mane that distinguished the likes of Vitas Gerulaitis,
Bjorn Borg, and Andre Agassi.

Mats Wilander surprised the world in a couple of ways when, as an
unseeded seventeen-year old, he won the French Open in 1982. Instead
of running out and buying a red Maserati or a Finca the size of Texas,
Wilander went out and got himself a monkish buzzcut. For the next

eight years Wilander was a superb competitor and an absolute gentleman. Maybe it was all coincidence, maybe not.

Women have a tougher time with hair than men do because taking
two or three showers a day isn't hairdo friendly. Most of them go with
bobbed hair or long locks that can be braided or gathered in simple variations on the ponytail. In an environment increasingly dominated by
gender-bending and sexual ambiguity, women who wanted to send a
traditional message often did so by becoming ponytailers. These
included young Chris Evert, Tracy Austin, Steffi Graf, and a host of
lesser players.

Evert's hair history is interesting in that she began her life in the public eye with a ponytail and eventually grew out of it in a way that
reflected her evolution from the simple "girl next door" into a symbol
of the independent, savvy woman. She frequently had her hair done and
color treated, but she never made the antifashion statement that many
of her peers did with their practical, butch cuts. Evert's career was a
long and bitter battle against bad hair days. She didn't always win, but
it was the good fight.

The most interesting thing about hair is that the tennis player's head
is one of the few commercial-free zones on his or her body, so it is one
of the areas in which players can express themselves authentically. But
even that condition has been challenged and sometimes compromised.
Back when Borg and Vilas brought the headband to its peak of popularity, Vilas's manager, Tiriac, realized that it was the ultimate vehicle for
advertisement. Tiriac put together an auction, with the bidding to begin
at $1 million per annum. The international division of Ford expressed
interest, but the deal ultimately fell through.

Much later, in 1991, Monica Seles had a hefty contract with the hair-
care products company Matrix Essentials. But as a fan of the pop star
Madonna and a budding student of high fashion, she was given to
experimenting with her hair. Matrix did not especially like the fact that
Seles had a different hairdo every fifteen seconds. (Robin Finn of *The
New York Times* pointed out that Seles had a record of sorts in that she
was the only woman to have won the French Open three times, with
her hair a different color on each of those three occasions.) But Seles's
hair fixation was hell on print and electronic ad campaigns which rested
on the assumption that you would recognize Seles from one day to the
next. So Seles and Matrix prematurely and amicably parted company.
Matrix then signed up a wife and mother to replace Seles, Chris Evert.

Seles was not the only one to discover that keeping your head free
from commercial exploitation requires a certain amount of sacrifice. In
the mid-1980s, flaxen-haired Peter Fleming abandoned his Prince

Valiant look in favor of a punkish cut with buzzed sides and a spiked top. The cut suited Fleming's personality and taste for New Wave music, but his agent pulled Fleming aside and told him that the cut made him much less marketable. As soon as Fleming's hair grew out, he grudgingly went back to his old helmet-head look.

Just a few years after Fleming was advised to toe the conservative line, Agassi burst on the scene. He was a hair renegade, and the degree to which his hair was perceived as a marketing asset rather than a liability indicated how much the game had changed. Forerunners Gerulaitis, Borg, and Vilas had long hair, but Agassi will be remembered as the man who made tennis safe for individuals with big hair.

Facial hair was once considered just as risky as big hair. But Stan Smith (no relation to Roger, the Bahamian Smith who pioneered radical hair with his bead-festooned mohawk) almost singlehandedly changed that. Smith's pencil-thin mustache bespoke Prussian severity, Christian temperance, and Dudley Doright righteousness.

John Newcombe's big Aussie mustache got him painted into one heck of a corner. "Newk" was boyish and charming, and the only criticism leveled at him was that he was bland. This made it difficult to market Newk until the rocket scientists working on this problem at IMG seized upon Newk's lavish mustache and turned it into his identifying attribute. Newk's mustache literally became his trademark, and it appeared as the logo on various products, including shirts, that he endorsed. This stroke of advertising genius did not become a problem until Newk awoke one morning sick and tired of having to trim and pick encrusted pieces of comestibles out of his mustache. He was told that shaving would destroy an image that had been painstakingly put together over the years to make him marketable. So Newk kept the mustache until he faded from the public eye.

Later, when the pop star George Michael cultivated perpetual stubble, some tennis players, including McEnroe, followed suit. The sparse beard grown by Boris Becker in 1992, combined with his severe Spartacus haircut, illustrated his increasingly monkish, philosophical tendencies.

The rest of a player's face provides slim pickings for the commercial establishment. Earrings have trade potential, but nobody has quite figured out a way to make a logo-freighted earring light enough not to give an endorsee a badly distended or torn ear. Pat Cash, an ardent fan of heavy-metal music and all-around Aussie rude boy, was the first top player to sport an earring. The affectation also suited the androgynous Agassi. But diehard McEnroe fans were distressed and his critics merely snickered when McEnroe decided to stick a diamond stud in his ear. This was a true fashion error from someone whose better attributes included a conspicuous lack of vanity. McEnroe wore perpetually wrinkled clothing and enjoyed unique status as a tennis player who never, ever had a suntan.

You could be forgiven for wondering why a top tennis player always wears a wristwatch on court. He never has a train to catch (although players have intentionally lost matches in order to catch a flight), and if he wants to know the time, he can just turn around and look at the scoreboard clock. Players wear timepieces on court as part of their "watch deals," but it doesn't do much for the image of tennis as a rugged sport when the combatants flail away wearing classic tank watches with alligator bands.

We covered shirts earlier, but I feel obliged to pay tribute to the three best examples of the garment. Once upon a time, no player's trip to Wimbledon was complete without a stop at the Fred Perry warehouse on Half-Moon Street in London. There players received free tenniswear, including the classic white Fred Perry shirt. Made of high-quality woven cotton, the best and worst things you could say about it was that the shirt was nearly as heavy as a bath towel. It had the Perry wreath stitched on the right breast, and if you were important enough, you could get your three-letter monogram right below the wreath.

The classic chemise LaCoste was created by one of France's legendary four Musketeers, René LaCoste. In his heyday in the 1930s, LaCoste had been called "*Le Crocodile*" because of his dogged style, hence the trademark logo. LaCoste took the Perry shirt and breathed Gallic style into it. It was made of lighter cotton and came in a dazzling array of colors. The buttons had beveled edges, the body was tapered, and the shirt had an extra-long tail.

The Borg-line shirt by Fila, once a company that specialized in making generic underwear, is my third choice. I don't think it compared with the Perry and LaCoste shirts because it was slightly overstyled, too fine, and too expensive. But it was perfect for Borg (who didn't have to fork over his own dough to buy one, or expect it to last him several summers). It also caught the essence of Borg and the sensibility of the budding professional era, pushing the conservative envelope as far as it could go. The tight-fitting shirt was made from finely woven, off-white cotton, pinstriped in a way that evoked the uniform of the legendary New York Yankees baseball team. It was splashed with red-and-blue trim on the collar and placket, and instead of buttons it had neat little snaps. The matching white shorts were brief, featuring a red-and-blue waistband. They fit Borg's lean legs and compact butt just so, but resembled bursting sausage casings on most other adult males.

"At the time, Americans still took their cues from European fashion," Marty Mulligan of Fila told me. "And at the time, European men were much more conscious of their physiques. Americans didn't buy the gear because it made sense. They bought it to identify with that trim, healthy European look."

Black socks were completely outre until the 1990s, but Peter Rennart wore them once during a doubles match in which his partner was McEnroe, wearing traditional white socks. Noticing this curious violation (not merely of taste, but of the official tennis dress code), the umpire suggested that the team repair to the locker room and return in reasonably matching outfits. Rennart and McEnroe just sat down and each of them took off and exchanged a sock, which brought them in line with the letter, if not the spirit, of the law. This anecdote may tell you all you need to know about McEnroe.

Finally, there are the shoes. The specialty footwear market is one of the great success stories in the sportswear business. Once there were sneakers, then a few variations on the theme, such as Chuck Taylor basketball shoes or Jack Purcell tennis shoes. Now there's a custom shoe to fit every niche in the market. I'm not going to bore you with the details of the shoe wars that have been chronicled elsewhere. Do you even want to know who started Nike, much less why he hates the guy over at Reebok? Trust me, it's dog-eat-dog, image-bang-image out there in shoe world. But understanding the nature of the turf lines helps to explain why Nike went apoplectic when Agassi did his "image is everything" shtick for Canon.

Since the inception of the company, Nike has tried to stake out the high ground of credibility, spending millions on images to show that their contract players were dedicated, passionate athletes obsessed with performance. Even when Nike came up with Agassi's "rock 'n' roll" tennis campaign, the message was predicated on the contemporary intensity of Agassi's style. So then Andre appeared in a black shirt and a baggy white suit, smiling impishly, advising television viewers on behalf of Canon that image is everything. This was an outstanding example of one hand not knowing—or caring—what the other one was doing.

The best shoe story of them all brings us back to the ground-breaking company Fila. The Italian firm began to reap big profits almost as soon as it changed from manufacturing underwear that nobody saw to tennis clothes that everybody noticed, and sales figures showed that signing top pro players to endorsement contracts was a powerful stimulant that triggered the all-important impulse buy. The Borg, Goolagong, and Vilas lines sold like hotcakes. Before long, Fila crossed the official line between tenniswear and sportswear with a Borg-line navy blue sweater containing almost no white at all, and it was off to the races. Other manufacturers got into the fray. In the ensuing rag wars, players changed sponsors so frequently that they damaged the foundation on which the whole enterprise was built—that the audience would associate specific players with the brand of clothes they wore.

"It's very, very difficult to cancel the image a previous company created for a player," Mulligan explained. "We were lucky when we picked Boris Becker up from Puma because that company was less and less active. When Boris went to Lotto after us, they probably had a much harder time breaking through the public perception that Becker was a Fila person. On top of that, the players were less and less inclined to do anything to help market the clothes, apart from wearing them in their matches."

The changing climate and its economic repercussions caused progressive companies like Fila to sniff around for new opportunities. Fila dabbled in golf, only to learn what you and I have known all along—that the typical golfer is the walking definition of a fashion error who would much rather spend his money on high-tech putters and little ducky club mittens than clothes.

Then there was yachting. The Italians, particularly those who go ballistic over anything with potential snob appeal (and there are a lot of them), discovered yachting in the late 1980s. (Christopher Columbus might insist that I use the word "rediscovered," but this new spurt of interest had more to do with deck shoes and horizontally striped sweaters than celestial navigation, charts, and Dramamine pills.) But in the end, Fila's upscale yachting line fared no better than the doomed America's Cup yacht that bore the company logo.

Fila did do well in skiing, although it was unable to crack the American skiwear market. The company wasn't even the top dog in Europe until it put its stretch suit over the slalom racer and legendary party animal Alberto Tomba.

No longer able to capitalize on high identification with specific players, Fila became just another player in an increasingly crowded, chaotic market. By 1990 tenniswear accounted for only about twenty-five percent of the company's earnings. Other leisurewear and licensed products, including watches bearing the Fila logo, raised another ten percent. So where did the other sixty-five percent come from? Shoes. And not tennis shoes, either.

Fila's biggest market in the early 1990s was basketball shoes, made in the Far East and sold not to the upwardly mobile, mostly white consumer that Fila has traditionally cultivated but to scores of African Americans. We've all heard the stories about inner-city kids shooting each other for $100 sneakers by Nike or Reebok, and some people have even challenged the definition of poverty in a society where the officially "poor" routinely spend a C note on footwear. But even in this bizarre climate, the notion that hundreds of thousands of black Americans, many of them poor, keep afloat a high-profile Italian company that aggressively courts la-di-da skiers and yachtsmen is a little mind-boggling.

Basketball shoes sold in the United States accounted for over fifty percent of Fila's profits recently, and they have become the backbone of the company. In 1992, Fila did over $250 million worth of business in the United States. More than sixty-five percent of that loot came from the pockets of black Americans purchasing basketball shoes. By contrast, Fila sells less than $1 million worth of its tennis shoes in the United States. Furthermore, unlike Nike (Michael Jordan) or Reebok (Shaquille O'Neal), Fila doesn't have a single superstar under endorsement contract. Fila's two big guns as late as 1994 were Hirshey Hawkins and Mark Jackson.

This phenomenon can be explained with two words, the first of which is "Gucci." Fila's basketball shoe became a powerful status symbol to African Americans, much like the Gucci handbag and spinoff products did in the late 1970s. Such items take on a life of their own, which is the point at which their makers sit back and feel like genii. But there's another word that comes into play: "luck." As Mulligan said, "It was just plain dumb luck that it worked out this way."

CHAPTER 9

CHRIS EVERT
The Cold and Absolute Fire

IT's OFTEN SAID that you can't have it all, but boy-oh-boy, has Chris Evert ever come close. She survived the perils of being a prodigy, amassed a record that makes her one of the top tennis players of all time, and also managed to lead a robust emotional life, unmarred by the kind of scandals that so often haunt celebrities and raise doubts about their judgment and conduct through the unattractive way in which they are played out.

Evert's companions included actors (Burt Reynolds), tennis players (Vitas Gerulaitis and Jimmy Connors, among others), pop stars (Adam Faith), the son of a U.S. president (Jack Ford), at least one talk-show host (Geraldo Rivera, if he is to be believed), and two husbands (not at the same time): British tennis pro John Lloyd and former Olympic skier Andy Mill. Not bad for a young woman who in her heyday was often called the "Ice Maiden," and who was repeatedly characterized as an unemotional, repressed, introverted, all-for-Daddy daughter of a strict Irish Catholic, public-park-teaching pro from Fort Lauderdale, Florida, Jimmy Evert.

As a young girl, Evert believed that she would play tennis for a few years, retire to a domestic life, and raise children by the age of twenty-five. She married John Lloyd at just that age, in 1979, but because of her champion's appetite for competition and public performance, as well as her celebrity and emotional independence, her first marriage turned out to be a dry run. As a result of that, Evert was able to wring every bit of potential out of her spare game. She became a beloved ambassador of tennis who spoke to a remarkably broad range of people. A Los Angeles divorcee who streaked her hair and spent every waking hour in "work-out" clothes related to her just as powerfully as an eastern dowager who never played tennis on any surface but grass.

All you need to know about Evert's attitude toward tennis was revealed in a brief locker room exchange that transpired at Wimbledon more than a decade ago. Having just lost a match, the amiable pro Paula Smith returned to the locker room and remarked to a friend, "Thank God that my happiness doesn't depend on winning or losing a tennis match." Evert, sitting a few feet away, did not miss a beat. She quipped, "Thank God that mine does."

Nevertheless, Evert got out just in the nick of time. In 1988, almost a decade after her own estimated time of departure from tennis, Evert married Mill. She was thirty-three at the time, and she would squeeze one more year on the circuit out of her surprisingly durable body. She then beat the biological clock and quickly had two children. All that and filthy rich, too.

As Ted Tinling once told me, the essence of being a star is wanting it both ways: the fame and the privacy, the privilege and the connection with ordinary life, the glamour and a sense of authenticity. But few female players have been able to combine the demands of a long and distinguished career with traditional feminine roles. Two other women who managed to accomplish that were early rivals of Evert's: the Australians Margaret Court and Evonne Goolagong Cawley.

Court, a largely forgotten champion who won more Grand Slam singles titles than any other woman, had no star quality whatsoever. Goolagang had plenty of star quality, but she never shared Evert's enormous appetite for competition, or her hunger for stardom.

"I never really enjoyed everybody making such a fuss over me," Evert once told me. "Being able to walk around without a crowd at my heels is just fine. But to be realistic, I also know that I wouldn't be happy if people were shoving me out of the way to get a glimpse of Gabriela Sabatini."

The key word there is "realistic." Evert was the most realistic and self-aware woman pro that I've ever known, but she was also haunted through much of her career by the issue of her image in a way that was often painful for her. She was called prissy, but she became earthy and worldly. She was thought of as cold, but she had a noteworthy capacity for empathizing with those who were different or even threatening to her. (She was, and remains, good friends with her main rival, Martina Navratilova.) She was accused of being tough, but, well, she *was* tough. At the same time, she was fair-minded and an exemplary sport.

For a long time Evert's only problem was that some people just didn't like what they saw, and so they were predisposed to believe that it couldn't be authentic. Evert certainly sent mixed and provocative signals. She highlighted the difference between two kinds of feminism—

the one that accepts, enjoys, and sometimes trades on the fundamental differences between the sexes while still insisting on equality, and the branch whose constituents believe that our traditional concepts of femininity are confining, socially imposed burdens.

Evert took great pride in her status as an athlete and in the strides taken in her time by her profession. She had nothing but contempt for knee-jerk sexism in tennis, of which there was a lot, and she worked arm in arm with the masculinists to get more money and more exposure for women's tennis. At the same time, Evert espoused traditional values and incessantly questioned the conflict between professionalism and her goals as a woman. She carefully avoided defining herself as a feminist, yet she was anything but a boy toy. She lived with one foot planted in each of two different worlds, and it took formidable skill and tact for her to survive and to retain a distinct identity. She was frequently chastised for managing that balancing act.

For instance, when journalist Barry Lorge was working on a tribute to Evert and her legacy, the best thing Billie Jean King could bring herself to say about Evert was: "Chris is very gracious. She's calculated. She thinks before she speaks. That is the way she was brought up, the way her father is, and the way she plays. She says and does the right thing regardless of how she really feels—unlike me or Martina [Navratilova], who made waves."

This backhanded compliment is not only curiously bitter, it also leaves the impression that thinking about things before shooting your mouth off is somehow base. But Evert certainly was different from King and Navratilova. She didn't harbor nearly as many controversial opinions, and she often bit her tongue and suppressed turbulent emotions because she didn't trust them, and because she had always believed that keeping them in check was a virtue. The "clean image" she projected was the result, not the goal, of her modus operandi.

Evert certainly was "image-conscious." How could she not have been, given her life experience? You can count on the fingers of one hand the number of times that anybody ever called Evert sensitive, but throughout her entire career she tried to avoid hurting the feelings of others. You couldn't necessarily say this about, say, King, who spent a fair amount of time going around telling other people, including Evert, how they should run their lives. At Wimbledon in 1987, late in Evert's career, King admonished her for not smiling more. She suggested that Evert ought to derive more enjoyment from her waning days in tennis.

"I could have killed her," Evert told me later. "I'm not Evonne [Goolagong], who can walk around singing. I told Billie, 'Geez, this is Wimbledon, and I'm intense.' But the whole incident was really interesting to me because who ever saw Billie Jean King smile when she was still a top player? When she smiled at Wimbledon, you knew it wasn't genuine. And it wouldn't have been genuine coming from me, either. I'm not a fake person, why should I go around smiling or trying to manipulate the crowd's emotions?"

Evert did have a lifelong desire to retain some semblance of privacy. She was especially insistent on the right to make mistakes in private, like the rest of us do. Having been observed, dissected, and analyzed by the media and the public since she skyrocketed to celebrity at age sixteen, Evert became a master not of giving the public what it wanted to see, but what she felt it was entitled to under her uneasy but voluntary pact with fame.

Evert refrained from blasting or criticizing opponents in public, but privately she never refrained from making her feelings known. She never evaded a question unless answering it would embarrass herself or another individual. Even then she would make her point, although she often made you read between the lines to dig it out. Decades of fame also taught her to avoid incriminating herself by taking the fifth amendment on a question. She had a remarkable way of saying a lot without telling you anything at all. She could also tell you all by hardly saying anything. That was good enough for me, but not always for everyone else.

During one period late in her career, rumor had it that Evert enjoyed smoking pot now and then. On one occasion during the Virginia Slims Championships in Madison Square Garden, when Chris was taking a break from tennis, I sat down next to her and said hello. She appeared to barely recognize me. Her eyes were red and lidded, and she had the slightly drowsy look of someone who was high. That was the impression I had, anyway, and the next time I formally interviewed her, I broached the "P" word in a discussion of her healthy, all-American image, and the conflicts it created in her private life.

"Well, that squeaky clean image was thrust on me at a very young age, when I *was* squeaky clean. And even though I pretty much lived it out, there are things in my life that I'd rather keep to myself. Doesn't everybody? But I won't ever deny something that I know in my heart is true. I don't lie. That puts me in some tough situations because I also believe that a person in the limelight should be free to choose how much he or she wants to reveal. That's a real conflict, and it's taught me to be diplomatic, which some people interpret as being 'calculated.' At least that's the word that always comes up.

"But to me there's nothing negative about 'calculating,' which is just thinking ahead. Let's say that somebody comes right out of the blue and asks me if I've tried drugs. Even if it *is* true, I'm not going to jump up and say, 'Yeah, I've smoked marijuana.' I'm going to think about how many kids I'd let down by admitting that. I'm going to think about fielding a thousand calls from the press. I'm going to think of the context that will appear in. I would say that my attitude about drugs is much more important than whether I've tried them or not, unless I'm doing drugs all the time and going around saying that nobody should ever try them. But we both know that if I come out and say I've smoked pot, that's what is going to be in the headline."

I believe that this was Evert's way of telling me that she had smoked pot. Whatever the truth, I let her comments stand on their own. Later, another reporter picked up on the theme, and the subsequent story generated just the kind of controversy Evert described and hoped to avoid.

Evert also had a good nose for pretense, an aversion to public displays of sentiment, and enough competitive pride to get herself into occasional bouts of trouble. At Wimbledon in 1986, Evert lost a titanic semifinal struggle to her rival Navratilova, 6–4 in the third set. As usual, Evert showered, put on a new sweater, fixed her hair, and applied a touch of makeup before she walked into the interview room below Centre Court.

After a loss like that, Evert was always loath to face anyone, including her devoted mother Colette. But only the veterans in the tennis press understood how disheartened and prickly she could be under those circumstances. After a few innocuous questions about the match, one of the reporters related the anecdote Navratilova had told in the same room just minutes earlier. She had told the press that near the end of the match, she had tears in her eyes. Those tears were for her friend Evert, Navratilova said, because it had suddenly occurred to her how nice it would have been for Evert to win one more Wimbledon title. For one of the rare times in her career, Evert reacted spontaneously. She rolled her eyes and smacked her lips. Her reply was a simple, incredulous, "Oh, yeah . . ."

A few reporters exchanged knowing glances. They probably felt that they had smoked out the real Evert—the tough, icy woman lurking behind the gracious, cool image. But I think Evert was showing her sensitivity, not her toughness. She felt that she was being patronized, and it made her angry that Navratilova was callous enough to violate the intimacy of their friendship by sharing the story with the world press. Besides, Navratilova was closing in on a record, nine Wimbledon singles titles. Evert had only three.

Evert's diplomatic ways were also a survival mechanism for a shy girl who became very famous, very quickly, and one who suddenly found herself immersed in a closed society where values different from her own had established a kind of shadow ethic.

At the time, many of the top women players were lesbians. The ethic of this older generation was fiercely professional, and Evert quickly learned that a pecking order existed in the women's game. She would have to learn to play politics with the best of them in order to protect her own interests. I'll tell one sad and weird story to illustrate the degree to which personal and sexual politics play a part in women's tennis a little more often than they should, and how no top woman player can steer clear of them and still be an active force in the establishment that runs the game.

Andrea Jaeger, the gifted prodigy, reached five Grand Slam semifinals and the Wimbledon final by the time she reached eighteen. We were friends, and I was sorry to see her become something of a lost soul on the tour—a rebellious, discontented, confused pilgrim whose increasingly erratic behavior sent silent but powerful shock waves through the women's tennis establishment. I liked Andrea's punk, rebel-without-a-pause attitude, her fire as a competitor, and her taste in dirt bikes. I didn't even mind that she took to carrying a switchblade. Shoot, I was eighteen once, too.

But the Women's Tennis Association was alarmed by her behavior and the image she projected. The knife proved to be a serious problem, as did the incident in which Andrea shoved another woman, Renee Blount, up against a locker. Jaeger was not only a loose cannon but a top player and potential superstar, a combination that made the WTA establishment (which is dominated by both active and retired players) really edgy. It all came to a head shortly before a shoulder injury sidelined Jaeger for good. When a top woman player with whom Jaeger had a close friendship suddenly took up with a tour official who happened to be one of Evert's friends, Jaeger sensed that she was suddenly getting the cold shoulder from both parties.

Feeling rejected, Jaeger became embroiled in a series of confrontations with her former friend, and other top women on the Tour. The other women closed ranks and, Jaeger said, encouraged her to embark on a lesbian relationship with another player, apparently as part of their damage-control strategy. This really upset Jaeger, who denied having any lesbian inclinations. Jaeger had always admired Evert, and she was crushed by what she described as Evert's complicity in this crude ploy. Feeling betrayed on all fronts, Jaeger caused a fair bit of trouble before it all got sorted out. Among other things, this episode illustrated the dangers of exposing a child who may have been wrestling with typical problems of gender confusion to an atmosphere supercharged with sexual ambiguity and politics.

I was also disturbed by Chris's alleged role in all of this, and I discussed the imbroglio with a number of women players. Most of them said that Jaeger was misinterpreting events and expressing her feelings of rejection in irrational ways. They maintained that Evert was just trying to mediate. And being heterosexual herself, Evert wouldn't be inclined to steer a young player toward lesbianism. Whatever the truth was, I found myself thinking about the whole steamy mess as symbolic of the politics and personal rivalries that cause so much tension on the women's tour. Evert, along with many of her peers, had to contend with those issues every day.

So while Evert may have looked like a tennis player to the manor born, the manor had changed by the time she claimed her birthright. Nevertheless, she was too bright, ambitious, and competitive to stand aside from the battles waged in the new era of women's tennis. She was a player in every sense of the word. And she did such a good job negotiating the quagmire that it's easy to forget how much antagonism and criticism she had to deflect on her way to becoming fully realized as a player, as an activist who played an important role in the governance and promotion of the game, and as a woman whose expectation had always been to be a wife and mother.

When you come right down to it, Evert spent much less time cultivating an image than in dumping one. And, as any celebrity will tell you, an image is a lot harder to lose than it is to acquire.

The noun "professional" is commonly used to describe a person who bears the demands and responsibilities of his or her work effectively, with grace and consideration for others. In that sense, Evert was the consummate professional. As a result we developed the same kind of fondness for each other as good neighbors who often meet along the fence between their properties. Chris always made time to see me privately, even if she wasn't the subject of whatever article I was about to write. She also did so during the two or three occasions when she was angry about something I had written.

Chris was one of the few players who bothered to contact Bjorn Borg when, less than a year after Borg quit the game but before he officially announced his retirement, the tennis establishment insisted that Borg couldn't return to the pro tour without participating in lowly qualifying tournaments. Evert wrote Borg a letter of support and encouragement.

My friendship with Evert's great early rival, Evonne Goolagong, was a real obstacle to developing a similar relationship with Evert. She kept score in such matters and interpreted them as a realist. But while she thought of me as part of the Goolagong camp, she also appreciated a spirited defense I wrote about her in one of my first articles for *Tennis*. She was eighteen at the time, and many people had characterized her as a chilly bitch goddess who played a lethal but boring game. My take in that article was that Evert was only boring to boring people who could not look beyond the conspicuous components of sporting genius—the athleticism, the flashy strokes, or the sheer power that you expect to see in tennis champions.

I argued that Evert was a neurological miracle whose consistency was the product of extraordinary but not necessarily "athletic" gifts. The signal sent from Evert's eye to her hand was almost never interrupted by its passage through her mind, where anxiety or fear or overeagerness so often blur the message and lead to a flubbed forehand or a weakly netted volley. Even when she was exhausted, Evert's strokes remained silken, perfectly timed, and, above all, purposeful.

I still stand by that analysis because, while other women often made more spectacular shots from difficult positions or reeled off longer strings of unanswerable winners, Evert had the almost preternatural ability to avoid having to do those things. In tennis as in life, Evert was first and foremost about poise and control. She rarely showed an impressive burst of speed or the kind of acrobatic skill that Navratilova made her stock in trade. Yet you can count on the fingers of one hand the number of times that anybody overpowered Evert, jerked her around the court, or exposed her shortcomings as a pure athlete.

Evert always seemed to be on top of the ball, prepared to make the most use of her riposte. This was partly because of her precision, which enabled her to control any given point from the outset. But it was also due to her powers of anticipation and a unique sense of knowing at all times where she was and where she had to be next. She did not make the game look easy in the way that a natural like Goolagong or Ilie Nastase did, but she sure made the court look small.

Evert had only one technical weakness, and it was the same one that has haunted numerous other women players from successful professionals on down to country club hackers. One of the radical, definitive differences between male and female pros is in the serve. Countless men have survived the pro tour mostly because they had outstanding serves, while countless women have had otherwise sound games hampered by an inability to serve effectively. Evert's serve was effective, but it wasn't good. Her delivery was strikingly labored and self-conscious, as if she had remained an earnest twelve-year-old trying hard to serve exactly the way her father had insisted she should. Nevertheless, Evert shared an interesting quality with other great champions: a formidable ability to blank out any consciousness of a weakness. This is an issue that truly shows the degree to which tennis matches—even whole careers—are played out in the psyche just as much as on the court.

Jimmy Connors never acknowledged that he had real trouble lifting a forehand approach shot from the forecourt over the net. Stefan Edberg pushed his forehand with a bizarre and reluctant shoveling motion but insisted that he felt confident hitting the stroke. Tracy Austin's overhead always looked like an adventure. So it was with the studied serve of Evert. The stroke never really crumbled under pressure because Evert did not dote on its vulnerability or try to do too much with it.

Navratilova did finally develop the confidence to capitalize on Evert's serve, using aggressive returns (including textbook chip and charge tactics) to take control of a point before Evert could do it with her first ground stroke. That was one of the chief reasons the Czech expatriate was able to turn her competition with Evert into the greatest rivalry in women's tennis, perhaps even in all of sports.

Evert and Navratilova stand tied for third place on the all-time list of Grand Slam singles championships with eighteen titles each. Second place is occupied by Helen Wills Moody, who collected nineteen titles. But the most prolific champion of all time is Margaret Court, whose career spanned both the amateur and pro eras. Court has an untouchable record of twenty-four Grand Slam singles titles, and in 1970 she became the second woman to achieve a Grand Slam, winning all four major titles in the same year (the feat was first accomplished by Maureen Connolly in 1953). There is an interesting footnote to these statistics.

Because of their commitments to World Team Tennis, Evert and Navratilova both skipped the French Open in the mid-1970s. Playing WTT was a particularly unwise choice for Evert, who won two consecutive titles in Paris and then declined to play the event three years running. When Evert returned to Roland Garros, she took up where she had left off, winning the next two titles. She might easily have won the French title in the years that she avoided the event, 1976–78.

Evert once held an enormous head-to-head advantage over Navratilova. In 1977, Navratilova had won only four times out of twenty meetings. But she gradually chipped away at Evert's lead and finally pulled even at thirty wins each in the 1984 Wimbledon final, which she won, 7–6, 6–2. Navratilova then nosed ahead for good and led 35–32 at the time Evert retired in 1985. Not long thereafter, Evert presented her friend Navratilova with an internally illuminated globe featuring a lighted pinhole commemorating every city where Navratilova had captured one or more of her staggering 161 career titles.

Trying to decide whether Evert or Navratilova was the greater player involves many variables. Navratilova dominated Wimbledon to about the same degree that Evert dominated the French Open, primarily because Navratilova was at her best on fast grass courts and Evert was formidable on slow clay ones. Evert's advantage on clay was apparent as early as 1972 when, at age eighteen, she rocked the tennis world by beating Billie Jean King on clay in Florida, 6–1, 6–0. That was one of the most astonishing results of the Open era because that year King won three Grand Slam titles and didn't play for the fourth one, at the Australian Open.

The most interesting way to compare Evert and Navratilova is to break down their head-to-head records on their respective, preferred Grand Slam surfaces as well as on the surfaces that gave each of them the most trouble. Evert went 9–2 against Navratilova on clay, and she holds a 2–1 edge at the French Open. Navratilova's record against Evert on grass was 7–5, with a 4–2 edge at Wimbledon. Overall, Evert enjoys a 14–9 advantage on the combined surfaces, but Navratilova holds a 5–4 lead in their key meetings at Wimbledon and the French Open.

Evert played the French Open thirteen times. Her worst performances at Roland Garros were a third-round defeat in the last year that she played (1988), and three semifinal finishes. She reached the final in nine out of thirteen years, winning the title on seven of those occasions. Navratilova played the French Open eleven times. She missed two more meetings that Evert did during the WTT era, and she stopped competing at Roland Garros after a fourth-round loss in 1988, mostly to improve her chances at Wimbledon. Navratilova's worst performances at the French Open were two fourth-round losses and three quarterfinal finishes. She reached the final on six occasions, winning twice.

Now for Wimbledon. Evert played eighteen times, and her worst loss was a third-round defeat suffered in 1983. On every other occasion she reached at least the semifinals. She played in the final ten times, but she won the title only three times. Navratilova played Wimbledon twenty times. She lost before the semifinals on five occasions, but she reached the final eleven times, capturing nine titles.

In the big picture, Navratilova has a more glamorous record, while Evert has a more consistent one. Navratilova also played her best at the most prestigious tournament of them all, Wimbledon. Evert's resume at Roland Garros is the capstone of her career, but her record at Wimbledon is a great tribute to her versatility as well as a powerful testament to her competitive powers.

After all, Wimbledon is the domain of the attacking, serve-and-volley player. It is also the domain of the pure athlete. The success of baseliners like Borg, Steffi Graf, and Jimmy Connors at Wimbledon was not predicated on their technical prowess at grass-court tennis but on their mobility, reflexes, anticipation, and a flexibility that allowed them to deal successfully with the unpredictable nature of tennis on grass. Evert was neither an attacking player nor a particularly athletic one. Yet only Navratilova, who was both of those things, prevented Evert from ending up with six or eight Wimbledon titles.

Evert was a surprisingly complete player from day one, but her development into a complete human being was a much more incremental process. The novelist Thomas Mann once said that the best stories were all long stories, which is a natural claim coming from a man who specialized in writing novels as thick as telephone directories. If you take Mann at his word, Chris Evert was one of the best stories in tennis.

One of the chief reasons Evert's career lasted so long is that she paced herself, an ability long lost on successive generations of players. Early on, it was Jimmy Evert who was careful not to expose his teenage daughter to the pressures, demands, and itinerant life-style of the pro tour. The most positive feature of her decision to play team tennis was the stability it helped bring to her personal life.

Later on, Evert would take a number of extended breaks from the tour, for preventative rather than curative reasons. At one point in the early 1980s, she decided to skip altogether the dreary, claustrophobic indoor tour that moved from one arena to another, one late night after another, in winterbound cities. Navratilova accused Evert of ducking her in order to protect her World Number One ranking. Evert frostily answered, "Tell Martina not to worry. She'll have nine whole months to play me."

Another contributing factor to Evert's longevity was her early training on soft, forgiving clay courts that not only forced her to develop consistency, concentration, and patience, but were less punishing to her developing physique. In stark contrast, Tracy Austin, a Californian whose game was modeled on Evert's, grew up playing on cement courts. Her career was cut short by chronic lower back problems.

Evert could have turned pro at age fourteen, after she first made shock waves by posting wins over perennial top-ten player Françoise Durr and, even more shockingly, Margaret Court, in her first foray onto the circuit. But Evert didn't become a pro until three years later, on her eighteenth birthday. That was more than a full year after her sensational run to the semifinals of the U.S. Open. By then she had also reached the semifinals at two other Grand Slam events, the 1972 Wimbledon and U.S. Open tournaments.

One of the main factors in Evert's decision to wait was that she wanted to finish her studies at Saint Thomas Aquinas High School back in Fort Lauderdale, Florida. The other big reason was Jimmy Evert, who exercised complete control over his daughter until she turned eighteen. From the get-go, Jimmy Evert mistrusted the agents of professionalism, from tour officials to racket manufacturers to managers who began to promise him the moon when Evert was fourteen. Even when Evert did turn pro, Jimmy recruited his brother Chuck and a close family friend who lived down the road to help manage her business affairs. His decision to keep it all in the family was not based on a reluctance to give professional managers a piece of the action. He understood the built-in conflict of interest between business managers and the players they represented. Mostly, Jimmy wanted to keep any threat to his daughter's commitment to tennis at bay. As Chris has often admitted, she spent most of her career playing for her father. And he was participating not for his own celebrity or hers, or for money; he was participating merely for distinction. The only big change in Jimmy Evert's material life after his daughter became famous was that, as a result of her prodding, he raised the rates he charged for a tennis lesson at the public courts from $6 to $10.

"There were three big things in my father's life," Evert once told Curry Kirkpatrick of *Sports Illustrated*, "family, tennis, and religion. All the other things that came with my success didn't make him happy, they just aged him."

At that time it was easier to just say no to the temptations of turning pro as soon as possible. Even Jimmy Evert agrees with that assessment. On the other hand, he was a man of absolute values, so I think that even today he would have brought a different sensibility to the table than do most contemporary tennis parents.

One of the best examples of a battle that he lost was Chris's decision to play World Team Tennis. At around age twenty-one Chris wanted to enjoy the camaraderie and security of participating in a team sport. And WTT, with its goofball, quasi-serious ambience and astronomical wage scale, provided the perfect opportunity. But in the end, WTT may have cost Evert an exclusive place behind Court in the Grand Slam record book.

Jimmy also fought hard to keep Evert in the traditionalist camp when the USTA created a women's circuit that was perceived in some quarters as a threat to the new, burgeoning Virginia Slims tour. Many of the pioneering female pros (King, Rosie Casals, and others) were hostile to the embattled amateur establishment and fiercely committed to the new tour. They were critical of the two youngest stars of the game, Evert and Goolagong, when both of them decided to support the USTA tour. The phrase that kept coming up was that they should "play with the big girls." The guardians of Evert and Goolagong, Jimmy and Vic Edwards, certainly were old-school types, but each of them was also reluctant to expose his real or surrogate daughter to the pressure and naked professionalism of the Virginia Slims circuit. And the girls—which is exactly what they were at that point—were not all fired up to join the Slims tour, either. They felt that the "big girls" were a little scary, a little tough.

In comparison, the USTA circuit was an amiable, low-key operation, and the women who played on it tended to be products of the tennis mainstream. Like Evert and Goolagong, many of them did not see themselves as tennis players for life, and they had a greater interest in the overall social environment of tennis than in the game's potential as a source of income or as a vehicle for social change.

Evert's ambivalence toward the new tour, compounded by her formidable talent, made her a threat to the new order emerging in the pro era. And when I asked the firebrands of professionalism about Evert and what she represented, they spoke guardedly, with a deference demanded by her talent. But if you knew them well enough, they would express their reservations about the apparent "selfishness" that kept Evert from throwing her weight behind the Slims tour. And any discussion of Evert's girl-next-door image was punctuated with pregnant pauses, colored by thinly veiled cynicism. When the older pros talked about the new kid on the block, they rolled their eyes—often.

Evert's personality did nothing to alleviate the pure fear her game inspired in her older peers. If anything, it exacerbated it. Her sangfroid as a sixteen-year-old during that enchanted U.S. Open of 1971 not only scared the bejesus out of her rivals, it moved the crowd to support her to an extent that automatically turned many people, including many female players, against her.

It certainly wasn't Evert's fault that the crowd cheered her opponent's errors and swept her along on a wave of encouragement. But to many of the other women players it still didn't seem fair. They quickly came to feel threatened by Evert's apparent remoteness, and by the way she seemed to trade on her femininity.

"I know that I wasn't very friendly or warm toward people," Chris once told me, "but you know, I was *afraid* of them. Fans and players, too. They were looking at me like I was a little bit of a freak, like how can this girl be so unemotional and cool? People weren't exactly very friendly and warm toward me, either, and for a long time that included many of the other players. I was lucky in that I was the first really feminine, big-name player of the Open era, at least in America. And I carried that to the hilt. I made sure my earrings and makeup were always perfect. But I wasn't trying to intimidate the other women with that, I was just, well, impressionable. It sounds too simple to be true, but my friends in high school had a lot to do with it. My mother had a lot to do with it. I think it also became a little bit of a reaction when people began to say and write that I was kind of cold. That bothered me, it made me feel insecure."

It did not help that when the reticent prodigy did speak, her comments revealed acute self-consciousness. As a debutante at the U.S. Open, Evert survived six match points in her second-round match to beat Mary Ann Eisel. When she was asked what she had been thinking during the match points, she said, "I was thinking how I would look during the handshake at the net. Would I be cute? Sad? Tired? Then when the ball came up, it looked so big, just like a huge balloon."

That remark galled many people, and it helped to implant the notion that Evert was obsessed with her own image. It was easy to forget that in many ways Evert was just another out-to-lunch sixteen-year-old, apt to wonder, "Who am I?"

The media had a big hand in quickly bending the public's fascination with Evert toward ambivalence. One of the most damning and accurate charges that can be brought against the press is that it is institutionally indisposed toward taking into account the age of its subjects—as if managing to accomplish something newsworthy constitutes a de facto waiver of the right to be young, confused, and stupid. This proclivity has especially hurt tennis, a game full of sheltered, undereducated children and callow prodigies.

Another typical example of the type of problem Chris experienced occurred shortly after she burst on the scene. After a close match with Billie Jean King, who had once again flung herself all over the court trying to intercept Evert's pinpoint passing shots, Evert was asked if she was ever tempted to throw all caution to the wind, abandon her poise, and, as King would put it, "just go for it." Evert replied, "I don't think any point is worth falling down over."

In an increasingly hot war between the sexes—and among women themselves—that reply was interpreted as a confession of vanity. King was seen as a woman who had the courage to compete with the same abandon that is considered virtuous in men . By renouncing that mentality, Evert seemed to be defining herself as gender inhibited.

Shortly before Chris retired, I found myself sitting with her in some lounge at a tournament, just killing time. I brought up that ancient remark, and she immediately remembered the controversy it had initiated. She told me that the remark had been pumped full of false significance. She had only meant that until match point arrived, no single point in tennis ought to be so important that you would fling yourself after it. And if it was, you just didn't have control of a match.

Evert's extraordinary abilities created an almost immediate backlash.

The new American tennis princess soon became the Ice Maiden, once again demonstrating that Shakespeare had it right: Humankind cannot stand too much perfection. The mischievous British press, who at the onset disliked this all-American girl in roughly the same measure that they embraced her after she married the English player John Lloyd, dubbed her "the Metronome."

At Wimbledon in 1972, Evert also discovered that the rousing welcome that greeted her just a year earlier at Forest Hills could not be taken for granted. It was different in England, where the Yankeephobes were no less vocal than the Yankeephiles. The press and the public in England were enthralled by Goolagong, and Evert suddenly found herself cast as the villain—the Mary Ann Eisel or Billie Jean King—when she faced Goolagong in a historic semifinal. Goolagong won the match, after which Evert marched into the locker room, let her rackets fall clattering to the floor, and declared, "Now I hope *they're* happy."

Evert was acquiring an education quickly. As the realities of her situation sank in, she began to understand that she would not float through life on a magic carpet of adulation, or be spared by virtue of her talent from having to make hard, practical decisions. She would have to learn how to make her way and to take her place in the burgeoning pro establishment represented by the Virginia Slims tour.

The new Slims tour projected glamour that was more evocative of show business than athletics. The media was hot for it, because it appeared to be a social phenomenon, not just another tennis circuit. The commercial expertise of the promoters generated ever-escalating prize money and state-of-the-art administrative and public relations departments. When Evert and Goolagong decided that it was time to play with the big girls, the USTA women's circuit was left dead in the water. Securing the loyalties of Evert and Goolagong put the final stamp of legitimacy on the new Slims tour. While the character and nature of the tour would often be at cross-purposes with Evert's goals and desires, it became the environment in which she was finally socialized.

Over the years she would learn to live in close quarters with a baffling array of characters, including rivals who were apparent clones, lesbians, anorexics, ingenues, unfulfilled heterosexuals, and, as time went on, a parade of flinty, gifted youngsters who would exist outside of the tour establishment in a germ-free atmosphere, under a transparent bubble erected by a family entourage and financed by the tennis bucks that Evert and her peers had helped to generate.

Evert's emotional history may be a long story, but at heart it's the relatively common one of the fairy tale(s) that didn't quite work out. Early in her career Evert allowed that she couldn't imagine being married to a man who wasn't a "great" tennis player. In what could be interpreted as punishment for her pride, God sent Evert a man named Jimmy Connors. He that was calleth Jimbo. The pairing of Connors and Evert was mortifyingly predictable. Connors was perceived by many as a punk, and Evert's infatuation with him seemed to confirm the suspicion that she was just a silly girl. Cynics delighted in the liaison because it allowed them to vent contempt for two conveniently joined targets. Jimbo and Chrissie were portrayed, in different ways and not entirely without reason, as a pair of tennis brats. Their happiness, while short-lived, really got people's noses out of joint.

In the big picture, Evert's relationship with Connors allowed her to break away from her powerful father without threatening the hopes and dreams that they had invested together in tennis. This loyalty to her father was typical of Evert. When she hired Bob Kain of IMG as her manager, he became her agent for life. She also stayed with the same racket and shoe manufacturers as well, instead of periodically turning herself over to the highest bidder.

Evert made her first, dramatic statement of independence shortly after she began dating Connors at age eighteen. Eager to see Connors, she booked a flight to visit him in Los Angeles. Knowing that her parents would never approve of her actions, she wrote them a tender but firm note explaining what she was doing. Jimmy and Colette Evert were wise enough not to confront Chris when she returned.

It was impossible to expect the romance between Connors and Evert to work out, even though the two were briefly engaged. They were too young, and each of them was brimming with tennis ambitions. Connors was also devoted to his mother and coach Gloria, just as deeply as Evert was devoted to her father and coach Jimmy. The spice in this bubbling Freudian stew was that Jimmy Evert and Gloria Connors themselves had dated briefly, back when they were two young tennis nuts at Notre Dame University.

One of the main reasons the relationship between Chris and Jimmy collapsed was that she was not truly prepared for independence. She tried to transfer her dependence on her family to Connors, but that ultimately made him feel stifled and restless. After the two parted, Connors took up with a colorful assortment of women, a few of whom might still be listed in Andy Warhol's *Encyclopedia of Famous-for-Fifteen Minutes People*. They included someone called Mean Mary Jean (she was in TV commercials for Dodge cars), actress Susan George, and a former Miss World, Marjorie Wallace.

One of Evert's chief talents was her ability to sublimate any personal difficulties she was experiencing in a positive way. When Evert was unhappy, she was a holy terror on the tour—a relentless, unforgiving, highly focused competitor who punished her opponents for the difficulties she was experiencing. In the years between her liaison with Connors and her marriage to John Lloyd, Evert enjoyed a robust emotional life. But tennis always came first, and while a young Evert often turned to other women for her feminine cues, she did not really tolerate anyone's encroaching on her own stardom. These conditions made it difficult to be a genuine and lasting friend to Evert.

The former player Kristien Kemmer Shaw was an important influence when Evert was famous but still socially awkward. Evert took immediate notice of Kemmer at a tournament. She was a very pretty girl, in granny glasses, with her braided hair tied up, reading a book (my guess would be *The World According to Garp* by John Irving). The two quickly became friends, and after Kemmer married New York banker Rick Shaw, she also became Evert's confidante, World Team Tennis teammate (on the Phoenix Racquets), and style counselor. Evert visited the Shaws at their Riverside Drive digs often, and Kristien introduced her to the myriad delights of Gotham. These included shopping at Saks Fifth Avenue, dining at the Palm, having her eyebrows bleached by "Laszlo," and getting her hair and nails done by another superstar whose name was hyphenated to boot, Jean-Pierre.

The intense friendship between Evert and Shaw ended quickly, partly because Shaw made some indiscreet revelations to Kirkpatrick in a long profile of Evert in *Sports Illustrated*. Among other things, Shaw apparently told Kirkpatrick that when Connors took up with Mean Mary Jean, a television journalist cornered Evert and broke the news to her during an interview. Evert handled the revelation with aplomb, but, according to Shaw, she later broke down in "a sobbing and moaning fit." Stung by this indiscretion, Evert had a falling out with Shaw. But, ever the quick study, Evert had absorbed a lot. As her independence and sophistication flowered, tennis remained her hedge. She said, "My family was my first source of security. But when I started to be truly on my own, tennis became my security. If I couldn't make it work that way, I probably would have become a basket case."

Evert endured a number of emotional crises and weathered periods of discontent, but instead of negatively affecting her game, they seemed to energize it. But in 1980, at age twenty-five, the basket seemed to beckon. This had less to do with unhappiness (which she could always handle) than joy. In 1978, Evert took a four-month break from the game to refresh her attitude. Soon thereafter she met and began to date her first husband, John Lloyd.

Lloyd was a popular, blond-haired, blue-eyed British heartthrob who had reached the final of the Australian Open at age twenty-three in 1977. He was fleet, skillful, and blessed with a smooth and attractive game. He lacked power, however, and without a weapon, he had to be highly motivated in order to grub out matches and live up to his potential as a Top Twenty player. By that time Evert had done a little more math regarding whom she could marry. He would no longer have to be the number one or three or five player. He didn't even have to be a great player; a good one would do.

As Evert's romance with Lloyd blossomed, she declared that while she would probably continue to play the game after she wed, it was not vitally important for her husband to be a top player. She would be happy with a good ranking, number three or even five.

"How about him being number thirty-two?" she was asked.

She answered, "Let's not get ridiculous here."

Looking back on her decision to marry Lloyd, Evert would later say, "All my life I pictured myself as one day becoming a cute little housewife. It was another variation of the way I saw myself in tennis, as a little, walking, talking tennis doll. So when I grew disenchanted with tennis, I grabbed for that other little idealized image."

Lloyd recognized and stood in awe of what he would call the "absolute fire" of champion players, including Borg, Connors, McEnroe, and the woman he would marry. But Lloyd also knew himself well enough to admit that he lacked that fire. He came from a thoroughly middle-class British family of tennis nuts for whom Wimbledon represented the perfect world. But a typically British concept of his own place in the grand scheme of things—a by-product of Britain's class system—inhibited him.

"If I had been born in the States, where it's so much more competitive, where success alone is so much more the be-all and end-all, I might have been forced to work harder and maybe I would have become a better player," Lloyd once explained. "On the other hand, I also might have been lost in the shuffle. I was lucky to be born in England where I was among the top two or three players at every level. I was handed things on a plate, and I was very successful in the scheme of things. In the States, I'm not even sure I would have survived the college game to become a pro."

Lloyd was going great guns when he met Evert. He had reached a career-high ranking of number 23 in July 1978. Less than a year later, he married Evert. He was twenty-six and she was twenty-five, and one of the first issues facing the young couple was just which of them was going to end up the tennis player and which one the significant other.

That decision seemed an easy one at first because Evert was finding it increasingly hard to convert emotions into rocket fuel for her career. And then along came Lloyd to further complicate matters by suggesting that she might draw motivation from a novel source—happiness. Evert had often wondered if she could retain her competitive intensity if she found herself happily married. She soon found out.

There was another important element in Evert's crisis, one that showed the extent to which tennis players can develop the same behavioral habits as fading movie stars or divas. For the first time in her life Evert was hearing footsteps. They were made by a rapidly maturing young woman who had been on the cover of *World Tennis* magazine, racket in hand, at age three, Tracy Austin. Navratilova may have been Evert's lifetime rival, but she was different from Evert in every aspect, from her game to her emotional makeup. This created a pleasant distance between the women and a contrast that both of them enjoyed trading on. But Austin was unnervingly similar to Evert, and she represented the nightmare scenario: being replaced by someone who was a younger, better version of herself.

Austin was so like Evert that she was even forced to deal with similar criticisms. She was frequently described as a coldhearted tennis doll in gingham. These complaints were transparently sexist (nobody ever slighted Borg or questioned his sexuality when he appeared coldhearted), but Austin dealt with them differently from Evert. Instead of becoming withdrawn, Austin became more aggressive. She was a regular spitfire, and all her rivals were fearful.

To make matters worse for Evert—but more interesting for others—Austin was also a traditional girl who enjoyed capitalizing on her femininity. To top it off, Austin also played from the baseline, employing a two-handed backhand. The superficial similarities were so striking that Austin was often insultingly referred to as a "Chrissie clone," which would be the last android that Chrissie—or anyone else in her shoes—would feel comfortable having to play.

Evert handled Austin's gradual rise graciously, but when the younger girl came within striking distance of her role model, Evert dropped her racket and lit out for the hills. The first important tournament Austin won was the Italian Open in Rome in 1979 when she was sixteen. En route to that victory, Austin ended Evert's record 125-match winning streak on clay.

In September of that same year, Austin beat Evert, 6–4, 6–3, and became the youngest U.S. champion in history at sixteen years and nine months. Early in 1980, Austin demolished Evert in three successive matches in a ten-day span. After the last of those encounters, Evert declared that she was "burned out" and taking an indefinite rest to reassess her future. In April 1980, Austin was the first woman other than Evert or Navratilova to be ranked number one since 1975.

I'm not cynical enough to suggest that Evert married Lloyd because of Austin, but conjugal bliss did seem to offer Evert a nice way out of a spooky quandary. Evert promised that if her appetite for tennis did not return, she would travel with her husband and provide emotional ballast for him in much the same way that he had through her difficult 1979. So Evert fulfilled her remaining tournament commitments after the three losses to Austin and then joined her husband in Palm Springs, where he was working on his own comeback.

For a while Evert took a whack at what Lloyd called "the housewife bit." For three weeks, she swung a mop instead of a racket. Then she began to turn up at the court to watch her husband work out. Then she decided to play for an hour each day, just so she wouldn't get completely out of shape. Soon it was ninety minutes and, by late April, with the Grand Slam season coming up, Evert was once again the lean, mean, fighting machine of yore. Lloyd not only accepted this turn of events, he was magnanimous enough to encourage his wife's aspirations.

Evert entered the Italian and French Opens, and won both events in 1980. At Wimbledon, Evert reached the finals but lost to Goolagong, 6–1, 7–6. Lloyd bombed out in the first round at that same Wimbledon, which brought him to the following realization: "I was going nowhere fast." At that point, Lloyd quietly put aside his own ambitions and completed a dramatic and rapid role reversal. Not only did he realize that he was more valuable as the horse than the cart, he flat-out admitted it. And he believed that he could make the marriage work despite the profound change in his role.

Evert won the U.S. Open in 1980, beating the Czech Hana Mandlikova, 5–7, 6–1, 6–1. She turned in a masterpiece of a semifinal victory over Austin in the process. This may have been both the high point and the breaking point of her marriage, because it sealed the issue of whose career would come first in the Lloyd household. As Evert's confidence and ranking grew, Lloyd's declined. The fate that Chris had speculated about so recently was beginning to operate, but not in the way that she had anticipated. (I guess that's why they call it "fate" in the first place.)

A year of traveling and catering to Chris's needs left Lloyd out of shape and poorly motivated. He couldn't defend the computer points that had created his respectable ranking, and he went into a permanent tailspin. His ranking dropped as low as 356 during his marriage to Evert, and there were numerous painful milestones along the way. At the 1981 U.S. Open, Connors outraged his former fiancée and friend by destroying Lloyd, 6–0, 6–0, 6–2. Chris did not object to the humiliat-

ing score (after all, she was a tennis player) as much as the obvious relish with which Connors performed the execution.

Lloyd remained unfailingly amiable, polite, and supportive of his wife,
but he was ridiculed by tennis insiders for his fascination with erotic
videos. He got great satisfaction out of the success of his wife, but the
other players whispered about how completely he had been sucked into
the gravitational field of his wife's burning star. When Lloyd did make an
effort to rekindle his own career, he became a juicy target for mean-
spirited opponents and critics—a habit that wasn't entirely discouraged
by John's image as a snappy dresser who, thanks to pastel-mad Ellesse,
had matching his-and-hers contracts with his wife. Soon Lloyd was
reduced to having to play in the qualifying tournaments held for hope-
fuls, journeymen, and also-rans vying for a place in upcoming tour
events.

"I'd show up for some event with Chris, and we'd stay in the best
hotel. I had a nice car, nice clothes, all that. Then, at nine next morning,
I'd have to go out and play some guy, and most of the time I could tell
what he was thinking: 'What's this guy doing here? He's got the cozi-
est setup in the world, and here he is, trying to take bread out of my
mouth. I'm going to whip his ass.' "

Lloyd had no appetite for playing under such ugly conditions, and
often he merely went through the motions. He failed to live up to his own
standards, and he couldn't help but notice that he also failed to live up to
those of his wife. "It hurt Chris more than anything to see me put in a bad
performance. It killed her to sit there watching me not put in the effort,
even though I was always encouraging her to put in a high degree of
commitment. To tell you the truth, I think she felt humiliated."

Chris, who had drawn great strength and confidence from her husband, was unable to provide the same kind of support for him. That's a
tough call, but I'll never forget a remark made by the former tour player
and coach Dennis Ralston, who worked with a variety of players including Evert, Sabatini, and Noah. Although he had a fine relationship with
Evert, he also knew that she had one thing in common with other great
players. "Every last one of them is a taker," Ralston said. "That's just
how it is, and you have to live with it."

Witnesses said that soon little things, such as the fact that Lloyd
didn't even know how to drive a car when they married, suddenly
seemed emblematic to Evert. During an otherwise idyllic sojourn on
Amelia Island Plantation where the Lloyds had a "touring pro" deal,
Evert was disgusted when a harmless snake appeared on their doorstep
and Lloyd was too timid to slay the beast.

As Chris's career thrived again, John Lloyd seemed to succumb to the lure of life in the fast lane. The Lloyds went through an unappeal-ing phase together, during which they began to hobnob with a variety of Hollywood celebrities and hipsters.

The Lloyds were invited to dinner at the Beverly Hills home of Ron Samuels, who was the personal manager of his own wife, the star of the popular television series "Wonder Woman," Lynda Carter. Samuels was a tennis nut, but he also had a reputation as a manipulator of women. Chris was still undecided about her future when she met the Samuelses, but they encouraged her to keep playing. When she decided to do so, they became part of her entourage, although they derived some pleas-ant—and profitable—side effects from their friendship with the Lloyds. Thanks partly to the offices of Evert, the Lynda Carter/May-belline Tennis Classic became part of the official calendar of the women's tour, and it attracted many top pros.

Few players have endured a Hollywood phase without ending up looking like guppies in a shark tank, and the Lloyds were no exception. At the time, Navratilova was getting a load of grief for trailing around a bewildering assortment of trainers, advisors, and gofers. Yet after Navratilova beat Evert in the 1983 U.S. Open final, it was Evert who trooped into the press interview room with half a dozen retainers, including Samuels and Carter. I described the scene in some detail in *Tennis* magazine, referring to Samuels, about whom I then knew virtu-ally nothing, as "some guy in tight jeans and pointy cowboy boots."

When I next saw Chris a few months later, she sent word through a public relations staffer, Ana Leaird, that she wasn't speaking to me. I wrote Chris a note saying that both of us had been around a little bit too long and had to work together too often to engage in a silly cold war. I gave Leaird the note, but after reading it, she decided that pass-ing it along would only exacerbate the situation. John ultimately broke the impasse by seeking me out and venting his displeasure. He told me that Chris was mostly upset by my characterization of their good friend Samuels. I stood by my point but apologized for any embarrassment I caused Chris by the acerbic way I had made it.

Eventually Samuels and Carter divorced, as did John and Chris. Somewhere along the way their friendships quickly dissolved. Samuels soon took up with fitness-video star Kathy Smith, but by then he was seen less often on the circuit.

The Lloyds also became good friends with the former South African player Johan Kriek and his wife, Tish, a couple of swingers who were part of the nouveau riche scene in Naples, Florida. Tish Kriek was an exhi-bitionist who used to walk around at tournaments with a serpent in her handbag, and although she knew nothing about tennis, she once sought me out and hit me with both barrels for daring to suggest in print that her husband, who was in his mid-twenties, probably was no longer a legitimate contender for a Grand Slam title. As it turned out, there was no Grand Slam title in Kriek's future, but he did get a Florida ditch named after him (Johan Creek) as well as a reputation for living fast, loose, and loud.

At the beginning of 1982, Chris decided that she and John should spend more time apart, partly so that he could rekindle the flame under his own career. But as she would wryly observe later, "Absence doesn't make the heart grow fonder. It just makes it grow colder." At the Australian Open at the end of 1982, Evert had a fling with British pop star Adam Faith. Lloyd, like everyone else in tennis, heard the rumors. He agreed to a trial separation in January 1983, shortly after his wife returned from Australia.

In the ensuing months, John Lloyd became a tennis player again. He reached the round-of-16 at the 1983 Australian Open and the third round at Wimbledon the following June. John and Chris reunited briefly after the 1993 Wimbledon, and Lloyd played a fine U.S. Open. He made the quarterfinals, beating Kriek along the way. Although Lloyd was again punished by Connors in the quarterfinals, he suddenly found himself back in the top twenty. "He was hurt and angry when he began to play well again," Chris ruefully told me at the time, "so if I get any credit for his comeback, it's in a negative way."

The marriage was on the rocks, even though Lloyd and Evert limped along as a couple until 1986. Apart from being confused, they knew that the staunch Catholic Jimmy Evert, who loved John like a son, would be devastated if they divorced. Both players were also loath to wage an ugly divorce battle. They stayed together long enough to work through whatever resentments each of them felt, and to find a common ground as friends. I don't think that had as much to do with "image" as it did with their mutual decency and compassion.

Ultimately, the settlement was negotiated by the firm that represented both of them, IMG. The marriage was dissolved gracefully and quietly in 1986, at about the time that an unexpected loss to Helena Sukova in the U.S. Open semifinals, and a troublesome knee injury, led Evert to take another break from tennis.

That break would last for over five months, a good bit of which Chris spent visiting her friend Navratilova in Aspen. Evert's bum knee did not stop her from skiing and snowmobiling, and her divorce from John had been so slowly and carefully consummated that she was emotionally up to the task when she met the handsome skier Andy Mill.

In a way, Mill satisfied Evert's lifelong desire for a man strong enough to support her without succumbing to domination. He was also full of the classic male qualities that Evert held important. Mill had skied a demanding Olympic downhill race on a painfully injured ankle, finishing sixth. He was also a fly-fisherman, and he not only knew how to drive, he liked racing through the Colorado mountains on a dirt bike. The only thing you could hold against him was his impossibly good looks, which of course many people did.

You could say that it took Evert an entire career to find the kind of man who fulfilled her, or you could say that her career never allowed her to find a suitable man in the demanding environment of pro tennis. You could even say that a deep "taker's" instinct in Evert ensured that even her traditional desires would not get in the way of her career until she was good and ready—meaning the age at which she had to get out while the getting was good. She did draw new competitive energy from Mill, but the obstacles represented by Navratilova and an assortment of newcomers, including Monica Seles and Steffi Graf, prevented Evert from winning another Grand Slam title. It may have been the best thing that ever happened to her.

Lloyd was unable to sustain his good results in 1984, but he had enjoyed a giddy ride and gotten off the roller coaster set for life. He went on to marry an attractive California girl who would bear him two children, and prove to be a partner in every way that Evert was not. In the end, everybody seemed to win, which is a lot more than can be said for a lot of other people, a lot of the time.

Reflecting on his life with Chris, Lloyd told me, "Chris is probably the most gracious champion tennis has ever had. But that external sophistication hid the fact that she had a lot of growing up to do. With me, I think she wanted it both ways. And it took her a long time to realize that you couldn't have it both ways—you can't have the macho guy and then the polite, considerate, supportive husband all rolled into one. Jimmy was more the macho guy, and that didn't really satisfy her. I was more the other way, and that didn't do it in the long term, either. She wanted it all, but then she was a person used to having it all.

"But you know, I still don't regret the way I handled it. Sure, I let my tennis go after our marriage. Sure, the celebrity, the publicity, everything suddenly got so much bigger after we became a couple. But the thing is, she had something, that absolute fire, that I didn't. And I truly enjoyed bringing that out in her. Even at the worst of times, I felt satisfied helping my wife. There were wonderful moments at that time when I felt as if we were really a team, accomplishing something that I never could have accomplished alone. I wouldn't trade that for anything. It really was satisfying."

Don't try to figure it out. You'd have to be a tennis player to understand.

PART III

CHAPTER 10

WIMBLEDON
Bath Buns, Bad Bounces, and Why Nigel Can't Play

THE SIMPLEST WAY TO TELL whether or not somebody knows anything about tennis is by the way he pronounces the name of the most important tournament of all, Wimbledon. A person who pronounces the "d" in the name ought to be listened to, but when the alleged tennis nut in question says, "Wimbleton," write him off. This is as close to a universal law as I've discovered in life, but of course there are those sticky, rule-proving exceptions. Pete Sampras says "Wimbleton."

The Brits who run the All-England Lawn Tennis and Croquet Club (Wimbledon is the name of the community where this grandest of all Grand Slam events transpires) have a lot of things in common. They all wear suits and the green-and-mauve official club tie every blessed day of the tournament, and many of them seem to have an aversion to trimming their nose hairs. And they all call the tournament "The Championships," as if there is nothing else in quite the same league on God's green earth. There is only one socially correct variation of "The Championships," which is "The Fortnight." The Fortnight has a nice Shakespearean ring to it, and Shakespeare is a British enterprise in which every Englishman owns common stock. (And just in case you're keeping track of such things. you pronounce it "fowtnight." Otherwise you're just a bloody Yank putting on airs.)

Wimbledon, Wimbleton, The Championships, The Fortnight. The colorful, populist American journalist and television commentator Bud Collins has made a nice living out of goofing on Wimbledon. He calls it the Big W. The former touring pro Peter Fleming christened the place "Wimby," and the name stuck with some players. Ivan Lendl called it

"Vimbledon," and his sworn enemy John McEnroe called it "the pits of the earth."

Boris Becker, the youngest-ever male champion of The Championships, likens the tournament to heaven, but Vimbledon reminds Lendl of a place considerably farther south, below even the pits of the earth. Bjorn Borg owned the place for a brief while, and then Martina Navratilova rented it—apparently on one of those typically English ninety-nine-year leases.

As for me, I just call the place . . . well . . . *irrelevant.* I'll be the first to admit that Wimbledon is also incomparable, preeminent, charming, riveting, dramatic, and fun. But alas, since day one of the Open era, Wimbledon has not only become increasingly prestigious but has also grown increasingly anachronistic. It is at once the most important of events and also the least representative, a condition that exists nowhere else in Sportsworld.

The chief reason for this is the surface on which Wimbledon is played, grass. At the dawn of the Open era, three of the four Grand Slams were still contested on natural turf, and the nations where they took place also held a number of warm-up events in which the players could prepare for the big meetings. These days there are only two notable grass-court events other than Wimbledon: the official warm-ups for The Championships staged for the men at Queens Club in London and for women at Devonshire Park in Eastbourne.

So while winning at Wimbledon remains the ultimate dream of every aspiring tennis player, the simple act of playing on grass is as novel and exotic an experience for them as it is for you. The nature of the surface and even the way the game is played on grass have absolutely nothing to do with the way tennis is played during the other fifty weeks of the year. To truly appreciate the irony and the absurdity of this, imagine the National Basketball Association playoff finals being played at the birthplace of basketball, Springfield, Massachusetts, on a court of dirt and straw, using a wooden backboard and peach baskets with the bottoms cut out.

Still, Wimbledon manages to be all kinds of things to all kinds of people, and it has been extraordinarily successful in changing with the times without appearing to have done so. The tournament has succeeded in keeping its preeminent position in tennis while making the fewest compromises with the new era, proving the value of football's good old end-around theory: When everybody else is going left, there's an automatic value in going right. Wimbledon became ever more distinguished by resisting change, or seeming to do so, and therein lies its genius.

Wimbledon has reaped the rewards of increasing commercializations with more integrity, sophistication, and discretion than any other major event. Wimbledon's abundant charm translates well in print and television advertising. The public never appears to tire of endless courses of strawberries and cream, and the theory that you run the risk of boring people with endless photo montages of the Chelsea Pensioners in their dress reds, or close-ups of a Pimm's Cup sprouting all kinds of flora, has yet to be proven. People like Wimbledon in the same way they like blue jeans or even their own spouses: for the pleasure yielded by their reliable sameness.

This overwhelmingly traditional image obscures Wimbledon's many concessions to professionalism. The tournament is about great players and lousy courts, wooden scoreboards and electronic line-calling devices, Kevlar-boron-ceramic killer rackets, and white Slazenger tennis balls.

Wimbledon is also about rain, black tea, well-hidden corporate marquees, closed-circuit TV on many courts, and shivering ball boys and girls—all of whom are recruited from local schools—in flimsy shirts and plimsolls (shoes). It is about retired colonels who served in India (you'd better go now because they're disappearing fast) and teenagers with the Swedish flag painted on their faces. Wicker chairs in the Royal Box and majestic bathtubs instead of plebeian showers in the locker room. Wimbledon has gone to digital clocks, and it has very quietly struck deals with a handful of major sponsors. The most ubiquitous advertising logo of them all, with the possible exception of a red light in a window, appears oh-so-discreetly on the cooler next to the umpire's chair on Centre Court: that unmistakable script, "Coca-Cola."

But all you may need to know in order to truly understand Wimbledon is that even the clout and money of the Coca-Cola company has not persuaded Wimbledon officials to give up their timeless loyalty to a local product called Robinson's Barley Water. For ages, a bottle of that orange drink has occupied a special place on the umpire's chair, tastefully and exquisitely casting its subliminal message over the television airwaves. It sits there still, as much a part of Wimbledon as Big Ben is of Westminster. If that bottle could talk, it would undoubtedly say something supremely condescending about its new neighbor, Coke.

When it comes to the soul of Wimbledon, the word that first comes to my mind is "prohibition." Wimbledon is an autocratic place, and it has a bewildering number of rules. Although Wimbledon has made many concessions to the public and generally provides it with good services, you always have the sense that your presence is at the leisure of someone else, any of a number of pleasant but remote men wearing green-and-mauve ties.

Although the Centre Court was scheduled for gradual renovation beginning after the 1994 championships, it is unlikely that the look or flavor of the place will change very much. On the outside, the most famous tennis stadium on earth is all ivy and balconies and window boxes full of hydrangeas.

On the inside, the multileveled structure is more like a fortress than a stadium. The design of the place might be called Empire Erector set because it is all steel girders and slab concrete, painted very dark green or gray. There is something gloomy and institutional about it, a feeling that is exacerbated by the plethora of pleasantly menacing signs dedicated not to telling you where you are but in keeping you out of places where you're not supposed to go.

In fact, everywhere you turn at Wimbledon there are signs telling you what you can't do. These range from the laudable stricture against removing your shirt in the stands, to elaborate instructions on how to go up and down any of the Centre Court's myriad staircases, to a prohibition against walking your dog on the lawn at the refreshment area— just in case you were daft enough to waste a precious Centre Court ticket on your rottweiler.

Wimbledon has a wonderful Centre Court press box that was designed and built in proximity to the Royal Box in an era when the relation between the media and royalty was considerably more friendly. The press box has old wooden benches and canted, eight-inch writing boards that run the length of each row of seats.

But this modest press box can accommodate only about 150 of the 700 or so accredited print journalists who descend on Wimbledon during a typical Fortnight. Thus, the vast majority of reporters experience Wimbledon just as you do. They watch it in front of a television set situated just a stone's throw from the live action on Centre Court.

The media "overflow" room in the Centre Court complex is a dark air-conditioned bunker dominated by a wall of television screens trained on every conceivable point of interest at Wimbledon. Even journalists with press box seats often spend a lot of time in the overflow room, because most of the courts at Wimbledon are "wired," along with the interview rooms, BBC studios, and even the main electronic scoreboard. You can see everything that is happening at Wimbledon simultaneously. The various monitors provide vast amounts of information—easy information. You can just sit back and write down what you see and hear, and then write it up as though you were right in the thick of it. The proximity of the press bar encourages this type of coverage.

I was in the overflow room once when the late beloved BBC commentator Dan Maskell, a proper gentleman, said, "Miss Sabatini is under the Royal Box now, and she appears to be breathing quite heavily." The remark went off like an alarm clock among the napping multitudes.

Of course, journalism at Wimbledon has gone electronic, too. The only exception to this is the Beastie Boys of Fleet Street, who provide London's notorious tabloid newspapers with fodder for their monumentally vulgar headlines and so-called news stories. The Beasties still rush to the telephones to dictate their lurid, cliché-ridden match reports as well as tidbits of information pertaining to Fergie's weight, Agassi's chest hair, or the secret significance of the time at which Princess Di chooses to adjourn for tea. If you visit London during Wimbledon, I can guarantee you one thing besides the frustration you'll experience trying to find real ketchup: Former prime minister Ted Heath will attend Wimbledon and sit in the Royal Box. He will fall asleep during the matches. The tabloids will capture this on film, throw it on the front page, and trot out the doomsday type to declare: TED SLEEPS. It's just one of the reasons that I love to pore over the tabloids every morning during Wimbledon.

One of the most thoroughly English characters at Wimbledon was the former chief press officer Roy McKelvie. He was a florid-faced man with a mane of white hair and watery eyes, and he ran the press operation in much the same way that bureaucrats stuck in the backwaters of India once administered the empire.

Some of you will know that the English have this thing about Germans, for entirely understandable reasons. I enjoyed hanging around McKelvie's office when some poor German reporter needing a break went to petition him. On one occasion a kid named Henry Henning, from *Welt Am Sontag,* a leading paper in Germany, found himself with an expired credential even though his main story interest, Steffi Graf, was still in the tournaments. So Henning went to ask McKelvie for a credential extension.

Upon hearing Henning's explanation, which was delivered in the direct German manner, McKelvie said dryly, "Oh, I'm afraid it has nothing to do with me whether your pass gets extended or not."

"So who can work here, only the British?" an exasperated Henning retorted.

"Oh, no, no, no. There are thousands of Germans here."

"*Ja?* Which papers are working here?"

"You have to look that up in the media log book, I'm afraid," McKelvie said, pretending to clean his glasses. "Which paper is yours, anyway?"

After the reporter told McKelvie, the Englishman rendered his opinion. "Peanut paper."

"What is this meaning?" Henning asked. "Peanut?"

"It's a peanut paper," McKelvie roared, leaning across his desk.

Henning turned to me. I shrugged and told him all about peanuts and elephants and all that.

"Just some small paper," McKelvie muttered.

"Small paper. You think so?" Henning was getting hot under the collar. "One million readers. You can buy this 'small' paper anywhere in London."

"You told me seven hundred thousand if I recall," McKelvie said. He then leaned forward and boasted, "*Our* papers average ten million."

This comedy continued until McKelvie's eventual successor, Richard Behrens, came over to sort things out. The funny thing about it all was that Henning had misread his pass. It was valid for the entire tournament. When Behrens pointed that out, Henning grew furious and stormed off.

"Maybe they'll win the *next* war," McKelvie said, "but until that happens, they have to go through me. And it won't ever be easy. Let's try a nip of that scotch then, shall we?"

It's funny, but through all the years I visited Wimbledon, I never once was invited into the Members' Enclosure opposite the Centre Court, a place whose tiny thatched roofs resemble those of some Polynesian village plopped down in the S.W. 10 section of London. This strikes me as meaningful only because the nature of my work or social life always takes me into those kinds of places, everywhere else.

But at Wimbledon you go hop-scotching around the social game board only under unusual circumstances. That is to say, you don't enter the Member's Enclosure at Wimbledon unless you're an international pop star who happens to be friends with a titled, heroin-addicted twit whose father is an AELTC member. Most of my colleagues in the *British* press haven't been in the Member's Enclosure, either, despite their generally do-or-die loyalty to The Championships.

I once had to meet an aging and infirm Slew Hester, a former president of the USTA, at 3 P.M. Hester happened to be a guest that day in the International Box, a DMZ of sorts between the Royal Box and Wimbledon's press box. A short hallway under this complex connects all three areas, but only kitchen staff and club officials are allowed to use it. Despite my most persuasive arguments (which included Hester's advanced state of arthritis), the usher at the Royal Box wouldn't allow me to meet Hester in the hall that was only twenty feet from the seats Hester and I respectively occupied. Instead, we both had to take two flights of stairs, leave the Centre Court, and rendezvous in front of the entrance to the club. Everybody at Wimbledon has an assigned place, and is tacitly advised to save himself the embarrassment of asking that an exception be made to the rule.

Back in the good old days, circa 1976, entrance to the Players' Lounge by anyone but players, their guests, and club officials was strictly verboten. Of course, that's where all the action was, and if you knew the right people, you got to take part in it. The guard at the foot of the stairs to the tea room was a doddering, capital chap called Harry. On the first day of the tournament, every member of the media cognoscenti would approach Harry, greet him effusively, and shake his hand—allowing the five-pound note folded therein to pass to Harry in civilized fashion. It was customary to renew your friendship with Harry at the beginning of the second week of the tournament. This pleasant and thoroughly civilized system collapsed as advancing age caused Harry to lose a great deal of his hearing—along with most of his short-term memory. There were a lot of folks standing around screaming Harry's name on the first day of Wimbledon, and even more who were puzzled when Harry refused them entry to the Players' Lounge just twenty-four hours after having collected a crisp fiver from them.

Harry's successor was an odd, cold fellow called Curt. He looked like a member of Britain's right-wing National Front Party, complete with buzz-cut hair that was dyed a different color each year. Curt refused to accept any tithe, but by that time—the late 1980s—the AELTC had adopted a nice system whereby there were six entry badges available to journalists who needed to go to the Players' Lounge. You had to sign in and out for the badges, so Wimbledon regulars did get to know Curt over the years. Sometimes you even got a nod out of him as you flashed your badge and bade him good morning.

One day in 1991 I was coming down from the Players' Lounge when I saw the former British player Ann Jones approaching, in the midst of an animated discussion with the American journalist Steve Flink. He listened and kept up with her as they waded through the usual throng. She invited Flink into the lounge to continue their conversation, but as he had just bumped into her, he didn't have a badge. Naturally, I offered to give Flink my badge, explaining in front of Curt that I would go back to the press center and sign myself in and him out.

Flink gratefully took the badge, but Curt blocked his path with an arm. He said, "Can't go in with his badge, mate. Sorry."

So Flink and I walked around the corner ten feet away, and I gave him the badge again. This time Curt let him through, for reasons I have yet to figure out. The amazing thing about all this is that all of us were Wimbledon veterans who had known each other for years. Strange are the ways of the lords of Wimbledon.

The most remarkable thing about the arrogance and condescension that you can find so easily at Wimbledon is that Nigel Q. Public not only puts up with it, he laps it up. There's some kind of weird reverse psychology at play here, with the pleasure you derive from being let into The Championships increasing in direct proportion to the extent to which you are treated as an earthworm. I've never seen so many people get so fired up about going to a place where most of them won't even get into the stadium. Wimbledon issues separate, numbered tickets for the "show courts" (Centre Court, Number One Court, and Court Number Two), which guarantee you seats only at those respective places. Many of the Centre Court seats are reserved for the elite "debenture holders," who are in effect Wimbledon's shareholders. But the rest of them, along with many seats for the other show courts, are distributed in a fairly enlightened way—doled out to thousands of British tennis nuts who belong to the official Lawn Tennis Association and put up for sale through a lottery.

Most of the public gets in through some twenty thousand "ground passes" that are issued daily. These tickets allow you in, but that's about it. You then roam around the outside "field" courts, hoping to find a seat, or you settle for standing room in the jammed walkways beside the courts. Your chance of seeing a top player out in the hinterlands was once pretty good, but that isn't true anymore in the age of superstar tennis players. Doubles was once an excellent vehicle for allowing spectators to get a close glimpse of top players, but the big guns hardly play doubles anymore.

The typical spectator does have the option of waiting in a queue for up to three or four hours for a seat in the small, unreserved section at each of the "show courts." So here's another Wimbledon tip: If you're determined to see top players from a seated position, for God's sake don't drink any liquid for at least forty-eight hours before you get to Wimbledon. The last thing you want to do after standing in line for three hours to get a seat is have to go to the toilet after witnessing just three games.

After a day at Wimbledon, you will understand Britain's obsession with "sensible shoes." And if you don't have a prized Centre Court ticket and aren't willing to spend half the day waiting in line, the only way you will see the inside of tennis's most illustrious court is if you find an usher compassionate enough to allow you to run up to the top of the stairs at his portal for a quick peek inside. Don't bother to tempt the usher with some feeble bribe. It doesn't work.

There are people who have trooped to Wimbledon for twenty years and have never been able to sit down and watch a tennis match on Centre Court. Until just a couple of years ago Centre Court didn't even have seats for fans who were willing to spend hours in line in the hopes of getting inside. They had to watch standing up, on the "terraces" along either side. This form of cruel and unusual punishment was eliminated when the blight of soccer violence led the sponsors of athletic events to rethink their age-old method of accommodating general admission spectators.

I used to have long and lively debates with Ted Tinling about whether or not Wimbledon was full of bad vibes and weird, foot-on-the-neck games of social status. We disagreed on many things, but I did buy his explanation as to why the Brits tolerated—indeed, they seem to adore—the Wimbledon experience.

"The English have always loved excursions in general, especially the ones that posed some kind of hazard," Tinling told me. "Look at all that bloody mucking about they did in Africa. The provincials get a great sense of accomplishment out of coming to Wimbledon, coming to the *south,* and making it back home. It's a kind of pilgrimage, and it's considered that much more memorable *because* of the difficulties. Everybody wants to come to Wimbledon, everybody wants to see tennis on grass, which has enormous charm precisely because it *is* doomed and outdated.

"Never forget, we English actually *love* to stand in line. We're basically an amicable nation, but we also have a high degree of class consciousness. People who wouldn't say hello to each other if they happened to be from the same neighborhood get very chatty standing in a queue. It gives them the excuse to start a conversation. People going away from Wimbledon are thrilled to have done that. It's one of those occasions on which they can really mingle and communicate without feeling all sorts of social restraints."

So that's the big picture—the view of the psychic landscape of Wimbledon. But as you reduce the image, focusing ever more closely on the microenvironment that is Wimbledon, the aesthetics and the ambience of the club supersede most other issues. This is true even when it's raining, and most sensible Englishmen are wise enough to sit at home cradling mugs of strong English tea with two hands.

I would be remiss if I moved along to the nature of tennis on grass without telling you about the Battle of the Bath Buns because that, too, was very English, very Wimbledon. The adventure began innocently enough when I stopped by for one of my routine chats with Tinling, who was seventy-seven at the time. I found him all worked up over what he and Wimbledon chief executive Chris J. Gorringe agreed was a decline in the quality of the buns that had originated in the city of Bath.

Elders like Tinling knew that Bath buns were much more of a Wimbledon tradition than the *arriviste* strawberries and cream that have been so heavily hyped. A relative to the common Danish, a Bath bun is a pastry made with sultanas (small raisins imported from Smyrna) and candied peels to give it a lemony taste. The proper Bath bun is pale yellow and sprinkled with sugar crystals. When people went to Wimbledon decades ago, Tinling told me, they wanted a nice bun and a cup of tea after the long rail journey. Many of them couldn't afford the considerably more expensive strawberries and cream.

Thus, Tinling was dismayed by the state of the Bath buns at Wimbledon in 1990. He said they had lost their tart, lemony flavor, they weren't light enough, and the sugar crystals on top were like wet sand. According to Gorringe, they were "too bloody big." The men agreed that the latter condition couldn't be helped anymore. It was the American influence. But Tinling mounted a campaign with the bakers. He offered himself as a taste tester and lobbied vigorously to have the buns presented in baskets instead of the glass-doored cooling compartments in the various dining rooms around the grounds. I found Tinling just as he was about to dash off to test the latest batch of Bath buns, and he invited me along. So the two of us went racing through the crowd to taste the fruits of his labor.

We chose to do the test in the press dining room where they're apt to feed you anything that has stopped moving. One bite was all that Tinling needed to approve the changes. The buns were indeed light and airy. The sugar crystals were properly crunchy, there were just enough sultanas, and the hint of lemon was fresh and strong. The buns were still big, but being American, I didn't complain.

That's how things are at Wimbledon. It's one of the few places on earth where a return to prewar standards is considered progressive, where the future is inextricably bound up with the past.

A foreign visitor to Cambridge once remarked on the lush beauty of the lawn around an old chapel there. This fellow was curious about how to cultivate and maintain a lawn that looked as dense as it felt, even when it was cut to within a millimeter of the earth.

"Oh, there's really not that much to it," a caretaker explained. "You just give them plenty of water and roll them every day for two hundred years."

That same formula was employed to create Wimbledon's courts, which are of striking beauty at the onset of The Championships. Their greatest distinction is the way they rebound from year to year after the players destroy the courts over the fortnight.

During the occasional dry and hot Wimbledon meetings, the turf gets so bald at the baselines and near the service box intersection that groundsmen have to paint the sod. Try dumping a gallon of quick-dry Latex on your lawn someday, and you will understand the problems the tournament poses and appreciate the extraordinary way Wimbledon's lawns bounce back to sylvan beauty year after year.

Grass is the most unpredictable surface of all. It is always fast, which puts a premium on power—especially the power of the serve. But as a natural surface, grass can vary tremendously from court to court, not to mention by country and even continent. This helps to explain why the Swede Mats Wilander often had good results on Australian grass in Melbourne, (he won the Australian Open on grass three times) but never managed to reach the semifinals at Wimbledon—not even in 1988, when he became the last man to win three of the majors in the same year.

The brutal Australian sun always baked the courts at Kooyong, and in the dry heat of the winter they became as hard as parking-lot cement. Thus the Aussie grass courts played true, and they yielded a nice, high bounce—much like the hard courts on which Wilander's all-purpose game was so effective.

Another interesting and maddening feature of grass is that it changes character with the ambient conditions. During wet and cool weather, the ball stays low, squirting off the turf like a watermelon seed. Dry, hard courts yield a higher bounce that serves to slow down the game just enough to suit the quicker baseliners. Spin serves have more pronounced slice on damp courts, but flat bullets are more lethal on dry courts. One of the main disadvantages of dry courts is that they create more bad bounces, and the number of bad bounces produced by worn grass courts can be astonishingly high.

Add up these variables, and the Wimbledon phenomenon becomes that much more interesting. The tournament may be anachronistic, but for a variety of reasons it is also the most challenging and difficult tournament to win. Thus, the preeminence of the Wimbledon title is entirely justifiable, and the players who have won at Wimbledon are a varied group. Champions at The Championships do not conform to a surface-dictated stereotype, an accusation that can be leveled at the French Open, where baseliners tend to dominate, and even, to a lesser degree, at the cement-based events in Melbourne and Flushing Meadow.

Over the past decade or so, the winners at Wimbledon have included baseliners such as Borg and Agassi, all-court players like Jimmy Connors, serve-and-volley disciples including Boris Becker, John McEnroe,

Stefan Edberg, and Pete Sampras, and even a counter-punching, serve-and-volley player, Pat Cash. On the other hand, two prominent number one players, Ivan Lendl and Wilander, have never won Wimbledon.

The mental and emotional flexibility required to win at Wimbledon is surpassed only by the physical flexibility that most successful Wimbledon players show. This helps explain why such apparently likely candidates for success as Lendl and even Guillermo Vilas never did win The Championships. Both men liked to plant their feet and throw heavy body punches, but successful tennis at Wimbledon demands nimbleness, and the ability to make incessant split-second adjustments in stance and swing. But the best case study in the deceptive nature of tennis on grass was a good Australian player, John Alexander.

From the time he was one of the world's top junior players, Alexander was touted as the Aussie who would finally pick up at Wimbledon where Laver, Hoad, Emerson, and others left off. He had all the credentials: a big serve and a sharp volley, physical size and strength, solid training on grass, and the psychological benefits of being the heir apparent to a great tradition. Not only did Alexander fail to emerge as a threat to win Wimbledon, but the high points of his career turned out to be a few unexpected titles he won on, of all things, clay.

Alexander lacked the athleticism that is a requisite for winning Wimbledon, but he had the patience and consistency to succeed on clay, on which he was able to better manage the shortcomings posed by a lack of foot speed and quick reflexes. I think Lendl's problems at Wimbledon had similar roots, but then he came so close, so often, that his failure to capture a Wimbledon title can be partly attributed to fate. He never did get that one lucky break that most accomplished Wimbledon champions consider essential to success there.

In 1986, Lendl led the American journeyman Matt Anger by two sets to one and 4–2 in the fourth set on the Centre Court. In what seemed like the blink of an eye, Anger got back the service break and forced a tiebreaker. He then held three set points before Lendl regrouped and eked out the tiebreaker, 13–11. According to the scores, it was a routine win for Lendl, but the Czech player knew how close he had come to losing control of the match in a way that is so typical of tennis on grass.

"That game I served while leading 4–2 is a classic example of what can happen on grass," Lendl later explained. "He hit a bit of a lucky shot on the first point. Then I got a bad call. Next, he hit a great return—nothing I could do. Just like that, it's love-40. I fought back to 30–40. Then I served and went for a volley down the line. But I saw him heading that way, so at the last moment I tried to adjust, to hit the ball a little shorter, and I blew it. That's *exactly* how a match changes on grass, in three or four strokes. And that's why nobody wins big on this surface without that little bit of luck."

Lendl's analysis articulates the oxymoronic but accurate proposition that tennis on grass is a minimalist exercise of great complexity. On no other surface is the difference between the so-called bit points and the routine ones so deceiving. Hitting an ace on grass when you're down break point is just not that big a deal unless you have a lousy serve. But making a silly volleying error off your serve at the modest 0–15 point can be the key moment that ends up changing the result of a match, just as Lendl's example suggested.

Grass is considered a "fast" surface, but most players will tell you that indoor carpet can be faster—by far. Grass is also considered an "easy" surface because of the soft footing and short rallies. Heck, you can play barefoot on the stuff, which isn't something you'd want to try on cement. But as the former pro Bud Schultz once pointed out, "The softness of grass makes it that much more effortful to make decisive movements. After a tough grass-court match, you end up with a lot of pain in your lower back, buttocks, and quads."

Most fans of clay-court tennis believe that the game on dirt is more grueling because of the long points and incessant rallies. But Tim Mayotte, who posted his best results on the grass at Wimbledon, knows better. "The wear and tear of a five-set match on grass is remarkable, and a big part of it is the pure psychological tension created by the potential importance of every point. Nothing requires the same sequential intensity, point after point, and nothing leaves you as exhausted as a tense, close match on grass."

The big serve is commonly considered a sure ticket to success on slick grass, and it has certainly given countless journeymen players who upset superior players at Wimbledon their fifteen minutes of fame. But the second serve may be more important on grass, and the quality of Borg's second delivery accounted for a great deal of his success at Wimbledon. Borg's reliable second serve was much more of an asset than the big first serve that some of the more erratic players possess, no matter how much excitement they generate by turning in the occasional upset on those rare days when their serves work perfectly.

Questioning the merits of the big, flat serve on grass is a little bit like pooh-poohing the merits of the Tomahawk cruise missile in a sticky international showdown. Nevertheless, second serves do wonderful tricks on grass, with minimal effort. "All you need to do is snap your wrist and the second serve does unbelievable stuff on grass," Tim Wilkison once commented. "It's an instant knuckleball."

The flip side of the serve is the return, and the biggest change in the nature of Wimbledon tennis in the age of high-tech rackets that give almost every player lethal power has been a shift of emphasis from the serve to the return. In the days of the standard-sized wooden racket, it took an exceptional day for a journeyman player to just plain rip through the match on the strength of a serve. These days almost any player with a good serve is capable of doing that—unless the player is facing an opponent with an extraordinary return.

Connors set the standard for the service return in the Open era. Here was a man whose serve, by grass-court standards—make that any standard—was mediocre. Yet, mostly on the strength of his sharp returns, Connors appeared in six Wimbledon finals as well as four semifinals. Connors's lethal returns often inspired anxiety and doubt in proficient servers even when their deliveries were up to snuff.

Andre Agassi won Wimbledon in 1992 because of his mastery of the return game in an age dominated by lethal power servers. His victory over the hard-serving Croat Goran Ivanisevic was achingly simple and, to some observers, unspeakably one-dimensional. Agassi simply got more balls back into play than any of Ivanisevic's previous victims, a surprise that rattled the losing finalist and led him to relinquish control of the match.

Fred Stolle believes that contemporary players return much more accurately and aggressively than he and his peers did during the Australian dynasty. But Stolle also contends that the top Aussie players had a more impressive mastery of the second most important offensive weapon (after the serve) of the grass-court game: the volley. In the era of wooden rackets, even the best servers had to back up their deliveries with sharp, decisive volleys. The number of serves put back into play was so high then that you were better off having a good serve and a great volley than a great serve and a decent volley. During the Open era, the only volleys that were comparable to those of the Australian legends belonged to McEnroe, Edberg, and Cash.

Tony Roche may have had the best volley among all the Australian players, which helps explain why Ivan Lendl hired Roche as his coach in his quest to win Wimbledon. The southpaw Roche helped Lendl improve his volley measurably, which was one of the chief reasons Lendl reached back-to-back Wimbledon finals in 1986 and 1987. But Lendl's volley, while sharp, was not quite sharp enough. And it may not have been as effective as Borg's volley, which could easily be called a travesty.

Borg's volley was a cross between a slap and a poke, with so little of the requisite "punch" spoken of in Tennis 101 that the stroke gave his opponents fits. Going to the net was always an adventure for Borg, and once there he would wave at the ball with all the grace of a man wielding a flyswatter. He'd get some string on it, maybe a little wood, too, and the ball would land feebly across the net just a few feet away, with no pace on it. I'm not sure that Borg ever hit a crisp textbook volley to the corner of the far court, but the odds suggest that he must have done it at least a few times. But those short, dying quail volleys cut down the potential angle available for his opponents' subsequent passing shots. They offered the opponents no pace to use, and they rarely bounced high enough to be played comfortably. Borg's volleys consistently forced his opponents to dig up junk and try to turn it into jewelry.

You can throw ground strokes out the window on grass—at least you can in men's tennis—except for the passing shots that are so vital on a surface in which almost everybody's strategy is to get to the net as soon as possible. Yet as racket technology advanced and made grass-court tennis even more suited to attacking serve-and-volley players, two players who preferred to operate from the baseline dominated Wimbledon less than a decade after the advent of Open tennis.

When Connors and Borg appeared on the scene, the old guard insisted that they were not fated to do well at Wimbledon. Connors's serve was suspect, and Borg was considered a clay-court specialist. Furthermore, each man hit an unorthodox two-handed backhand that was less versatile than the one-handed version, partly because it reduced the reach of the player employing it. The record clearly proved the critics wrong.

In Connors's case, the skeptics underestimated the degree of penetration that the hawk-eyed Connors would achieve with his ground strokes. He had no interest in the ground stroke as a tool used in a conventional rally. Both his backhand and forehand were sharp, probing, exact placements that simultaneously served to run opponents ragged and allow Connors to get to the net without relying on textbook approach shots. The key to Connors's success was the relatively flat, quick ball that he hit. Not only did his opponents find themselves with insufficient time to make a good reply, they were incessantly having to dig the ball up from a low bounce.

Borg's vaunted groundies were not as useful as those of Connors's at Wimbledon, but one facet of them was critically important to his success at The Championships. Borg's passing shots were classic—at least in terms of where they went, if not in how they were struck. Borg was disposed to use tons of topspin, which can be notoriously counterproductive on "slow" (damp) grass. Players who rely on topspin usually have a long backswing and exaggerated shoulder rotation, along with an extended follow-through—all of which take time. Also, overspin on damp grass often causes the ball to lose pace and sit up instead of taking a high, accelerated bounce toward an opponent, the way a ball struck with topspin does on hard courts. Finally, consistent baseliners often have a finely grooved swing that isn't tailored to making last-minute adjustments for the surprises offered by grass. For those reasons, the majority of steady, accomplished clay-court players who use heavy topspin always experience frustration at Wimbledon.

But Borg was blessed with exceptional speed, a compact backswing, and quick wrists—qualities that drastically reduced his prep time and gave him a great facility for adjusting to the erratic bounces that so trouble long-stroke topspinners. And when it came to the vital passing shots from which service breaks are built, Borg's topspin gave him a distinct advantage.

The radical topspin that Borg used caused the ball to travel in a parabola, dipping sharply as it crossed the net. This prevented his opponents from punching through on the ball with a high-to-low volley, and it also prevented them from making full use of the angles of the court. Facing a Borg passing shot was like trying to meet, control, and redirect a bottle rocket.

The strength of Connors's pass was accuracy that let him go around opponents rather than through them in the manner of Borg. But he did "roll" the ball frequently on the forehand side, especially when he needed to make a sharply angled pass or when he wanted to pull an opponent far off court.

So while the two men used their ground strokes in different, unconventional ways, each found a weapon that in other hands was just a modest tool used to set up an approach shot. But even more importantly, each of them also possessed the first ingredient required to control the tempo of a match: the ability to arrive at the ball early. This was largely a matter of athleticism, which on grass courts more than any other surface is a virtue unto itself.

If you want to win on grass, it also helps to have an excellent lob to keep a net-rushing opponent at bay. For all of his power serves and crisp forehands, the Aussie John Newcombe had one of the best and sneakiest lobs in the business. The tradition was carried on by Connors and, to a lesser extent, Borg. Cash used his lob well, as did McEnroe. Ilie Nastase, who performed well at Wimbledon but lost in finals to Stan Smith and Borg, had a marvelous lob.

The footing on grass poses a major challenge to the athlete-tennis player, and if successful Wimbledon players have one thing in common, it is lightness of step. It was a key element in Cash's quest for the title, and the only thing quicker than McEnroe's hands was McEnroe's feet. The same goes for Edberg. In fact, the only recent Wimbledon champion who occasionally appeared to have heavy feet has been Becker.

As Bud Schultz, a student of the game, said, "The better athletes tend to win on grass because there is so much improvisation. The bad bounces, the tricky footing, the changing conditions—all of them put a premium on versatility."

Versatility, flexibility, quick feet, and—the last element required for success on grass, which doesn't always go hand in hand with those mercurial qualities—patience.

Service breaks are few and far between on grass. On grass it's easy to fall into a state of quiet desperation (not to mention ennui) as the blacksmith across the net pounds in heavy serve after heavy serve, holding one love game after another. But great grass-court players don't get discouraged or mesmerized by that drill. They may appear to, but they are actually biding their time, remaining alert and poised to strike quickly, often at seemingly innocuous opportunities, to create unexpected service breaks.

Of course, there are those Wimbledon matches—most of them, in fact—in which the subtleties of the game on grass are barely evident because of the power revolution. These days the typical grass-court encounter is more like a rock fight than a tennis match. The game has been reduced (at least on the men's side) from what was universally called serve-and-volley tennis to serve-and-return tennis. Nothing with the possible exception of almost any pro soccer game is more boring than a bad tennis match on grass.

I'll give the last word on the soporific nature of bad tennis on grass to Rex Bellamy, who distinguished himself for decades as the quirky, poetic, ever-reaching tennis correspondent for *The Times* of London. Commenting on yet another match in which two men took turns trying to serve each other off the court, Bellamy wrote: "Watching certain matches on grass is rather like watching a friend's dachshund sit up and beg. It is indeed impressive, but after five minutes it becomes a little tedious."

Writing in the *London Evening Standard* in July of 1991, British player Nick Brown described his upset victory over the Croatian Star Goran Ivanisevic like this:

> *The feelings I experienced when four thousand people were willing me to win that match against Goran Ivanisevic at Wimbledon last year were breathtaking, unforgettable. Their expressions of emotions when I had achieved my task were quite unbelievable. The biggest moment occurred at 4:45 on that first Saturday of the tournament.*
>
> *After three and a half hours on Court 13 against Ivanisevic, one of the favorites for the title and the tenth seed, I found myself at match point.*

I felt calm. The crowd [was] suddenly very quiet. Today was going to be the day when I buried the ghosts of all those matches where I had missed my chance.

I served . . . the crowd erupted with applause. I had served an ace, and the match was over. The crowd [was] giving me a standing ovation, cheering. I turned to all four corners and clapped back. I just wanted them to know how much their support had meant to me. They were superb. They made me proud to be British.

Ah, to be proud. To be British. To turn to the crowd with an erect back and a moist eye. To return their salute. To applaud. It was indeed a moment of glory in July 1991 for Nick Brown, an Englishman's Englishman. It was indeed a moment of glory for England. And under the circumstances, it would be mean-spirited to quibble. But there is a down side.

Brown, who was thirty at the time, was competing in his seventh Wimbledon, and he needed a wildcard to get in every single time. Shortly after being upset by Brown, Ivanisevic said it was the first time that he had ever lost to a player who "walks like an invalid." At the time, Brown was ranked number 2 in Britain but number 591 in the world. At Wimbledon that year, no British male was ranked in the world's top 200, and thus not a single one was entered in his national championships on merit. On the women's side, Jo Durie and Sara Gomer were at least in the top 100. Things have not improved since the beginning of this decade; in fact, they have gotten worse.

Although Brown would win another match after his upset of Ivanisevic in 1991, he would lose in the third round to Theirry Champion, a Frenchman whose best surface is slow red clay. Thus ended Wimbledon of 1991, with one giant step for Brown, one small step for mankind— or at least the portion of it that packs a British passport.

As the status of Wimbledon swells, television revenues continue to go through the roof, and men in green-and-mauve ties contemplate what to do about the antiquated main scoreboard, one thing does not change either substantially or superficially: The Brits can't play for squat.

This is an intriguing state of affairs. Tennis was allegedly invented in France, but it was popularized on British lawns. The game still clings stubbornly to many of its Anglo values and longstanding traditions. Wimbledon remains the most important tournament in the world, a condition that presumably would inspire millions of youths to dream of winning The Championships no less than their American counterparts dream of winning the World Series. But they don't.

Thus, the demise of British tennis remains one of the most baffling and surreal issues in the world game. It has become a problem with a thousand solutions and no solution at all. A riddle wrapped within a riddle. An enigma wrapped in contradiction, stuffed into a dilemma, stamped with a paradox—and lost in the mail. It is tennis's very own version of the ageless question, "Daddy, why is the sky blue?"

So let's run through some of the theories: (a) The United Kingdom, with a population of millions, has too few people; (b) the British climate is too cold and wet; (c) Britain has too few tennis courts, particularly indoors; (d) the British are an island culture that exists outside of the European and North American traditions; (e) the British are too poor to develop champions; (f) the British don't have the staff or facilities to create a generation of top players; (g) the British don't have the right "social" attitude for creating the next Jimmy Connors or Monica Seles.

Let's begin by noting that at the time of Nick Brown's heroic achievement, Holland (population 12,000,000) had three men and four women in the World Top 100, Sweden was not exactly tropical, Russia was short of everything (including tennis courts), and the last time I checked, Australia was an island, too. Yet those nations, not to mention small, temperate, dollar- and court-poor Czechoslovakia, all produced prominent players in the 1980s. So that takes care of theories a through d. The rest take some explaining.

The British have had their economic ups and downs, but the British tennis establishment has been happily immune to them. This is because Wimbledon has shown mind-boggling largess, supporting the British Lawn Tennis Association to the tune of some $15 million annually. This is a fascinating dole queue of the old-boy network, meaning that everybody standing on it went to a good school, wears a tie, serves on a committee, and seems remarkably incapable of converting Wimbledon megabucks into the homegrown Wimbledon champions that the British so crave.

In 1985, the LTA launched a "five-year plan" to restore British tennis. The massive budget earmarked some $3 million for training players of national and international status. Astonishingly, the British are in worse shape today than they were at the onset of the five-year plan.

David Wynne-Morgan, a successful advertising executive and an outspoken critic of the LTA, told me that the LTA has a staff roughly three times the size of its American counterpart, the USTA, so the annual administrative fees for the LTA are roughly the same as the entire budget for the national training program. "We Brits do certain things terribly well," says Wynne-Morgan. "We're good at coronations. We shine at state funerals and trooping the colors. And we're really tops on making up committees and spending money on keeping them going."

Richard Lewis, a former British player of little distinction, was the head of national training at the beginning of the 1990s. He reported to Ian Peacock, the head of the LTA's developmental effort, who in turn reported to nine committees, many of which had subcommittees but none of which benefited from the service of even one former world-class player. Contemplating this hierarchy and the bureaucrats who control and operate it, Wynne-Morgan said: "Making Tony Pikard [a British Davis Cup captain and lifetime personal coach of Stefan Edberg] report to Richard Lewis is like making Horatio Nelson report to Popeye."

John Lloyd, the best British player of the 1980s, has been a biased but keen observer of Britain's plight. Lloyd's brother David, an energetic guy who was a feisty, overreaching pro (just the kind that so often makes an ideal coach), pulled out all the stops in his attempt to get the job as the LTA's head of development. Not only was David Lloyd qualified as a coach, but he also knew about business, having run England's most prosperous indoor tennis club. But Lewis got the job anyway. As John Lloyd told me with uncharacteristic vehemence: "Lewis got the job for keeping his mouth shut and working for the LTA for three years. It's the old-boy network again. Nobody rocks the boat. The LTA has a lot of well-meaning people in positions they can't fill. It's all bullshit."

Most parties agree that David Lloyd was always too outspoken in his criticism of the LTA ever to be embraced by that body. But nobody issued a more bizarre explanation for why Lloyd didn't get the job than Peacock, who with a straight face told me: "David offered to give up his other day-to-day activities, everything. He was so keen on the job that he even offered to do it without a salary. Well, that's not a way to hire somebody."

Peacock did preside over a successful effort to build a tennis infrastructure in England. There's a nice Maoistic ring to the LTA's "five-year plan" of the early 1990s, and an equally Big Brotherish element in the tracking system it has produced to keep tabs on all active players. The five-year plan also called for a dramatic increase in the number of covered (indoor) courts, which grew from 190 to 500. And open tournaments have burgeoned from 400 to 980.

In a matching-funds scheme, local communities have contributed some $40 million to the LTA, mostly for facility construction. Almost half of the LTA's planned fifty regional centers were completed by 1993, and a grass-roots coaching system was in place. But England's plight suggested that producing champion players had less to do with slick facilities and welfare-state training programs than it did with who chooses to play tennis and why.

"In our tradition we learn to settle for a good effort," John Lloyd told me. "We're not supposed to get all carried away and obsessed with winning. And down deep we still believe that you're missing the point if winning is all-important. We *say* we admire winners, but we don't really mean it. So we end up focusing on the controversial winners and use their behavior to justify our suspicion of total commitment to winning. But the way I see it, what's wrong with having a son like Stefan Edberg?

"And the British are still squeamish about all the money offered in tennis. I'll never forget the year I got to the final at the big indoor tournament at Wembley. I lost to Bjorn Borg, and when they announced to the crowd that I was getting a check for ten thousand pounds, the fans actually groaned. I was almost embarrassed to accept it. The amateur mentality is still with us in lots of hidden ways."

The notion that athletics are a part of a well-rounded life rather than the focus of a narrow one still lingers in the British mind. As Peacock put it, "It's still more acceptable in the middle class to earn your living with your brain rather than your brawn."

Furthermore, tennis still bears the stigma of a snob sport in a nation where class values and antagonisms have not died, but merely gone underground. Wynne-Morgan attended one of England's better schools, Branston. He played schoolboy tennis on grass courts that, he said, are second only to those of Wimbledon (a claim that is lodged by every tennis venue in Britain except Wimbledon). Oddly enough, the typical match against another school when Wynne-Morgan was a schoolboy consisted of three doubles matches, with no singles competition at all. He told me, "The British mentality is that it is all about teamwork. Encouraging individualism is wrong, and wrong in direct relation to how rampantly that individualism is expressed."

England's last and perhaps greatest male singles champion was the late Fred Perry, whose status as a hero was institutionalized when Wimbledon renamed one of its entrance gates after him, and also erected a handsome bronze statue of him at the choicest site on the grounds. But Perry was, like Wimbledon, an anomaly.

Perry's father was a Labour MP, just the kind of working-class proto-socialist who spent his life in bitter conflict with the privileged world represented by Wimbledon. His son was a fierce competitor—a prototype for Jimmy Connors. Perry's individualism and unbridled competitiveness were such that the privileged class rebuffed him until they no longer had to suffer his working-class ethic at play on Wimbledon's

lawns. When Perry scored a sensational victory over the German aristocrat and sportsman baron Gottfried von Cramm some sixty years
ago, the president of the AELTC actually apologized to von Cramm.

The English are quintessentially team players and a people accustomed to a strict social hierarchy, even in the milieu of club tennis. Any
number of Brits like to point out that English juniors are considered a
blight at most clubs, where the prevailing sentiment is that kids should
be seen and not heard.

"The seniors couldn't give a snuff about kids," John Lloyd told me.
"So the kids are pushed off the courts routinely, and they're lucky if
they can nip back on for a little hit at nine or ten at night."

The restricted social mobility in England also militates against a talented kid of West Indian, African, or Indian origin taking up the game.
Such kids would much rather succeed in soccer, an egalitarian game of
unrivaled international popularity.

The real dilemma of British tennis has a lot more to do with various
social conditions than it does with logistical ones such as court availability. Which brings us back to Wimbledon. British kids don't really
aspire to becoming tennis stars because the premier event in tennis isn't
really about athletics, it's about England and about being British. It isn't
a sporting event as much as it is a social phenomenon, a quirky, ritual-
ized, national event that has more in common with the American celebration of the Fourth of July than it does with the World Series.

There may be plenty more courts on the horizon as well as improved
training techniques and opportunities, but the ceiling is still low, and
beyond it lies a vast expanse of blue sky—one part of the moribund
British Empire over which the sun still has not set.

CHAPTER 11

RACE
The Hard Road to Tennis Glory

ONE EVENING ABOUT TEN YEARS AGO, the 1982 French Open champion and incipient pop star Yannick Noah and I were leaving the grounds of a tennis tournament at the Boca West resort near Boca Raton, Florida, to grab a bite to eat at a local fish joint. I was writing about Noah at the time, and we had spent a good part of the afternoon talking about race. Noah's father was a native of Cameroon, and his mother was French. After having been discovered by Arthur Ashe, Noah was whisked from Cameroon to France by the French Tennis Federation, which underwrote his development into a solid top ten player.

Noah became the first male French national to win at Roland Garros since Marcel Bernard in 1946. His 6–2, 7–5, 7–6 victory over Mats Wilander in that final was an upset, *un miracle,* that even the passionate French had not dared imagine. Noah's win was inspired, rooted in a brave commitment to attacking the seemingly impregnable defenses of a cool, consistent counterpuncher.

Noah's attitude about race was sophisticated, clear-eyed, and well-reasoned. He was a confident person blissfully free from the resentments, suspicions, and animosities bred by racial friction. This may have been partly because his mother was white and partly because Afro-Europeans, so much fewer in numbers than their American counterparts, often are more assimilated. But in his heart as well as his appearance, Noah still saw himself as a black man—which explains why, on that sultry evening in Boca Raton, he spontaneously stopped, turned to face me, and, in an anguished tone, declared, "God, I *hate* these places. I hate this phony country club existence. There isn't a black face anywhere except for the man picking up the garbage."

I would never forget that interlude because it communicated the sense of dislocation that black tennis players must contend with almost every day on the tour. Oddly, Wimbledon would seem like the ultimate bastion of white values, but it's so whacked out on tradition that everyone considers it some version of never-never land, where racial distinctions seem less important.

These days, inclusion is the buzzword and exclusion is the dirty word. The engineers of the Open era traded heavily on this cultural change, promising that there would be room on board for everyone in the new era. So why is it that tennis hasn't become substantially more multiracial, most contemporary black players don't feel any more comfortable in the tennis environment than their predecessors, and a black player still can't walk through the player entrance at a tournament without getting checked for his or her credentials while any white bozo in short pants and moonboot tennis sneakers can come and go like the wind? These and other common questions raise the granddaddy of them all: Is tennis by nature a racist sport?

Yes, it most decidedly is. But while this admission might thrill egalitarians, it also raises an uncomfortable question for them: Whose fault is it that minority communities still haven't made a significant impact on pro tennis in this so-called new, democratic era? In fact, while the pro game is over twenty-five years old, only one of the four minority players to win Grand Slam titles can be considered the product of the Open era. Althea Gibson, the first black person to win a Grand Slam title (Wimbledon, 1957), predated Open tennis. Arthur Ashe won the first U.S. Open (1968), but he did so as an amateur, and an Army man to boot. Evonne Goolagong, as we have seen, was discovered and taught by an old-guard type, Vic Edwards. That leaves only Yannick Noah, who was the product of a French pro-era initiative to develop talent. Curiously, Ashe discovered Noah in Cameroon during a State Department–sponsored goodwill tour. This kind of noblesse oblige exercise was common during the amateur era, but it has all but vanished in the new, professional age.

Noah did develop his talents through a sophisticated program financed by the windfall profits of the pro era, but that program was created and administered by amateur-era types—Philippe Chartrier and his minions in the French Tennis Federation. In fact, most of the search-and-develop programs existing today are still administered through the vestigial amateur organizations affiliated with the ITF.

One of the critical failings of the Open era, as far as minorities go, has been the way that groups like the ATP and WTA are led around by the nose—or pocket—by sponsors, promoters, and tournament directors who are essentially indifferent to the challenge of recruiting minorities. The pro bureaucrats talk a good game, and the black players who make it to the pro tour are welcomed. Sometimes they are treated with even greater deference and accorded more privileges than white players of equal status by the game's administrators (if not the security guards). But the bald truth is that the ruling bodies of pro tennis do not spread the tennis gospel to minorities.

But two things must be said in defense of the Open era. It has not had as much time behind the wheel of the game as the amateur establishment did, and the new era has undoubtedly produced a broader spectrum of players, including many more journeymen from minority communities. While many of those players were developed by ITF affiliates, the color-blind ranking and tournament entry systems of the pro era have certainly leveled the social playing field.

These revisionist speculations support the notion that the appeal of tennis has always been rooted in its exclusionary nature, and there's nothing wrong with that. Exclusionary organizations draw like-minded—not like-complexioned—people, and the strength of exclusionary systems depends on who is included and why. Likewise, their weakness or ultimate failure is determined by whom they exclude and why; exclusionary organizations fail and become repugnant when their standards for inclusion become morally insupportable.

Whenever I think about these issues, I think about Sarah Allen, whose daughter, Leslie, distinguished herself by becoming the first black woman since Althea Gibson to win a sanctioned pro event when she won the Avon Championships of Detroit in 1981. Sarah, a statuesque, charismatic woman, once told me, "I played tennis back when a black player couldn't get into USTA tournaments. Yes, it was wrong. Yes, it could be painful. But I'll tell you something—tennis had more class then. It had great beauty and elegance."

Now there is a woman whom you ought to have in your country club—that is, if she would tolerate your company. Allen understood that the fundamental human urge to identify and pursue beauty and distinction is by nature a discriminatory act. More importantly, it was this vision of tennis as a game of beauty and elegance that led Sarah Allen to urge her daughter to play tennis. The tennis establishment may have been mired in overt as well as subconscious racism, but the game it promoted was exclusionary in the best sense. Tennis in the amateur era had strict ethical standards based on a largely unwritten but universally accepted code of conduct. And, of course, amateurism itself was not a tool used to keep people from earning a living at something they loved (as many of the revolutionaries of the Open era would have you believe), but a device intended to ensure that tennis remained a means, rather than an end—a means to good health and the cultivation of virtues that would be useful later in life.

A great deal of discrimination and prejudice undoubtedly went unchallenged during the amateur era in tennis. These days no form of discrimination—real or imagined—seems to go unnoticed and uncontested. An incident that occurred a few years ago between Zina Garrison-Jackson and Pam Shriver, who shared a lifetime of friendship as well as an Olympic doubles medal, is relevant. During a closely contested doubles match in which the women were paired against each other, Shriver took exception to the enthusiastic and unremittingly boisterous crowd that had turned out to support Garrison-Jackson. The crowd eventually got to Shriver, who finally asked Garrison-Jackson to tell her supporters to "shut up." Garrison-Jackson, a sensitive and introspective woman, felt insulted, and she had words of her own for Shriver. Later, the media quizzed Garrison-Jackson about this incident, and before long somebody asked if there was perhaps a racial component to the controversy. Garrison-Jackson, who has always had high racial consciousness, suggested that there probably was—an allegation that cut Shriver to the quick. "That's ridiculous," she told me. "Zina's friends were just out of line. They were making too much noise, and it impaired my ability to concentrate. They could have been white or blue or yellow, and I would have done the same thing. They were just rude."

The conflict between Shriver, the product of a WASPy, patrician family, and Garrison-Jackson, a player from the Houston, Texas, ghetto, was not racial. It was ethical, and it occurred because there is no longer unanimity about what does and doesn't constitute correct behavior.

The old values in tennis may seem silly or repressive to both black and white fans who grew up hooting or hollering at an athlete trying to make a free throw, but scores of African Americans adopted them when they were still in use. That's why Sarah Allen loved tennis, and it helps to explain why Gibson and Ashe bothered to endure the down side of an exclusionary, predominantly white sport. They and other people of character, regardless of race, creed, or color, wanted to buy into an aesthetic and a sensibility that elevated tennis above other sports and pastimes, even though the value system of tennis was often a conduit for snobbery and racial discrimination.

It seems clear that the price of inclusion in tennis for minorities has been awfully high. At one time that cost was measured mostly in intangible psychological and emotional factors. These days, despite the broad cultural mandate for inclusion, and the assistance available from some organizations, including the USTA, the price can also be measured in the ever-escalating financial cost of training a tennis player. And to make matters worse, many of the cultural issues and obstacles to minority involvement in tennis remain with us, albeit in different dress.

My gut response when the issue of minority involvement in tennis is raised is to play the devil's advocate: Why *should* typical African Americans want to take on all the obstacles presented by this complex, difficult, expensive, and predominantly white sport, this elitist sport that is still in some ways the manifestation of a dated and defeated Anglo-Saxon ethic? Popular team sports undeniably offer more camaraderie, plenty of fame and money, and a much more familiar cultural environment for aspiring minority athletes. They also impose far fewer financial burdens on parents, given the role scholastic and collegiate sports programs play in developing the future stars of the pro sports leagues. On top of that, many of the "traditional" benefits of playing tennis no longer obtain.

Aspiring pro tennis players no longer have to cultivate the kind of discipline that Arthur Ashe did, except in the narrow sense of putting in the court time to develop their games. Aspiring tennis players can no longer look to tennis to provide them with a formal education similar to the one Ashe received by virtue of his tennis scholarship to UCLA, because the pro establishment is intrinsically antagonistic to the collegiate game.

And finally, top tennis players in the Open era may be celebrities, but that's all they are anymore. They no longer have the social or political cachet that led the State Department to recruit tennis players like Ashe for their goodwill tours. (Can you imagine a contemporary player giving up a few weeks of his time, for no money to speak of, to fulfill such a missionary role?)

The doors of many banks and brokerage houses were once wide open to former world circuit players, because the value system in tennis was thought to provide good training for adult life and work. And it did not hurt that tennis players—not just the well-known competitors, but almost all players—were perceived as well-mannered, well-rounded, sophisticated individuals who would be assets in any enterprise.

These days, the best a tennis player can hope for is to make a lot of big money fast, and to get famous enough to trade on his or her name and image later in life. But only a handful of very famous players in every generation reaches that level of public recognition. And even for them, the opportunities constitute a subtle form of dehumanization. There's something sad about being a person whose usefulness begins and ends with his visage, his name, or even his reputation, while there is no demand whatsoever for his intelligence or imagination, or any of the other qualities by which the rest of us make our way.

So if you want to be a real pencil-neck and do one of those "cost-benefit analysis" things on this issue, you come up with lots of reasons for discouraging your black child from playing tennis—conclusions that support the idea that tennis is a "racist" sport, but not for the obvious reasons. Still, if you ask someone why a minority child should play tennis, the most common, reflexive one-word answer you get is: money. Bad reason. Bad word. Bad idea.

One of my favorite people in tennis, and one of the game's unsung heroes, is John Wilkerson. If you don't know his name, it's a pity. Wilkerson single-handedly developed Zina Garrison-Jackson and Lori McNeil, two women from the Houston ghetto. Although their families had no tennis history whatsoever, Garrison-Jackson, the runner-up at Wimbledon in 1990, was the finest black female player since Althea Gibson. She was consistently ranked in the Top Five and was rarely far from the top of the game for most of her career. Lori McNeil was a solid tour player for about a decade, with upsets of Chris Evert and Steffi Graf at important tournaments to her credit. Garrison-Jackson and McNeil made history when they contested the first pro tournament final featuring two black women, at the Eckerd Open in Tampa in 1988. McNeil stole the spotlight from her childhood friend and won that title.

As a country boy growing up near San Antonio, Texas, Wilkerson picked cotton to earn money—a backbreaking stint of which he remains resolutely proud, saying, "I got strong by picking cotton. It's nothing I'd ever be ashamed about."

Wilkerson also read the Bible as well as the *Autobiography of Malcolm X*, whose influence changed and shaped him without leading him to renounce his identity as a southern black Christian.

At eighteen, Wilkerson took a fancy to tennis and taught himself to play. Some years later he won the national championships of the ATA—an extraordinary accomplishment in and of itself for a man with conspicuously homemade strokes. But then, Wilkerson is the sort of man who would set about building a jumbo jet in his basement using directions found in a back issue of *Popular Mechanics*. Such can-do types popped up frequently in the ATA and USTA.

Wilkerson eventually moved to Houston. When he began to slow down as a player, at about age forty, he set up shop in MacGregor Park, a public facility, and launched a tennis training program. Initially he charged a fee, but when nobody showed up, he offered the program for free. Parents soon flocked to the program and continued to do so after Wilkerson reinstituted the charge.

According to Wilkerson, those parents were not obsessed with visions of their children becoming rich and famous pro players. They saw tennis as a healthy recreation as well as a good way of constructively getting rid of the kids for the day. As he told me, "The great thing about that was that the parents didn't interfere with us. Back then, they didn't have that glint of money in their eyes, to make them full of crazy demands."

Eventually, Wilkerson and his two assistants took thirty of the most promising youngsters and invited them to participate in a year-round program. McNeil's mother, Dorothy, got her talented daughter into the program straightaway. It took Wilkerson a little longer to see the potential in Zina Garrison, and he might have overlooked her completely if it were not for Garrison's brother, Rodney. A basketball junkie at MacGregor, Rodney approached Wilkerson one day and told him that he had an athletic kid sister. Soon after, Wilkerson noticed a shy little girl sitting by the fence, intently watching him conduct a training session. When the girl was still there an hour later, Wilkerson deduced that it must be Rodney's sister. He invited her to join the group, and to this day she remembers the first tennis ball she ever hit.

"I took a baseball-style swing, with two hands," Zina told me. "The effort pretty near twirled me around. But I made contact. Boy, did I make contact. The ball sailed clear over the fence."

Garrison-Jackson would become Wilkerson's star pupil, so eager for tennis that when Wilkerson arrived to unlock the gates to the tennis courts at 7:30 every morning, little Zina would already be there, sitting along the fence, waiting for him.

Like so many of the best coaches, including the Australian Harry Hopman, Ashe's coach, Dr. Robert Johnson, and Boris Becker's former coach, Bob Brett, Wilkerson nurtured talent by building character. He was a moralist whose program was short on fancy training techniques and the New Ageish psychobabble in which so many of today's coaches traffic. Wilkerson instilled discipline and demanded that protégés toe the line. Years later, Garrison-Jackson still felt guilty if she stepped onto a tennis court with chewing gum in her mouth.

The kids in Wilkerson's program were separated into groups according to ability, and their daily regimen consisted primarily of hitting drills, running, and some stretching. Attendance was mandatory. Saturdays were reserved for the much anticipated chance to play matches, and Sunday instruction was optional. The unique part of the program was that it was coeducational. Long before male hitting partners became de rigueur on the women's tour, Wilkerson's girls were benefiting from playing with boys. One of the other advantages that Wilkerson's group enjoyed sprang from the homegrown, inner-city nature of his program. Most of the kids attended the same school, and because they traveled together, Wilkerson's kids were spared the feelings of aloneness and dislocation when they began to test themselves against the competition at USTA sectional tournaments, age-group events that attracted an overwhelmingly white, fiercely competitive crowd.

After little more than one year of training, Garrison-Jackson was one of the top juniors in Texas. By the time she was fourteen, she was the dominant player in her age group. Wilkerson began taking his students to USTA sectional tournaments just two years after launching his program. He himself was shocked by the kids' poise, determination, and aggression. He thought, "I've grown a monster."

"Everything came so fast," Garrison-Jackson would say later. "One day we were playing park tennis, and overnight we were out in California playing national events."

McNeil also hit the ground running, and although she appeared to have more natural talent, Wilkerson never could get her to overcome her chronic lack of concentration and casual demeanor. Wilkerson interpreted those tendencies as the elaborate defense mechanisms of a girl who was reluctant to put herself on the line. Making an observation that would apply long after McNeil was firmly established as a dangerous but inconsistent pro player, Wilkerson said, "If Lori ever lets go and allows her *real* self to get involved, if she just gives her being to the game, she will be one hell of a tennis player."

In the big picture, both Garrison-Jackson and McNeil had flourishing careers, yet according to Wilkerson, each woman might have accomplished more. Garrison-Jackson, a solid top five player for some years, had a lethal attacking game that could have earned her a Grand Slam title, but she fell just short in that quest. McNeil played some great matches, but she never did put together the succession of top performances needed to win an important title.

Garrison-Jackson reached the semifinals of each Grand Slam event but the French Open at least once. Her best chance to win a Grand Slam title materialized in 1990, when she played brilliantly in the quarterfinals and semifinals to score successive upsets over Monica Seles and Steffi Graf. But after battling Martina Navratilova in a tight first set, Garrison-Jackson's focus evaporated. The second set flew by like a dream, with Navratilova winning 6–4, 6–1.

Analyzing McNeil's and Garrison-Jackson's results presents the age-old question about a water glass and whether it is half-full or half-empty. That question can be particularly—and unfairly—haunting to any person who traveled a very long road to success. When Wilkerson engages it, he does so with the stubborn pride of a self-taught perfectionist, and with the conviction that judging McNeil or Garrison-Jackson by anything other than the same absolute standard that applies to their rivals is patronizing as well as symptomatic of the most powerful racial problem in tennis. So while Wilkerson was proud that Garrison-Jackson reached the Wimbledon final, he felt frustrated when his former protégé returned to Houston as "a conquering hero." And he was further dismayed when Garrison-Jackson appeared to have her head turned by all the attention.

"I told Zina, when you go into the losers' locker room after the Super Bowl or an NBA game, there is no celebration. If Monica Seles or Steffi Graf lost in the final, she would be sad. It all depends on what standard you set for yourself and what you want to achieve. All I'd like is for my kids to expect as much out of life and out of themselves as those who went in with greater advantages. Anything short of that means they're not getting or giving themselves a fair deal."

You could take exception to Wilkerson's attitude on the grounds that many other players of either sex or any race would have been equally proud to reach the final of the greatest tournament in the world—especially on the wings of wins over such players as Seles and Graf. And you could argue that Garrison-Jackson's glass is not half-full, but almost up to the brim.

Wilkerson's exacting standards ultimately began to grate on Garrison-Jackson, and coach and pupil were drifting apart at about the time she began to date the man she would eventually marry, Willard Jackson. And while the 1993 WTA media guide told you that, among other things, Garrison-Jackson's favorite musical producer was Narada Michael Walden, that she enjoyed making her own painted T-shirts, and that Chinese and Mexican were among her favorite foods, the book contained no mention whatsoever of Wilkerson.

After his split with Garrison-Jackson, Wilkerson soldiered on with McNeil, even though that relationship also showed signs of strain—particularly at the time McNeil began to pal around with Robin Givens and her former husband, the ex-heavyweight boxing champion and convicted rapist Mike Tyson. McNeil leaped from the sports pages to the gossip pages after Tyson allegedly punched her in the nose during a domestic altercation with Givens.

Wilkerson showed forbearance through that period, and he continued to fight the good fight, working tirelessly to improve McNeil's game, and to keep her from spinning off into the void that seems to threaten quasi-celebrities. And in the end that's what made Wilkerson such a rare individual—his larger, moral perspective, his conviction that how a life is lived is just as important as what it produces and that the way one lives can affect what one produces.

Paraphrasing a discussion he often had with McNeil, Wilkerson once told me, "The way I see it, values can make your forehand fly into the fence or lead you to hit a double fault. Every time a player makes contact with the ball, her value system is put on the line. What does she care about? Why is she doing what she's doing? How does she feel about herself, her habits, her friends? And a pressure situation is nothing more than a strong test of that value system.

"I'm not saying that the great players, pressure players, have good values because some people just have an abundance of natural ability, and a powerful desire to win. But someone who doesn't have that clarity and confidence is going to be either really hurt by having a faulty value system, or really helped by developing a good one. That part I'm sure about."

Such homilies are difficult enough for anyone to follow, but they are particularly challenging for inner-city kids bewitched by the wealth.

"It is very, very hard to convince kids that they're looking for gratification in the wrong place," Wilkerson told me. "That's why I tell every kid who comes my way to hit the ball well, first of all. Think of the matches, then the titles, then the big titles. And if you do that, all the rest of it—the money, the fame, the celebrity—will take care of itself.

"Over the years, it's become much harder to convince kids of the wisdom of that. You see, I was taught that money doesn't mean anything, and I *still* think it doesn't mean anything. But the money mentality has become so pervasive in tennis, especially as an incentive for minority kids, that I'm not even sure I'd want my own daughters to play pro tennis. If you look around, it's easy to come to the conclusion that pro tennis is a dead-end street for most kids. Money is like drugs—it can bring ruin to the life of anyone, rich or poor, black or white. It's amazing to see how much material success tennis players have and how few of them come out of the experience healthy.

"You know what I tell my nine-year-old students? I just tell them that God loves them and that they should love themselves. If they don't do that, they won't ever develop the values that might protect them from all the pitfalls along the way."

Wilkerson may be the descendant of sharecroppers and a man who took up tennis at eighteen, knowing as little of the game's traditions as he knew of its technique. But he fit right into the traditional tennis community. He may sound like an idealist, but his approach was a proven one. Many great champions came out of households where tennis was a way of life for reasons that had nothing to do with money: Chris Evert, Jimmy Connors, Ivan Lendl, Tracy Austin, and a host of other champions were motivated principally by the urge to excel at a game their parents loved. If the best reason to pursue a career in tennis is because you love the game, the next best reason to like tennis is that it is a proven vehicle of self-improvement and upward mobility. Ashe, Noah, and Goolagong could have told you that, as could countless others going back to the amateur era when white players such as Frank Parker and Fred Perry used tennis to improve their stations in life.

But the more tennis becomes just another sport offering little more than a huge payout for a successful pro, the crazier it is to place your hopes and dreams into it unless you have money to burn. As the ante for potential pro players in tennis keeps going up—even while the game purportedly grows more inclusionary—minority players face more, rather than fewer, obstacles. As Wilkerson said: "What stops a lot of potentially great black tennis players is a general process of conditioning. All their lives they've been taught or told or lived in situations where they had to settle for less. In that sense the playing field is never level, because poor black kids already come to a tennis program conditioned to not have all that much."

This process of conditioning causes the most damage at the bottom of the ladder, ensuring that many kids will never even reach the journeyman level, much less a Grand Slam final. Wilkerson has coached kids whose parents bought them all the expensive brand-name tennis equipment they wanted but balked at paying for lessons because, as he put it, "nobody can see a lesson later; it has no status value comparable to the tag on a pair of designer jeans."

Similarly, Wilkerson has observed as well as coached kids whose idea of success is getting onto the "free list" of equipment manufacturers, or attracting sponsorship. The free list is a potent marketing tool for equipment manufacturers hoping to implant brand identification in the public and brand loyalty in the players. Given the spiraling cost of clothing, shoes, and rackets, along with the status value with which they are imbued, getting on the free lists of manufacturers is one of the first steps in the validation of a prospective player. But for many minority youth it is also the last step, and one beyond which they cannot see.

"Given where they're coming from," Wilkerson said, "you can see how these kids feel as if they've made it in tennis because they get free shoes, clothes, and rackets. For them, reaching that stage is like winning Wimbledon, so how can you expect them to want Wimbledon?"

In Philadelphia during one tournament, Wilkerson noticed that a nine-year-old girl kept smiling at him while she was playing a junior match. After it was over, she ran over to him and asked, "Can you help me get free equipment or a sponsor?"

"You already have a sponsor," Wilkerson replied. "God."

"Where did she get that mentality?" Wilkerson later wondered. "How can a nine-year-old come up and say that? She was bold, and you know that's great—if she learns how to use her boldness in the right way. That's that value thing again. What is important to this girl? There's one kid who needs to tap into what is and isn't important, but that has gotten harder as time goes on."

Unfortunately, the rate of attrition among gifted minority youth is awfully high. Skip Hartmann, an operator of indoor tennis clubs and president of the New York Junior League, is an expert on the subject. Hartmann has invested enormous time, energy, and money into creating feasible talent identification and development programs for minority youth in New York. Hartmann has had little trouble finding talented kids willing to endure long bus rides, cold indoor practice facilities, and a host of other obstacles and frustrations that come with mastering a sport that requires a high level of skill and discipline. But inevitably, something happens to the kids. With the onset of puberty, they become hormones in sneakers, and the impact is felt in every area of their lives.

"That's when we lose most of them," Hartmann told me. "At puberty. That's when they start to feel peer pressure. They also begin to develop social awareness. A lot of these players begin to take flack back in the neighborhoods, where basketball and football players have all the status, because they pursue a sport that isn't played on the streets, one that's associated with rich white people. Like any other kids, they want to fit in but not necessarily conform. So they drift away. The ones who rebel often do so against tennis. It's an obvious outlet."

Long after Wilkerson rode to the top of the game with Garrison-Jackson and McNeil, he still had hopes of going back to the future by creating and running his own tennis training facility, designed to tutor the same kind of children who originally came to him so long ago in MacGregor Park. Thus far, Wilkerson's efforts have not panned out. This is partly because Wilkerson is adamant about retaining control of the operation—a demand that does not fly well with organizations such as the USTA, or with some potential private investors. Some critics also suggest that a self-taught privateer who did not compete at the highest level of the game can't succeed in the increasingly competitive field of tennis training, yet Nick Bollettieri's history as a player is even less impressive than that of Wilkerson. Bollettieri, however, did develop a much stronger game on the vital playing fields of self-promotion and corporate schmoozing, and he did so without citing moral imperatives that are bound to make some people uneasy.

When we last spoke, Wilkerson was discouraged about his prospects. But as he said, "Every morning I say a simple prayer: 'Here I am, God, use me as you wish.' Meanwhile, I'm just holding my ground. I know I'm a stubborn person, but I'm willing to stick it out rather than compromise what I believe. I've gotten plenty of criticism for not bending my values, but the way I see it, that's just the price you pay for having values to begin with."

It's very difficult to write directly about Arthur Ashe. There's the practical problem presented by the volumes that have already been written about Ashe, many by his own hand. And then there's the emotional problem posed by trying to write about a great man, a consistent and sensible man whose story ended so abruptly and insensibly.

So I'm going to write about Ashe obliquely, which is not as tough an assignment as I expected. For one thing, Ashe himself was oblique—owlish, complex, dispassionate and even remote. For another, Ashe's impact on the world was oblique in that even at the best of times he did not enjoy the luxury of operating on a purely unilateral intellectual level. Because he was an African American, Ashe lived every day of his life in a world environment where race was always an issue.

If there was once such a thing as the "white man's burden," Ashe demonstrated there is now a "black man's burden." And that one may be a hell of a lot heavier. That burden consists partly of two curious forms of racial oppression, and identifying them is central to understanding some things about Ashe: First, a black man cannot succeed in a white society without having to become a spokesman for all black men and women. Second, in the recent social climate it has been all but impossible for a black man to be conservative in his social and political views without having to face the accusation that he is a traitor to his race.

Ashe accepted those two burdens without complaint, as part and parcel of his quiet mission to combat racism. But sometimes they were also intellectual and emotional shackles for Ashe, who had a ubiquitous, free-ranging mind. Furthermore, Ashe had to struggle with the conflicts they posed differently than did his fellow Afro-American personages.

While Ashe was politically and socially a liberal, personally he was a conservative. He emanated complicated and sometimes mixed signals throughout his life, and that was one of the reasons he did not really become a national hero until he was forced to confess that he had AIDS, an affliction that he contracted through transfusions of contaminated blood when he underwent open heart surgeries in 1979 and 1983. When Ashe realized that he was suffering from AIDS in 1992, in the last year of his life, he suddenly found himself on the same footing in the public eye as another AIDS-afflicted athlete-celebrity, Magic Johnson. For a man as distinguished in as many areas as Ashe, that footing represented a giant step not up but down. Ironically, if it were not for his illness—his specific illness—Ashe probably never would have gotten the popular widespread recognition and accolades that he deserved. Not until he disclosed that he was suffering from AIDS did Ashe earn universal recognition as a "role model."

The battle against AIDS was not Ashe's battle of choice. If it were, Ashe would have begun to fight it in 1988, shortly after brain surgery revealed that he had AIDS. We may all be potential victims of AIDS, but Ashe was not of the community in which the disease took its heaviest toll. And as much as he sympathized with the afflicted and saw the general menace posed by AIDS, nothing in his way of life imbued Ashe with passion or fury for the cause.

The great irony in the death of Arthur Ashe is that he was brought low by a disease that put a final, chilling punctuation mark on the very era that in some ways allowed him to rise above and leave his mark on his times. Ashe had the bad luck of living on the seam of two generations. He was a product of the 1950s, which accounted for his discipline, traditional values, patriotic sentiments, and a lifelong dedication to civilized discourse. He was not prepared for the cultural upheaval of the 1960s, and their substance was foreign to him except in one very important way. Ashe was both shaped and empowered by the civil rights movement. Otherwise, Ashe just did not fit into a culture that celebrated promiscuity, made an institution of drug abuse, deified the antihero, and discredited religion while elevating feel-good spiritualism to new heights.

So by the early 1970s, as Ashe was reaching his peak as a tennis player, many of the very principles that guided his life were under heavy fire. And he became a representative of a culture under attack—the culture of quiet striving diplomacy, and communication rather than confrontation.

In the tennis community, where the likes of Ilie Nastase and Jimmy Connors were creating shock waves as the first pros freed from the patrician traditions of the game, Ashe was considered a member of the old guard. He embodied the tennis ethic, honorably observing all of the game's unwritten rules of gentlemanly conduct. His sangfroid was as legendary as his wickedly sliced serve or whiplash backhand. Ashe had such a store of dignity and such a formidable command of himself that he was rarely berated for embodying "white" values and virtues. But at a time when militant rhetoric was the norm, he was not considered much of an activist, either. Ashe preferred to expend his activist urges diplomatically, within the framework of an establishment in which he fundamentally believed until the day he died.

Another reason that Ashe did not transcend the elitist image was the company he kept. Along with Stan Smith, Tom Gorman, Bob Lutz, and others, he was a client, close friend, and staunch ally of superagent Donald Dell. Despite his ambitions and the bullish way he often pursued them, Dell was essentially a member of the old guard. In light of the changes that have transpired since those years (circa 1974), Dell probably represented the most realistic compromise between the traditional and the progressive forces in tennis. Unfortunately, Dell was such an abrasive and arrogant operator that he filled many people with loathing for the traditional tennis community. Thus, Dell's clients (including Ashe) were often perceived as straitlaced minions, blindly and uncritically loyal to a man who manipulated them in order to achieve his own commercial and imperial ambitions. There was a lot of truth to the charges: Dell did try to manipulate everyone around him, often with a startling degree of success. And there really was an arrogance about the Dell faction—a self-righteousness that, while it may have been justified, did nothing to attract people to the traditional standards it represented at a time when such standards were under attack.

I will say this for Dell: His relationship with his clients often transcended the commercial alliance on which it was based. Dell may have manipulated his clients, but it was in a common cause. And nobody could question the genuine friendship and sense of fraternity that existed in the Dell cadre.

Bob Kain of IMG, the man who replaced Dell as the most powerful agent in the professional world of tennis, rarely enjoyed the same relationship with his clients. I once asked Kain if he had ever longed to enjoy a more intimate friendship with clients, or if he was disappointed by his own lack of influence when Bjorn Borg began to flounder, or when Vitas Gerulaitis fell into the throes of cocaine addiction. "It was a different world by the time I got into it," Kain told me. "Those guys didn't really want to be friends with me, and I didn't have any particular desire to share their life-style, which was a new and different lifestyle. We liked each other, but they wanted me to be nothing more or less than a good, honest business manager."

Dell, Ashe, and others were an especially hard sell to the younger generation at a time when the notorious, ever-widening "generation gap" could be measured in paltry installments of five or seven years. Those of us who were between the ages of fifteen and eighteen during the middle of the 1960s were very different from many people less than ten years older than we were. This was true in a broad cultural sense, and it was also true in the tennis environment, as a host of talented young reporters came flooding into this hot, new, reconstructed game called tennis.

Most of this generation—my generation—were from outside the

traditional tennis community, so we didn't properly understand or appreciate the tennis ethic. My generation was bewitched not by the game of tennis and the things that it traditionally represented but by the antics of Nastase and the punk, iconoclastic fury of Connors. There was something too squeaky clean about the Dell constituents in those days, and we took silly pleasure in charting the battle between the conservative and revolutionary factions in tennis. Our sympathies lay mostly with the revolutionaries, on the grounds that they were more "real" or more "honest" or more just plain exciting to watch and write about, as they turned the elitist, exclusionary sport of tennis on its ear.

Ashe, more than anyone else at that time, was an enigma. He was erudite, thoughtful, and polite. But he was also part of that organism vaguely called "the establishment." He had been a collegiate tennis star and then an Army man—a good soldier at a time when countless young people thought the expression was an oxymoron. Ashe was also an apologist for that rough power-monger Dell. He wore short hair and spoke the king's English, a language that many of us couldn't speak or didn't want to understand. But because he was black, white liberals were careful not to criticize him, while African Americans respected his achievements without embracing him wholeheartedly.

For all of those reasons, most people found it hard to get a handle on Ashe. He worked tirelessly for the cause of his people, but he did so mostly in boardrooms, Beltway offices, and other establishment venues. Thus, he existed in a vacuum. He was not inclined to perform on the large, popular stage except on rare occasions, such as the one on which he was arrested while taking part in an anti-apartheid demonstration in Washington. But because of his measured activism and his intellectual pursuits (among other things, Ashe wrote a definitive three-volume history of Afro-American athletes and athletics, *A Hard Road to Glory*), Ashe was beginning to emerge as a man of great distinction if not massive, popular celebrity by the time the smoke left by the revolution of the 1960s was beginning to clear.

And then came AIDS. The disease finally brought Ashe into sharp focus in the public eye, but in a way that did not do justice to his unique personal and intellectual journey.

The terrible truth is that popular culture, for all its cant about racial equality, is still willing to embrace only a certain kind of African American. Ashe was not the kind of man it wanted until the very end, and then only because of a tragic medical accident. Others who do not fill the role demanded by popular culture—General Colin Powell, former U.S. president George Bush's chief of staff, is the best example—must wait for history to pass judgment. Or they must find a way to shock the world into recognition, as Ashe inadvertently did. It was not easy growing up with Arthur Ashe, and it's going to be even harder growing old without him.

I can't really say that I knew Arthur Ashe, and I'm not sure that anybody—with the exception of his immediate family—did, either. I can say that most of the people who said they knew Ashe did so in about the same way they might claim to know a senator, because the man once happened to be invited to the same dinner or cocktail party. Billie Jean King had the honesty and sensitivity to offhandedly acknowledge this during the memorial service held for Ashe in Saint John the Baptist Cathedral on a bleak and snowy morning in New York in the winter of 1992.

King disavowed having any inside track on the "real" Arthur, other than feeling that the real Arthur was a reserved man disinclined to let very many people get close to his person, even though he had no trouble sharing his intellect with anyone. She went on to tell a charming story about Ashe's "cute" ears—a story that provided comic relief from the weighty, wooden testimonials that preceded it. Those testimonials revealed how few people really were close to Ashe, and how thoroughly he had cultivated a complete and handy public self that did not impinge on his private being.

As my friend Marion Gengler and I took our places in a pew at that service, I saw only one active pro player in attendance, Lori McNeil. The turnout of active name players at Ashe's funeral in Richmond, Virginia, a few days earlier, had been even more disappointing. Zina Garrison-Jackson was the only active player among the four thousand souls gathered there. She broke a tournament obligation in order to attend, a sacrifice that none of her male or female peers saw fit to make. This probably tells you as much about the nature and values of the pro tennis community today as anything else you're likely to read in this book.

The single electric moment of the service occurred when John McEnroe and his brother, Patrick, arrived, all eyes regarding them as they walked down the broad aisle of the cathedral. John was all scrunched up in a tailored overcoat, wearing the special scowl he reserves for most public occasions.

We sat with Peter Fleming and his wife, Jenny. Fleming and McEnroe, one of the great doubles teams of the Open era, played Davis Cup under Ashe on many occasions. They were rash young men of a different generation, and they frequently clashed with Ashe on issues ranging from conduct to coaching to appropriate dress. Ashe and McEnroe happened to be the two most successful Davis Cup singles players in U.S. history. McEnroe, whose Davis Cup career spanned fourteen years, broke Ashe's record in the most prestigious category, singles victories. McEnroe won forty-one matches, while Ashe won twenty-seven. McEnroe played the most singles matches, forty-nine, followed by Vic Seixas (thirty-six) and Ashe (thirty-two). The one department in which Ashe led McEnroe was the only one in which McEnroe still has a chance of eclipsing Ashe—the captaincy records. McEnroe has yet to serve as Davis Cup captain, while Ashe's tenure as captain lasted for five years, from 1981 to 1985. He won the third-highest number of ties as a U.S. captain, thirteen, trailing two men who each held the captaincy for seven years. Tom Gorman accumulated seventeen victories while Tony Trabert led the U.S. to fourteen wins.

Ashe's top player during his years of captaincy was McEnroe. Nevertheless, the relationship between Ashe and McEnroe was always a fragile one, held together by Ashe's diplomatic abilities and McEnroe's absolute dedication to the Davis Cup. Unlike his rival Jimmy Connors, McEnroe tried to set aside politics and personality conflicts when he was asked to represent his nation in the Davis Cup. He also took special satisfaction from the ensemble nature of the competition, which Connors did not.

One of the great differences between Ashe and McEnroe was that Ashe believed in two things that were anathema to McEnroe. Throughout his career Ashe believed in observing standards of good conduct, and he felt they were particularly important in Davis Cup competition, in which a player was not representing merely himself but his nation. And Ashe was by nature a man who always believed in working within the establishment to exert his influence and achieve his ends. McEnroe was notorious for his bad temper, and he had nothing but contempt for the establishment in which he operated (in the case of Davis Cup, the USTA) unless its ends were compatible with his own personal goals.

Most of the time, these vital differences and their dramatic manifestations did not become a source of conflict between Ashe and McEnroe. For one thing, McEnroe was always acutely conscious of his conduct, even when he appeared to be in the throes of a purple rage. By and large, he kept his temper under control in Davis Cup matches. And Ashe, conversant with McEnroe's behavioral disorders, had a fine feeling for allowing slack in the reins without letting them go. But their separate peace was not destined to last, and a controversy finally put them on the outs and prematurely shattered a great U.S. Davis Cup renaissance in 1984.

That year, the Swedes hosted the final round at Christmastime in Gothenburg. They had a fine squad led by Mats Wilander and Henrik Sundstrom, while the United States had a great one featuring McEnroe and Jimmy Connors. But Connors was preoccupied with the pending birth of his second child back at his California home, and he was too much of a lone warrior to fit comfortably into the U.S. team—a squad whose leader was his hot rival, McEnroe.

As for McEnroe, he was coming off a three-week suspension for an ugly outburst during a tournament played just months earlier in nearby Stockholm. To top things off, the Swedes had chosen to install a slow indoor clay court in the hall where the tie was to be played, an ambush tactic that made the Americans edgy.

The United States lost the first three matches (and thus the tie) in short order, but the real crisis was germinated in the way the United States lost. In the first match of the tie, Connors versus Wilander, the American came within a hair's breadth of being defaulted. He was censured and fined $2,000 for his frequent audible obscenities and generally appalling behavior. McEnroe did not behave badly during his matches, at least not by his own standards, but he was incommunicative, surly, and rude at the "official" functions that are part and parcel of the Davis Cup competition. Peter Fleming, McEnroe's doubles partner, and Jimmy Arias, who would replace Connors in the meaningless fifth match of the tie, were also accused of arrogant and insolent behavior. Lined up for the opening and closing ceremonies, the Americans chewed gum, laughed, joked, and fidgeted around as if they found the proceedings laughable. In short, they were perceived as the quintessentially Ugly Americans, making a mockery of the pageantry and dignity of Davis Cup competition.

The behavior of the American team—a team whose captain was the impeccable sportsman, Ashe—sent shock waves through the sports world, moving even those observers and commentators who didn't pay much attention to tennis at the best of times to censure the team as a national disgrace.

This sentiment was shared by the sponsor of the team, the wood products company Louisiana-Pacific. Its president, Harry Merlo, left Gothenburg claiming that the experience there made him "embarrassed to be an American." He subsequently wrote a letter to the USTA threatening to withdraw Louisiana-Pacific's sponsorship if the organization did not institute a code of conduct. Merlo released the letter to the press shortly after sending it off to USTA functionaries and Davis Cup team members. The players, including McEnroe and Connors, claimed that they learned about the letter from media reports. They felt that the matter should have been settled behind closed doors, and they accused Louisiana-Pacific of "grandstanding" for public relations reasons.

Ashe, ever sophisticated, knew that the players' complaints rested on a curious combination of cynicism, naïveté, and arrogance. In the aftermath he told me, "The players are used to everybody kowtowing to them, and they're accustomed to having their own way. But Harry Merlo is a CEO, a big shot. He's used to doing anything he damned well pleases, at any time he chooses. And in this case he was driven by his own sense of right and wrong. As team captain I can't side with Merlo, but I completely understand his position. He basically stood up and said that he doesn't have to take this kind of embarrassment, not with the kind of money he's putting up, and for the reason he's putting it up. The man feels like he has egg on his face."

Brian S. Parrot, Louisiana-Pacific's Davis Cup point man, also made a few astute remarks. "The appalling behavior in question occurred in public and before millions of viewers. So why should it be discussed behind closed doors? We've seen too many tennis sponsors get fed up and quietly withdraw. The changeover is bad for the game. The popular logic suggests that the top players don't care about public opinion, but I maintain the opposite. Public opinion is all they care about. That's why they're so upset by the stand we've taken."

That final observation was both a gem and a signal that the sponsor meant business. The USTA embraced the hard line, drew up a formal code of conduct, and announced that henceforth, all Davis Cup nominees would have to sign and abide by the document. The players were outraged, insisting that Merlo's demand was a publicity stunt, and that the code was silly, redundant, and demeaning.

No crisis in tennis ever put Ashe in a more painful, conflicting role than the Davis Cup standoff. He took pains to point out that McEnroe's on-court behavior was, if not charming, at least acceptable. ("He got painted with Jimmy's brush," Ashe said. "I think when people heard about the tie, they were still thinking about the way John had behaved in Stockholm and assumed that he made a similar scene in Gothenburg.") Fleming observed that during the winter following the debacle in Gothenburg, Ashe was "walking a tightrope."

Others perceived a larger, sad truth about the American squad: It was a team that did not know how to be a team in either spirit or formal behavior. And its captain was hamstrung between enforcing standards imposed from above (but standards in which he also deeply believed), and trying to run a successful team built around a proud, selfish, unyielding individualist, McEnroe. Gene Scott, a former Davis Cup player and publisher of the newspaper *Tennis Week,* even found a legalistic compromise based on the legally binding nature of some verbal contracts. If the players pledged to support the code, they would be spared the embarrassment of having to sign the document.

My own question was a simple one: If the document was so silly and redundant, why not just sign the stupid thing—as an act of atonement

and good faith, and a concession to an offended sponsor—and get on
with the successful campaign to bring the Davis Cup competition back
to national prominence in the United States? When you come right
down to it, the egos simply got in the way, and the budding American
dynasty came crashing down. Neither McEnroe nor the USTA would
back down. Thus, the United States played its first tie in 1985 against
undergunned Japan in Tokyo, with a team that consisted of Eliot
Teltscher, Aaron Krickstein, and the outstanding doubles team of Ken
Flach and Robert Seguso. The United States forged an easy 5–0 win.

But the next stop for Ashe and company was Germany and a date
with a team led by an explosive new talent, Boris Becker. The emerging
star defeated Eliot Teltscher in straight sets in the opening match of the
tie, and then Hansjorg Schwaier, Germany's number two singles player,
upset Krickstein, 8-6 in the fifth set, to give Germany a 2–0 lead. The
United States climbed back into the tie on the backs of Flach and
Seguso, and Teltscher's subsequent win over Schwaier. But in the decisive fifth rubber, Becker decimated Krickstein, 6–2, 6–2, 6–1.

The loss to Germany ended Ashe's tenure as Davis Cup captain. You
could argue that he was a casualty of McEnroe's hubris and that the two
men had too little in common to make a sincere effort to find a way out
of the quandary. The only mitigating circumstance was that at the time
McEnroe was spinning toward a personal crisis. Although he reached
three quarterfinals and a final in Grand Slam events in 1985 (he lost the
U.S. Open championship match to Ivan Lendl), he would soon declare
that he was burned out, cash in his chips, and head out to Hollywood
to woo the woman he would marry, the actress Tatum O'Neal.

For the next few years, the U.S. Davis Cup team would limp along
under the able leadership of Ashe's successor, Tom Gorman, losing to
the likes of Australia (1986) and Paraguay (1987). Andre Agassi would
lead the team to the championship in 1990 and 1992, but McEnroe
never played singles on a winning team after the debacle in Gothenburg.

You can accuse McEnroe of being many things, but he has never been
a hypocrite. That helps explain why, when I called to ask him for an official comment on Ashe's death, he declined to give me one. I had also
asked Fleming to think about his relationship with Ashe and to give me
a comment or an anecdote that would shed light on him. Fleming never
got back to me, either, and he later told me over a friendly dinner that
he just couldn't think of anything that would have been appropriate.

McEnroe must have entertained a plethora of conflicting emotions
and thoughts as he sat in his pew at the memorial service for Ashe. He
paid attention during the entire service, as one distinguished speaker
after another recited the litany of Ashe's achievements, causes, and

interests. Afterward I chatted with about a dozen people, all of whom had at one point or another been struck internally by the same question: What could McEnroe have been thinking, and how was he to measure his own life and achievements against those of Ashe?

On that day, I would not have wanted to be in McEnroe's shoes. To tell you the truth, I wasn't even all that comfortable in my own. And while I don't know what McEnroe was thinking on that doleful occasion, I do know that since that time he has become a formidable, silent backer of many of the institutions and programs created by Ashe. And he has never made a public pronouncement about his activities unless it was to advance and publicize the cause.

But back to Arthur. When I first began to spend a lot of time around tennis, in my mid-twenties, I didn't have very strong feelings about Ashe. A journalist thrives on spontaneous engagement with his subject, and that was almost impossible with Ashe. For all his erudition and eloquence, Arthur was too aloof to be a great "communicator." He was acutely aware of the weight his words carried, so he doled them out carefully, in a restrained tenor voice. He learned early on how to budget his time, so he also developed an auto-pilot function that I always described as "interview mode." At such times his eyes would get slightly glazed, and his ears would only half-listen for those things that he needed to pick out in order to satisfy the interviewer. He was so damned accustomed to explaining things, from his tennis to his background to his social and political convictions, that he tended to recite.

Also, for many years I saw tennis as little more than an attractive, esoteric, chaotic game that kept churning out a bizarre assortment of characters. And whatever else Ashe may have been early or late in his life, bizarre was not one of them. On the whole, it was a lot easier to skip over Ashe and go running off, pen in hand, to pick the brain of Nastase, Connors, Eddie Dibbs, Harold Solomon, or any number of other jocks who were inclined to shoot off their mouths, often delivering outrageous bon mots and observations.

But later, when I began to define and appreciate the tennis ethic, I became much more interested in Ashe. And over the years I got to know him well enough so that at times I did walk away from him feeling not as if I'd merely been granted an interview, but had actually shared a conversation with the man.

For many years Arthur was on the masthead of *Tennis* magazine. After one meeting in Connecticut, we drove back to our Upper East Side neighborhood together. We had a wonderful conversation during those two hours, and I finally got my chance to ask Arthur how he reconciled his conservative nature and his liberal political beliefs. Arthur told me that while he sometimes felt trapped by his role as an activist for African-American progress, rejecting that role would cause him even more problems—problems of conscience as well as problems of public perception. "But you know, there's something liberating about the situation I'm in, too," he mused. "It's similar to the security you feel in the armed forces. You know what your job is, the job is pretty strictly defined, and you believe in the cause. It brings a certain amount of meaning and order to your life."

What struck me most powerfully on that occasion was Arthur's thorough familiarity with political and social philosophy, including a broad knowledge—and appreciation—of conservative African-American writers and thinkers. Reflexively liberal people living in a society dominated by liberal thinkers and media are always vulnerable to the charge that they are intellectually lazy and disinclined to put their convictions to the test. That could never be said of Ashe. I realized during that trip that he was neither a political animal nor an intellectual. He was an inquisitive, open-minded, practical thinker—a keen social observer rather than a mere partisan.

Although Arthur was not a man known for his humor, he had a dry wit and a fine sense of irony. I had one brief interlude with him that not only demonstrated that but, despite its superficial nature, defined the essence of Arthur Ashe as well as anything he ever wrote or said.

I found myself standing with Ashe up in the top deck of the media center in Flushing Meadow at the U.S. Open of 1991, during a match between Jimmy Connors and Aaron Krickstein. I inquired about Ashe's health, and he told me that he was "up and down" and still dealing with complications related to his brain surgery. Those "complications" were his infection with HIV.

Nineteen ninety-one was the year that Connors, at the unlikely age of thirty-nine, enjoyed his riveting, sensational run to the semifinals at Flushing Meadow—a run characterized by a series of remarkable comebacks against the likes of Patrick McEnroe, Paul Haarhuis, and Krickstein. Round after round, Connors's escapades whipped the crowd in Louis B. Armstrong Stadium into a frenzy. So Ashe and I stood there in the bright sunshine watching as Connors clawed his way back into his match with Krickstein before a vociferous, SRO crowd. After yet another display of his acrobatic shotmaking, Connors pumped his arms and began grinding his hips in that delicate way that we all know and love. The crowd went ballistic. Arthur chuckled, shaking his head.

Early on, Ashe and Connors had been as close as you can get to being enemies without one having shot the other. Ashe had often been openly critical of Connors's rudeness and vulgarity. Connors had often expressed contempt for Ashe's behavior and etiquette, citing him as exactly the kind of tennis player the game had to be rid of in order to achieve mass popularity. Part of the antagonism between Ashe and Connors had to do with their managers. Bill Riordan, Connors's agent, was a Barnumesque character who never tired of taking cheap shots at the conservative faction in tennis, and he harbored a special loathing for Dell. So when Connors emerged as the top American player among a host of Dell clients, Riordan took every opportunity to denigrate Dell—and vice versa.

There was also the little matter of the 1975 Wimbledon final, in which Ashe reached the high point of his career at Connors's expense. At the time, Connors was the best player on earth, and he was playing with confidence and unbridled fury. Anybody who picked Ashe to win that final did so not out of conviction or insight, but on the slim chance that if the unthinkable did indeed occur, he would be dubbed either a genius or a psychic.

Ashe went into that match and executed the most brilliant bit of strategic thinking and playing that I've ever seen. He figured out that Connors had trouble returning a soft, low ball in the midcourt area on his forehand side. He also knew that Connors thrived on pace and relished the challenge of hitting on the run, from the corners of the court, where he had plenty of options to exploit with his precise, powerful ground strokes.

So Ashe decided to handcuff Connors by taking the pace off the ball and preventing Connors from hitting on the run. He achieved this by employing a dazzling array of dinks, chips, drop shots, and slices. Connors reacted like a skittish horse tied up in a stall during a thunderstorm. He snorted, pawed, bucked, and tried to force his way into a running and hitting match. Ashe kept that from happening, and he won, 6–1, 6–1, 5–7, 6–4.

And then there were odds and ends, including the Davis Cup fiasco under Ashe in Sweden.

So my question to Arthur that day during the Connors-Krickstein match was a simple one, and I'll ask you to forgive its intrinsic vulgarity on the grounds of accurate testimony: "So, Arthur, what's the bottom line? Is Jimmy Connors really just an asshole?"

Ashe pondered the question for a few moments before he replied, "Yeah. But he's my *favorite* asshole."

My last private encounter with Ashe occurred before an exhibition match staged on behalf of his own Safe Passage Foundation, a charity for troubled kids. The event took place in Mahwah, New Jersey, as part of maverick promoter John Korff's exhibition in July 1992. After shaking hands and making the rounds during an informal dinner reception, Arthur joined my party of three at our table. Both Arthur and his wife, Jeanne, enjoyed fishing, and I happened to be sitting with my buddy and fellow fisherman, Joel Aronoff. So we spent a good part of the dinner hour talking about the excellent striped bass fishing in Long Island Sound, near Ashe's Westchester digs. Arthur became very enthusiastic about the prospect of taking Jeanne and their daughter Camera out striper fishing, and we offered to take the Ashes out for a day on the Sound in Joel's boat. We picked a few tentative dates, and Arthur gave me his unlisted number so that we could finalize plans.

When I called a few days later, our first date proved unworkable. Ashe had to go to Washington for an unexpected, important meeting. It was not the first time that Arthur had been forced to cancel a fishing trip, but it was the last time. Our fallback date didn't work out because Arthur's health took a turn for the worse, and it proved to be the beginning of his end. Thinking about it later, I realized that the worst thing about being Arthur Ashe was not that he had to give up some things that he truly enjoyed, but that he had grown so accustomed to sacrifice that it hardly seemed to bother him. I shudder to think of how much of himself Ashe gave away as he trod his own hard road to glory.

But along the way, he also developed fierce intellectual honesty. At Mahwah, he also told me about a dinner party he had recently attended at the home of a prominent Beltway African-American family. One of the boys in the family was a university student on a special minority scholarship. According to Arthur, the dinner became the setting for an intense debate. Playing devil's advocate, Arthur suggested that the student, whose family was wealthy, was probably depriving a poor African-American student who may have been no more deserving, but was considerably more needy. Arthur's position triggered an animated discussion of the values embraced by the bourgeois African-American community, and I'll never forget the excitement in his voice as he described the ideas bandied about that evening. The conversation occurred at a time when it seemed that the excitement was long gone from Arthur's voice, and person. Funny how wrong you can be.

CHAPTER 12

The Gals of Babylon,
Part Two

JANE BROWN, a former head of the Women's International Tennis
Council and the International Tennis Hall of Fame in Newport, Rhode
Island, was invited a few years ago to the wilds of New Brunswick,
Canada. She was to fish for the prized Atlantic salmon at Runnymeade
Lodge, the splendid camp owned by Joseph B. Cullman III of Philip
Morris Inc., the company that manufactures Virginia Slims cigarettes.
The other lucky guests invited to fish on the Restigouche River that
week included Chris Evert and Pam Shriver.

Cullman had the women flown up in the Philip Morris company jet.
Shortly after the women disembarked at Charlo Airport—a modest
airstrip where an impressive, unlikely fleet of corporate jets stands
parked wing to wing during the height of salmon season—they were
trundled into one of the camp station wagons for the sixty-minute run
to Runnymeade. Lorne Mann, Cullman's camp manager, began to drive
and soon lit a cigarette.

Evert coughed. Shriver cleared her throat.

A short while later, Lorne fired up another butt. One of the tennis
players rolled down her window. The other one made a remark under
her breath. If you have fished with salmon guides in New Brunswick
(and I have, often), you will know that they are not big on indirect communication. They aren't even particularly big on direct communication.

By the time Lorne lit up yet another smoke, Evert and Shriver were
making oblique, audible remarks about having to share a car with a
smoker. Brown, a sophisticated woman, became embarrassed. She made
an elliptical reference to something that both of her companions knew
all too well—that Philip Morris had not only been the largest sponsor
in the history of women's professional tennis but the key player in the
very genesis of that tour.

"That has nothing to do with it," Shriver said.

"It smells terrible in here," Evert added.

"Well, let's try to be a little tolerant," Brown said. "We're almost there anyway."

When Brown related this story to me later, she was still amazed that neither Shriver nor Evert, two women who had been politically active in women's tennis, seemed to understand the vital link between cigarettes and their own lives, or the way each of them had been a de facto marketing agent for Virginia Slims in exchange for having made personal fortunes as a result of Virginia Slims sponsorship. Each of the women existed in a state of denial, willfully or subconsciously suppressing fundamental facts of their professional lives. In the end, Philip Morris may have done its job too well, Brown felt, and become so entrenched in the women's game, in so subtle and powerful a way, that even the most famous of players perceived Virginia Slims less as a product and company than the entity called women's tennis.

Obviously, the partnership between cigarettes and tennis is a bizarre one. But the nature of that relationship is not nearly as interesting as the story of how it came about in the first place, and the nature of the organism that this critical, revolutionary partnership ultimately created, the women's pro tour.

In the early 1960s, the amateur game of tennis was in a state of stagnation. One of the most perspicacious witnesses to that condition was Gladys Heldman, founder of the magazine *World Tennis*. She was an energetic, outspoken, provocative, special-interest journalist, much like Philippe Chartier had been early in his career. The crucial difference between them was that Chartier championed the spirit of amateurism, while Heldman was a visionary proto-professional.

Heldman was a creative, intelligent Houstonian armed with a robust entrepreneurial spirit. But her "progressive" views posed an implicit threat to the amateur establishment, and as a woman she was at a distinct disadvantage when dealing with the conservative male-dominated hierarchy that ran the USLTA (back then, "Lawn" was still part of the U.S. Tennis Association's official name). She needed a male patron, and she found one in the future head of Philip Morris, Joseph Cullman. Both spirited tennis nuts, Heldman and Cullman were doubles partners, close friends, and like-minded entrepreneurs. They were youthful, energetic, and highly impatient with the elephantine workings of the amateur tennis establishment. Owen Williams, a former South African player and tennis promoter who would, among other things, serve as tournament director of the U.S. Open under Cullman, put it this way: "Joe and Gladys were just full of ambition and fire. They loved tennis, and they saw the potential it had as a pro sport. They also saw how the sleepy, conservative establishment was an impediment to the growth of the game. So they got on their wagon, and soon they were riding along, lobbing firebombs into the tennis community to wake people up."

It did not take Heldman long to demonstrate her promotional proficiency. At the onset of the 1960s, the U.S. National Championships (also known as the U.S. Open) appeared to be moribund. Over the years, fewer and fewer foreign players, who were still subject to amateur regulations, had chosen to make the costly trip to New York in order to compete in the nationals at the West Side Tennis Club in Forest Hills, Queens, even though it was one of the four gilded Grand Slam events.

Heldman came up with a brainstorm that she ran by the president of the WSTC, Augie Millang. She suggested that the club charter a plane to airlift eighty-five of the best international players to New York. Millang flew the idea by USLTA president Ed Turville, who was amenable to it. Heldman then raised the money for the plane by leaning on nine friends, each of whom wrote an $1,800 check to cover the cost of the charter. If the tournament could recoup that amount in profits, Heldman and her friends would be repaid their investments.

The next step was procuring living expenses for the players. Heldman decided that the cost would be $125 per player, and she wrote 130 letters to friends and acquaintances, asking each of them to sponsor a player. She also hit on the novel idea of selling corporate boxes and marquee seats, throwing a variety of social activities into the package. As a result, the U.S. Championships of 1962, in which Rod Laver became only the second man in tennis history to complete a Grand Slam, was an enormous success. The tournament raked in about $100,000 more than it had during the previous year, and Heldman and her fellow investors were paid back.

This was one of the early, key battles to establishing professionalism in tennis. Those struggles would grow increasingly savage over the next few years as a novel, energetic commercial spirit appeared in the tennis community, infecting all who came into contact with it. The establishment (the leaders of the ITF and its affiliates) disdained the "commercialization" of tennis, but they could not withstand the allure of the money, expanded public interest, and power promised by a vigorous professional game. They often talked one game and played another. They wanted entrepreneurial types to revive the game, but they were deathly afraid of losing power to them.

One of the establishment's greatest practical fears was the prospect of being held hostage by professional players who enjoyed unilateral freedom to play where and when they wished. The establishment wanted to protect its own status as the principal power and promoter in organized tennis. Thus, through much of the 1960s, as the inevitable professionalization of tennis picked up steam, the establishment kept fighting a rearguard action to retain control of the players, thereby ensuring that they would support ITF events.

The establishment's bargaining tools were its ownership of the pre-eminent Grand Slam events and the prestigious Davis Cup and Federation Cup competitions, and its status as the organizer and administrator of the game. For instance, the "official" national rankings were issued by ITF affiliates, and they were the last and only word on the matter since day one of tennis history.

Thus, in the 1960s, the establishment came up with guidelines that players had to observe in order to remain in "good standing" with their tennis associations. These usually demanded that the players be available for Davis Cup duty and also compete in a modest number of domestic tournaments. Otherwise, they were free to do as they wished—provided their actions did not threaten the well-being of the association. If the players refused to comply with the association's demands, they could be suspended and thus denied the chance to play in Grand Slam events. They would also be ineligible for inclusion in the all-important national rankings.

Most of the activist ITF types felt that if this system could be made to work, the establishment would reap the rewards of increasing com-mercialization without jeopardizing its power in tennis. The die was cast when the All-England Lawn Tennis and Croquet Club declared in 1967 that it would not ban professional players from Wimbledon. The USLTA fell into line with the AELTCC and promptly accepted the offer of Philip Morris sponsorship of the first U.S. Open in 1968.

Joe Cullman, who had been elected chairman of the board of Philip Morris by then, immediately became the most powerful man in Amer-ican tennis. And the Marlboro Man, riding high on his horse over the vast western prairie, became a fixture above the delicately manicured lawns at the effete, eastern, WASP stronghold, the West Side Tennis Club. Ah, the Marlboro Man. The rugged, outdoorsy, steely-eyed icon of two generations, the enduring, quintessentially masculine symbol of independence and self-reliance, the most identifiable advertising image ever created, and the most powerful tool in marketing history.

Although it was not very long before the bow-legged Marlboro Man was replaced by the stick-legged flapper Ginny, the Virginia Slims logo, the original smoking cowboy was a key player in the evolution of ten-nis. This condition abounds with ironies, but the most delicious one of all is the element of gender bending that occurred in the evolution of the product long before it occurred in the evolution of the tennis tour that would market it.

Marlboro cigarettes were introduced in the 1920s, behind the ad theme, 'Mild as May." Their target audience was women, but the cigarettes never really caught the public's fancy. The makers then added an ivory tip, but women complained that it became unsightly when it was smeared with lipstick. Philip Morris's clever riposte was to change to a red tip. Sales climbed, but not enough to keep the company from pulling the product during the war years. After the war, Marlboro returned. It had the ivory tip once again, but this time wrapped around a filter. At the time, filter-tipped cigarettes were considered effeminate, and the appeal of the brand was limited to female smokers.

Stymied, Philip Morris executives took their problem child, Marlboro, to the Chicago image therapist and ad wizard Leo Burnett in 1954. After studying Marlboro's case history, Burnett offered a drastic diagnosis. He felt that the only way to defeat the "effete" image of the brand was to cut it loose from all previous associations and to couch its appeal in the bold, individualistic, rugged elements of the traditional "masculine" sensibility. The result of this drastic redesign was the now immortal Marlboro flip-top box, in striking red and white with black lettering. Burnett also suggested that the ads feature male cowboys who inhabited a place that would come to be known as Marlboro Country, a place that suggested all the things with which Marlboro cigarettes wished to be associated.

It was pure, distilled marketing genius, as the remarkable, continuing success of the brand proves. But one of the most astonishing and unpredictable effects of the campaign was the appeal that Marlboro cigarettes held for women. Without knowing it, Philip Morris had tapped into a powerful, broad cultural movement that would soon express itself much more overtly in the feminist movement. As it turned out, almost everybody wanted, as the slogan suggested, to "come to Marlboro Country."

In a 1988 article in the magazine *Advertising Age,* Fred Danzig noted that up to that time, Marlboro had enjoyed twenty-two consecutive years of growth and, in 1988, delivered more than $6 billion in sales. Thus, Marlboro cigarettes alone would have ranked somewhere in the mid-sixties on the Fortune 500 list of mega-companies. And when Marlboro launched a line of outdoor work and leisure apparel, company executives were shocked to see how many women eagerly snapped up the product, just as they had Marlboro cigarettes. Three Texas women even called the clothing company and tried to buy three mail-order cowboys.

The antismoking movement in the United States has recently thrown some massive roadblocks into the path of the tobacco industry, but Marlboro Country knows no boundaries. Tobacco companies have been targeting more smoker-friendly nations, and it appears that hundreds of thousands of Chinese, Filipino, and Latin American folks also identify with the sensibility of the Marlboro man. Marlboro Country has proven to be a state of mind that transcends gender. It is at once a quiescent lotusland and a wild and woolly frontier, open to all who aspire to be like the Marlboro Man. And the crowning touch is that, despite the masculine, frontier values projected by the Marlboro Man, the original model for the campaign was gay. And he died of lung cancer.

Cullman's sponsorship of the U.S. Open was such a success, and the lobbying efforts of Heldman on his behalf were so powerful, that the following year he was asked to be tournament director at Forest Hills. According to his contemporaries, Cullman's only condition for accepting the job was that he would not have to answer to the USLTA bigwigs who appointed him. He was far too intelligent and successful a man to put himself at the mercy of patrician volunteers who were largely ignorant of the rough-and-tumble world of big business. The USLTA acquiesced, and as a direct result, the 1969 U.S. Open was the first of our national championships to receive nationwide television coverage, on the CBS network. This deal was struck on the golf links by Cullman and the president of CBS. Presto, pro tennis was off and running in the new era, its future all but secured by a commitment from a national network television.

Suddenly, Heldman and Cullman were no longer outsiders but vital players in the emerging establishment of pro tennis. Cullman was in the forefront, but Heldman's own opportunity to leave her mark on the evolution of tennis occurred in year three of the Open era, 1970.

At the time, the general prize-money ratio favored the men by roughly $2 to $1. But the figures varied, and they were to some degree relative. For instance, the prize-money ratio favored the men by three to one at the U.S. Open, yet the winner's check for the female singles champion ($7,500) represented a bigger payday than the male champion enjoyed at an even more important tournament, Wimbledon.

When Billie Jean King won the 1970 Italian Open in Rome, she collected $600. Her male counterpart, Ilie Nastase, took home $3,500. King and her fellow players decided that the disparity was unacceptable, and they decided to take matters into their own hands. A few months later the female pros called a press conference at the U.S. Open to protest the prize-money ratio. They threatened to boycott the upcoming Pacific Southwest Open in Los Angeles, where the ratio in prize money would favor the men by ten to one.

The women received little support from the outside until Heldman stepped in and offered to promote an all-female tournament in Houston, offering $5,000 in prize money, with the winner receiving $1,500. The establishment was not quite sure how to react to Heldman's bold stroke. It might placate the women, but it also posed a potential threat to the nascent USTA women's tour. This was one of the first and most important occasions on which it was vividly clear that the commercially driven pro game by its nature posed a threat to the status quo. The prospect of the women pros boycotting an "official" USLTA event and playing instead in a nonaffiliated maverick event in Houston represented the nightmare scenario for an establishment that was neither designed nor inclined to push the marketing envelope. It was also the handwriting on the wall, written in bold script.

Just three days before Heldman's tournament was to begin, the establishment moved against her. The USLTA announced that it would not sanction the event. If Heldman went ahead with the tournament, the players, officials, and even the host, Houston Racquet Club, could be banned from national affiliation. The establishment was playing its final hole card, implying that the women who played in Heldman's event would be banished from Grand Slam events and ignored in the official national rankings.

Heldman responded by creatively exploiting an interesting legal loophole. Instead of merely staging an unsanctioned tournament, she hired the players as employees—offering each of the nine women in the field bona fide, one-week "personal service" contracts. Each woman was paid exactly one dollar for her services, but each of them would also compete for the prize money offered by the tournament. If the USLTA subsequently suspended the players, they would have an antitrust grievance that might very well hold up in civil court, where only the owners of major league baseball teams enjoyed a special exemption from restraint-of-trade regulations.

At that critical juncture, Heldman turned to an old ally and cashed in some of the chips she had accumulated. She asked Cullman to step in as a sponsor of her new event. Cullman probably would have gone to Heldman's aid out of friendship alone, but a tournament featuring just women—particularly outspoken women fighting for equal pay—was about as good a hook as anyone could imagine for a relatively new Philip Morris product, Virginia Slims cigarettes.

Cullman agreed to contribute the prize money and raised the pot to $7,500 in the process. Heldman then went public, unveiling the first Virginia Slims Women's Pro Tournament. At an elaborate press conference, the nine players signed their one-dollar contracts. Two of the women,

Kerry Melville and Judy Dalton, were Australians. The other seven were Americans: Peaches Bartkowicz, Rosie Casals, Heldman's daughter Julie, Billie Jean King, Kristy Pigeon, Nancy Richey, and Val Ziegenfuss.

The very next day, the American players were notified by telegram that they were suspended from the USLTA. They could be locked out of the Grand Slam events of 1971, and they would no longer be eligible for national rankings. This meant that the "official" U.S. number one player could conceivably be the eighth-best American woman. Nonetheless, the women showed great solidarity. Heldman's inaugural event was a resounding success. She quickly lined up two more events, one in San Francisco and one in Richmond, Virginia. The women players unanimously—make that ecstatically—voted to sign contract extensions that would be good until the end of the year. Legally, the establishment couldn't touch Heldman, and any move it made to lock her contract players (her employees) out of the circuit could be effectively challenged.

The Virginia Slims events were so well received and they attracted so much general attention as a socially progressive phenomenon that Heldman had little trouble putting together an "official" circuit of twenty-four events for 1971, each one offering at least $10,000 in prize money. She generously and wisely slotted the events around the Grand Slam championships, should the USLTA back off the hard line that it had taken on Virginia Slims players. She offered Cullman the title sponsorship to the tour, and he instantly accepted.

Early in 1971 the intransigent USLTA appeared to change its position and lifted the suspension on the U.S. players. With tennis booming, the three most prestigious Grand Slam events coming up, and the potential for a nasty legal case brewing, nobody really wanted war.

All in all, the timing that created the Virginia Slims circuit was perfect. The growing feminist establishment was bewitched by the fiercely independent spirit and entrepreneurial expertise shown by the women players, chiefly Billie Jean King. Heldman was hailed as the architect of the first significant, exclusively female tennis tour. The public at large was captivated by tennis in general and by the bold new concept of women's pro tennis. Virginia Slims was generally perceived as an enlightened sponsor that had courageously stepped in to advance the cause of women's rights—or at least women's opportunities. Nobody gave much thought to the product that was being marketed, not when the effort seemed to be so vitally linked with progressive social politics in one of the most liberal periods in the history of the United States.

You don't have to be an antismoking advocate or the anxious parent of a promising young female tennis player on the women's pro tour to look at the history of the women's game and come to the conclusion, "That was then, this is now."

"Now" is a crisis point in women's pro tennis, and now is about stabbings, child abuse, teenage drug abuse, and a shocking rate of attrition among players who often appear to be little more than child entertainers, richly compensated for their brief turns on the public stage.

Through most of the 1970s, the Virginia Slims tour was an arresting, exciting entity as well as the most successful all-female sports enterprise in history. But that glory was remarkably short-lived—an eternity in marketing time, perhaps, but a mere blip on even the narrow graph of sports history. Two decades after its inception, the Virginia Slims tour has lost much of its cachet, and the sponsor, hounded by the anti-smoking lobby, has essentially pulled out of tennis.

The first generation of Slims players were pioneers, mature women who fought the good fight for equal wages and led lives of struggle and achievement. But the subsequent waves of players increasingly seemed like nothing more than tennis players, incrementally younger and younger ones created and shaped in a curious, irrelevant, self-contained world revolving around the sport of tennis.

Another reason the tour lost some of its luster is the "life-style" element. As the women's tour evolved, it became a milieu featuring a strikingly high degree of lesbianism. At one period in the heydey of the tour, the majority of the top ten women were homosexuals. It's impossible to quantify the impact of this statistic on the popularity of women's tennis, but, if nothing else, it's an extraordinary sociological tidbit. This is doubly true when a comparison is drawn to the men's tour, on which the incidence of homosexuality is so negligible that it may even be under the general social norm.

In the pro era, the female player's way of life rapidly began to militate against her cultivation of traditional heterosexual relationships. Often, the only available choices for a female player were forming a sexual relationship with a fellow player or the only man who was even a semi-regular fixture in her life—her coach. Exercising either of those options posed obvious problems, not the least of which was the corrosive effect of having your professional and emotional life intermingled.

Traditionally, the incidence of lesbianism is higher among female athletes than women in more mundane walks of life. Undoubtedly, there is a biological component present in that condition. But more recently I've noticed another factor that contributes to the high incidence of lesbianism on the pro tour: Given the high income of the top 50 or so players and the cushy, insular lives they enjoy as one tournament after another bends over backward to accommodate them, the only significant problems female tennis players face are emotional ones. In the long run it's much easier to simply eliminate that problem—as well as that can be done—than to make career-threatening choices that would solve it in more traditional ways.

Many women who may not be biologically programmed as lesbians make their lives complete, if not necessarily whole, by becoming gay. This decision represents a total surrender to the demands of the profession. If totalitarian man or woman is by definition one-dimensional, then allowing one's already pervasive occupation to dictate sexual conduct is the epitome of one-dimensionality.

I raise all of these issues because the gender bending that occurs on the pro tour is to some degree the product of the thinking that shaped and gave substance to the women's tour. The most convenient way to approach that mentality is historically and practically, through the Virginia Slims looking glass.

The overwhelming issue that led to the creation of the Virginia Slims tour was an uncomplicated one: the desire for equal pay. There are some debatable points, however, in the application of the equal-pay-for-equal-work mandate in tennis. Some critics argue that the women do not deserve equal prize money because, at least at Grand Slam events, they play best-of-three instead of best-of-five set tennis matches. They also say that the conspicuous lack of competitive depth that usually characterizes the female game makes the top female pro's typical workday much shorter than that of the top male pro.

In the broader perspective, the equal pay concept may be no more relevant to tennis than to the entertainment industry where wages depend on such practical considerations as marquee value. You've probably noticed that many members of the tennis cognoscenti (most prominently Billie Jean King) constantly stress the nature of pro tennis as "entertainment." Yet they ignore the fact that show business may be the most economically capricious and unpredictable enterprise of them all.

To say that the women are "worth" the same as the men is probably a non sequitur to anyone who has a decent grasp of free-market economics. More importantly, it is insidiously sexist because it assumes that women should be judged comparatively, by the standard set by men. It also denies women the opportunity to carve a niche or create an enterprise that relies on their unique talents and sensibilities. If you feel that men and women are in some inherent way different, then those qualities that can be identified as "feminine" should be identified, cultivated, celebrated, and exploited intelligently in an enterprise like pro tennis. The failure to acknowledge or act on the different nature and different needs of women is at the very root of the crisis that plagued tennis in the early 1990s. Since the inception of the women's tour, "equality" has been synonymous with "identicity." This has had some harmful effects on the women's tour in both practical and substantial ways.

The U.S. Open provides an interesting example of the practical problems of identicity. There, the Women's Tennis Association has successfully lobbied for equal time. That's why the women's final is sandwiched between two men's semifinals on the infamous Super Saturday. Not only does this overload of tennis violate the principle of providing too much of a good thing, it is grossly unfair to both the men and women competitors.

The men who contest the third major feature of the day, the last men's semifinal, may have to begin play as late as 7 P.M. If the match is a doozy, the winner finds himself having to bounce back to play the championship match less than twenty-four hours later—a tough assignment on the harsh, unforgiving cement courts of Flushing Meadow.

As for the women, they never know what time they will be taking the court for the all-important championship match. At every other Grand Slam event, the women and men play their finals at prearranged times, on separate days. The women's establishment is not wholly to blame for this sorry state of affairs—at least not anymore. CBS television grew fond of the idea of Stupor Saturday, and the USTA immediately fell in line and continues to protect it. But it's still odd that the women would rather share a crowded stage than take the chance of going it alone.

One of the other regrettable side effects of the socially correct condition at the U.S. Open is that the prime-time weekday evening schedule always offers a singles match between women first (starting about 7:30 P.M.), followed by a men's match. Thus, the five-set men's match often doesn't begin until 9 P.M., and it frequently lasts until well after midnight. This routinely creates scheduling nightmares and supportable charges of unfairness, particularly when rain wreaks havoc with the first few days of the event.

Worse yet, the chronic inability of the women's tour to create competitive depth means that the national viewing audience is routinely subjected to a benumbing series of "prime- time" matches in which a star (for television executives want stars, not great match-ups) is seen mercilessly beating up on some hapless journeywoman by the traditional 6–1, 6–2 scores.

The problem is compounded by the fact that the only reason some journeywomen are on the tour at all is that the women insist on fielding the same number of players as the men, even though they cannot produce as many competitive players. Just why the women seem unable to produce the same competitive field as the men is the subject of incessant debate. I once embraced the *Psychology Today* school of thought, which relied on theories of "social conditioning." But clichés of that theory are easily refutable, starting with the notion that women are "socially conditioned" to be less competitive. If anything, the competition on the women's tour has been far more cutthroat, unbridled, and often personally motivated than anything you find on the men's tour. Countless female players, from Virginia Wade to Andrea Jaeger, have told me that. Women don't compete less well, they compete differently, and why they do so is a complex question.

So I've come around to the *Biology Today* school of thought. Given a certain amount of physical power, or power derived from ever more advanced rockets, the game of tennis between highly trained male players becomes something of a crap shoot. On a good day the "average" male pro presents a legitimate threat to a top player even when the favorite is performing well. But the vast majority of women players are physically incapable of generating enough force to simply overpower anyone, much less the superior players. Even when the top players are the victims of upsets, their own momentary incompetence is often the major reason.

Given these realities, I'm amazed that the women's tour hasn't seen the folly of mimicking the men's tour. So what if the women decide to field half as many players and begin their Grand Slam tournaments after the men have already been at it for a week? So what if the women decide to abandon the unfriendly "world tour" concept and go with some kind of team tennis concept that both levels the playing field and provides a much more normal environment for young girls? Neither equal prize money nor size of field does anything to elevate and distinguish women's tennis. People want to see great players and/or great matches, period.

The economics of tennis in the Open era were skewed, and driven by social philosophy as much as market forces. Through the 1980s, the game lived on the fat accumulated over the years of plenty. By the time the 1990s got under way, tennis was no longer a growth industry. It had a new establishment, richly compensated stars, and a core, albeit a dwindling core, of supportive, upscale sponsors. But the game was in a curious state of stagnation, and the women's game was in nothing less than crisis.

I don't know if the women's tour will ever project a healthy, wholesome image again, and I don't know how long it can survive and generate public support if it doesn't. In order to do so, it has to deep-six the pervasive, masculinist agenda that it developed early in its history.

Many of the issues I've discussed came to a head at the U.S. Open in

1994, at a press conference held by the Women's Tennis Council to reveal the long-awaited findings of a comprehensive age eligibility study. The Age Eligibility Commission was formed in 1993 to address the increasing number of problems caused and experienced by prodigies on the tour. It may just as well have been called the Capriati Committee. Many of the reporters gathered in the room were baffled, then outraged, by the commission's declarations. The overwhelming sentiment expressed—generated by some three thousand pages of evidence, statistical surveys of the relation between age and playing longevity, and congressional-hearing-style "testimonies" from over ninety individuals from all segments of the tennis community—was that fourteen-year-old girls should not play on the pro tour. Under the system in place at the time, fourteen-year-olds were allowed to play a whopping twelve WTA Tour events, plus the Virginia Slims Championships.

The commission recommended that while fourteen-year-olds should be barred from playing in WTA Tour and Grand Slam events, they should be allowed to play a maximum of five ITF Futures events (low-key tournaments offering $25,000 to $100,000 in prize money) and one exhibition match. Fifteen-year-olds would be allowed to participate in nine events, including some WTA Tour events, but no Grand Slam championships. The formula goes on like that until young women reach the age of eighteen, when they can play without any restrictions.

Furthermore, the two best-known prodigies on the scene at the time, the Swiss youngster Martina Hingis and the African-American Venus Williams, each of whom was fourteen, were to be grandfathered into the "old" system, as would a number of others who could be restricted by an arbitrary new body of regulations.

Given the nature of this inquiry, it was almost fitting that the meeting degenerated into as rowdy and infantile a gathering as a second-grade class left unattended by a teacher.

Mary Carillo, the former player and popular TV commentator, led the charge: "You guys [sic—the three representatives of the AEC present were all women] are going against all of your findings. . . . All you're doing is tweaking a system that doesn't work to begin with. . . . Under your 'new' regulations, you're still going to have six-year-old girls out there running wind sprints and doing push-ups and sit-ups, still aiming for the same thing."

As the debate raged on, I found myself in disagreement with both Carillo and the AEC, a body that increasingly seemed to be one of those dreaded "independent committee of renowned international experts" that specialize in generating voluminous reports, burning tons of money, and constructing elaborate, ineffective bureaucracies.

The AEC had also laid out a remarkable proactive agenda aimed mostly at policing the rogue parents who brought the game to the brink of crisis. In order to achieve that unattainable end (how on earth can the WTC prevent a prodigy from playing three hundred exhibitions a year at fourteen if her parents encourage or allow her to do it?), the AEC revealed a robust willingness to punish the innocent and gifted as well as the guilty. Prohibiting a legitimate prodigy from playing at a Grand Slam tournament until she is sixteen, as the commission proposed, was not only unfair to talented players, it was downright stupid.

Wimbledon, more than any other tournament, protects players from the kind of media circus that sprang up at Jennifer Capriati's pro debut at the Virginia Slims in Delray Beach, Florida. Furthermore, the two most important Grand Slam events (Wimbledon and the U.S. Open) take place during the traditional summer school vacation. And lastly, not a single prodigy, from Chris Evert to Tracy Austin to Jennifer Capriati, has ever said that playing at Wimbledon at fourteen or sixteen was a distasteful or damaging experience.

The harm done to Capriati, the most badly damaged prodigy, was the result of all the things that transpired after her youthful adventures at major championships. Most of them had to do with the strategy of her parents, who turned her into a cash cow pastured on the WTA Tour and on exhibition circuits. Granted, Capriati's exploits at Wimbledon and the U.S. Open made her famous, thereby creating special problems for her. But the same could be said for Evert and Austin, who weathered them very well.

Pressure? A prodigy at Wimbledon has nothing to lose. Pressure materializes after, not before, a player has put together a resume—when critics begin to compare and analyze promise and results, and when the tour establishment begins to lean more and more heavily on the kid in question.

The AEC appeared utterly blind to these important facts of tennis life. What's worse, it put on the table an agenda aimed not at reducing the role of professional tennis in a young woman's life but actually enlarging it. The AEC suggested that the WTC develop seminars, counseling, "mentor" relationships—a whole panoply of dull, artificial, cradle-to-grave programs that are de facto alternatives to such traditional notions and institutions as parental authority, schools, churches, or even the Girl Scouts.

When Anne Person-Worcester, CEO of the WTC, suggested that massage therapists and athletic trainers could also double as "psychological counselors," I couldn't help but remember an anecdote from my friend John Feinstein's recent book *Hard Courts*. He told the story of how young, happy-go-lucky Jennifer Capriati once bopped into the training room and was shocked to see the masseuse on duty locked in a romantic embrace with one of the other female players.

The thrust of the AEC's recommendations was that young women need to be better "socialized" to life on the tour, which was a very telling premise. For all of the commission's cant about the loneliness and pressures bred by the tour, there was not a smidgen of criticism of the tour system itself. This was an extraordinary oversight, considering the formidable problems embodied in a single-gender tour that hops all over the globe and militates against young women developing healthy, lasting relations with anyone who is not a part of that small, inbred organism.

Further, that vaunted "independent commission" was not so independent after all. It was, wittingly or not, a creature of the WTA Tour, lacking either the expertise or the mandate to do the most sensible thing of all, which was to examine the structure in which tennis players had to function. If it had done so, it might have decided that the cure for the ills of women's tennis lay in making the tour more player-friendly. Example: Don't offer prize money to kids under the age of eighteen. Stop giving greedy parents everything they want, all the time, absolutely free. Don't allow kids to play indoor pro tournaments during the winter months. Require kids to win amateur age-group events as a condition for participating on the tour.

Nobody ever went to Wimbledon at fourteen and had a lousy time. Not even Jennifer Capriati.

Early in 1994, contemplating the plague of problems visited on the women's tour, Billie Jean Moffitt King offhandedly remarked that her solution to the crisis would be "to blow the whole thing up and start again." This suggestion was odd and yet typical, coming as it did from one of the two women most responsible for the creation of the women's tour (the other being Gladys Heldman). It was also bombastic and enterprising, coming as it did from a woman whose lifelong adult dream has been the transmogrification of tennis into a team sport. It was also positive and full of abnegation, and that's probably because it emanated from a remarkably positive but painfully complex person in whom honorable striving and self-loathing have always been freely mixed, and whose compulsive honesty coexists with a remarkable willingness to manipulate and obfuscate issues as trivial as tennis politics, as essential as her own nature.

King was a ranking masculinist who became a certified feminist hero. She ascended to that place because she courageously took on a male establishment and, with the help of a few male allies, broke free of its control. And while her place in the record and history books remains intact, she took a nasty tumble from the pedestal she once occupied because of an unsavory sex scandal. First and foremost, Billie Jean was a magnificent tennis player, the kind of player who communicated her deep love of the game. A courageous competitor who relied on quickness and an enterprising serve-and-volley game, she won each of the Grand Slam titles at least once. Ironically, she played her best tennis at the major tournament that most offended her egalitarian sensibilities, Wimbledon, where she won six singles titles. She may not have been the best player of all time, but she certainly was the most important one.

This remains true even though so many of her grander dreams, including the success of World Team Tennis and the emergence of a women's tour that has all the competitive depth of the men's field, remain unrealized. Even though she has recently come under heavy fire for her continuing willingness to serve as an apologist for Philip Morris. Even though she often seems to be a cipher free-falling through a tennis community that still pays lip service to her accomplishments but has also slowly edged her out of the locus of power.

In the fall of 1994, after a painful restructuring of the leadership of the women's tour, the WTC had yet to select a CEO and find a tour sponsor to take over on the heels of the pullout by Philip Morris. King and the management company that represents her, IMG, made an aborted attempt to seize control of the women's tour. The swift, embarrassing failure of that coup attested to the solidarity of the newly constituted WTC—and proved that IMG and its allies had grossly overexaggerated King's personal clout.

In the aftermath of that debacle, I couldn't find one principal who was willing to go on record criticizing King's role in the proceedings. Privately, almost every one of them expressed dismay at the position she had taken. According to them, she was willing to destroy the nascent, inclusive organization that intended to govern by broad consensus, and turn women's tennis over to the agents. Backpedaling after the aborted coup, King claimed that her actions were a response to the slow rate of progress shown by the WTC in its search for a new leader and a tour sponsor. But they may also have had a lot to do with her position as the prime mover in team tennis, and IMG's status as the chief investor in team tennis. You don't have to be a rocket scientist to figure out the implications of those realities.

The inclusion of the ITF in the new WTC alignment was a particularly bitter pill for King to swallow because of her lifelong conviction that the amateur establishment was an impediment to the professional growth of tennis.

At the peak of her fame, thanks to the good offices of her buddy Elton John and a pop song that he wrote about her ("Philadelphia Freedom"), King was dubbed and often referred to as Mother Freedom. But in a sports column that appeared in *The New York Times* in December 1993, columnist Ira Berkow likened "Mother Freedom" to an ostrich playing with her head in the sand because of her fealty to Philip Morris. Maybe this is just one of those "what goes around, comes around" things. At any rate, these historical details all suggest that Mother Freedom has always relied on alliances with men, from the executives at Philip Morris to the bigwigs at IMG, indicating that in the end maybe it really is a man's world. And that may have as much to do as anything else with the problems and frustrations King has experienced every step of the way. I do know that Billie Jean, armed with egalitarian fervor, ready to play ball with any ally who appears to support her agenda, still stands far from having her vision of tennis realized. And I think it's partly because there are some key flaws in that vision, and complex inconsistencies in the woman harboring it.

Some of these inconsistencies are created by King's dedication to the here and now. It made her too willing to be defined by the whim of the moment, and thus subject to the cruelty of shifting times and values. Like some pop stars and many politicians, she enjoyed a unique, explosive moment of universal fame from which it is very difficult to recover. That moment was her storied match against the aging male player Bobby Riggs, which was held in Houston's Astrodome, drawing more live bodies (30,429) and more television viewers than any other encounter in tennis history.

That match was an undeniably riveting, quasi-cultural phenomenon that assumed a life of its own on the hot, smoky battlefield where an ever larger battle of the sexes was being played out. Everybody was interested in the match between Riggs and King. Everybody had an opinion and a prediction, a hero and a villain. On that day, Billie Jean probably got 80 percent of the American population momentarily interested in something that was marginally about tennis. And that is a heck of an achievement.

But the important question is: Was that Battle of the Sexes a significant event in the growth of tennis and society's march toward equality and female empowerment, or was it a chimerical happening that evaporated not long after the last ball was struck? Billie Jean herself said, eighteen years later, "It was actually pretty stupid, a twenty-nine-year-old woman against a fifty-nine-year-old man. No logic, all emotion, but that's okay."

King had another flaw that was even more damaging than her dedication to the historical moment, rather than the historical continuum:

a debilitating class-consciousness that imbued her with a lifelong resentment of the traditional tennis establishment and all it stood for. That resentment often undermined her unbridled optimism and the attractive, can-do confidence she brought to the struggle to promote women's tennis.

King's class-consciousness and intensity accounted for her strange, unsatisfying relationship with Wimbledon, and they were also motivational factors in her extraordinary success there. She burst out of nowhere at age seventeen and, with her eighteen-year-old American partner, Karen Hantze, won the doubles from an unseeded position at Wimbledon in 1961. She was effervescent, enthusiastic, and tomboyish. The reserved British could live with that, but not with the flinty ambition and competitive ruthlessness that King would come to manifest as she matured into a great singles player. King was too blatantly aggressive for the audience at Wimbledon, the sport's bastion of restraint, etiquette, and conventional social roles. They never did embrace her or she them, but King was fired to great accomplishments by the mutual freeze-out. She accumulated more Wimbledon titles (twenty) than any other female player in history.

But in the end, everybody lost. King ought to be an icon at Wimbledon. Instead, she is the tournament's forgotten champion.

King's intensity did not sit well with many of her rivals, either. She dominated friends and allies such as Rosie Casals and, later, Martina Navratilova. But she had uneasy relations with other top players who cultivated restraint and traditional politesse. Early in her career, Chris Evert quickly adopted a policy that she would adhere to until the day King retired, which was to avoid making eye contact with King during a match. As Evert said, "She can be *that* intimidating."

The mixed blessing of King's intensity also affected her forays into coaching. Over the years she has worked with a variety of players, including the male pros Ben Testerman and Tim Mayotte. In most cases her legendary intensity, along with her celebrated powers as a "motivator," backfired. She was such an intimidating person and coach that she often seemed to damage the confidence of her protégés.

One of the most interesting coaching episodes of the Open era occurred when Martina Navratilova, who has enjoyed a long and special relationship with King, asked the older veteran for help in her quest to win the 1991 Wimbledon title. King drastically altered Navratilova's service motion for the tournament, citing "biomechanical" reasons that were so abstract and technical that listening to them would have made the average physicist's head swim. The result was a highly forced, complicated, and extremely unnatural-looking delivery that left even veteran Navratilova watchers slack-jawed. The extent to which Navratilova's "official" coach and hitting partner, a pleasant young man named Craig Kardon, supported this experiment was a testament to the untouchable nature of the relationship between King and Navratilova.

As it turned out, Navratilova's new service motion was a disaster. Serving awfully, she lost to Jennifer Capriati in the quarterfinals, 6–4, 7–5. The interlude was extraordinary, and probably the key factor in the outcome of the tournament. Yet nobody bothered to write about it, and when the smoke cleared and Navratilova had wiped the last tear from her eye, she resolutely refused to blame her disappointment on the altered service motion.

Socially, King's intensity was vented as enduring antagonism toward those whom she perceived as upper-crusty types (a class that included most of the USLTA hierarchy during the amateur era). The source of her resentment has been articulated on many occasions in a famous anecdote that occurred at the Los Angeles Tennis Club during a junior tournament in 1955. Billie Jean Moffitt was eleven at the time, and crazy about tennis, a game that was foreign to her family. Moffitt's father was a fireman, and he knew from the moment his daughter showed an interest in the game that it was a sport dominated by patrician types. He didn't appear to have a problem with this, other than feeling slightly out of place and underfinanced at the exclusive tennis clubs where his daughter played many of her tournaments. In fact, Moffitt encouraged his daughter to "fit in" and to act more "ladylike." But Billie Jean, a stubborn tomboy, had no use for that advice. She attended junior tournaments carrying her lunch in a brown paper bag and preferred wearing shorts to tennis dresses—a habit that led to her oft-cited "formative" experience at a tournament run by the czar of tennis in Southern California, Perry Jones.

Jones decided to exclude Moffitt from a routine group photograph of the junior players because she had insisted on wearing shorts. King would never forget that slight, and it only fanned the flames of her rebelliousness. She described her reaction years later to Ted Tinling: "Who cares, was how I felt. It was small time. I decided I would show them anyway. I despised the whole junior system, and although I wasn't sure what I would do, I knew even then that I would change it. Eventually, I did play a part in changing the system, and as I get older, it still gives me great gratification to know I did."

My reaction to that anecdote has always been the same: What a pity. Perry Jones may indeed have been an imperious snob, but that's no reason to dedicate the rest of your life to destroying anybody even remotely like him. Besides, doesn't everyone have an analogous experience, and isn't the humiliating anecdote part of everyone's childhood legacy?

The end result was that Billie Jean spent a great deal of her adult life getting revenge for having been born into a perfectly fine, ordinary, blue-collar family. Others in her shoes welcomed the opportunity to improve their lot in life through tennis, but armed with great talent and a sense of justice, King resolved to destroy the class implications of tennis. She won the first stage of that battle swiftly and brilliantly, winning her own economic independence from those whom she mistrusted by leading the charge toward professionalism. But her assault bogged down in the second stage.

The most important failure that can be attributed to King's class resentment was the demise of the marvelous idea that she helped spawn and continues to promote: World Team Tennis. I've always felt, and still believe, that many of the sacrifices tennis players must make to play the pro tour these days would be alleviated by rejecting the idea of an exhaustive, year-round international circuit. Instead, the sport should revolve around the Grand Slam events, Davis Cup and Federation Cup—and some workable form of World Team Tennis.

The advantages of team tennis are the same conspicuous ones offered by any team sport. The players can enjoy stable home lives, along with the camaraderie available in a team sport. But the greatest obstacle facing any attempt to create viable team tennis is the aftertaste left by a major effort that failed in the late 1970s. It was a matter of unsound business, but I also think WTT collapsed because it was too radical. King was too intent on destroying tennis as we knew it to produce a version of the game that had sufficient credibility, relevance, and appeal.

World Team Tennis was a great idea cloaked in grotesque raiments. WTT staged matches on multicolored courts. The league encouraged the audience to behave like a bunch of bozos at a pro wrestling contest. It devised a scoring system that was simultaneously too streamlined and too complicated. It was part circus and part zoo, ensuring that in the long run nobody would take it seriously. And to top it off, the starstruck owners overpaid for the services of players (including almost all the top guns) who were too selfish and myopic to realize the potential of the format.

Billie Jean King created or endorsed most of the distinguishing characteristics of team tennis, and she helped install her husband, Larry, as president of the fledgling league. She wanted tennis to be as popular as baseball (after all, King's brother, Randy, was a pitcher for the San Francisco Giants), but she forgot that despite the universal popularity of baseball, a good deal of its appeal lay in its own traditions, history, and nostalgia quotients. King simply didn't take into account that many of the genteel traditions of tennis were actually appealing to the large numbers of new spectators flocking to the game. Apparently she didn't believe that ordinary Americans could ever accept a sport in which they couldn't scream at the top of their lungs and wave around big mitts of colored foam with a single digit sticking up: "We're Number One!"

The success of team tennis might well have prevented the development of the worst features embodied in the professional movement that King so vociferously promoted. It also might have invested King with the authority and distinction that she had earned in her inspirational up-from-nothing struggle to become one of the great champions of tennis.

The desire to be all things to all people, including herself, was another self-imposed obstacle in Billie Jean King's path. Ted Tinling was as proud as a peacock about having dubbed King "Madam Superstar," and I always felt that his reasons for doing so were much more interesting than that hokey moniker. I've already quoted Tinling's definition of a star, which hinges on equal competitive desires to be private and public, famous and anonymous, adored and treated as an equal. In his own book, *Sixty Years of Tennis,* Tinling elucidated just how ambivalently even he sometimes felt about King: "I nicknamed her Madame Superstar because it implies the full gamut of her emotions, from great loyalty, great professionalism and warm affection, all the way to deceit, bitchery, and, at times, self-destructiveness."

King's personal and professional lives were hazardously and often haphazardly intertwined, and her image and aspirations affected the way she conducted—and projected—her personal life. For a long time she lived the life of the closet homosexual. Given her background, this was understandable. Homosexuality is a great liability when it comes to marketing and endorsement opportunities. Finally, Billie Jean had a right to some semblance of a private life, although her pursuit of power and celebrity qualified that right.

One of the more memorable examples of King's desire to transcend tennis and to exert her sociopolitical influence occurred in 1971, and it helped to precipitate the crisis that nearly drove her into retirement. That year, the feminist Gloria Steinem's brainchild, *Ms.* magazine, published a list of fifty-four signatures beneath a bold headline that read; WE HAVE HAD ABORTIONS. One of the more surprising and popular signatories was Billie Jean King. Now the curious thing about the episode is that many of King's friends and associates knew she was a lesbian. Her marriage at an early age to lawyer-promoter Larry King was widely considered a convenient outgrowth of their shared ambition, friendship, and various business partnerships. As the years went on, some tour insiders took malicious pleasure in charting the liaisons that Billie Jean and Larry each pursued—his heterosexual, hers homosexual.

This arrangement blew up in the Kings' faces when "L'Affair Barnett" broke. It was a tawdry mess, and I'll give you the details in shorthand: Marilyn Barnett, former Beverly Hills hairdresser turned "personal secretary" to superstar tennis player and feminist icon, sues King for palimony. Superstar appears at press conference in the company of her understanding, doting husband, Larry, confessing to hairdresser's allegations. Hairdresser wants beach house and pots of money. Superstar wants understanding and sympathy, and gets a measure of it by doing the Barbara Walters show.

Sponsors and friends rally to star. *People* magazine publishes an upbeat story on the Kings, featuring Billie Jean and Larry frolicking on a king-sized bed.

Hairdresser and superstar settle out of court for an undisclosed sum of money paid to Barnett in 1980. Lawyers get rich.

Sponsors and friends abandon superstar as soon as firestorm of publicity dies down. Two years later (1983), superstar files lawsuit seeking $55 million for hairdresser's alleged breach of an agreement "to get out of Mrs. King's life." Lawyers get richer.

One sad postscript: the people who really suffered as a result of L'Affair Barnett were King's parents. According to a friend of the family, they felt so ashamed that they packed up and moved out of Long Beach, California, where they had lived most of their lives.

Anyway, years after King's signature appeared on *Ms.* magazine's list of the liberated fifty-four but two years after Barnett blew the lid off King's secret life, King announced to reporters that she and Larry really wanted a child. Claiming that she did not want to risk pregnancy at age forty, King said the couple would try to adopt. She even said that she was considering taking a "hard-to-adopt" child (code at that time for a minority or handicapped child), and she added, "I want this [child] to be a gift to my husband who has sacrificed so much in his life for me."

You know, I understand realpolitik. I understand the concept of damage control. I even understand the awful, vertiginous feeling that a homosexual must have when he or she feels rejected by society. But to hold a press conference and work a minority or handicapped orphan into some feeble attempt to recapture lost power and glory? It was too much. Most members of the tennis community reacted with tears, laughter—or nausea.

By the early 1990s the Kings knew that they would never recover from L'Affair Barnett. Billie Jean King soldiered on with her live-in girlfriend, and Larry drifted off and married a pleasant, former Virginia Slims staffer, Nancy Bolger. The couple quickly had a child in 1992.

All of this may seem as tawdry to you as it does to me, but the details of King's emotional life can't be ignored, not when they're flung into the public's face by a personality with grand public ambitions. The important thing about L'Affair Barnett was not that Billie Jean was a lesbian, but that she had conducted her affairs in a way that ultimately created a shocking mess. Madame Superstar wanted it all, and like many people saddled with a similar craving, she has had to settle for a whole lot less. Given her talent and drive, she had a remarkable ability to shoot herself in the foot. I can think of lots of reasons to mistrust Billie Jean and even some for resenting her in the same way that she always resented almost all of the tennis establishment, but it's kind of pointless because in the end Billie Jean was bruised as much as she bruised, manipulated as often as she manipulated.

It is shocking and it's sad, too, because there is no denying Billie Jean Moffitt King's greatness, her contribution to the history of the game, or the pure, vibrant power of her personality. With that, let's bid a melancholy, Shakespearean "adieu" to the girls of Babylon. For now.

CHAPTER 13

Martina of Starwood

MARTINA NAVRATILOVA is not only the most versatile and accomplished tennis player that I've had the pleasure to watch, she's also my favorite comedienne, especially on those frequent occasions when she tackles some great social or political issue—homelessness, Republicanism, racism, homophobia, whatever—that makes her heart burn, leaving sympathetic souls swooning in admiration and giving serious conservative types heartburn.

Navratilova never met a cause she didn't like, which is an understandable and even predictable reflex in an inquisitive, undereducated woman who grew up in the hellishly repressive climate of Czechoslovakia in the 1960s. Navratilova is also openly and actively gay, a condition that currently demands adherence to a special-interest agenda. I've always accepted Navratilova's sexual identity and respected the basic honesty with which she's handled her nature and the issues it has raised.

There are a host of other qualities that help make Navratilova a complex and intriguing personality, beginning with her remarkable adaptability. For instance, most of the successful, self-made people I know from Navratilova's part of the world (Eastern Europe) tend to be conservative, more like Ivan Lendl than Martina. They're deeply aware of the opportunities afforded them in the United States and, unlike fourth- or fifth-generation Americans, they know what it's like to live with a boot grinding on their faces.

Although Navratilova defected to the United States in 1976 and became a U.S. citizen in 1981, she skipped an entire generation or two in those short years. Even before her defection, she was enthralled by American manners and habits. She picked up the English language with dazzling facility and speed, and her penchant for slang was alternately touching, comical, and bizarre. Soon after her defection, Martina developed a robust appetite for junk food of all kinds. She began spending almost all her disposable income in the mall. Navratilova was more like the child of some fabulously successful immigrant, saddled with the same idealism, naïveté, and misplaced sense of guilt as any sensitive, overprivileged kid who thinks that the problems of this world can be solved without anyone's ever having to do any dirty work.

Martina's talent catapulted her right into the rich and cushy tennis environment. She was the most promising tennis player of her generation at the time that she defected, so she didn't have to work her way from the bottom up but from the top to the pinnacle. Her generational leap also had a great deal to do with her nature as a celebrity. In fact, there may be no better way to understand Martina than through her distinguishing characteristics as a celebrity. She is appealing, emotional, driven, wacky, turbulent, and charismatic, and she has often seemed as deeply and existentially uncomfortable as any Hollywood starlet. Here is the short list of the traits that identify Navratilova as a bona fide celebrity:

She adopts the interests, passions, and politics of whomever she happens to be emotionally involved with at any given time. She lived in a development called Starwood in Aspen, Colorado, until her spurned lover Judy Nelson's palimony action stripped Navratilova of the home. She likes to travel and live with an entourage. She throws her money out the window. She is most attracted to other celebrities. She has serial, overlapping relationships that affect her work, her pocketbook, and her emotional stability. She buys lots of cars, for herself and other people. Those closest to her insist that she's really smart. And vulnerable. And honest. And generous. Things that are supposed to be self-evident in ordinary schmoes, but must be revealed about celebrities.

Martina of Starwood is also a master of Celebthink, which is why I described her earlier as a comedienne. For all of their faults, most tennis players rarely feel a compulsion to speak out on social and political issues that they are ill-equipped to understand. They cheerfully acknowledge that they're too wrapped up in their careers to even understand, much less take a stand, on the burning issues of our times. But Martina was always different. She has the celebrity's sloppy penchant for taking the moral high ground on issues in which she has no real stake or significant experience. You know how it goes: Wealthy celebrity builds enormous, fossil-fuel-heated, multi-million-dollar home of exotic wood and then turns into an antinuclear fanatic dedicated to saving what's left of the rain forest after all the pretty people have built their homes.

I'll give you a good example of Navratilova's penchant for Celebthink. In a question-and-answer interview with David Higdon of *Tennis* magazine, Navratilova ripped an Iowa town whose residents were afraid that a program of forced integration would bring gangs, drugs, and guns into their community. "This whole stigma about blacks is attached to it," Navratilova commented. "They [presumably, the Iowa burghers] don't know. People are always afraid of what they don't know, and they always think they're better than the other guy."

Navratilova's comments contained the typically weird mixture of compassion and callousness that distinguishes Celebthink. You have to ask: If she's so fired up about racial injustice, why does she insist on living in a place like Aspen where you have to take an airplane trip to even bump into a black person who isn't a domestic employee—that is, unless Whitney Houston or Eddie Murphy or Diana Ross is in Aspen to hit the slopes and to mingle with other beautiful people for a couple of days.

And then there is the ever-fine line between altruism and self-interest. Navratilova has supported many charities and foundations. In 1986, Martina's representatives at IMG even set up one of her very own, The Martina Navratilova Youth Foundation. The organization quickly announced that it would award a college scholarship grant to a needy youth during the high-profile Virginia Slims Championships in Madison Square Garden. I thought I might even write something about this nice gesture, but I was dissuaded by a conversation I had with a disillusioned mole in the Navratilova camp. It seems that just days before the grant was to be awarded, nobody had bothered to do anything about finding a worthy recipient. So a number of Navratilova's minions were hurriedly dispatched to scour the streets, under orders to find someone—anyone—qualified for the scholarship. The mission was a success, and Navratilova awarded the lucky young lady the scholarship in front of twenty thousand tennis fans at the Garden. Watching the presentation, I imagined that the recipient, an African-American girl, felt as surprised as any winner of the American Family Sweepstakes on the day Ed McMahon marched up and knocked on the door, bearing a giant cardboard check for $10 million.

I suppose it ended up well enough. Some deserving kid got a free ride at college. Martina of Starwood got her tax break. And in an era of random violence, it was refreshing to witness what can only be described as an act of random charity.

Let me give you one more example of Celebthink before I move on to look at Navratilova's brilliant career and turbulent life. At the Virginia Slims Championships in 1992, Navratilova created a controversy with some comments she made about the AIDs-infected basketball star Magic Johnson. She essentially said that Johnson had received little flack for pursuing the promiscuous life-style that probably led to his

infection and that if he were a woman, he would not have gotten off as
easily—nor received such uncritical public support. I thought she was
dead right about that.

The controversy generated by Navratilova's remarks turned her next
post-match press conference into another sociopolitical inquiry ranging far afield from tennis. Navratilova went on a rant, making some
tasteless remarks about then-President George Bush because of his
alleged "insensitivity" to the AIDs crisis. Navratilova also blamed a rise
in sexual harassment on her conviction that Supreme Court Justice
Clarence Thomas "got away with it" and described the prospect of a
conservative Supreme Court and president as "scary."

And when a reporter, sensing that Navratilova was on a roll, mentioned that a USTA official had recently attributed the increase of male
coaches on the tour to the fact that parents were afraid that, without a
male presence, their young daughters would be more vulnerable to lesbians, Navratilova suggested that people harboring those fears were living in "the dark ages."

As Navratilova segued into full social crusader mode, I just couldn't
resist the urge to put her "moral awareness" to a test where few celebrities like it, close to home. I resolved to ask her about the tennis and
tobacco connection. After all, she had carried off many millions of dollars in prize money and bonuses from a Virginia Slims establishment
whose product was increasingly perceived as an insidious health hazard.

I glanced around the crowded pressroom and saw the faces of many Virginia Slims personnel. Most of them were women who had always been
gracious, charming, and helpful to me. My question would undoubtedly
embarrass those friends and acquaintances, and asking it would certainly
embarrass me, but I knew in that moment that if I didn't ask it, I would
feel cowardly. So I forged ahead, pointing out that many people who
shared her enlightened views were also very critical of the tennis and
tobacco connection. How did she feel about that?

I quote Navratilova's answer from the printed, rough transcript,
altering it only to recreate the halting nature of her response:

> Well . . . that has been a problem for the women, and we have been try-
> ing to address it the best way we can, but at the same time, you have to
> have some loyalty to people . . . people that brought you to where you
> are today. And Virginia Slims was there when nobody else gave a damn
> about women's tennis, and also it is . . . difficult. I mean—obviously,
> sports and cigarettes don't go together, but Virginia Slims and women's
> tennis are synonymous, and we are here because of them. . . .
> You know . . . this is a tough one to answer . . . and it ruffles people's

feathers, but I always—my answer was always—I don't tell people to start smoking, I just tell them, if they smoke, they might as well smoke Virginia Slims . . . which is probably not a very good answer, but that has been my answer for years.

It was not an unreasonable reply, but it was a verbatim repetition of the Slims' party line that every player coming on the tour was schooled to give when the unpleasant issue arose.

Martina Navratilova may or may not be the greatest female player of all time. In the pro era alone, there are two other claimants to that distinction: Margaret Court and Chris Evert. Martina, however, turned in the most preemptive, masterful performance I've ever seen a woman produce against a top-quality opponent in an important final. It occurred in January 1980, in the Capital Center in Landover, Maryland, when Navratilova met seventeen-year-old Tracy Austin in the final of the Colgate Series Championships. The tournament featured the top female performers of 1979, each of them having earned a place in the draw by points awarded for their yearlong performances. The tournament favorite was Austin, the prodigy who had come to dominate the women's game by late 1979. Since the U.S. Open of that year, Austin had beaten Evert three consecutive times without the loss of a set, and she had posted four consecutive victories over Navratilova.

The only trouble with the final between Navratilova and Austin was that it could hardly be called a match. It was an exhibition in which Austin, for all of her ascendant confidence and talent, was reduced to a foil for Navratilova's commanding, aggressive style and breathtaking abilities as a shotmaker. I've never seen anybody come as close to playing perfect tennis, or a match that so conclusively demonstrated that, on the right day, an aggressive, serve-and-volley stylist is unbeatable. Austin played beautifully. Navratilova won, 6–2, 6–1.

The problem for aggressive players, of course, is that the right day comes along about as often as the "right" anything else. The rest of the time, which is most of the time, a talented baseline player can exploit any weakness or inconsistency in the attacking player's repertoire—including the mental fragility with which an inordinate number of artistic, aggressive shotmakers like Navratilova are saddled.

That brings us to Navratilova's greatest achievement, the conquest of her temperament. No player, with the possible exception of her countryman Ivan Lendl, overcame a reputation as an anxiety-prone and thus ever-vulnerable opponent as completely as Navratilova.

Navratilova did not win her first Grand Slam title until the Wimbledon championships of 1978, by which time she had been on the pro tour for six years—long enough to convince most astute observers that she was destined to be remembered more for the blown titles and opportunities than the realized ones. But Navratilova got a grip on herself and her game in 1978, and rose to a new competitive level. She won Wimbledon and then reached at least the semifinals in the next five Grand Slam events she entered. (She did not play the Australian Open in 1978 or 1979, and she also avoided the French Open from 1978 to 1980.) At the end of 1980, Navratilova faltered in the fourth round of the U.S. Open, but it would be her last misstep for quite some time. Navratilova entered her golden age in 1981, reaching the final in twenty-two of the next twenty-eight Grand Slam events she entered. She won fifteen of those twenty-two championship matches.

Over those glory years, Navratilova also availed herself of the services of a variety of specialized trainers, including nutritionist and diet guru Dr. Robert Haas, author of *Eat to Win*. Depending on whom you listened to, Haas was either the Prophet of Pasta or a New Age snake oil salesman. Even Navratilova's own coach, Renee Richards, dubbed Haas "the nitwit nutritionist." Haas may have gone out of fashion as quickly as the mood ring, but he certainly built an impressive resume during his brief moment in the spotlight. Both Navratilova and Lendl, whose makeover as a champion so closely paralleled that of Navratilova, swore by Haas. He indisputably played a part in their success, offering physiological help, psychological help, or both.

The lengths to which Navratilova went in her pursuit of perfection ranged from the inspirational to the comical, but she completed a remarkable makeover from a pudgy, emotional organism into a lean, mean fighting machine. But her baffling assortment of specialized trainers had less to do with her transformation than did her willingness to embrace broad but simple discipline. Navratilova radically altered her career by becoming a realist—a pragmatist who accepted the idea that if she immersed herself in working her buns off and improving her technique and strategy, mental and emotional stability would follow.

And follow it did. By the end of 1994, her last year as a full-time competitor, she had won 167 singles titles, more than any other man or woman (Evert finished her career with 157). From January 16 through December 6, 1984, Navratilova won 74 consecutive singles matches, breaking the 55-match record Evert had held since 1974. In fact, Navratilova holds 3 of the 5 longest singles winning streaks in the modern era.

Navratilova's greatest asset was her athleticism. At her peak she was distinctively feline; she loved to pounce on the ball and had a seemingly inexhaustible appetite for exertion. Oddly enough, though, Martina never developed the full potential of her serve. The common quality shared by all fine servers is fidelity to their basic service motion. It's impossible to think of John McEnroe without visualizing his radical corkscrew service motion, and the same can be said about Billie Jean King, whose signature was the arched back and the parallel, out-stretched arms.

But I have trouble conjuring up a strong mental image of Navratilova's serve, which tells me more about her serve than about my memory. Navratilova never settled into the foolproof motion that char-acterizes accomplished servers. She did not consistently exploit her nat-ural advantage as a left-hander, producing the vicious, swerving slice that is such a devastating asset to the southpaw. This shortcoming prob-ably resulted from a glaring technical flaw, a failure to toss the ball as far forward into the court as the masters of the left-handed slice. When she did, her serve achieved greater movement and penetration, and her momentum gave her a valuable half-step to the net. And that was when she played her most authoritative tennis.

In other ways, Navratilova was a more typical left-hander. For instance, she always seemed more comfortable hitting her backhand than her forehand. The slice backhand was second nature to her, but she relied on it too heavily early in her career. Renee Richards was the first coach who truly tapped the potential of Navratilova's backhand, help-ing her develop fine flat and topspin drives that brought Navratilova to the zenith of her game.

The forehand side was another story. In tight, pressure-filled situa-tions, an opponent like Evert could at one time exploit Navratilova's tentative forehand. She sometimes lapsed into guiding the ball, espe-cially on passing shots—a tendency that caused her (and anyone else) to miss wide. At other times she took a quick and short swing, swiping it into the net. The root of both problems is the same: the lack of a grooved stroke, impervious to anxiety.

Navratilova's volley was generally superb, but there, too, she could be vulnerable at times on the forehand—especially on high, apparently routine put-aways. This problem plagued Navratilova until 1982. Botched forehand volleys cost Navratilova a number of important matches, but none more painful than the U.S. Open final of 1981. Tracy Austin came back from match point down to win that one, 1–6, 7–6, 7–6, thanks partly to some awful forehand volley errors by her oppo-nent—including a failed put-away at match point for Navratilova.

"Everybody said that I choked," Navratilova would say of that final two years later. "But I missed those crucial forehand volleys for a rea-

son. I was swinging at them from my ear, which is no way to hit a solid
volley."

That Navratilova could look back and analyze her failure in the 1981
Open so rationally was a tribute to the woman who set into motion the
process that would transform Navratilova from a talented but unpredictable contender into a champion. Renee Richards, the transsexual
ophthalmologist who played briefly on the women's tour, took that job
during the 1981 Open, by which time two factors had put Navratilova
into the mood to listen to advice. First, the steady success of Evert and
the new threat posed by Austin made Martina realize that while she
could sleepwalk to victory over the majority of women on the sheer
strength of her athleticism, she was not enough of a tennis player to
consistently defeat the two or three other women vying to dominate
tennis. Second, a new friend, the collegiate basketball star Nancy
Lieberman, convinced Navratilova that she ought to adopt a strict general training routine. Because Lieberman was not a tennis player, she
could address only Martina the athlete. But at the same time, Richards
was able to address Martina the tennis player. She introduced
Navratilova to the topspin backhand, changed her forehand grip to
make the stroke more reliable, and prevailed upon her to develop her
advantage as a left-hander by hitting the sharp slice serve. Richards also
fixed Navratilova's forehand volley.

Good coaching almost always calls for some ego-massaging and self-
image building. Richards convinced Navratilova that she could not only
compete with baseliners but beat them at their own game. She also
taught Navratilova, a shotmaker and crowd pleaser, how to tighten up
her game and tough out matches at times when the miraculous drop
volleys weren't falling and the acrobatic overheads were errant. Under
Richards, Navratilova learned how to win when she wasn't playing particularly well.

When Navratilova and Richards split up in the spring of 1983 (more
about that later), Navratilova was a much more complete player than
ever before in her career. And that was when Mike Estep, a former journeyman on the pro tour, stepped in and put the finishing touches on
Navratilova. Estep felt that in trying to develop Navratilova's full
potential, Richards had flattened the peaks of her protégée's game.
Coming from the men's tour, Estep knew the power and value of
attacking tennis.

If Richards was the idealist seduced by the challenge of making
Navratilova all that she could be, Estep was the pragmatist who wanted
Martina to win as often and as quickly as possible. Why should
Navratilova prove that she could beat Evert from the baseline when she

had the kind of attacking game that could potentially overwhelm any baseliner? After an experimental practice session and meeting at the Eastbourne grass-court tune-up for Wimbledon in 1983, Estep told Navratilova that it was time for her to chisel away the fluff and fat in her game, and to return to the things that she did best.

Intrigued by the idea, Navratilova persuaded Estep to sign on as her coach. Shortly after he did that, he laid out his philosophy to me, and I was struck by the unconventional wisdom of his approach. He perceived one condition that nobody else had paid much attention to, and built his entire strategy on it. Even at her best, Navratilova was cast as the shotmaker—the woman who won or lost on the strength of her ability to make the right shot at the right time.

But Navratilova was such a good athlete and such an accomplished player that she didn't have to be in that risky position. As Estep put it, "The idea is for Martina to make the other person hit the great shot, something that very few women can do consistently. Martina should get in there and force her opponent to play well. She should be there to be beaten, not to have to show that she can win. Great players win when they aren't at their best because they still have a way of making their opponents do things they can't or don't like to do."

Estep and Navratilova set to work on that mission. The strategy was for Navratilova to get to the net as quickly as possible, thereby challenging her rivals to exploit the small areas that were beyond the reach of her rangy, lethal volley with passing shots. Most players hate to be victims of passing shots that leave them standing flatfooted at the net. Passing shots are crowd pleasers and confidence builders for opponents, and one of the cardinal rules of attacking tennis is to treat such unnerving and even humiliating ripostes as accidents of nature. Instead of worrying about Navratilova getting passed, Estep insisted that if Navratilova wasn't getting passed, she wasn't going to the net often enough.

Estep's approach represented a new twist on the old concept of "percentage tennis." It worked so well that at the 1983 U.S. Open final, Navratilova slashed and sliced and volleyed her way to a 6–1, 6–3 win over Evert. Afterward, Evert inadvertently paraphrased Estep's theory.

"I don't feel consistent with Martina because I have two choices when she approaches. I can hit right at her, or I can go for the risky pass. If I hit anywhere near her, she'll end the point. So I end up going for the winner, which puts me under a lot of the kind of pressure that I'm not accustomed to. Martina doesn't let me play my game."

That 1983 Open was the last of a number of turning points for Navratilova. The rest was, as they say, gravy. And there was an awful lot of it—enough to drown all of her former critics. But one opinion about Navratilova voiced at the time stuck in my mind.

In 1984, Helen Hull Jacobs, a former Wimbledon and U.S. Open singles champion (vintage 1935), suggested that Navratilova was not an entirely complete player. "She could make one important addition to her game," Jacobs told *Tennis* magazine. "Navratilova has yet to produce a truly flat drive on either side. It may be the influence of champions like Bjorn Borg, Chris Evert, and others, but the flat drive is overlooked as a devastating shot and as an attacking weapon. Only a handful of players today hit a first-class flat drive." (Jacobs cited Jimmy Connors, John McEnroe, and Hana Mandlikova.)

It was easy to write Jacobs off as another old tennis nut badmouthing contemporary players. But Monica Seles demonstrated the validity of Jacobs's contention when she quickly and furiously blasted her way to the top of the game. Martina was no longer at her peak when Seles burst upon the scene. Nevertheless, the younger woman's minimalist, flat drives proved to be the best weapon against an entrenched volleyer, as well as devastating tools for keeping an opponent off balance. Even at her acrobatic, artistic best, Navratilova may not have been able to handle Seles's sheer, flat firepower.

This epigrammatic qualification doesn't diminish Navratilova's achievements or her remarkable transformation. She was a player who remade herself and ultimately fulfilled her extravagant potential. She accomplished that with more help, from a greater variety of people, than any other player in the Open era. There's nothing wrong with that, but the same tendency to simultaneously use and rely on a series of companions in her personal life often had different, less happy consequences.

The degree to which Martina Navratilova remained intellectually and emotionally malleable throughout her phenomenal career is nothing short of extraordinary. This hurt her in many ways, even as it helped her grow as a tennis player.

Just as Martina the player became an embodiment of the successive coaching philosophies of Richards and Estep, Martina the person also has a history of adopting the attitudes, habits, interests, and even the living conditions of her succession of companions. The proof is in the number of homes Martina has owned, in so many different places, throughout her career. Properly speaking, Navratilova is homeless. This may have psychic roots in her defection experience, but I think it has more to do with one of her great tools (flexibility) and one of her outstanding weaknesses (inconstancy).

Like so many other professional athletes, Martina of Starwood has the classic attributes of a taker. Often, the friends and companions who pointed her in a series of new directions became gracious victims of her basic lack of commitment. They wistfully waved good-bye as she bolted for a new person with a fresh and often different agenda.

Navratilova's itch to remake herself, often in the image of someone else, was a dominant theme in her life. In 1991, *Tennis* magazine published a picture of Navratilova taken during a duck hunt with her former doubles partner and buddy, Pam Shriver. Martina was dressed in camouflage, and she was holding a shotgun and a brace of ducks (she had often named Peking duck as her favorite dish). Not long afterward she met and became friends with the vegetarian lesbian country singer k. d. lang, and the next time I saw Navratilova, late in 1993, she was proselytizing against the meat-producing industry.

After her defection in 1976, Navratilova quickly settled into the Los Angeles home of tennis promoter Fred Barman, whose daughter, Shari, was an avid camp follower, friend of Rosie Casals, and functionary in the women's game. This placed the young, impressionable, gifted Czech right at the epicenter of the power elite in the women's game—Casals being a longtime associate of Billie Jean King, and a ranking member of the old-girl network that had emerged on the Virginia Slims tour.

Navratilova soon began to impersonate King in her rhetoric, her dress, and even her hairstyle. But despite her talent, Navratilova at that time couldn't play with any consistency. The press reveled in chronicling her consumer habits, her nouveau riche life-style, and the fragile, anxiety-prone temperament that made her a viable target for players who otherwise couldn't beat an egg.

I got to know Navratilova in that period, and we hit it off well thanks to a profile that I wrote about her for *Tennis* magazine. Bucking the tide, I argued that her flamboyant behavior and extravagant habits were not those of a superficial person but one who was compensating for the emotional shock and trauma of her defection. I also predicted that with stability she would overcome the flaws in her tennis psyche. She appreciated the support, and told me as much.

The person who eventually brought Navratilova out of that painful phase was not King but a pro golfer from Texas, Sandra Haynie. Not long after the two met in 1976, Martina left Los Angeles and bought a house to share with Haynie in Dallas, where Navratilova quickly molted into a typical suburban golf and tennis nut. Haynie was the first in a series of women who demonstrated that the content of Navratilova's relationships was almost invariably reflected in her tennis. If Haynie didn't exactly turn Navratilova into a champion, she at least pointed her in that direction. A cool, composed competitor and proponent of self-control, Haynie brought Navratilova out of her post-defection funk. She helped Navratilova curb the self-destructive freak-outs that caused her to lose so many matches. For Martina the player, life went along productively, if blandly, until she met the author Rita Mae Brown in 1978.

Being a writer, Brown used one of the oldest tricks in the book to meet Navratilova. She asked to pick her brain for a book on which she was working. Brown would later describe their first meeting as "a lunch that never ended." Soon after the New Year of 1979, Navratilova packed her bags and bought a regal home in the town where Brown lived, Williamsburg, Virginia. Navratilova quickly became a culture vulture.

Unfortunately, hopping onto the literary fast track had a negative effect on Martina's career. Brown's greatest flaw in an otherwise stimulating relationship was a cavalier indifference to the unfortunate but real demands of Navratilova's profession. When they traveled to tournaments together, their days were often a whirlwind of cultural search-and-absorb missions at theaters, museums, and art galleries, social engagements, and literary gabfests that often left Navratilova exhausted for the evening matches she had to play on the indoor circuit. A number of times Navratilova almost missed her match because of those other activities.

Soon the tension between her life and her profession was real and impossible to ignore. Enter, Nancy Lieberman.

Navratilova spotted Lieberman in the gallery while she was playing a match at Amelia Island, Florida, in April 1981. The two women were introduced later that day. Lieberman, a tough redhead with street manners to go along with her street smarts, was the best female basketball player in the United States at the time, and she was playing for the Dallas franchise of a pro league that would soon go belly-up. With her forthright *machisma*, Lieberman pushed all the right buttons in the floundering athlete Navratilova. Books about Henri Matisse and volumes of lesbian poetry were soon brushed off the coffee table as Navratilova cultivated her new friendship with Lieberman. Brown didn't pay the situation much mind until Navratilova declared that she was going to move into Lieberman's Dallas digs for a while, at which point Brown realized that she had been jilted.

After settling into the Dallas town house that Lieberman occupied, Martina once again went house hunting. This time, she decided to buy a new home in Virginia Beach, near the school where Lieberman had played basketball, Old Dominion.

Lieberman whipped Navratilova into physical shape and imbued her with the desire to concentrate on tennis. As a result, Martina began to assemble the small, goofy army of trainers, friends, advisors, technicians, dogs, and gofers that would set out to conquer the tennis kingdom under the flag of team Navratilova.

Enter Renee Richards, née Richard Raskind, a former male amateur player. Raskind had become a woman through the miracle of surgery at about the same time that Martina became an American through the miracle of defection, but the two did not form an alliance until 1981, just a few months after Navratilova had moved in with Lieberman. It turned out to be good timing because Navratilova needed somebody in her camp who knew and understood the actual game of tennis. As a former player and female pro, Richards had a vast store of experience.

But when Richards signed on as Martina's coach, she faced formidable problems and inevitable confusion over roles, mandates, and responsibilities in Team Navratilova. Richards, a tennis purist, had little use for most of Martina's entourage, and the inevitable tensions developed. Lieberman, who had come to Navratilova knowing nothing about tennis, had the good sense to learn from Richards before any serious confrontation transpired. As Navratilova's game reached new heights and disparate egos clamored for attention, Richards grew disgusted. Hedging her bet, she quietly slipped off in 1982 to try to reestablish her once flourishing ophthalmological practice. Thus, Richards did not arrive at the French Open of 1983 until the morning when Navratilova would play her fourth-round match against the fine American clay-court player Kathy Horvath.

Although Navratilova had played attacking tennis to win her first three matches handily, Richards advised her to stay back against the baseliner Horvath. By the time Navratilova and Horvath split sets, Lieberman had abandoned her seat alongside Richards and taken up a new post. From there she sent Navratilova a variety of coaching signals. Confused by this amoebic split in her camp, Navratilova lost the third set, 6–3.

Navratilova believed that Richards's strategic advice was disastrous, but she probably would have forgiven her coach. However, a distraught Richards left Paris the following morning without even having spoken to Navratilova. She left behind a note containing an ultimatum: If she was to continue as Navratilova's coach, she wanted absolute and unilateral control in that area. Navratilova rejected the ultimatum, leaving Lieberman the winner of the power struggle. But Lieberman, who was by then collecting a paycheck from Navratilova, probably underestimated her friend's growing independence and confidence.

Navratilova flew home after the loss to Horvath, but she graciously returned to Paris just two days later to attend the ITF's annual ball. She met Estep at the party and was so impressed by their conversation that she asked him to prepare her for the upcoming Wimbledon. By the time Martina returned to the United States, she was already having second thoughts about the degree of control Lieberman had seized over her life—power that she was wielding to alienate people as diverse as Chris Evert and Peter Johnson, Navratilova's business agent at IMG. Lieberman made disparaging remarks about Evert in the press and urged Navratilova to work up a hate for her rival and friend.

Wimbledon proved to be a sticky wicket for Navratilova in 1983, but only behind the scenes. She would win her fourth Wimbledon singles title handily, crushing Andrea Jaeger in the final, 6–0, 6–3. But her more formidable opponent during that fortnight was Lieberman, who was growing increasingly obsessive. Camp followers had taken to calling Lieberman "Agent Orange" because of her red hair and lethal tongue, and even Martina began to resent the degree to which Lieberman was trying to isolate her from her former friends.

But thanks to Estep, whose sound coaching and genuine friendship offset the machinations of Lieberman, Navratilova cleared her final and perhaps most difficult hurdle in the summer of 1983. For all of her prowess on the grass at Wimbledon and the fast carpets of the Virginia Slims circuit, Navratilova had experienced only frustration and failure at the U.S. Open. She still hadn't entirely shaken the "choker" label that once haunted her, but she won the 1983 U.S. Open impressively, beating Evert in the aforementioned final, 6–1, 6–3.

Eventually, in 1984, Navratilova broke with Lieberman and allowed her friend to claim she had initiated the break on the grounds that she stood in danger of being "overshadowed" by Navratilova. That was a genuine hoot, given the brief time and dim place Lieberman had occupied in the sports firmament. Weirder yet was Lieberman's almost immediate "offer" to help Evert, the very person she has so vigorously bad-mouthed for so long. Evert politely declined the offer.

Finally, Lieberman went after Navratilova's money, holding vague claims to having been a partner in some of Navratilova's business deals. Navratilova settled out of court and was finally rid of Lieberman for good. By then Martina had moved on. She was in love again, this time with a Texan whose yearning for celebrity was so strong that she was willing to abandon her own identity as the married mother of two boys. That woman was Judy Nelson.

If Richard Wagner had only lived one century later and had been a tennis nut, he might have written a fin de siècle tennis opera about

Navratilova's adventures. It might have been called the "lunch cycle" and contained as much greed and intrigue as his monumental Ring cycle. The first installment, The Never-Ending Lunch, would have been about Navratilova's relationship with Brown. The second installment, The Free Lunch, might have been about the Lieberman (gee, it even sounds like Niebelungen) episode in Navratilova's life. And the third and final opera in the trilogy would have been about the Nelson affair. She brought less to the table than either Brown or Lieberman, and she walked away with a whole lot more. Call it The Expensive Lunch.

Navratilova and Nelson began living together in Fort Worth. This presented a number of problems, not least of which was Nelson's proximity to the family she had left behind. Besides, Martina had already made and abandoned a life in Dallas, and more than once. So the two lit out for Aspen. The couple settled in the aptly named, exclusive community of Starwood. Navratilova took to horseback riding, skiing, and wearing truly awful cowboy hats. She made friends with lots of other celebrities, including the pro skier Cindy Nelson, but she lost some friends along the way, too.

One thing became very clear shortly after Navratilova and Nelson got together: The Fort Worth hausfrau certainly had her own ideas about the turf Navratilova occupied and how she ought to handle her manifest destiny as a celebrity. I experienced that firsthand just about a year after Nelson began to travel the tour with Navratilova. In fact, the incident caused my theretofore pleasant relations with Navratilova to suffer a blow from which they never did recover.

Once or twice a year in those heady times for women's tennis (circa 1986), I would write a general essay on the women's tour and its condition. To do that well for a magazine, I usually needed to speak to some of the top women players privately about the issues I would address in the essay. Most of them were more than happy to take twenty minutes or half an hour to share their views with me. I had always enjoyed easy access to Navratilova as well. So in the spring of 1986 I went to a tournament in Florida to do some interviewing for a story. I missed a chance to see Navratilova after one of her post-match press conferences, so I asked one of the public relations functionaries to tell Navratilova that I wanted to have a chat with her for my article. The young woman came back with a verbal message from Navratilova. She said she was sorry, that it was nothing personal, but she was no longer doing one-on-one interviews. Navratilova's decision may not have been "personal," but she was flouting the basic professional etiquette that dignifies the always tenuous relationship between newshounds and their subjects. I tell this story to illustrate the extent to which Martina, after she hooked up with Judy, developed an overinflated sense of her own status. She suddenly seemed to think that she had "outgrown" the small tennis community, and she no longer had any use for its conventions, or many of the people who had helped make her life pleasant in it.

"When Judy got into the act, the whole thing became a rock 'n' roll show," one disgruntled associate of Navratilova's told me. "That's when I learned the difference between a limo and a *stretch* limo."

Navratilova's peers also noticed the change. Many of them complained of the arrogance she exuded as an opponent. Granted, Jimmy Connors, John McEnroe, and Ivan Lendl also thrived on intimidating opponents once they set foot on the court, and they were often lauded for it, but the women have traditionally been more sensitive about and to such things.

Most women players during Navratilova's heyday knew that they were destined to be humiliated by 6–1, 6–2 scores anyway, so the last thing they wanted was to be made to feel as if their very presence on the court was an affront to Navratilova's genius. "It can be really uncomfortable," Andrea Land once told me. "When you play Martina, you feel like just nothing out there, like you have no right even to be there. . . . And a lot of that feeling is created by her attitude."

Pam Shriver and Navratilova were probably the greatest women's doubles team of all time (they won 79 titles together, 20 of them in Grand Slam events, and they were undefeated in 109 consecutive matches, from April 1983 to July 1985). But Shriver also became a victim of Navratilova's imperious ways, and a target for the possessive Texan, Nelson. The experience was doubly painful for Shriver, who had always cultivated Navratilova's friendship despite profound differences in everything from their political beliefs to their sexual identities.

Late in the 1980s, Nelson and Navratilova decided that they would design and market a line of tenniswear under Navratilova's name. It wasn't the worst idea, because Navratilova's open lesbianism kept her from pulling in the kind of lucrative endorsement contracts that women like Evert and Graf held. At a banquet shortly before Navratilova launched her new line overseas, Shriver offered to help out her friend by wearing the Navratilova line of clothing for their doubles matches in an upcoming tournament in Japan. Shriver then left the table, whereupon Nelson proceeded to warn Navratilova that Shriver was probably trying to get in on the ground floor of their great enterprise. She would probably want to be paid for wearing the clothes, too. Unbeknownst to Nelson, someone at the table happened to a guest of Shriver. You can imagine Shriver's reaction when the story made its way back to her.

Later, in 1989, Navratilova announced just three weeks before the U.S. Open that she would not be playing doubles with Shriver but with her Czech countrywoman Hana Mandlikova. That was an interesting decision in a variety of ways, and it allowed a peek into the complex world of personal politics in women's tennis.

Mandlikova was a highly gifted player who won three Grand Slam titles but she also had an unquenchable appetite for self-destruction. She would play beautiful attacking tennis one moment, clipping lines left and right, and then undergo a vicious mood swing that left her hitting the fence and railing at any handy scapegoat, from linesmen to ball kids. Mandlikova won the Australian Open in 1980 and reached the semifinals of the French Open and the finals of the U.S. Open that same year. She won the U.S. Open in 1985, and remained a constant if unpredictable threat until 1987, when she again won the Australian Open. Then she appeared to burn out, reaching only one quarterfinal in the next nine Grand Slam events she played.

Mandlikova dropped out of sight for a while and then emerged on the tour as the coach and companion of the promising young Czech player Jana Novotna. Mandlikova's own longtime coach and companion, the former Dutch pro Betty Stove, was conspicuously absent. The idea that Mandlikova, who was perhaps the most erratic and uncoachable top player yet produced in the pro game, would wind up as a coach herself was nearly as hilarious as the sham wedding she staged in 1986 in order to acquire Australian citizenship. Many veteran tennis observers were nonplussed to learn that Navratilova had ditched Shriver and taken Mandlikova as a partner before the U.S. Open of 1989. Those who were familiar with the sexual politics and the lethal role played by significant others on the women's tour saw a certain amount of sense in the move—although there was no sexual rivalry between Shriver and Nelson, there was a fair measure of antipathy.

Shriver was stunned and hurt by Navratilova's decision to drop her, particularly because it was made just three weeks before the U.S. Open. "I guess she decided to give me a kick in the butt," Shriver said. "If she was just a friend, I would have said, 'You're a rotten friend.' But this is our business, too, so it was extra rotten." Shriver then teamed up with Mary Joe Fernandez, and they reached the final, where Navratilova and Mandlikova were waiting. It was a tense and unpleasant match. At one point Fernandez, a gentle soul, kicked a ball in frustration. She didn't kick it hard, but the ball passed near Navratilova, who had her back turned. Navratilova whirled around and glared at Shriver, who threw up her hands and protested that she'd had nothing to do with it.

In the equally tense post-match conference, some newshound suggested that Shriver had fired a ball across the net near Navratilova, and asked if Shriver had meant to hit her former partner with it.

"No," said Shriver, adding, "If I had wanted to hit her, I would have done it."

It was a sad, final comment on an epochal partnership.

Navratilova had been at her zenith when she fell in love with Nelson, but less than three years later she would fall from the number one ranking and never hold it again, thanks mostly to the emergence of Steffi Graf. By then, Estep was long gone. Tim Gullickson, another fine tennis mind, took a crack at coaching Navratilova in 1988, but when she failed to win a Grand Slam title that year, the partnership dissolved. Navratilova then hired as her new coach the Dallas teaching pro Craig Kardon. He was quickly absorbed into Team Navratilova, and he proved to be a staunch loyalist, hitting partner, and cheerleader.

All in all, Nelson was lucky that the fulfillment of Navratilova's potential was not really a dangerous issue in their relationship, as it had been in so many of Navratilova's previous liaisons. At the same time, Navratilova suddenly had more time on her hands to enjoy her life and celebrity. By 1990 the relationship between Navratilova and Nelson was beginning to show signs of strain.

In 1991 rumors were flying about liaisons between Navratilova and other women. Navratilova sent Nelson a letter dissolving their relationship. Regrettably for Martina of Starwood, Nelson was in possession of a "non-marital cohabitation agreement" signed by the two women in 1986 and videotaped for posterity. In true celebrity fashion, Navratilova claimed that she had signed the agreement hastily, without even bothering to read it.

Nelson claimed that she had "explored every possible avenue to avoid litigation and the resulting publicity without success," and she then filed a suit asking for a whopping $10 million settlement. Navratilova claimed that she had spent nearly $2 million on Nelson and her family during their relationship, and she felt that Nelson deserved zilch. The lawyers went to work, dealing with such crucial issues as Nelson's demands for visitation privileges with Navratilova's dogs. The rumor mill churned on. Nelson and Navratilova finally settled for an undisclosed sum of money, and Nelson got the house in Starwood.

Celebrities. They're always eating lunch. In fact, they're often eating each other's lunch. Wagner would have gotten a kick out of it all.

CHAPTER 14

FROM GENTLEMEN TO JERKS
Sportsmanship in the Open Era

SHORTLY AFTER THE TROPHY PRESENTATION following the junior girls final at the U.S. Open in 1989, a tournament official was approached by a sheepish ballboy holding, of all things, the cut glass runner-up trophy. "Rachel McQuillen [who had just been beaten in the final by Jennifer Capriati] gave me this," the ball boy reported. "I don't know what I'm supposed to do with it."

After the presentation ceremony, McQuillen had simply handed him the trophy and told him to keep it. The dejected Australian girl then packed her kit and left the court. The ballboy didn't know what to do next. He certainly didn't want to get in trouble, so he dutifully reported the incident. The bewildered official got on the phone and made some calls. She finally contacted McQuillen's father in the players' lounge. She explained that his daughter had left behind her trophy and that it could be sent right over.

"If she gave away the trophy, she doesn't want it," Mr. McQuillen said.

"But this is the runner-up trophy to the U.S. Open," the official remarked.

"I told you," the man growled. "If she wanted the bloody thing, she would have kept it. Besides, she already got one of those last year. Now good-bye."

In tennis, a sport long associated with restraint and good manners, the final nails may have been driven into the coffin containing the concept of sportsmanship in the late 1980s. How could it have been otherwise, at a time when feeling good about anyone but yourself was passé? Come to think of it, it was an awful decade for feeling good even about yourself, unless you happened to finish number one at something and stood with your heel pressed into someone else's forehead. In such

313

times even the runner-up in the junior girls singles of the U.S. Open felt as if she were just another bozo with a heelprint on her forehead.

Being preoccupied with this subject of sportsmanship in 1989, I paid special attention to some of the other shenanigans that occurred at Flushing Meadow that year. They included these events:

- In a first-round match, an American kid named Paul Chamberlin tried so diligently to intimidate and hit Javier Sanchez with the ball that the young Spaniard finally became exasperated and quite dolorously complained to the umpire, "This guy is not just trying to hit me, he is trying to kill me." Fortunately for Sanchez, Chamberlin's talents were so modest that he could barely keep the ball in the court, much less find the considerably smaller target presented by Sanchez's head.
- The unpleasantly tense doubles match featuring good friends and former partners Pam Shriver and Martina Navratilova on opposite sides of the net, in the women's double final, took place at the Open of 1989 (the situation was described at length in the last chapter).
- Amos Mansdorf, tired of hearing Yannick Noah's sister cheering madly every time he made an error or struck an errant first serve in his match against Noah, sauntered over to the players' guest box and cursed out Noah's entire family. Consequently, Noah refused to shake Mansdorf's hand after the match ended. The two players then aired their grievances through the press.

And these were just the incidents I observed knocking around the tournament. Who knows the full extent of the bickering, backbiting, and mudslinging that went on during that Open of 1989—on court, in the players' lounge, behind the closed doors of the dressing room, or even in the corporate marquee.

The most striking feature of the controversies listed above is not the common thread between them but the lack of one. Clearly, there was a failure throughout the system, caused by a lack of consensus on the nature of sportsmanship, improperly channelled aggression, obsession with winning, failure of or disinterest in communication, partisanship gone rampant, and unwillingness to accept defeat graciously.

But to understand the new barbarism in tennis we have to understand the old notions of sportsmanship and gentlemanly conduct that peaked in the Anglo world from which tennis sprang in the first half of this century. Most of us think we know what good sportsmanship is, at least in the sense that even if we can't exactly define it, we can identify it when we see it. But the following anecdote, told to me by Don Budge, may leave you wondering about that.

In 1937, Budge was a raw, well-intentioned youth of twenty-two, and rapidly developing as a player of uncommon talent. At Wimbledon that year he had to beat Bitsy Grant in the semifinal to reach the Championship match against a German player renowned and celebrated for his lofty standards of conduct, Baron Gottfried von Cramm.

The semifinal between Budge and Grant produced an unfortunate officiating error. Down by two sets to one and playing a point at deuce at four-all in the fourth set, Grant hit a drive to the baseline. A puff of chalk indicated that the ball had caught the line, but the linesman called the ball out. Budge was loath to reach a potentially decisive break point through an injustice, so he made a flagrant error during the next point to redress the mistake. He still went on to get the service break, and he quickly served out the match.

Later, von Cramm approached Budge in the players' tearoom. As the two had not yet met, von Cramm graciously introduced himself. He complimented Budge on the quality of his game and then asked to have a word in private with him outside. They sat down on a bench on the grounds, and von Cramm good-naturedly chided Budge for acting in an unsportsmanlike manner in his match against Grant. Puzzled and deflated, Budge asked von Cramm to explain. "That break point you gave back with an obvious error, do you realize what you did with that? You embarrassed that poor linesman in front of ten thousand people by bringing even more attention to the error he had made." Von Cramm went on to insist that in the final they must play every ball the way it was called, regardless of the effect it might have on the result. According to von Cramm, that was the surest way to vouchsafe the dignity of the game and all of its principals.

"And that was just what we did," Budge told me almost fifty years later. "And it all worked out fine. I never forgot that incident because I learned a lot from it. It made me aware that sportsmanship didn't necessarily have to do with justice. And it doesn't have that much to do with the immediate outcome of a point or a match. It has to do with how you treat people and how you accept the inevitable mistake or accident that could affect the outcome of a match. Mostly, that incident taught me that tennis in the end is just a game you play and to which you bring more or less beauty and dignity. From that day on, my attitude was always to play every point the way it fell without trying to intrude on the process for my own benefit or even for the benefit of my opponent."

As the sociologist E. Digby Baltzell once told me, "Sportsmanship has a lot to do with having empathy for others. Everybody makes a mistake now and then. Every official is going to make a bad call occasionally. Look at a professional baseball player. If he gets a hit one out of three times at bat, he's a superstar even though he failed to do his job properly two-thirds of the time."

This reminds me of the most startling and hilarious display of bad sportsmanship that I ever witnessed. Fittingly enough, it occurred at the last U.S. Open staged at the West Side Tennis Club, in 1977, before a packed house, in a semifinal match between Jimmy Connors and the Italian clay-court specialist Corrado Barazzutti. The Italian press had dubbed Barazzutti "Soldatino" (little soldier) for the hangdog way he went about his business, which was grinding down opponents on clay.

In the sixth game of the match, Barazzutti reached break point against Connors's serve. During a rally, Connors hit an unreturnable crosscourt forehand that landed on the green clay near the far sideline from the umpire. The linesman made no call, the point was apparently over, and Connors was back at deuce.

But in his typical Gloomy Gus fashion, Barazzutti made some hand gestures indicating exasperation. He frowned and shook his head as he strolled over to where the ball had landed. He examined the mark left in the clay and asked the linesman to come out and see for himself that Connors's shot had landed wide. Connors immediately took off at a trot. He went around the net post and over to where the aggrieved Barazzutti stood, hands on his hips, waiting for the linesman. Connors then proceeded to erase the mark by vigorously scuffing his tennis shoe on it. Barazzutti watched, slack-jawed. The umpire passed those uncomfortable moments gazing up at the pretty clouds in the blue sky.

As Connors returned to his side of the net, the crowd erupted with boos and catcalls. Connors turned to them, and in a reference to his status as the last American player left in contention, cried out, "I'm the last one you've got left, so you'd better pull for me."

The crowd was not convinced. Although Connors handily defeated Barazzutti, he was upset in the final by a paragon of good sportsmanship, Guillermo Vilas. The American crowd loved every minute of it.

I can't think of any anecdote or testimony that so vividly describes how far tennis has traveled from its roots. I know that even in von Cramm's own time his ethic was not universal, but he did pass it on to Budge, who passed it on to a succession of players from Rod Laver to Bjorn Borg to Stefan Edberg. But generally the ethic has been supplanted by a comprehensive, complex set of "rules" that are delineated in a formidable document, an entire book called the ATP Code of Conduct.

Tennis in the Open era featured a proliferation of rules and laws that, instead of ensuring good conduct, often seemed to exist in a symbiotic relationship with offensive or unsportsmanlike conduct. The claim made by almost all the players who violate the good sportsmanship mandate is that the tennis match they happened to be playing in was "too important" to be plagued by a bad call here or there. In other words, they just don't get it. Contempt for officials has been part of the pro credo from day one, and nobody ever had a more irrational and unpredictable aversion to officials than the fine doubles player Scott Davis.

This gifted Angeleno hit his zenith as part of a doubles partnership (with David Pate) dubbed "The Nasty Boys." Davis took his cues from his opponents, rendering them the same degree of respect that he felt coming from them. But Davis had no such patience for officials. He reacted to them the way Don Quixote responded to the sight of a windmill. Davis spent entire matches muttering at umpires under his breath (even when there were no questionable calls). He bickered with them, he provoked them. This ump-basher extraordinaire was so repulsed by the mere sight of an official that he made it a practice to avoid the traditional handshake that players generally exchange with an umpire after a match.

"I know I create things in my mind," Davis told me. "And when I talk to the ump, I'm not exactly getting him on my side. In fact, I always knew I was getting into risky territory the minute I began talking to an umpire. First I talk, then I begin to see red. It's weird."

In 1988 during a singles match in Cincinnati, Davis was slapped with what he felt was an unjust point penalty that put him down 4–5, 0–30, with his opponent serving. Incensed, he hit his next service return as hard as he could, right at the chair umpire. "I lost the match and I got fined $500," Davis said. "It might have been worth it if I had actually hit the guy, but I missed."

Davis was just one of a number of players who underwent a remarkable transformation the moment they set foot on a court. For them, the beginning of a match did not signal a demand to be on good behavior but license to indulge their most spontaneous aggressive instincts.

One of the most interesting and important controversies over sportsmanship occurred during the doubles final of the U.S. Open in 1985 between the popular French team of Yannick Noah and Henri LeConte, and the brilliant new American pairing of Ken Flach and Robert Seguso. The match was a corker, with each team winning a set in a tiebreaker. In the third set tiebreaker, Noah and LeConte reached 6–4 and thus held a set point. During the ensuing point, LeConte drilled a volley that clipped the net cord, whizzed perilously close to Flach's head, and sailed beyond the baseline. Noah and LeConte were sure that the ball had ticked Flach's shoulder, which would have made it their point—and set. Seguso seemed to think so, too, because he started walking off the court as if the set were finished.

But umpire Zeno Phau did not overrule the baselinesman's call of "out." He gave the point to Flach and Seguso, and the Frenchmen immediately asked Phau for an overrule. The umpire said he didn't see what had happened. Noah called across the net, asking Flach to give up the point. Seguso asked Flach what had happened, and Flach replied, "If anything, it brushed my hair." By the rules, that would have made it Noah and LeConte's point. But Flach would not surrender the point, claiming that he wasn't sure that the ball had touched him. He may have just "felt" it whiz by his long locks. He insisted that the call had to come from the umpire, who had already admitted that he was not sure the ball had touched Flach.

The Frenchmen were stunned, and they just quit, losing the tiebreaker and letting the next set go at love. Flach and Seguso won the championship, the first of their many Grand Slam doubles titles, 6–7, 7–6, 7–6, 6–0. During the trophy presentation after the match, CBS-TV analyst Tony Trabert asked Flach over an open microphone if the disputed ball had hit him. Flach reiterated his position, and the crowd of twenty thousand jeered his reply.

The post-match press conference was an inquisition that went off in all directions at once. I had only one question, and it had less to do with the Code of Conduct than its precursor, a USTA pamphlet simply called The Code. This was a considerably less byzantine document, written by the former dean of tennis officials, Colonel Nick Powell. It was distributed to all kids, including Flach, who took part in organized competition. Essentially, The Code set down guidelines for competition between players who make their own line calls. And The Code clearly stated that when a player wasn't sure if a ball was out or in, he was ethically obliged to give the benefit of the doubt to his opponent.

When I brought this up at the press conference, Flach's reply was telling. "I wouldn't think that would apply on the professional level. That's why you have umpires and linesmen."

The debate raged on for the rest of the day: in the stands, in the press box, and in the locker room. Flach's reply may have been honest, but the general sentiment was that he was taking refuge in the rules and refusing to face a demand of conscience. Given the evolution of tennis, this was the surprising eruption of an ethos that had been driven underground. The concept of sportsmanship has not completely vanished from the pro game, but it has been redefined endlessly and altered from a simple, straightforward code into something that, like contemporary religion, many people make up as they go along to accommodate their desires or actions. For instance, Connors always felt that in order to succeed with the general public, tennis had to be a spectacle, filled with colorful and controversial characters. And McEnroe often justified his boorish behavior as a by-product of his desire to take tennis to "the next, exciting level as a sport."

Some feel that good sportsmanship is a matter of following the letter of the law spelled out in the Code of Conduct—no more, no less. Others believe that righting a perceived wrong is the essence of sportsmanship. The deconstruction of the relatively simple concept of sportsmanship explains the development of the elaborate Code of Conduct. But the guidelines in the code could not promote a general, universal ethos, they could only spell out specific rules and prohibitions. Still, veteran players developed more or less traditional notions of sportsmanship, and aspiring players often ran headfirst into them. These players constituted a new class, the Tennis Jerks.

One of the most vivid examples I stumbled upon in my quest to define the Tennis Jerk in 1989 occurred at a tournament played in the idyllic Green Mountains, near Stratton, Vermont, the Volvo International. I watched a match that featured Pieter Aldrich, a South African who was ranked 108 at the time, against a qualifier, Eric Amend, a college player who did not have a world ranking. But he had wicked ground strokes—lashing, hissing, smoking groundies—that he was putting to good use against Aldrich.

Amend reached set point early in the match and promptly hit a sizzling backhand service return winner. When the ball fell good, Amend cried out ecstatically and pumped his fists. Up on the player's patio, Aldrich's countrymen did not like what they were seeing at all. Like the Aussies, the South Africans spend less time at home than European or American players. Thus, they cultivate closer friendships and develop fraternal pride and group notions of conduct.

In the first game of the second set, Aldrich made a point of chiding Amend for his histrionics. But there was no stopping the kid. He was on a roll, he was pumped. He was all those things he thought Connors and McEnroe were at the time they began their rapid ascent to the top of tennis.

The match was a cliff-hanger. It went to a third-set tiebreaker in which Amend was down four match points at 2–6. But the American came back to win the tiebreaker, 10–8, whereupon he flung his racket so high that it nearly came down with ice on its strings.

The South Africans on the patio slowly got up and adjourned to the locker room. One of them observed, "Look at the guy. He acts as if he's just won Wimbledon."

Amend gathered up his things and floated off to the locker room, where he suddenly came plummeting back to earth. "That locker room should have been the greatest place on earth," Amend ruefully told me later, "but when I walked inside, I felt all those eyes all over me. I felt these cold stares coming at me from everywhere."

Of course Amend was just a kid, and a pretty nice one at that. He had no idea that the pros he wanted to emulate clung to a code that had never been spelled out for him—and then he read it in the eyes of the tour regulars in the locker room. The code said that when you're beating up on a guy with a higher ranking, you don't rub his face in it. You kill him as quietly and deferentially as possible.

"I was like a kid in a candy store," Amend told me. "There I was at Stratton, in the same locker room with guys who basically were my heroes. I was winning matches in qualifying. I was winning sets in a real big-time tour event. Sure I was excited. I just didn't know that there were okay ways and unacceptable ways to show what I was feeling."

At the Lipton Player's International Championships on Key Biscayne that same year, Mats Wilander played the American touring pro Todd Witsken. Steady, lethal Wilander was trouncing Witsken so soundly that on one changeover the frustrated Witsken loudly and childishly questioned Wilander's gender and disparaged the Swede's precise baseline game. It was a little bit like some tomato can telling Mike Tyson that even though he was the heavyweight champion, he sort of had a sissy voice. Wilander proceeded to win every game.

There was little sympathy in the locker room for Witsken. If you're getting whipped and can't do anything about it, you're supposed to keep quiet and take it like a man. It is also taboo to "personalize" a match by allowing your frustration to erupt as anger toward another player, unless he's having his way with you because of gamesmanship, or cheating.

The tennis tour has always had a pecking order, but some of the changes in the Open era altered the way it was manifested. As top players became celebrities and multimillionaires, they often lost all sense of fraternity with their peers and lost touch with the general tennis community. They often demanded special treatment, and usually got it from most, but not all, quarters.

Brad Gilbert, a very funny, gregarious fellow who wrote an interesting book called *Winning Ugly*, ran afoul of John McEnroe on a few occasions—most notably at the season-ending Masters playoff in January 1986, a time when McEnroe was a frazzled, burned-out champion about to take a hiatus from the tour.

Gilbert, a solid, Top 10 player whose artfully mild game frustrated and outwitted many power players, had an 0–7 career record against McEnroe going into their match, but he quickly began to exploit McEnroe's general fatigue and impatience. By the time the men split sets, they were jawing at each other during changeovers. And as Gilbert took control of the match, McEnroe delivered the ultimate insult, shouting, "You don't deserve to be on the same court with me."

Uncowed, Gilbert went on to win, 5–7, 6–3, 6–1. Afterward, Gilbert said, "The top guys get away with a lot more when it comes to their conduct and tactics. You've got to be ready to stand up for your rights if you have any hopes of beating the top guys. You just can't go out there feeling intimidated."

"The top guys are very territorial in a psychological way," the hard-hitting Texan Steve Denton once told me. "They don't like to have their mental space invaded. Question their antics, challenge their mental control of a match, and they tend to get saucy."

This wasn't mere pop psychology from Denton, because he tested the theory himself on a few occasions against McEnroe. They once had an altercation during a doubles match at Wimbledon and continued their debate in a locker room shouting match afterward. A few weeks later, in Toronto, Denton again found McEnroe's behavior objectionable. He put down his racket and invited McEnroe up to the net for a more intimate confrontation. The next time the two men played singles, Denton beat McEnroe to reach the final of the ATP Championships in Cincinnati.

In fact, during his years on the tour, Denton took it upon himself to be a one-man jerk patrol, refusing to tolerate antics that most other players accepted as an occupational hazard. In the early 1980s, Denton and his partner Kevin Curren formed one of the best doubles teams of the time. They once lost a match to Chip Hooper and McEnroe's good friend Peter Rennart, 7–6 in the third, at a tournament in Milan, Italy. Feeling that Rennart had acted like a jerk, Denton pounced on him in the locker room. He had him by the throat when Curren and Hooper intervened and separated the two men.

On another occasion Denton was so annoyed at Jimmy Gurfein's antics that he said, "If you come into the locker room after this match, I'm going to give you a whipping." Gurfein decided to go straight from the courts to the hotel without taking a shower or changing clothes.

Some of you may deduce from all this that Denton was a violent, angry person who couldn't contain his aggression. Actually he was just carrying out the mandate of a traditional code of honor, one which implied that the cleanest and simplest way to end some kinds of disputes was with a good shot to the kisser. This can be a lot more satisfying, not to mention simpler and cheaper, than lodging a complaint with an administrator, or filing a lawsuit.

As a matter of fact, Denton's fellow players voted him the ATP Sportsmanship Award for 1982. He was also one of the very few players who ever expressed the most unfashionable sentiment of the pro era: empathy for officials.

"I think that having a certain amount of respect and showing support for umpires is an aspect of sportsmanship," Denton said. "I try to catch myself when I get carried away, when I get overdemanding. I mean, how often do you hear a player say, 'Hey, that was a great call'? But then, I never did agree with the 'anything to win' mentality. I need to feel that I have a clear conscience out there and that I haven't violated the standards of my profession. Also, I'm probably more affected by what other people think of me than some of the top guys. More and more, they actually seem to thrive on adversity."

One of the strange things that happens when players begin to develop custom definitions of sportsmanship is that the urge to be a nice guy and a crowd pleaser often backfires. Nobody likes to be patronized or upstaged by an opponent.

Early in his career, Andre Agassi performed a startling faux pas during a Davis Cup match in Argentina, in July 1989. Leading Marin Jaite by two sets to love and 4–0, Agassi made a barehanded catch of Jaite's serve to give the Argentinean a game in the third set. The cavalier gesture incensed the ever-sensitive Latin fans, and Agassi's mentor McEnroe soon sorted him out.

"Andre pulls some stuff that doesn't feel too good to the other guys out there," McEnroe said. "Actually, it's the opposite of what I'm always been accused of doing, but it amounts to the same thing. Nobody likes to be bullied out there, and nobody likes to be crowded off the court. If you hog the whole show by playing great and making a spectacle of yourself, one way or another you're disrupting the balance."

Gamesmanship has a rich and colorful history in tennis, and even the Code of Conduct cannot monitor a player's penchant for playing mind games. Take Ros Fairbank, a mild-mannered South African who had full command of all the tricks in the gamesman's bag. Paula Smith once appealed to a tournament referee for a ruling on Fairbank's insistence on standing inside the service line when receiving a serve. Fairbank nearly upset Navratilova at Wimbledon in 1989 in a match in which she tried to pull every trick in the book. She repeatedly caught her service toss without striking the ball. She began jumping around when Navratilova prepared to serve, presumably to distract her. She employed some delaying tactics.

"With Ros, it's entirely possible that she was doing all that to upset Martina," another woman player told me. "She's known on the tour for playing little mind games. It's all kind of silly in the long run. Nobody pays it much mind."

When I asked Pam Shriver for a short list of tennis jerks, she replied, "Actually, the person who stands out the most in my mind for jerky behavior is me." Shriver felt that her supreme moment as a jerk occurred at the U.S. Open of 1984 when she was twenty-two. She was upset in the quarterfinals by Wendy Turnbull, after which she blithely told the world press that it was a shame "for tennis" that Turnbull had beaten her. Shriver felt that she would have given Martina Navratilova a much better match in the next round than Turnbull.

"I said it with a straight face," she told me years later, "and I still wince whenever I think of it."

Anne White, a slender, attractive girl who turned Wimbledon on its collective ear one year by playing a match in a tight, form-fitting white body suit, had an extensive repertoire of facial expressions and sarcastic cracks. Before playing a doubles match against White, some opponents agreed that whoever managed to hit White with the ball would get a free dinner for her markswomanship.

You might think that the genteel enterprise of mixed doubles would be free from bad sportsmanship, but mixed doubles in the Open era often had a curious way of bringing out the worst in players, particularly male players. Anne Henricksson once played the mixed doubles at Wimbledon with the Dutchman Michiel Shapers. In one match their female opponent, Laurie Feld, fell down during a point. Shapers promptly drilled her in the back with an overhead. Feld's partner had to be restrained from going after Shapers.

Gilbert had an interesting take on the lack of respect that characterized relations between the players in the 1980s. He said, "By winning Wimbledon at seventeen, Boris Becker spread this feeling that it was not only okay to win big titles at that age but necessary in order to make a big splash and get in on the big money and publicity. So you've got eighteen- and nineteen-year-old kids out there who are like animals.

"These kids never lived anywhere but at home, so they don't know what it's like to have to get along with other people. They have these new, big rackets that they can use to fire aces or to drill the ball through your forehead. These guys, they don't respect the top players. In fact, they don't respect anybody, maybe not even themselves. The bottom line is that nobody is untouchable anymore."

Oh, the perils of living in a dog-eat-dog—whoops, make that puppy-eat-puppy—world.

The degradation of the concept of sportsmanship in the Open era had at least one pleasant side effect, the creation of a handful of players who could be called heroes. This chapter would be incomplete if I didn't try to identify at least some of them. There isn't enough space to mention the scores of fair-minded, dedicated men and women who played in the pro era—the Dentons and Brian Gottfrieds and Manuela Maleevas—but they were there.

First, some kind of definition of a hero is in order. The first and perhaps most important attribute is courage. In tennis, a largely psychological game, the most workable definition is one that Ernest Hemingway gave us when he defined "guts" as the ability to show "grace under pressure." Outstanding Open-era players who have projected that form of courage—and enjoyed the ensuing public adoration—include Evonne Goolagong, Chris Evert, Tracy Austin, Rod Laver, John Newcombe, Stan Smith, Arthur Ashe, Stefan Edberg, Mats Wilander, and, of course, Bjorn Borg.

But the two players who most consistently projected grace under pressure on the great stage that is the Open-era game were undoubtedly Evert and Borg. One of the key differences between them and some of the players who never quite achieved hero status is that an astute spectator could sense it wasn't very easy for Evert and Borg to behave as they did. Yet both of them routinely triumphed over any urge to abandon their self-control.

Heroes never look trigger-happy (the Navratilova problem) or bloodthirsty (the Connors problem). They don't berate older women sitting in chairs watching lines, or slam chairs around when things aren't going their way (the McEnroe problem). And we want heroes to project exemplary self-control without appearing remote (the Lendl problem).

Stan Smith did not amass a record that even approached that of Borg; in fact, his highest world singles ranking was 3. But Smith defined the conventional hero at a time when society seemed more interested in rebels and iconoclasts. Smith achieved that honor despite often seeming rigid, distant, and even arrogant. There were striking parallels between the careers and personalities of Smith and his lifelong friend Arthur Ashe. But while Ashe's unique place as an African-American champion automatically invested him with distinction, Smith was an almost stereotypical WASP among many, and he still somehow rose to hero status.

Smith consolidated his status on two important fronts: through his Davis Cup record and in his rivalry with Ilie Nastase. Like Ashe, Smith was a Davis Cup stalwart, amassing a 15–5 record in singles and a 20–3 mark in doubles, with two prominent partners: Bob Lutz and Erik van Dillen. Smith provided the U.S. team with the clinching third point in sixteen ties—thirteen times in doubles and three times in singles.

But the high-water mark in Smith's career was the Davis Cup final against Romania, which was contested in the hostile environment of

Bucharest in late 1972. The site of the tie was the Progresul Sports Club, where Ilie Nastase had grown up and subsequently amassed a streak of twenty straight Davis Cup singles victories. The surface at Progresul was the same slow red clay that had prevented Smith, a serve-and-volley player whose game was tailored to fast, hard courts, from ever getting beyond the quarterfinals at the French Open. Nastase, by contrast, was a former French Open champion, the holder of the U.S. Open title, and, at the time of the tie, the number one player in the world.

As always, the referee was from a neutral nation, but the referee has almost nothing to do with the mechanics of matchplay, and he gets involved in matters such as the integrity of line calls only after the umpire has lost control of the proceedings. In this case, the Romanian chair umpires never lost control of a match because they swiftly backed up every shamelessly partisan call made by the Romanian linesmen.

Smith opened the tie by winning the most important singles match of his career. He upset the heavily favored Nastase in straight sets, 11–9, 6–2, 6–3, under nerve-wracking conditions that subsequently led him to complain, "I had to concentrate so hard, I got a headache."

In the second match, Ion Tiriac used all the wiles that would later help him become a highly successful coach and entrepreneur, along with an appalling amount of gamesmanship, to upset Tom Gorman. After the United States won the doubles to take a 2–1 lead in the match, the Americans' hopes seemed to rest on Smith's shoulders. If the crafty Tiriac could find a way to beat Smith, shell-shocked Tom Gorman would have to play the match of his life in the tiebreaking fifth rubber of an away match against the number one player in the world.

As soon as Tiriac and Smith got under way, the Romanian began to orchestrate the boisterous hometown crowd. The spectators chanted Tiriac's name and greeted each point he won with ecstatic outbursts. They showered Smith with boos and catcalls, called out and banged on pots while he was trying to serve, and pulled out all the stops in their attempt to rattle the American. In addition, a reliable witness counted at least fourteen flagrant bad calls, all of which benefited Tiriac. But Smith persevered in the tense match, 4–6, 6–2, 6–4, 2–6, 6–0, giving the United States the vital point in one of the most controversial and memorable ties in Davis Cup history.

But the rivalry between Smith and Nastase was not defined by anything as simple as nationalistic loyalties or competitions. Although Nastase, Newcombe, Smith, Ashe, Laver, and others were all professionals by then, Nastase was the first great player of the Open era to flout the amateur ethic. Thus, his encounters with Smith took on the dimensions of neat morality plays.

Smith was the very model of a blond-haired, blue-eyed Christian soldier, a product of the amateur values that still obtained during his formative years, and an army man to boot. To the public he represented the forces of light, whereas Nastase—swarthy, puckish, volatile, and vulgar—represented the forces of darkness. He was a street urchin from a nation where the totalitarian communist rule had institutionalized amorality, creating a culture of cheaters. Because the empowered bureaucrats stole from the nation with impunity, the oppressed population viewed beating the inhumane "system" a worthy and even honorable pastime.

On top of all that, Nastase had loads of charisma. He appeared to be part buffoon, part demon, and part genius. He would give his opponents points after bad calls against them, and then turn around and attempt to steal calls on his own behalf. He threw distracting tantrums, poked fun at his opponents, and never knew where to draw the line between harmless fun and ugly gamesmanship. What often began as joshing often degenerated into mean or cruel conduct. Tiriac, Nastase's mentor, described him best with the famous remark: "Ilie doesn't have a brain, he has a bird flying around inside his head."

Moreover, Nastase played a game of sublime beauty. No other player in the Open era has his fluid grace or imagination. Nastase played as if that racket was not a cumbersome impediment but a limber, magical extension of his arm. By contrast, Smith's game was deliberate and wooden; *his* racket was a tool that had to be controlled and used with care and patience to perform a limited number of mundane tasks.

Say what you will about the great rivalries between Connors and Borg, McEnroe and Lendl, or even Evert and Navratilova. None of them had as much resonance as the confrontations between Smith and Nastase. This quality can't be quantified by statistics, but some numbers are worth examining.

Neither player was able to maintain his place at the top of the game for very long, and Smith never did manage to reach the number one ranking (the closest he came was number three, in August 1973). Smith won thirty-nine career titles in fifteen years of competition on the official circuit, but only two Grand Slam events: the U.S. Open of 1971 and Wimbledon of 1972. Smith also won the title at the first of the season-ending "playoff" events, the Grand Prix Masters of Tokyo in 1970, although under the round-robin format he did not have to play a proper "championship" match.

Nastase won fifty-seven singles titles and held the world number one ranking for about six months, beginning in August 1973. He survived on the tour for a remarkable seventeen years, beginning in 1968. But

Nastase's period of greatness was also compressed into roughly five years. He won the same number of Grand Slam titles as Smith, capturing the U.S. Open of 1972 and the French Open of 1973, but Nasty won the Masters four times (1971, 1972, 1973, 1975).

The record gives Nastase a 7–3 edge over Smith in tour events, including wins in two of their only three meetings in Grand Slam events. Nastase defeated Smith in the second round of the 1969 U.S. Open and in the quarterfinals of the 1971 French Open. But Smith won their crucial meeting in the Wimbledon final of 1972, and he had a perfect 4–0 record against Nastase in Davis Cup play. Thus, the singles head-to-head becomes a symmetrical 7–7. Additionally, Smith and his Davis Cup doubles partners put together a 3–1 record against Nastase and Tiriac.

This is curiously appropriate because the striking similarities in the resumes of the two men suggest that while they often appeared to be bitter enemies who represented wildly different sensibilities, they had a symbiotic relationship and brought the best out in each other.

As the Open era evolved, it became increasingly difficult to be identified as a hero. One of the promises of the revolution that created the ATP Tour was that tennis would be made "respectable"—more "professional," if you will, than in the heydays of Nastase, Connors, and McEnroe. This change has undoubtedly occurred, but with side effects that were accurately prophesied by one of the men who inspired it: Connors.

Connors always claimed that once the bureaucrats got control of the game, they would suppress the expressive personalities who brought droves of fans to tennis early in the Open era. There's often a very fine line, of course, between a "colorful" character and a lout, but Connors's point is well taken.

Possessing heroic virtues doesn't necessarily make a player morally superior, either. In the end, tennis is just a game. Some of the ageless kids who play it happen to be savvy and mature enough to manage and control their emotions, while others are not. In a way, both sportsmanship and winning have a lot to do with self-control, and among all the great players, only McEnroe appeared able to routinely elevate his game while losing control of his emotions.

Heroes also are probably more image-conscious than villains, yet less inclined to reveal their innermost feelings. That can be a real liability these days when the media and public exalt in personal confessions and controversies. McEnroe was always a man of singular honesty, liberally mixed with qualifying doses of self-interest and, occasionally, delusions. In his own way he clung to a conviction as firm as any moral position, even if it is not as defensible: "With me," he has said, "what you see is what you get."

There is often a touch of arrogance in heroes, and skeptics will always argue that Smith was smug, Borg supremely indifferent, and Evert calculating. But even cynics can't dispute the fact that whatever their motivation, the heroes of tennis set a standard and infused a measure of dignity into the game at a time when dignity was often in short supply. Besides, a player who seems to have no flaws often ends up having no advocates, either. Just ask the least heralded hero of the Open era, the most reluctant hero of the Open era, Mats Wilander.

Wilander was one of the finest players of our time until the achievement of his goal—the attainment of the world's number one ranking—left him depressed, spent, and convinced that the ranking was worth reaching but not defending. As he once told me, "It was like blowing up a big balloon for many years, and then when it was full, there was nothing left except for the air to go out of it." The extraordinary combination of Mat's ambivalence to success and the degree of success that he enjoyed, puts him in a league all by himself. He was the last great amateur in that he was far more interested in process than result.

In 1982, at the age of seventeen, Wilander became the youngest man to win a Grand Slam tournament when he outlasted Guillermo Vilas (1–6, 7–6, 6–0, 6–4) on the slow red clay of Roland Garros. This was in the year following Borg's premature retirement, but he never did bother to offer Sweden's new champion his personal congratulations.

Unlike his predecessor, Wilander thrived on his relationship with his fellow Swedes. To this day he feels that having been part of a commercially sponsored team (along with Joakim Nystrom and Anders Jarryd) was a key element in the success that he enjoyed, as well as his ability to take that success lightly. The team provided Wilander with fraternity, kept him from becoming obsessed with his own career, and lifted his game. It gave him the one thing Borg never had: roots.

Wilander was far more representative than the loner Borg of their common national heritage, and if Borg launched the Swedish tennis boom, it was Wilander and company that brought it to fruition in a way that quickly made Swedish players role models of tennis.

In the 1980s, eight different Swedes finished in the world's top ten, beginning with Borg. In 1984 and 1985, four of them were simultaneously among the elite ten: Wilander, Andres Jarryd, Joakim Nystrom, Henrik Sundstrom (1984), and Stefan Edberg (1985). In relative terms, the Swedes of the 1980s were as successful as Australians of the 1950s and 60s. Furthermore, the group ethic of the Swedes flew in the face of the prevailing winds of individualism and bad conduct. Not only did they enjoy great camaraderie, they also behaved like gentlemen from the amateur era. This was no less true for the journeymen Swedes than for the two great Swedish champions of the post-Borg era, Edberg and Wilander.

Digby Baltzell explained the Swedes' group ethic and national pride with the following characterization of Swedish society: "The Swedes are a very liberal state but a very conservative society. They're very self-denying, and they have a rigid social structure. People come out of it knowing how to get along, and with a great deal of discipline."

Wilander epitomized the word "classic" in tennis at a time when classic virtues were in rout. He was the game's equivalent of the tank watch, the wooden sailboat, or the white cable-knit sweater. He was a great champion and a team player. Wilander was the leader of the Swedish generation, but he may have been only the second-best player in that group. Wilander won seven Grand Slam titles, compared to Edberg's six. But Edberg collected two Wimbledon and two U.S. Open singles titles, while Wilander won only one title at those two preeminent events, the U.S. title in 1988. Edberg held the number one ranking for a longer time than Wilander, but Mats was the first man since Jimmy Connors in 1974 to win three of the four Grand Slam titles in the same year.

Edberg and Wilander had a spirited rivalry, but only in the battle for ascendancy in Swedish tennis. They had a cordial, if cool, relationship. That Edberg dated and eventually married Wilander's former girlfriend, Annette Olson, only added a little spice to the competition between the men.

Under Wilander's leadership, Edberg became something of the odd man out on Team Sweden. As Edberg himself liked to say, he had a classically phlegmatic Swedish temperament, but he did not have a typically Swedish game. Unlike the rest of the Swedes, Edberg played serve-and-volley, attacking tennis. And he hit his backhand with only one hand on the stick. Edberg never had quite the same degree of esprit de corps as his fellow Swedes, either. But nobody held it against him.

Wilander was the pivotal singles player on the Swedish Davis Cup teams that won the event three times (1984, 1985, and 1988), with a 4–2 singles record in those matches. On court, Wilander's conduct was so exemplary that even McEnroe tended to be on good behavior in his matches against the placid Swede. "I think Mats and I could have been a great rivalry," McEnroe once told me, "especially when Borg just disappeared. But in a funny way, I never felt that passion with Mats. He was just like *there*—a good guy, great tennis player, but I never felt this personal thing pushing it up to the next level."

Early in his career, Wilander played a match at Roland Garros against the formidable clay-court player José-Luis Clerc. Wilander appeared to win the match when a forehand hit by Clerc fell near the line and the linesman briskly called "out." Wilander approached the chair umpire and asked him to overrule the match point decision because he felt that Clerc's ball was good. The umpire obliged Wilander, and everyone's sense of justice was served when Wilander quickly won the replayed point.

Wilander projected an arresting combination of serenity and fierce competition, but unlike Borg, he did not have a mysterious, charmed aura nor a fatal flaw that made his demise fascinating. For a champion, Wilander was a remarkably well-adjusted, balanced, thoughtful individual. He was shy but not taciturn. Intelligent but not outspoken. Intensely dedicated but never obsessive. Those virtues helped account for his image as "just another Swede," albeit the most talented one. The media and public never did take to Wilander in a big way. This indifference was partly the result of Wilander's struggles at the only two tournaments that matter to people outside the tennis community: Wimbledon and the U.S. Open. Wilander routinely reached the Wimbledon quarterfinals, and just as routinely succumbed there. And in his first few years at Flushing Meadow, Wilander never managed to stir the crowds that only sit up and take notice of winners.

The other liability Wilander carried was the very nature of his baseline game. Many people found it boring, but I never did. It was compact, flexible, precise, and subtle. Wilander's game had to be all those things, because without those virtues and without a superior temperament orchestrating them, Wilander would have been just like a typical Swede: an underpowered baseliner doomed to journeyman status on the world tour. Wilander's great distinction as a player is that he was a middleweight whose intelligence, confidence, and courage enabled him to beat many of the heavyweights. Wilander was solid all around.

Until Wilander's charmed year of 1988, the cognoscenti considered him just a beat off the standard set by the very top players. His best performances occurred on the slow red clay of Roland Garros. In the three years following his precocious victory in Paris in 1982, Wilander lost in the final, lost in the semifinals, and won the tournament a second time—all before he turned twenty-one in August 1985.

Wilander played like a human backboard in his first French Open final, wearing down a man who specialized in wearing down others: Guillermo Vilas. But when Wilander won for the second time in 1985, it was with uncommon intelligence and verve. Facing Ivan Lendl in the final, he played very aggressively, attacking the net every time he had the opportunity to hit a serviceable approach shot. The strategy seemed to rattle Lendl, and it most certainly kept the Czech from getting into the groove he liked. Wilander won in an upset, 3–6, 6–4, 6–2, 6–2.

It was an omen of things to come.

Wilander also fared well at the Australian Open, even when it was played on grass. In his first appearance Down Under, as a sixteen-year-old, he lost in the first round. In his next four appearances, a span that lasted until 1988, he won the title three times (1983, 1984, and 1988) and lost a straight-set final to Edberg in 1985.

Wimbledon posed particular problems for Wilander, partly because of the toll taken by his consistent success at Roland Garros. Unlike Borg, Wilander seemed unable to bounce back with fresh legs on grass with only a two- to three-week break between the two events. He also lacked the winning tradition that would inspire him to do so. Wilander did not have the go-for-broke service return that is so valuable on grass, or the power that comes in so handy when you need to club an unreturnable serve at 40–30. And he wasn't quite explosive enough to play from the baseline as efficiently as either Borg or Connors did.

Wilander reached the late stages of the U.S. Open every year that he played, never losing before the fourth round. At the onset of 1988, he knew that it was time to make his move. Until that time, Wilander had always been ambivalent about targeting the number one ranking. He always felt that it was supposed to be a lifetime ambition, sort of like becoming the president, or getting an invitation to the *Playboy* mansion from Hef. He saw what becoming number one at a young age had done to a number of players, including Borg and McEnroe. He didn't want to spend his time fighting off rivals, with no place to go but down. On a number of occasions he told me that he only wanted to become number one when it felt like the right time. He didn't want to back into it, he didn't want it to fall in his lap, and he didn't want to attain the top ranking before he was mature enough to understand what it really meant.

The quest that could be put off no longer began at the Australian Open of 1988. Wilander managed to squeak by Pat Cash in a superb final contested on the brand-new rubberized asphalt courts of Flinders Park, 6–3, 6–7, 3–6, 6–1, 8–6. In the final of the French Open, Wilander had an easier time with mercurial Henri LeConte, 7–5, 6–2, 6–1. Once again Wilander hit the traditional wall in the Wimbledon quarterfinals, losing to Miloslav Mecir, the smooth Slovak nicknamed "the Big Cat," 6–3, 6–1, 6–3.

As the U.S. Open approached, Wilander was deliciously close to the top of the game, but no closer than he had been on a number of other occasions. The key difference was that in 1988, Wilander decided that he really wanted it. And it just so happened that a win over Lendl in the final would pass the World Number One singles ranking from Lendl to Wilander. Thus, the Swede found himself in the ultimate do-or-die scenario.

Lendl and Wilander ended up playing the best tennis match that I've seen in the Open era. Even the most exciting of tennis matches contain peaks and valleys, along with clearly discernible shifts of momentum, but in this encounter the score was so close the entire way that each point assumed crucial significance, and each one was a minor drama. It was "take no prisoners" tennis at its finest.

The big question hanging over the proceedings was whether or not Wilander, the middleweight, could outwit, outrun, outmaneuver, and outthink the heavyweight, Lendl—a man who up to that time had held the World Number One ranking for 156 weeks. Wilander eventually succeeded by mixing it up like a general conducting a number of battles on different fronts under divergent conditions.

It was the longest U.S. Open final on record—four hours and fifty-four minutes of unrelenting tension during which neither man held enough of an advantage to take even the most cursory of breathers. The final score was 6–4, 4–6, 6–3, 5–7, 6–4. You could say that the match was closer than the scores indicate. As a result, Wilander received the number one ranking on September 12, just a few days after the U.S. Open final. In 1989, he lost in the second round of the Australian Open. On January 30, Ivan Lendl, with the Australian title in hand, reclaimed the top spot. Wilander reached the quarterfinals at Roland Garros and Wimbledon, but he lost in the second round at Flushing Meadow. He took a lot of grief for vanishing from contention just months after he reached the pinnacle of the game, but by then Wilander couldn't care less about anyone else's expectations. He had made his point.

Wilander had enough intelligence, courage, and self-awareness to know that he had neither the strength nor the desire—perhaps not even the pure, easy talent—to defend that exalted position. So while Wilander will not be remembered as the greatest player of the Open era, he deserves to be remembered as the wisest—a heroic achievement in Babylon.

CHAPTER 15

Boris Becker
Herr Doppelgänger in Babylon

THE EASIEST WAY to understand Boris Becker, a young man who frequently caused his army of sympathetic fans and armchair psychologists to lose sleep over the state of his soul, is through familiarity with a phenomenon that was discovered, appropriately, by a German scientist, Christian Doppler. The Doppler effect has to do with the frequency of sound, light, or radio waves, and the way they sometimes trail the object projecting them, depending on the speed of that object. Any bright object (a comet, a Roman candle going off at night, and so forth) that leaves a discernible trail at speed demonstrates the Doppler effect.

Being whacked out on LSD is a proven way to experience as much of the Doppler effect as you can handle, but it isn't mandatory.

There is an apt relationship between the term Doppler effect and the German word *doppelgänger,* which means "the ghostly counterpart of a living person." That is where we get back to Becker. Until about the age of twenty-five, Becker spent a lot of time trying to catch up to the quickly moving object that was his own celebrity. The chase took a great deal out of him, and it made him the subject of constant speculations that only increased his fame.

Although he traveled from peak to valley to peak in his checkered competitive career, this struggle was not always as futile and self-injurious a battle as some critics suggested. Becker knew very well how to take a reading of his own bearings, and he proved it on a number of occasions. Yet he couldn't avoid the Sturm und Drang, having realized early on that the price he had to pay for his stunning, precocious success at Wimbledon was the inevitable clash between public expectations (particularly in his native Germany) and his own desires. This conflict was exacerbated by Becker's own nature. He is fundamentally a seeker, and while great tennis champions are often many other things, they are rarely seekers. Champions try to make things easy for themselves; seekers find ways to make them more complicated.

In 1985, Becker won his first Wimbledon title, beating Kevin Curren in the final, 6–3, 6–7, 7–6, 6–4. This was before he turned eighteen and after less than a year on the pro tour. Seven years later he would look back on that experience and say, "The only big mistake I ever made as a tennis player was at the very beginning. I won the biggest prize of all after being for only nine months a tennis player. I don't know how I could top that, but I've felt all these years that people thought I should."

Ion Tiriac, Becker's mentor and former manager, assessed the impact of his achievement another way: "Winning Wimbledon at age seventeen formed and deformed Boris."

Becker successfully defended the Wimbledon title in 1986, proving that he was no fluke. But events over the next few tempestuous years convinced some people that the operative word in Tiriac's analysis was "deformed." In 1987 and 1988, Becker reached only one Grand Slam final, losing the championship match at Wimbledon in 1988 to Edberg. In 1989 he won Wimbledon and the U.S. Open, but a loss to Andre Agassi in the semifinals of the season-ending ATP Tour World Championship kept Becker a whisker away from the number one ranking. The following year, 1990, Becker's best Grand Slam performance was at Wimbledon, where he again lost to Edberg in the final.

By then a pattern seemed to have emerged: Becker never fell far from the peak of the game, but he performed in fits and starts. He hired coaches but wouldn't always listen to them. He was sometimes distracted by extra-athletic interests in philosophy and social and political affairs. At his inspired best, Becker was virtually unbeatable (at least on fast surfaces), but you could not tell from week to week whether or not Becker would be sufficiently motivated.

For instance, on the morning that he was to play his fourth-round match at the Australian Open of 1989, against Jonas B. Svennson, Becker rolled over in bed, looked out at the sunny blue sky and the gleaming eucalyptus trees of Flinder's Park, turned to his girlfriend at that time, Karen Shultz, and asked, "Why am I playing tennis?" Later that day he still hadn't come up with a satisfactory answer. He played listlessly and lost to Svennson. And when Becker slipped into a real funk, not just a momentary loss of interest, he would play strings of matches looking nothing less than tormented.

But the blues came and went. Early in 1991, Becker won the Australian Open. It was his fifth Grand Slam title, and, more important, it earned him the number one singles ranking, getting a monkey that had grown into a gorilla off his broad back. Edberg reacquired that ranking some three months later, and Becker lost another shot at it when he was upset by a surprise finalist at Wimbledon, his countryman Michael Stich.

In 1992, Becker faltered in the third round of the Australian Open, missed the French Open due to injury, and lost in the quarterfinals at Wimbledon. Although he lost a tight five-set match to the eventual champion, Agassi, the quarterfinal finish was his worst result at Wimbledon since 1987 (when was upset in the second round by the Australian journeyman Peter Doohan). Becker faltered in his quest for a singles gold medal in the Barcelona Olympics, but he joined with Stich to win the doubles title. It was hardly enough to silence the voluble chorus that demanded to know what was wrong with Becker.

By then Becker was increasingly given to throwing fits and delivering loud, lengthy monologues in his native German. After missing a routine forehand, he would tense up and shriek like a spooked exotic bird. His nervous, dry cough became as pronounced as a facial twitch. Delivering one of his soliloquies, with his eyes sunk deeply in their ashen sockets, Becker sometimes tempted you to conclude that his nerves were shot, and that he had nothing left to give the game but the image of a burned-out champion. This condition was so marked by 1992 that it had to be addressed in *Tennis* magazine, but it was an assignment I didn't exactly relish. I had been with Boris at a small dinner attended mostly by family after he won the doubles gold medal in Barcelona, but that wasn't the appropriate place to plumb his psyche. So I ended up going from Barcelona to a tournament in Indianapolis, Indiana, just a few days after the Olympics, to find out what was really going on.

There's something surreal about conducting an interview with a friend, especially when the conversation doesn't promise to be entirely cheerful. The atmosphere in Indianapolis was relaxed and easy, but in spite of that, Boris looked haggard. And when we finally got down to business, he spoke about the doppelgänger wisely, sadly, and wearily.

"There's something that I think a lot of people don't understand because I was such a wunderkind. They think I must be miserable if I'm not winning or when I am going crazy on the court. I know what everybody is saying about how I look on the court, a little bit crazy, but all I can say is that when I am like that, I'm just having a bad day on the job. Nothing more dramatic than that. Sometimes I think that everybody talking about me retiring or quitting, and people speculating about my happiness, will make me leave tennis faster than my results, my feelings, or the real amount of happiness or sadness that I feel.

"I don't think you can compare me to Lendl or Connors or Edberg, or read that much into the fact that they don't seem to struggle while I do. Well, I just put more emotions into it, or at least different kinds of emotions. And that's my biggest strength and my biggest weakness. That's why I can beat them sometimes when everything is on the line, and that's why sometimes I lose matches I should win. The others don't get as down as I do, and maybe not as up. They make it more of a job, while for me tennis was always more my identity, my definition, even when I don't want it to be.

"That is always the problem I have to face, and the other Boris Becker that I have to live with. But there is another way to look at it. If in my shoes I wouldn't be basically content, there would be something *really* wrong, much more wrong than the problems I have on court now. I'm twenty-four, and I have all the freedom anybody can want. At twenty years old I was asking myself, 'Why am I doing this?' At least now I know why I'm doing it. I'm doing it because I am a tennis player, even if that is not the kind of tennis player that everybody else wants me to be.

"It's funny, but a lot of people say I should hide my feelings more. They say I shouldn't give away what I am feeling because it will help the other guy. But I'm not that kind of person. I prefer to show pain when I am feeling pain. When I'm down, it hurts and I show it. Is it good or bad? In what way? Who knows. I know only that I am not faking it. Not faking anything. Sure, seeing me struggle gives the other guy energy sometimes. That's fine. I never really cared about that because I always believed that when I'm full of energy physically and mentally, it doesn't matter how the other guy plays.

"People don't understand that even after the craziest match, I'm fine. I really am. Back at the hotel or in the shower, I think, 'What a fool I made of myself today!' But I'm fine with it. I don't have anger about it inside of me. So my way costs me a match here and there, but it doesn't cost me more.

"The only thing wrong with Becker is that sometimes he is losing a tennis match. Otherwise, he's young, healthy, he has enough money, and he has a girl he loves. I am not a machine. If I became one, I would probably have quit the game by now. That's why it's so strange to hear or read the speculation about me quitting or being burned out. I am just now feeling and believing that I can be a tennis player without being just a tennis player. I'm trying to make it more of a nine-to-five job, but a job that I really care about. I'm trying to take it as just a normal part of my life, with its ups and downs. And I can only create that balance by being the way I am now, because of the way I am inside."

One of the main reasons I quoted that conversation at length is the sincerity radiating from it; that ingenuousness is one of the qualities I like most in Becker. It also accounts for the sympathy, compassion, and goodwill that Becker seems to generate everywhere he goes. He is neither the first nor the last tennis player to strive to hear the hum of human decency above the siren song of privilege, but he appears to listen to it more intently and more often than most of his peers.

Becker is everybody's kid brother; he gets knocked flat and then picks himself right up, often spurning the offer of a helping hand because he wants to prove that he can do it, just like everybody else, on his own.

As Tiriac put it, "Boris, like many very famous people, is disabled. But unlike many of them, he knows it. And for that reason he is interesting, even beloved."

The best example I can give of Becker's sincerity and decency occurred at the 1992 Australian Open. On the first Tuesday of that event, Marchetti's of Melbourne was transformed from a fine Italian restaurant in a sleepy metropolis into the dining hall of Tennis Valhalla with all the titans of tennis on the feed.

John Newcombe, accompanied by his ever-present lager, sat with friends in one quiet corner. Edberg, sharing a banquette with his doubles partner Anders Jarryd, studied a menu. McEnroe was present, chowing down with his associate Sergio Palmieri and the South African doubles specialist Gary Muller. There were plenty of others who had won a paltry Grand Slam doubles title here, a big-but-not-big-enough singles title there, but nothing good enough to get them seated immediately.

I was with Becker and Barbara Feltus, whom he would marry late in 1993. When McEnroe paused on his way out to say hello to us, Becker invited him to join us. John was depressed about the way he had been playing, and he was taking no joy from the game in the twilight of his career.

The ensuing dialogue, in which Boris tried to convince John that he should just relax and enjoy the game, was a match as enthralling as any final they've played. We were one of the last parties to leave Marchetti's, and as we said good-bye to McEnroe under a street lamp, he pointed out that he might end up meeting Becker in the third round of the tournament if he got that far.

Becker responded with a crooked grin: "If we both get that far."

As it turned out, both men kept their date. And McEnroe played as well as he ever had to upset Becker in a match that generated headlines worldwide and inspired McEnroe to play fine tennis through the rest of the year—his last as a full-time tennis player.

I felt bad for Becker and slipped into the locker room after the match. I thought he might want to unwind with a drink at a Melbourne bar that we frequented, LeMonde. The only mention Boris made of the match later in the bar was to say, "John's on the way out, and that's tough. I hope he has a good year."

After being blown to bits in a match against Becker a few years ago, the zany and wildly talented Frenchman Henri LeConte went on an interview-room roll about Becker's qualities as a competitor. He wound up his monologue by jabbing his finger at the crook of his arm and excitedly claiming, "He is German. To fight and kill is in his blood—in the blood!"

Although that impression was easily cultivated by the fearless, free-swinging way young Becker played, over the years he proved that the Teutonic bent of his temperament drew much more heavily on the Faustian tradition than the militaristic one. This was well disguised in the potent, aggressive package of his tennis game.

Boris, the son of an architect in the prosperous, conservative town of Leimen, was something of a misfit even as a child. His schoolmates teased him about his red hair and he didn't know if it was good or bad to have red hair, because he was the only kid in his class so endowed. "People always laughed at me because of the way I looked, the way I talked, the way I was. Even the way I thought about things. But I was also very good in sports; that was the thing I had over them."

Becker spent most of his youth around older people who seemed to understand him better. By the time he was fifteen, that included someone who could easily be mistaken for the oldest man on earth—the obdurate, shrewd realist who had been a coach to his Romanian countryman, Ilie Nastase, and a Svengali to Guillermo Vilas: Ion Tiriac. He entered Becker's life when Gunther Bosch, a tennis coach and childhood friend of Tiriac's, called to suggest that Tiriac have a look at this unusual boy in Leimen. Tiriac remembered the experience vividly:

"Boris was moving like a little elephant. No running, just pushing and fighting and bouncing everywhere. This was maybe the worst athlete I ever had looked at. He couldn't do anything. And he was bleeding all over everything, like a bad boxer. Bleeding on the knees, bleeding on the mouth, bleeding in every bloody place. This was because he wanted it so badly.

"Boris was throwing himself all over the court and it made me think maybe the little elephant can be a player someday. I knew by that time that I could make a player out of anything, but I couldn't make a *champion* player out of even the most talented guy if he wasn't hungry for the important things—the struggle, the effort, the work.

"By then I thought I would never coach another tennis player. I thought I was finished with all of that. But something inside me said that this was the real one."

Tiriac guaranteed the Becker family a healthy minimum income for the right to manage Boris. He assigned the day-to-day training of Becker to Bosch, but supervised the proceedings closely. Less than a year later, at sixteen, Becker decided to leave school and concentrate on tennis.

Becker had personal qualities that were no less vital to his early success than his atomic serve and devastating forehand. He was headstrong and not only able but eager to swim against the tide. His competitive courage was forged in the crucible of sound advice not taken. As he once explained, "When I was told that at 30–40 I shouldn't hit my second serve very hard, my reaction was always to wonder, 'Why not?' I mean, I was feeling good, the birds in the trees were singing, and I really wanted to make that point. So why not go for it?"

Two elements were crucial to Becker's initial success at Wimbledon. Both were created by the new conditions and sensibilities of the Open era.

It's hard to imagine that Becker would have won his first Wimbledon without the help of Tiriac, and not only because the tennis veteran had entered his life at such a young age. Like a good cornerman in boxing, Tiriac orchestrated Becker's victory in 1985 by helping to keep him at an even keel, with his eyes focused not on the big win or even on a semifinal performance, but on the biggest prize of them all, the title. The other crucial factor was a technical one: Becker's midsize graphite composite Puma racket. The sudden popularity of tennis, which went hand in hand with the professionalization of the game, drove entrepreneurs into an orgy of development that, in a few short years, drastically altered the shape and composition of what was once the simple wooden tennis racket.

Players armed with the new rackets could survive on sheer power, without having fully developed games. Holding serve easily, they could pour their efforts into breaking down their opponent's serves. This was an important asset for Becker whose ability to hold serve easily allowed him to exploit his natural inclination to rise to the challenge presented by a "big point." Time and again, from the very start of his career, Becker would receive a serve at a crucial break point and send back a winner that came off his racket sounding as if it was fired by a deer rifle.

These advantages don't detract from Becker's achievement. By then, the tour was already awash with both superior coaches and superior rackets. But the terms of the game had shifted almost overnight. Remember, Becker's friend McEnroe had also made a stunning debut in 1977 at Wimbledon, as an eighteen-year-old amateur unaccompanied by a coach and armed with a stiff, standard-sized wooden racket, the Wilson Pro Staff. He did not falter until the semifinals.

In 1987, Becker suddenly emerged as a complex human being destined to represent something other than a one-dimensional, powerfully efficient tennis player who by eighteen had already won back-to-back Wimbledon titles. Showing the first flashes of genuine temper, he went ballistic during a fourth-round match against Wally Masur in January at the Australian Open. Annoyed by line calls, warned by the chair umpire about receiving coaching signals from Bosch, Becker proceeded to spit water and hit balls toward the umpire. As Masur, a gifted grass-court player, gained control of the match, Becker became increasingly unglued. He ultimately shook the umpire's chair, broke three rackets, and accumulated $2,000 in fines.

Becker lost to Masur, and he was deeply hurt by the criticisms that Bosch subsequently voiced about him to the world press. Three days after the loss, Becker declared that he was through with Bosch. Apart from feeling betrayed, Becker was by then in the throes of rebellion against the coach who insisted that he be called "Mr. Bosch" and that Becker put on a jacket and tie for dinner. Bosch was also none too pleased that for about three months leading up to the Australian Open, Becker had been traveling to tournaments in the company of a twenty-two-year-old Monacan, Benedicte Courtin. In those three months, Becker had uncharacteristically begun to miss training sessions and to ease up on his conditioning drills. He had also declined to show up in Melbourne until less than a week before the tournament began, while such stalwarts as Ivan Lendl had been in Australia for up to a month, getting accustomed to the grass courts and nearly tropical heat.

Becker's first statement of independence was a powerful rejection of the exclusionary male relationships for which he seemed tailor-made. By the standards of the day, Bosch was conservative to the point of being puritanical. Tiriac was also a no-nonsense "guy's guy," but he was perspicacious enough to see that his protégé was not cut from the same cloth, destined to hang around the locker room exchanging salacious tales with his fellow players.

From the earliest time, Becker was intent on having challenging relationships with independent, headstrong women. Those liaisons would cause plenty of tension in the life of a young man who had been groomed to assign women a clear, secondary role in his life. Unlike Bosch, Tiriac picked up on that quickly, and he wisely steered clear of Becker's emotional life while working to maintain his status as a manager who was also, as Becker often said, "my best friend."

Naturally, Becker's tempestuous performance at the Australian

Open of 1987 had powerful repercussions in Germany, whose older generation was captivated by their native son. At seventeen he was the very picture of the clean-cut *Überjungen*. A little different, perhaps, because of his red hair. A little goofy, maybe, because of the impression created by his large, elastic features, and the odd blond frosting on his eyebrows and arms that made him look like a giant pastry sprinkled with confectioner's sugar.

But oh, that serve. Oh, that confidence. Oh, that seductive Germanic will.

But the notion that Becker was a typical youth who personified rigid atavistic virtues was swiftly undercut in 1987. Oddly enough, this surprising development gradually made Becker a much more powerful symbol, a representative of the "new" multidimensional Germany.

Becker's generation came of age in the throes of German revitalization, which was driven only partly by unquenchable cultural impulses toward order, hard work, and success. Young Germans in the 1970s and 1980s were an odd lot. They were handcuffed by history and yoked to liberal, left-wingish pieties—"politically correct" attitudes that led to rebellion and even disturbing signs of a neo-fascist movement.

As it turned out, Becker was more and less than the Germans bargained for when he became the nation's greatest and most intriguing postwar sports hero. At Wimbledon the popular British press, ever afflicted with a nickname disorder, took to calling Becker "Boom-Boom." Becker reminded them that he was not a soldier but an athlete and that he was offended by his British neighbors' unremittingly lurid references to blitzkriegs and panzer divisions whenever Becker happened to produce his own brand of power tennis.

After 1987, Becker sometimes got himself into trouble by expressing sympathy for such diverse groups and causes as the squatters in Hamburg, Amnesty International, and the Green movement. Ivan Lendl, among others, contemptuously began to refer to Becker as "the limousine radical."

I was privy to that side of Becker on many occasions. I almost always disagreed with his opinions, but he was always open-minded when I challenged his assumptions. Some critics forgot that Boris was callow when he vented some of his more controversial opinions. More than any other tennis player I know, he should have had the opportunity to be a college student, to sleep until noon and loiter in cafes, proposing lunatic solutions that would probably ruin the very society they were intended to save. Talking about that rocky period, Becker once explained: "In the beginning I wasn't able to clearly express that I probably wasn't the typical, conservative German. I probably screamed that out too loudly for a time. I also tried to get away from that right-wing stereotype, and I found myself a little further left than I felt comfortable with. And there was something else. Certain groups tried very hard to use me as a symbol for themselves. Part of the problem is that because my generation thinks a little differently than the last one, we don't have many role models."

Becker's struggles eventually humanized him in the eyes of his own nation. I don't think he ever tried to be all things to all people, but he has come close to achieving that kind of status to many Germans. He is still their Teutonic paragon, not merely because of his twin distinctions as Wimbledon's youngest and first-ever German champion, but also because of his stellar record in that quintessentially nationalistic competition, the Davis Cup.

In 1988, Becker led the German team to a final contested in Gothenburg, Sweden. The number two German, Carl-Uwe Steeb, opened the proceedings with an upset of Wilander. Becker beat Edberg in the second match. The following day Boris teamed with Eric Jelen to win the doubles, giving Germany an insurmountable 3–0 lead—and its first Davis Cup championship.

The following year, in Stuttgart, Germany, Becker turned in one of the finest Davis Cup performances in history, once again against a fine Swedish team. Steeb lost a five-set match to Wilander in the first rubber. Then Becker subdued Edberg, 6–2, 6–2, 6–4. The following day Becker teamed with Jelen to beat Jan Gunnarson and Anders Jarryd in a tense, tiring five-set match, 6–4 in the fifth. Becker then had to return to play his third match in three days, and the early match to boot. Showing no sign of fatigue, Becker routed Wilander, 6–2, 6–0, 6–2, to clinch the match. Considering the quality of the opposition, Becker's performance ranks right up there with the best in Davis Cup history.

Some of Becker's most memorable Davis Cup matches occurred against Americans, although never in the final championship round. Becker played three matches against U.S. teams and led Germany to victory each time.

Two of Becker's singles victories against the United States were particularly noteworthy. He toppled McEnroe in Hartford, Connecticut in 1987, 4–6, 15–13, 8–10, 6–2, 6–2. In Munich in 1989, Becker came back from two sets down to beat Agassi, 6–7, 6–7, 7–6, 6–3, 6–4.

Davis Cup play underscored Becker's remarkable nature as a "clutch" player. His statistics in final-round matches (singles and doubles) in which the final result was not yet determined was 7–1, for a winning percentage of .875. It's the finest record since H. L. Doherty of Britain went 9–0 between 1902 and 1906. The number three man on the list is McEnroe, who was 9–2, for .818.

Becker's results as a Davis Cup player had less to do with his patriotic feelings (although they were a factor) than his love of leadership and the nature of team competition. But most of all the three-day, three-match Davis Cup format suited Becker's emotional nature perfectly. At two-week Grand Slam events he was less able to maintain his resolve and intensity.

Unfortunately, Becker's passion for the Davis Cup was dampened by the emergence of his domestic rival, Michael Stich. After Stich upset Becker in the 1991 Wimbledon final, he challenged Becker for leadership of the squad. The two players just didn't get along, and the potent Davis Cup combination of Becker and Stich was stillborn, with Becker deciding that he had no desire to play Davis Cup under such strained conditions.

Becker's results satisfied traditional Germans, but over the years a very different kind of German has also come to love him, accepting his occasional wrong-headedness, his lapses to less than heroic conduct, and, despite a significant amount of racist backlash, even his relationship with the daughter of an African-American GI and a German mother, Barbara Feltus. My feeling is that he won Germans over because Germans are pretty much like everyone else—they are moved by sincerity and they can tell honesty from evasiveness. Many of them have kid brothers, and many of them like seekers.

I never expected that Boris would become a good friend, partly because I'm almost twenty years older. But I also saw right away that he was not the typically unaware young champion in the making when I first met him in the California desert. That was in the spring of 1989, when Tiriac and his coach at the time, Bob Brett, prevailed upon Boris to sit for an interview with me—something he had no desire to do because of the media frenzy that accompanied his every move in Germany.

So I found myself parking before a condo at one of those quiet, squeaky clean, luxury golf-and-tennis resorts, PGA West, in Palm Desert, California. From the moment I set foot inside, I was struck by how odd a domicile it was for Becker and his girlfriend, Karen Schultz. Sitting on a sofa, they both looked absurdly young and, well, much too interesting for a place where retired insurance executives and their wives languished amid oatmeal-colored furniture, chrome-and-glass tables, and pastel prints of floral still-lifes in aluminum frames. I made some remark to that extent, and we were off and running.

Scenes with Boris Becker admirers occurred almost every time I was out in public with Boris, and the remarkable thing about them was that despite their frequency, and Becker's awareness of his own popularity, he often didn't seem to know how to handle them. It was as if he for-

PETER BODO

got his own identity and was thus obliged to watch the scene unfold like some baffled bystander, some doppelgänger. The condition made for some funny encounters.

On one occasion in Australia, a big galoot who looked like a Rugby player approached Boris and me as we were about to leave some trendy Melbourne pasta joint. He was very drunk. He extended his hand and launched into the customary obsequious paean to my friend's virtues. I noticed a strange look creeping across Boris's face, and by the time the fellow finished his speech, it was an expression of panic. Looking down, I realized that the guy still had hold of Boris's hand, and he wasn't about to let go. I finally intervened and literally pried them apart. The big guy stood, swaying, as we made our getaway. Then he pitched over like a piece of big timber.

Boris and I spent a fair amount of time over the years on Miami's famous South Beach strip in March, during the Lipton Championships on nearby Key Biscayne. The fashion industry congregates on South Beach at that time of year, shooting their print ads and catalogs against the backdrop of the funky art deco buildings on Ocean Drive, or right across the street at the beach. If you stay on Ocean Drive in the winter months, you can't leave your hotel without tripping over a model—or some tourist ogling one.

One evening Boris and I were having a drink outdoors at one of South Beach's many sidewalk cafes. We were engaged in conversation when we were interrupted by two young women who recognized Becker. They boldly plopped right down in two empty chairs. One of them was a beautiful, leggy model, a six-footer as well as one of the mononomial elite whose name was something like "Aja." As soon as she sat down, she began babbling about the actor Mickey Rourke, who had recently opened a bar on South Beach and allegedly was a friend of Aja's. The other woman, who was also very attractive, engaged Boris in conversation in German. Boris's eyes grew wider and wider as she spoke.

When the waitress finally came around, Aja began to blurt out an order, but Boris tersely said, "No, no drinks, thanks." As the waitress departed, I looked ruefully at my empty whiskey glass. Boris sat, a stony expression on his face. The girls finally got the hint, stood up, and melted into the pedestrian traffic.

As he signaled for the waitress to return, Boris remarked, "I didn't want to order drinks because then they would never leave. Unbelievable, eh, that they just sit down? The one I was talking to, she was a stomach dancer."

"A what?"

As Boris explained, I cast a last look at the backs of the model and the belly dancer. They didn't for one moment appear to tempt Boris.

He was only twenty-three, but even at that age he had no desire for that kind of thing.

Although Becker had done his fair share of dating, the first woman to travel with him regularly was Karen Shultz. The daughter of a university professor, a former model and student, Karen met Boris while she was working as a waitress in the players' lounge at a tournament in Hamburg in 1988. She was part of the liberal, trendy youth culture in Hamburg, and she had a lot of trouble squaring the wealth and privilege she saw in tennis with the poverty and homelessness she saw elsewhere. She thought the tennis scene was vulgar and boring, and she always seemed anxious and restless in it.

Shultz introduced Boris to life at ground level, in the cafes and streets of Hamburg. This often put her at cross purposes with Becker's coach, Bob Brett. Although Brett had no more use for the dross of the pro tour than did Shultz, he was much too conservative for her idealistic, marginally bohemian nature. Both an astute psychologist and passionate tennis nut, Brett always found a link between a player's character and his results. He believed Boris was first and foremost a tennis player, and thus he was less likely to find contentment by dabbling in politics or hanging out with bearded poets and performance artists than through the offices of clean living, hard work, and discipline.

So while Brett began laying the groundwork for Becker's run at the number one ranking, Boris was being pulled in an entirely different direction by Karen. The strain on him was such that at one point, at the end of 1989, he admitted that he was seriously thinking of quitting the game. He almost folded up his tents after a solid performance in the season-ending Masters of 1989, after he beat McEnroe and lost the final to Stefan Edberg.

Boris stayed in New York for a few days after that event. I could tell that he needed a break from the world of tennis, so on one bitterly cold morning I took him on a tour of a part of New York he would otherwise never have seen, the Lower East Side. Getting off the subway, he stopped to mug before a video camera set up in the window of an electronics store. Watching himself on the monitor, he repeated the question, "Who is this man? Who is this man?"

We made our way down Second Avenue, through the seedy, colorful East Village, heading for Alphabet City, where the Avenues are named A, B, C, and D. I knew this dangerous urban frontier from another time in my life. Although the "dope shops" that operated out of abandoned tenements didn't open until late at night, the streets were full of addicts and predators. Here and there, junkies hawked "works" (syringes), while others huddled around roaring blazes set in oil barrels. When a scuffle broke out between street people, Boris turned to me and said, "I haven't felt fear—real fear—for a long time, until now. Maybe it's better that we go now."

During a long lunch at Telephone Bar, I realized that Boris was seriously thinking about quitting the game. I also realized that while his profession gave him staggering wealth and fame, it denied him many essential liberties—including the freedom to change jobs. He had no formal education to speak of, so he couldn't decide to go to, say, law school. He was famous, so he couldn't very well apply to be a night manager at Burger King. He could have learned to manage the fortune he'd already earned, but he wasn't interested in finance.

It took me a few days to come up with something that seemed somewhat appropriate or possible: the movie business. With his assets, his reputation, and his intellectual curiosity, Boris eventually might have been able to make his way as a movie producer—even if that did mean spending more time with belly dancers and mononomial models turned aspiring starlets.

These tensions in Boris almost always occurred when the tennis champion in Becker came into conflict with the doppelgänger. The champion almost always prevailed, as it did on this occasion. Over the next few months Becker decided to renew his commitments to tennis, and Brett was waiting by the phone for the news.

Gunther Bresnick, the shrewd Austrian who later briefly coached Becker, once remarked, "With Boris, you have to make him think that a change is his idea. You can't say, 'Do this now.' You have to suggest it and give him a few days to absorb it. Then when he feels that it's his own idea, he may try it."

That process could be agonizing, but Brett was an astute man with a good feel for the complex, sometimes intransigent champion who had been unwilling to fully accept the authority of a coach ever since his experience with Bosch. But the partnership began to work, albeit in its own bizarre way, with Boris questioning and second-guessing every step of the way.

Becker had a solid year in 1990, culminating in a surge of brilliant play. He won the major fall indoor clashes in Sydney, Paris, and Stockholm. That left him poised to seize the number one ranking if he reached the final of the season-ending ATP World Tour Championships in Frankfurt. But he lost to Agassi in the semifinals.

That evening Becker ducked the postmatch press conference and walked some forty blocks back to his hotel. "It was November and very, very cold," he told me later. "It was raining wet snow, but I couldn't face seeing anybody—not coach, not manager, not press, not even my dri-

ver. So I just started walking, still in my tennis shorts. I was so confused, so gone mentally from the sheer effort. Later, when my doctor
tried to inject me with vitamins, I couldn't tense my muscles for the
shot. The injection made me cry for half an hour."

But after a few weeks' rest, Becker grew angry at himself for the
missed opportunity. He decided to go to Melbourne in mid-December
and train for almost a month in order to make a last-ditch effort to
claim the top ranking at the 1991 Australian Open. He succeeded, beating Lendl in the final, 1–6, 6–4, 6–4, 6–4. As soon as Becker converted
that match point, he dropped his racket, raced out of the stadium into
Flinder's Park, and howled back at the spirits that had been baying at
him since 1985.

But the triumph cost Becker. His relationship with Karen had eroded
badly, as Karen felt increasingly lost, isolated, and powerless. She had
developed a deep dislike for what Boris did best, the habits that it
demanded, and the people who populated a world that she continued to
perceive as "unreal." Over the next few months Boris and Karen tried
to patch things up. I think she wanted the old Boris back, the one who
was in rebellion against tennis, the one who was willing to live like a student in Hamburg, speaking out on social issues when he wasn't running
off to fulfill some professional obligation in the decadent world of pro
tennis. I think the one she loved was the doppelgänger.

The other casualty of Becker's success in 1991 was the very man who
had helped engineer it, Bob Brett. The coach had been on board since
late 1987, but by the time Boris played for the number one ranking in
Melbourne, the two were bickering and feuding over the smallest of
things. If Brett suggested that Becker drop his string tension by six
pounds, Boris would dig in his heels and raise the tension by two
pounds. If Brett suggested that Becker slice his backhand return down
the line against a certain player, Boris would hit it with topspin, crosscourt. Brett thought he knew what Boris needed to do to win. Becker
wanted to win on his own.

All of this was not nearly as counterproductive as it may seem. In
fact, Becker's desire to prove to Brett that he could claim the top ranking without turning himself over to a puppeteer had a lot to do with
Becker's outstanding play in Melbourne in 1991. Boris had always gravitated to older and, presumably, wiser people. He saw the value of what
they had to offer, but he was too strong and stubborn to turn himself
over to them. As late as 1991, Boris was still young enough to have outgrown people, even good people like Brett.

Moments after Becker won the match that earned him the top ranking, the television focused on Brett. He had tears in his eyes. But soon

thereafter his bags were packed. Fathers probably would understand all this better than anyone else.

Severing those two important ties hurt Boris. He was hobbled by injuries and adrift for much of the rest of the year. At the U.S. Open he lost in the third round to the Dutchman, Paul Haarhuis. We met for a late dinner that night in the Soho restaurant Lucky Strike. My friend Isabelle Fritz-Cope was to join us later.

It was a somber dinner during which I could sense the loneliness plaguing Boris. He felt that he was back at square one, struggling to figure out just what to do next. Shortly after midnight Isabelle showed up. We all started chatting, and she spontaneously reached over and tousled Boris's hair.

"Don't do that," he said, sharply drawing back. "Please."

But Isabelle was fascinated, and she mussed his hair again.

Boris became really angry, protesting that he wasn't a dog. All his life, he said, people had been tousling his hair. He didn't like it. It made him feel like a child, and he was anything but a child. Mussing his hair was an invasion, a liberty that people didn't have the right to take.

The subject died an awkward death, leaving everybody gloomy and out of sorts. After we said good-bye outside, I watched Boris walk off to his car. He looked huge. He was hobbling on a sore foot, and his shoulders were all hunched up. He looked like anything but a puppy or a child, but in some ways he was still a little bit of both.

The next time I spent any time with Boris, in Australia early in 1991, he was in considerably better spirits. He had been dating Barbara Feltus for a few months, and they both felt it was best to make their relationship public as far as possible from Germany because of the inevitable media circus it would create.

After the lively dinner with John McEnroe described earlier, Boris, Barbara, and I headed back to their hotel. Bad news was waiting there: Robert Lubonoff, chief tennis writer for Germany's largest news service, had made special arrangements to have copies of the major newspapers flown in, because they contained the first official news of the relationship between Becker and Feltus. Most of the papers focused on the racial difference between them, and many did it in an ugly way. A group of us sat down in the lounge to examine the papers. One headline pleaded, WHY, BORIS? WHY NOT ONE OF US? Another paper had transposed the heads of Boris and Barbara on a picture of a couple exchanging wedding vows. Yet another one offered an artist's rendering of the couple holding a conspicuously brown child.

Barbara excused herself and went upstairs. She cried for fifteen minutes, then returned, cool and composed. It was an impressive show of character from a woman who appeared to be a bundle of nervous energy, an aspiring singer and actress who, I at first suspected, might have all the temperamental glitches bred by those professions.

There were some striking similarities between Karen Shultz and Barbara. Both were highly strung, lean, and mannish, but Barbara was athletic (she had excelled at track) and Karen was not. Both were emotional, compassionate women, but while Karen's life was rooted in the liberal, bourgeois society of Hamburg, Barbara's had been considerably more complex and, ostensibly, difficult.

Apart from the problems faced by any child of an interracial marriage, Barbara had come from a broken home. She had developed great poise and strength, she could be hard when she needed to, and she was fundamentally a realist. She was willing to take Boris at face value, as a tennis player with a remarkable history who was struggling with the demands of his position and profession.

Barbara did things that brightened up Boris's life in a way that no amount of supportive attentiveness or coddling could accomplish. During the U.S. Open of 1992, the couple was bewitched by a homeless man who played the saxophone every day at a corner near their hotel. Early one morning, Boris woke up to the strains of a mellow jazz tune emanating from the foot of the bed. Barbara had hired the homeless man and then persuaded the hotel staff to allow him up to Becker's suite to play for him.

A year later, during the unseasonably cool 1993 U.S. Open, Boris and Barbara took to donating articles of clothing to yet another homeless man encamped near the Peninsula Hotel. By the second week of the Open, hundreds of daily passersby were astonished by the sight of the bum, who was dressed from head to toe in expensive, dazzlingly clean Diadora tennis togs.

As it turned out, 1993 was a year full of transitions for Becker. The most significant was his decision to break with the longest-standing friend and associate he had, Ion Tiriac. The break was accelerated by the growing importance of the relationship between Becker and Feltus, who understood Tiriac's role in Becker's life but also felt that it had grown stale.

For a number of years Becker and Tiriac had been drifting apart. Becker trusted Tiriac implicitly and allowed him a free hand in managing his money. Tiriac would bring "deals" to Becker, who would either approve or reject them. Tiriac would take his percentage and go about his business, which gradually came to encompass such diverse interests as the creation of the first post–cold war private bank in Romania and promotion of the Davis Cup (for Germany) and the World Amateur Swimming Championships.

As a father figure, Tiriac had grown redundant over the years, but he was still hurt and shocked when Boris announced shortly before the U.S. Open of 1993 that he was breaking with the only manager he had ever employed. One of the main reasons for Tiriac's dejection was the identity of the man Becker had chosen to replace him. Axel Meyer-Wölden was Tiriac's most serious challenger in the lucrative business of tennis promotion in wealthy Germany. Meyer-Wölden's main event was the richest of all tennis tournaments, the ITF-sponsored Grand Slam Cup.

For complicated political reasons stemming from the rivalry between the ITF and the ATP Tour, Becker, along with some other top players, had declined to support the Grand Slam Cup despite the $2 million payout it offered to the winner, and despite the fact that the tournament took place in Becker's domicile, Munich. And as long as Becker held out, Tiriac had a trump card over Meyer-Wölden.

But after Becker and Feltus became serious about each other, a new element entered the picture. Meyer-Wölden, a highly respected, conservative entertainment lawyer and concert promoter, also lived in Munich, and he happened to be married to an African beauty who knew the challenges facing any interracial couple. Inevitably, friendships and business became intertwined. Taking a hard look at his joint affairs with Tiriac, Becker decided that his manager had been taking undue advantage of him because of the long-standing nature of their relationship.

Tiriac did not take kindly to the news of severance. When he showed up at Flushing Meadow, he asked for one of the highly prized stadium parking lot passes on the grounds that he was Becker's manager. He was politely but firmly refused. Shortly before Becker played his fourth-round match against Magnus Larsson, Tiriac strolled into the locker room. He greeted Boris effusively, slapped him on the back, and then slapped into his hands legal papers charging that Becker's dismissal of Tiriac violated their contract.

Becker was upset by Larsson, an event that paled alongside the other issues at play for Becker during that Open. Tiriac was Becker's last link to his roots—a man who, for better or worse, was also partly responsible for the creation of the doppelgänger. And by then, Barbara was pregnant and beginning to show it.

Over the years Becker had developed the habit of hosting a dinner or breakfast meeting with a handful of Germany's top journalists as soon as a Grand Slam tournament was over for him. The breakfast meeting at the U.S. Open of 1993 posed special problems for Boris because of Barbara's condition. The couple did not know how to confirm Barbara's pregnancy. They felt very strongly that having a child was a private matter, but they had not made any decision about getting married. Of course, Boris had to handle the matter delicately because of his status. If he just happened to mention in passing that, yes, Barbara was pregnant and, no, there were no wedding plans, the press could easily paint a picture of the young tennis star casually dropping the bombshell while his girlfriend, barefoot and pregnant, remained sequestered in the lavish hotel suite. The idea that the baby might appear to be a love child created by a careless couple troubled Boris and Barbara, because they had consciously decided to create a baby.

The three of us had a long discussion about the subject. Boris and Barbara finally decided that it would be best if Barbara, who shunned the limelight, accompanied him to the breakfast meeting and answered questions for the reporters. She had a terrible case of the flu that morning, and she used up nearly every cocktail napkin in the bar of the Peninsula. Otherwise, the proceedings went smoothly and with the appropriate dignity.

That night Boris, Barbara, and I went to see Lenny Kravitz at Radio City Music Hall. Over a leisurely dinner and long into the night we talked about what the future held. Tennis came into the conversation only tangentially. We talked mostly about marriage, what it really meant, what it really did for, or to, people. It struck me as both odd and ironic that the happy young couple had given plenty of serious thought to becoming parents, but little to the notion of marriage. This was partly because of the myriad practical details and special problems it posed for a celebrity like Boris. Still, while they could have had any kind of marriage they wanted, the one that appealed most to them was a simple civil affair in a town hall. And when they decided a few days later to marry, that was exactly what they planned.

I regret that because of my mother's terminal illness, I was unable to attend their wedding. I was tempted to catch a plane at the last minute to surprise them, and it's a good thing that I couldn't. The ceremony was scheduled for Kitzbühel, but on the morning of the event the guests were whisked away to Becker's home town, Leimen, where the ceremony went off quickly and smoothly.

I also regret not having made the wedding because it may have been my last chance to see the Doppelgänger. Just for old times' sake.

PART IV

THE U.S. OPEN
Flesh-Eaters, Price-Gouging, and
the Strangelove Solution

KEVIN CURREN, a Wimbledon finalist in 1985, lost in the first round of the U.S. Open just two months later to a young Frenchman, Guy Forget. Afterward, the disappointed South African remarked, "I hate New York. I hate the environment, and I hate Flushing Meadow. The USTA should be shot for the setup they have here. They should drop an A-bomb on this place."

Granted, Curren was an introspective, moody fellow. Granted, he was still smarting from having missed out on the chance of a lifetime at Wimbledon, where he had lost to a seventeen-year old German kid named Becker. And sure, Curren had been distracted during his match with Forget by jets roaring overhead, shadows creeping across the court, and the commotion created by a restless audience. None of that means that Curren didn't mean what he said or that he wasn't right. In fact, countless folks in the tennis community felt that Curren's suggestion was altogether reasonable. Being a New Yorker myself, I wasn't all that eager to become nuclear toast. Nevertheless, I agree that the USTA has managed to turn the U.S. Open into the most calamitous and infuriating of Grand Slam events.

All of which gives the U.S. Open the distinction of being the most realistic Grand Slam event of them all. Wimbledon may trade heavily—almost exclusively—on this British thing with tradition, but the U.S. Open cuts right to the heart of what the host city is all about. The tournament brings out the best and worst in everybody, but in this era the worst is usually far more interesting. You can't help getting absorbed in the U.S. Open any more than you can help staring transfixed at some horrible car wreck.

If the U.S. Open were a coat, it would be a leather jacket. If it were a tool, it would be a chain saw. If it were a vanity plate, it would read FUK U 2, and if it were a tennis player, it would be that boy from just down the pike in Douglaston, John McEnroe. Like its local son, the Open features an unremitting, unapologetic, in-your-face, what-you-see-is-what-you-get kind of authenticity. You might have a problem with this if you think that what you see is brutal, graceless, undistinguished, and unnecessarily hostile, and don't particularly think that "authenticity" has anything has to do with it.

McEnroe has been party to almost as many hijinks at Flushing Meadow as that other consummately raw American, Jimmy Connors. Of course, Connors isn't from New York, but as he himself has said time and again, he should have been. A savvy, street-smart kid from the depressed suburb of East St. Louis, Illinois, Connors figured out quickly that no matter what they say, most New Yorkers love watching train wrecks, dope deal shootouts, and fistfights. New York is full of flesh-eaters. It's a thumbs-up, thumbs-down kind of town. Start spreading the news, but watch your back. The dude's got a Glock.

Connors understood and tapped into the vulgarity of New York very early in his career when he made some remarks that foreshadowed, like those of many another martyr, his inevitable canonization. That occurred late in Connors's career, during the brutally hot summer of 1991 when the thirty-eight-year old patched together the most unlikely and inspirational series of performances in the Open era. Injury-plagued and written off, Connors kicked and clawed his way to the semifinals of the U.S. Open, and in the process he forced an increasingly indifferent public to focus on tennis again—just as it had when Jimbo was an eighteen-year-old hellion.

The words he had uttered as a babe rang across the land anew in 1991: "The people in this town love to see blood, and I'm willing to spill my guts for them."

But, actually, a match involving McEnroe and Nastase was probably more emblematic of the character of the Open than most of Connors's heroic triumphs at the New York championships. The principals in this tragicomedy were Nastase, McEnroe, and three officials with long histories in the game. In ascending rank, they were umpire Frank Hammond, tournament referee Mike Blanchard, and tournament director Billy Talbert. Some ten thousand mostly blotto fans also played their small parts in what came to be known as "the Wednesday night massacre."

In 1979, Nastase was thirty-six and clearly in decline, but he was still a big drawing card. He scored an unexpected first-round win that earned him a date with twenty-year old McEnroe. Although McEnroe had yet to win his first Grand Slam title, everyone in tennis—including Nastase—was awestruck by his unique game and intrigued by his volatile temperament. The match was a promoter's dream, a pairing of the oldest and the youngest hellbenders in tennis.

The media played up the match in advance as a New York–style happening, and the referee not only scheduled the meeting as a night match but the second one on the evening program. This ensured that the spectators would be restless and intoxicated from anticipation, booze, or both. Knowing that the proceedings might get raucous, Blanchard assigned the veteran umpire Hammond to officiate the show. Hammond, a rotund tennis nut who had been involved with the game from day one, successfully straddled the amateur and early pro eras, but he was a throwback who believed that officials, players, and promoters were all in it together for the good of the game. He had no use for the idea that an official should be a briefcase-toting, remote bureaucrat who observed strict rules about everything from fraternization with the players (which was forbidden) to rule interpretation.

Hammond perceived himself as, in his words, "a maestro conducting an orchestra." He enjoyed the challenge of handling each player and his personality quirks on an individual basis, and when he was assigned to oversee a match between two rambunctious types, he usually handled it like a father trying to mediate between two unruly, different, but equally loved children. The worst things you could say about Hammond was that he was slightly starstruck and inclined to give preferential treatment to the mercurial marquee names. His bulk and his experience also made him a celebrity in his own right, a condition that violates the old saw about the best official being the one you least notice.

By the time Nastase and McEnroe took the court, well after 9 P.M., the crowd was all juiced up and ready for anything. As ever, Nastase did not disappoint them. He quickly began to use all of his formidable tactics for throwing off an opponent, from stalling to clowning to arguing and chatting with the spectators. McEnroe did not merely rise to the bait, he exploded on it. Nastase set the tone for the farcical proceedings early on when he said to Hammond, "McEnroe keeps calling me a son of a bitch. Please make him call me Mister Son of a Bitch."

The big difference between the players was that McEnroe lacked the charm and humor of Nastase. He was alternately surly, whiny, and mean-spirited, but Nastase was sharper, and he knew how to exploit McEnroe's shortcomings. This was no simplistic conflict between the forces of good and evil but a bizarre throwdown between an aging, talented clown and a young, deadly serious punk. Nastase, who was responsible for almost all the problems, also cornered most of the sympathy. That emotional windfall propelled Nastase to ever greater heights of outrageousness. Soon even his long-suffering and ever-forbearing buddy Hammond could no longer handle him. In the fourth set, with McEnroe leading two sets to one and prepared to serve at 2–1, Hammond lost control of the match.

Nastase was futzing around at the baseline, and the crowd, returning from a quick changeover beer run, was not yet settled in when Hammond ordered McEnroe to serve. McEnroe obeyed and hit an ace.

"Fifteen-love," Hammond called.

Nastase bounded toward the chair, protesting the apparent quick serve.

"I thought it was all like a big joke until I heard Hammond call the score after I served," McEnroe said later.

The crowd went into a frenzy as Nastase, who had already used up a point penalty, protested for so long that he was hit with the requisite game penalty.

Suddenly it was 3–1 McEnroe, but the crowd would have no part of it. Fans showered the court with plastic cups and any other handy projectiles. A resounding chant rose up: "Two-one, Two-one, Two-one . . ." The ensuing mayhem lasted for eighteen minutes.

Ordered to serve at 1–3, Nastase just paced the baseline, holding the balls. The crowd wouldn't give it up, insisting that it was still 2–1. Discombobulated, Hammond began begging Nastase, "Come on, Ilie, you have to play right now. Please. Let's go."

By that time the referee, Blanchard, had come out of his courtside foxhole and stood in the wings watching. As the din continued, he took the next step mandated by the rules. He signaled for Hammond to start the clock. If Nastase refused to serve in the next thirty seconds, he would be subject to the next, final step in the disciplinary process—disqualification.

Fifty-eight seconds elapsed with no sign of cooperation from Nastase, prompting Hammond to bellow, "Game, set, and match, McEnroe."

It was over. Well, almost. As trash and catcalls rained down on the court, the tournament director, Talbert, purposefully strode across the Deco-Turf to Hammond. The two men exchanged a few words, and then the crowd was treated to the spectacle of watching Hammond struggle to get down out of the tiny seat that bore a striking resemblance to a high chair. Fearing a riot, Talbert had taken matters into his own hands. Making it up as he went along, Talbert disqualified not Nastase but Hammond. He then put the puzzled Blanchard in the chair and ordered the players to continue. But by then the fun was over, and McEnroe put away a meek and distracted Nastase in no time at all—for the second time that night.

The ugly mess helped teach a young, opportunistic, and presumably impressionable McEnroe that the rules of tennis are eternally flexible and that promoters generally were loath to spoil a crackling good show by booting a crowd-pleasing marquee name. The fiasco also showed that the notion of officiating by virtue of an unwritten "gentleman's agreement" among basically amicable, friendly principals was no longer supportable. Nastase clearly left Hammond skewered on his own conductor's baton.

The travesty also demonstrated that the Flushing Meadow crowd was anything but a typical tennis audience. It had come for a show, and it got theater of the absurd—participatory theater of the absurd, like one of those awful 1960s productions that many New Yorkers attended, fearing or hoping that they might have to hop on stage, strip naked, and join in an orgy with a bunch of frizzy-haired freaks.

The way the evening played out, it was also clear that most of the spectators did not know from one moment to the next what was going on, a flaw that demonstrated the inadequacy of the complicated disciplinary system. The fiasco also proved that the enormous stadium was just plain too big for tennis, although it was just about the right size for venting emotions that any number of Manhattan shrinks would probably urge you not to feel guilty about.

The change of venue of the U.S. Open was probably the most significant and telling event of the Open era. The "new" U.S. Open was created during the egalitarian frenzy that accompanied and accelerated the professionalization of tennis. In the mid-1970s a new wave of USTA officials, eager to take the game public and to tap into the cash cow that their tournament potentially represented, felt that the U.S. Open had outgrown the confines of the exclusive and historic West Side Tennis Club in Forest Hills, Queens. By 1977, the last year that the event was held there, the ten-plus acres at the club were entirely in use. If a fire marshal happened to show up, you couldn't have squeezed him in there. The grounds were packed, the walkways between the field courts were jammed all day, and the 13,500-seat stadium was routinely filled to capacity. There was no room for corporate entertainment marquees. The clubhouse and player locker rooms were overcrowded, and the concessionaires and merchandise vendors were cramped. In 1976, the last year the Open was held at Forest Hills, the twelve-day crowd hit the record number, 250,880.

In 1976 and 1977, USTA officials negotiated with representatives of the club, trying to find an expansion plan suitable to all parties. The record will show that despite all the populist rhetoric about the future of tennis, the pivotal issue was nothing more philosophical than, well, parking. Although the West Side Tennis Club was an easy subway commute from midtown Manhattan, the USTA wanted to provide better service for the new breed of tennis fan—the upwardly mobile, suburban, car-driving, quiche-eating folks in the greater metropolitan area.

This condition raised a number of contradictory problems for the USTA. New fans of tennis were flocking to the game, but there was no room left for them. They were also descending on Forest Hills because of, rather than in spite of, its aura of exclusivity. Those fans were willing to put up with plenty of discomfort in order to enjoy the unique, touchy-feely accessibility of the pros and the game they played, on both the field courts and in the modest-sized stadium. The West Side Tennis Club and the pro game were a nice but tight fit—just as they were at Wimbledon and Roland Garros. Expansion of the site seemed to be the logical solution.

When negotiations broke down over the WSTC's unwillingness to drastically alter its character and grounds just for the privilege—and payoff—of hosting the U.S. Open, the USTA struck out in a bold new direction. Anticipating a massive grass-roots explosion of players as well as new fans, the USTA decided to build the National Tennis Center on seventeen acres in nearby Flushing Meadow, ostensibly to serve as the greatest public tennis facility in the land as well as the new home of the U.S. Open. The architect of this plan was the USTA president at the time, W. E. "Slew" Hester. Ole Slewfoot was not the typical USTA type. He was an outsider from the Deep South (Jackson, Mississippi), and although he was a successful "wildcat" (oil-industry patois for an independent entrepreneur in the oil and gas exploration business), he had a good ole boy's habits. His long service in the USTA defined him as a member of the establishment, but he felt a certain measure of well-concealed scorn for the eastern establishment types.

Hester was a populist visionary, but he was also a practical leader in the finest, uniquely American "can-do" tradition. Some people thought that Hester would be dismembered and devoured in the shark pond of the Big Apple's construction industry and civic bureaucracy, but Hester embarrassed them with his abilities as a horse trader and his easy way with what the blazer boys would call "rough trade." He managed to get the National Tennis Center built on time, in less than a year, at a cost estimated at only $500,000 over the projected $9 million price tag of the Center.

Okay, so there were a suspicious number of lemon-ice trolleys (and almost no water fountains) on site during the first few years of the new Open. That doesn't prove anybody ever put the head of a decapitated horse in Hester's bed, does it? Granted, the new place had a raw, unfinished look in 1978. It featured twenty-seven outdoor Deco-Turf hard courts made from rubberized asphalt. The walkways between the courts were macadam, with no landscaping. The stadium, a steep bowl with a capacity of twenty thousand, was a maze of concrete and exposed steel beams. Approaching it before one of the night matches that became standard fare at the new Open, you could easily mistake the stadium for a coal-fired hydroelectric facility somewhere in the Ukraine.

I had a few niggling problems with the new facility. In 1978 I counted seventy-six flags flying on and around the grounds, and every one of them was the American standard. There was something clumsy, inhospitable, and xenophobic about this at a Grand Slam event, because the major championships traditionally pay tribute to the international nature of the competition in much the same way as the Olympic Games. And despite the USTA's populist agenda, I had to search high and low to find a good old-fashioned hot dog among all the exotic and overpriced foods offered. I was also troubled by the conspicuous lack of aesthetics at the new site, given the ambience of the other Grand Slam events.

Still, I certainly wasn't going to be cast as the deadbeat at the dawn of an exciting new era in tennis. I supported Hester's bold leap from the country club to the public park, and I backed the alleged USTA agenda to broaden both the base and the appeal of the game. On a walking tour of the new facility with Ole Slewfoot, I did express some of my reservations about the featurelessness of the place. He clapped me on the back and said, "This is just the beginning, boy. By 1979 the U.S. Open is going to be more beautiful than Wimbledon."

Nevertheless, 1979 came and went with few tangible changes at the house that Slew built. So did 1980, by which time Hester, his tenure as president over, had vanished into the brush of the Mississippi bottomlands. And the next year passed, and the year after that. Nothing seemed to change except the escalating prices and the diminishing availability of tickets.

By 1985, when Curren called for the Strangelove solution, the shape and substance of American tennis in the new era was manifest. The much-heralded "tennis boom" was grinding to a halt, bogged down by the unfortunate fact that it took more time to get good at the game than most people were willing to give to the effort. But Connors, McEnroe, Evert, and Austin were packing in the fans; however, these fans weren't the cabbies, plumbers, and jelly salesmen that such visionaries as Hester, Connors, and Billie Jean King wanted to bring to tennis. The new order was essentially a continuation of the trend established at Forest Hills. It was composed of the upwardly mobile professional class: doctors from Parsippany, New Jersey, Manhattan corporate entertainers, and scenemakers. And their instincts told them that the U.S. Open was less important as a place to see than as a place to be seen, and to ogle others. This explains why so many people flocked so eagerly to a place so short on ambience and aesthetics.

In fact, the wilting heat, the uninspiring facilities, and the general mayhem of Flushing Meadow hastened this development. Unless you brought along a pith helmet, an IV rig full of hydrating fluids, and a good set of earplugs (neighbors, you know), it was nearly impossible to sit through a couple of matches at the Open. If you wanted to survive, you had to keep moving, mingling, buying drinks.

The U.S. Open gradually developed into a New York happening comparable to the opening of a new show by a hot artist in Soho or one of the big charity balls at the Metropolitan Museum of Art. People will do anything to get inside those gates at Flushing Meadow, even though the gates are nothing more than two black swinging Cyclone fences that get padlocked each night when the evening session is over.

In 1993, a record 530,764 people attended the Open. Most sessions were sold out long in advance, although only a small number of general admission tickets (*All* of them lousy, if not cheap, seats) were available to the general public after the corporate biggies and series ticket holders took their dibs. It isn't fair to single out the U.S. Open in this regard because by the 1990s it was clear that at most sporting events "Joe Fan" was an increasingly endangered species. And while there's no law saying that Joe's money is any better than that of a suburban tennis nut who is willing to shell out in advance for a block of tickets and divvy them up among friends, the system has created a unique spectator base at the Open. Almost the entire bottom half of the stadium, meaning almost all the best seats, are sold as series boxes to corporate interests. The holders often throw these tickets to clients or friends, many of whom show up late and leave early. Sometimes a ticket gets passed on and on and on until the guy who ends up in the choice hundred-dollar seat looks suspiciously as if he were recruited in the men's room of the Greyhound bus station in Syracuse. Well, that's one ordinary schmo who got in, anyway.

The thriving business in scalped tickets and the brisk bribe economy driven by all those portly ushers in their Mets caps do have one great benefit for the USTA: They prevent the development of the real-life scenario in which the entire bottom half of the stadium is empty while day-trippers sit packed in the nether reaches of the stadium. The USTA knows this, which is why the shadow economy flourishes. By contrast, a large number of tickets for Wimbledon are distributed to clubs affiliated with the Lawn Tennis Association, which sell them (at face value) to local tennis nuts.

U.S. Open tickets have become status objects, a condition that cuts right to the heart of the real revolution that occurred in tennis in 1968. First of all, the populist revolution (like almost all revolutions) was not one pitting have-nots against the haves. It was the have-somes against the have-mores. And if the revolution was "democratic," it was only so in a narrow, curious way. The ultimate message of the new U.S. Open was not "Power to the people" but the grotesque one that some of you may have hoped never to see in these pages again: "Money talks, bullshit walks."

At the U.S. Open, more than any other Grand Slam event, the dollar rules. And that development is almost preordained in an egalitarian democracy committed to leveling traditional social and cultural hierarchies. The funny thing is that every society needs a least common denominator, as well as some standard by which its constituents measure themselves. Once you chuck everything else out the window, the least common denominator becomes the ever enduring, glorious, absolutely necessary buck.

Of course, that doesn't mean that the new U.S. Open is less fun; in fact, it's probably more of a hoot. And that's doubly true if, instead of being some cranky tennis nut who gets all bent out of shape by the distractions of Flushing Meadow, you enjoy playing a pilgrim at the vanity fair. This is the recommended attitude at Flushing Meadow. If you're more interested in how Richard Krajicek generates pace on his serve than in hearing all about how the two guys sitting next to you feel about being indicted for insider trading, you came to the wrong place. You came to the wrong place if you thought that Flushing Meadow was an inclusionary, populist heaven. The U.S. Open at Forest Hills had two "exclusive" dining rooms (meaning the kind from which outsiders were excluded): the clubhouse itself and the U.S. Open Club, which was open only to the holders of expensive blocks of tickets. At Flushing Meadow all four of the dining rooms (the U.S. Open Club, Slew's Place, Racquets, and the Presidential Lounge) are restricted, either on the grounds of status or money. In other words, shelling out the $25 to $55 it costs for even the worst seat in the house, provided you can snag one of the few available to the public, doesn't entitle you to eat in any of the dining rooms. *Plus ça change, plus c'est la même chose.*

As a matter of consolation, I'd like to add that the tyranny of the

buck is universal. Gene Scott, a former Davis Cup player and the publisher of the newspaper *Tennis Week,* has always been just as comfortable in the chaotic confines of Flushing Meadow as he was among his
fellow patricians at Forest Hills. But in the early 1990s even the most
loyal, to-the-manor-born tennis nuts at the U.S. Open were growing
disillusioned with the USTA's appetite for price-gouging. In three short
years the price that Scott was asked to pay for his choice six-seat box at
one corner of the stadium court more than doubled, from $8,700 to
$18,500. As a lawyer and tennis promoter, Scott knows about market
economics, but even he took umbrage at the price hike.

   "There are scenarios in which the generally sound principle of charging what the market will bear is not really appropriate," Scott told me.
"Let's face it, the lumber industry could have quadrupled prices and
really cleaned up in the aftermath of Hurricane Andrew, but the industry refrained. In the big picture, the USTA's policy has been capricious
and arbitrary. The organization has a very short memory when it comes
to dealing with people. Like a lot of other people, I supported the Open
when it moved. I bought my box in 1978, at a time when the boxes were
virtually unsalable. A good management plan takes those kinds of
things into account."

   Granted, the guy with the great seat at the U.S. Open isn't Whitney
Paleface III anymore. But guess what: It isn't you or me, either, buddy.
It's Donald Trump, and if the other 19,998 people watchers get really
lucky, he'll have Marla Maples on his arm. Maybe that's a better deal,
maybe it's not. I will say this: Having been around in both eras, I think
that the ordinary tennis nut without a single drop of blue blood in his
veins consistently got to see more appealing tennis, under more attractive conditions, from better seats, often with better neighbors, than
that same spectator gets to see at Flushing Meadow. And it cost a whole
lot less, too.

   The U.S. Open is a goose that lays golden eggs, accounting for about
80 percent of the USTA's annual revenues. We're not talking about big
money here, we're talking huge money: The 1993 operating budget of
the USTA was a whopping $80 million, and there was plenty left over
to stuff into the mattress. The "easiest" money hauled in by the USTA
comes from its various television contracts with, first and foremost, the
CBS network. Both CBS and the USTA guard the numbers ferociously,
but the contract is worth an estimated $60 million. The USA network,
which broadcasts weeknight, prime-time matches, ponies up another
estimated $91 million. Throw in a few more million for sundry interna-
tional broadcast and rebroadcast rights, and you see where the goose
gets its stamina.

The USTA is often accused of abusing the goose, at which times it takes shelter behind a handy escutcheon. Like all the other national ITF affiliates, the USTA is a not-for-profit organization whose charter calls for the development and promotion of tennis in the United States. Thus, the organization's officers will tell you, the more money the USTA makes, the more it plows right back into the game of tennis. The only hitch in that defense is that money plowed back into the Open is not really money plowed into the game at large. This has been corroborated over the years by disgruntled USTA sectional officers who privately but frequently expressed dismay about how little of the USTA's formidable revenues trickled down to programs designed to expand the grass roots of the game. The USTA did not even implement a serious development program until the late 1980s, when a lull in the steady stream of American champions finally forced the organization to get up off its butt and do something besides crow about the imperial greatness of the U.S. Open.

Early in 1994, at the annual mercantile convention in Atlanta called The Super Show, a number of panel discussions were called to address a crisis in tennis. Equipment, clothing, and shoe manufacturers all lamented the lack of growth in the game. They all warned that if tennis didn't get moving again, their "industry" would inevitably shrivel up and die.

Okay, so it isn't all that easy to work up sympathy for people who brought you the $300 tennis racket, the nausea-inducing tennis shirt, and the ski boot masquerading as a tennis shoe. But their basic message was nonetheless a disturbing one: The tennis boom may have been an act of spontaneous combustion, but despite the growth of the U.S. Open and the vast riches mined by the USTA from the event, the national association had failed strikingly to broaden the base of the game.

Jim Baugh, an enterprising delegate from the venerable Wilson Sporting Goods Company, did a little homework and came up with some astonishing numbers. Funding for programs intended to attract new players to tennis received only $1.8 million from the USTA in 1993. Baugh conservatively estimated the additional administrative and miscellaneous costs attached to those programs, and even then the investment accounted for no more than 4 percent of the annual USTA budget. This was an implicit indictment of the USTA, whose delegates to the panel either remained mum or reflexively cited the success of the U.S. Open as a de facto example of making the game grow. The trade boys did smoke some numbers out of Kevin Loftus, a USTA marketing honcho. On the record Loftus said that 70 percent of the USTA advertising budget was directed toward "championship" promotion, an area in which the U.S. Open is the big-ticket item. Only 20 percent of that same budget was designated for advertising the "recreational" game.

Of course, even if the USTA did plow most of its money into tennis development schemes, there's no guarantee that they would work. But recent USTA history has certainly made one thing clear: The organization is Open-centric, and increasingly resembles one of those sprawling so-called charities whose revenues are consumed not by their intended beneficiaries but by ever-escalating administrative and marketing budgets.

All of this suggests that the very fact the U.S. Open is a tennis tournament has become almost incidental. It's as if the USTA owned the rights to an immensely successful TV game show and is so busy running that business, it hardly has time for anything else. And a heady business it is, one that intoxicates the USTA leadership and, for two brief weeks during the year, allows it to bask in the public limelight. The agenda of the USTA has shifted far afield from anything that is spelled out in the organization's charter, and the secrecy with which the USTA conducts its affairs suggests the modus operandi of a start-up company in a viciously competitive private enterprise much more than it does the civic-minded workings of a not-for-profit organization.

As a result of all that, the U.S. Open has presented a potential nightmare scenario of professionalism. The tournament continues to grow, but the game of tennis continues to shrink. It is more expensive to play and to watch than ever before, and it no longer seems to attract new players. It is also rapidly losing its cachet (not merely its snob appeal, but its genuine beauty), the very thing it once traded on in the struggle to expand the game. The USTA still has a whopper of a television contract, but, regrettably, it generates dismal ratings. The math just doesn't add up, but never fear, the USTA has a fix for this. If you're plugged into the weird logic of it all, you can guess what the solution is: expansion.

The USTA is going to make the Open bigger and better than ever before, with a massive reconstruction and renovation of Flushing Meadow. I honestly hope it works. Meanwhile, I keep going back to the answer that people like Scott received from the USTA when they protested the hike in box and ticket prices. They were told, "If you won't pay it, we have somebody else who will."

Money talks, all right, but when it runs out, things get mighty quiet, mighty fast. But don't start spreading that news.

The attitude of the majority of pro players toward Flushing Meadow can be described as a diatribe against the heat, the noise, the fans, the location, and the atmosphere of Flushing Meadow, but the well-documented challenges of playing on the asphalt-based courts at the new U.S. Open are also very much in tune with the spirit of the city where the tournament is held.

No tournament is as demanding in as many different ways as the U.S. Open, but complaints about ambient conditions ring hollow, because no matter how challenging the conditions get, they're the same for all players. Still, someone occasionally does get a particularly raw deal; his or her consolation is that the next person may get one that's even worse.

Take the players who had the misfortune to be assigned to play on Court No. 3, until it was paved over in 1992 to provide more space for the "food court." For fifteen years Court No. 3 was situated much too close to a busy intersection between the concessions and a main entrance of the stadium, meaning that there was an endless stream of traffic and noise at one end of it. Worse yet, when the lunch rush occurred during a lull in the action in the stadium, Court No. 3 was enveloped in a unique atmospheric phenomena. As lines formed at the kiosk selling charbroiled hamburgers, billowing, juicy clouds of burning fat and meat would surround Court No. 3 and its unfortunate occupants. Combined with the usually stifling heat and cloying humidity, the routine smokeouts brought new meaning to the McDonald's slogan, "You deserve a break today."

The cumulative effect of all this was that the man and woman who won the U.S. Open singles titles had to overcome more distractions, hazards, scheduling curveballs, and ambient changes than at any other tournament. There's a certain allure to seeing all this transpire, although I'm not sure it's all that healthy.

In 1978, the first year that the U.S. Open was played at Flushing Meadow, the first four rounds of the men's singles were contested in a best-of-three set format. This was a break from the best-of-five set system that separated Grand Slam events from ordinary tour events, but even under the streamlined format, the searing heat and the soaring humidity index of typical late-August weather in New York proved debilitating.

During a first-round, three-set singles victory over India's Sashi Menon in 1978, the American player Gene Mayer lost more than fifteen pounds (weighing in at 155, and out at 139). Mayer was almost incapacitated by cramps in the late stages of his match. When he finally walked back into the air-conditioned locker room after winning, he seized up and collapsed. Doctors had Mayer rushed to nearby Booth Memorial Medical Center where Mayer, hallucinating and unable to perform even the most rudimentary of motor skills, was given muscle relaxants and hydrating fluids. Fortunately, Mayer recovered in time to continue in the event. I caught up with him a few days later as he was getting ready to go out to play a doubles match.

"Just wait until the format shifts to five sets," Mayer cheerfully observed. "Guys are going to be dropping dead out there."

Mayer's experience on day one of the new era in U.S. tennis was not unique, either. Ruta Gerulaitis experienced an unexpected surprise during her first-round match when her racket hand cramped so badly that she was unable to relax her grip on the handle. "I was going to pry my fingers off the racket," she said later, "but then I got scared that I'd break them off."

Such incidents, stories, and complaints resounded for the duration of the tournament and at almost every U.S. Open thereafter, becoming part of the lore and legend of Flushing Meadow. The conditions did do wonders, however, for the towel-laundering service as well as the lemon ice industry. At the end of each day thirty-five hundred towels had been tossed into the hampers in the locker rooms.

The USTA has made innumerable puzzling decisions that affect the way tennis is played at Flushing Meadow, starting with the choice of an architect who incorporated a striking feature into the stadium/grand-stand complex. Every afternoon the massive shadow cast by the stadium inexorably creeps across the floor of the grandstand, much to the consternation of the combatants, and the frustration of TV crews and spectators alike. The equivalent of this error in the automotive world would be designing a car with an opaque windshield.

But none of the decisions that went into the creation and development of Flushing Meadow is quite as richly puzzling as the choice of Deco-Turf II as the surface for the U.S. Open. I can think of only two reasons for that—one of them supremely metaphorical, the other allegedly practical. Hard courts represent the least common denominator of tennis surfaces in the same way that the buck represents the same at the Open. Hard courts are also the "traditional" surface of American tennis, insofar as they are ubiquitous in the hotbed of the game, California, as well as at public tennis facilities. But think about this: In the past few decades, revolutionary changes have swept through all levels of tennis, most particularly in the design, construction, and material of tennis rackets. Yet the American establishment in tennis insists on continuing to promote and play the game on the ultimate low-tech surface, hard courts.

The USTA faced a thorny problem when it decided to go ahead with the Flushing Meadow project. The organization justifiably wanted a surface that gave American players the same advantage that clay gave

Europeans at the French and Italian Opens. It also wanted a surface that was different from those at the other Grand Slams, and it wanted to send a populist message to a nation in which all-weather asphalt courts were the norm at public parks and schools.

Arthur Ashe and Stan Smith, both fast-court players and former U.S. Open champions, lobbied very hard on behalf of hard courts. Their opinion carried considerable weight, but there was another important factor that influenced the USTA's decision: So much of the soil at Flushing Meadow was wet, marshy landfill that installing clay courts with reliable drainage posed insurmountable obstacles.

The USTA therefore chose hard courts for a variety of reasons that ignored the fundamental perils of the surface. Your basic hard court has much more in common with the parking lot at the local Wal-Mart than with "natural" surfaces (clay and grass). It's also unlike the variety of high-tech, synthetic surfaces available today. Hard courts take a devastating toll on players, especially frequent singles players. Todd Snyder, an ATP Tour trainer, once told me, "There are more traumatic injuries on hard courts than on any other surface. Hard courts lead to chronic back problems, arthritic knees, problems with the ankle and foot joints, and with the hips. Nobody can play for three or four weeks in a row on the stuff without putting himself at risk."

Snyder conducted a study a few years ago on the rate of common foot and ankle injuries on different surfaces. Synthetic surfaces, including indoor Supreme Court and outdoor asphalt, accounted for 55 percent of the injuries, grass courts logged in at 12 percent, and clay courts at 8 percent. The evidence is clear: Tennis on natural surfaces is a much less punishing exercise.

Beyond that, hard courts don't look very appealing, and even the cushioned, rubberized brands such as Deco-Turf or Rebound Ace (the Australian version) either hold or retain much more heat than natural surfaces. Yet the two Grand Slam events that feature the hottest weather also feature hard courts. Both in Melbourne and New York, on-court temperatures routinely soar to more than 100 degrees, and the rubber that cushions the court can turn so soft, the players' shoes stick to it.

But there is an even broader issue at play here. Ever since grass-court tennis ceased to matter, except at Wimbledon, the superiority of players bred on clay was swiftly and incontestably established. There have been many champions schooled on fast courts, but almost all of the great champions in the Open era were developed on clay. Here is the short list: Ilie Nastase, Bjorn Borg, Chris Evert, Ivan Lendl, Martina Navratilova, Mats Wilander, Boris Becker, Monica Seles, Stefan Edberg,

Arantxa Sanchez-Vicario, Steffi Graf. Even John McEnroe developed his game on Har-Tru.

When you come right down to it, the great advantage of hosting the Open on hard courts is not the edge that it gives American players but the discomfort so many Europeans feel playing on the stuff, at a tournament already brimming with player-unfriendly elements. But the USTA achieved its objective at Flushing Meadow. Americans won only three of the last nine U.S. Open titles contested at Forest Hills (Connors had two titles and Smith one), while Connors and McEnroe combined to win the first seven titles offered at Flushing Meadow.

But the new American tradition of hard courts has had one unfortunate ramification. By virtue of a domino effect, the focus on hard-court tennis has pretty much killed the clay-court tradition in the United States. This has made the development of domestic blue-chip champions, rather than players capable of winning their premier domestic tournament, that much more difficult.

The player whose name dominates the American championships in the Open era is Connors, but he's the subject of the next chapter. Instead, I'd like to say a few words here about two players whose success at the U.S. Open was in different ways more remarkable than that of good old, fist-pumping, finger-wagging, gut-spilling Jimbo.

Ivan Lendl had a remarkable record at Flushing Meadow, a place that almost every other European player of his generation regarded with fear and loathing. Lendl appeared in the U.S. Open final a record nine consecutive times, from 1982 to 1989, winning on three occasions. Even the redoubtable Connors did not come close to that mark, managing "only" five successive trips to the final, from 1974 to 1978. However, Connors had three victories in those five tries. Nothing says so much, so unequivocally, about Lendl's basic toughness as a player than his record at Flushing Meadow.

But for my money, the most interesting success story at Flushing Meadow was the one written by mild-mannered, phlegmatic Stefan Edberg who has won the U.S. Open twice, in 1991 and 1992. To appreciate this, you not only have to look at the big picture but take in the wall on which it hangs.

The unique conditions at Flushing Meadow and Bjorn Borg's failures there easily convinced a generation of Swedes that the game in New York was not worth the candle. As Anders Jarryd once told me, "Bjorn gave a signal to many of us. It was that we Swedes could do great in Paris and London but that New York was maybe too rough, too American, for us to feel confident there. A lot of us didn't really think we had much of a chance in that crazy Flushing Meadow place, and we didn't put much pressure on ourselves to perform. If you did well in Melbourne, Monte Carlo, and even Indian Wells or Indianapolis, you were fine. You got great rankings, great money, and respect. We could afford to do badly at the Open, so a lot of us did."

Edberg was an outstanding sportsman and a shy individual surprisingly prone to discouragement. Although he rarely appeared to experience emotional highs during a match, he often seemed susceptible to lows, at which times he was visibly hangdog. Although Edberg was a fearless attacking player, even his style often looked curiously passive. In short, while Edberg's game was well designed for hard-court tennis, nothing about the man ever suggested that he had the guts and gumption to tackle and prevail over the sublime and ridiculous challenges posed by Flushing Meadow. Furthermore, Edberg quickly developed a discouraging tradition at Flushing Meadow. Pundits often overlook the vital impact that past history has on the performances of players at most tournaments.

In his first eight years at Flushing Meadow, Edberg bombed out in the first round twice, lost in the second round once, and reached the fourth round on three occasions. He appeared to have maxed out when he reached back-to-back semifinals in 1986 and 1987. Wilander beat Edberg on the latter of those occasions and then won the title one year later—a breakthrough that must have been a bitter pill for his main domestic rival to swallow.

Worse yet, Edberg's failure in 1988 was as dramatic as Wilander's success. He met resurgent Jimmy Connors in a fourth-round match that evolved into a classic Flushing Meadow throwdown. The conditions were awful: The match was played at night before a prime-time crowd juiced up on watery beer and stricken by the swamp fever that Connors always spread at Flushing Meadow. As winds swirled paper cups and napkins around the stadium, Edberg grew increasingly frustrated and disconsolate. He seemed unable to do anything right. Once again he resembled a naive tourist doomed to return home from Gotham in his clogs, with nothing more to show than a badly overpriced electronic gadget or the tale of how his wallet had been lifted on the subway by an apparently friendly nun. Connors mauled him, 6–2, 6–3, 6–1.

And when the Russian Sasha Volkov hammered Edberg in the first round of the U.S. Open the following year, it seemed like the final nail had been driven into Edberg's coffin at Flushing Meadow.

But then Edberg—the meek Edberg who always hated the stifling humidity, the vulgar crowds, the made-for-TV scheduling, and, yes, even the official bird of the U.S. Open (the Boeing 747)—did some-

thing not only unexpected but downright mind-boggling, something
reminiscent of all those B-movies in which John Q. Public, discovering
the vigilante lying dormant in his all-too-socialized urban being, takes
justice into his own hands and begins to shoot back. Accurately.

Edberg won the 1991 U.S. Open and repeated the performance in
1992. His feat in 1992 was particularly heroic in that he survived three
consecutive five-set battles before he pinned down Pete Sampras in four
sets to take the title.

Looking back on that reversal of fortune, Edberg told me, "It took
me a few years to get more or less comfortable at the Open. There's a
lot to deal with there, especially for a foreign player. But you know, in
other places I always did okay in the heat, and my game is pretty well
suited for the hard courts. So in my mind I never gave up on the U.S.
Open. In the past few years I tried just to accept all the distractions and
play my best tennis."

And then he added: "Maybe I also needed to have a little bit more
confidence, a little more fire inside me. I don't think too much of the
opinion of other people, but I hear it, you always do. And I didn't like
hearing that I was too nice a guy or not strong enough inside to handle
New York, to win at Flushing Meadow. I think I proved that I am."

For a long time I couldn't figure out why the site at Flushing Meadow
always looked so, well, incomplete. Ole Slewfoot's claim that by 1979
the NTC would be more "beautiful" than Wimbledon turned out to be
a comical, empty boast. If anything, the basic facilities at Flushing
Meadow only got shabbier and more decrepit over the years.

Nobody ever bothered to clothe the stadium. The smell of trash fil-
tered in everywhere. The skeletal superstructure of the stadium became
a dimly lit mixture of cables, crates, and boxes. And then there was the
"Great Hall," the main corridor that encircles the stadium at ground
level. It sounds grand, it makes you think Camelot or Valhalla, but it
never evolved into anything more than a bleak cinder-block corridor
lined with concession stands. It was crowded, noisy, and redolent of
cheap disinfectant and spilled beer.

I might have had some inkling of the future back in 1978 when,
shortly after Hester made his aesthetic prediction, I went to visit the
marketing director for the Open, Bob Arrix. He was a beefy, direct,
New York type of guy who told me, "Those gargoyles and stuff like that
are a thing of the past. This is the Shea Stadium era."

Still, I didn't figure out the reason for the anti-aesthetic of the U.S.
Open until about the time that Curren suggested the Strangelove solution for Flushing Meadow. All you need to know about Flushing

Meadow is that the second most important word there is "television." And if you've ever seen the set of any TV program, even one of the most popular and star-studded TV series, you will note the similarity it bears to Flushing Meadow. To wit: Anything that is "on camera" is dressed up and presentable. Everything else is cobbled together with duct tape, wire, and veneer.

Television has a lot to do with tennis watching at Flushing Meadow and a lot more than it should with tennis playing. Two of the monumental problems of the U.S. Open are that the live audience often gets stiffed because of telecentric scheduling and that, because of the inordinate amount of power that television interests hold over such vital matters as scheduling, the players have come to view the event with disillusioned, contemptuous eyes. They don't feel that way about the other Grand Slams, and that's reason enough to worry.

Charges against the Open are serious ones, and they cut to the heart of the integrity of the game in New York and the validity of the results it produces. As part of its lucrative deal with CBS, the USTA virtually allows the network honchos to dictate the schedule. And the network does all that it can to provide a "viewer-friendly" show—meaning a "name" player, preferably an American one, for every telecast. Ironically, the U.S. Open still gets ratings that are meager by the standards of a popular sitcom or a typical NFL Sunday football game. In the eight years between 1985 and 1993, the best cumulative rating CBS managed was a 4.8 in 1985, with a low of 2.6 in 1993. The average over those years is about a 4.0, which is about as good as a weekday morning show such as "Good Morning, America." The ratings for the men's final are higher, although CBS broke the 7.0 mark on just three occasions in that eight-year span: in 1985 (when Lendl beat McEnroe), in 1989 (when Becker beat Lendl), and for one brief, shining moment in 1991 during Jimmy Connors's enchanted run to the semifinals. Connors's theatrics boosted the USA network's weeknight ratings by 75 percent over 1990.

The other Grand Slam events also have lucrative broadcast contracts, but none of them gives television producers the same leeway over such key elements as starting times, order of play, scheduling, and even general format. The first sign that the USTA was going to manage the U.S. Open any way it saw fit appeared in 1978 when a desire to cut to the car chase in early round matches led the USTA to adopt the best-of-three format. Sixty-six of the seventy players polled voted against this break from the Grand Slam tradition, but the USTA implemented it anyway. This was not only a telegenic decision, it was also a transparent attempt to stack the deck for American serve-and-volley players, giving them a chance to unleash their firepower and make a quick kill over superior opponents on the fast hard courts. The best-of-three experiment was stupid and dangerous, and the USTA had the good sense to abandon it.

Night sessions also became a tradition-busting feature of the U.S. Open at that first Flushing Meadow meeting. This move immediately sent ticket revenues soaring, and it ultimately made tennis a prime-time, weeknight entertainment. But in order to provide the most telegenic matches and in order to meet the Women's Tennis Association's demands in 1979 for equal exposure, the USTA's myriad, conflicting interests often produced schedules that violated both common sense and the ethical mandate of fairness.

Because of the duration and nature of Grand Slam events, tradition dictates that the competitors play on alternate days. These tend to be the "men's" and "ladies'" days, designed to lead to a women's final on Saturday and a men's final on Sunday. It can be tricky to keep the rotation intact, especially when the weather is unpredictable, but it isn't exactly rocket science. At Flushing Meadow the USTA has thrown that format out the window in its attempts to capture two different television audiences (day and night) and to keep television executives and the women players happy. Here's a simple example of what I mean.

In 1993, Boris Becker informed the tournament office before the event that he was willing and able to play as soon as the tournament saw fit to put him on court. Edberg, the defending champion, was also prepared to play on the first day. And rightly so, because the male and female defending champions at Grand Slam events traditionally play on the first and second days of the tournament, respectively.

Yet when the order-of-play for the afternoon session of opening day came out, only one of the many marquee names in tennis was on it: Steffi Graf. Eager spectators on what should have been a festive banner day were furious. But the USTA had apparently decided to hoard its resources. Who cared about the crowd? There was no daytime telecast. As it turned out, Becker was kept hanging until the first Thursday, the fourth day of the fourteen-day Open, partly because of inclement weather. But he was delayed for that long only because the USTA and its partners in television wanted to slot him in an "appropriate" time. Thus, after his first match, Becker faced the prospect of having to play three best-of-five matches in three days—just to catch up with the field.

Each year the Open seems to come up with more, rather than fewer, scheduling snafus, a sure sign that the USTA is increasingly pressed to give its partners their share of the pie. Detailing all the inequities foisted on the players and the live, paying public would be a long and boring undertaking for me and for you, so I'll just say a few things about the U.S. Open's Super Saturday, or Stupor Saturday.

In traditional Grand Slam scheduling, the women play two semifinals on Thursday and the final on Saturday. The men play their semifinals on Friday and the championship match on Sunday. This sensible format presents some unfortunate problems. The day of the men's semifinals is often the most attractive day of the tournament. But Friday is a working day when spectators and potential viewers are bound to desks and time clocks. So CBS's desire to put together a big weekend package was frustrated by the Grand Slam format and also by the final Sunday's coincidence with opening day of the football season. To further complicate matters, until 1994, CBS's own sporting plum was the broadcast rights to the National Conference of the National Football League. This therefore dictated that the men's tennis final be scheduled for sometime after the early football games concluded, at around 4 P.M.

The combined weight of these problems created Stupor Saturday, which CBS has tried to turn into a one-day tennis happening—an event within the event called the U.S. Open. It takes advantage of a good Saturday time slot and features both men's semifinals and the women's final. Stupor Saturday is either the greatest single day of tennis or a broadcast orgy that ruins a good thing by providing too much of it.

For my money, Stupor Saturday is both of those things. It has become a tradition but not a very good or sensible one. It has turned television watching into a team sport, with fans taking turns watching the proceedings and sleeping. But more important, it just isn't fair—and that counts.

The men players have the most serious grievances. Because of the marathon program, the first men's semifinal starts at 11 A.M., often with a nearly empty stadium that robs a Grand Slam semifinal of any sense of occasion. At just about the time that things get interesting, the arriving crowds create a formidable distraction. And we are talking about a potent, critical crowd here, because Super Saturday has become *the* day on which everybody who thinks he's anybody absolutely, positively must be there, albeit not necessarily on time.

One of the wackiest Stupor Saturday scenarios was played out in 1987. Because rain was forecast for the late afternoon and evening, the starting time of the first men's match was inched forward to 10 A.M. So the tournament referee had to decide which of two matches to put on first: Ivan Lendl versus Jimmy Connors or Stefan Edberg versus Mats Wilander.

At the time, Wilander led the rivalry with his fellow Swede by 6–4 (although Edberg had won their only previous meeting of the year), and they were separated by only a few meager percentage points in the computer rankings (Edberg was 2, and Wilander, 3). Connors, on the other hand, had lost thirteen matches in a row to Lendl, dating back to October 1984. Lendl was the top-ranked player in the world, and Connors was ranked 6.

Furthermore, Lendl and Connors hadn't played matches since the previous Wednesday, while the Swedes had both played singles on Thursday, and Edberg had played a five-set doubles final the previous day, Friday. If you're plugged into USTA-think, you can guess who was picked to play the 10 A.M. match.

"This is an American tournament," Grand Prix supervisor Ken Farrar commented. "We had to go by which was likely to be the more popular match for the more desirable TV time slot. That was Connors and Lendl. Let's face it, we're selling a product here."

The Swedes, hearing that they had the early start time, had a long locker room discussion of how to protest. Although they initially threatened not to play at all, they backed off and settled on a short "strike" that delayed the start of the match for about fifteen minutes. Wilander ended up beating Edberg in a tight, bright four-set match. Connors got only eight games off Lendl in a straight set loss.

Stupor Saturday features one other conspicuous inequity. Although both winning semifinalists have to bounce back to play at around 4 P.M. on Sunday, the starting times for the semifinals, sandwiched as they are around the women's final, often have an inordinate impact on the final. Nobody has a great deal of stamina left after two weeks in the searing heat of Flushing Meadow, yet the winner of the second, late semifinal has to bounce back to play for the championship of the second most important tournament in the world in less than twenty-four hours. Throw in the urge to stage-manage the competition on behalf of an American competitor—and the most telegenic one at that—and you have a nasty package that sometimes blows up right in the faces of the USTA and CBS.

John McEnroe's last appearance in the U.S. Open final occurred in 1985 when he played the man he had beaten for the title the previous year, Ivan Lendl. On Stupor Saturday in 1984, McEnroe and Wilander fought tooth and nail for almost four hours in the early match, on a court where the temperature registered 118 degrees, before McEnroe prevailed in five sets. Lendl and the USTA's prime-time darling, Connors, contested the late match under much cooler temperatures. Connors twisted his ankle badly in his afternoon warm-up, and his lack of mobility was evident in his straight-set loss to Lendl.

Up to that point Lendl had reached three consecutive U.S. Open finals and, looking nervous every time, lost each one. True to form, Lendl got off to a painfully slow start against McEnroe, spraying ground strokes all over the stadium. But once McEnroe's initial rush of Sunday adrenaline subsided, he looked conspicuously leg-weary and awkward. Lendl hung in there to win a first-set tiebreaker and then made short work of his nemesis, 7–6, 6–4, 6–4.

With all due respect to Lendl, I can't remember another Grand Slam final in which unwise and ultimately unfair scheduling played such a glaring role. With the championship ice broken, Lendl would go on to win three successive U.S. Open titles. No wonder the guy's such a flag-waving, red-white-and-blue, all-American nutter. A round of thanks is in order to the United States Television Association. Hold that bomb until we hear from our sponsors.

CHAPTER 17

JIMMY CONNORS
Forever Punk

NOBODY REPRESENTS the Dickensian nature of the Open era—the best of times, the worst of times—better than Jimmy Connors, whose life experience seemed handily summed up by his bombastic nickname, Jimbo. Any number of players, managers, administrators, and camp followers will tell you that Jimbo was a selfish, vulgar, uncharitable, and often unsportsmanlike champion, a man who not only raised tennis to new heights in the public consciousness but on just as many occasions dragged the game down to crotch, if not ground, level.

But I still like Connors, and a lot of other people who had more reason that I ever did to dislike him feel the same way. Some of my affection for Connors goes back to an incident at the U.S. Clay Court Championships in Indianapolis in August 1978. The host club was at the edge of town, in farm country, and the lights of the tiny stadium attracted a dazzling variety of moths and insects, many of which took inquisitive passes at the competitors. During Jimmy Connors's first-round match, a large moth briefly fluttered near him and then very dramatically flew just inside the court and swooned to the clay, like some heartbroken operatic hero. Connors walked into the court, nudged the creature onto the face of his steel racket, and then gently deposited it out of harm's way at the back of the court.

A few evenings later, Guillermo Vilas was the marquee name on the stadium court. A formidable clay-court player known for his work ethic and fierce concentration, the long-haired, brooding Vilas was also a published poet. His countryman, the Nobel Laureate writer Jorge Luis Borges, once remarked that Vilas wrote poetry about as well as Borges, who was blind, played tennis. Nevertheless, in tennis circles Vilas was considered an *artiste,* and he was generally described as "soulful" or "sensitive"—accusations that were never brought against Connors.

Anyway, a moth interrupted Vilas's elaborate, ritualistic service preparations; for all I know, it was the same creature, hamming it up again for the packed galleries. The poet patiently observed the antics of the moth. After the moth settled on the Har-Tru in another grand finale, Vilas walked out to it, his eyes fixed on his own shoes the whole way. Then he very deliberately and soulfully ground the moth into powder with his right foot.

Jimbo had a gentle side, although he was loath to allow it to show on the court.

I also liked Connors's penchant for clean, simple living, a habit that was buried in the avalanche of bad press he got for his vulgar antics and hellacious zest for competition. At heart, Connors was a goofy, naive midwestern kid whose second most potent addiction (the destruction of opponents being his first) was for nothing more evil than the soft drink Dr. Pepper. Every morning for a good part of his career, Connors began his day not with coffee or tea but with a few cans of Dr. Pepper.

I wouldn't be surprised to find out that Jimmy even sang the brand's jingle to himself in the bathroom mirror: ". . . How'd you like to be a Pepper, too?"

I was often struck by the fastidious side of Connors's personality but never as surprisingly as during the 1980 tournament at Wimbledon, at a time when cocaine abuse was just as popular in the tennis community as the rest of society.

One evening, I had a telephone message in my room at the official tournament hotel, the Gloucester, from a fellow I'll call Nigel—a small-time gofer and drug dealer who often showed up at the trendy London discos and restaurants that name players frequented. The message rather cryptically suggested that I might want to show up for a "party" in room 456 at 11 P.M.

I went to 456 at the appointed hour and knocked. Nigel cracked the door and, seeing that it was me, opened up. Only two of the dozen or so people in the room were players, but there were seven or eight coach and manager types, including a former tour player whose protégé was a handsome, highly gifted South American player who had top five potential. There was a peculiar, creepy kind of gravity to the occasion, as there always is when drugs are the common denominator.

Nigel's boss sat at a table, his open briefcase containing packages of coke in various quantities. Nigel played the host, doling out samples. Another dozen people came and went over the next half hour. Some customers did their business briskly. The deadbeats hung around, engaging in the stilted, sham conversations that go on when people are basically just waiting for the offer of another free line. I stayed for about an hour, killing time like everybody else.

The following day, I stopped by to watch Connors playing a match on Court No. 3. He was snorting and taking huge drafts of breath between points. On the changeover he discreetly went to an inhaler wrapped in his towel and serviced both of his nostrils. I knew what it looked like when people snorted cocaine out of small glass or steel cylinders called Blasters, and I couldn't believe my eyes.

I looked over at the seats reserved for coaches and spotted Connors's friend, hitting partner, and frequent traveling companion, the Las Vegas pro Lornie Khule, a fellow who was always derided as a gofer because of his fanatical loyalty to Connors. A stranger materialized out of the crowd and passed Lorne a brown paper bag.

Connors snorted and chuffed his way to a win. Afterward I felt obliged to say something to Lorne because of the flagrant carelessness of Jimmy's behavior and Lorne's transaction. I found Khule standing on the balcony overlooking the grounds outside the players' tea room.

"Lornie," I said, "it's none of my business what Jimmy does, but, jeez, anybody with eyes in his head could see what was going on out there."

"What are you talking about?" Khule asked, surprised.

When I explained everything I'd seen, Khule laughed.

"Jimmy's got terrible hay fever," he said. "He couldn't breathe out there without taking a decongestant on every changeover." Khule's tone turned flinty. "Jimmy would never fool around with that dope. He hates drugs. He hates everything about them."

A moment later Khule pointed down into the crowd. The South American player and the coach who had been in room 456 the previous night were making their way through the usual crush on their way to the court. "Those guys are the ones who have the problem, not Jimmy."

I never did learn what was in the brown paper bag. Khule and Connors did share a healthy appetite for gambling at backgammon, if not cocaine, but for all I know the bag was full of Dristan.

If you could get by the toilet humor and Connors's alternately cocky and defensive persona, he was nothing less than a real square: a kid who listened not to the Rolling Stones but Paul Anka, a boy who was captivated but never seduced by the tawdry, high-rolling glitter of Las Vegas, a player who stuffed every nickel he earned into a mattress and allowed himself only one frivolity: small-time gambling. Connors also was refreshing devoid of the professional patina that made so many of his less controversial rivals appear remote, uninterested, and unknowable. He often appeared defiant and prickly, but if you knew him well, you couldn't help but be struck by his happy-go-lucky, cheery nature. He never got depressed—he simply didn't see what there was to get depressed about.

Jimbo was the rude boy of Babylon, a young punk who became an old punk with a penchant for heroic, age-defying, and crowd-pleasing adventures that served to wipe out the memory but not the impact of his numerous earlier transgressions.

James Brady, editor-at-large for *Advertising Age*, articulated that point of view shortly after thirty-nine-year old Jimbo's improbable performance at the 1991 U.S. Open. In an editorial, Brady wrote:

> Connors has always been a vulgarian, groping at his crotch and performing obscene little on-court bumps and grinds. He believes this to be funny. He has always been selfish, refusing to play Davis Cup tennis. . . . He has always been self-pitying. Did you hear that Labor Day exchange with the chair umpire?
>
> "You son of a bitch, get out of the chair," Connors said, after he was the victim of a controversial decision by the umpire, Dick Littlefield. "Get your ass out of the chair. I'm playing my butt off here at thirty-nine years old and you're pulling that crap?"
>
> I think that had Littlefield climbed down off his chair right there and then and clocked this punk, the city's "love affair" might well have been with the umpire, rather than with Connors."

Brady made no attempt to conceal the subjective nature of his commentary, but for better or worse, Connors's performance at Flushing Meadow in 1991 undoubtedly reflected a "love affair" with New York, and everything from the attendance figures to the startling television ratings bear that out.

More important, Connors' impassioned, courageous efforts not only outweighed his lapses to vulgar or unpleasant theatrics but were intimately bound up with his very being. This was one of those "take the good with the bad" scenarios, and the overwhelming number of witnesses was more than willing to accept the bad because the good was both inspired and inspiring.

Connors inarguably cultivated vulgarity like some men cultivate a taste for power neckwear. With a few choice words or hand gestures he could mortify a full stadium, acutely embarrassing everyone but himself. Connors was also loath to explain his behavior to the press, much less apologize for it. Jimbo was a consummately visceral man, a windy, Barnumesque showman. A simple, common man who actually did live life at crotch level, for better or worse, come hell, high water, or Bjorn Borg.

Connors's love of tennis was so fundamental and burned with such a pure and bright flame that it ultimately rescued him from the ennui, confusion, and identity crises that have plagued other top players. Connors was the purest tennis player of his generation. He may have been a vulgar man, but he was only marching in lockstep with the era that produced him, as well as the peculiarities of his own unusual history.

Connors was the first great American player spawned in the Open era. Unlike so many up-from-nothing tennis players from the amateur era, Connors was neither imbued with, nor interested in, the tennis ethic. Right from the start of his career, he dismissed most of the traditions in tennis as frivolous affectations of a class to which he did not belong, and would rather subvert and conquer than join. In that sense, he was similar to Billie Jean King.

He inherited this fundamentally antisocial attitude from his mother, Gloria. She was the one who shaped his attitude and game, with help from her own mother, Bertha Thompson (Connors's beloved "Two-Mom"). Gloria was an attractive tennis nut, tournament player, and teaching pro. If anyone seemed to be the type who would love to become the resident celebrity at the country club, it was Gloria Connors. But Gloria was made from tougher stuff than that. She was trapped in an unsatisfying marriage and stuck on the wrong side of the tracks in East St. Louis, Illinois. Her estranged husband, James Scott Connors, Sr., was never anything more than a remote influence in the life of his two sons, John and Jimmy. Gloria's two children were her single hedge against a disappointing and unreliable world. She poured all of her ambitions and dreams into the boys, teaching them to play as soon as they were toddlers. "Jimmy was swinging a racket pretty much as soon as he could walk. And he just took to tennis like it was part of him. He had his game together by the time he was five."

John did not take to tennis the way Jimmy did, and when his precocious kid brother began to upstage him, John quit the game at twelve and quietly went his own way. This did not appear to trouble Gloria, who bluntly said, "John just didn't have the guts for competitive tennis." At that time, the vision of an organized professional game was barely a gleam in the eyes of disgruntled amateur players. Unlike the parents of the next generation, Gloria could not have anticipated the riches that tennis in the incipient new era would offer the players. She was a purist.

Single mother. Tough life. Favorite son. Elite sport. Add the ingredients and bake at high temperature for a dozen or so years, and you get an obsessional casserole, full of succulently radical personality and even behavior. For instance, the sight of Gloria sitting courtside never prevented Connors from grabbing his private parts or uttering a stream of obscenities. In fact, her presence often seemed to wake his demons as well as lift his game. At such times Gloria sat impassively, looking lost in thought. I often found myself wondering what she was thinking. Perhaps she was entranced by Jimbo's status as an Oedipal avenger come to life, a raging, mother-loving, foul-mouthed son who unabashedly, even gleefully, fondled himself like an infant in front of his mother. Maybe she was just tracking his game, coolly indifferent to all that came with it. I don't know, but it sure was weird. The one thing I do know is that Connors never offended his mother, which may help to explain why he never seemed to care if he offended anyone else.

Parents at junior tournaments were often astonished when, lingering by a phone at the tournament desk, young Jimbo would call home with his results. As soon as Two-Mom Gloria would answer the phone, Jimmy immediately regressed to baby talk. Later, when Connors's world-class potential became manifest, Gloria and Jimmy moved to Los Angeles, where Jimmy could find better practice and take advantage of the help offered by the wily old pro Pancho Segura. In Los Angeles, Gloria Connors began to give tennis lessons again. She shared a modest two-bedroom apartment with her son, cooking his favorite dinners of short-rib stew and chicken-fried steak.

In 1975 I went to Las Vegas to cover a garish Heavyweight Championship of Tennis match pitting Connors against John Newcombe, with $400,000 for the winner. Connors won the match, and later that evening I attended his victory celebration in a bar in Caesar's Palace. Gloria sat on Jimmy's lap, cuddling with her son throughout most of the evening. You might find all of this distasteful or even mortifying. But the extraordinary thing was that Gloria and Jimmy's relationship was not only remarkably positive but wildly successful. Tweak a screw here and a bolt there, and Connors might have come to hate tennis by age fifteen or become a terminally maladjusted character. Instead, he became one of the great tennis players of all time and the father of two in a conventional, if occasionally problematic, marriage. A lot of tennis players have done worse.

By the time Jimmy began to fulfill his promise, whatever personal dreams Gloria had appeared to be spent. She rarely left St. Louis. When she did show up at a tournament, she seemed aloof and icy. She never assumed the prominent position that she had earned in tennis society.

Although Gloria initially didn't give a hoot about money, Jimmy quickly learned upon moving to Los Angeles that even if there wasn't much money in the game, tennis players enjoyed a great measure of status among wealthy and influential people. "At the time, when I was about sixteen, I had friends who would drive up in Ferraris or Lamborghinis to the club where I was practicing," Connors told me, "friends who came from houses that had pools in the ground and even private tennis courts. I sat back and thought, 'Hey, how do I get some of this for me?' Tennis was my entree to everything. And in my own eyes I couldn't see it as being just a little tennis. It had to be great tennis, top-of-the-pile tennis. So I just ate, breathed, thought, talked, and dreamed tennis. For as long as I can remember."

Meanwhile, the dawn of the Open era had pushed tennis to the forefront of the public consciousness. Connors took his cues from the game's egalitarian revolutionaries and decided that tennis players were first and foremost entertainers. The word "entertainer" is bandied about so easily and so often, it's easy to forget the radical proposition that it embodies. The entertainer's only real mandate is to captivate and amuse. No code of conduct or value system applies; in fact, the entertainer often thrives on flouting such conventions. When you come right down to it, an athlete who chooses to project himself as an entertainer has embraced the least common denominator. This role has little distinction, but it has almost universal appeal.

The entertainer's universe is one driven and ruled with mechanical precision, by the equivalent of one of those television game show "Applause-O-Meters." Throughout his career Connors played to that appliance, and I found it noteworthy when, near the end of his period of ascendancy in tennis, Connors gave me an eloquent silent answer to the question of what he would miss most about the game when he retired. It wasn't going to be the rush of adrenaline provided by competition. It wasn't going to be the lavish hotel suites or exotic sites. It wasn't going to be the camaraderie. Jimmy just looked at me and in slow motion, without allowing his hands to touch, mimicked clapping. That was what he was going to miss most.

Yet Jimmy never compromised the nature and quality of his tennis. He talked a good game about being an entertainer, but he played an even better one as a pure athlete. Even the most dedicated tennis players sometimes tanked matches, but Connors never gave less than his best as a player.

Although Connors certainly came to love the money, he wasn't driven by it. As he said in 1991, "Because of the money in the game, getting to be number one doesn't mean much to a lot of the guys out there. When I first started [1971], there wasn't much money. So the main concern was to go out and win Wimbledon or the U.S. Open. The real reward in tennis was the top ranking."

A year later, in 1992, Connors told Robin Finn of *The New York Times* how he felt about the most recent crop of pros: "They all play great tennis, they do the job. But I mean, I shouldn't have been beating those guys a year ago, at age thirty-nine. What disappoints me about tennis today is that for most of them, tennis is just about doing the job. There's nothing else behind that."

Connors's criticism of the pro establishment always revolved around the same themes: the loss of color, passion, and commitment in the structured game. Ironically, the very rules of conduct that he so despised and mistrusted were partly created because of his own frequent transgressions against taste and the concept of sportsmanship. He seemed willing to compromise all the things for which tennis once stood in order to bring more people into the stadium or to generate better television ratings. Despite that, it seems that trapped inside Jimmy Connors was an amateur tennis player striving to get out. Above all else, he played because he loved the game. He happened to come along at a time and from an environment characterized by confusion and debate over the very nature and purpose of tennis. But ultimately, dedication saved Connors from becoming just another entertainer, an ex-clown who once traveled with the circus.

Jimmy Connors played tennis like a girl. This observation may smack of gender prejudice or awaken painful memories of schoolyard taunts, but it's a rich, multifaceted fact that is not merely a provocative comment on Connors's psyche and style, but is also a testament to the value of the flat, all-purpose, all-court game that Connors learned from Two-Mom and Gloria. It is also exactly what Karolj Seles had in mind when he developed his daughter Monica's tennis game, and the results speak for themselves.

"My grandmother and mom were big fans of the compact, flat game," Connors told me. "Minimal backswing, pretty flat stroke. Their whole idea was to hit forcing balls from the baseline, which meant having to do two things—take the ball on the rise and keep the pace on it by keeping it flat. Serving and volleying just isn't too important to me except in the sense that you need the ability to finish points with sharp volleys.

"It's basically a woman's game, but I was able to get the power to open up the court with it. I was strong enough to push people all over the court with my game, with my pace and accuracy, even if I wasn't strong enough to overpower them with big serves or outright winners like Lendl did. It was drilled into me from the start that every stroke should be aggressive, attacking, designed to get my opponent out of position so that I could cruise in and finish the job off with a good volley."

Connors employed that game to dominate defensive baseline players
as well as aggressive practitioners of power tennis. He stood only five
feet ten inches and weighed in at just over 150 pounds. He was consistently outweighed if not outmaneuvered, outmuscled, and outrun.
Fleet, alert, and feral, he reached the pinnacle of tennis with a versatile
game, a lithe body, and a remarkable stroke of good fortune delivered
by technology.

Hanging around one sunny morning at the Orange Bowl, one of the
premier international junior championships, twelve-year-old Jimmy
Connors saw a man showing off an new experimental racket, the Wilson T-2000. It was a dazzling thing made of bright steel and featured a
round "lollipop" face and a unique stringing system that had more in
common with a snowshoe than a wooden tennis racket. The experimental racket glittered in the sunlight, and many years later, Connors
remembered thinking, "Boy, I like that! I want one of those."

The Wilson rep promised to send Connors a few frames as soon as
the racket was ready for production. The chemistry was classic: a slender boy with ambitions his physique could not yet satisfy, and a futur-
istic instrument that gleamed with the promise of heroic deeds and
lethal power. It was Arthur and Excalibur all over again, every kid's fantasy. In Connors's case, the fantasy would be fully realized. When the
Wilson rep made good on his promise, all Connors had to do was convince his mother to allow him to change from a wooden frame to the
new, unconventional, and unproven racket. Fortunately, Gloria Connors was wise enough to see that the extra power promised by the steel
racket could be a great asset to her son.

Throughout Connors's junior career, he was hounded by the theory
that, with his skinny arms, concave chest, and spindly legs, he just
wouldn't have the power or stamina to play at the top level. This
remained true even after Connors moved to Los Angeles and prevailed
on the wily Ecuadorian pro Pancho Segura to put the finishing touches
on his game. Segura knew better than to tamper with Connors's unconventional style, but he was a master strategist who could teach his protégé the finer points of tactics. "I worked with Jimbo because I believed
in him," Segura told me. "Everyone who saw him play said he was too
small and that he didn't have enough of a serve. But they didn't see that
Jimbo was a killer. In his head, he had everything. It didn't matter how
big you were. He wasn't afraid. He could destroy you."

Connors's notorious killer instinct was implanted early by Gloria,
who once told me, "I taught him to be a tiger on the court. Even when
he was really little, I would hit the ball down his throat if he gave me the
opportunity. Then I would call him up to the net and tell him, 'See that,

Jimmy? Your own mother will do that to you. Everybody will do that to you if they have the chance."

By the time Connors moved to Los Angeles, he had learned to harness and exploit the power of the T-2000. This was a powerful testament to his neurological superiority because many other world-class players found that the extra power offered by the racket came at the expense of consistency. If you hit the ball on the sweet spot, it flew. If you hit it off-center, the resulting underpowered shot often fell short. Billie Jean King, Clark Graebner, and a host of other outstanding pros had flings with the T-2000, but all except Connors quickly gave up on the explosive, unpredictable frame. Connors played with the T-2000 for nearly all of his career, even after it was rendered obsolete by more powerful, mid- and oversized rackets made of graphite. Connors's devotion to the steel racket outlasted the product itself; he played with it long after the frame was no longer sold, which cost him millions in endorsement monies.

Over the years, Connors learned how to fine-tune the racket by adding strips of lead tape to various parts of the frame and he developed an odd technique for neutralizing the frame's unpredictability. Connors basically "aimed" his ground strokes for a spot three feet inside the far baseline. The closer he came to making perfect contact in the sweet spot, the closer the ball landed to the line. And when he was in a groove, which was more often than not, the ball flew with the power and accuracy of a shot from a well-tuned rifle.

The extra firepower was crucial to Connors's success because his game and sensibility were radically different from the norm. He developed his game at a time when tennis largely belonged to practitioners of Aussie-style serve-and-volley tennis, the "big game" style that was deadly at a time when three of the four Grand Slam tournaments were contested on grass. The foundation of the big game was a powerful serve. You followed it to the net and volleyed the service return to one corner or the other. Then you were set up, close to the net, ready to intercept and put away your opponent's defensive attempt at a passing shot or lob. Long before it was clear that Connors would never have an overpowering serve, he was playing the kind of game that didn't require one.

But Connors's style was enhanced by two qualities that were athletic rather than technical. He had remarkable timing, a function of eye-hand and eye-ball coordination, but unlike other players with those gifts, he also had something like eye-body coordination. He could get most of his body weight behind most of his ground strokes most of the time. Nobody pivoted as precisely and completely on the ball as did Connors. He generated a lot of his pace from the rotation and thrust of his

hips and legs. Other players, such as Nastase, had amazing arm and
hand control. But Connors hit his strokes with his entire body. Anybody foolish enough to give Connors a waist-high ball on either side
could just as well forget about it. His other great asset was his limber
body. Half-contortionist, half-acrobat, he almost always found a way to
hit a solid shot from an awkward position.

Connors's backhand was his bread-and-butter stroke, and his physical flexibility compensated for the classic disadvantages of the two-
handed stroke: poor reach on balls low and away, and the danger of
getting jammed on balls, particularly serves, coming at the body. Connors could get out of his own way quicker than any other player, and
even when he was out of position, his backhand stroke was truly
grooved and almost always accurate. The same wasn't true of Connors's
forehand, although plenty of opponents got eaten alive by trying to
exploit the inconsistencies that sometimes crept into his stroke. On an
off day, he had trouble with the timing of his forehand, but he eventually learned to take off a little pace and roll over the ball with a bit more
topspin.

A great deal was always made about Connors's tendency to err with
his low forehand approach shot. He was in a deep state of denial about
this condition, upholding a cardinal rule of tennis: A stroke is only as
bad as you think it is.

Nevertheless, Connors did not like to roll over the ball with topspin
when he was moving forward. On bad days his forehand approach shot
would not clear the net, or it would fly deep because Connors couldn't
get the trajectory that would lift the ball and still allow it to fall in the
court. It was amusing to watch his opponents doggedly trying to work
this flaw and Connors laboring mightily to fend them off.

Connors also needed the pace of his opponents' shots to generate
the velocity he liked, and wily players were sometimes able to frustrate
him by denying that pace. It was possible to chip and dink your way to
a win over Connors, as Ashe proved in the course of his great strategic
victory over him in the Wimbledon final of 1975. Still, most players
who tried that bold gambit were quickly and mercilessly ripped to
shreds.

Few players hit their forehand volleys with the same authority as
Connors. He simply pounced on the ball, body outstretched, and
crushed it. Although the first volley is often considered a setup for the
put-away, Connors usually eliminated it. He would take a volley just
inside the service line and punch through it with a stroke that was more
like a ground stroke than a proper volley.

Although Connors hit his backhand volley with two hands, the stroke was extremely effective. He was a master of striking half-volleys despite his grip, and he hit swinging volleys off balls at the proper height.

Connors's serve was a weakness that he disguised and compensated for artfully. He almost never hit a flat serve, preferring to set up for his first ground stroke with a topspin, slice or kicker that traveled more slowly, giving him ample time to prepare for a ground stroke. The tendency to hunch under his serve, instead of reaching up and out to it, was a conspicuous weakness that cost Connors some matches.

By contrast, Connors's service return was a formidable weapon off either wing. With his sharp eyes and quick reflexes, he generated such velocity that his return often appeared to travel faster than his opponent's serve, leaving the bizarre impression that Connors had greater control of, and a more aggressive approach to, games in which he was the receiver rather than the server. It was just another way in which Connors turned the game upside down.

Connors holds the all-time record for singles titles with 109, culled in fifteen countries on five continents. He played only twice in the Australian Open, winning the title in 1973 and losing in the final to the Aussie John Newcombe the following year. Connors did not play in the French Open during his glory years between 1973 and 1978 because of political infighting in the game. But in seven years beginning in 1979 he reached four semifinals and three quarterfinals in Paris. His overall record on clay, which includes a Grand Slam title at the U.S. Open when it was contested on green Har-Tru, proves that he was a top player on that surface.

Back in 1974, Connors's manager, Bill Riordan, was engaged in a long war against both the establishment (ITF and USTA) and rival managers such as Donald Dell. Connors himself insisted on retaining freedom to play World Team Tennis in addition to participating on the official circuit.

In 1974 the French Tennis Federation issued the equivalent of a nuclear strike, banning WTT participants from competing at Roland Garros. Riordan filed a massive lawsuit, but Connors was forced to sit out the French Open in a year when he absolutely dominated the game, winning the title at each of the other three Grand Slam sites. Thus, he was denied the opportunity to complete the first Grand Slam in men's tennis since Rod Laver did it in 1969.

With Connors absent, the French Open title went to the youngest male champion up to that time, seventeen-year-old Bjorn Borg. Although Borg soon became unbeatable on clay, I would have given Connors an edge in a meeting with his emerging Swedish rival for three reasons: At twenty-one, Connors had four years on Borg at an age when being older is still an asset; subsequent meetings also proved that Borg was intimidated by Connors until 1977; and, finally, Connors was an unexpectedly mature player in 1974.

While there's no telling how the pressure of chasing a Grand Slam would have affected Connors—or the resolve of his opponents—as the year progressed, Connors had no greater grasp of such refined notions than would a shark in the midst of a feeding frenzy. I'm not kidding about that, either. He was an eating machine, driven by aggression and hunger that I haven't seen before or since.

In 1974, Connors won 99 of 103 matches and 14 tournaments, including 3 Grand Slam events, the U.S. Clay Courts, the South African Open, and the U.S. Pro Indoor. It was the best single-year record of the Open era until John McEnroe won 13 titles and compiled an 82–3 singles match record in 1984.

The only glaring weakness on Connors's resume is his Davis Cup record. For a man who took so much pride in being an American that he often became flustered and even furious when fans at the U.S. Open dared to support his foreign opponent, he was an infrequent Davis Cup performer who played in only seven ties: two in 1976, one in 1981, and four in the year of the debacle in Gothenburg, 1984. His overall record as a singles player was an impressive 10–3—or 6–2 if you discount meaningless matches played after a match had been decided—but his two failures were more noteworthy than most of his triumphs.

There were a number of reasons for Connors's patchy Davis Cup record, including the relatively meager payouts offered by the USTA, an aversion to the establishment, mistrust and antipathy toward his major rival, the Davis Cup stalwart John McEnroe. But the connecting thread among them all was Connors's nature as a radical individualist— a quality so strong that it subverted even his deep and sincere patriotic feelings, and colored the decisions he made in all aspects of his career.

Early on, Connors reveled in his reputation as a maverick sweeping through the placid game with the gale force of a midwestern tornado. His manager and surrogate father, the late Bill Riordan, encouraged him to buck the tide and also seemed unable to resist using Connors to further his own personal and political ambitions in tennis.

Connors had serious social problems during his early years on the tour. When he vaulted to the top of the game in 1974, Dell and his clean-cut minions were the ruling clique in American tennis, and they were allied with the no less traditional Aussie champions. Those men, from John Newcombe and Rod Laver to Stan Smith and Arthur Ashe, were appalled by Connors. They saw him as a blight on the game, an arrogant, selfish, antisocial punk, and they uniformly gave him the cold shoulder. Connors just took a bite out of it, and delighted in pounding his critics into oblivion.

The standoff hardly invited Connors's participation in the Davis Cup under a captain who was a member of the clique, Dennis Ralston. Although Ralston was a notorious hothead in his playing days, he had become a member of the conservative establishment, a no-nonsense disciplinarian, and a born-again Christian.

At that time, Connors did have a deep desire to play Davis Cup. He proved it when affable, easygoing, apolitical Tony Trabert succeeded Ralston as captain in 1976. Connors led the United States to an easy victory in the first-round tie against Venezuela, but in the squad's next assignment—a tough, away tie in Mexico City—Connors was stunned in the fifth and decisive rubber by one of the best players never to win a Grand Slam title, the mercurial Raul Ramirez.

Stung by the loss and not entirely comfortable with the unique demands of Davis Cup play, Connors did not make another appearance until five years later. Setting aside a history of antagonism with John McEnroe, he joined his rival to quell the threat represented by Ivan Lendl and a strong Czech team in a tie contested at Connors's beloved Flushing Meadow. But Connors, looking to make a renewed assault on the number one singles ranking and wary of the personal dynamics on a U.S. squad led by McEnroe and captained by Arthur Ashe, begged off further duty. He might not even have played against Czechoslovakia if the tie had been staged anywhere but in New York.

Still, Connors made one more effort to fit into the team picture. In 1984 he was part of what might have been the American Davis Cup all-time "Dream Team" built around Connors, McEnroe, and McEnroe's regular doubles partner, Peter Fleming. The United States swept past Romania, Argentina, and Australia, winning the first three rubbers in each, and entered the final against a promising but green Swedish team with a perfect record in singles. But the Dream Team was upset in a tie described in a previous chapter.

The bulk of Connors's reputation rests on his performances at the two most important Grand Slam events, Wimbledon and the U.S. Open. Although he was overshadowed by Borg and later McEnroe at Wimbledon, he won the Wimbledon title twice (1974 and 1982) and lost in the championship match on four other occasions, falling once to Ashe (1975), twice to Borg (1977 and 1978), and once to McEnroe (1984).

Connors played best at the tournament that he loved most—the U.S. Open. Connors won more matches in the American championships (ninety-eight) than any player in the modern era, missing the event only once in twenty-two years. That was in 1990, and we saw just how much he missed Flushing Meadow in the following, charmed year of 1991. In a twelve-year span from 1974 to 1985, Connors reached at least the semi-finals at every U.S. Open, winning the final five times (1974, 1976, 1978, 1982, 1983) and losing in the championship round on two other occasions.

Connors's versatility was incontestably established by a unique feat, a "Surface Grand Slam" of sorts that he achieved by winning the U.S. Open on three different surfaces—grass, Har-Tru, and cement. That accomplishment stands right up there with the Grand Slams of Don Budge and Rod Laver, and Borg's five consecutive Wimbledon titles.

Writing on the day after Connors inflicted a savage beating on Bjorn Borg in the 1978 U.S. Open final, Bill Nack, a thoughtful columnist for *Newsday*, produced an elegant eulogy for the mild-mannered, gracious loser. He wrapped up his speculations on the two finalists with this paragraph:

"There will come a time when Connors is fifty that he will be sitting alone in an airport between flights, over a cup of coffee, faced with the shards of his past. He will be a man then and he will wish that as a boy he had done it better, as Borg had done it. Borg will never so suffer his past. In fact, the last Open between them will be won there."

Connors is not quite fifty yet, but it doesn't appear that Nack's prophecy has even the slightest chance of coming true. Yet more than any other player, Connors often seemed to be existentially and exclusively bound to his profession in a way that disturbed many people, a way that filled armchair psychologists with forebodings and many critics with loathing. But Connors's legion of critics often seemed to overlook two vital aspects of Connors' character: He loved to play the game of tennis, and no matter how much he raged and rampaged, tennis ceased to be a matter of life or death to him the moment he left the court. He said as much on many occasions, but few people believed him.

Connors's greatest performance in a tournament undoubtedly occurred at that 1978 U.S. Open. He may have played better at other events and turned more heroic tricks at still others, but the 1978 U.S. Open was full of significance for Connors. It was the first American championships held at Flushing Meadow. It was the first Grand Slam event and the first U.S. Open since 1974 at which Connors was clearly the underdog. That was mostly because after three years of trying, Borg finally seemed to have wriggled out from under Connors's thumb. He was the champion of France and Wimbledon, and the buzz was that he was en route to a Grand Slam.

The challenge facing Connors was compounded by the presence of two other players in the draw, a streaky, artistic Italian player, Adriano

Panatta, and Connors's emerging American rival, John McEnroe. Connors beat both of them in superb matches before he completed his quest with a 6–4, 6–2, 6–2 upset of Bjorn Borg.

Shortly after Connors won that 1978 U.S. Open, he secretly wed Patti McGuire in Tokyo. The couple soon had their first child, a boy named Brett. This radical change in Connors's life affected his tennis, and by 1981 it appeared that he might become another one of those players for whom domestic life would be a pleasant decompression chamber.

The fine psychological line between winning and losing at the championship level was vividly demonstrated in three matches that Connors played in 1980 and early 1981. He lost a bitterly contested semifinal to McEnroe at Flushing Meadow in 1980, 7–6 in the fifth. In January 1981, Connors lost to Borg in the Grand Prix Masters because of an inexplicable third-set lapse of concentration. Later that year, at Wimbledon, Connors won the first two sets against Borg, but he let the Swede back into the match and eventually lost, 6–4, in the fifth. Connors squandered chances to win in each of those matches.

So, by the fall of 1981 even Connors's sympathizers felt that he was fading out of the picture and that McEnroe had come to replace him as Borg's chief rival. When I went to visit Jimmy late that summer, I felt apprehensive. I expected to find him defensive and angry, but he was happy and optimistic.

"It's amazing what goes through your mind out there sometimes, even in milliseconds," Connors told me. "You flash on your kid, remembering how three months ago you let him fall out of the couch on his head. You have to learn how to deal with those kinds of things. You have to learn how to shut them out when it really counts out there. I've always felt that when everything else is right, my game will come around. And it's not like anything big is wrong, either. I've got a great wife, a fine little son. My problems are minute compared to some people's. When I lose a match like I did to Borg at Wimbledon, I can't let it wear on me, cramping all the good things in my life. Look, I'd hate losing to my *son* after being up two sets, but I can't worry about it.

"I still have a need to be number one. Once that's in your system, the other numbers don't count, whether they're number two or one fifty-two. That goal, the one that makes me want to win, is still burning down there. But I can't let it set fire to my family life. Sometimes it's hard not to take out my frustrations on my family, but that's absolutely taboo. I'd rather quit tennis than do that. But I'll tell you this: Before I quit or before I die, whichever comes first, I'm going to win Wimbledon or the U.S. Open again. It might kill me, too. But you know what? I'm going to do it."

The following year, 1982, Connors won Wimbledon and the U.S. Open. At Wimbledon he beat McEnroe in the final, 3–6, 6–3, 6–7, 7–6, 6–4. At Flushing Meadow he stopped Ivan Lendl, 6–3, 6–2, 4–6, 6–4. Once again he became the number one player in the world.

By returning to the summit of the game, Connors proved that he was one of a precious few, great Open-era players who could balance the conflicts between his game and his life, between Jimbo and Jimmy. If those two sharply different identities within Connors had gone to war against each other, I'm sure that Jimbo would have won because Jimbo was the assassin. And you might have bumped into Jimbo one day when he was fifty, a broken man sitting in an airport, hunched over a cup of coffee, and so forth.

The funny thing about all this is that Jimbo and Jimmy didn't really merge, either. They just learned to coexist, which is why you can't exactly say that Connors "matured," at least not in any classic sense of the word. The events that occurred at the Davis Cup final of 1984 and on the numerous subsequent occasions when he pumped and cursed his way through tennis matches that he was supposed to lose testify to that. If Connors had matured, he probably would have vanished as a force in the game by age thirty. Instead, he remained forever punk, which is exactly why he was able to perform the way that he did at thirty-nine at the 1991 U.S. Open. If you think about it, it really isn't all that complicated. How many forty-year-olds do you know who are willing to hump the air like hormonolly supercharged puppies in front of twenty thousand strangers?

Connors had ups and downs, of course, in his life as well as in his career after 1982. In fact, just a few short months into 1983, Patti Connors served her husband with a petition for divorce. Although her claims to Connors's substantial fortune were limited by an explicit prenuptial agreement, she appeared to be more interested in securing custody of Brett. It seems that it was conflicts over the kind of childhood that Brett would have that initiated Patti's action. She did not like the plan Jimmy had for making Brett the next great player called Connors.

The news got me thinking. I imagined a court hidden away in Southern California somewhere, a modest court with a few cracks in the asphalt, far from the plush lounges, attended locker rooms, and valet parking of trendy L.A. tennis clubs. Gloria Connors, still keen and sprightly in 1982, patiently waited on that court, accompanied only by her shadow in the heat of the day, with a visor, her racket, and a bucket of balls. She knew how to wait. She was quite used to being alone. She could wait almost forever, just in case her son and daughter-in-law changed their minds and decided that once was not enough.

CHAPTER 18

BELIEVERS IN BABYLON
The Rise and Fall
of the Christian Ministry in Tennis

THE NEWS CAME early in 1987, clattering over the Associated Press tele-type machines that stand in almost every office of every daily newspa-per in the United States. The eye-catching dateline read Lagos, Nigeria, and the exotic contents of the story did not disappoint the night editors who got a first look at it.

During a Challenger Series tennis tournament in Lagos, three jour-neymen tennis players, apparently in the throes of religious fervor, went on a rampage that was more characteristic of a heavy-metal rock-and-roll band, snowbound in some Holiday Inn, than of a trio of born-again Christians in Equatorial Africa. While engaged in a Bible study and fellowship session, Skip Strode, Bud Cox, and Jimmy Gurfein col-lectively snapped. Convinced that they must rid themselves of material possessions, Strode and Cox shredded their money, their passports, and their airline tickets. They tossed the remnants out of the window and pitched their tennis rackets after them. Gurfein, convinced that he was possessed by the devil, jumped through the glass window. Fortunately, the room in which all this transpired was on ground level. Gurfein sus-tained only minor injuries.

After I read the story, which alluded to the players being part of the born-again movement in tennis, I decided to follow up on the incident with a column in *Tennis* magazine. Mostly, I was curious to find out the extent to which the group freak-out in Lagos was inspired by the nature and methods of the Christian subset on the tour. To do that I needed to speak with a variety of players and spokesmen for an entity called the "ten-nis ministry." This proved to be a lot more difficult than I anticipated.

I knew that there was a number of fundamentalist Christians on the tour, including such successful players as Stan Smith, Sandy and Gene Mayer, and Terry Moor. At many tournaments, announcements of Bible study sessions had begun to pop up, posted on the message boards in players' lounges and locker rooms. I soon learned that in 1985 some of the Christian players had set up the tennis ministry, partly financed by their own out-of-pocket contributions. Gurfein, Strode, and Cox were part of a group of Christian players who met regularly for prayer and Bible study meetings. The ersatz pastor was Fritz Glaus, a thirtyish tennis teaching pro who in 1975 experienced the biblical injunction to be born again.

After spending some six years teaching tennis abroad and casually evangelizing to his students, Glaus returned to the United States, spent two years at a seminary, and soon was recruited to serve as minister-on-tour by Smith. I took it as a good sign that I had never met the man or even knew what he looked like; whatever he was, Glaus certainly wasn't a publicity hound. If anything, Glaus avoided the media—so much so, that at the U.S. Pro Indoor tournament in Philadelphia, an event we both attended, I was unable to get in touch with him, either at the official "player" hotel or at the venue.

Exasperated, I began to call the board members of the Christian ministry, including Sandy Mayer and, eventually, Smith. I had known them both for a long time, but they were still apprehensive. Because of what had happened in Lagos, the Christians were sitting ducks. Anyone who felt antagonistic toward the Christian movement could have a critic's field day in the pulpit of public opinion—a place in which secular notions of "morality" had come to carry more authority for many people than the mandates of religious belief.

I trotted out all of the persuasions that a good reporter brings to bear on the situation. However the ministry felt about the press or even about me, refusing to address the issues raised by the incident in Lagos would make it look as if the ministry had something to hide. It would also make it look as if the ministry acknowleged no public accountability whatsoever. Furthermore, the ministry's intransigence could be interpreted as proof that it operated in a furtive manner, with a hidden agenda that, especially after Lagos, might appear sinister. After all, when I discussed the Christian movement on the tour with one player, he had said, "Hey, don't quote me on any of this. I mean, you just never know who's dabbling in this stuff."

This could be doubly controversial because the tennis ministry also had an evangelical function. A number of players had told me that on occasion they felt that they were being recruited to Christianity. This made some of them uncomfortable. Some felt hounded or prevailed upon; others were spooked by the intensity projected by some Christian players when the "G" word came up, even on the most fleeting or casual occasion.

Glaus finally agreed to meet with me. By then I was a little apprehensive about how things would go. But when we finally met, I could tell right from the start that he had no interest in recruiting me. He probably thought that a reporter was beyond reach even for him. Anyway, he spoke by rote, a little too quickly and a little too generally, ruling out real conversation. Glaus struck me as a zealot put into the difficult position of practicing damage control.

Still, I ultimately resisted taking the easy, sensational way out. Instead of a interpreting the incident in Lagos as a lesson in the hazards of fanaticism, I suggested that the three players had collectively succumbed to the stress of playing in a strange exotic environment under the extremely competitive conditions that typified the minor leagues of tennis. Without the tennis ministry there to provide a safety net, they began to make it up as they went along, feeding off one another's spiritual hunger and anxieties in an unhealthy way.

What remarks I used from Glaus were banal. He told me that he had spoken to Strode and Gurfein, and told them that in the future it would help if they all worked "more closely." Glaus also said that the ministry did not "endorse" anything that happened in Lagos and insisted that it had nothing to hide. He also said, "The main thing we learned from Nigeria is to be more open with the media. If this is the way people find out about the ministry, it's no good."

The column generated a surprising amount of mail, ranging from nutty denunciations of Christianity to letters that were uncritically and almost pathetically thankful for the simple fact that something—*anything*—about Christianity had made it between the covers of *Tennis* magazine. But one letter made me angry at first, then it got me thinking. The letter was a comment on the first few paragraphs of my column in which I related the peculiar conversation between Gurfein and another player, Larry Scott, immediately after Gurfein lost his first-round match in Lagos.

Scott was shocked when Gurfein, apparently unaffected by the loss, breezily told him, "It didn't matter whether I won or lost, I felt free out there. I felt I played for Jesus."

Evaluating that remark, I wrote, "When a tennis player says something like that, he is on his way to being no tennis player at all."

The letter addressing that passage came from Rochester, Minnesota, from a wrestler who had won a gold medal in an event called the National Sports Festival. The pertinent part read: "The article . . . was both disturbing and insulting. A writer in a publication the quality of yours should not write about something he does not understand without properly researching the subject. . . . To say that anyone who plays tennis for Jesus is on his way to being no tennis player at all is absurd. . . ."

The striking thing about this was the accusation that I didn't "understand" Christianity. How could someone raised as a Christian and educated at a Catholic university *not* understand? Well, I eventually came to understand that the answer to that one was, "Pretty easily."

Before we get into the ozone-ranger Gabriela Sabatini, the power-eating and power-believing Mayer brothers, devout Michael Chang, and "the little fetus that could," Andre Agassi, some elements of Christian doctrine need to be spelled out because typical secular individuals, including highly educated ones, often don't understand them. They see Christianity as a bewildering jungle of arbitrary, antiprogressive doctrines (doctrines that some, particularly fundamentalists, take literally). This attitude is shared by nominal Christians who basically think that believing is a good "idea" for its social and moral value, but find fundamentalism scary and arrogant. These prejudices prevent lively and productive debate, and they make it difficult to grasp the problems with which believers grapple. So let's take a quick look at some of the most troublesome claims of Christianity and the defense that believers make for them.

CLAIM: Christianity is not *a* way but *the* way to spiritual salvation

DEFENSE: Despite the existence of other great, lasting religions and personages, including Muhammad and Buddha, only Jesus Christ made the explicit claim to be the Son of God. Of course, a lot of other people have also subsequently claimed to be the Son of God, but they did not become what Christ did—an important, if not *the* most important, and well-known figure in world history, an achievement nearly as mind-boggling as Christ's claim.

This puts Christ in a very different league from other religious figures. To paraphrase the Christian author C. S. Lewis, this claim made Christ one of three things: a good, albeit deeply deluded, man, a manipulative crackpot, or, well, the Son of God. Anybody who would take religions seriously must choose one of those three descriptions and figure out the consequences.

CLAIM: The Bible contains literal truth.

DEFENSE: If Christ was just another teacher and moralist, the Bible is just another old book full of symbolism, poetry, and moral guidelines set down at a time when different problems, values, and needs obtained. But if Christ was indeed the Son of God, the Bible is by far the most extraordinary document ever written. Instead of interpreting the Bible by the standards of our time, our time must be judged by the standards of the Bible.

CLAIM: Homosexuality (substitute abortion, infidelity, and so forth) is wrong.

DEFENSE: The Bible is a book full of restrictions and prescriptions, but the Christian God is not only all-knowing but all-loving and all-forgiving. That's why, unlike some other tyrant, he really does have the authority to tell you how to live. And that's what makes him God, instead of just another three thousand-year-old dog who speaks to you through the medium of some guy working out of a mall in Santa Monica. The essence of Christianity is love and forgiveness, so its mandate to believers is to "hate sin, love the sinner." And even those who most flagrantly violate biblical mandates can be saved through belief.

CLAIM: An individual's way of life and actions have less to do with his or her salvation than whether or not the person believes.

DEFENSE: Accepting this has something to do with Christian humility, in that it implies that even the most murderous serial killer, may ultimately end up saved. This may not seem fair, but fairness itself is a temporal notion based on the very shaky premise that you and I can be the ultimate judges of our brethren. The preeminence of believing also ensures that nobody can buy his way into heaven. Anybody who has ever wondered why Donald Trump or Aristotle Onassis seemed to have all the luck will appreciate this. The paramount importance of belief offers universal access to salvation, and the fact that so many people still choose not to believe is a confirmation of the flawed, stricken condition of human nature.

CLAIM: It is possible to have a personal relationship with God.

DEFENSE: This is the bonus baby that bothers so many people. God is like Michael Jackson. Some people know him, others don't. Some will, some won't. Some want to, some don't. The key difference, however, is that a lot of people who want to know Michael Jackson never will, but anybody who wants to can know God. Thus, Christianity is not only remarkably exclusive but breathtakingly inclusionary. It is open to every person who fulfills its single, overwhelming demand to believe.

And, finally, knowing God doesn't give you a leg up on anyone else. And it isn't any easier getting along with him than with Michael Jackson, your wife, or your boss. In fact, if you don't have problems with God, you don't have any more of a relationship with him than you do with your wife or boss.

During the U.S. Open of 1993, I was working on a tribute to two of the outstanding sports in tennis, Edberg and Sabatini. This required doing long interviews with each of them in order to discover the source of their values and their exemplary comportment.

Edberg was easy. He came from a highly socialized, secular society. His father was a policeman, and his mother was a full-time housewife. Edberg characterized his parents as "kind," which is how many people would characterize Edberg. Like most tennis pros, he occasionally grew tired of traveling and the individualistic, sometimes lonely life of a player. But one big hedge against those problems was the rest of Team Edberg: friend and coach Tony Pikard and Edberg's wife, Annette (née) Olson, both of whom traveled with Stefan. In 1993 a baby was added to Team Edberg.

Overall, Edberg was a well-adjusted, successful, happy tennis player. His identity as a Swede and his wholesome background taught him to manage and properly channel his aggressions. He had a great, modest talent for not appearing to ask more of life than it offered in the most tangible, primary way.

Gabriela Sabatini was different. She was an idol who could do no wrong in her native Argentina and an appealing, universally loved world star. She was also a kind person and a gentle soul. In her very first Grand Slam outing, at fourteen, Sabatini reached the third round of the U.S. Open. The following year she reached the semifinals at the French Open and the third round at Wimbledon. Great things were expected of and predicted for the popular Gabby.

But while some very good things happened for Sabatini—victory in a number of tournaments, a Grand Slam semifinal here, a final there—great things did not. This undoubtedly had something to do with the vulnerable nature of her second serve and with her radically overspun strokes, but I think they also had something to do with the nature of life on the tennis tour.

Sabatini ascended swiftly in the rankings and maintained her position in the top five over the years, but by 1990 it was clear to many people that she was sleepwalking through her matches—perhaps even through her life. Although she was cordial, Sabatini often seemed remote. She was unfailingly polite but generally aloof. And she seemed to take shelter in her omnipresent family, represented most regularly by her father, Osvaldo.

Then the clever, lighthearted Brazilian former touring pro, Carlos Kirmayr, came into the picture. With the help and guidance of her managers and family, Sabatini decided to hire Kirmayr at around the time of Wimbledon in 1990. Kirmayr immediately breathed fresh life into Sabatini's stale game. He convinced her to play more positive, aggressive tennis, partly so that she could use her accomplished volley to both threaten and confuse her opponents.

Sabatini suddenly became a different player in the summer of 1990. With a fresh mind and a multidimensional game, she won her first Grand Slam title at the U.S. Open. She gave Kirmayr his due but also attributed her success to a new attitude founded on an ability to separate her identity as an individual from her identity as Gabriela Sabatini, superstar. Soon she had her very own perfume, called Sabatini, and there was even talk of a Gabby doll.

But then a curious thing happened. Over the course of the next few years, Sabatini once again appeared to lose her focus and enthusiasm. And while she was generally successful, gracious, and unfailingly sportsmanlike, that thick layer of transparent material seemed once again to envelop her like the shrink-wrap on a record album.

Anyway, Sabatini agreed to be interviewed for the tribute piece on her and Edberg. She told me to meet her on a Sunday morning at the the Lowell hotel in Manhattan. She had never been an easy interview, and I wondered if she would be at all stimulated by questions about her background, values, and beliefs. As I approached the Lowell, church bells sounded in the distance, and I knew instantly what I would ask Sabatini as my first question.

Gabby met me in the lobby and led me up to her room. She was already dressed in tennis gear, ready to go off and practice as soon as our interview was through. When we sat down, I said, "Right about now, most good South American girls are coming out of church, ready to sit down to a nice Sunday meal with their families. Do you think you miss out on something by not being one of them?"

"It's not possible with the life I have," Sabatini replied. "I am always away or playing in a singles or doubles final on Sunday—ever since I was a child. I have no religious training. I am Catholic and I believe in God, but I don't practice. Religion isn't something that I rely on very much."

We went on to talk about various things: conflicting emotions she felt when the omnipresence of her family began to feel stifling, the blurring of her twin identities as person and player, the problems posed by being a woman from a culture in which it was still unseemly for women to appear aggressive or tough. In fact, as a heralded prodigy who had devoted herself almost exclusively to the tennis culture since her childhood, traditional elements of Latin culture had only minimal impact on her.

I left that pleasant interview with all I needed to know about Sabatini's sportsmanship, but I felt I also knew more about a considerably more complicated subject: her disengaged, almost mechanical being, the eerie absence of a personality that could be cleanly and easily peeled away from her identity as a tennis player. It seemed pretty clear to me that Sabatini had come to exist in a vacuum, cut off from most of the conventional sources of motivation and inspiration, cut off from foundations other than those provided by her family. She had developed something very much like the penal system's "institutional personality."

In all the times that I spoke with Sabatini, I don't think she once cited the joy and satisfaction of winning big tournaments as a source of motivation, as would Connors or even Evert. In fact, winning the U.S. Open of 1990 seemed more important to her as a therapeutic tool than as a feat accomplished in the professional area of a multidimensional life. By late 1993, the women on and around the tour noticed that Sabatini again appeared to be going through some kind of crisis of motivation. It didn't surprise me, because in a fundamental way her life seemed to lack moorings besides those provided by her family or tennis.

Sabatini's condition was further clarified for me by a long conversation I had with another sweet, exemplary player, Mary Joe Fernandez. The parallels between the two young women were striking. Each had been a prodigy (although Sabatini was much more of an international "star"), and each came from a Latin background long on family togetherness. Both of their fathers were dominant presences who began to take it easy soon after their daughters began to make the big money. And like Sabatini, Fernandez had trouble cracking the top level of the game. But Fernandez seemed firmly grounded. There were several interesting reasons for this. Unlike Sabatini, Fernandez had insisted on finishing high school, resisting even parental pressure to turn pro at fourteen. Thus, she built lasting relationships with a number of her childhood friends. Fernandez also had been raised a Catholic. In fact, she was such a good Catholic girl that when she was required to go to confession in grade school, she would often run to her friend Marilupe Lopez with a unique request: "Quick," Fernandez would say, "help me to think up some sins."

Up to the age of twenty-two the greatest act of rebellion committed by Fernandez was quietly to renounce her Catholic background and embrace fundamentalist Christianity—a decision that dismayed both of her parents. But I think the portable nature of her new "personal" faith, and the strength she claimed to draw from it, were very powerful assets that helped to make her a well-adjusted young woman reconciled to the demands of her often harsh profession.

"If tennis is all you have, if it's all you live for," Fernandez told me, "then you're bound to get hurt. You're not going to win every tournament, and even if you do, there comes a day when you're still young that you have to stop. I don't like to go around preaching about it, but my faith has become my foundation. It helps me to keep everything in perspective, and it helps me to see that the bad times are as much of the ultimate plan as the good times.

"Faith even gives me motivation, it's one of the main reasons I play. There are a lot of corrupt things about tennis, from the amount of money to the life-styles it creates. But a Christian isn't supposed to live in isolation. I see my tennis partly as a way to advertise my beliefs and to have an influence on people, especially children. That's why I'm big on good behavior. Faith also make me thankful for my talent, and it gives me a responsibility to employ it in a positive way."

I contrast these two women to illustrate the challenges, conflicts, and consolations posed to a Christian who happens to be a professional tennis player, and to cite the grave dangers lurking in the professional way of life, particularly for a person as malleable and uncritical as Gabriela Sabatini. It's funny, but the women's tour, which has featured so many controversies and problems, has never engaged religious issues. There has been no Christian ministry on the women's tour or anything like the number of believers that are found among the men. I think it's another example of the way pro tennis has dehumanized women.

By the early 1980s religious inquiry and belief were slowly creeping back into mainstream American culture. Many players, mostly on the men's tour, were trying to find a greater meaning in life and finding it difficult to satisfy that quest. The incessant travel required by the pro tour, the privileges, perks, and riches bestowed on the players, and the celebrity and individualism that were part of being a tennis pro all worked against many of the mandates and principles of active Christian belief. The secular activism of the state had also undermined traditional expressions of belief, as did the broadly accepted notion that religion is a very private thing. Those trends drove conservative believers underground.

But the growing number of Christian players also faced two practical problems. Scripture encouraged shared worship and even evangelical activity. And on a more philosophical plane, Christian belief is based on a body of accessible, revealed truths that were subject to some interpretation but not revision. To Christians, the idea that religious beliefs were such private matters that you settled them in your own conscience was dangerously akin to saying that your physical health was such a private, intimate matter that you should cure your own ills.

Thus, the tennis ministry was born—to a large extent through the offices of Smith. Glaus was hired by the board of the ministry, and his salary and traveling expenses were paid from contributions from the players and the budget of the non-denominational church with which Glaus was affiliated: The Chapel, in Akron, Ohio. His main job was to serve as a minister on the hoof, traveling the tour and conducting Bible study sessions and fellowship meetings for Christian players.

The core group of Christians numbered about thirty, including founding members Smith, Sandy and Gene Mayer, Mike Cahill, and Terry Moor. A number of younger players, including Ken Flach, David Wheaton, and Andre Agassi, came into the fold a little later. Michael Chang, a devout Christian, remained at the fringe of the tennis ministry. At one time the Christians on the tour could have formed a formidable Davis Cup team and filled a typical tournament draw exclusively with believers.

The Mayer brothers were two of the more interesting people in the Christian movement. Their father, Alex Mayer, Sr., a former Yugoslavian Davis Cup player, had immigrated to the United States after World War II. Mayer knew what he wanted for his sons from the moment they were born, and it was embodied in something he rather grandly called "pre-tennis court education." While the boys were still in the crib, they were encouraged use tiny paddles to swat at a little rubber ball suspended on a string above them. With that head start, the Mayers became top national junior players. Sandy was the older son, but Gene had more natural talent. Alex Sr. was a steely, bombastic disciplinarian who often spoke as if he had invented the game of tennis, imposing on his sons standards and pressures that not only fueled their sibling rivalry, but eventually led each of them to bang heads with their peers and with Alex Sr. himself.

Sandy and Gene both attended Stanford and became Top Ten pros. (Gene eventually climbed as high as number 4). But en route they also developed reputations as contentious, opinionated, highly cerebral, and slightly eccentric fellows. But even their imposing intellectual appetites could not bear comparison to their physical appetites. At seventeen a slightly overweight Sandy went on a fast and lost fifty pounds. When he began to eat again, he never stopped. Maybe the fast changed his metabolism. Maybe Sandy needed to vent anxiety and avenge himself on his taskmaster father, who envisioned his sons as trim fighting machines. Whatever the reason, Sandy became a trencherman of abnormal proportions, and Gene followed right in his big brother's footsteps.

"Every day was a new record," Gene once explained. "When we were both at home we'd eat three or four omelets with a dozen eggs in them, along with a pound of cheese and ham and every type of other thing that goes into an omelet. Then we'd each have two dozen English muffins, a box of cereal, and a gallon of orange juice. Then we'd go out and practice and come back and have a whole loaf of bread apiece with cold cuts. We'd eat that and come back for something else. And then we'd have dinner—five or six pounds of steak, a bag of potatoes. An hour later we'd be starved, and we'd hit the kitchen for a snack. Then about midnight, before going to sleep, we'd eat a dozen donuts apiece. My mother was in the kitchen twenty-four hours a day. We had six meals a day plus snacks. For a while we were completely out of hand."

In fact, when the Mayer boys went away to Stanford, the local grocer took up a collection for the family. He was under the impression that the Mayers had just plain run out of money to feed the boys.

At Stanford, Sandy's physical appetite was suddenly transformed into spiritual hunger. He was born again in 1971, although he said he wasn't a fully realized Christian until about the time of his graduation in 1974.

"I realized at that time that my own efforts were not resulting in the kind of reactions from people and the kind of personality I wanted," Sandy told me. "I really didn't feel I was disagreeable or difficult to get along with, but I think other people saw me that way. I didn't like that, and I didn't like the way I was on court. Getting close to Christ and letting him make changes in me was the only way I could change."

A few months after his conversion experience, Sandy Mayer's tennis results improved dramatically, and he was named Rookie of the Year by *Tennis* magazine. Perhaps because of the Christian injunction against gluttony, even Mayer's legendary eating habits changed. Soon, following a meal with his brother Gene, Sandy would say, "I don't like to eat with Gene. It makes me sick. I start thinking, 'Is that what I look like? Did I eat this much?' "

Following Sandy's lead, Gene and even Alex Sr., who had been without religion for most of his life, also became born again. And while the brothers left behind their physical appetites (although Gene was given to backsliding), they brought their spiritual hunger along on the tour.

The Mayers were not always the best advertisements on the tour for Christianity. Gene was given to throwing fits of bad behavior. He was accused of occasionally giving less than his best effort in matches, and also of taking too much of an interest in the "easy" money that could be made in exhibitions that often undermined the integrity of tour events by luring players away from them. Gene Mayer addressed his shortcomings with classic Christian logic: "I've won some tennis matches and come off the court thinking, 'I've won in the eyes of the world, but I failed as a Christian and disappointed God.' I've also lost and felt good in the eyes of God, even if I was a jerk in the eyes of the world. One time in Hong Kong, I had a fever of a hundred and three on court in a match against Chris Kachel. I went nuts over a call, and I was really ranting and raving the entire rest of the match. I was a total jerk, but I won in three sets. I can only imagine what Kachel thought of me, especially in light of my professed beliefs."

A Christian may suggest that Stan Smith, the driving force behind the tennis ministry, provided a better example of the Christian sensibility at work in the pro tennis environment. But he did not face the same temptations and obstacles that greeted the younger, more individualistic generation of players in a drastically changed game.

"Stan came from a generation that had a lot more camaraderie," Mayer told me. "For that reason, and because he believed in Christian fellowship, he was able to bridge the generation gap. There's a definite caste system on the tour, but that was broken down in the early days of the Christian ministry. Stan would be happy to practice with other Christian players even if they were players of a different level.

"There was still this feeling that it didn't matter if you revealed or worked on weaknesses in your game with a guy you might have to play. It was like, 'So what, we're all in this together. If he beats me because of this inside knowledge, I just have to work harder to eliminate the weakness.' But as the stakes in the game went up, that began to change.

"The tennis circuit magnifies many of the unwholesome elements in life. In fact, tennis began to be all about some things that fly right in the face of Christian belief—rampant individualism, obsession with success, the desire to make a lot of money, suspicion of others. One player, Brian Page, even came to believe that in good conscience he just couldn't continue to play the circuit.

"As time went on, the attitudes of players, especially top players, really changed. Even among the Christians the feeling came to be that if you were top ten, you wanted to appear remote, uninvolved, a little mysterious and threatening. But even journeymen players didn't really want to let down their guard in front of others, and having spiritual fellowship is about letting down your guard and getting intimately involved with others at a spiritual level. The things that we were getting bombarded with made it increasingly difficult to maintain Christian principles and to cultivate Christian relationships with others."

Despite these problems, the ministry managed to function, and it even attracted players from the next wave of pros. One of them was David Wheaton, a tall Minnesotan with a rangy, all-court game. Wheaton's parents were from the pious, puritanical wing of Christendom, so much so that many other, committed Christians often found them overzealous. Parsimonious and abstemious, the Wheatons were the sort who frowned on drinking wine despite the healthy role played by the beverage in the Bible.

One tennis agent recalled an experience he had with the Wheaton family when he made a deal to get David into a pro event in Ohio. He was still an amateur who could not accept prize money, but the tournament could pay all his expenses, which included travel and lodging for his family. When David, his manager-brother John, and their father Bruce asked the agent what they should do about their bills, he just waved his hand and told them to submit a simple invoice. That seemed to be the end of it until Bruce Wheaton asked, "What about tolls? Can we put in for them, too?" "You mean you all *drove?*" the startled agent asked.

Not long after that conversation, Wheaton won $2 million as the singles champion of the Grand Slam Cup, a year-end event sponsored by the ITF in Munich, Germany. Added to his prize money and the big endorsement contracts Wheaton pulled down thanks to his fast start on the pro tour, it ensured that the Wheatons would never have to worry about toll money again.

Wheaton played a major role in bringing Andre and Philip Agassi, another player-brother/manager combination, into the fold of the tennis ministry. But according to Philip, Andre had a good reason to believe right from the start. He told me, "When I was about eight years old, we had a crisis. Our mother, Elizabeth, had come to Christianity through Billy Graham. She had been a Christian for years when she found out that she had to have a hysterectomy. But at the time, she was pregnant with Andre. That presented complications, and four out of five doctors advised her to abort. She didn't feel she could do that because of her religious beliefs, and the operation nearly killed her. But that was how Andre came to be born, because of her convictions."

The Agassi boys attended a Christian school in their native Las Vegas, but as Andre reached high school age, he was shipped out to develop his striking talents at the Nick Bollettieri Tennis Academy near Bradenton, Florida. By the time he was sixteen, Agassi was, at least superficially, about as unlikely a candidate for success in tennis as he was for status as a conservative Christian.

Agassi favored radical haircuts featuring pink, green, and blond streaks. His penchant for wearing makeup suggested gender confusion, as did his habit of painting lightning bolts on his fingernails and wearing jewelry. He often practiced shirtless, wearing jeans, his makeup in stark contrast to his hirsute chest. Andre also did a fair amount of teenage binge drinking. Yet he still managed to explode in the tennis scene in 1987, ultimately rising to a world ranking of 3 by 1988.

By that time Agassi had become the most complex personality in tennis. He was the most iconoclastic and showmanlike player since young Jimmy Connors. But where Jimmy had been snarly, Andre was puckish. Where Jimmy had been obscene, Andre was wholesome. Where Jimmy had been intimidating and antagonistic, Andre was spritelike, commiting only one sin against his fellow players: Sometimes his playful stunts made his opponents look bad or, even worse, silly.

Agassi was also a declared Christian, which many people just could not square with his persona. I don't think any player in all the time I covered tennis was subject to as much unfair criticism and ridicule as young Agassi was, despite the obvious surge of public interest that he precipitated, and his colorful babe-in-toyland presence.

A good part of Agassi's image problem was easily explained by the mad, commercial scramble to capitalize on his highly marketable personality. All of the rewards for which other players worked hard and long were basically dropped in his lap before he even earned the attention by winning a Grand Slam tournament. Thus, he was a perfect target for cynics. But there was nothing false or hypocritical about Andre's youthful commitment to belief.

Andre's first girlfriend, Amy Moss, was a devout Christian. At one point Andre and Amy did not want to create the impression that by traveling together they were flouting Christian sexual mores, so they consulted Glaus. He suggested that they take separate rooms, not only to ward off temptation but also to observe the biblical injunction to avoid even the appearance of wickedness.

Wheaton first took Philip and Andre Agassi to a Bible study session conducted by Glaus in 1985. Initially, the Agassis had resisted overtures from the Christian community, insisting that they were already believers. But when they went along with Wheaton, they were so moved that they returned for the next ten consecutive days.

With such promising players as Wheaton and Agassi on board, the tennis ministry appeared to be headed for a renaissance. But by then some of the problems that Mayer cited began to poke through the thin wall of fellowship. The Christian core group also seemed to grow increasingly insular and unable to accommodate someone who was as worldly and extroverted as Andre Agassi.

"I think some of the Christian players tended to get into a bubble with each other and God, and they wanted to live in there," Philip Agassi told me. "In one prayer meeting, one of the guys wanted all of us to pray about a leak in his roof. I mean, God gave him a brain and he gave him money; I don't see why the guy didn't just put the two of them together, get the Yellow Pages, and call a plumber."

By 1988 the Agassis had also struck up an independent friendship with a Las Vegas pastor, John Parenti. A talented musician, Parenti wrote three songs that topped the charts of Christian music. Andre, a car nut, once gave Parenti a red Corvette to use for a week while his own modest Honda was in the garage. A good portion of Parenti's congregation was offended by the sight of their pastor tooling around in a little red Corvette, but that was only the beginning of it.

"John Parenti was a married minister with short hair and a four-door Honda when he met the Agassis," Philip told me. "Now he's divorced. He has long hair, he drives a sports car, and he lives in Southern California."

It's easy to see how the Agassis' free-flowing interpretation of Christianity did not sit well with any but the most liberal of believers.

"Fritz ran really good Bible studies," Philip Agassi told me shortly after the Agassis pulled away from Glaus, and thus drove the last nail into the coffin of the tennis ministry. "But if only he had educated himself on the outside the same way he was inside, he would probably still be around the tour. But he tended to get his faith in at the first opening, and he kept hammering away at it. I think he just wore thin."

By that time, around 1990, the changing nature of the tour also made it increasingly difficult to sustain a daily ministry.

"People just got scattered all over," Mayer said. "The tour grew bigger. You could play for six months and not bump into one of your Christian friends. More and more, fellowship and competition just didn't fit in any way. And the players got younger and younger, coming up through a system in which the emphasis from all quarters, from agents to press to coaches and parents, was on winning. From a Christian perspective, winning is not the ultimate measure of success. But try telling that to a sixteen-year-old phenom and his people. Without a core group, the ministry splintered. The message is: 'I don't need a church. I don't need fellowship. My life is about other things.' "

Michael Chang, the defending champion at the French Open in 1990, sat in the interview room in Paris after winning his fourth-round match. In the early part of the interview, when players usually talked about how they felt about winning or losing, Chang said, "And I'd like to thank God because without his help I couldn't have won this match."

Christian athletes often make the same comment as Chang did in Paris, and they are almost always considered arrogant by nonbelievers. They take it as a statement of moral superiority over a beaten and unfortunate opponent, as if God had nothing better to do than take sides in a stupid tennis match. But the Christian makes that statement as a tribute to God and as a check on his own noisy pride. He is acknowledging that whatever glory informs his feat is not entirely of his own making, and that he was not playing merely for his gratification but to honor God.

If you can buy that, then hearing an athlete thank God is no more offensive than hearing the Academy Award acceptance speech made by an actor who thanks his parents, his agent, his psychiatrist, his (current) spouse, and a couple of native American tribes for their support.

In the early 1990s, Chang often seemed to be the last Christian left standing on the tour. He certainly was the one who had the best ranking, and the persistent willingness to make public acknowledgments of his faith. This put the Chinese-American dynamo with the slender shoulders and the sturdy legs into a unique position of being maligned on two fronts—as a vocal Christian and as one of those "inscrutable," impassive Chinese who seem to lead insular, almost antisocial lives built on the cult of the family.

The rap on the Chang family was generally harsh. Many people accused the Changs of being, among other things, inordinately money conscious and tight-fisted. According to friends of Jose Higueras, the former top ten pro who coached Chang when he became the youngest male Grand Slam champion at Roland Garros in 1989, Michael's mother, Betty, approached Higueras and handed him a "present" in an envelope shortly after the tournament. The "bonus" was a gift of cash: fifty bucks.

Curious about the Changs, I went to Beijing, China, and Hong Kong with Chang and his brother, Carl, in late 1993. Michael was playing in the first sanctioned professional tennis event ever held on mainland China. I didn't really know Chang at the time as anything other than a dedicated player, an amateur ichthyologist who bred tropical fish, and a soft-spoken, devoutly religious young man. After winning the French Open of 1989, Chang took up permanent residence in the top ten. He was always a factor at Roland Garros and Flushing Meadow, and because of his determination and poise, Chang was always a threat when he reached a final. In 1993 he won five tournaments. Although he had a ranking of 8, only three players won more sanctioned events.

The true measure of Chang's talent and character was his ability to survive and even prosper in a game that was increasingly dominated by bigger, more powerful men. Chang stood five feet eight and weighed 145 pounds at the beginning of a tournament (he lost an average of 10 pounds during an event, despite forcing himself to eat four meals a day). He lived by his wits, relying on quick feet, precise ground strokes, reserves of stamina, and a surprising willingness to play as much attacking, aggressive tennis as his modest power allowed. Tim Gullickson, Pete Sampras's coach, once observed that more than any other top player, "Michael can play outside of his own comfort zone."

The key to this proclivity was Chang's constant attempt to use his defensive tools—speed, anticipation, and stamina—as offensive weapons.

On one sunny afternoon early during our swing through the Orient, Michael and Carl Chang invited me to join them on an expedition to one of Beijing's local markets, on a hunt for exotic fish. In the car I couldn't resist bringing up one of the more conspicuous issues at hand. Chang certainly was proud to be of Chinese extraction, yet as a Christian he must have had problems with the official atheism of his homeland. Fittingly, he answered with a parable.

"There was once a group of five Christian families in Beijing, and they would get together for prayer and fellowship," Chang told me. "When the news got out and people started talking about it, the local government officials had to do something. So they took four of the families and relocated them in different provinces. Those five families were spread out all over China. But the officials weren't really killing the Christian movement, they were just sowing seeds throughout the country."

Soon after our official driver dropped us off, we were lost in the teeming Chinese market. The vendors made the most use of what little space they had, coming up with novel solutions to the problems posed by having to transport live fish to and from the market. Some of them just made a square of bricks, draped a thick piece of oiled canvas over it, and created a pool in the middle for their wares. Others kept their fish in buckets, pouring water back and forth to sufficiently oxygenate the pails.

We stopped before a man who stood beside a picture of a handsomely striped fifteen-inch fish surrounded by Chinese writing. Chang read the poster. He explained, "That's an arowana. They can go as high as $35,000 because they're rare. The fish is worth so much that the man can't risk bringing it to the market. You'd have to go to his house to see it."

I asked Chang if bringing exotic fish into the United States posed the same formidable problems with customs as agricultural products.

"Not really," he replied. "Fish exist in a strictly contained environment, so they don't pose any risk of transmitting diseases through the typical mediums of air or touch. There's really no threat of exposure to humans or other animals."

Suddenly, Chang's innate sympathy for fish did not seem at all exotic or quirky. I realized that the fish's "strictly contained environment" was no strange concept to Chang. In fact, over the ensuing days I would come to realize that he was, by choice, no less contained than the fish, only in his case the medium was not water but his beliefs and his family. As he would tell me later, "If anybody wants to know me, they have to pass through my family and my religion. Those are the most important things to me."

Carl and Michael were both doted on, loved, and perhaps unusually sheltered. But the struggles faced by Joe and Betty Chang ensured that the children also developed a fair amount of self-reliance. Betty was a working mother, and Joe was a student who worked nights until he obtained his master's degree from Stevens Institute of Technology, in Hoboken, New Jersey. By the time Carl was six, he was in the habit of babysitting his brother, a responsibility that served to make the boys allies rather than rivals.

Michael was always quieter, more cautious and focused than his brother. He liked Tonka trucks and teddy bears, many of which he kept into adulthood as reminders of his happy childhood. He ate all his vegetables because he wanted to be like his hero, Popeye. And when he went to the barbershop, he asked if he could have his hair cut like Superman.

But Michael's happiest memories were of the fishing trips that the Changs took after they left gritty Hoboken for the greener pastures of St. Paul, Minnesota. On Saturdays, the entire family would go down to the outlet where a power station discharged warm water, and they fished for carp and silver bass.

The Changs were living out an American dream that even most Americans had forgotten, but their extraordinary closeness would make them the objects of suspicion and snide criticisms in the world of junior tennis and even later on the pro tour.

"The criticism we've tended to get was always based on a misunderstanding of our Asian concept of family bonding," Michael told me. "I think it can be a very difficult thing for a 'typical' American family to understand these days. In the United States, kids are *supposed* to leave the nest when they get around college age. But in a Chinese family there's nothing unusual about even a thirty-two-year-old single man living with his family. One of the key issues is the role of the father. He just isn't the supreme authority in a Chinese family, so you don't get some of the stresses and tensions that that situation creates. Most people find it surprising, but Asian families don't have nearly the same hierarchy of authority. We tend to put more emphasis on group discussion, and our decisions are more collective. When it works that way, there's less motivation or need to rebel."

The circumstance that enabled Michael Chang to become a pro tennis player instead of, say, a software engineer in some grain-processing plant in rural China was religious. Before the Maoist revolution, when religion was still tolerated in China, the vast majority of Chinese were Buddhists. Chang's forebears were interested in Christianity, but they did not formally convert untul Michael's paternal great-grandmother made a miraculous deathbed recovery from an apparently terminal illness.

Then came the communist revolution, whose official prohibition of religious worship led Michael's grandfather, Ken Wu Chang, to immigrate to the United States. Ken Wu founded a Chinese-American Christian church in Thousand Oaks, California. Carl and Michael were baptized there, and they remain part of that congregation.

Even model sons in tightly knit Chinese-American families often feel a need to rebel, and when Michael did so, it was against the church and religion that had been such a decisive force in the life of three generations of Changs. At fifteen, Michael did not find much relief from teenage pressures in strict Christian worship. He told me, "I wanted to be out playing tennis or fishing. Instead, I was sitting in church with a bunch of adults."

He wasn't cured of his restlessness in church until he heard a sermon by a substitute preacher, a woman known to the congregation as Aunt Betty. She was light, engaging, and witty. She seemed to be talking to him. Michael suddenly found himself genuinely believing, which was probably a good thing. Pretty soon he would need all the guidance the church had to offer.

In 1987, at just about the time that Chang was grappling with his rebellious impulses, he won a handful of important U.S. junior titles. Moonlighting as a pro, he reached the semifinals of a satellite event, the second round of the U.S. Open, and the semifinals of the Scottsdale Open. In six weeks he went from being an unranked fifteen-year old junior to the number 163 player in the world.

This burst of success put the Changs in an unexpected quandary. Initially, Joe and Betty thought that tennis proficiency was just a good way for the boys to earn college scholarships that would allow them to become engineers or lawyers. By late 1987 it looked as if their younger boy might not even be able to graduate from high school. The commercial market was hot for Chang, and the money that sponsors were offering seemed like a good hedge against the risk of turning pro. So Michael took the money and became a full-time pro at sixteen. If his faith helped him to maintain a steady keel in those heady times, it also landed him in some unexpected controversy.

Chang shocked the tennis establishment when he won the French Open after just one full year on the pro tour; he was seventeen years and three months. His pivotal match in that event was a fourth-round encounter with the top player in the world at the time, Ivan Lendl. Chang lost the first two sets but doggedly struggled back into the match. In the fifth set he was stricken by cramps and suffering from general exhaustion to such a degree that at one point he even threw in an underhand serve. When he faced the media after winning the four-hour, forty-three-minute match, 4–6, 4–6, 6–3, 6–3, 6–3, he did not hesitate to bare his religious feelings or to ascribe his success to them.

"I came across straight and said what I really believed," he told me many years later. "And I got a lot of heat for it. Some people thought I was cheating when I threw in that underhand serve. They even suggested that my cramps were some kind of ploy to throw Lendl off. Even the major respectable newspapers were pretty ambivalent. Some of them even mocked me. But it was funny that at the same time they were throwing in biblical allusions, things like the story of David and Goliath. It struck me as weird and very confusing."

There was more confusion in store for Chang. After a hip injury in late 1989, he got off to a slow start in 1990. To prepare for his defense of the French title, he entered events in Munich, Hamburg, and Rome, as well as an exhibition in Marseilles. Chang didn't win a single match in those events, but he did manage to reach the quarterfinals at Roland Garros in 1990. He felt discomforting pressure, however, and the fun was seeping out of tennis for him. In some ways it was a typical "sophomore slump," although Change worked his way through it in atypical fashion.

"I saw that I was putting too much emphasis on winning matches, which I guess is a typical reaction to my unexpected success in 1989. But for me it went deeper than that, down to a flaw in my religious feelings. I thought that in order for God to do his work, I had to be winning. It became a lot easier for me when I realized that it just isn't like that. It's never that clear-cut or obvious. In my faith, God doesn't judge you by what you do. The only thing that counts is believing in him and accepting him as your savior."

Chang's very survival on the pro tour required a great deal of faith in practical as well as spiritual ways. Whomever he faced, Chang was always in danger of being outgunned, overrun, and overwhelmed if his wheels and his wits were not in perfect working order. This forced him to have a remarkably high work ethic.

Just how hard he does work was evident to me in Beijing, where he was eager to earn a place in history by winning the first pro tournament held on mainland China. He did so by surviving tense three-set clashes with a strong Japanese player, Shuzo Matsuoka, and with Canadian Greg Rusedski.

The curious Chinese who attended the tournament or who watched Chang on the Asia-wide telecast were delighted with him. Not only was he of Chinese origin, but he played a game to which they could respond. As he put it, "Tennis is a thinking man's game, and the Chinese put a very high value on cleverness. That background is in me somewhere, and it helps me all the time. My own best asset is the ability to move quickly and think clearly, often at the same time."

Chang mingled with the spectators very little during most of the event, but immediately after he tamed the explosive Rusedski in a touch-and-go final, Michael climbed into the stands and spent forty-five minutes signing autographs—something that he does with the same courtesy and patience everywhere. And he always signs the same way, "Jesus loves you—Michael Chang."

No matter how you cut it, Chang is one of the most centered, purposeful pros the tour has produced, especially among those saddled with the burden of prodigy. He's a young man of extraordinary specific gravity. If I didn't know better, I would guess that although he barely stands five feet eight, he must weigh nine thousand pounds. Maybe there are advantages to being a Christian in Babylon.

CHAPTER 19

The Gals of Babylon,
Part Three

I KNOW WHAT YOU'RE THINKING: more bad news, more idol-bashing, more criticism of the women's tour as a radical entity that chews up and spits out young women, leaving them a few million bucks richer, a life-time poorer.

Well, the good news is that, from about the time Tracy Austin appeared on the scene in 1977, there has been something that can broadly be called an alternate, "traditional" movement, one in which many players have rejected the sweeping claims made on them by the pro women's estab-lishment and even the cant of sexual politics. Players such as Austin, Pam Shriver, Steffi Graf, and Monica Seles made it clear that they wanted to be women who happen to play pro tennis, not tennis players who happen to be women.

The bad news is that for a variety of reasons, including the young age at which women become physically mature enough to play on the world circuit, many of the more traditional women players have had sadly abbreviated careers, traumatic setbacks, or career-threatening crises.

Austin was forced off the tour by back problems combined with an awakening to the joys of normal life; Steffi Graf was dealt a severe blow by her father's unsavory philandering, and an ugly paternity contro-versy that resulted from it. Jennifer Capriati quit pro tennis in 1993 because she just wanted to do goofy kid things, such as attend school, paint her fingernails black, and go shoplifting at the mall. And then there was Jennifer Rhodes. This ranked junior and talented pro prospect was the object of a kidnapping attempt early in 1993 by a man who had once coached her, Gary Wilensky. And a few weeks later Mon-ica Seles, who had won more Grand Slam titles in a shorter period of time than any other woman in Open era history, was attacked on the court and stabbed in the back by a deranged fan of her chief rival, Steffi Graf.

The attack on Seles was the most sensational and unexpected example of the abuse of women tennis players. But the attack on Jennifer Rhodes probably provided a more vivid illustration of the broader issues faced by most young women and their parents in tennis—because if it happened to Rhodes, it could happen to anyone. Rhodes was not an international star like Seles, capable of inspiring hostility in almost any deranged individual with an appetite for recognition or a resentment of those who have earned it.

Rhodes was playing in a junior tournament in upstate New York when fifty-six-year-old Wilensky struck. I'd met Wilensky a few times and found him forgettable, just another ordinary guy who, perhaps for lack of any other ambition, had immersed himself in the local tennis microculture and established himself as a teaching pro despite a lack of any noteworthy credentials. Wilensky had been coaching Rhodes for about eighteen months when his growing obsession with her, manifested in inappropriate correspondence and incessant telephone calls, began to make Jennifer feel uncomfortable. She complained to her mother, Sonya, who promptly dismissed Wilensky in February 1993. He then wrote them a tortured letter of apology but secretly hatched the abduction scheme that transpired in April.

Wilensky attacked Jennifer and Sonya Rhodes with a cattle prod outside the motel where they were staying. Apparently he had plans to whisk Rhodes away to a cabin in the nearby Adirondack Mountains, a place he had equipped with gruesome sado-masochistic devices, sexual paraphernalia, and enough armaments and security devices to keep an army at bay. But when the women fought him off, Wilensky ran off to his rental car, drove a short distance, and then blew his brains out.

On the surface, it would seem that Wilensky's assault on the Rhodeses, as well as Gunther Parche's attack on Seles, were acts of passion. But I think they were characterized by a dearth rather than an overabundance of emotion. These two brutal incidents demonstrate the extent to which women tennis players have come to be seen as objects. As long as that condition was merely implied in traditional, noncoercive ways that served to enrich the young women and their families through pro tennis, nobody thought much about it. But when Wilensky and Parche crossed the line of social acceptability, a line that is very clear, the results shocked everyone.

Young women in our era have increasingly become tools with which parents, coaches, entrepreneurs, and, occasionally, deranged individuals exercise their ambitions and powers. It isn't that complicated: At ten or twelve or fifteen, these girls are just too young to understand what others are doing to them. Often they are unaware of their own need for attention and approval, and thus, they are easily manipulated.

One reason all of this has come to pass is that the traditional roles young women and older men had once been expected to play have been thrown out the window. Girls in their early teens habitually spend inordinate amounts of time with coaches, and they sometimes develop abnormal attachments to them. Many girls gain confidence, pride, and self-esteem from their success at tennis, but those triumphs are often linked to the coach. At an age when most girls have a deep and powerful need to develop relations with members of the opposite sex, a young tennis player often has nowhere to turn but a domineering father or a middle-aged male coach.

Any parent who believes that his or her daughter can have an intense, pupil-mentor relationship with a male coach without the danger of sparks flying is dehumanizing that child. Is she supposed to engage in the often banal and always excruciatingly repetitive process of training for its own sake, with no emotional engagement, at a time in life when most youngsters are seething with emotions and exploring relationships? Many parents also fail to realize that coaches aren't simply ball machines, either. They are men, older men with sexual drives, fantasies, and considerably more experience in the cat-and-mouse games that sometimes characterize human relationships. Some of the most well-known and respected coaches in pro tennis have had intimate relations with one or more of their pupils.

One of the other, subtle dangers in the relationship between an adult coach and an adolescent players is the false sense of empowerment that a successful player may develop. Savvy kids quickly figure out that coaches are not merely authority figures and teachers but also dependent employees.

Take Pam Shriver, the vivacious, intelligent pro who reached the U.S. Open singles final at age sixteen in 1978 and went on to win twenty-two Grand Slam doubles titles. Shriver's game was developed by the Australian former world-class player Don Candy. When Shriver vaulted to the top of the game, she took a remarkable degree of control over her own affairs. Although Candy was ostensibly her coach and authority figure, he found himself holding a comet by the tail. All he could do was hang on for the ride, even though the complex emotional nature of his relationship meant also that Shriver needed Candy.

"My parents weren't a very big factor in my development in tennis," Shriver told me some years after her long relationship with Candy had gone stale. "In a way that was great because I was also spared the experience of playing to please them or having them try to run my life. I was outgoing and curious, eager to make my own decisions. When I started to play well, people were falling all over me, which gave me a real sense of power. I probably would have been lost without Don, but he was there all the time with his general experience and knowledge. So with his help I was off and running at sixteen. I love my parents as much as anyone, and I get along with them great—better than a lot of women whose parents were involved in their careers. But they weren't really a big factor in my career, not ever.

"It was funny, but on the night before I played the final in that 'magic' U.S. Open, a shoe company called and offered me $10,000 to change the logo on my shoes. You would think that a sixteen-year old, unexpectedly in the U.S. Open final, wouldn't even be exposed to that kind of stuff. A parent or a coach would deal with it. But I was different. I wanted control, and I was the one who ended up making a decision about it. I declined the offer, figuring it wasn't fair to the company whose shoes I'd worn to get that far in the tournament. But I think I was a little sharper than most sixteen-year-olds."

The same maturity that enabled Shriver to reach the U.S. Open final at such a young age also helped her solve the special problems created by the combination of her youth, her talent, and her long relationship with Candy. But Shriver is a striking exception.

Tracy Austin was the first great prodigy after Chris Evert to have to deal with the nature of an all-female world tour. Her mother, Jeanne, accompanied her everywhere and even made her presence felt in the locker room—habits that were resented and ridiculed by many of the women players.

In seven years on the pro tour, Austin never played in all the Grand Slam events in a given year. She also played a streamlined schedule on the world pro circuit, qualifying for season-ending championships on the strength of her performances in the tournaments she did play rather than the force of the number of events she entered. Austin won the U.S. Open twice (1979 and 1981) and reached the singles final in five season-ending championships (meetings sponsored at various times by Colgate, Toyota, Avon, and Virginia Slims), winning on three occasions. She played in only 101 sanctioned events in her career but won an impressive 29 titles. On two occasions in 1980 she interrupted the Evert-Navratilova monopoly on the number one ranking.

Tracy was sheltered, inexperienced, and devoted to her large family of tennis nuts (Austin's sister, Pam, and her brothers, John and Jeff, also played on the pro circuit). She was a little hellcat who refused to be intimidated by her formidable rivals, and neither her impudence nor courage sat well with the women who ruled the game. Once Evert and Navratilova realized that the other woman wouldn't just go away, they struck up a unique friendship that eventually enabled them to divide the tennis kingdom and create one of the most intriguing multidimensional rivalries in the history of sports. But early in this process, Austin appeared as both the third wheel and the squeaky wheel.

Austin took on and tormented both women. Up until the Toyota Championships that concluded the 1981 season, Austin had an 8–7 winning record against Evert. Navratilova had a better record against Austin in the same period (17–13), but Austin defeated Navratilova on some key occasions, including the semifinals of the 1979 U.S. Open and the final of the 1981 event at Flushing Meadow.

But by the time the chronic sciata, a condition that may have been caused by playing too much tennis at too young an age on the traditional California surface, hard courts, began to threaten Austin's career in 1982, she was also becoming interested in boys. She began to date a fellow player with a name right out of a pulp novel, Matt Anger. Tracy never was the same player after those two factors disrupted her life of unconscious, hellbent prodigy, even though she would make a few comeback attempts in ensuing years. She certainly loved the game, but she didn't feel nearly the same amount of affection for the tour and all the baggage that went with it.

Austin had one other important function that became clear as the years passed and she faded from the public imagination. She was the canary in the mine, the first of a series of prodigies whose careers would be foreshortened or rendered asymmetrical by injury, emotional struggles, or a combination of the two.

During a tournament in 1991, the Hungarian reporter Eric Siklos gave me an article that had appeared in a newspaper in Budapest. It was a guest column written by a man who lived in the Hungarian enclave in Novi Sad, Croatia. It was a spooky, poignant reflection, part of that modest narrative genre whose stories are about mysterious people who live downstairs.

The author rented the flat above the Seleses for some years, and he recalled sitting in his rooms night after night, month after month, listening to the pounding of a tennis ball against a wall downstairs. He had not gotten to know the Seleses very well. They mostly kept to themselves, saying little more than "good morning" as they came and went with their tennis gear.

The name of the little girl downstairs was Monica, and by the time

she was only eight or nine, the steady tattoo of the tennis ball was punctuated by long periods of silence. At those times, the man learned,
Monica was away from home, playing in tennis tournaments. Then in
1986 the man returned home after work one day and noticed that he
had not heard the thud of the tennis ball against the wall for a few days.
In fact, there was no noise whatsoever from downstairs. The Seles family had vanished.

I still picture this man sometimes, sitting down at a bare wooden
table in the evening, the dying light filtering through the windows, pon-
dering the silence in the months after the Seleses vanished. Knowing
that he would never hear the beat of the tennis ball again. Pouring
another Palinka. Wondering what would become of the little girl Monica, wondering what would become of himself and, as darkness fell,
whether or not he should have done something differently, as had the
mysterious people who once lived downstairs.

Well, we know where Monica Seles went, along with her father and
mother, Karolj and Esther, her brother, Zoltan, and her dog, Astro.
They went to the Nick Bollettieri Tennis Academy in Bradenton
Florida, at the invitation of Bollettieri himself. The famous coach had
seen Seles, then twelve, in action at the Orange Bowl, the premier tournament for international juniors. He immediately recognized that she
had extraordinary potential.

Karolj Seles had no money, no job, and no English. All he had was his
family. Bolleteiri gave the Seleses a place to live, and he gave Esther Seles
a job bussing tables and washing dishes in the dining facility at the academy. Bolletieri said he spent tens of thousands of dollars on room,
board, travel expenses, and other amenities for the Seleses and "thousands of hours" coaching and honing Monica Seles's game. The Seleses
would dispute that last claim when they abruptly packed their bags in
March 1990 and parted from Bollettieri. They claimed that Bollettieri
was spending an inordinate amount of time with his other star protégé,
Andre Agassi. Furthermore, they insisted that he never really had been
Monica's coach—Karolj Seles was Monica's first and only coach.

But for all the mystery, controversy, and speculation surrounding the
Seleses, one thing was becoming abundantly clear by 1989: Monica
Seles was a remarkable player, a stick figure of a girl who used two hands
off both wings to hit remarkably flat, hard, accurate strokes. There was
a fiercely minimal quality to her game, and it preempted almost any discussion of a potential strategy that could target her weaknesses.
Granted, she did not have much of a volley. But the pace and depth that
characterized her ground strokes were such that there was no way to
draw her in to the net. About all an opponent could hope to do against

Seles was hit a winner off her middling serve. But if it wasn't an outright winner, Seles would fire back a laser that put her opponent on the defensive.

The only player to whom Seles could be compared was Jimmy Connors. Relatively speaking, she had more power than Connors, but she did not quite share his compact build or lightness of foot. A lot of women sat around hoping that as Seles matured she would develop wide hips, substantial thighs, and enough height and bulk to cause her problems. Their hopes were realized by the spring of 1990 as Seles sprouted to five feet nine and began to fill out her frame. But the spurt of growth hardly affected her tennis. She won her first Grand Slam title in Paris in 1990, beating Steffi Graf in the final, 7–6, 6–4. She would win seven of the ten Grand Slam titles she contested from that point on, until she was stabbed in April 1993. The only Grand Slam title she did not win was the one offered at Wimbledon, where she had played only three times.

Monica Seles was officially on her way to becoming the greatest player of all time when she was stabbed. Although any number of other things might have interrupted her career, her record up to 1993 is nothing short of astonishing. To understand her greatness properly, you have only to compare her numbers to those of the top players of the Open era. Beginning with the French Open of 1990, Seles won seven of the ten Grand Slam events she entered. Overall, she won eight of the fourteen Grand Slams she played until she was stabbed. Martina Navratilova did not win a single Grand Slam title in her first fourteen attempts. Chris Evert was five for fourteen. And Steffi Graf won but one of the first fourteen Grand Slams she played.

The media had a particularly hard time deciding just who Monica Seles was, alternately casting her as an airheaded fashion victim, a Madonna wannabe (based on Monica once having said that she admired the pop star), or a manipulative brat who self-consciously generated mystery and controversy about herself in order to steal the limelight from her rivals.

Seles was a smart kid who came from relative poverty, and may have spent more time than she should have worrying about slipping back into that condition. She was also a decisive girl who wanted to control her own destiny—an impulse so strong that when she was not sure of how to handle a situation, she simply refused to deal with it, no matter who was waiting or what was at stake. And she was an imaginative kid with a sense of style that few of her peers shared or bothered to develop.

Heather MacLachlan, a partner in Ion Tiriac's tennis business, remembers a meeting that occurred when Seles was fourteen. Monica had been invited by Tiriac to play in his lucrative exhibition in Essen,

Germany, and had won the tournament. Shortly after the final, Seles showed up at the tournament office and asked MacLachlan about the prize money. The older woman told her that her parents could come around for the $400,000 check in half an hour. Thirty minutes later MacLachlan was surprised to see not Karolj or Esther at the door but Monica again. MacLachlan was reluctant to give such a large sum to a child, but Monica insisted. She proceeded to pick MacLachlan's brain about local taxes, wire transfers of large sums, interest rates, and other banking miscellanea. Then she took the check, folded it carefully, and slipped it into her pocket. She said, "Thanks for everything. I'll let you know how it works out."

Monica also had an advanced sense of style. After she won the final at the Lipton Championships on Key Biscayne in 1989, at age fifteen, she insisted on going back to the locker room before attending the postmatch press conference. She showed up in the press tent about thirty minutes later, freshly showered, wearing a black cocktail dress and a string of pearls. She was animated, and the only way to describe the way in which she answered even the most simple of questions was "stream of unconsciousness."

But a combination of Seles's unique sense of style and her method of making or avoiding decisions soon created problems for her, and they ultimately raised questions about her ambitions, credibility, and motivations. The most telling incident occurred in 1991, when, at seventeen, she abruptly and mysteriously withdrew from Wimbledon shortly after winning her second consecutive French Open title. Ostensibly, she was suffering from a leg injury that may have been as benign as a case of shin splints. While doctors were attempting to determine the nature of her injury, Monica declared that she would skip Wimbledon and then went into deep seclusion. As Wimbledon approached, everyone from WTA administrators to the international media tried to reach her, to no avail.

At one point Monica was holed up in Donald Trump's Palm Beach residence. At another she was spotted by photographers as she and Karolj, both wearing wigs, scrambled into a getaway car. As Seles continued to play hide-and-seek, resentment of her began to mount. She was clearly flouting WTA rules pertaining to the proper procedures for withdrawing from tournaments. She was embarrassing corporate types such as WTA president Jerry Smith, who had to admit to the media that seventeen-year old Monica Seles simply wasn't returning his urgent telephone calls. Seles was accused of damaging not only her own credibility but that of the women's tour—striving for autonomy and power she didn't deserve.

Layer upon layer of speculation and innuendo was heaped on the banal facts. According to one report, Seles was pregnant with the child of an Italian hitting partner. According to another, she was in the midst of a passionate affair with Donald Trump. Others claimed that her absence was an attempt to extort more money out of the people who held her racket contract.

Monica was soon dubbed "the Mystery Girl" at the vortex of an international sensation. She generated reams of publicity for the women's game and left hundreds of thousands of otherwise oblivious folks asking, "So just who *is* this Monica Seles?"

But they weren't about to cancel Wimbledon simply because Monica was missing in action. Somebody else would win, everybody would have a great time, and the only person to suffer would be Monica herself. (As it turned out, Seles won the other three major championships of 1991 and thus missed a chance to complete a Grand Slam by virtue of her absence from Wimbledon.) And that's how Wimbledon passed, with Graf winning the title of a fine, exciting tournament.

Seles continued to hold out, refusing to make a public appearance until an exhibition event staged in late July in Mahwah, New Jersey. She came out of seclusion on an unbearably hot, humid day. Two hundred-plus representatives of the international media descended on the scene, a tournament site erected on the parched ballfields of a community college.

One of those reporters was a Brit who had marched right up and banged on the door of the Seles house late one night at the height of the crisis, only to have Karolj Seles call the police on him. Rivers of sweat ran down his forehead as we waited, sweltering, for Seles to make her way into the giant tent. Like most British reporters, even the ones who work for cheesy tabloids, the fellow was impeccably dressed, but his shirt was soaked through and his tie was loosened and askew. He leaned over and revealed the strategy: "We're going to hit her early, open her up, and cut her to pieces."

When Monica finally appeared, flashbulbs exploded throughout the tent. She wore a sleeveless blue top and was carefully made up. She held her beloved Astro in her arms. She was too smart for the press, conceding nothing more than that her actions were the result of the conflicting diagnoses and her own fears for her career. She fielded the rumors that had developed and dismissed them one by one.

Later, while riding in a car with Monica, I told her that I had never witnessed such a bizarre and intriguing story in women's tennis. There wasn't a publicist on earth who could have orchestrated such a riveting, electric, and prolonged happening. Monica laughed and said, "I never planned it to happen this way, no matter what anybody says. I swear that to you. It was just a case of not realizing what a heavy presence I have and how much my words count. It may look like I was having fun with it, but that wasn't the case—at least not in the beginning. At first it was just very tough and very scary for me."

If you think of Monica as one of the mysterious people who lives downstairs, the incident makes a certain amount of sense. I think it also taught her that being one of those people doesn't have to be just scary, it can also be fun.

Monica Seles was a prodigy in the grand tradition of Chris Evert in that the parental influence on her career was positive and low-key. Seles wasn't damaged or abused by the misplaced ambitions or conduct of the man who shaped her game, her father Karolj. It was hard to come to that conclusion from cursory exposure to the mysterious people who live downstairs. At tournaments, the Seleses were unfailingly polite, but partly because of their difficulty with the English language, they did not socialize much. They appeared clannish, and in a way I suppose they were. I thought they suffered some dislocation and accepted it as a family sacrifice made to advance Monica's career. I don't think they ever expected to be understood, but there were some complex reasons for that, beginning with their ethnicity.

Although Seles was born in land claimed by Serbia, her family was ethnic Hungarian, a group that did not see the Yugoslavian conflict as its own war. The Seleses had no patriotic or emotional stake in the atrocities that the Croats, Serbs, and Muslims were busy visiting on each other, other than their fears of becoming victims of those horrors. That fear was entirely justified. Monica was a far bigger fish in the pool of potential terrorist targets than even the outspoken Croat Ivanisevic. She was certainly more famous, but, more important, she was nominally a Serb. Thus she was part of an "oppressive majority" against whom revolutionary minority Croatians felt entitled to take action in the name of freedom.

Seles received a number of death threats from fanatical Croatians during her career. As a result she often booked hotels under assumed names and frequently made last-minute changes in her travel plans. Long before Gunther Parche made his chilling mark on tennis history, Seles knew what it was like to live in fear of physical violence, a moving target for political extremists.

Being Hungarian myself, I had no trouble becoming friendly with Karolj Seles. He was a shy, warm, intellectually hyperactive man. He remembered the postwar years in Yugoslavia as a time of utter want and told me on a number of occasions that his experience of growing up had left him indifferent to the kinds of material wants and desires that people from more comfortable backgrounds harbored.

Karolj did not travel on the tour because he enjoyed the limelight, and he studiously avoided getting mixed up in his daughter's affairs at tournaments. Other parents conspicuously trouped to postmatch interviews and made themselves available to the media, but Karolj preferred to sit patiently with Esther in the players' lounge, waiting for his daughter so they could all go home together. In fact, one of the few times that Karolj did consent to sit for an interview, a live session with the telecast giant Eurovision, he came to me in a panic and asked if I would *please* agree to accompany him and serve as translator.

Karolj was a decent man and a good father, a worrywart, perhaps, but a man who did not push his daughter or live out his own dreams through her except in the sense of accomplishment he felt in shaping her game.

"My mom and dad let me me make most of my own decisions from the time that I was eight, but they drew the line about the amount I was allowed to play. At fourteen, I could only play three pro events. I remember begging my father to let me play more. I really wanted to try to get a wild card to play the U.S. Open, and I wanted us to push to get one. But Dad said no. And that was that. I was so sad. He explained that I had plenty of time to play in plenty of U.S. Opens, but it didn't help then. I cried."

Monica's driven, restless nature sometimes troubled Karolj. At various times he expressed worries that she would burn out, forget to become a woman who might one day start her own family, or lose sight of the fact that, in the end, the only reason to play tennis was because you loved the game, because it was fun. Karolj was concerned for the state of his daughter's tennis game, which the Seleses insisted that only he understood, and her physical well-being. He became resigned to the nomadic life.

I didn't see Seles after she was stabbed until early in 1994 when she invited me to interview her in Bradenton, Florida. True to form, Seles's whereabouts and even the precise nature and extent of her injuries were shrouded in secrecy, mystery, and rumor. All anybody knew, even months after the attack was that Seles had been stabbed with a curved, serrated, nine-inch boning knife. The knife entered just below her left shoulder blade, and although it left "only" a two-inch-long wound, the puncture narrowly missed her spinal cord.

Soon after Seles was released from the hospital, she flew out to Vail, Colorado, checked into a hotel, and embarked on a five-month, closely supervised rehabilitation and therapy program at the Steadman-Hawkins Clinic. She did not even hit a tennis ball until September when Dr. Steadman allowed her to hit only two balls into a net set up in his office. She experienced some pain on the follow-through and decided to give her shoulder three more weeks of rest.

In the interim Seles held her first public news conference, on the first day of the U.S. Open. Cynics noted that Seles just happened to meet with the press while Graf, who had taken back the number one ranking during Seles's absence, was playing her first-round match on the stadium court. Seles's spokesmen said that she had refrained from holding her press conference the day before the tournament because she didn't want to upstage the charity event mounted that day by the Arthur Ashe Foundation for the Defeat of AIDS.

That mean-spirited controversy underscored a truly sad state of affairs. Although Graf had visited Seles in the hospital in Germany shortly after she had been stabbed (a meeting that Graf described as "very emotional"), there had been almost no contact between the women afterward. According to Seles, a variety of girls had made an effort to stay in touch, including Jennifer Capriati and Mary Joe Fernandez, who wrote Seles a long letter after attempts to reach her by phone failed. Seles said she was very disappointed that Graf had not once communicated with her after their meeting in the hospital. Later, Graf said that she had tried to call Seles but had no luck getting through. Whatever the truth was, the reality of the situation was a damaging and ugly comment on the lack of compassion and bonhomie at the top of the women's game.

During that press conference, the situation quickly began to look like Wimbledon 1991 all over again. Seles and her representatives at IMG were accused of revealing too little about her injury. Seles was taken to task for choosing to remain in seclusion, unavailable to the press. There was no tangible evidence of damage to Seles other than a small scar on the left side of her back that nobody could see (Seles herself said that she couldn't bring herself to look at it in a mirror). That scar simply would not bear the weight of unanswered questions and percolating rumors.

When Seles refrained from giving a timetable for her return to the pro tour, some people suggested that she was being coy. Others suspected that she was busy playing various promoters off against each other to see who would offer the biggest appearance fee, knowing that her return would provide any tournament with more publicity than any amount of money could buy outright.

And then there was the matter of her ranking. Seles had been forced out of the game by an act of violence intended to benefit her chief rival, Graf. The only thing that would stop that plan from working out perfectly was intervention by the WTA. If the WTA froze Seles's ranking at number one until her return to competition, the best Graf or any other rival could do was earn a co-ranking at the top.

The WTA put this issue to a vote of the rank-and-file. In a sad and telling decision, the women players declined to freeze Seles's ranking because of the many "technical" problems the unusual but morally courageous decision would pose. Only one of the women bridled at this, Gabriela Sabatini. She refused to vote, out of compassion for Seles. When Seles heard about Sabatini's stand, she broke down in tears.

The ranking controversy would simmer for months, leading some camp followers to conclude that Seles was blackmailing the WTA, refusing to play again until she was accorded satisfaction. As usual, Monica did nothing to dispel such speculations. I think that was because Monica was ill-equipped to handle the challenges of her own absolute authority. As a result, she was free to just keep on making it up as she went along until she either painted herself into a corner or somehow saw herself clear. In 1993, as in 1991, her puzzling actions and comments were the fruit of her private fears, her insufficiently developed sense of accountability, and her boundless power. But in 1993, she was also reeling from having been stabbed in the back twice—once by Parche, and once by her fellow players.

By late 1993, Monica was also struggling with the unquantifiable, psychic repercussions of the terrible thing that had happened to her in April. If that weren't enough, her father was suffering from cancer, and Monica wanted to keep Karolj's illness a secret. She wasn't a natural liar, so she simply chose to avoid the pressing questions of the tennis establishment and the media. I think Monica was running scared, as she had been in different ways for so much of her young life. And this time she was running alone.

As it turned out, reports that Seles would return to tennis at the Australian Open of 1994 were unfounded. At about that time, I went to see Seles in Florida. She had asked that we meet at a Hyatt hotel at noon, and I waited for her in front of the place. Ten minutes after the appointed hour, she came strolling up the driveway, alone. She was modestly dressed in black workout tights and a sweater. Her hair was pulled back, but unruly strands surrounded her oval face. She looked a lot older and slightly haggard. And she had reason to be. Just the previous day the skater Nancy Kerrigan had been attacked by an assailant who had been recruited through the offices of her chief rival Tonya Harding's bodyguard and her ex-husband. Monica told me that she had tried to call Kerrigan but, failing to get through, had left her a message. The events almost caused her to beg off seeing me.

The attack on Kerrigan had caused Monica's own recent experience spring to mind with fresh force. She had been attacked before a huge crowd, in broad daylight, by a deranged, morbidly obsessed loner. Apparently the German judicial system didn't find anything particularly sinister in the tableau. They had let her assailant go virtually scotfree under the theory that he was unlikely to attempt anything so destructive again.

"It's funny, but he got exactly what he wanted," Seles said of Gunther Parche, "and he also got to walk away. It cost him nothing."

She was often troubled by the idea that Parche might strike again. In a recurrent nightmare, a man with a red face stood just behind Seles with a raised knife. Having already stabbed her once, she could see in his eyes that he was about to do it again. This was one of those art-imitates-life scenarios because Parche had in fact been trying to stab her again on that cold, bright day in Hamburg, when spectators in the crowd managed to wrestle him to the ground.

We talked about her rehabilitation regimen, and we talked about how she had dealt with the emotional and psychological residue of the assault. Monica had become part of a network of people who had been stabbed and who were all members of an informal hot line that was open day and night, seven days a week. "It's not a celebrity thing, although there are a few known people who are in it because they've been stabbed," Seles said. "But mostly, it's just other victims who understand what you're going through. They're there to help, and to be helped."

As we chatted, I couldn't help but notice how much more mature Seles seemed. In a few short hours I once again came to see Seles in a different light—an unpredictable process that was becoming routine, proving that whatever else Seles may or may not have been, she sure was interesting. To wit: At the moment Seles was stabbed, she was within an inch of death. But from the moment her assailant was subdued, she came within an inch of life. Normal life, anyway.

During her long rehabilitation, Seles tried many things she hadn't done before, including hiking, fly-fishing, and camping in the Colorado Rockies with friends. Later she took classes in painting and grappled with James Joyce's *Ulysses*. She became accustomed to having a home and fretting over her ill father.

"One of the big changes in me is that I'm not all that cautious anymore, I'm not as afraid of living," she said. "I guess that's ironic because I heard all the rumors about how I was in a mental institution, how I'd become an emotional wreck. But it's almost like the opposite is true. I don't spend much time looking over my shoulder, and I'm open to more things than ever before. I used to just shut out anything that went against my routine as a player. I wouldn't even think of going skiing or ice-skating because I might fall down and get hurt. I just don't worry about things like that anymore.

"Sometimes I find myself wishing that I could have started playing three or four years later. I would have had a little more time to experience 'normal' things and to prepare myself for becoming number one. But I had this gift, and in that I was very lucky. I couldn't give somebody else that ranking and say, 'Here, hold this for a while. I'll come for it when I'm good and ready.'

"I withdrew a little when I became number one. I remember my very first reaction to reaching that spot. I thought, 'Oh, God, I'm only seventeen. What do I do now?' It was a really weird feeling. I can see now what I did: I withdrew into myself. I tried to manage and control everything, and I was scared that if I let go, it would all slide away through my fingers.

"I've had a lot of time to think since that day, a lot of time to decide about my priorities. They've changed. My family comes first. My life comes next. Then comes tennis, but I'm not sure where yet. I know that I don't want to play just to get my number one ranking back. I don't want to play for more attention or for more money. I don't even want to play because the world wants me to, even though it's nice to know that the world is interested. I only want to play because I love the game itself, which is the reason I began to play in the first place when I was just seven. Somewhere along the way I forgot about that. There were too many other responsibilities, too many other pressures."

I asked Seles about all the rumors, about the way she seemed to make things harder for herself than they had to be during the Wimbledon crisis of 1991 and again in the aftermath of having been stabbed. Would her actions in the future continue to be clouded by rumors, speculation, and obfuscations?

"After you endure something like what happened to me, the single, *absolute* thing you have to be is clear with yourself. And while there are things that I really want to keep private, I know that I just couldn't live with myself if I was hiding something, if I was trying to manipulate situations the way some people claim I do. It's not just an attitude, it's a matter of survival. I have to be clear with myself. And if I am, I'm going to be clear with everybody else, too."

It wouldn't be fair to bid *adieu* to the women of Babylon without taking a closer look at the young lady whose reputation as a player will always be clouded by the attack on Seles, at the player who has shown a remarkable ability to pick and step her way through the maze of prodigy and the mine field of the women's tour: Steffi Graf.

Ah, Steffi Graf, the shy, leggy golden girl. The Uberfrau, winner in 1988 of not merely a Grand Slam but a Golden Slam, adding an Olympic gold medal in singles to her sweep of the four Grand Slam titles. The dog lover, the family lover, and, perhaps most of all, the lover of winning—of rolling on through scandal and violence, through good times and bad, through sunshine and thunder. And even more than a lover, a survivor. The last woman left standing, the queen bee of Babylon.

But by 1994 it seemed suspiciously like the only thing that Steffi Graf liked about tennis was the winning, and it was impossible not to notice that she conspicuously lacked the measure of the joy that someone in her position was supposed to feel.

This was manifest in a multitude of habits and unspoken discontents: the way Steffi showed up for matches and, shortly after winning (usually in less than an hour), beat it home. The way a look clouded her face when she was accosted in a hall or players' lounge. The way she remained utterly unconnected to the issues, traditions, and social milieu of the game she played so well. The truth of the matter is that, for a girl who ostensibly had so much going on, she was a presence in tennis only on the court when the ball was in play.

I got to know Graf in 1985 when she was sixteen and rising quickly to the top of the game. I spent a lot of time with her and her father, Peter, at the Family Circle Cup on Hilton Head Island, South Carolina, that year. I learned that Steffi started playing at age three, partly because her father, having taken up the game out of the blue at age twenty-seven, was a maniacal recreational player. He was too busy with his own game to spend too much time with Steffi, but he did allow her to create a makeshift court by running string between two chairs in the basement of their home in Bruhl, Germany.

Steffi did not make it out of the basement into the daylight until she turned five, and by that time she had developed extraordinary powers of concentration. Soon she would also show the athletic ability that eventually made her the female equivalent of the fleet male player Bjorn Borg.

Peter Graf proudly told me that he had never pushed his daughter, that she had pushed him. At the age of nine she had been invited to a birthday party at three in the afternoon. She said she didn't want to go because it would interfere with her tennis. "I had to make her go to the party," Peter told me. "I was always trying to make her slow down in tennis."

In 1987, Steffi vaulted to the summit of the game, winning eleven singles titles including the French Open. She also reached the finals at Wimbledon and Flushing Meadow, but she lost the title match at each of those Grand Slam events to Martina Navratilova, who won only two other singles titles in 1987.

At the time, the computer had not yet become the sole authority on year-end rankings. The rankings issued by *Tennis* and *World Tennis* magazines still carried some authority. As a member of *Tennis* magazine's international ranking panel, I felt obliged to give Navratilova the top ranking based on my order of priorities.

Soon after the rankings appeared in print, I covered a tournament in Florida. I was killing time in the press tent when a WTA functionary told me that Peter Graf was waiting to see me at the door. I thought that he just wanted to say hello. Instead, when I approached him, he looked at me and said, "So now we see what kind of a friend you are." Peter turned on his heels and walked away without saying another word. Peter had put a cramp in what had been for me an otherwise pleasant and promising relationship with his daughter. He did this with many other people as well. He alternately wooed journalists and then turned on them if they did not become fanatical partisans of his daughter. He did the same thing with tennis officials and functionaries, including the highly esteemed veteran tournament referee Lee Jackson.

By the time Peter Graf, an amateur boxer and former used-car salesman, arrived on the scene, the conduct of obsessive tennis fathers had forced the WTA to enforce the fairly strict and clear rules against coaching from the sidelines, either audibly or through tricky body language reminiscent of signals in baseball. Even Chris Evert, who was much more inclined to finesse tricky situations, felt impelled to go public with her complaints about Herr Graf. "It's obvious that he coaches her during matches," she told me. "He speaks German to her, and he's got a whole system of hand signals. The rules clearly say that no coaching is allowed, so if you're an opponent playing by the rules, his actions are difficult to accept. They're just plain unfair."

The guerrilla war that ensued between Peter Graf and various officials reached comical proportions on some occasions, as Peter Graf furtively moved from one post to another during a match, always staying one step ahead of the posse. After one Graf victory, Steffi walked off the court and said to Peter: "Where were you? I was looking all over, but I didn't see you."

Still, people tried to work around Peter because they liked Steffi. Early in 1990 I found myself standing in the back of a press conference, right alongside Peter, with whom I'd spoken very little since his outburst over the rankings. I turned to him and said exactly what I was thinking as I watched his daughter speaking to the press: "You know, what I like about your daughter is that there's no baloney about her. She's natural. What you see is what you get." Peter nodded approvingly. He said something about letting bygones be bygones, and he expressed an eagerness to resume friendly relations. But the scandal that would soon erupt over his own affairs ultimately prevented that from happening.

From 1983 until the spring of 1990, Graf amassed a record that, among women in the Open era, only Seles could match. She made her debut on the tour in 1983 at age fourteen and didn't reach a quarterfinal until she made the semifinals of the last Grand Slam event of 1985, the U.S. Open. The following year Graf played only two Grand Slam events, reaching the quarterfinals of Roland Garros and the semis at Flushing Meadow. Then, in 1987, she caught fire. She reached the final in the next thirteen consecutive Grand Slam events she played, winning nine titles including her Golden Slam. The streak of finals ended at Wimbledon in 1990, although she did bounce back to reach the final at Flushing Meadow.

Graf accomplished all that while harboring a big secret, which was that she couldn't play tennis. What I mean is that nobody in his right mind would teach someone to play tennis the way Peter Graf taught Steffi. Graf didn't win because of her game, she won in spite of it. Unlike Evert, Austin, or Seles, Graf's ability to win tennis matches had much less to do with the way she addressed the ball than with her assets as an athlete and her fine, strong mind.

Graf's service toss was much too high and much too far back over her head, and there was a noticeable hitch that robbed the stroke of some power. But because of her natural strength, Steffi still managed to hit one of the better serves in the women's game.

Graf's slice backhand was a crude stroke, although the addition of topspin later in her career did improve the product. But during the glory years of 1988 and 1989, she almost always sliced the backhand. The function of slice is control, and if a player applies just the right amount of slice, he or she can achieve a marvelous combination of power and control, along with penetration, à la Ken Rosewall.

But, like many lesser players, Graf built her backhand around the defensive uses of underspin. As a result, her ball tended to float, and it rarely achieved penetration. But because of her stamina and speed, Graf was able to engage in long rallies, relying on the safety factor afforded by her slice. She could maneuver her opponent out of position, waiting patiently for a chance to run around the backhand, and then clock a forehand winner. In that sense the tendency of Graf's slice to "dig in" became a technical as well as a practical asset, because it robbed her opponents of pace and forced them to play shots off very low bounces.

Graf's trademark forehand led me to dub her Fräulein Forehand, but even that stroke was by no means classic. She committed the cardinal sin of waiting too long to begin her backswing. As a result, she often played the ball late, off her back hip, her stroke clearly rushed but still explosive.

Faced with Graf's confidence, power, and accuracy, few women challenged her forehand. But while Graf could blow them off the court with the forehand, the technical flaws in that stroke also left her vulnerable. It did not always hold up well under pressure or as a rallying tool. Graf liked to set herself up for the forehand put-away, and when she was denied the combination she liked (three backhands to open up the court and then—*poof!*—forehand winner), she often became error-prone and ineffective.

The most vivid example of that occurred in the semifinals of the French Open in 1992, against Arantxa Sanchez-Vicario. The bouncy, puckish Spaniard came out firing directly at Graf's big gun, the forehand. Aggressive, sharp service returns certainly helped her cause, and so did Arantxa's ability to run down Graf's shots without giving up court position. She confused and frustrated Graf by working her forehand. Graf's timing appeared to be off, and having to use her forehand as a basic tool rather than an ultimate weapon revealed the hit-or-miss character of the stroke. I'm not suggesting that anybody who played to Graf's forehand could run through a first set 6-love, but in that match Sanchez-Vicario did.

Then Arantxa made a silly and ultimately disastrous decision. With a set in hand, she figured she could sit back, stop taking chances, and desist from messing with Graf's forehand before it made an ugly mess all over her face. She began to play to Graf's strength, the backhand-forehand combination. Free to use the forehand in exactly the way she liked, Graf slowly found her rhythm. Being one of the few women who could run all day with Sanchez-Vicario, Graf won the last two sets, 6–2, 6–2.

After Graf lost the final to Seles two days later, I had dinner with Graf's coach, Heinz Gunthardt, who had been a friend of mine for years. I knew that Peter Graf, inordinately concerned with "leaks" from the Graf camp, insisted that the various coaches who had worked with his daughter traffic with the media as little as possible, and after assuring Heinz that I wouldn't quote him, I asked what he thought would have happened if Sanchez-Vicario had maintained her successful first-set strategy.

"Actually, I don't want to think about that," Heinz answered, smiling enigmatically.

Graf was living proof that a gifted athlete and a fine competitor can hide and protect almost any number of technical weaknesses. It's one of those Abe Lincoln "most of the people, most of the time" things. But a shielded weakness is still a flaw waiting to be exploited, and one of the things that Seles was able to accomplish with her power and accuracy was to push Graf out of the combinations she used to win most matches.

But there was another, perhaps even larger factor in the astonishing speed with which Seles was able to destroy Graf's domination of women's tennis, beginning at the French Open of 1990. That brings us back to Peter Graf.

At the beginning of 1990, Steffi Graf was twenty and sitting on top of the world. She seemed decent, down to earth, and content to go about her business in the most fundamental, live-and-let live fashion. Granted, she had developed few outside interests, but that could easily be explained by her spectacular success and the demands it created. Despite her wealth and age, Steffi still lived at home in 1990, and her father was an omnipresent force in her life.

At the Australian Open that year, I sensed that something was not quite right in the brilliant saga of Steffi Graf. I began to pay attention to what Graf projected as well as how she was perceived, both in her own words and those of the local media, each of whom had patiently lined up for the obligatory "exclusive" interview that top players granted to the main local reporters. One of the articles tried to portray Steffi as an ordinary girl with a hearty appetite for "normal" life. The best support for this contention was Steffi's claim that she had taken an afternoon off from practice earlier that week in order to go to the beach. A different reporter tried to play up the "Lifestyles of the Rich and Famous" angle. Graf found herself having to explain her relationship with men. Asked if she had been out with any Australians, Steffi said, "Sure, but only people I know, some friends I have here. Not like some *young boys* or anything like that."

Steffi was pushing the right buttons, talking about how much she loved her family, how much she loved animals. She told the Aussies that one of her ambitions was to visit the Great Barrier Reef, but, regrettably, she never had the time to do so.

I couldn't help but wonder about that. By 1990, Graf had been Down Under on six different occasions, and she had won the Australian Open twice. If she was so fired up about seeing the Great Barrier Reef, why hadn't she just gone after one or another tournament, instead of catching the first flight back to Germany, win or lose?

At that Australian Open I also found myself on a balcony overlooking a hotel lounge in Melbourne. Down below, Peter Graf was drinking, holding forth for his new best friends, an entire Lufthansa crew. He had promised them Steffi, but she was still up in her room. The party waited patiently. When she finally arrived, with the look of duty engraved on her face, Peter effusively declared, "Here she is, my Steffi."

I suppose those were the people with whom Steffi was preoccupied, rather than those young boys she had alluded to in the press. In fact, Peter Graf had a curious habit of inviting all his new best friends to the victory party whenever Steffi won a tournament. As a result, Steffi was forever celebrating with strangers, older people whom she didn't know, much less care about. Steffi seemed willingly mired in a life dictated by her tennis celebrity and orchestrated by her obsessive father, one that offered her nothing but domestic security. This was a condition that Graf's advisors took great pains to deny.

Phil De Picciotto, Graf's fiercely partisan agent at Advantage International, insisted that Graf had keen, extra-athletic interests that included politics, cooking, and animal husbandry. He said that only her acute sense of privacy kept those interests from public view, although I didn't really understand how any desire Graf had to bake a soufflé that didn't collapse figured as a profoundly private matter. Granted, one major function of an agent in the pro era is to act as a spin doctor. For all I know, De Picciotto may even have believed what he was saying. But Steffi's game didn't lie, and there was a surprising element of inconsistency and staleness in her tennis in Melbourne in 1990.

Graf had beaten Patty Fendick in the quarterfinals, 6–3, 7–5. Fendick had led in the second set, 5–3, and then double-faulted twice in the next game to allow Graf to pull even. I saw two different Grafs in that match: the familiar, overpowering one, and a very different player whose game was bubbling with petulance and impatience. More important, Fendick had noticed the difference, too. She said, "Steffi's not as sharp as she has been in the past. I don't know if it's something with her, or the fact that she's played so well that she's slowly pulled all of us up to her level and made life tougher for herself."

In the semifinals, Helena Sukova forced Graf to a third set in an intriguing match that ended in a stunning anticlimax. On service at 4–5 in the closely contested third set, Sukova made four mind-boggling unforced errors, including a double fault at deuce, to abruptly end the match.

Afterward, Graf lamented, "I don't feel 100 percent, technically or mentally. It's not the right time, the right feeling. I'm far away from playing good tennis."

Although Graf won the final with a neat 6–2, 6–4 win over Fernandez, the signals she sent were clearly mixed. Graf reportedly broke her thumb in a skiing accident shortly thereafter and vanished from tennis until April. Upon her return she was asked if she had missed the game. She answered curtly, "No. I was a little surprised at how *little* I missed it. I learned that I could live without tennis if it ever came to that."

Given Graf's curious attitude early in 1990, I find myself wondering just when she first learned that her father was embroiled in a scandal that erupted publicly in the spring of that year, creating sensational headlines around the world at just about the time that she returned to the game after her reported thumb injury. The facts of the case were sordid and a matter of public record. Nicole Meissner, a twenty-two-year-old model who fraternized with many shady characters in the German underworld of gambling and prostitution, claimed that she had an extensive liaison with Peter Graf. Claiming that he was the father of her child, she filed a paternity suit. The scandal soon worsened. A civil paternity case took on potentially criminal overtones as German authorities began to investigate whether or not the $424,000 collected by Meissner and her manager from Peter Graf (guess whose tournament earnings provided that tidy sum?) constituted criminal extortion.

The press was all over the story like a cheap suit. It was hardly surprising that Graf subsequently lost to Seles in the French Open final, or that Graf would not win another Grand Slam title until Wimbledon in 1991, a tournament at which Seles was not present.

Graf maintained an extraordinary degree of self-control during the painful, embarrassing days that the story was being played out in the tabloid newspapers. It probably helped that she adopted a "shoot the messenger" mentality, accusing the press of trying to "destroy" her family. She promised, "I will never stop hating the press after this."

I had to write about Graf late in 1990 when it was clear that her untroubled, enthusiastic persona had been shattered. She declined to sit for an interview, a decision that led to an interesting twist. If she had agreed to meet with me, my first priority would have been, as it always was, the articulation of her point of view. But without her cooperation, the long essay I wrote was a speculative one based not on her opinions and feelings but on the facts and my own observations. And the simplest, clearest fact I unearthed was the difference on the scorecard for the final of the first big Grand Slam meeting after the Meissner affair had broken. In the championship match at Roland Garros, Graf lost to Seles, 7–6, 6–4. It was the first Grand Slam title for Monica and the first big loss for Steffi since the beginning of her ascendancy. It was an odd match in which Graf led the first-set tiebreaker by 6–2, holding four set points. When she uncharacteristically failed to capitalize on any of them, the tide turned for good. In the end, the margin of victory in Seles's straight-set victory was a single point. She had won seventy-four points to Graf's seventy-three.

Graf's results in 1990 and for a brief period thereafter indicated that she was subconsciously exacting revenge against the man whose consuming obsession was her success, Peter Graf. There was no more effective way for Steffi to make her father feel guilty or to communicate the anger, hurt, and damage done to her by his actions.

The piece I wrote raised lots of eyebrows in tennis and earned me some unexpected compliments. It probably also ruined any chance I had of developing a better relationship with Steffi, perhaps forever. When a willful, strong person like Graf says that she will hate someone "forever," I wouldn't sit around waiting for her to change her mind.

But from mid-1990 up until six months after Seles was stabbed, Graf never was the same player she had been before the scandal. Sure, she won tournaments—she even had a fine win over Seles in the Wimbledon final of 1992—but the record will show that time and again, Graf was in a position to be beaten, and the only thing that allowed her to escape and retain her position right behind Seles was the inability of the rest of the women to play with sufficient courage, skill, and determination to beat her.

Time and a succession of wins helped to slowly repair Graf's drive and confidence. By early 1994, with Seles still off the tour, Graf once again began to look like Fräulein Forehand. The record book will show that she had a smooth, astonishingly successful career, the graceful curve of her accomplishments interrupted only by a curious downward spike between 1990 and 1993.

Here are some additional thoughts on that period. When Peter Graf disgraced himself, Steffi found herself at an important crossroads at age twenty-one. She could have struck out in a new direction, taken a greater degree of control over her own life. It was both a natural and an ideal time to grow up. To break, forgive, and repair.

Instead, Steffi drew back even further into her family, swallowing back whatever bitter taste lingered in her mouth. She wasn't going to let the press destroy her happy family. She wasn't going to take a good hard look at the toll her identity and talents had taken on those closest to her, or even herself. Steffi ducked her head and weathered the storm.

Peter Graf quickly climbed back in the saddle, too, no less a presence at tournaments than he had been in the past. In a little over three years, Steffi was entitled to feel a measure of vindication. She was number one again and adding still more titles to her hefty resume.

It was like old times again but without the joy. That was an element that never reappeared in Steffi's game. But so what if there is no apparent joy in Steffi Graf? She achieved something that few women in her shoes could match. She became something that even the formidable Monica Seles could not claim to be in 1994. She became a survivor in Babylon. Joy has nothing to do with it.

CHAPTER 20

JOHN MCENROE
Rebel with a Cause
or Lawyer without a Brief?

ONE DAY AT THE U.S. OPEN during the heyday of John McEnroe, the British reporter Richard Evans accosted me in the so-called Great Hall in Louis Armstrong Stadium. Evans was one of the most passionate McEnroe partisans in the press, and the author of a book about McEnroe, *A Rage for Perfection*. Essentially, the book was an extended apologia for McEnroe, based on Evans's theory that McEnroe's boorish and often ugly behavior was the result of his own nature as a genius and a perfectionist surrounded by dullards and incompetents. The book was interesting, and utterly offensive to those people who believed that McEnroe's talent or personality did not exempt him from having to observe the same standards of conduct and decency as anyone else, in or out of tennis.

Anyway, Richard was clearly agitated. He asked, "Did you see the new McEnroe poster put out by Nike? It's fantastic, absolutely fantastic. It gets right to the heart of what John is all about. It's brilliant, just brilliant."

He went on his way, and I sauntered over to the Nike booth to see what the fuss was all about. The grainy black-and-white poster was a spinoff of a widely known picture of the late actor James Dean: McEnroe was walking down a New York street bundled in an overcoat. In faux movie-poster lettering, the poster declared, "Rebel with a Cause."

The idea of a tennis poster that had nothing to do with tennis was certainly innovative, but my own feeling was that it was a little silly. For one thing, it suggested that McEnroe was some kind of James Dean wannabe. For another, I wasn't sure that the connection between the tormented juvenile delinquent portrayed so movingly by Dean in the movie *Rebel Without a Cause* and the millionaire tennis player McEnroe was all that strong.

Rebel with a Cause. And what cause was that, you may wonder.

The closest I can come to answering that is a declaration McEnroe made to me in 1989 when he was turning thirty and recovering from the general exhaustion that had caused him to take an extended break from the tour: "Once I became a top player, I got this idea in my head that I wanted to take the game to a new level. We tennis players had always been looked down on in a certain way, as upper-class, country-club types, a little soft, a little quick to complain or whine. I thought I could lead the way in erasing that image, in showing people that we're truly great athletes. We've never had that kind of respect, and one way to get it was by raising the level of the game. I wanted to raise it through the roof. I wanted it to be supercharged with intensity and passion and an incredible level of performance, night after night. I wanted to raise the game to a level that the average fan couldn't even understand so that all he could do was sit back, watch, and say, 'Wow. This is awesome.' "

That was the Cause. In a way it was selfless, and tinged with artistic integrity. There was also something appropriately Dionysian and self-immolating about it.

McEnroe's first great rival, Bjorn Borg, did a great deal for tennis without ever looking beyond his own nose or interests. Jimmy Connors, another rival of McEnroe's, expressed sentiments similar to those of McEnroe. But Connors was coarse, down to earth, and practical. He aspired to being a showman, not an artist. Ivan Lendl, McEnroe's third great rival, seemed content to just play his best tennis, letting the chips fall where they may, while he raised his income to a new level that the average fan was hard put to understand.

The Cause espoused by McEnroe certainly was worthy, but the way he went about advancing it often damaged his efforts in the same way that IRA partisans hurt their cause when they blew out the brains of elderly policemen whose most political assignments were crosswalk duties at the local school.

Of course, John's problem was his behavior. And if he didn't so often overstep the boundaries of decency, good taste, sportsmanship, and basic human civility, there's no telling how universally popular and beloved he would have become. Like my colleague Richard Evans, I once thought that with McEnroe you had to try not to let the distasteful outbursts and controversies cloud his general accomplishments. But looking back on his history and his legacy, I can't help but think that they did.

McEnroe's behavior prevented him from becoming a cherished and distinguished ambassador for the game, and by the time the memories of his conduct fade, so will the immediate, compelling aura of his greatness. Rod Laver, Arthur Ashe, and Chris Evert each made a smooth transition from player to ambassador, but McEnroe has had to do some time in purgatory. He has been serving it as a Soho art dealer, which a wag might interpret as a sentence not to purgatory but to a considerably warmer place.

This isn't just idle conjecture. For instance, the main reason that McEnroe didn't get the job of Davis Cup captain in 1993 is that the USTA officers who made the selection had long memories and obvious fears of the image that his captaincy would project for tennis. In many ways McEnroe is meeting the same people on the way down as he did on the way up, and many of them have been waiting a long time to collect a little payback.

Over the years I was frequently accused of being a McEnroe partisan who overlooked the issues raised by his conduct and allowed him to put his own spin on the issue when it did come up. The accusation is true. I was always fond of him, and much more interested in his basic sensibility and vision than in passing judgment on his behavior. I still believe that McEnroe's temper is not something that bears a lot of analysis, except perhaps on the couch of some shrink who gets big money for telling people that anything they do is okay. I still see McEnroe's temper and his subsequent conduct as a regrettable character flaw that at a very early stage in his career proved to be a natural condition, like halitosis.

But what is interesting in a variety of ways is how John was able to get away with his outrageous conduct and how being able to do so reflected flaws in McEnroe *and* the tennis establishment. Let's take the easy one first. McEnroe became a big star and a top drawing card so fast that nobody was willing to incur either the loss of income or, more important, the long-term wrath of McEnroe himself by chucking him out of a tournament for behaving badly. The very same promoters and officials who sat around condemning McEnroe for his behavior put up with everything that he dished out when their own self-interest was at stake. Furthermore, the burgeoning administration of the professional establishment elevated the survival and success of the bureaucracy and the tour itself above all other things. The administrators of the game knew that adopting a clear and swift concept of justice was not in everyone's best interest, least of all their own.

Let's say that McEnroe was entered in three successive tournaments in the month of March. If he was disqualified from the first event and subject to the immediate disciplinary sentence of two weeks' suspension, the promoters of the two subsequent tournaments would also suffer. So would those fans who bought advance tickets because they hoped to see McEnroe. As a result of such considerations, the tennis administrators developed a complicated, compromised disciplinary system that players could play like a pinball machine. And McEnroe was a young man who could play pinball with Tommy, the protagonist of a rock opera of the same name created by one of McEnroe's favorite bands, The Who. In the course of a very frank conversation near the end of his career, McEnroe told me, "There were occasions when I should have been defaulted from a match, but the system wasn't set up that way. It was a damage control kind of thing based on accumulated fines and deferred punishment. There were times when, because of the fines I'd already accumulated, all I had to do to get suspended was toss a racket, which in the big picture just isn't that big a deal.

"I've been suspended sometimes when I've done nothing that would be considered offensive enough to warrant it. And I've kept on playing in some tournaments where I went nuts. Really, tennis should be more like baseball. If you go too far, you should get thrown out. And if you go really nuts, you should get suspended.

"I'll be the first to admit that I did play the system. I manipulated it more than some people realized. In fact, I kind of got caught up in it all; it was like a big game. In most cases I was fully aware of what I was doing on the court during an outburst, and I knew how I was—or wasn't—going to have to pay a price for it."

The best example of the game played by McEnroe and the bureaucracy occurred at the only pro tournament from which McEnroe was ever disqualified, the Australian Open of 1990. The incident took place late in McEnroe's career and, ironically, at a time when the calming influence of his marriage to actress Tatum O'Neal, along with the joys and responsibilities of fatherhood, had inspired him to make a new effort to improve his image.

McEnroe was playing tennis reminiscent of his heyday. His fourth-round opponent was the dangerous, streaky Swedish player Mikael Pernfors. Anxious and agitated from the start, McEnroe was defaulted in the tight third set (after the players had split the first two sets) for a series of violations that included breaking his racket and cursing the umpire in the wake of a controversy created by a line call. But the key to the default was a rule change that had been made a few months earlier in which the disciplinary procedure culminating in disqualification had been reduced from a four-step to a three-step process of warnings and penalties. Although the rule change had been publicized and posted, McEnroe was not aware of it. He simply miscalculated and assumed that he could not be disqualified until after he committed his fourth official violation.

At the chaotic press conference afterward, McEnroe was subdued, remorseful, and introspective. As he had so often been in the past, McEnroe seemed torn between feeling guilty, as might any other naughty Irish-Catholic boy in his shoes, and taking the legalistic offensive, as might any cagey attorney who specializes in defending the indefensible.

The remorseful Irish-Catholic boy said that the incident was the logical, natural culmination of a long story. The lawyer argued that technically he had uttered just one little four-letter word, adding, "The guy could have let me off."

The remorseful Irish-Catholic boy said that he honestly could not say he was surprised. The lawyer argued the rules had been made up just for him and that they proved the players had no power in the game. (Of course the rules had been made by the official players' organization, in an attempt to police themselves.)

The remorseful Irish-Catholic boy said that he was careful not to throw his racket so hard that it broke (thus incurring an automatic penalty) and that it was bad luck the racket landed in such a way that it cracked. The lawyer insisted that McEnroe could and would have played with the cracked frame, so the automatic penalty was questionable.

And so on.

I didn't distinguish between these two dimensions of McEnroe for the common and simple pleasure of bashing lawyers, either. Those two disparate aspects of personality defined McEnroe as a complex individual often at war with both himself and the tennis establishment. He was simultaneously a rebel with a cause and a lawyer without a brief.

McEnroe's father, John Sr., was a brusque, self-made man who learned all too well how to play hardball at the Manhattan law firm where he was employed. And if there was a lot of the temperamental artist in young McEnroe, it didn't always offset his domestic legacy. And for all of the cant about McEnroe being a tough, street-smart, abrasive New Yorker, he is more easily understood as a kid from an upper-middle-class, thoroughly suburban, upwardly mobile environment. His father was shrewd, tough, and demanding. By McEnroe's own admission, his delightful mother, Kay, was his most impassioned and loyal ally, a woman who would refuse to forgive critics of her son long after even he had buried the hatchet. You could say he was spoiled. You could also say he was schooled in the tough art of survival in a harsh, competitive environment where lawyerly skills could come in very handy.

In the last year of McEnroe's career, we collaborated on a lengthy first-person reflection by him on his career. The article appeared in the April 1992 issue of *Tennis,* and I began it with an anecdote which is worth quoting verbatim:

Now that I'm playing my last full year as a totally dedicated tennis player, let me tell you how I became the person you know or think you know.

The first time I ever questioned a line call was at Wimbledon in 1977 in my quarterfinal match with Phil Dent. Up to that point I was still this unknown kid who had qualified and won a couple of rounds at Wimbledon. No big deal. But they scheduled my match with Dent for Court No. 1, which is second in importance only to the Centre Court. While it wasn't exactly a pressure-packed situation for me, it was like the first real test of my legitimacy.

Dent was a good grass-court player. If I beat him, I'd be the only qualifier—and the youngest guy ever—to make the semifinals, where I'd get to play Jimmy Connors.

Having to play Dent in that crucial match was a bizarre twist of fate. Just a couple of weeks earlier I had played Dent in the second round of the French Open. I was up two sets to one and a break, but I eventually lost. There were lots of bad calls in that match. For instance, Dent would hit a serve and it would be like a foot in and the linesman would call it out. So I'd say, "No, that was good. Play a let."

All through the juniors I would play anything that was even close because I hated the idea that somebody would think I cheated him or wasn't fair and square. But in Paris, after giving Dent six or eight calls, I couldn't help but notice that he wasn't exactly returning the favor. And that got me totally confused. Then, after the match, Dent pulls me over and says, "Listen, sonny. This is the pros here. We don't play that way. We play the calls, and we don't converse."

So the last thing I was going to do at Wimbledon was be like this naive rookie guy again—especially against Dent. There were a couple of funny calls, and I lost a close first-set tiebreaker. It got me really sore. After the last point I tried to break my Wilson wooden racket, but it just bent and bent, it wouldn't break. It was funny. The picture of me bending that racket is semi-famous. And while I'm trying to break that racket, I hear some boos. My first thought was, "What are *they* booing about? I'm the one who just lost a set, not them—what do they give a darn about?"

I actually thought it was funny, so I dropped my racket and kicked it along the turf from the service line all the way to my chair. And they started booing even louder. I was really into this match, but still—in my mind—I figured this is humorous. Of course, I had no idea of how the world was going to react. But I would find out soon enough, after hanging in there and getting a win over Dent.

In the next days and weeks the press was all over me. I went from being nobody to this young upstart, questioning calls. Plus, I was Irish, which doesn't always go over too big in England. Although Jimmy beat me easily in the semis, I was suddenly this big deal. . . .

Shortly after the story appeared, John Parsons of London's *Daily Telegraph* approached me. Parsons, the dean of British journalists, was known as a committed establishment man and an apologist for Wimbledon, as well as one of the staunchest advocates of all the embattled values that the British championships represented.

"Enjoyed the story," Parsons said. "Awfully good read, but it wasn't quite accurate, you know."

"Really?" I asked. "How so?"

"McEnroe said that the first time he acted up was in the match with Dent, didn't he? As a matter of fact, he received three official warnings for bad conduct while he was still at the qualifying tournament for Wimbledon, down at Roehampton."

"Are you sure?"

"Quite," Parsons replied. "I went back and looked it up."

I didn't know what to say.

"It's very like John to rewrite history that way, isn't it?" Parsons said, ending our conversation.

I suppose you could argue that being a qualifying event, Roehampton was not really a proper pro tournament. Or the antics McEnroe had indulged in there may have been different, in substance or appearance, from the ones he pulled at Wimbledon. Maybe he merely cracked his racket on the soft sod of Roehampton, another freak accident caused by the laws of physics, rendering a warning questionable. That is, you could argue it any of those ways if you wanted to get all lawyerly about it. And knowing that is probably what kept me from feeling that John had duped me. Hey, do I look like the kind of rummy who is not familiar with the old Latin saw that informs so much of the law: caveat emptor?

McEnroe's game was no less complex and intriguing than his personality, and while he appeared to play the brand of classic, serve-and-volley tennis perfected by his illustrious Australian predecessors, his style was unique, an inimitable mélange of unconventional strokes that challenged the fundamentals of the big game.

Arthur Ashe described the nature of McEnroe's game perfectly after losing to the nineteen-year-old in the Masters championship early in

1979: "McEnroe doesn't overpower or overwhelm you. He nicks you here, cuts you there, slices you somewhere else, and before you know it, you've bled to death."

McEnroe played in Grand Slam events and Davis Cup for sixteen years, winning seven titles in eleven championship matches, at Wimbledon (three) and Flushing Meadow (four). Those results were compressed into a five-year span between 1979 and 1984. He did not win a Grand Slam title after that.

His best year was 1984 when he posted the best twelve-month record that any player has enjoyed in the Open era. That year McEnroe won thirteen singles titles, including those offered at Wimbledon and the U.S. Open. His match record of 82–3 constituted the best annual winning percentage of the Open era.

McEnroe did not enter the Australian Open in 1984, but he played brilliantly on the winter indoor circuit and in the first outdoor events of the spring. He entered the French Open with a winning streak of thirty-three matches and quickly set the tennis community abuzz. No American male player had won the singles title on the French clay since Tony Trabert did it in 1955, and despite McEnroe's brilliant form early in 1984, he was not expected to stop the drought. He was a serve-and-volley player at a tournament dominated by all-court or baseline stylists. He was not big, strong, or exceptionally fit, so it was unlikely that he would have the stamina to keep his game at its highest, freshest level over four or five long sets against the masters of the passing shot, the topspin lob, and the penetrating service return.

But over the course of two inspired weeks, McEnroe slashed and chipped and charged his way to the final. In the championship match he led Ivan Lendl by two sets and 4–2 in the third. But McEnroe's complaint over a motor drive whirring in the photographer's pit led to a ruckus, after which neither McEnroe nor Lendl was the same player. Lendl worked his way back into the match and eventually won in five punishing sets, 3–6, 2–6, 6–4, 6–4, 7–5.

Many years later McEnroe would tell me, "I was five points away from winning the ultimate clay court title, and I let it slip away. It hurt, and it still hurts, at a couple of levels. It was undoubtedly my biggest loss ever. Having said that, I also believe that the match helped me put together my overall record in 1984. It was such a shock. It woke me up. It made me determined to win Wimbledon and the U.S. Open, and it got me focused like I hadn't been before. For the rest of 1984 I felt that every time I stepped on the court I was on a different level, above what anybody could handle. It was a truly amazing feeling."

McEnroe's radical service motion was the best example of his idiosyncratic style. Then there was the odd forehand that McEnroe often played late, turning on the ball with his entire upper body, racket head dangling and arm trailing, almost as if the appendage was atrophied.

McEnroe often drove his topspin backhand off his rear foot, falling away from the ball, and he rarely leaned into his sliced backhand with a long, leisurely stroke and follow-through. Inside every one of McEnroe's underspun backhands was a drop shot dying to be played.

The radical essence of McEnroe's game was not fully revealed until the emergence of the first truly classic stylist among the top players of the Open era, Pete Sampras. He had barely turned nineteen when he won his first Grand Slam title at the U.S. Open in 1990, and his quarterfinal match against a rejuvenated and still dangerous McEnroe was something of a revelation. Sampras played the game like one of the big cats—like a Pancho Gonzales or a Lew Hoad—with an arresting combination of explosive power and ease that almost suggested indolence. In contrast, McEnroe was quick, feisty, deceptive, and unpredictable. In other words, Sampras was a predator, and McEnroe was prey.

I believe that the extraordinary intensity and nearly paranoid focus McEnroe needed to maintain his place at the top of the game, with a game that lacked some of the big game essentials, had as much to do with his flameout and subsequent hiatus from tennis in 1986 as did the cumulative toll of his notorious episodes and the self-image problems he created for himself. McEnroe dominated the game for a relatively short period, winning seven Grand Slam titles in eleven championship match attempts over sixteen years. By contrast, Borg was eleven for sixteen in just nine years, Connors was eight for fifteen through twenty-two years, and Lendl was eight for eighteen over sixteen years. Even the forgotten champion, Mats Wilander, won the same number of titles and reached more finals than McEnroe (twelve), despite playing six fewer years.

But McEnroe had a great sense of timing and a remarkable ability to turn his matches against the champions mentioned above into intense rivalries. He went after each of them, with the exception of Wilander, with the gusto of a kid who loves to fight even when he is getting the tar beat out of him. And McEnroe treated them as successive challengers to a supremacy that he took for granted shortly after his twenty-first birthday, before he had been on the tour for three full years. McEnroe ascended to Olympian heights in the eyes of the tennis public and his peers swiftly and convincingly through his conquest of the invincible Borg. And from the time he wrested the top ranking away from the Swede in 1981, he seemed to believe that he carried the game on his shoulders, like Atlas.

By the time McEnroe burst onto the scene, even the most diehard

American chauvinists had to admit that Borg had subdued Connors and forced him to settle in as a strong if restless world number two. Borg was potentially the greatest player who ever lived and a good candidate to become the first man to win a Grand Slam since Laver last accomplished that feat in 1969. But suddenly, McEnroe turned the scenario upside down. He was only nineteen when he first played Borg and whipped him, 6–3, 6–4, in the semifinals of a tournament staged on Borg's home turf, Stockholm. The men traded wins until the summer of 1979 when Borg launched a three-match winning streak beginning at the Canadian Open and ending at Wimbledon in 1980, in what many pundits consider the greatest Wimbledon final of all time. Borg won, 1–6, 7–5, 6–3, 6–7, 8–6.

The first of three key victories by McEnroe over Borg occurred at an indoor tournament in Milan, Italy. In their next meeting in a Grand Slam final, McEnroe ended Borg's five-year reign at Wimbledon in the championship round, winning 4–6, 7–6, 7–6, 6–4. McEnroe delivered the knockout punch two months later at Flushing Meadow, beating Borg in the title match, 4–7, 7–6, 7–6, 6–4. A stunned silence enveloped the tennis community. McEnroe's reputation skyrocketed. Borg decided to quit tennis, leaving their career rivalry deadlocked at seven wins each.

If McEnroe's command of the game spooked Borg, the Swede's abrupt retirement in 1982 also had a profound affect on McEnroe. Near the end of his career, McEnroe told me how he learned of Borg's decision: "A month or two after I beat Borg in that 1981 Open, Vitas [Gerulaitis], Bjorn, and I were playing an exhibition in Australia. We're sitting in this room at the stadium when Borg just looks at me and says, 'I'm retiring from tennis.' I just looked at him. I didn't think he was serious. When he didn't smile, I said, 'You're kidding me, right?' Vitas just looked back and forth, at me and Borg. I must have started laughing, just out of the pure shock of it, because I clearly remember Bjorn saying, 'No, no, no. I'm dead serious. I'm sick of it.' I can still hear the words.

"The surreal thing was that five minutes after Bjorn says this to me, we had to go downstairs and do a joint press conference. Of course, everybody starts asking Bjorn how he feels about the upcoming year, and he just says, 'Well, I'm really looking forward to 1982. I'm really pumped up about it.' I mean, he said exactly the opposite, *verbatim*, of what he had just told me. So then the reporters got me into it, wondering how I felt as the new number one, and what it meant for the new year, and I'm thinking, 'Man, I don't know what to say. I don't get it.' So I just said more or less the same thing Bjorn had said, even though I knew that 1982 was going to be really different if Bjorn was quitting. It was truly bizarre."

Although Borg couldn't have realized it, his decision to quit was the second most powerful form of revenge he could have inflicted on McEnroe. From the time that McEnroe set his sights on peeling the top ranking away from Borg, he had anticipated that their rivalry might attain historic proportions, might "take the game to a new level." When Borg quit, McEnroe suddenly felt a void develop. He told me: "It was as if the great Lakers [basketball] team had decided as a unit to retire in the 1980s. Where would that have left the Boston Celtics? How would Larry Bird have felt if Magic Johnson quit? It's funny, but after Borg retired, the issue of my behavior seemed to snowball. You could accuse me of rationalizing, but maybe that helped to fill the void left by Bjorn quitting."

McEnroe was also troubled by Borg's retirement because, unlikely as it may seem, the two men had a good relationship based on mutual respect. This was partly because Borg was always attracted to flamboyant, charismatic types who seemed to transcend tennis in a way that he did not, like his best friend Vitas Gerulaitis and McEnroe. It was also because Borg was cool enough to regard McEnroe's outbursts with bemused indifference and, in a way that was untypical for a man as literal and simple as Borg, able to empathize with a man radically different from himself.

When Borg packed it in, leaving McEnroe confused, the ever-tough, patient Connors got the chance to step out of the wings to torment McEnroe on a few choice occasions. Connors won their first four meetings, but beginning in the summer of 1983, McEnroe went on a run of ten straight wins that carried him all the way to the end of 1986, a streak that served to obscure just how close his rivalry with Connors had been once upon a time. In typical Connors style, Jimbo got in his last licks, winning two of his last three matches against McEnroe. But at the end of the day, McEnroe led the rivalry 20–13.

McEnroe's rivalry with Borg transcended scores and records; there was genuine symbiosis. The chemistry with the rest of his rivals, however, was unsatisfying. Connors kept to himself, ever the loner, uninterested in sharing the limelight even when it served to make his own achievements shine. But McEnroe did feel that his rivalry with Connors was also characterized by the most prized consideration anyone could show him: respect.

Regrettably, the rivalry between McEnroe and another player, Ivan Lendl, was sour from the start, and it got worse. A cynic might say that this was principally because McEnroe could tolerate the notion of losing to Borg or even Connors, but he absolutely, positively would not entertain the idea of playing second fiddle to Lendl. That cynic would be dead-on.

There was an irrational element in McEnroe's antipathy toward Lendl, but it was based on real elements in Lendl's character. Early in his career, Lendl appeared to be cold and arrogant, in a way unlike Connors or the Swedes Borg and Wilander. But worst of all, Lendl did not know the "R" word, respect. He refused to pay homage to McEnroe. Unlike Borg or Connors, he did not acknowledge his rival's genius or cut McEnroe some psychological slack when it came to his conduct. The mutual antagonism between McEnroe and Lendl was so strong that even those critics who loved controversy often found McEnroe-Lendl confrontations well played but unpleasant, sullied by the iciness of Lendl and the surliness of McEnroe. It was a pity, because the rivalry between them might have become as rich and enjoyable as the extended symbiotic competition between Evert and Navratilova.

But the realist in me says that all of this unappetizing nonsense had something to do with the fact that Lendl was the only rival of McEnroe who ended up owning a superior career record against him, 21–15.

Although Wilander and McEnroe shared a passion for rock music, and the ability to win big without having big power, they didn't meet often enough on important occasions to develop an intriguing rivalry. They played thirteen times, with McEnroe holding the edge, 7–6. Each played his best tennis at the places where the other felt least comfortable. Wilander was never a real factor at Wimbledon, and he did not reach a U.S. Open final until 1987, by the time McEnroe was in decline.

Furthermore, only three of their meetings occurred in the championship round, and none in a Grand Slam final. Wilander won two of those three matches (Cincinnati, 1983, and Brussels, 1987), while McEnroe, ever the spoiler for Swedes, beat Wilander in the Stockholm final of 1984. McEnroe also won both of his Davis Cup matches against Wilander, including an epic confrontation in St. Louis in 1982. The match was the longest in Davis Cup history, six hours and thirty-two minutes. McEnroe won, 9–7, 6–2, 15–17, 3–6, 8–6.

And that brings us to hole card in McEnroe's quest for greatness—his record in Davis Cup competition. Not only was his record brilliant, but it was one that none of his four rivals could even approach, no less match.

It's always risky to throw Davis Cup records in with tournament results because of some fundamental differences between easily quantified individual performances in tournaments and national team competitions.

Before 1971, the Davis Cup had a Challenge Round format, with the defending champions sitting out the competition until the last team left standing earned the right to challenge for the cup. While McEnroe is third on the all-time list of leading Challenge or final round Davis Cup players, he is the top player in the final round era—ahead of such luminaries and Davis Cup stalwarts as Laver, Roy Emerson, Bill Tilden, and Frank Sedgman.

McEnroe played in the final round six times between 1978 and 1992 (the only year he played only doubles). The United States won the cup on five of those occasions. The only final round loss in which McEnroe participated was the debacle in Göteborg, Sweden, in 1984.

McEnroe won nine of ten singles matches and three of four doubles matches in final round play. If you eliminate meaningless rubbers played after matches were decided in the final round era, he trails only Boris Becker as a clutch performer. Becker won seven of eight matches (singles and doubles) while the outcome was still undecided. McEnroe won more matches (nine of eleven), but his winning percentage is slightly lower (.875 for Becker, .818 for McEnroe).

Given the fact that the United States was always competitive in Davis Cup play and blessed with a deep, continuous stream of talent, the domestic records held by McEnroe are a great testament to his passion for cup competition as well as to his abilities. He played the most number of years (twelve), the most team matches (thirty), and the most singles matches (forty-nine). He played more total matches (singles and doubles) than anyone else (sixty-nine). McEnroe won the most singles matches in American Davis Cup history (forty-one) and ranks third on the winning list for doubles (eighteen). He has the highest combined total of victories (fifty-nine), twenty-one more than his nearest rival, Vic Seixas.

McEnroe's Davis Cup record compensates for some of the shortcomings apparent on his Grand Slam resume. At his peak, McEnroe was nearly unbeatable in Grand Slam play, but his peak was brief. In Davis Cup, McEnroe wrote records that will be difficult to surpass.

In December 1988 I went out to Los Angeles to prepare a story about McEnroe for the occasion of his thirtieth birthday in February of the following year. At the time he was recovering from a collapse brought on by the stress that began to accumulate when he first seized the number one ranking in March 1980.

McEnroe held sway for almost four years. He heard Ivan Lendl's footsteps behind him almost all that time and was finally overtaken by Lendl in 1985. By then, McEnroe was little more than a bundle of raw nerves with a very short fuse, suffering from comprehensive exhaustion that diminished his playing skills and ultimately forced him to take a six-and-a-half-month hiatus from tennis at the beginning of 1986.

McEnroe's ambivalence about holding the number one ranking was well documented, and to some people, including his nemesis Lendl, it was unfathomable. As Lendl once told me, "John was always so busy defending the top ranking, worrying that somebody was going to take it away from him, that he never seemed to enjoyed just plain having it. I did enjoy being the top player, and that let me relax and appreciate it. John didn't burn out because he played too much, he burned out because he worried too much. What's the point of being number one if you're just going to get an ulcer over it?"

I didn't really understand why McEnroe felt so beleaguered by his preeminence until that visit to Los Angeles in 1988. The day I arrived and logged in, John and Tatum invited me to join them and friends for dinner at Tribeca, a basic art nouveau lunch foxhole for the rich and famous in Beverly Hills. Since I hadn't seen McEnroe in many months, I was a little worried that he'd show up with a ponytail, in the fashionably correct attire that could only be called downtown monastic. Fortunately, he wore blue jeans and a black T-shirt, not by Kenzo but Fruit of the Loom. And over appetizers he eyed the clams something-or-other suspiciously, as if they were going to bite back.

The conversation rolled along easily, turning to the Christmas vacation that McEnroe and his wife were about to take at a ski resort in Idaho. John, who had previously spent down time from tennis in late-night rock and roll joints and other urban environments, had reservations. Basic reservations.

"What if there's no snow?" he asked Tatum. "What if there's no snow *at all.* What then?"

"Of course there's going to be snow," Tatum answered, laughing. "How could you *not* have snow at a ski place in Idaho at Christmas?"

"It happens," McEnroe replied, although God only knows how he would have known. He went on ominously: "All kinds of things happen, you know. You'd be surprised."

Tatum reached across the table and ran her fingers through John's thinning hair. She chided him almost maternally, "You're such a pessimist sometimes."

"Me?" McEnroe feigned outrage. "A pessimist? How can you say that? I'm an optimist, I'm like a serious optimist."

"You, an optimist?" Tatum laughed again. "Boy, that'll be the day."

The McEnroes were off and running. At that time they already had two kids, Kevin and Sean, meaning that at times the McEnroe household consisted of four children. John was getting all worked up. If he had been on a tennis court, he would have plucked at his shirt, tugged at his shorts, and touched a dozen places that didn't really itch.

"Just because I've got reasons to question things doesn't mean I'm

THE COURTS OF BABYLON

not an optimist," John said. When Tatum conceded that that was true, John calmed down and segued into his closing argument: "Let's put it this way. I'm an optimistic pessimist. That's what I am."

"What you are," Tatum said, "is a realist. That's the real bottom line."

Actually, I liked John's theory better, and it seemed to explain a great deal besides his unnecessarily gloomy meteorological ruminations. It was a key element in his big personality, which included many fine qualities, including a gift shared by few tennis pros—a good sense of humor often driven by self-deprecation. On one occasion McEnroe requested that Cyclops, the electronic service-line calling device, be turned off because of its erratic performance. "I'm not paranoid," McEnroe remarked. "But that machine knows who I am."

McEnroe was unpretentious despite the volatile combination of his competitive spirit and his talent and charisma. He frequently felt betrayed and broke off cordial relations with reporters who criticized him in print, including some who had been kind and forgiving toward him for years. But he also brought a measure of "what you see is what you get" honesty to press conferences that he faithfully turned up for, even after he had created some embarrassing controversy that would incur the wrath of his critics.

McEnroe was not always good to the important "little people," but then he wasn't good to the "big people," either. Nor did McEnroe live like an athlete, which was another compelling thing about him.

In the mid-1980s when Lendl went on the fitness kick that ultimately helped him wrest the number one ranking from McEnroe, Lendl incorporated the computer-generated "Haas Diet" into his training regimen. Upon hearing that, McEnroe declared that he was on the "Häagen-Dazs diet," a reference to a popular brand of rich, fat-laden ice cream.

McEnroe enjoyed his beers, and it was also rumored that, like any suburban kid who wore sleeveless T-shirts and listened to The Who, McEnroe was not adamantly opposed to occasionally blowing a "doobie."

Although the McEnroes have consistently denied such rumors, things did turn ugly briefly when reports published in the *New York Daily News* had McEnroe covertly checked into a drug rehabilitation center in New Jersey. The report was never confirmed. In fact, John McEnroe, Sr., told me in a private conversation that it was patently untrue. But the story did send shock waves through a tennis community that had its fair share of marijuana, cocaine, and alcohol abusers.

McEnroe wasn't much of a womanizer, having had only two serious relationships before his marriage to Tatum O'Neal. One of them was with the tennis pro Stacey Margolin, and the other with the attractive, down-to-earth model Stella Hall. In fact, McEnroe once complained to me that the handsome Italian star Adriano Panatta—a man who affected a look based on Borsalino hats and costume directions from any number of Alain Delon movies—was furious with him because he felt that McEnroe was putting the moves on his striking Italian mistress. "I'm not into that stuff," McEnroe said. "Nothing bugs me more than being around women who I *know* are hanging around because of who I am."

Whatever aspirations McEnroe had as a lothario were also hampered by his basic shyness, a quality that often translated to gruffness and public moods that were powerful, unmistakable, psychic equivalents of a DO NOT DISTURB sign on a hotel room door.

McEnroe's status ensured that he did not exactly have to beat the bushes to find women who regarded him with some measure of interest. My favorite rumor along those lines came to me secondhand but from a good source—something about McEnroe and Alana Stewart, the former wife of rock star Rod Stewart, whiling away some time together at a time when the Stewarts were committed to separation but still sharing the same home. When Rod, the man who gave us the popular sexual travelogue and hit "Every Picture Tells a Story," came home unexpectedly, McEnroe was forced to gather up his things and climb out a bedroom window in the Stewarts' home, much like a character in one of those appalling British "Adventures of a Window Cleaner" films.

That adventure transpired during McEnroe's 1986 break from tennis. During that period he spent a great deal of time in Los Angeles. Although he was the quintessential New Yorker accustomed to playing rough, he would soon learn that people in laid-back Los Angeles could play rougher in unexpected ways.

I met McEnroe in Hawaii early in 1992 to collaborate with him on the first-person article that I mentioned at the beginning of this chapter. We had agreed on Hawaii because McEnroe was going there directly after the Australian Open, on a busman's holiday of sorts, as a doubles player on the U.S. Davis Cup team that would play Argentina on the island of Maui. McEnroe had done well at the Australian Open, upsetting Becker and reaching the quarterfinals after a poor start to the new year, his last on the tour. It would also be the last happy year of his marriage, and Tatum O'Neal and their three children, Sean, Kevin, and Emily, flew out to Maui for the Davis Cup match.

I'd always liked Tatum, and I'd had some amusing conversations with her that left me feeling she was complex and difficult, opinionated, willful, and absolutely accustomed to speaking her mind and baring her true feelings. In other words, she was just like her husband. A lot of people had been cynical about the relationship between John and Tatum, predicting that it couldn't last. I'd always felt that there was something very romantic about the match. They were like runaways, two hard-headed delinquents who had somehow found each other and decided to take the plunge into parenthood and eventually marriage, in defiance of social conventions, the will of their parents, and a general feeling among many that it would never work out. The pessimists felt that one household was too small to accommodate two difficult celebrities.

One of the most striking features about my conversations with McEnroe in Hawaii was the love and devotion that colored everything he said about Tatum. I don't really know what tensions existed in their marriage at the time, and there certainly were moments during that trip when it seemed like something was troubling one or both of them, but I do know that John never uttered an unkind word about her, and that he was still amazed and even angry about many particulars of her past. Most of those centered on the conduct of her father, Ryan.

"She had no real female figures in her life from the time she was six, and she went to live with her father," John told me. "That is, none unless you count people like Cher or Margaret Trudeau or any of the other women that came and went in Ryan's life. It was like life was one long party for the guy."

Neither John nor Tatum seemed to have much use for their in-laws, and by all accounts those feelings were mutual, a situation that created a bizarre if not entirely agreeable compromise. Nevertheless, John did tell me that Ryan O'Neal once approached him with an offer to play himself on screen. Ryan was to appear in the same picture, playing the role of an older man who would sort out McEnroe's behavior. "The psychology was bizarre, to say the least," John said. "And besides, it was a really crummy script."

The first two days in Hawaii passed pleasantly enough, with John and me chatting casually on the beach when I wasn't rolling tape for our collaboration. Tatum seemed indifferent to the allure of the sun, which was another odd thing that she had in common with her husband. John was that rare tennis player who couldn't care less about getting a sun-tan, and even at the peak of the summer had a complexion like that of an oyster.

I had told McEnroe days earlier that *Tennis* magazine was really keen on publishing some exclusive photos of him and Tatum. He didn't know how she would feel about that, but he promised to work on it. She finally agreed to do it, but I could tell as we prepared for the shoot that she was not exactly fired up about the idea.

Tennis magazine's photographer, Steve Surlej, was all set up on the hotel beach when I knocked on the McEnroes' door at the appointed time. No sooner was Tatum out the door than she looked me square in the eye and asked, "We're not going to do one of those corny kissing under the palm trees pictures, are we?"

I laughed and told her that we wanted to shoot the two of them from above, while they lay in a hammock.

"Eeeech," Tatum said. "That's almost the same thing."

"Actually, I was thinking that maybe you could lie with your heads at opposite ends."

This seemed to take Tatum by surprise, and she didn't say anything else until I suggested that we take the two flights of stairs down instead of walking all the way around to catch the elevator.

"My knee's hurt," Tatum said, bridling at the idea.

"Sorry," I said. "I didn't know."

"It's okay. I don't care. Let's take the stairs."

"No," John interjected. "We'd better take the elevator."

"The stairs are fine," Tatum said.

This debate went on for a little while longer, with John still mumbling about the elevator as we made our way down the stairs. I think Tatum just didn't want to be taken for a sissy and would have crawled down the stairs with a broken leg flopping on each riser just to prove she could do it.

I felt that we had a genuine disaster in the making, but a funny thing happened when we arrived at the photo shoot. The photographer said he wanted to start by shooting a few simple portraits with an ocean backdrop. Tatum said she thought that was kind of "boring," but as soon as Steve trained the camera on them, she changed. She just turned on whatever it is that photogenic people have, and she looked terrific. Clearly, the woman was a pro.

Tatum lodged only one other objection. After Steve fired off the first few frames, she chucked John in the ribs. "Don't smile," she said. "I *hate* it when you smile. I love it when you look straight into the camera. That's how I love you best. Serious." John knew better than to disobey.

Tatum registered no more complaints for the duration of the shoot. She popped right into the hammock alongside John, their heads alongside each other's feet. It turned out to be a fine, interesting shot that we spread over two pages. In fact, the story and pictures worked out so well that we decided to make a giant, high-quality print of the photo and give it to John and Tatum as a token of our appreciation. By the time we got the print made and I got around to delivering it across town to the McEnroes' residence on Manhattan's Upper West Side, many months had passed. I left the print with the doorman at their grand old building, and I was mildly surprised when I never received any acknowledgment that they had received it. Soon I heard that John and Tatum were estranged and that John was working double-time to keep their imminent divorce from becoming a messy public thing.

Naturally, there were all kinds of reports and theories about what had gone wrong. One of them suggested that Tatum was finding it impossible to get her movie career back on track because John was unwilling to make the logistical sacrifices it would require. That seemed odd, because McEnroe had told me in Hawaii that as soon as he stopped playing at the end of 1992, he was going to support Tatum's effort to rekindle her career. He seemed sincere and even passionate about that.

But unlike Tatum, John was the product of a traditional household in which his father worked and his mother took care of the house and children. And while John was a doting father, he was also a high-profile celebrity and public figure, accustomed to the limelight and to doing as he pleased. I think he wanted Tatum to be a "wife" in the classic sense. Unfortunately, John and Tatum did not have to face the obvious challenges confronting a young couple with three children. They were rich and had a dizzying array of options and no practical pressures to bind them. They were perhaps a little bored, even as they felt insecure about their personal prospects for the future.

Soon there were reports that John was spending a lot of time just hanging out with the guys. And tabloid newspapers reported that Tatum had expressed her discontent by taking up with a hunky young surfer from the West Coast.

In any event, Tatum was quickly accused of doing just what her own mother had done—abandoning her family while it was still in its infancy. It was a bitter blow for John and an apparent rejection of the most selfless and positive thing he believed he had brought to Tatum's life: the security and stability of the family life that she had never experienced.

Maybe it never occurred to him that because Tatum had never had those things, she didn't particularly need them—at least not in the traditional way he had envisioned providing them. If so, there was something deeply romantic and surprisingly naive in McEnroe. Funny, but it wouldn't surprise me one bit.

On the last afternoon that I saw John and Tatum together, the day before I left Hawaii, we drove a convertible Ford Mustang out to a remote beach. John and Tatum had a date with a friend of John's from the year he spent at Stanford, a football player named Ken Marjorem. John and I still had one segment to tape, having to do with his legacy in tennis. We wandered off to complete the interview while Tatum, Ken, and his companion, Joy, went bodysurfing. The surf was substantial, and as we talked, John kept casting anxious glances at the bodysurfers.

Later, while we were all sitting around chatting in the golden, late-afternoon sun, John finally decided to go for a swim. He peeled off his T-shirt. As always, he was pale. His chest was smooth, with only an odd reddish hair sprouting here and there on it. He was a lefty; his right arm looked like a stick. The surf had abated some since earlier in the day. The tide had gone out, and McEnroe had to walk quite a distance to where the waves were breaking. The water was barely over his knees when he stopped. He couldn't have been cold, but he looked it. He also looked as if he didn't really know what he wanted to do, head back or go on.

As I watched him, I realized that John McEnroe had ridden incredible waves of public adulation—swells matched only by angry rollers of villification and controversy. He had also balanced on the crest of his own genius, riding it as masterfully as a surf bum. But in McEnroe's case the thrill and the memory would not vanish as the wave broke and receded, seething, into the sea. His achievements would become part of history, even if it was just the history of tennis. But for all of that, one thing became increasingly clear: John McEnroe did not know how to bodysurf.

AFTERWORD

Jim Courier and Pete Sampras, a doubles team that won the Italian Open in 1989 and then broke up because both American players wanted to concentrate on singles, represented the United States at the Barcelona Olympics in 1994. Because neither had played any doubles in the year preceding the Olympics, they were unseeded. Both were weary from having played long singles matches on the slow red clay when they met the outstanding veteran Spanish doubles team of Emilio Sanchez and Sergio Casal in the second round of the competition.

Courier and Sampras quickly won the first two sets, but the home team, inspired partly by a delirious crowd of Latin partisans, bounced back and beat the Americans in a thrilling match, 5–7, 4–6, 6–3, 6–2, 6–1.

As Courier and Sampras, exhausted, dazed, and bitterly disappointed, wandered back toward the locker room, a fan who had been furiously cheerleading for the Spaniards ran up to Courier and thrust at him an empty cardboard pizza box and a pen. "Autograph," he begged. "Please. Autograph per Italia, per Italia."

I was surprised when Jim paused to acknowledge the man. He took the pen and very deliberately signed, "Fuck you, Jim Courier."

Our eyes met and Jim managed a weak grin.

I knew I couldn't use the anecdote in *Tennis* magazine, partly because of its intrinsic vulgarity and partly because I couldn't preface it with a disclaimer suggesting that it not be taken as an exposé of the "real" Jim Courier. I didn't even feel that I could share it with some of my colleagues because one of them might write it, and it would become part of a case that was being built against Jim by some members of the media.

The antagonism between Courier and the media had roots at the French Open of 1991 where Jim unexpectedly reached the final and upset Andre Agassi to win the title. Courier had been a little surly in official post-match press conferences, perhaps because he had to contend with mildly insulting questions about his "legitimacy" as a Grand Slam title contender. Courier's on-court behavior had been good and

459

clean, and yet a number of articles that appeared in the wake of his victory, particularly one published in *Sports Illustrated*, cast the twenty-year-old Courier as an unpleasant boor.

"That really hurt me," Jim told me months later. "I had grown up reading *SI*, it was like my bible. And I finally do something worth writing about, and I just get ripped apart and made to look like a jerk."

Courier subsequently established his legitimacy by, among other things, winning three other Grand Slam titles and earning the world's number one ranking. He would also charm many people, including the fickle Parisian crowd, when he successfully defended his French title in 1992 and then struggled through a victory speech given entirely in French. But the die was cast by that first bout between Courier and the media in 1991, and Courier never did get the respect he deserved as an intelligent, thoughtful, inquisitive individual.

In the big picture, Courier was part of a new breed of American player who, in the early 1990s, moved into the vacuum left by John McEnroe and Jimmy Connors. This group, which included Andre Agassi, Michael Chang, and Pete Sampras, represented a return to more traditional tennis values. Sampras, Chang, and Courier were reminiscent of the great Australian players of the 1950s and 1960s. They were brilliant players, outstanding sportsmen, and friends. Agassi was a bit of a loose cannon, but I thought he was a sensitive, interesting kid who had to cope with a number of formidable challenges, including overnight stardom.

Regrettably, this revolution of ethics within the men's pro tennis community was rarely acknowledged and never examined in any depth by the media. Instead, Agassi was villified for having become a vastly popular, overmarketed star who lacked dedication to his career. Courier was cast as a lout. Sampras was often described as bland and boring. A surprising number of commentators waxed nostalgic for the days of Connors and McEnroe, conveniently forgetting that they had spent good portions of their own careers bashing those two American individualists.

Although I've mentioned or written briefly about the members of this new generation in this book, they were too young—too close to the beginning rather than the end of their careers—to warrant more extensive treatment. I only wish that my colleagues had refrained from pigeonholing those youngsters so quickly and ignoring their potential as important players in the battle for the soul of tennis.

The very appearance of this new generation suggests a dramatic, unexpected shift of sensibility. Although the current crop of top American players (Todd Martin is the newest member) generally faced the same handicaps as the first wave of cradle-to-grave professionals, they seem to have handled the stresses better. This is probably because their parents, coaches, and advisors have a better grasp of the hazards of professionalism, and because the chaos that attended the birth of professionalism has given way to a semblance of order.

In any event, there is reason to hope that a new day is dawning and that some of the more destructive and dehumanizing elements of professionalism are being curbed. Ironically, this may be occurring at a time when tennis is widely perceived as a game in crisis, which says a lot about how people, and particularly the media, see the game—what they have come to expect of it and how well they know its history.

I'd like to close with a few quick thoughts on what I think the game of tennis needs in order to flourish:

- a streamlined circuit revolving around Grand Slam events;
- a points race for an annual world's number one ranking in which all tournament results count and in which everybody begins fresh on January 1. Some form of the current computer rankings should be kept in order to generate seedings;
- some form of team tennis that is more like Davis Cup competition or the popular Bundesliga competition in Germany rather than the radical World Team Tennis concept pioneered by Billie Jean King;
- a radically restructured womens' tour to alleviate the current crisis in the game;
- the playing of Davis Cup finals every two years, during non-Olympic years;
- the sanctioning of a Davis Cup–style competition, the Hopman Cup, in which women and men players represent their nations on the same team; with a slightly richer format than the present one of two singles and one mixed doubles match per tie;
- the creation by the establishment of some age restrictions for participation on the tour, without unfairly punishing legitimate prodigies who are capable of competing on the highest level. This should be done for the men as well as the women;
- the revival of the collegiate game, which is still struggling to survive in the United States;
- a more attractive and available game for minority players;
- the resolution of differences between the ITF and the ATP, an agenda for the common good of the game.

I know, I know, it's quite a wish list. But even if none of these things occur, I like the fact that the game seems to be righting itself, sailing along on calmer seas than it traveled just a few years ago. And I'm glad I finally got to use my Jim Courier anecdote.

INDEX